NURSING MANAGEMENT
IN CANADA

JUDITH M. HIBBERD
MAVIS E. KYLE

W.B. SAUNDERS CANADA

A division of
Harcourt Brace & Company Canada, Ltd.
Toronto Philadelphia London Sydney Tokyo

W.B. Saunders Canada
A Division of
Harcourt Brace & Company Canada, Ltd.
55 Horner Avenue
Toronto, Ontario M8Z 4X6

Nursing Management in Canada

ISBN 0-920513-18-2

Made in Canada.

Canadian Cataloguing in Publication Data

Hibberd, Judith M. (Judith Mary), 1934–
    Nursing management in Canada

Includes bibliographical references and index
ISBN 0-920513-18-2

1. Nursing services - Canada - Administration.
I. Kyle, Mavis E. II. Title

RT89.H52 1994   362.1'73'068   C94-930399-2

Design/technical art/desktop publishing: Blair Kerrigan/Glyphics
Editing/production: Francine Geraci

Printed and bound in Canada at Webcom

Last digit is print number: 9 8 7 6 5 4 3 2

Contents

Foreword

Many people think of Florence Nightingale only as "the lady with the lamp." But, as historical accounts and her own writings testify, she was much more than that, for she was the first truly professional health services administrator.

Nightingale's administrative practice exemplified the process of determining what nursing care needed to be done, where, why, when, how, and at what costs—within immensely complex, unpredictable, unparalleled situations. To do this, she used her general and practical knowledge about administration and her special knowledge about nurses and nursing. She evolved ways and means of collecting data and using statistics to document needs and intervention outcomes. And she did all this keeping in mind factors affecting health and illness of people—and keeping in mind what was going on and not going on, and what could be achieved and not be achieved, within the larger social context of those times.

Even beyond Nightingale, nurses were at the vanguard of health services administration. For example, it was nurses who established the first university program for "administrators of care," *Hospital Economics for Nurses*, in 1899, at Teachers College, Columbia University, in New York City. It was not until some 45 years later that the first graduate course in hospital administration was established, at the University of Chicago. Since that time, there has been an increasing tendency for health services administration to be taken further out of the hands of nurses and put into the hands of those who rely on business administration methods with no knowledge of the basics of care of humans.

The value of this text is not limited to nurse managers. Other health services administrators, politicians, civil servants, and health sector specialists from such areas as political science, economics, and sociology need to be aware that administrative practices, policies, and priorities must no longer be based on what, by the 1970s, had become an "old boys' network" often bypassing nursing input. Efficacious administrative practice in health care requires interfacing practice, theory, and research from many disciplines, with many levels of government, non-governmental organizations, and the community at large. As this book shows, the nurse manager is of pivotal importance in that interface and throughout the health care system.

In many ways, today's nurse managers and nurse administrators, at all levels, are facing challenging situations equal to those of Nightingale's times, for their work is highly complex, historically unparalleled, and increasingly overlooked. They are facing unpredictable futures, individually and collectively, personally and professionally. That is why this introductory text is extraordinarily timely, for it includes practical advice, sound theory, and recent research that all nurse managers—not only novices—need to know. This text introduces nurse managers to a general and practical knowledge of administration so they will be better able to relate on those many levels where administration and nursing combine. They will be prepared to carry on the important role of nursing administration in a rapidly changing health care system and within a rapidly changing broader social context.

Shirley Stinson, RN, EdD, LLD, DSc
Professor Emerita, Faculty of Nursing & Department of Health Services Administration & Community Medicine
University of Alberta

June 1994

Preface

As teachers of nursing management, we are constantly looking for a suitable textbook with content relevant to the Canadian health care system. It is more than nine years since such a textbook was published in Canada. It is our hope that *Nursing Management in Canada* will not only fill a gap in the literature, but that it will serve as an educational resource for first-level nurse managers as well as for nursing students.

When we talked about our tentative plans to edit a nursing management text with students and with colleagues in service agencies and educational settings, there was instant and unanimous support for the project. Not only was there support for the idea, but nurse experts offered to write chapters for us. Our plan was to incorporate a nation-wide perspective, and so we invited health care practitioners, educators, administrators, and academics from across the country to share their special areas of knowledge and experience with us. Readers will find contributions from some of the most distinguished leaders and writers in our field, from Newfoundland to British Columbia. These authors represent a diversity of health care settings, including community health, home care, ambulatory services, long term and acute care, professional associations and private practice, and they bring a variety of perspectives and a wealth of wisdom and experience to bear on their topics.

In organizing the content of the book, we chose a framework developed by the Canadian Nurses Association (CNA). In 1988, CNA published a conceptual model of nursing administrative practice in a document entitled *The Role of the Nurse Administrator and Standards for Nursing Administration*. This model, together with the standards for nursing administrative practice, assisted in the identification of material to include in the book, and served as a common conceptual base for contributing authors.

This book has taken a little over three years from initial concept to publication. Much has happened within the health care system during that period. When we started planning, we knew that the cost of health care services had exceeded the rate of inflation for nearly three decades, and that transfer payments from federal to provincial governments would be gradually reduced. We did not know then how persistent the prevailing economic recession would be, nor the impact such economic forces would have on public policy in relation to health care. Since then, regionalization has emerged in several provinces, health care agencies are being restructured, and work processes redesigned to promote cost-effective, patient-centred services. There are signs that the health care system will undergo the reforms that have been advocated in numerous commissions and task force reports. No one knows yet how effective these changes will be in reducing costs and improving services. There have been layoffs of nurses and nurse managers which, until recently, would have been regarded as unconscionable. Indeed, latest figures show a decline in overall numbers of nurse administrators and managers in Canada by almost 20% since 1988.

Historically, competent nurse clinicians have been promoted into managerial roles, often without any additional management preparation. To function effectively in the current climate of uncertainty and turmoil, management nurses need, in addition to a sound knowledge of their own discipline, a broad-based understanding of management theory, as well as health care economics, finance, informatics, and labour relations. In particular, they need to understand the politics and process of change at all levels of the health care system; how policy decisions are made; how to articulate the needs of patients and clients; how to involve both nurses and consumers in decisions affecting them; and how to promote a work environment that supports professional practice. Nurses are committed to patient and client care, and they strive for high standards and quality of care, but they do so with diminishing resources. More than ever, they need expert nurses who will work with them as effective leaders, and involve them in shaping health care services for the 21st century. We hope this book will help prepare such leaders.

This book is a joint endeavour of many people, and we acknowledge the assistance of them here with a deep sense of gratitude. As novices in the business of editing a book, we were especially fortunate to have Glennis Zilm, a nurse and a copy editor, on the team. We depended on her for advice, positive reinforcement, and wise counsel as the project progressed. Her ability as a copy editor is first rate, and her background as a nurse was invaluable. She has a special ability to make a sentence, a paragraph, or an entire manuscript infinitely clearer without loss of meaning.

Our publisher, W.B. Saunders, encouraged us throughout the process. Darla Clark, former regional representative, supported this project from the beginning, and Gerry Mungham, Manager of Marketing and Acquisitions, and Kathleen Davidson, Vice-President, have encouraged us in many ways. Francine Geraci, in charge of editing and production, patiently and diligently pulled the finished product together, despite the deadlines we missed.

Our colleagues and friends provided advice and reassurance, and they willingly served as chapter reviewers. The contributors to this text are all busy, committed professionals, but they responded to the demands we placed on them with tolerance, dignity, and good humour. Our employing agencies were supportive, and they contributed to this project in many ways including the provision of secretarial and office resources. Liz Carpenter, Janis Winters, Tom Hall, and Angela Canonaco deserve a major vote of thanks for their secretarial support. We also wish to thank the reference librarians at the Woodward Biomedical Library at the University of British Columbia who assisted in verifying information and checking numerous references. The project was supported in part by a grant from the Publications Fund of the University of Saskatchewan.

Judith M. Hibberd
University of Alberta
Edmonton, AB

Mavis E. Kyle
University of Saskatchewan
Regina, SK

June, 1994

C H A P T E R 1

Introduction and Overview

Judith M. Hibberd and Mavis E. Kyle

Judith M. Hibberd, RN, PhD, CHE, and Mavis E. Kyle, RN, BSN, MHSA, teach nursing administrative practice to undergraduate and graduate students at the Universities of Alberta and Saskatchewan, respectively. Both have held first-level nursing management positions, Hibberd in orthopedics and Kyle in the operating room, and they consider these positions among the most rewarding of their careers. Both authors are graduates of the master's program in Health Services Administration at the University of Alberta.

The first-line manager of any organization is in a key position to influence day-to-day operations, the quality of the product, and the work lives of employees. Nurses have occupied such positions in the Canadian health care system since the earliest hospitals and health services were established. The first-line nurse manager's role is a complex one, and responsibilities vary depending on the type of service, the setting, and the culture of the organization. The position, traditionally referred to as head nurse, is situated at the interface between client services and the rest of the organization—the point where changes in health care and in nursing often have their greatest impact (Duffield, 1989). The position is sometimes viewed as a linchpin of health care organizations (Eubanks, 1992), and it is one that will involve more authority and more responsibility if health care agencies are to adjust to current trends. This book is about the work of nurses who manage the front line in the Canadian health care system.

The health care system is currently undergoing intense scrutiny. The principal reason for this scrutiny relates to the state of the national economy and the attendant debt burden confronting federal and provincial governments. Diminishing sources of funding are stimulating realignment among health care agencies, as well as retrenchment and internal restructuring. Health agencies are attempting to reduce costs without jeopardizing the quality of care and treatment of clients. At the same time, medical technology and changing treatment protocols are contributing to greater intensity of inpatient care and earlier discharge of clients to the community. Financial resources, however, are not necessarily being reallocated to support the shift in care from institutions to homes and health agencies. Meanwhile, consumers (a growing proportion of whom are getting older and living longer) are better informed about the capabilities of health services. Increasingly, they value the system and expect to be involved when changes are proposed. To appreciate the full significance of this turbulence, current trends and issues in the health field need to be viewed from a broad perspective.

Society at large is in the throes of a transition that is changing the political, economic, social, and moral landscape of the world, not merely the Western world. As noted by Haines (1993): "In a few seemingly short years, the combined forces of technology, financial constraint and global competition have generated a rate of change unseen in history. That change has touched every society and every level of society—shaking convention, creating uncertainty, creating opportunity" (p. 9). Drucker (1993) predicts a fundamental transformation to a society whose principal economic resource is knowledge. Theoretically, influential social groups in a transformed society will be knowledge workers who know how to allocate knowledge and put it to productive use. According to this view, managers of the future will be expected to provide a generic and vital service to a society of organizations. Common assumptions of the past that underlie health care may no longer be true. New ways of thinking, especially "systems thinking" (Senge, 1990), and new ways of doing must be found. Traditional managerial roles and functions will become secondary to the ability to provide visionary leadership in an emerging post-capitalist society.

In the view of Fernande Harrison (1992), president of the Canadian Nurses Association (CNA), there has never been a greater need for nursing leadership. What is needed are people who can cut through the ambiguity and uncertainty of the immediate future and offer a vision to their followers, and an ability, according to Murphy and De Back (1991), to "manage the dream." Nurses need to exert leadership at all levels of health agencies because authority is being diffused throughout organizations. Many of the traditional leadership positions in nursing are disappearing along with the dissolution of functional departments such as nursing and rehabilitation services. In view of the complex interplay of current trends and the uncertainty that it creates, this book constitutes a summary of current practice rather than a prescription for future nursing administrative practice. Nurse managers need to understand the immediate past, as well as current administrative practice, if they are to play a constructive role in shaping the future.

This introductory chapter describes the organizational framework for the book. A model of nursing administrative practice developed by the Canadian Nurses Association (1988) was selected as a conceptual basis for planning and organizing the book because of its applicability to any nursing practice setting in the health care system. The book is divided into four parts or sections, corresponding to the major concepts of the CNA model. This introduction briefly describes the pertinent chapters in each section. The chapter concludes with some comments on educational requirements and individual preparation for careers in nursing management.

The CNA Model

One of the first challenges in planning a management text is to decide on an organizing framework and the content to be included. The Canadian Nurses Association published a model of nursing administrative practice in 1988 after several years of studying the educational requirements and the practice of nursing administration. Like models in general, it is a simplification of reality in which broad concepts and their relationships are clearly indicated. The model is sufficiently general for it to endure over time, and to remain relevant even though major changes are taking place in the system it represents. This model appears in Figure 1.1 (see page 4).

The CNA model is based on systems theory. The central concept is nursing administrative practice, which takes place within the context of both internal and external environments. In this model, nursing administrative practice comprises professional and corporate dimensions with roles and functions integral to both.

As noted above, the current external environment of health care organizations is characterized by turbulence and uncertainty. It is not surprising to find that external forces have had an impact, not only on the internal context and culture of health care organizations, but also on the roles and responsibilities of nurses in management positions.

It has been customary to identify three levels of nursing administration (CNA, 1988) depending on the size, complexity, and type of health care service being administered. Common titles for these levels are: chief executive nurse (director, vice-president);

Figure 1.1
Nursing administrative practice.

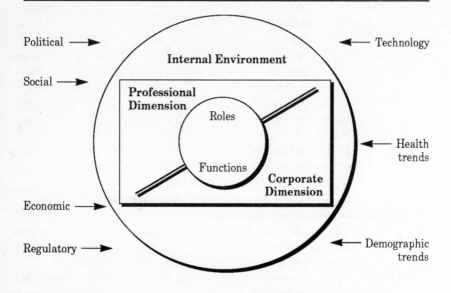

Source: Reprinted, with permission, from Canadian Nurses Association (1988), *The role of the nurse administrator and standards for nursing administration* (Ottawa: Author), p. 7.

middle nurse manager (supervisor, coordinator); and first-line manager (head nurse, nurse manager). In general, the more senior the role and function of the nurse administrator, the greater the corporate dimension of his or her practice. For example, executive nurses are usually involved in decision making and policy development at board and senior executive levels of the organization. Thus, if strategic planning and priority setting are on the agenda of the governing board and senior management, a nursing perspective is added to the deliberations. On the other hand, nurses practising in a management role close to patient care have more direct responsibility for the professional dimension of the role. In the CNA model, the line that represents the division between the professional and corporate dimensions of the nurse manager's role is free floating, and this denotes the dynamic interaction and interdependency of the two dimensions.

The bureaucratic hospital structures of the past are being replaced with more flexible organizational designs such as program or product line models. With these designs, senior and middle nursing administrative positions have been eliminated (Deutsch, 1992). In such cases, organizational structures tend to be flatter, replacing traditional pyramidal designs; the accompanying decentralization of decision making and authority to first-level managers has greatly expanded their corporate responsibilities. Also, as hospitals downsize and streamline management functions, head nurses have found themselves responsible for more than one patient care unit. In addition to being accountable for the professional practice of nursing and the quality of nursing care, they carry out all the traditional management functions of planning, organizing, directing, controlling, and evaluating, as implied in the CNA model.

Providing leadership in the nursing discipline is what distinguishes *nursing* management from other types of management. Although there are situations in which non-nurses have been appointed as directors of nursing, nurses generally want their leaders to be nurses, in much the same way that physicians want their medical directors to be physicians. It is important to be able to distinguish between the concepts of leadership and management. These two concepts have attracted a vast literature. Leadership is increasingly viewed as an empowering relationship between leader and followers. Bennis and Nanus (1985), for example, suggest that a leader "is one who commits people to action, who converts followers into leaders, and who may convert leaders into agents of change" (p. 3). Management, on the other hand, is usually defined as a rational process, such as "the coordination and integration of human and material resources to produce optimal goal achievement through the use of technical, interpersonal, and conceptual skills" (CNA, 1988, pp. 17-18). Although leadership and management involve goal-oriented activities, they are conceptually distinct, but to be truly effective as a manager, leadership is clearly an essential ingredient. Mintzberg's (1975) concept of managerial roles illustrates this point.

According to Mintzberg, management can be described as a complex set of managerial roles, including interpersonal, informational, and decisional roles. Leadership is viewed by him as an interpersonal role. The concept of multiple managerial roles has been applied in studies of nurse managers (e.g., Baxter, 1993; Jones & Jones, 1973), but as noted in the CNA (1988) document, it is only one approach to understanding the nature of management. Mintzberg's framework underscores the complexity and the challenge for nurse managers in providing leadership in their discipline.

Standards for nursing administrative practice accompany the CNA model, and these are listed in Table 1.1. These standards

Table 1.1
Standards for nursing administration.

Standard I
Nursing administration plans for and implements effective and efficient delivery of nursing services.

Standard II
Nursing administration participates in the setting and carrying out of organizational goals, priorities, and strategies.

Standard III
Nursing administration provides for allocation, optimum use, and evaluation of resources such that the standards of nursing practice can be met.

Standard IV
Nursing administration maintains information systems appropriate for planning, budgeting, implementing, and monitoring the quality of nursing services.

Standard V
Nursing administration promotes the advancement of nursing knowledge and promotes the utilization of research findings.

Standard VI
Nursing administration provides leadership that is visible and proactive.

Standard VII
Nursing administration evaluates the effectiveness and efficiency of nursing services.

Source: Reprinted, with permission, from Canadian Nurses Association, *The role of the nurse administrator and standards for nursing administration* (Ottawa: Author, 1988), p. 10.

were developed to assist nurse administrators in defining their roles, improving their practice, and evaluating their effectiveness. Individual nurse administrators are responsible for refining the standards so that they can be applied to their own particular work settings. It is assumed that ethical behaviour underlies all aspects of these standards (CNA, 1988).

In general, when the term "nursing administration" is used in this book, it refers to nurse executives. When the term nurse manager is used, it refers to first-level nurse managers, who are fiscally and clinically accountable for their patient care areas or programs on a continuing basis.

Organization of This Book

This book is divided into four parts, each part corresponding to a major component of the CNA model. Part 1 deals with the external environment of health care organizations; Part 2 is about the internal environments of health care organizations; Parts 3 and 4 contain chapters that focus on the professional and corporate dimensions of nursing administrative practice, respectively. In organizing the contents of this book, the placement of some chapters was somewhat arbitrary. One could argue, for example, that risk management belongs in Part 2 (internal environment) rather than in Part 4 (corporate dimension) because it has organization-wide implications, but discussion of the legal liability of the nurse manager as the employer's agent seemed to fit more precisely into the corporate dimension of nursing administrative practice.

A brief overview of each section of the book follows.

Part 1: External Environment

There are two chapters in this section. In Chapter 2, Storch and Meilicke outline the evolution of the Canadian health care system and the political, social, and economic forces that influenced it, and they discuss future policy implications. Preservation of the Canadian health care system, with its five fundamental principles, became an important political issue in the 1993 federal election because Canadians place a high value on this public service.

Knowledge of the community and the populations they serve is a requirement of all health care administrators. In Chapter 3, Knox reviews demographic and epidemiological trends and discusses how these will affect health care in the next decade. Although national health goals are not yet established, it is expected that health promotion, illness prevention, and the principles of primary health care will eventually become guiding principles in shaping future health services.

Other external forces referred to throughout the book include legislation governing hospitals, nursing homes, and public health services, and regulations required by various levels of government and professional bodies. Medical technology is a major force and has consequences for all health disciplines including nursing; as well, informatics has changed forever the way information is managed and communicated. The implications of these trends for nurse managers are addressed in several parts of the book.

Part 2: Internal Environment

In this section, six chapters focus on aspects of the internal organization and management of health care agencies. In many ways, the internal environment is a microcosm of the external environment, having governing structures, unique cultures, and groups of influential people typical of society at large. Structure in organizations, such as the size and composition of agency boards, are almost always influenced by politics. For example, major initiatives are currently taking place in several provinces where regionalization of health services is accompanied by the dissolution of individual health agency boards. Chapter 4 by Meilicke provides a comprehensive overview and synthesis of management theory essential for understanding and influencing internal environmental policy. Few changes within health care organizations occur without some impact on nursing services, a point that is well illustrated in this chapter.

Decisions being made by senior executive officers are increasingly influenced by economics and government policy regulations. In Chapter 5, Dick and Bruce discuss the impact of funding issues and cost containment strategies on health care organizations. Rodger provides a framework for understanding power and politics within organizations in Chapter 6, and suggests strategies for influencing policies to support patient care goals. Parallel structures such as medical staff organizations must be understood by nurses in order to foster constructive interdisciplinary relations in the interests of patients and clients, and this is the subject of Chapter 7 by Lemieux-Charles. Storch, in Chapter 8, applies ethical principles to nursing management issues and tasks, and notes that the ethical dimensions of nursing management are exacting, and require serious self-examination and a high degree of accountability.

Workplace design is addressed by Skene in Chapter 9. It is included in this section to emphasize the necessity of nurses' involvement in the planning process of construction and renovation projects. Too often, efficiency and effectiveness are marred by poor planning for the needs of clients, and hence quality of care is jeopardized.

Part 3: Professional Dimension

The professional dimension of nursing administrative practice refers to the "area in which an administrator demonstrates knowledge and expertise with respect to professional nursing, exerts leadership in relation to the discipline, and acts as an advisor on nursing matters" (CNA, 1988, p.17). Leadership is the critical concept in this definition. In Chapter 10, Wylie examines leadership and leadership theory, and explores implications for future leadership styles. In Chapter 11, Monk discusses the issue of governance by nurses, including models for enhancing professional practice, and addresses the implications for nurse managers. Chapter 12 by Kyle and Donnelly introduces nurse managers to concepts and theories of nursing and their importance as a foundation for practice. Unless nurse managers can articulate the nature of nursing, and interpret it to other health care disciplines, they are unlikely to be effective professional leaders. Similarly, as noted by Pepler in Chapter 13, nurse managers must understand the research process and the contribution that nursing research can make to cost effectiveness and outcomes of nursing care.

The next three chapters deal with ensuring high standards of professional practice. Boulerice, in Chapter 14, traces the movement from quality assurance to quality improvement, which, next to cost containment, represents a major thrust in the internal environments of contemporary health care organizations. Richardson, in Chapter 15, reviews the literature on ways and means of offering clinical advancement opportunities for professional nurses. She notes that reward systems in the past were such that skilled nurses seeking promotion tended to move away from services to the client into administrative or educational roles. In Chapter 16, Vollman and Hartin-Avon provide a comprehensive account of one of the most challenging functions of management, evaluating staff performance. Increasingly, this responsibility is shared among managers and staff. More peer review systems are likely to be used for professional staff in the future.

The organization of work is one of the fundamental functions of management. The evolution of methods has been influenced by the professionalization of nurses, and, as Lendrum notes in Chapter 17, new opportunities for autonomous practice for nurses continue to emerge, including case management. Justifying staffing levels and the appropriate mix of professional and auxiliary nursing personnel has been complicated by the difficulty of measuring what it is that nurses do for their patients. Giovannetti discusses workload measurement in Chapter 18 as an important administrative tool for allocating sufficient nursing resources to meet the requirements for care. The practical implications of staffing and scheduling hours of work are presented by Beed and Rigby in Chapter 19, and the implications for managing a predominantly female work force are addressed by Valentine in Chapter 20.

Perhaps the most underrated responsibility of nursing administrative practice is the promotion of a practice environment that maximizes the quality of nurses' work lives. This is the focus of Chapter 21 by O'Brien-Pallas, Baumann, and Villeneuve. Institutional nursing has historically been plagued by such problems as shortages of nurses, turnover, and dissatisfaction (CNA/AHA, 1990) to the point where provincial funds have recently been earmarked specifically to enhance the work lives of nurses. One of the repetitive themes in studies of nurses' job satisfaction has been the lack of continuing education programs. In Chapter 22, Spiers discusses the role of the nurse manager in creating a practice environment where learning flourishes.

It should be clear from the chapters in this section that professional leadership is a critical ingredient in the management of health care organizations, to ensure that internal environments are conducive to providing the best nursing practice possible. There is mounting evidence that nurses play a critical role in maintaining and improving quality, in understanding patient care needs, and in balancing costs in a reformed health care system (Prescott, 1993). Health care policy makers need to be informed of this kind of evidence in a timely manner.

Part 4: Corporate Dimension

The corporate dimension of nursing administrative practice refers to participation "in the organization's administrative team for the purpose of determining policies, priorities, allocation or resources, and general management issues" (CNA, 1988, p. 17). The chapters in this part of the book tend to deal with the traditional functions of management, as implied in the CNA model (1988).
McHutchion, for example, in Chapter 23, presents a blueprint for strategic planning, and similarly, in Chapter 32, Ready, Johnston, Gray, and Paege bring a community health perspective to program planning and evaluation. Managing change is probably the most challenging of management activities at the present time, and this is discussed by Montgomery in Chapter 24. Thorpe defines and differentiates decision making, problem solving, and critical thinking, and applies two models of decision making to nursing situations in Chapter 25. Although preparing a budget involves planning, it also represents a control function of management. As noted by Elliott in Chapter 29, budget reports permit nurse managers to compare actual expenditures with predicted or budgeted expenditures, and to make adjustments accordingly. Another control function is risk management. In Chapter 30, Mrazek brings a legal perspective to corporate liability, describing approaches to minimizing risk, and outlining the legal liability of nurse managers.

In view of the labour intensity of health care, human resource management is a particularly important function. One of the most difficult responsibilities is the successful recruitment and hiring of personnel. In Chapter 26, Acorn and Walker provide an overview of human resource management with a specific focus on hiring and termination. As the majority of health care workers are unionized in Canada, it is essential for nurse managers to practise effective employee relations. In Chapter 31, Hibberd discusses the administration of collective agreements, and the role of unions in the work place. Computerized information systems were originally designed to support corporate functions such as accounting, but increasingly they are used for the collection, organization, storage, and retrieval of clinical information. In Chapter 28, Hannah and Anderson discuss recent developments in the nursing component of health information, and the importance of identifying the data essential for managing patient care and defining the specific contributions of nursing to particular health services.

Corporate activities are increasingly undertaken by task forces and ad hoc committees and, as Wylie points out in Chapter 27, collaborative interdisciplinary teams are an essential requirement for meeting current and future needs of patient populations. Thus, nurse managers must understand the dynamics of group process if they are to develop effective teams.

There are numerous other important skills that nurse managers need to develop, four of which are discussed in the final chapters of the book. Managing available time, both the manager's time and staff time, is a critical skill to master given the complexity of health care agencies, the competing demands for the nurse manager's time, and the labour intensity of the work; this is discussed in Chapter 33 by Hibberd. As resources become more scarce, nurse managers may find themselves bargaining over anything from office space to unit supplies, and so, as Clark notes in Chapter 34, they must understand the dynamics of negotiation. She focusses on day-to-day interactions designed to achieve specific objectives and points out that the dynamics of such negotiations are essentially the same as those employed in collective bargaining. Communication skills are integral to all roles and functions of managers, but, in Chapter 35, Smith raises several issues that are unique to managerial communication. Finally, as the staff of any health agency, whether nurses or others, represents a significant corporate investment, managers must develop human relations skills, including the ability to identify individuals in trouble. In Chapter 36, Kirk outlines the responsibility of nurse managers in relation to identifying and assisting employees who may be undergoing personal difficulties.

Preparing for Management Roles

The CNA model and standards for nursing administrative practice provide an indication of the extensive scope of knowledge required for nursing administrative practice. The chapters of this book collectively capture significant portions of that knowledge. In view of the rate at which new knowledge is being developed in health care, nurses with leadership and management responsibilities need to cultivate self-directed learning skills so that they can remain adequately informed in their field. The final section of this chapter contains a brief discussion about management as a career option for nurses.

Career paths for nursing administrative practice are changing rapidly. There will be fewer traditional nursing management positions as a result of changing organizational designs. For example, program and matrix structures, with their emphasis on cross-functional teams, are substantially changing the nature of nursing management. In the future, most, if not all, first-level nursing management positions will be called patient care or program managers, and their positions will probably not be part of employee bargaining units. In fact, Peters (1987) suggests that all first-line supervision as it is understood today will be eliminated. This may seem like a radical view, but there is already evidence of a decline in the overall number of administrative nurses in Canada. In particular, the number of head nurses dropped from 15 872 to 9746 between 1988 and 1992, which is a decrease of 39% (Table 1.2).

Nevertheless, there will continue to be opportunities for nurses to compete for administrative positions in the health field. Indeed, Aburdene and Naisbitt (1992) suggest that appropriately prepared nurses are particularly well situated for competing for top jobs in health care.

> *Nursing Directors will increasingly break through into top hospital posts, successfully competing with finance directors and other executives for the chief operating officer job. But other executives will not match the depth of knowledge about hospital operations the chief nurses have. To win that competition, however, nurse/managers should start now to round out their administrative know-how with new skills in finance and marketing. (p. 73)*

Table 1.2

Nurse administrators by type of position and educational preparation: 1988 and 1992.

	1988	1992
Director/Assistant	**5160**	**5320**
	%	%
Diploma	67.8	64.0
BScN	25.8	29.0
Master's/PhD	6.4	6.9
Supervisor/Coordinator Assistant	**10 834**	**10 443**
	%	%
Diploma	77.7	74.5
BScN	20.6	23.7
Master's/PhD	1.7	1.7
Head Nurse	**15 872**	**9746**
	%	%
Diploma	87.1	79.3
BScN	12.0	19.0
Master's/PhD	0.9	0.9
Nurse Administrators: Total	**31 866**	**25 509**

Source: Compiled from information in L. Lemieux-Charles and D. Wylie (1992), *Administrative issues.* In A. Baumgart and J. Larsen (Eds.), *Canadian nursing faces the future* (Toronto: Mosby Year Book), p. 254, and from *Registered nurses management data 1992* (1994) (Ottawa: Canadian Centre for Health Information, Statistics Canada), prepared by the Research Department, Canadian Nurses Association. Information used with permission.

The same can be said for management nurses in community-based health care organizations because they have tended to be better educated than their hospital counterparts. As an example, even at the beginning of the 1980s, 46% of directors in public health nursing in Canada held graduate degrees compared to 28% of their colleagues in teaching hospitals and 21% in large hospitals (Leatt, 1981).

The number of nurses seeking additional education for managerial roles has increased, but as Lemieux-Charles and Wylie (1992) observe, a large percentage of nurse administrators have no administrative preparation beyond a basic diploma in nursing.

In Table 1.2, figures cited by Lemieux-Charles and Wylie (1992) for l988 are compared with 1992 figures available from Statistics Canada (1994). Although there has been an increase in the proportion of nurses with university education at all three administrative levels, the majority still have no administrative preparation.

Educational Preparation

In view of the profession's goal of university-level preparation in nursing for all beginning practitioners by the year 2000, first-level nurse managers should have, at minimum, a baccalaureate degree in nursing. Many undergraduate nursing programs offer an introductory course in management but, although this is valuable preparation, it is not adequate to meet the educational needs of most of today's nurse managers. It is abundantly clear that not only do nurse managers need to have advanced knowledge in their own discipline, but they need additional knowledge of the corporate dimension of their roles. This includes knowledge of health economics, finance, informatics, and labour relations. Specific aspects of the educational requirements for first-line nurse managers remain controversial (Fullerton, 1993), but to compete for emerging health care management positions, nurses will need to prepare themselves at graduate levels.

There is considerable debate as to the clinical and administrative content of graduate programs for nurses pursuing management careers. Not the least of the difficulties is, as Stinson (1989) notes, that few nursing faculty members are experienced in nursing administration and thus not well equipped to make substantive nursing linkages between management content and nursing service objectives. According to the American Organization of Nurse Executives (AONE), the nurse manager requires:

> *finely honed clinical, leadership, and management abilities in such diverse areas as finance and budgeting, information systems applications, organizational theory and development, human resources management, strategic planning, and marketing. Nurse managers also balance the divergent needs of staff, patients, families, physicians, support services, and top administration. They empower and influence bedside caregivers to exemplify and expand the profession of nursing.*
> (AONE, 1993, p. 26)

When selecting a program of management education (whether in nursing administration, health services administration, or business administration), it is important to examine the curriculum in the light of one's professional and personal goals, as well as prevailing labour market conditions. This is where mentors can provide helpful advice.

Mentors

Nurses contemplating a career move into management would be well advised to seek a mentor. Experienced nurse administrators who have reputations for excellence and who can serve as role models should be consulted. Although a mentor relationship may not necessarily evolve, nurse executives should be willing to coach their staff, to listen to them, and be supportive in providing guidance (Orth, Wilkinson, & Benfari, 1990). It is important to learn first hand about the realities and implications of leadership and management roles, rather than to proceed on the basis of some idealized notion of management. There is evidence that successful business executives have had mentors and coaches in the past, although as Colvin with Light (1990) note, there have been fewer mentors and role models for female executives. A mentor can guide a protégé in evaluating strengths and potential for leadership, in exploring motives for choosing a management career, and in accessing wider networks in the health field.

Career Planning

In addition to a mentor, it may be wise to consult a career counselor. A career counselor can advise the potential nurse manager on how to prepare a résumé or curriculum vitae, and can discuss such aspects of the job search as marketing oneself, preparing for employment interviews, and negotiating employment contracts. Once an offer of employment is obtained, it will be necessary to do some assertive bargaining about the terms of the appointment. Many Canadian nurses have enjoyed the services of their unions to do this for them in the past. An important part of the employment contract, after settling on salary and other benefits, is provision for severance of employment or "involuntary turnover" (Blouin & Brent, 1992). Although nurses may find negotiating a termination package distasteful, it is part of normal business practice. It would be a good investment to ask a lawyer to evaluate the employment contract before agreeing to it or signing it. Professional associations may also provide assistance in the career management process and may supply educational materials, and information on management salaries and terms and conditions of employment (e.g., Canadian College of Health Service Executives, 1993).

Conclusion

In summary, this chapter provides an overview of the book and an introduction to nursing administrative practice. The discussion focusses primarily on first-level nursing management because of its significance within health care agencies, and because of its importance in creating work environments that support the professional practice of nursing. Effective performance in such roles will increasingly require appropriate education in nursing *and* in management, as well as leadership skill. In the words of Wylie (see Chapter 10), "nurse managers need to be knowledgeable, be articulate, possess self-esteem, have an image of where the profession and the situation are heading, and inspire, challenge, support, and enable others " (page 189).

Fundamental changes currently underway in the health care system create both problems and solutions. As Roch (1992) suggests, however, opportunities abound if the nursing profession views itself as part of the solutions.

References

Aburdene, P., & Naisbitt, J. (1992). *Megatrends for women.* New York: Villard Books.

American Organization of Nurse Executives. (1993). In celebration of nurse managers. *Nursing Management, 24*(5), 26.

Baxter, E. (1993). Head nurses' perceptions of their roles—Parts I & II. *Canadian Journal of Nursing Administration, 6*(3), 7-16.

Bennis, W., & Nanus, B. (1985). *Leaders: The strategies for taking charge.* New York: Harper & Row.

Blouin, A.S., & Brent, N.J. (1992). Nurse administrators in job transition: Negotiated resignations and severance agreements. *Journal of Nursing Administration, 22*(7/8), 16-17.

Canadian College of Health Service Executives. (1993). *A guide to career management for health service executives.* Ottawa: Author.

Canadian Nurses Association. (1988). *The role of the nurse administrator and standards for nursing administration.* Ottawa: Author.

Canadian Nurses Association & Canadian Hospital Association. (1990). *Nurse retention and quality of worklife: A national perspective.* Ottawa: Author.

Colvin, J., with Light, P. (1990). Women in middle management. In S.A. Ziebart (Ed.), *Feeling the squeeze: The practice of middle management in Canadian health care facilities* (pp. 73-81). Ottawa: Canadian Hospital Association.

Deutsch, N. (1992). Chief nursing officers: Here today, gone tomorrow? *Canadian Nursing Management Supplement,* No. 54, 6-8.

Duffield, C. (1989). The competencies expected of first-line nursing managers—An Australian context. *Journal of Advanced Nursing, 14,* 997-1001.

Drucker, P.F. (1993). *Post-capitalist society.* New York: HarperCollins.

Eubanks, P. (1992). The new nurse manager: A linchpin in quality care and cost control. *Hospitals, 66*(April 20), 22-29.

Fullerton, M. (1993). The changing role and educational requirements of the first-line nurse manager. *Canadian Journal of Nursing Administration, 6*(4), 20-24.

Haines, J. (1993). *Leading in a time of change: The challenge for the nursing profession. A discussion paper.* Ottawa: Canadian Nurses Association.

Harrison, F. (1992). Leadership through alliances. *The Canadian Nurse, 88*(6), 20-23.

Jones, N.K., & Jones, J.W. (1979). The head nurse: A managerial definition of the activity role set. *Nursing Administration Quarterly, 3*(2), 45-57.

Leatt, P. (1981). *Education for nursing administration in Canada: A discussion paper.* Ottawa: Canadian Nurses Association.

Lemieux-Charles, L., & Wylie, D. (1992). Administrative issues. In A. Baumgart & J. Larsen (Eds.), *Canadian nursing faces the future* (pp. 241-257). Toronto: Mosby Year Book.

Mintzberg, H. (1975). The manager's job: Folklore and fact. *Harvard Business Review, 53*(4), 49-61.

Murphy, M.M., & De Back, V. (1991). Today's nursing leaders: Creating the vision. *Nursing Administration Quarterly, 16*(1), 71-79.

Orth, C.D., Wilkinson, H.E., & Benfari, R.C. (1990). The manager's role as coach and mentor. *Journal of Nursing Administration, 20*(9), 11-15.

Peters, T. (1987). *Thriving on chaos.* New York: Knopf.

Pedersen, A. (1993). Qualities of the excellent head nurse. *Nursing Administration Quarterly, 18*(1), 40-50.

Prescott, P.A. (1993). Nursing: An important component of hospital survival under a reformed health care system. *Nursing Economics, 11*(4), 192-199.

Roch, D. (1992). Overview of health care restructure within current resources. *Canadian Journal of Nursing Administration, 5*(2), 8-11.

Senge, P.M. (1990). *The fifth discipline: The art & practice of the learning organization.* New York: Doubleday.

Statistics Canada. (1994). *Registered nurses management data 1992.* Ottawa: Canadian Centre for Health Information.

Stinson, S.M. (1989). Education of nurse administrators in Canada: Implications for practice, theory, and research in nursing administration. In B. Henry, R. Heyden, & B. Richardson (Eds.), *International administration of nursing services* (pp. 112-125). Philadelphia: The Charles Press.

P A R T   1

External Environment of Health Care Agencies

C H A P T E R   2

Political, Social, and Economic Forces Shaping the Health Care System

Janet L. Storch and Carl A. Meilicke

Janet L. Storch, RN, BScN, MHSA, PhD (Alberta), is Dean, Faculty of Nursing, University of Calgary. She was previously Program Director of the Health Service Administration Program at the University of Alberta and author of numerous articles on health care policy and on ethical issues in health care and nursing.

Carl A. Meilicke, BComm (Saskatchewan), DHA (Toronto), PhD (Minnesota), is Professor Emeritus, Department of Health Services Administration and Community Medicine, University of Alberta, where he was founder (1968) and Director of the Program in Health Services Administration until 1980. He was seconded to the Alberta Department of Health until 1982 as the first Associate Deputy Minister, Policy Development, and returned to the Department at the University of Alberta from 1982-1993.

This chapter is a modified and expanded version of the authors' Introduction to their text, *Perspectives on Canadian Health and Social Service Policy: History and Emerging Trends* (Ann Arbor, MI: Health and Administration Press, 1980).

In this chapter, the Canadian health care system is briefly described, with attention to the political, social, and economic forces that have shaped it. To trace the causes and consequences in the development of the Canadian health care system, an historical analytical approach will be adopted, beginning with the period predating Confederation. The chapter will include a discussion of current issues and trends and of future policy implications relative to the Canadian health care system.

Nature of the Canadian Health Care System

Knowing the general types of health care systems across the industrialized nations assists in placing the Canadian health care system in context. Four general types ("ideal types") of health care systems are apparent, ranging from those in which governments play a residual role in a system governed by a market orientation (private health insurance systems), to the opposite extreme in which governments define health care as an essential service (socialized health care systems) (Najman & Western, 1984). In private health insurance systems, preservation of the autonomy of physician, health institution, and client take priority. The fact that a substantial minority of people might be without health care in such a system is viewed as unfortunate but unavoidable. In socialized health care systems, minimal autonomy of health provider or client is accepted since the goal of the health care system is to preserve the collective good by ensuring optimal productivity of citizens.

Between these two opposite types of health care systems are two other approaches to the delivery of health care. In one of these system types, the role of government in health services is viewed as a necessary vehicle for reasonable social distribution of resources (national health service). Health services are seen to be a natural resource that should be available to all based on need, not on ability to pay. Physician, institution, and client autonomy are secondary to meeting the public's need. In the final general type of health care system, government attempts to balance autonomy with the collective good through public insurance programs (national health insurance). In this type of system, physician, institution, and client autonomy are preserved but within a context of equitable access to health services for all citizens.

If the private health insurance system is typified by the general approach to delivering health care in the United States, and the national health service system is typified by the approach of the United Kingdom, then the Canadian health care system (the National Health Insurance System) can be viewed as a blend of the American and British approaches. By encouraging health professional and health agency autonomy, while ensuring relatively equal access to health care by all individuals regardless of their ability to pay, two important values in Canadian society are protected.

In an attempt to protect and preserve autonomy and equity, the Canadian health care system has been built upon five main principles: universality, accessibility, comprehensiveness, portability, and public administration. Provincial tax revenues, and to a declining degree federal tax revenues, fund medical and hospital service delivery in all provinces provided the five essential principles are honoured. Only two provinces (Alberta and British Columbia) levy premiums to assist with the cost of health services and, for the most part, there are no user charges or extra billings for services considered medically necessary; such charges are seen to violate the principle of accessibility. Thus, coverage of basic hospital care, including X-ray, medications, diagnostic testing, and other such services, and of physician care, is provided "free" of charge to all Canadian citizens. Private health insurance (e.g., Blue Cross and other insurers) covers only supplemental benefits, such as private accommodation, ambulance, and out-of-country costs not covered under the public plan.

The Canadian health care system is part of a broader network of social security programs that have developed over time. This network of programs, made accessible to all, is a remarkable achievement for a relatively young nation. The range of programs reflects the basic values that have evolved during more than 200 years. Some of the most notable commitments developed in the early part of the 20th century, particularly in the province of Saskatchewan, where a number of innovative approaches to health care occurred. These innovations became part of the background for establishing a national blueprint of Canadian Social Security in the mid-1940s. The values underlying the innovations continue to shape health care policy and programs in the 1990s. As Deber and Vayda (1992) noted, "Historically, Canadians have accepted government intervention in social programs and have welcomed sponsorship of health care" (p. 3).

Readers should note that although the phrase "Canadian health care system" is commonly used, it is important to remember that Canada does not have a federal health care system; it has 10 provincial health care systems, plus two territorial systems (Deber & Vayda, 1992). The federal government plays a more direct role in care in the northern territories, although the territories also are moving toward more autonomy. However, because the federal government has taken a major role in initiating and coordinating health care insurance funding and because the provincial and territorial systems do have common themes, it is possible to take a national perspective.

Understanding how the network of programs took shape is critical to understanding the strengths and the challenges of the health care system in the 1990s. Therefore, an historical perspective on the system will be presented, outlining six main eras of health policy and program development and highlighting the nature and dynamics of the changes that shaped its evolution.

Each era is characterized by distinctive concerns and activities spanning the time periods from the days of the earliest settlements until Confederation in 1867, from Confederation to the mid-1940s, from mid-1940s to mid-1960s, from mid-1960s to mid-1970s, from mid-1970s to the 1990s, and from 1991 to some point in the future. The time periods are approximate, of course; multidimensional historical dynamics defy precise categorization into unidimensional time periods.

Era One:
Pre-Confederation

In the young and developing Canadian nation predating Confederation, self-reliance was valued: self-reliance in providing for the necessities of life, in looking after one's family, and in attaining health care. The natural outcome of this focus on self-reliance was the belief that there should be limited government involvement in social security, other than a modicum of services for the sick, the mentally ill, and delinquents (Cassidy, 1947; Splane, 1965). Typical examples of the limited legislation and existing programs were acts (in the early 1700s) to control sale of meat, to establish quarantine stations, to deal with foundlings, and to make provision for sick and disabled seamen (Gelber, 1973; Gregoire, 1962; Heagerty, 1934). Buildings were provided for the insane (lunatic asylums), provisions made for the care of lepers, and procedures implemented to handle epidemics of cholera, typhus, and smallpox (Cameron, 1962; Hastings & Mosley, 1966). The procedures for dealing with epidemics were ad hoc measures, with no permanent boards of health established. This ad hoc approach was typical of a government choosing not to develop proactive policies, as these might be viewed as interfering with self-reliance. Instead, governments reacted only to the major crises of the day. As Wallace (1950) notes, Canada's population was rural, and problems that might now be defined as social problems were then viewed as problems for families, the local community, or the church to address, rather than for the state.

These were among the reasons that the British North America Act (BNA Act), one of the constitutional acts of Canada, made provision for only residual needs; the authors assumed that the family, community, or church were capable of handling the major concerns. Thus, Section 91 of the BNA Act outlines federal responsibilities as raising of money by a mode or system of taxation, provision for the census and statistics, provision for quarantine and establishment and maintenance of marine hospitals, and responsibility for Indians and lands reserved for Indians. The only items relevant to health care are in Section 92, which outlines provincial responsibilities. These are responsibility for the "establishment, maintenance, and management of hospitals, Asylums, charities, and eleemosynary institutions in and for the province, other than marine hospitals," and "generally all matters of a merely local or private Nature in the Province" (Van Loon & Whittington, 1976, p. 483). The short-sighted delineation of legal responsibilities left virtually all health service provision in the hands of the provinces, which had an insufficient tax base to support extensive services to meet the needs of the Canadian public. As Deber and Vayda (1992) note, "The fathers of Confederation proved to be poor prophets. The resulting imbalance between fiscal resources and constitutional responsibilities has made federal-provincial relations the primary concern of Canadian politics" (p.3).

Since the BNA Act contained such limited provisions for determining federal and provincial responsibilities in matters of health and welfare, and with the lion's share of responsibility resting with the provinces, only three options were open to federal or provincial governments to deal with this anomaly: (1) they could go ahead on their own; (2) they could push for a constitutional amendment; or, (3) they could enter into cost-shared programs (Taylor, 1987). All these strategies are evident in the system that unfolded during the ensuing years, as described and analyzed below.

It is important to note that the division of power and the use of these strategies are not only historically interesting but are important in understanding the Canadian health care system of the 1990s since these same provisions prevail today. In 1982, the BNA Act became part of a constitutional package under the Constitution Act, which added the Canadian Charter of Rights and Freedoms and a domestic amending formula.

Era Two: Confederation to Mid-1940s

The second era was characterized by a growing awareness that organized action was necessary to deal with the social security needs of an increasingly urbanized and industrialized nation. This awareness led to extensive developments in governmental and voluntary programs and, eventually, to a profoundly important clarification of federal versus provincial authority in matters relating to social security. The era is characterized by the increasing significance of government involvement and a slow but steady progression from reactive and ad hoc programming to at least beginning efforts to effect planned change.

In the years between Confederation in 1867 and 1920, municipal and provincial programs in health and social security were considerably expanded and many important voluntary organizations were formed. Organizations that now are known as the Toronto Children's Aid Society (1891), the Red Cross (1896), the Victorian Order of Nurses (1897), the Canadian Mental Health Association (1918), the Canadian Institute for the Blind (1918), and the Canadian Council of Social Development (1920), for example, were organized during this time (Armitage, 1975).

The growth in municipal and provincial government activities during this period occurred because the BNA Act (as noted above) was silent on matters of health and welfare services, reflecting the conviction that these matters, in so far as they were the responsibility of government, were of proper concern only to local and provincial authorities (Splane, 1965; Wallace, 1950). Representative of such activities was the substantial expansion of welfare services in Ontario, implementation of municipal doctor plans and union hospitals in Saskatchewan (1914-1916), an income support plan for widowed mothers in Manitoba, and municipal hospital plans in Manitoba and Alberta (1920) (Gelber, 1966; Morgan, 1961; Rorem, 1931; Splane, 1965; Taylor, 1949).

These municipal and provincial developments proceeded apace through to the 1940s when the federal government, in response to growing public demand for social services as well as to the social disruptions caused by World War I and the Depression, began to consolidate its health responsibilities and to respond to new needs deemed to require federal assistance. These initiatives were largely reactive rather than planned (for example, a grants-in-aid scheme for venereal disease control, the Soldiers' Settlement Act of 1920) and relatively few programs were actually established. One program, however (the Old Age Pensions Act of 1927), was significant in being Canada's first nation-wide income support plan and the first major, continuing, federal-provincial cost-shared social security program (Bryden, 1974; Cameron, 1962; Morgan, 1961). Various ad hoc unemployment measures were also undertaken by the federal government during the Depression of the 1930s because thousands of individuals could no longer be self-sufficient and self-reliant, and neither municipal nor provincial governments were capable of financing the relief programs required (Bellamy, 1965; Gelber, 1973).

The problems inherent in an ad hoc approach were dramatized in 1937, when the Employment and Social Insurance Act of

1935, designed to provide an extensive federal program for dealing with the economic and social problems created by unemployment, was declared unconstitutional because the federal government did not have the power to levy direct premiums on provincial residents in order to attend to health and welfare issues
(Taylor, 1987). A Commission was established to deal with this
first major federal-provincial controversy and was charged with
determining areas of federal-provincial jurisdiction in a wide variety of fields, including social security. In this case, the strategy of
pressing for a constitutional amendment was employed, but was
not effected until 1940 when federal responsibility for unemployment insurance was added to Section 91 of the BNA Act.

The end of this lengthy period characterized as Era Two was
dominated by efforts by the federal government to evolve a
planned approach to long-range policy and program development
based on a careful definition of national needs, a plan that was to
founder on the problem of federal versus provincial authority. The
passage of the Unemployment Insurance Act in 1940 permitted
the federal government to implement a compulsory, contributory
insurance program at the national level. Stimulated further by a
wide variety of pressures including serious concern for the social
and economic stability of Canada attendant upon the dislocations
caused by the Depression and World War II, as well as a commitment to the Atlantic Charter of 1941 (which stressed the concept
of individual freedoms and rights), two major reports were undertaken by the federal government, commonly known as the Marsh
Report and the Heagerty Report (Collins, 1976; Heagerty, 1943;
Marsh, 1975).

The Marsh report, which was prepared in 1943, has been
cited as the "single most important document in the development
of the post-war social security system in Canada" (Collins, 1976,
p. 5) because it was informed by a long-range perspective and it
outlined a comprehensive national plan for social security for
Canada. The Marsh plan included social insurance for interruptions of earning capacity (such as unemployment insurance), occasions requiring special expenditure (such as major accidents or illness), and greater continuous budgetary needs than the family
income could accommodate (such as chronic poverty). Marsh also
emphasized the need for integration of social security programs.

The Heagerty report was more limited in scope than the
Marsh report but more specific in its proposals. Heagerty considered it essential that everyone in Canada should be provided with
health insurance, but that no compulsion should be placed on
provinces other than that all indigents be included in the plan.
Health program benefits were to be broad in scope, including

medical, dental, and pharmaceutical benefits, and additional program grants to the provinces were proposed, including grants for tuberculosis, mental health, and professional training. Heagerty stressed the integration of public health and medical care, as well, with the goal of "raising and maintaining the standard of health care of the Canadian people" (Heagerty, 1943, p. 5).

The only apparent immediate result of these remarkably prescient reports, however, was the passage, in 1944, of the Family Allowance Act. It provided for payment by the federal government of monthly allowances for every child under 16 years of age. The prime reason that even this program went forward was the perceived urgent need for its expected economic stabilization effects through income redistribution (Bellamy, 1965; Lindenfield, 1959). The problem of federal versus provincial authority was to dictate that it would be many years before the bulk of the Marsh and the Heagerty concepts were to be effected and, ultimately, a great deal of the leadership was to come from the provinces rather than the federal government.

Both the Marsh and Heagerty reports formed the basis for a major document considered at a Dominion-Provincial Conference on Reconstruction, which was held in 1945 to foster strategic postwar planning. Proposals in the document stressed the need for cooperation among all levels of government and groups in the country to attain high levels of employment and increased welfare and security. The proposals also outlined strategies to address three main gaps in the system: health insurance, national old age pensions, and unemployment assistance (Dominion-Provincial Conference, 1945).

Because the social security proposals were part of larger proposals relating to financial matters upon which there was not provincial consensus, the innovative concept of comprehensive, integrated, and coordinated national programming for social security was eventually abandoned. This unfortunate outcome impelled the federal and provincial governments to seek ways independently in which to influence health policies. However, the extensive investigations and discussions associated with the conference had established political and social pressures for action that were not to be denied (Taylor, 1987). This pressure toward action in integration of health and welfare services led to the amalgamation of health and welfare under one common federal department in 1944. The act to do so charged the Minister of the new Department of Health and Welfare with responsibility for "all matters relating to the promotion or preservation of the health, social security and social welfare of the people of Canada over which the Parliament of Canada has jurisdiction" (Cameron, 1962, p. 1).

Era Three:
Mid-1940s to Mid-1960s

The third major era in the development of social security policy and programs in Canada, from the mid-1940s to the mid-1960s, was marked by consolidation of a dominant government role in social security and by remarkable progress made at both the federal and provincial levels in establishing a wide range of new programs and in improving those which already existed (Taylor, 1956). With one outstanding exception, it was a period of what might be called "disjointed incrementalism," in the sense that the order in which new programs were implemented, and the relationships between them, were not guided by a formal, rational plan, such as had been conceived at the federal level through the Marsh and Heagerty plans.

The one exception was in the province of Saskatchewan, which was to lead health care planning and programming for all of Canada during the next 20 years. In 1944, the Cooperative Commonwealth Federation (CCF) party came to power. This democratic-socialist, agrarian protest movement put forth a platform promising a "complete system of socialized health services" (Sigerist, 1944, p. 3). Dr. Henry Sigerist of John Hopkins University was then commissioned to develop a formal plan to guide health policy and program development in Saskatchewan.

The most dramatic immediate action of the Saskatchewan government was the establishment, on January 1, 1947, of the Saskatchewan Hospital Services Plan, the first compulsory and comprehensive hospital insurance plan in North America. During the next three years, provincial plans were also implemented in Alberta, B.C., and Newfoundland (Taylor, 1987). As a result of these developments, the provinces requested that health insurance be placed on the agenda of the 1955 federal-provincial conference. Subsequent federal-provincial negotiations resulted in federal proposals to pay approximately 50 per cent of the costs of insured hospital services, based on a cost-sharing formula (Taylor, 1973). By 1958, the federal Hospital Insurance and Diagnostic Services Act was implemented in five provinces; the remaining provinces had all joined the plan by 1961.

Several other important federal programs were also developed during this time. In 1948, the National Health Grants, designed to enable the provinces to establish the foundations for comprehensive health insurance, were introduced. Public health, tuberculosis control, mental health care, venereal disease control, crippled children's diseases, cancer control, professional training, and public health research were targeted by this grants-in-aid program, as were hospital construction and health survey capability (Martin, 1948). A number of positive modifications were also made to income security programs during this era. The majority of these programs had first been recommended in the Marsh and Heagerty reports.

In 1962, Saskatchewan again took the lead in health care when, on July 1, 1962, a medical insurance plan was introduced in the face of adamant opposition from the medical profession, opposition which resulted in the famous "doctor's strike" (Badgely & Wolfe, 1967; Meilicke, 1967; Tollefson, 1964). The fact that public opinion moved against the striking doctors ensured that medical insurance plans could be introduced in other provinces, and eventually at the federal level. In 1964, the Report of the Royal Commission on Health Services headed by Chief Justice Emmett Hall (the first "Hall Commission") was released, and it recommended that the federal government enter into agreements with the provinces to assist them in introducing and operating a "comprehensive, universal, provincial program of personal health services" (Royal Commission, 1964, p. 19). This led, in 1968, to the federal Medical Care Act, which provided for federal sharing of approximately 50 per cent of the costs of a provincial medical insurance plan if it incorporated comprehensive medical coverage, a universally available plan, portable benefit coverage, and public authority administration (the principles of medicare).

Several other federal programs began in the 1960s, including: National Welfare Grants in 1962; a Youth Allowance program in 1964; the Canada Pension Plan in 1965; the Canada Assistance Program in 1966 (a comprehensive program for federal sharing of provincial expenditures for public assistance and for welfare services on a conditional cost-sharing basis similar to that in health); and the Health Resources Act in 1966. This latter provided federal payments over a 15-year period for construction, acquisition, and renovation of facilities for the training of persons in the health professions or occupations associated with health and for research in health fields (Hacon, 1967).

In only 20 years Canada had moved from what has been described as a "backward position in welfare state development by international standards" (Collins, 1976, p. 6) to a level at which at least the major social security programs necessary for a modern industrial nation were in place. The speed of progress, and the scope and range of the programs established, generated a vast array of new problems, which were to become the focus of the next time period.

Era Four:
Mid-1960s to Mid-1970s

The 10-year period from the mid-1960s to the mid-1970s was characterized by the commissioning of special inquiries and reports designed to examine the numerous and complex social security programs established in the previous 20 years, to reassess needs, and to make recommendations for improvements in services, organization, financing, and cost control. One of the most ambitious investigations began in Québec in 1966 with the establishment of the Commission of Inquiry on Health and Social Welfare (the Castonguay-Nepveu Commission). Ontario also established the Committee on the Healing Arts and the Ontario Council of Health in that year. In the years following, almost every province instituted one or more mechanisms of inquiry into general or specific aspects of their respective social security services. (For extensive listings and notes on the most significant of these reports, see Storch and Meilicke [1979] and Browne [1980].)

At the federal level, a range and variety of inquiries were established: a Task Force was set up to look into the costs of health services and attempted to suggest ways to restrain the costs of health care (National Health and Welfare, 1969); a Special Senate Committee on Poverty (1971) highlighted the finding that poverty reflects a social attitude translated into economic and political policies; the Community Health Centre Project suggested people-centred primary care centres (Hastings, 1972); the Health Minister Marc Lalonde (1974) developed *A New Perspective on the Health of Canadians,* which maintained that an emphasis on human biology, environment, and lifestyle, equal to traditional emphasis on health care delivery, was necessary to further improve the health of Canadians; and his *Working Paper on Social Security* (Lalonde, 1973) upheld proposals similar to those of the Marsh Report of 1943 (i.e., the need for an employment strategy, a social insurance strategy, an income supplementation strategy, a social and employment services strategy, and a federal-provincial strategy).

An extremely important reappraisal process began in December 1970 when the federal government initiated a series of discussions regarding new federal-provincial cost-sharing formulas. Dialogue between the federal and provincial governments continued on a rather sporadic basis and, in the summer of 1975, the federal government served notice of its intent to terminate the existing formula for hospital cost sharing. After drawn-out negotiations with the provinces, this led, on April 1, 1977, to the Established Programs Financing Act, whereby federal cost-sharing for both hospital and medical insurance was changed from a conditional grant to a modified block grant system. The intent of this change was to provide a greater provincial flexibility and to facilitate the containment of costs to the federal treasury (Van Loon, 1978).

This fourth era in the development of the Canadian social security program was a time of extensive reappraisal. Although few definitive solutions were found, many problems and issues were more clearly identified and a rich variety of ideas and proposals were generated. Among the themes most frequently heard were that a comprehensive and integrated approach to planning, organizing, administering, and evaluating social security was required, that costs must be controlled, and that quality had to be better defined and controlled.

Era Five: 1977 to 1991

The fifth era was characterized by the federal government's attempts to uphold the principles of health care while reducing its cost commitments to the health enterprise. Still operating within the context of the provisions in the BNA Act, the federal government's only real enforcement mechanism to maintain the principles of accessibility, universality, comprehensiveness, portability, and non-profit administration was the power of withholding grant moneys to coerce conformity. With the change in funding involving block grants and tax point transfers, the financial transfer to the provinces became less valuable than that realized during the period of conditional cost-sharing. Thus, even the threat of withholding a portion of the block grant was not as serious as it once might have been.

By the late 1970s, there were numerous allegations that the provinces were diverting federal moneys that should be spent on health care to other services. There was also a growing practice by physicians to extra-bill (charge patients more than the amount covered by the provincial medical service), a practice potentially in violation of the principles of accessibility to health care. In 1979, Justice Emmett Hall was commissioned by the federal government to investigate the effects of these allegations and these practices on the health services in Canada. In examining the health care system that he and his fellow commissioners had recommended in 1964, Hall chose to broaden the scope of the review to include a focus on lifestyles and health care and on frontier and outpost services. He also incorporated a chapter on nursing proposals, which essentially summarized a brief developed by the Canadian Nurses Association (1980) for this second Hall Commission. The nursing proposals included recommendations for all health professionals to be salaried, for more community health clinics, for nurses as primary care workers, and for nurses as new points of entry to the system. Hall discovered in his review no evidence that federal dollars for health care were being diverted to other programs, but that extra-billing by physicians inhibited reasonable access to services. His findings on the latter issue paved the way for legislation to reinforce the principles of health care (Hall, 1980).

In 1984, the federal government introduced the Canada Health Act, which was intended to replace the Hospital Insurance and Diagnostic Services Act and the Medical Care Act and to re-establish the five principles of medicare. The act was bitterly opposed by the provinces and by organized medicine. The provinces resented intrusion into what they considered their constitutional domain, as did organized medicine. The penalty for lack of adherence to the act was the ability to withhold funds from the block grant transfer; for example, the federal government proposed to withhold one dollar for every dollar the provinces allowed to be paid through user fees or balance billing. The medical profession opposed this constraint on extra-billing and user fees, contending these represented a means for raising health revenues and a means for physicians to express their professional freedom (Taylor, 1987).

The 1980s were witness to endless challenges to this act across the provinces, with a particular challenge from within Ontario in the form of a physicians' strike in 1986. Again, public opinion moved against the doctors in this strike and the medical profession failed to sustain a united front. Ontario banned extra-billing shortly thereafter, and the last province holding out on such a ban (Alberta) banned the practice five weeks later.

During the late 1970s to the late 1980s, numerous government commissions and inquiries were again carried out to examine ways in which health care might be delivered in a more cost-effective manner. The growing cost constraint brought about by a downturn in the economy forced the provinces to a deeper level of consideration of the structure of the health care system and the necessity for major reforms to effect an affordable system. *The Rainbow Report* in Alberta and the *Closer to Home* report from British Columbia are only two of the numerous reports (Angus, 1991) produced at this time calling for fundamental changes in the delivery of health care with a stronger emphasis on health promotion and primary care and repeated suggestions for care outside of institutions.

Era Six: 1990 and Onward

By the 1990s, a dramatic change had occurred in the way health services were to be planned and financed. The federal government had basically restricted its role to the maintenance of five medicare principles and the provincial governments were left with the main responsibility for funding. In the face of growing budgetary deficits, this placed immense pressure on provincial and territorial governments to economize on health expenditures. In turn, this created a climate for change in the organization and management of health services that transcended anything since the foundation for the current system was completed in 1968.

Changes were evident throughout the system, including the frequency of mergers, amalgamations, and regional planning. There was growing activity to refine the operational mission and role of health care organizations and minimize costs associated with inappropriate or unnecessary distribution and utilization of resources. Provincial and territorial funding agencies moved to funding systems that more directly encouraged efficient management of resources, such as funding hospitals based on measurement of severity of illness (Meilicke, 1990). There were also modifications made to narrow the definition of basic health services under the Canada Health Act.

Paralleling these activities were efforts to rationalize technology assessment and distribution, and to improve hospital information systems. This was done to allow more precise definitions of intra-institutional responsibility, to improve the appropriateness of patient placement relative to care alternatives, and to develop guidelines for clinical decision making in physician practice. Health promotion and prevention activities were also expanded, although the investment of funding to elevate the status of these activities was still modest. Changes in delivery systems to focus on community-based services, including family health and preventive programs, and to move health promotion to a more central role in health care were only beginning.

Different patterns of governance, such as regional planning agencies and area health authorities, were also being discussed, planned, and/or enhanced in most provinces. In Saskatchewan, for example, plans were underway to replace the existing 400 separate hospital and agency boards with 30 autonomous health district boards to administer the province's health care budget. Such planning for "health districts" was reminiscent of the work of the Sigerist Commission in the mid-1940s (Sigerist, 1944).

Accepting their fundamental responsibility for health, the provincial ministers of health and their deputies began meeting to share their approaches to health care reform and to unite in their common struggle for cost containment. Once again, the intensity of these deliberations was similar to meetings in 1945, with the distinction that the agenda had changed from one requesting the federal government's assistance in funding health care to an agenda that assumed provincial responsibility and was designed to provide mutual support and consultation to effect health care reform.

The common fundamentals of reform included a desire to improve health status, to reaffirm the principles of the Canada Health Act, to ensure a more cost-effective system, and to provide a continuum of services characterized by a shift from institutional to community-based services, healthy public policy, and health promotion (*Background Paper ...* , 1992). A prime example of unity across the provinces and territories was evident in the commissioning of a study on physician manpower in Canada (Barer & Stoddart, 1991). Not only were the provinces instrumental in examining the numbers of physicians in the system and entering the system, but they also took action to deal with recommendations of the report, such as reductions in medical school enrolment.

By 1993, some clear signals were evident that health care reform was more than rhetoric and that virtually all policies and services were vulnerable to change. As the provinces accepted increasing responsibility for health care, they began to reconsider consumer needs in a more orderly manner—needs for first access care, for continuity of care, for care in emergency, for community care, and for social welfare. In many respects, a return to the ideals promoted in the Marsh and Heagerty reports was becoming evident.

Although history rarely repeats itself, it is clear that similar problems in health care delivery emerge in different contexts across the years. Knowledge of the past, therefore, allows for a respect for that history and a certain degree of wisdom in searching creatively for new solutions while avoiding repetition of past mistakes. A thorough knowledge of the development of Canadian health care delivery is critical to understanding the social, political, and economic forces that have shaped the system and that will continue to influence future changes in the system.

References

Angus, E.E. (1991). *Review of significant health care commissions and task forces in Canada since 1983-84*. Ottawa: Canadian Hospital Association.

Armitage, A. (1975). *Social welfare in Canada: Ideals and realities.* Toronto: McClelland & Stewart.

Background paper on health care reform initiatives (1992). Health Reform Paper for Provincial Health Ministers Meeting in Newfoundland. Saskatchewan: Health Planning & Policy Development Branch.

Badgely, R.F., & Wolfe, S. (1967). *Doctors strike*. Toronto: Macmillan.

Barer, M.L., & Stoddart, G.L. (1991). *Toward integrated medical resource policies in Canada*. Winnipeg: Manitoba Health.

Bellamy, D. (1965). Social welfare in Canada. In *Encyclopedia of social work*. New York: National Association of Social Workers.

Browne, J. (1980). Summary of recent major studies of health care in Canada. In C.A. Meilicke & J.L. Storch (Eds.), *Perspectives on Canadian health and social service policy: History and emerging trends* (pp. 293-305). Ann Arbor, MI: Health Administration Press.

Bryden, K. (1974). *Old age pensions and policy-making in Canada.* Montréal: McGill-Queen's University Press.

Cameron, G.D.W. (1962). The department of national health and welfare. In R.D. Defries (Ed.), *The federal and provincial health services in Canada* (2nd ed.). Toronto: Canadian Public Health Association.

Canadian Nurses Association. (1980). *Putting "health" into health care: Submission to the Health Services Review '79*. Ottawa: Author.

Cassidy, H.M. (1947). The Canadian social services. *The annals of the Academy of Political and Social Science, 253,* 191-198.

Collins, K. (1976, January-February). Three decades of social security in Canada. *Canadian Welfare, 51,* 5-7.

Deber, R., & Vayda, E. (1992). The political and health care systems of Canada and Ontario. In R. Deber (Ed.), *Case studies in Canadian health policy and management* (Vol. 1), (pp. 1-16). Ottawa: Canadian Hospital Association Press.

Dominion-Provincial Conference on Reconstruction. (1945). *Proposals of the Government of Canada*. Paper presented at the meeting of Dominion-Provincial Conference on Reconstruction. Ottawa: Queen's Printer.

Gelber, S.M. (1966, June). The path to health insurance. *Canadian Public Administration, 9,* 211-220.

Gelber, S.M. (1973). *Personal health services in Canada: The early years.* Address to the Association of University Programs in Hospital Administration, Faculty Institute, Ottawa.

Gregoire, J. (1962). The ministry of health of the province of Quebec. In R.D. Defries (Ed.), *The federal and provincial health services in Canada* (2nd ed.). Toronto: Canadian Public Health Association.

Hacon, W.S. (1967). Improving Canada's health manpower resources. *The Canadian Medical Association Journal, 97,* 1104-1108.

Hall, E.M. (1980). *A commitment for renewal: Canada's national-provincial health program for the 1980s.* Ottawa: Health & Welfare Canada.

Hastings, J.E.F. (1972). *The community health centre: Report of the community health centre project to the health ministers* (Vol. 1). Ottawa: Information Canada.

Hastings, J.E.F., & Mosley, W. (1966). *Organized community health services.* Report to the Royal Commission on Health Services. Ottawa: Queen's Printer.

Heagerty, J.J. (1934). The development of public health in Canada. *Canadian Journal of Public Health, 25,* 54-56.

Heagerty, J.J. (1943). *Report of the advisory committee on health insurance.* Ottawa: Queen's Printer.

Lalonde, M. (1973). *Working paper on social security.* Ottawa: Government of Canada.

Lalonde, M. (1974). *A new perspective on the health of Canadians: A working document.* Ottawa: National Health & Welfare.

Lindenfield, R. (1959). Hospital insurance in Canada. *Social Service Review, 33,* 149.

Marsh, L. (1975). *Report on social security for Canada: 1943.* Toronto: University of Toronto Press. [Original work prepared in 1943.]

Martin, P. (1948). A national health program for Canada. *Canadian Journal of Public Health, 39,* 220-223.

Meilicke, C.A. (1967). *The Saskatchewan medical care dispute of 1962: An analytical social history.* Unpublished doctoral dissertation, University of Minnesota.

Meilicke, C.A. (1990). International perspectives on healthcare: Canada. *Healthcare Executive, 5* (4), 25-26.

Morgan, J.S. (1961). Social welfare services in Canada. In M. Oliver (Ed.), *Social purpose for Canada.* Toronto: University of Toronto Press.

Najman, J.M., & Western, J.S. (1984). A comparative analysis of Australian health policy in the 1970s. *Social Science & Medicine, 18* (1), 949-958.

National Health & Welfare Canada: Task Force on the Cost of Health Services in Canada. (1969) *Report: Summary* (Vol. 1), (1969). Ottawa: National Health & Welfare.

Rorem, R.C. (1931). *The municipal doctor system in rural Saskatchewan.* Chicago: University of Chicago Press.

Royal Commission on Health Services. (1964). *Report: Royal Commission on Health Services* (Vol. 1). Ottawa: Queen's Printer.

Sigerist, H.E. (1944). *Saskatchewan Health Services Commission: Report of the Commissioner.* Regina: King's Printer.

Special Senate Committee on Poverty. (1971). *Poverty in Canada: Report of the Special Senate Committee on Poverty.* Ottawa: Information Canada.

Splane, R.B. (1965). *Social welfare in Ontario: A study of public welfare administration.* Toronto: University of Toronto Press.

Storch, J.L., & Meilicke, C.A. (1979). *Health and social services administration: An annotated bibliography*. Ottawa: Canadian College of
Health Service Executives.

Taylor, M.G. (1949). *The Saskatchewan hospital services plan.*
Unpublished doctoral dissertation, University of California,
Berkeley.

Taylor, M.G. (1956). *The administration of health insurance in Canada.*
Toronto: Oxford University Press.

Taylor, M.G. (1973, January-February). The Canadian health insurance
program. *Public Administration Review, 33*, 35.

Taylor, M.G. (1987). *Health insurance and Canadian public policy: The
seven decisions that created the Canadian health insurance system*
(2nd ed.). Montréal: McGill-Queen's University Press.

Tollefson, E.A. (1964). *Bitter medicine: The Saskatchewan medical care
dispute.* Saskatoon: Modern Press.

Van Loon, R.J. (1978, Winter). From shared cost to block funding and
beyond. *Journal of Health Politics, Policy & Law, 2,* 460.

Van Loon, R.J. & Wittington, M.S. (1976). *The Canadian political system:
Environment, structure and process* (2nd ed.). Toronto: McGraw-
Hill Ryerson.

Wallace, E. (1950). The origin of the social welfare state in Canada, 1867-
1900. *Canadian Journal of Economics & Political Science, 16,* 384.

Demographic and Epidemiological Trends

L. Jane Knox

L. Jane Knox, RN, BScN (Saskatchewan), MN (Dalhousie), was Executive Director, Community Health—Prevention Services Branch, Saskatchewan Health at the time this chapter was written. She has contributed to the health of the Canadian people as a community nurse, educator, manager, and senior government administrator. Her primary professional interest is to improve the cost effectiveness of health care by focussing on prevention.

Demographic and epidemiological trends of the early 1990s will influence health needs of the Canadian population well into the next century. Demography studies the characteristics of a people, including population growth, age, and mortality. Epidemiology analyzes disease patterns and appropriate interventions. Together, they are invaluable tools for all health professionals and policy makers.

Accurate predictions of the long term need and demand for various types of health care can be achieved only if demographic and epidemiological trends are used as a foundation for knowledge of health care needs. Use of these demographic and epidemiological trends helps to ensure that health care is relevant to society and effective in improving the health of individuals.

In this chapter, the author reviews some of the basic background for study of these trends and identify eight areas where current trends will affect health care in Canada during the next decade. These eight areas—population growth in general, and needs of various age groups, such as infants, children, youth, adults, and seniors, and of special population groups, such as immigrants and aboriginal peoples—will be discussed in some detail, with illustration of some of the factors that can be identified and have effects on health care. Nurse managers need to be conversant with these trends, keep abreast of new research in these areas, and recognize how these factors will affect planning of health services in their specific work areas.

Uses of Demographic and Epidemiological Information

Epidemiology is "the study of the distribution and determinants of health related states and events in specified populations and the application of this study to the control of health problems" (Last, 1983, p. 42). Epidemiology can be used to diagnose the actual or potential health problems of a community and to measure improvements or deterioration in the health of the population. It includes health hazard appraisal, assessment of risks to health, and search for causes of illness.

Determinants of health include both *causes* of illness and *risk factors* that influence the development of disease. The specific cause of a disease might be the tubercle bacillus or smoking leading to lung cancer or radiation resulting in leukemia. Factors influencing the risk of disease include personal susceptibility factors (e.g., age, sex, race, genetics, nutritional condition) and environmental factors (e.g., living conditions, lifestyle, occupation) (Tyler & Last, 1992, p. 12). Both personal and environmental factors are important in determining health, rendering epidemiology a highly complex field. However, each disease develops because specific determinants are present simultaneously. For example, there is considerable international agreement that the major risk factors for cardiovascular disease include smoking, dietary habits, physical inactivity, and lack of psychosocial support (Victoria Declaration, 1993).

A careful study of the epidemiology of a disease will identify risk groups and the services required to reduce disease and maintain health most effectively. Epidemiology can thus be used for both program planning and quality assurance.

Demography is "the study of populations, especially with reference to size and density, fertility, mortality, growth, age distribution, migration, and vital statistics, and the interaction of all these with social and economic conditions" (Last, 1983, p. 36). Policy makers, administrators, and nurses who make frequent use of demographic information can avoid health policies and services that are no longer appropriate for the populations they serve.

Unfortunately, demographic studies are rarely used,

resulting in an expensive, almost unmanageable Canadian health system. Thus, in the 1990s, despite a rapidly growing population of seniors, Canada has a health system that focusses on institutions, drugs, and "high tech" treatments for preventable diseases. Policy makers must use demographics and insist that health services respond to the needs identified by both the demographic characteristics and the epidemiological trends.

Population Growth

Dumas (1990) reported that the Canadian population was growing at a rate of approximately 1.3% in 1989. Both *immigration* and *births* contribute to growth in population. Canada's crude birth rate (live births per 1000 population) dropped from 26.1 in 1961 to 14.4 in 1987, followed by annual increases to 15.3 in 1991 (Wadhera & Strachan, 1992). The foreign born have represented approximately 16% of the Canadian population on a consistent basis since 1951 (Badets, 1990). Immigration is playing an increasing role as Canadian fertility rates are below the replacement level (Dumas, 1990, p. 1; Women in Canada, 1990, p. 11).

In *Charting Canada's Future,* Health and Welfare Canada (1989) projects that, if current trends continue, the Canadian population will reach a peak of 28 million in 2011, then will begin a long decline. However, Canada's population continues to grow at present, due in part to the large proportion of population currently of child bearing age. Since the late 1970s, the total fertility rate has remained fairly stable, at roughly 1.7 children per woman, less than in 1959 when it was almost 4 children per woman (Dumas, 1990, p. 21; Women in Canada, 1990, p. 11).

Canada's so-called "baby boom" began in the late 1930s with an upward swing in births and became more marked following World War II (Health & Welfare Canada, 1989, p. 17). The greatest number of births occurred between 1955 and 1970, so that by 1990 the oldest were approaching age 50 and even the youngest of the baby boom generation had reached age 20. As they entered the job market, baby boomers created fierce demand for available jobs and left behind an excess capacity in schools and pediatric wards (Kettle, 1980). Because this group of 20- to 50-year-olds now represents the largest proportion of people in the Canadian population, their views, health behaviours, and disease patterns will have a significant impact on the Canadian health system during this decade and into the early part of the next century.

Infants

One of the best measures of the health of a population is the *infant mortality rate* (children who die at less than one year of age). Infant mortality is declining in Canada, although there still is room for improvement. Dumas (1990, p. 27) reports that, excluding Japan, where the World Health Organization has questioned the methodology, Sweden has the lowest infant mortality at 5.8 per 1000, as of 1986. Canada has the second lowest rate at 7.2 per 1000. However, this rate fluctuates across Canada. Avard and Hanvey (1989) found that, in 1985, Newfoundland and Saskatchewan rates were 1.5 times greater than those in Ontario and Québec. In some provinces there are pockets of the population where the infant mortality rate rises to as high as 16 per 1000 from time to time (Statistics Canada, 1991, p. 71). Many of these are preventable deaths.

During the 1980s, the leading causes of death for Canadian children under one year of age were perinatal conditions and birth defects (Avard & Hanvey, 1989; Statistics Canada, 1990). Together, these two causes accounted for almost 75% of the infant deaths. *Low birth weight* remains the main risk factor associated with infant death. Statistics Canada's report *Children of Canada, Children of the World* (1990) states that "a constant average of 6 percent of Canadian infants of the past ten years have been born at or below 2500 grams" (the accepted World Health Organization definition of low birth weight) (p. 39). The critical factors associated with low birth weight include poor nutrition, use of tobacco, alcohol, or drugs, multiple births, and, most important, low socioeconomic status (Avard & Hanvey, 1989, p. 35; Millar, Strachan, & Wadhera, 1993).

Infant mortality continues to decline in Canada; early intervention is improving the survival rate for infants, but increasing numbers of these children have disabilities (Statistics Canada, 1991, p. 106). The effects of low birth weight, which include cerebral palsy, learning disabilities, visual and auditory defects, and other deficits in physical and mental development, are usually irreversible (Millar et al., 1993).

Most Canadian children are remarkably healthy, but some infants require hospitalization, most often for injuries or respiratory illnesses such as bronchitis, acute infections, and pneumonia (Avard & Hanvey, 1989, p. 28). Breast feeding is one of the most important preventive measures a family can take to avoid respiratory illness. Correct use of child restraints would also prevent some hospital admissions. A 1987 Transport Canada survey (cited in

Avard & Hanvey, 1989) found that only 38% of infants were properly restrained in Alberta compared to 70% in New Brunswick, and that the national average for safe use of child restraints was well below 50%. These epidemiological findings about infants indicate that nurses still have work to do in educating and motivating parents. Nurse managers in community health may need to consider such findings when planning new programs.

Children

Statistics Canada (1990) reports that, as of the 1986 census, there were 5.4 million children in Canada and these were evenly distributed across the age groups 0-4, 5-9, and 10-14. Children represented only 21% of the Canadian population in 1986, compared with 30% in 1971; there will be a further drop to 19% by 2001. Only 85% of children lived in husband-wife families in 1986, with 13% living in lone parent families and 2% living with relatives or friends (Crégheur & Devereaux, 1991, p. 4). Of the 13% living in lone parent families in 1986, about 1 in 5 had parents who were single and never married, while 3 in 5 had separated or divorced parents (Statistics Canada, 1990). In Canada in 1985, almost 1 in 2 marriages ended in divorce after a median duration of 10.9 years (Dumas, 1990, pp. 86-87); thus children coping with divorce may be very young, and face emotional stress, conflict, and confusion.

Preschoolers are beginning to walk, run, jump, and climb. Their constant motion increases their risk of injury, particularly as their language and cognitive skills are insufficiently developed for them to understand fully any potential danger. Accidents are the leading cause of death for children ages 1 to 4 (King, Gartrell, & Trovato, 1991), with motor vehicle accidents, burns, and drowning being the most frequent types of accidents causing death. In 1985, 54% of motor vehicle accident fatalities for this age group involved children who were pedestrians (Avard & Hanvey, 1989, p. 41).

For school-age children (5-14 years), the death rate from all causes dropped by 50% between 1970 and 1985, largely due to a reduction in deaths from accidents involving motor vehicles (Avard & Hanvey, 1989). However, in the late 1980s, school-age children still died at the rate of 24 per 100 000 children in this age group. Fifty-five per cent of these deaths were due to injuries, and more than half of the injuries were the result of motor vehicle accidents. Of the motor vehicle accidents that resulted in death, in 33% the child was an occupant in the car, in 31% a pedestrian, and in 20% a bicyclist (Avard & Hanvey, 1989, pp. 54-57).

Many children still do not wear seat belts or bicycle helmets or use other readily available methods of preventing accidents and injury. This is alarming when you consider that for every school-age child killed, 90 are injured, and many of these require hospital care (Avard & Hanvey, 1989, p. 57). Failure to use bicycle helmets is also common among teenagers. MacMillan and Jantzie (1993) found that only 17% of males and 11% of females reported helmet use in an Alberta study of 500 teens (average age 15.8 years). A vigorous multidimensional health promotion approach is needed to prevent disabilities and deaths caused by accidents.

In 1986, 5% of Canada's children were disabled; of these, 99% live in households rather than institutions (Nessner, 1990). The percentage of people who are disabled rises with each age group, by age 10-14 to 6.4%, by age 35-44 to 9%, and by age 65 and over to 46% (Nessner, 1990). The most common disabilities among children are learning disabilities, hearing, vision, or speech problems, mental handicaps, and psychiatric problems.

Teens

In a fascinating report of a study of the values and views of more than 3500 Canadian teenagers, Bibby and Posterski (1992) advise that there appears to be increasing emphasis on the individual over the group in Canadian society, and that there is a reduction in the value placed on interpersonal relationships, including the value placed on the goals of friendship, being loved, and recognition. However, as a source of enjoyment, friendships and music still rank highest. Friendship, love, and recognition are gradually becoming understood as significant determinants of health in Canadian society. Some researchers label them as psychosocial supports (Victoria Declaration, 1993). For teenagers who are in the midst of learning and earning an identity and lifestyle separate from their parents, psychosocial supports are critical for health.

Bibby and Posterski (1992) also report that sexual activity "has become fairly commonplace among Canadian young people, something taken pretty much for granted as an enjoyable part of life" (p. 27). Their research suggests that, after a few dates, approval levels are as follows: 99% for kissing, 96% for necking, 86% for petting, and 56% for intercourse. Considering the threat of AIDS, such views may be alarming for parents, especially those in Québec where young people were more likely to approve of both petting (95%) and sexual intercourse (70%) after a few dates. There were few other significant differences by region, but the differences between young men and women were pronounced, with about 75% of males approving of sex within a few dates while only 40% of the females would agree. Bibby and Posterski (1992) emphasized there has been "virtually no change in attitudes over the past decade for either males or females" (p. 28).

The rate of teenage pregnancies declined from 53.4 to 44.1 per 1000 teenage girls in the time period 1975 to 1989 according to Statistics Canada (as reported by Canadian Press, Ottawa, May 10, 1992). The rate of pregnancy among adolescents (15-19 years) in Canada has now stabilized at 38 per 1000 (Children of Canada ... , 1990, p. 39). Approximately 85% of 15- to 19-year-olds have taken sex education courses and 90% believe that they are "fairly knowledgeable about birth control" (Bibby & Posterski, 1992, p. 38).

In spite of extensive publicity given to AIDS in the late 1980s, this widespread reporting has not contributed to "an overall decrease in sexual activity. . . ; abstinence has not risen in popularity" (Bibby & Posterski, 1992, p. 38). Although teens reported that they thought awareness of AIDS had changed, only 2 in 3 of the 55% of teens who reported they were sexually active also admitted to having altered their sexual habits.

Unfortunately, alteration of sexual habits is lower in Québec than elsewhere. Only 3 in 4 Canadian teenagers who are engaging in sex are using some form of birth control and it is estimated that 2 in 4 are not using condoms as a means of engaging in safer sex (Bibby & Posterski, 1992, p. 47). These findings have enormous implications. Both pregnant teens and their infants are likely to be at risk of ill health in both the short and long term (Jacono, Jacono, St. Onge, Van Oosten, & Meininger, 1992). In addition, the danger of exposure to HIV is very real for sexually active teens as there is evidence that HIV has entered the Canadian adolescent population, particularly among intravenous drug users (Remis & Sutherland, 1993).

Not all sexually active teenagers are willing participants. In a 1990 survey of more than 3000 young people, most of whom were aged 13-16, Holmes and Silverman (1992, p. 19) found that almost 1 in 5 young women and 1 in 10 young men had been sexually abused. The same study suggested that denial and silence about sexual abuse contribute to the harm done by the experience. Therapy regarding abusive experiences may require special expertise, but every adult has a responsibility to be an alert, sensitive, and supportive listener.

King and Coles (1992) report that "by age 15 over a quarter of Canadian youths drink alcohol at least once a week, and 60% have been drunk at least once" (p. 95). The use of nonmedicinal drugs has declined but, by age 15, 24% of boys and 29% of girls say they smoke. However, the incidence of smoking among 15- to 19-year-olds has been dropping since 1978 (McKie, 1990, p. 88; Pederson, 1993, p. 92). King and Coles (1992) believe that smoking behaviour is most prevalent in subgroups of young people who are difficult to reach and do not respond to educational programs which are already in existence.

In the area of physical activity, only 40% of Canadian girls and 60% of Canadian boys expect to be involved in physical activity at age 20 (King & Coles, 1992). Canadian young people between the ages of 11 and 15 report that they spend their leisure time as follows: 61-65% watch at least 2-3 hours of television a day, 60-71% watch VCR movies for at least 1-3 hours a week, and 13-57% play computer games at least 1-3 hours a week. In each case, the range includes both male and female ratings and a breakdown by age group. Physical activity is essential for health and stress management. Advocacy for supportive environments is urgently needed in addition to education to raise the awareness of parents and children about the health benefits of physical activity throughout life.

Canadian youth experience strain in their relationships with their parents and with each other and this trend is especially pronounced with girls (King & Coles, 1992). Young Canadians tend to be aggressive in their relationships and experience more bullying than children in European countries. King and Coles (1992, p. 96) report that Canadian educators are investigating interventions designed to increase respect and understanding.

The strong links among health risk behaviours suggest the need to create supportive environments for health and then to focus health programs for particular target groups. King and Coles (1992) emphasize that smokers are drinkers and substance abusers, and are less likely to be physically active and more likely to have poor diets. They are also more likely to have poor self-esteem, difficulties in relationships with parents, and poor adjustment to school. They suggest that "this pattern contributes to the formation of peer groups alienated from school and home and to reaching out to each other for comfort and acceptance. These groups typically share anti-social values or participate in behaviours that put them at risk" (p. 96). Ultimately, children need more acceptance, understanding, and positive opportunities for success. Powerful group forces exist among young people and these must be considered both in planning comprehensive health programs aimed at high-risk groups and in targeting an array of complex health risk factors, including smoking, substance abuse, malnutrition, and lack of physical activity.

Adult Mortality and Health

In 1990, various kinds of cardiovascular disease represented the leading cause of death (39% of all deaths) for adults in Canada. Cancer continues to be the second leading cause of death (27%), with accidents causing 7% of all deaths. All other causes combined represented 27% of all deaths in Canada in 1990 (Cardiovascular disease in Canada, 1993, p. 4). Statistics Canada (1991) suggest that "preventive measures could reduce the incidence of lung cancer and heart disease by up to half" (p. 95).

It is strange that, although "more than 90 percent of Canadians recognize that heart disease is preventable" (Cardiovascular disease in Canada, 1993, p. 37), the direct and indirect costs of *cardiovascular illness* continue to be greater than for any other disease. Many Canadians do not recognize that a high fat diet, physical inactivity, hypertension, and oral contraceptive/estrogen therapy are all risk factors for cardiovascular disease; one risk factor that is recognized is smoking (Cardiovascular disease in Canada, 1993).

Cardiovascular disease results from a combination of risk factors, so when several risk factors are present a much higher risk occurs (Victoria Declaration, 1993, p. 18). These risk factors are part of the lifestyle and living conditions of large numbers of adults in Canada. Despite a gradual reduction in the prevalence of these risk factors over a 25-year period, the 1991 General Social Survey (Millar, 1992) found that, of Canadians aged 15 and over, 26% smoked daily and about 68% were not physically active. In the same survey, 23% of the population aged 20 to 64 were overweight, 6% more than those who were overweight in 1985. Overweight was more common among men (28%) than women (18%) (Millar, 1992). More weight reduction messages need to be targeted at men, including increased physical activity and decreased fat intake.

The International Heart Health Conference held in Victoria in 1992 emphasized the importance of using a public health approach with four cornerstones as the main thrust of heart health policy: reduced smoking, improved dietary habits, and increased physical activity, in combination with improved psychosocial support, "would lead to profound cardiovascular health benefits" (Victoria Declaration, 1993, p. 24).

More than 1 in 3 Canadians will develop some form of *cancer* in their lifetime; 1 in 4 deaths in Canada are due to this disease (Gaudette & Roberts, 1990). However, there are variations in the trends for major types of cancer. Gaudette and Roberts (1990) reported changes in the incidence and mortality of various types of cancers in Canada over the past 20 years. The incidence (new cases) of lung cancer is increasing rapidly, especially among women. Female deaths from lung cancer doubled between 1978 and 1988 (Statistics Canada, 1991, p. 97), although mortality rates are now fairly stable as a result of new drugs and treatment technologies.

The incidence of prostate cancer is rising, largely because of improved diagnostic procedures being used with elderly men. Breast cancer is now affecting 1 in 10 Canadian women during their lifetime, but the incidence rate is fairly stable. This is also true for cervical and uterine cancer. The mortality rate for both these cancers has declined in Canada during the past 20 years. The incidence for colorectal cancer and melanoma have been increasing. The incidence of melanoma is increasing sharply in spite of public knowledge of the dangers of exposure to the sun without sunscreen or other protection.

More people are living with cancer rather than dying from it, which is another factor contributing to the expense of cancer care. With the number of elderly Canadians rising and an increase in costly new drugs and treatment technologies, "the cost of caring for cancer patients is a major concern" (Gaudette & Roberts, 1990, p. 73). It is troublesome that the risk factors for cancer are not well understood. There is a need to act strongly against proven risk factors, such as smoking and low fibre diets, if rising costs of cancer care are to be controlled and suffering and loss of life from this disease are to be reduced.

Accidents, assaults, and suicides are also major causes of death and hospital admission among adult Canadians, with alcohol abuse being a significant risk factor associated with these events (Statistics Canada, 1991, pp. 95-97). Canadians are generally not heavy drinkers, and the proportion of those consuming 14 or more drinks per week has been declining even among males aged 20-24 (McKie, 1990). However, in 1991, 55% of the population aged 15 and over consumed alcohol at least once monthly with the peak of drinking frequency at ages 20-24 when 80% of men and 58% of women consume alcohol at least monthly (Millar, 1992). This is also the age group in which drinking is heaviest for men, with 19% of Canadians aged 20-24 consuming 14 or more drinks per week. Perhaps not surprisingly in view of dating patterns, heavy drinking peaks for women at age 15-19 (Millar, 1992). Drinking is least likely to be heavy for men aged 15-19 compared to older men (Millar, 1992).

Too many Canadian drivers are fatally injured in motor

vehicle accidents. According to Transport Canada (1992), in 1990 about 80.5% of fatally injured drivers were tested for blood alcohol concentration; of these, 49.6% of male drivers and 28% of female drivers had been drinking. The highest proportion of alcohol impairment (48.7%) occurred among 26- to 35-year-olds (Transport Canada, 1992, p. 2). Alcohol use was considerably higher among fatally injured truck or van drivers and motorcyclists than among automobile drivers. Fortunately, overall there has been a general downward trend, but in 1990, 41.7% of fatally injured drivers who were tested had been drinking (Transport Canada, 1992).

Deaths due to suicide have doubled since 1960. In 1986, suicide deaths were at an all time Canadian high of 15.1 suicides for every 100 000 population, well beyond the 10 suicides per 100 000 population recorded in the 1930s (Beneteau, 1990). Suicide rates for young adult men have risen dramatically and tend to be violent (such as from firearms, strangulation); the highest suicide rates for women occur in the age group 50-54 and more commonly involve medication or vehicle exhausts (Beneteau, 1990).

Although accidents, suicides, and myocardial infarctions are common causes of death and injury for men, *women's health conditions* tend to be associated with less dramatic chronic conditions that can lead to long term disability. The General Social Survey of 1985 reported (cited in Women in Canada, 1990, p. 127) that of Canadian women age 15 and over who were surveyed 1 in 4 had arthritis or rheumatism, 1 in 5 hypertension, and 1 in 10 respiratory illness. Only 1 in 20 had heart conditions, and 3 in 100 had diabetes.

In the 65 and over age group, 2 out of 3 were experiencing arthritis or rheumatism and 4 out of 10 had hypertension. Heart conditions, respiratory illness, and use of sleeping pills were each reported by 1 in 5 of the surveyed Canadian women 65 years and over. As Ferrence (1993) has noted: "Women live longer than men but have more health problems when they are alive. . . based on such measures as visits to physicians or prescriptions for medications" (p. 242). Such findings may be explainable by the chronic nature of health conditions experienced by women, including arthritis and osteoporosis. These diseases are more likely to result in regular physician visits and ongoing prescription medications.

Despite their frequent experience with these painful diseases, women report good health at the same rate as men but slightly more of them report activity limitation as early as age 40. This may be a result of their greater likelihood to have diseases such as cancer, arthritis, and anemia, which often cause physical limitations (Ferrence, 1993, p. 243).

Strike (1990b) presents a helpful summary review of the nature and prevalence of *sexually transmitted diseases* in Canada, highlighting dramatic increases in herpes and chlamydia, which are not life threatening, and in AIDS. Although Canada had a relatively small number of reported cases of AIDS in the early 1990s, it is expected that AIDS will soon begin to affect general mortality rates, even in this country. Already AIDS has become an important cause of death for males aged 20 to 40. According to Dumas (1990, p. 35), it is second only to accidents as a cause of death for Canadian males in this age group.

Most AIDS patients in Canada live in Ontario, Québec, and British Columbia, with men aged 20-49 making up 83% of diagnosed cases (Strike, 1990a). More than 80% of all cases of AIDS in Canada in 1987 were in homosexual or bisexual men, with only 3% being intravenous drug abusers and 5% being people from countries where HIV is widespread. Recipients of blood transfusions, heterosexuals, children, and people for whom risk factors were not identified accounted for a total of 12% of all cases in Canada in 1987 (Strike, 1990a). A multisectoral initiative is needed to prevent an epidemic of AIDS in Canada.

Experience in countries where the AIDS epidemic is in full force demonstrates that this disease attacks young people who are exposed to HIV as teenagers or young adults, are diagnosed as having AIDS in their early 30s, and are dead before they reach age 45. In developing countries where AIDS is widespread among the heterosexual community, the significance of these ages is great because young children are often left without both parents. This tragedy may soon be appearing in Canada as the number of heterosexuals with AIDS had doubled (to 4%) by 1992 (Quarterly surveillance update, 1993).

Mortality increases at all ages as *income* decreases (Dumas, 1990, p. 33), and the income of many Canadians is decreasing (Bramhan & Hamilton, 1993). Unattached seniors and female single parents are the most likely to have low incomes (Ng, 1992). Health and illness patterns are influenced by income in part because of living conditions and health hazards (both in the environment and in the work place), but there is also a relationship with risk factors, such as diet, physical activity, and smoking, which can be controlled by low income individuals. Green and Simons-Morton (1991) state that "behaviours and knowledge associated with increasing income and higher education level included lower prevalence of obesity and cigarette smoking, greater exercise and sports participation, greater use of preventive health services for PAP smears and breast examinations, and greater use of seat belts" (p. 189).

More than knowledge is necessary. Green and Simons-Morton (1991) point out that skills, resources, and motivation are also required for sustained behaviour change. In addition, health behaviours are closely associated with self-esteem and peer group membership (King & Coles, 1992, p. 96). Ineffective attempts to change behaviour can result in frustration, disappointment, and defense mechanisms, and these make individuals more difficult to reach on subsequent attempts. Managers of health promotion programs have a clear responsibility to "do it right the first time."

Immigrants

Immigrants are an increasingly important part of the Canadian population, bringing creativity, cultural richness, and hope for economic growth and stability. Immigrants continue to represent 16% of the total Canadian population, a percentage that has remained stable since 1951 (Badets, 1990). However, during those years, there has been a shift in the country of origin so that in the 1990s people born in Asia represent the majority of immigrants to Canada, followed by Europeans and those born in the Caribbean and Central or South America. Knowledge of the country of origin is important, as people bring with them dietary and other cultural habits (such as smoking) as well as other risk factors for disease. Most immigrants live in large cities in the provinces of Ontario, British Columbia, Alberta, and Manitoba (Badets, 1990; Dumas, 1990).

The 1986 census data (Badets, 1990) show the immigrant population as being older (17% were aged 65 and over compared to 9% of nonimmigrants). They are also better educated; 12% of those aged 15 and over had a university degree compared with 9% of nonimmigrant adults.

Immigrant women who participated in the 1986 census reported that they had relatively little formal education, with 26% having less than Grade 9 education compared to 16% of nonimmigrant women (Badets, 1990). More recent arrivals have higher levels of education. As a result of these educational differences, immigrant men are more likely to work in professional occupations or managerial and processing positions. Immigrant women are more likely to work in the garment industry or in service occupations. The Canadian Task Force on Mental Health Issues Affecting Immigrants and Refugees (1988, pp. 77-78) reports that lack of access to language training, lower education, and limited employment opportunities are contributing to special mental health needs for immigrant women.

These demographic and epidemiological trends should sound an alert for health system managers. Culturally appropriate care requires understanding of factors that influence health and illness behaviours. As Giger and Davidhizar (1990) state, "Culturally diverse nursing care must take into account six cultural phenomena that vary with application and use, yet are evidenced among all cultural groups: (1) communication, (2) space, (3) social organization, (4) time, (5) environmental control, and (6) biological variations" (p. 199). Quality health care is planned and implemented when professionals and health managers insist on an evaluation of the appropriateness of all of these elements of care.

Aboriginal Issues

For many Canadian health professionals, the most significant cultural group is the native population (status and nonstatus Indians, Inuit, and Métis). Perhaps the primary issue during the 1990s is a governance issue. Since 1984, Canadian policy makers have aimed to strengthen Indian autonomy, with Indian communities governing themselves (Statistics Canada, 1991, p. 77). The control of health care decision making has become a significant goal for First Nations people, particularly where aboriginal peoples represent 5-20% of the population, as in the Northwest Territories, Yukon, Saskatchewan, and Manitoba.

Politicians of all cultural backgrounds and political persuasions have been challenged to find ways to increase aboriginal involvement in decision making and control of health services because Canada's fiscal situation does not allow for duplicate, parallel health systems. In some areas, groups of Indian Bands have formed corporations called Tribal Councils. Among other functions, these councils may coordinate health care on reserves. Some are developing considerable expertise in the delivery of culturally appropriate health care (Scott, 1991).

Every health care manager who participates in discussions with First Nations people at *any* level must accept responsibility for learning about the issues. Ponting (1990) found that Canadians generally are not knowledgeable about aboriginal issues; his article contains a glossary of terms, which is a good place to begin this education process.

The 1986 Canadian census found that 3% of the total Canadian population reported native origins, whether Indian, Inuit, or Métis (Statistics Canada, 1991). Variations from this national percentage are considerable across the country and the figure has been questioned by aboriginal leaders, who feel that the participation rate of aboriginal people in the 1986 census was limited. It is also possible that some people do not claim their aboriginal heritage. Of Canada's 260 000 aboriginal children, in 1986, 39% were of North American Indian origin only, with 34% having origins in Indian and some other non-aboriginal culture (McDonald, 1991).

Regardless of the actual size of the aboriginal population in a particular area, Canada's aboriginal population has unique demographic characteristics. First, 58% of aboriginals are under age 25, compared to 37% in the total population (Statistics Canada, 1991, p. 77). Second, the birth rate of aboriginal women tends to be almost twice that of all Canadian women (Avard & Hanvey, 1989, p. 108). This is especially true in the prairie provinces. As a result, the Indian population is growing rapidly. By the late 1990s, the already urgent need for culturally appropriate health care will increase dramatically.

Canada's Indian, Inuit, and Métis people suffer much more ill health than the rest of the Canadian population, although measurement of the differences is difficult (Mao, Moloughney, Semenciw, & Morrison, 1992). For example, Canada's aboriginal peoples experience death rates from stroke 40% above the Canadian average (Cardiovascular disease in Canada, 1993). Aboriginal women experience higher death rates for ischemic heart disease and stroke, and for uterine and cervical cancer (Mao et al., 1992). During the 1980s, some of these differences began to disappear but the rate of ischemic heart disease among aboriginal women continues to climb. Risk factors for cardiovascular disease are observably higher among the aboriginal population, including smoking, obesity, diabetes, and high blood pressure (Cardiovascular disease in Canada, 1993, p. 9) and participation in cancer prevention programs may be as much as 30% lower (Hislop, Deschamps, Band, Smith, & Clark, 1992).

Suicide rates are also much higher for Canada's aboriginal people. Beneteau (1990) reports that, in 1986, the suicide rate for native women was 11.8 per 100 000 native women compared to 6.4 for all Canadian women. Native men died from suicide at a rate of 2.5 times the national average for men, 56.3 compared to 22.8 per 100 000. Young native men are particularly affected with 100 suicides for every 100 000 native men aged 15 to 29. Risk factors associated with suicide may include unemployment, low self-esteem, hopelessness, family stress, and loss of one parent (Kettle, 1980, pp. 110, 111, 143). Clearly the tragedy of suicide among aboriginal people will require action and cooperation from a wide cross-section of society.

Aging Society

Canada's population of elderly persons is expected to triple between 1986 and 2031 (Stone & Fletcher, 1986). This startling fact is already shaping the health system and contributing to health policies that promote mobility and general well-being rather than institutionalization. Such a welcome change is being readily accepted by the elderly, who see this as a quality-of-life issue, as well as by policy makers, who see it as a cost saving measure.

Tripling the size of the over-75-year-old population should not require a tripling in the supply of nursing home beds. It is essential, however, to ensure that supportive environments help the 50- to 60-year-olds of the 1990s to remain active and fit. In addition, more targeted programming (perhaps in the workplace) is needed for this age group, particularly for women, given their longer life expectancy. Small investments now will significantly reduce expenditures later. During the 1990s, Canada's seniors commonly require support services or institutionalization after age 75. Pushing that age to 85 is an important goal for Canada as the size and proportion of the seniors' population increases.

Burke (1991) discusses the social and pension implications of the rapid rise in the proportion of Canadians who will be over 65; that proportion will reach nearly 1 in 5 by 2021. In the meantime, the focus has been on the implications for health care costs of this shift in age of the population. Canada needs programs that help seniors to be independent, healthy, and active—with an emphasis on self-help, mutual aid, and coordinated volunteers. Supportive environments for independent living for the elderly require the attention of the food industry, housing officials, recreational professionals (Priest, 1990), and occupational therapists. In future, the Canadian health system will need to facilitate cost-effective care for seniors at home and will need to focus on maintaining mobility and independence even if institutionalization is required.

In planning for the aging of the population, a number of factors require attention. First, the proportion of elderly will vary across the country and within provinces. Stone and Fletcher (1986) report that Alberta and Newfoundland are expected to continue to have populations of seniors smaller than the national average while Ontario, Manitoba, and British Columbia will continue to have proportionately larger populations of seniors. This variation will also occur within provinces, resulting in an urgent need for decentralized health care planning and for programming highly responsive to special needs within communities.

Second, the nature of the seniors population is changing. Seniors are more informed, more assertive, and less deferential to health professionals than ever before. They increasingly are taking charge of their health and the decisions that affect their health. Inclusion of seniors themselves in decision making about their health is not optional; it is essential at the individual, group, and community level.

Third, seniors often choose to live in small rural communities where access to health care services is problematic because of travel distances (Stone & Fletcher, 1986). Seniors can establish car pools or an affordable volunteer taxi service. Caregivers, too, must look for ways to improve accessibility.

Fourth, there will be many more women than men, especially in the over-80 age groups (Priest, 1990; Stone & Fletcher, 1986). This demographic pattern was well established by 1980 and is expected to continue beyond 2030. However, the health system has been unresponsive to this change, perhaps because unisex warehousing of the elderly was the focus of seniors health care throughout the 1970s and early 1980s. As the 21st century approaches, effective health care managers will need to be highly knowledgeable about the health needs of older women and must design health programs with women in mind.

Fifth, life expectancy continues to improve, although survival chances diminish rapidly for men after age 92 and for women after age 94 (Stone & Fletcher, 1986).

Implications of These Trends

Policy makers in the Canadian health care system have been aware of the need for a broad approach to health promotion and disease prevention since Health and Welfare Canada published Lalonde's *A New Perspective on the Health of Canadians* in 1974. Awareness that health is influenced by a wide range of factors was strengthened again with Epp's (1986) *Achieving Health for All: A Framework for Health Promotion*. However, awareness is really not enough. Success in improving the health of Canadians requires that all managers and policy makers in the health system are knowledgeable about effective strategies and can evaluate their impact on health.

The key to successful health services is to ensure through regular evaluation that services meet the real needs of people in a way that is readily accessible, empowering, culturally appropriate, gender sensitive, and cost effective. The usefulness of such evaluations depends upon the availability of data collection systems (Psutka, 1992), outcome measures (standards, practice guidelines, health goals), and the degree of commitment to act on findings.

Although some policy makers fail to recognize nurses' contributions (Gottlieb, 1992), nurses play many and varied roles in contributing to the accomplishment of successful health services. Valverde (1992) complained that there has been too much emphasis on posters preaching how to live and insufficient resources available to support peer-to-peer messages. He states that although health promotion is now "consultation," with some participation from communities, it will become a truly empowering process only when implemented by the target group itself.

The internationally accepted definition of health promotion is given in the Ottawa Charter for Health Promotion (1986): "health promotion is the process of enabling people to increasing control over, and to improve, their health. . . health promotion is not just the responsibility of the health sector, but goes beyond healthy lifestyles to well-being" (p. 426).

The Registered Nurses Association of British Columbia (1992) has set an example by educating and supporting its own members, the public, and politicians with its background paper, *Determinants of Health: Empowering Strategies for Nursing Practice*. In it, the RNABC sets out a continuum of empowering strategies (see Table 3.1). It shows nurses how their current actions are already contributing to health promotion and identifies specific actions they can take to broaden the impact of their health promotion activities. Nurses are encouraged to get in touch with community organizers and policy makers in their communities so that all can appreciate the range of actions that are required to improve the health of the people of Canada.

Lassiter (1992) encourages a focus on citizen participation and partnerships at the local level and emphasizes that process and implementation methods must be suitable to the local community. Health and Welfare Canada (1992) takes a similar approach by encouraging community mobilization for improved health. The 1992 Health Policy Conference of the Center for Health Economics and Policy Analysis points out that citizens must also be involved in defining equitable access to health care because societal values influence perceptions of the appropriateness of care, no matter how accessible.

During the First National Conference on Chronic Diseases in Canada, seven major strategies were identified (Edwards, 1989, pp. 13-18). The strategies include developing and evaluating prevention goals and increasing the use of preventive measures, particularly for disadvantaged and high-risk groups. The involvement

Table 3.1.

A continuum of empowering strategies.

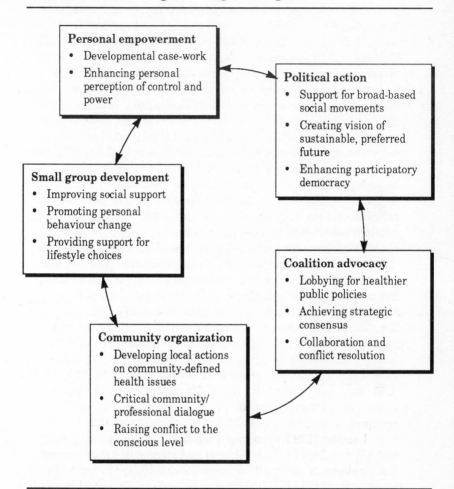

Personal empowerment
- Developmental case-work
- Enhancing personal perception of control and power

Political action
- Support for broad-based social movements
- Creating vision of sustainable, preferred future
- Enhancing participatory democracy

Small group development
- Improving social support
- Promoting personal behaviour change
- Providing support for lifestyle choices

Coalition advocacy
- Lobbying for healthier public policies
- Achieving strategic consensus
- Collaboration and conflict resolution

Community organization
- Developing local actions on community-defined health issues
- Critical community/ professional dialogue
- Raising conflict to the conscious level

Source: Adapted from Registered Nurses Association of B.C. (1992), *Determinants of health: Empowering strategies for nursing practice—A background paper* (Vancouver: Author, p. 10). Used with permission.

of these special communities in identifying health needs and their participation in selecting strategies is essential.

Health system managers and professionals have a primary role to play, both within their communities and provincially; they must advocate for and encourage health agencies and governments to identify health goals and use strategies that allow communities of people to determine their own priorities. Nursing may be the only profession that is always at the table during discussions of this kind, so the insistence of nurse managers on broad participation in the goal-setting exercise is critical for the success of this strategy.

After a review of six health promotion programs, Goodman, Steckler, and Hoover (1993) recommended a number of steps to ensure that community health promotion approaches are effective. An important first step, which is seldom mentioned, is an initial assessment of the capacity of the community to manage change. This simple first step would save many dollars and avoid considerable frustration. Too often, health managers and others move forward to address a health issue without realizing that the community is fully occupied in managing some other issue. Goodman and his colleagues (1993) also recommend that health needs assessments be analyzed and shared quickly with communities in a format that is useful to them. Technical assistance and flexibility are recommended, as are local input, coordination, and capacity building for future success. The use of multiple interventions is strongly encouraged and the list concludes by stressing that effective health promotion approaches need to be integrated into ongoing community programming in a way that ensures continuation and sustainability over time.

In summary, the role of health care managers in facilitating improvements in the health of the population includes at the very least:

- Decision making based on epidemiological and demographic trends;
- Insistence upon community participation in assessing and analyzing needs and in selecting appropriate priorities and strategies; and
- Regular program evaluations based on health goals and other outcome measures.

All health care managers can make their own decisions on the basis of these three steps and lobby strongly for these three actions by others. This would result in an immediate improvement in the effectiveness of health services, and shortly Canadians would begin to reap benefits in improved health status, which is nursing's ultimate goal.

References

Avard, D., & Hanvey, L. (1989). *The health of Canada's children: A CICH profile*. Ottawa: Canadian Institute of Child Health.

Badets, J. (1990). Canada's immigrant population. In C. McKie & K. Thompson (Eds.), *Canadian social trends* (pp. 7-11). Ottawa: Minister of Supply & Services.

Beneteau, R. (1990). Trends in suicide. In C. McKie & K. Thompson (Eds.), *Canadian social trends* (pp. 93-95). Ottawa: Minister of Supply & Services.

Bibby, R.W., & Posterski, D.C. (1992). *Teen trends: A nation in motion*. Toronto: Stoddart.

Bramhan, D., & Hamilton, G. (1993). The death of the middle class. *Transition, 23*(1), 10-11.

Burke, M.A. (1991, Spring). Implications of an aging society. *Canadian Social Trends, 20,* 6-9.

Canadian Task Force on Mental Health Issues Affecting Immigrants and Refugees. (1988). *After the door has been opened: Mental health issues affecting immigrants and refugees in Canada*. Ottawa: Minister of Supply & Services.

Cardiovascular disease in Canada. (1993). Ottawa: Heart & Stroke Foundation.

Children of Canada, children of the world: Canada's national paper for the world summit for children. (1990). Ottawa: Minister of Supply & Services.

Crégheur, A., & Devereaux, M.S. (1991, Summer). Canada's children. *Canadian Social Trends, 21,* 2-5.

Dumas, J. (1990). *Report on the demographic situation in Canada 1990: Current demographic analysis*. Ottawa: Statistics Canada.

Edwards, P. (1989). *Summary report, first national conference—chronic disease in Canada: Challenges and opportunities*. Ottawa: Canadian Public Health Association.

Epp, J. (1986). *Achieving health for all: A framework for health promotion*. Ottawa: Minister of Supply & Services.

Ferrence, R.G. (1993). Sex differences. In T. Stephens & D.F. Graham (Eds.), *Canada's health promotion survey 1990: Technical report* (pp. 238-241). Ottawa: Minister of Supply & Services.

Gaudette, L., & Roberts, G. (1990). Trends in cancer since 1970. In C. McKie & K. Thompson (Eds.), *Canadian social trends* (pp. 73-78). Ottawa: Minister of Supply & Services.

Giger, J.N., & Davidhizar, R. (1990). Transcultural nursing assessment: A method for advancing nursing practice. *International Nursing Review, 37*(1), 199-202.

Gooder, P.L. (1992). Targets—Are they sensible? *Health Policy, 21,* 223-231.

Goodman, R.M., Steckler, A., & Hoover, S. (1993). A critique of contemporary community health promotion approaches: Based on a qualitative review of six programs in Maine. *American Journal of Health Promotion, 7*(3), 208-220.

Gottlieb, L. (1992). Nurses not heard in the health promotion movement. *Canadian Journal of Nursing Research, 24*(4), 1-2.

Green, L.W., & Simons-Morton, D. (1991). Education and life style determinants of health and disease. In W. Holland, R. Detels, & G. Knox (Eds.), *Oxford textbook of public health* (2nd ed.). London: Oxford University Press.

Health & Welfare Canada. (1989). *Charting Canada's future: A report of the demographic review*. Ottawa: Minister of Supply & Services.

Health & Welfare Canada. (1992). *Health equality: Mobilizing communities for action*. Ottawa: Minister of Supply & Services.

Health Policy Conference (5th). (1992). *Beyond 'equitable access': New perspectives on equity in health care systems*. London, ON: McMaster University Center for Health Economics & Policy Analysis.

Hislop, T.G., Deschamps, M., Band, P.R., Smith, J.M., & Clark, H.F. (1992). Participation in the British Columbia cervical cytology screening programme by native Indian women. *Canadian Journal of Public Health, 83*(5), 344-345.

Holmes, J., & Silverman, E.L. (1992). *We're here, listen to us!: A survey of young women in Canada*. Ottawa: Canadian Advisory Council on the Status of Women.

Jacono, J.J., Jacono, B.J., St. Onge, M., Van Oosten, E., & Meininger, E. (1992). Teenage pregnancy: A reconsideration. *Canadian Journal of Public Health, 83*(3), 196-199.

Kettle, J. (1980). *The big generation*. Toronto: McClelland & Stewart.

King, A.J.C., & Coles, B. (1992). *The health of Canada's youth*. Ottawa: Minister of Supply & Services Canada.

King, M., Gartrell, J., & Trovato, F. (1991). Early childhood mortality 1926 - 1986. *Canadian Social Trends, 21* (Summer), 6-10.

Lalonde, M. (1974). *A new perspective on the health of Canadians*. Ottawa: Minister of Supply & Services.

Lassiter, P.G. (1992). A community development perspective for rural nursing: Topics in family and community health. *Journal of Health Promotion & Maintenance, 14*(4), 29-39.

Last, J.M. (Ed.). (1983). *A dictionary of epidemiology*. New York: Oxford.

MacMillan, S., & Jantzie, D. (1993). Young adults: Attitudes toward community health. *Wellspring, 4*(2), 1, 7.

Mao, Y., Moloughney, B.W., Semeniciw, R.M., & Morrison, H.I. (1992). Indian reserve and registered Indian mortality in Canada. *Canadian Journal of Public Health, 83*(5), 350-353.

McDonald, R.J. (1991, Winter). Canada's off reserve aboriginal population. *Canadian Social Trends, 23*, 2-7.

McKie, C. (1990). Lifestyle risks: Smoking and drinking in Canada. In C. McKie & K. Thompson (Eds.), *Canadian social trends* (pp. 86-92). Ottawa: Minister of Supply & Services.

Millar, W. (1992, Spring). A trend to a healthier lifestyle. *Canadian Social Trends, 24*, supplement.

Millar, W.J., Strachan, J., & Wadhera, S. (1993, Spring). Trends in low birth weight. *Canadian Social Trends, 26-29.*

Nessner, K. (1990, Winter). *Children with disabilities. Canadian Social Trends, 19,* 18-20.

Ng, E. (1992, Summer). Children and elderly people: Sharing public income resources. *Canadian Social Trends, 25,* 12-15.

Ottawa Charter for Health Promotion. (1986). *Canadian Journal of Public Health, 77,* 425-430.

Pederson, L.L. (1993). Smoking. In T. Stephens & D.F. Graham (Eds.), *Canada's health promotion survey 1990: Technical report* (pp. 92-101). Ottawa: Minister of Supply & Services.

Ponting, R. (1990). Public opinion on aboriginal peoples' issues in Canada. In C. McKie & K. Thompson (Eds.), *Canadian social trends* (pp. 19-27). Ottawa: Minister of Supply & Services.

Priest, G. (1990, Summer). The demographic future. *Canadian Social Trends, 17,* 5-9.

Psutka, D.A. (1992). Psutka on health care management. *Notebook on Data for Quality Management, 2,* 3-5.

Quarterly surveillance update: aids in Canada. (1993). Ottawa: Laboratory Centre for Disease Control.

Registered Nurses Association of B.C. (1992). *Determinants of health: Empowering strategies for nursing practice—A background paper.* Vancouver: Author.

Remis, R.S., & Sutherland, W.D. (1993). The epidemiology of HIV and aids in Canada: Current perspectives and future needs. *Canadian Journal of Public Health, 84,* supplement 1, S34-S38.

Ross, D.P., & Lochhead, C. (1993). Changes in family incomes and labour market participation in post war Canada. *Transition, 23*(1), 5-7.

Scott, J.K. (1991). Alice Modig and the talking circles. *Canadian Nurse, 87*(6), 25-26.

Statistics Canada. (1990). *A portrait of children in Canada: Target groups project.* Ottawa: Author.

Statistics Canada. (1991). *Canada year book 1992.* Ottawa: Author.

Stone, L.O., & Fletcher, S. (1986). *The seniors boom: Dramatic increases in longevity and prospects for better health.* Ottawa: Minister of Supply & Services.

Strike, C. (1990a). aids in Canada. In C. McKie & K. Thompson (Eds.), *Canadian social trends* (pp. 83-85). Ottawa: Minister of Supply & Services.

Strike, C. (1990b). The incidence of sexually transmitted disease in Canada. In C. McKie & K. Thompson (Eds.), *Canadian social trends* (pp. 79-82). Ottawa: Minister of Supply & Services.

Transport Canada. (1992). *Alcohol use by drivers fatally injured in motor vehicle accidents: 1990 and the past ten years.* Ottawa: Road Safety Division.

Tyler, C.W., & Last, J.M. (1992). Epidemiology. In J.M. Last & R.B. Wallace (Eds.), (1992). *Public health and preventive medicine.* Norwalk, CT: Appleton & Lange.

Valverde, C. (1992). Empowering communities makes third wave of health promotion. *Canadian AIDS News, 5*(4), 3 and 11.

Victoria Declaration on heart health. (1993). Ottawa: Minister of Supply & Services.

Wadhera, S., & Strachan, J. (1992). Births and birth rates, Canada, 1990. *Health Reports, 4*(1), 73-77.

Women in Canada: A statistical report. (1990). Ottawa: Minister of Supply & Services.

Women's Research Center. (1990). *Keeping on track: An evaluation guide for community groups.* Vancouver: Author.

World Health Organization & International Union for Health Education. (1992). *Meeting global health challenges: A position paper on health education.* Atlanta: Center for Disease Control.

PART 2

Internal Environment of Health Care Agencies

C H A P T E R 4

Management Theory: Critical Review and Application

Carl A. Meilicke

Carl A. Meilicke, BComm (Saskatchewan), DHA (Toronto), PhD (Minnesota), is Professor Emeritus at the University of Alberta, Edmonton. Throughout his career in health services administration, he maintained a special interest in the management of nursing services.

Knowledge about how to design and manage formal organizations has grown dramatically over the past several decades and this growth has resulted in its division into two categories. One is organizational behaviour, which focusses on the individual and small groups about such issues as motivation, leadership style, and interpersonal relations. The other is organizational design, which focusses on the organization about such issues as how the environment, technology, power, and human values influence management decision making.

This chapter provides an outline of what is known about organizational design theory and discusses how to make use of that knowledge in everyday management practice. The first section will provide an overview of basic theoretical concepts. The second section will provide a description of management as a process and present a conceptual framework that can be used by the reader to integrate the theory presented herein with other relevant knowledge. The third section will provide an example of the management process by using the conceptual framework in a critique of a hypothetical acute care nursing management situation. The fourth section is a concluding comment. The chapter ends with a brief annotated bibliography that identifies some essential background readings for health care managers.

Introduction to Organizational Design Theory

The evolution of contemporary organizational theory only began at the turn of the century and the most important developments have occurred since the 1930s. Even though a rich and varied store of ideas and concepts have been developed during this relatively short time, they can be grouped into four general schools of thought, or perspectives, as shown in Table 4.1 (pp. 66-69). The table, which originally was developed by Stephen Shortell and Arnold Kaluzny (1983), provides a brilliant framework for understanding organizational issues. The historical order in which these perspectives emerged is more or less from left to right in Table 4.1, but two other important elements are incorporated.

The first concerns basic or key assumptions underlying each perspective. The key assumptions reflect either a closed or open system perspective on organizations and, within each of these options, a rational or a natural approach. The closed versus open system perspectives reflect the degree to which it is believed that the external environment of the organization should and must be taken into account when managers make decisions. The rational versus natural approaches reflect the degree to which management is perceived to involve (rational) pre-planning of objectives and the means to achieve them, as opposed to a more (natural) dynamic process of ongoing adaptation to changing circumstances.

The second element incorporated into Table 4.1 concerns a comparison of the general conclusions about seven key organizational issues. How a manager deals with key organizational issues is profoundly affected by these differences in basic assumptions, as is outlined in the details in the table, and highlighted in the "limitations" section. For example, both of the closed system perspectives tend to support a "one best way" to manage, but this is largely the result of discounting or ignoring the impact that technical, political, and social factors in the environment can have upon the organization. To illustrate, the highly rational approach to organizational issues that is implicit in classical bureaucratic theory may seem to be the best way to deal with the control of cost and quality in a situation where the management issues are complex and the consequence of error is high. It is difficult to defend this position, however, if one recognizes that many employees have strongly negative feelings about rigid authoritarianism as a result of attitudes they form while outside of the organization.

Similarly, even though the human relations school recognized that workers often prefer more participation in decision making (and therefore concludes that the one best way to manage is an approach which emphasizes flexible accommodation to the workers' need for involvement), it failed to recognize that many workers do not wish to accept the responsibility that comes with participation because of commitments and interests they have outside of the organization.

By the early 1960s, researchers began to accept the importance of environmental variables and it was not long before a wide variety of technical, political, and social factors were considered to be potentially important to any given organization. These insights led to the idea of a contingency approach to dealing with organizational issues. This means that there is no one best way to manage and the most appropriate management action is seen to be contingent upon the particular combination of environmental variables that are significant to each specific organization at a given point in time. Within this open systems perspective, proponents of the rational approach argue that one can assess the environment and develop a plan to cope with its effects. Proponents of the natural approach believe that environmental complexity and rate of change are so great that the organization cannot plan for environmental changes and can only respond to them in an ad hoc fashion.

Needless to say, each of these orientations and approaches has some degree of usefulness, depending on the circumstances. The rational, pre-planned, and centralized authority techniques of scientific management (a subset of classical bureaucratic theory) are often of great value when the work is highly repetitive and routine, such as an assembly line. At the same time, some aspects of participative management will almost always enhance employee morale and some degree of contingency planning is necessary to protect the organization from sudden external changes (such as advances in robotic technology that could render much of the assembly line obsolete or a change in employee attitudes which could cause them to resist the tradition of highly centralized decision making).

This "mix and match" characteristic of a contingency approach to management leads to many different options, and it is helpful to think of them as falling on a continuum that extends from mechanistic to organic, with the intermediate range of the continuum being described as ambidextrous. A mechanistic style emphasizes rules, procedures, a clear hierarchy of authority, centralization, and a task-oriented approach to employee morale. It tends to incorporate many elements of the closed system

Table 4.1

Summary of theoretical perspectives on organizational issues.

Organizational Issues	Closed System	
	Rational Approaches	Natural Approaches
	Classical bureaucratic theory (Taylor, 1911; Gulick & Urwick, 1937; Weber, 1947; Mooney, 1947; Gouldner, 1954)	The "human relations" school (Barnard, 1938; Roethlisberger & Dickson, 1939; McGregor, 1960; Argyris, 1966; Likert, 1967)
Efficiency	**Classical/Bureaucratic Theory Position** May be obtained through application of work-study methods and predetermined principles of "good" management. Maximized through a hierarchically ordered chain of positions and specified procedures for operation.	**Human Relations Position** Best brought about by integrating individual aspirations with organizational goals. Involve workers in their job through participatory decision making, job enlargement, job enrichment, etc.
Effectiveness	As above.	In addition to profit, growth, and quality, individual member satisfaction in the organization is viewed as a major goal in its own right.
Conflict	Should be avoided. This can be accomplished by constructing appropriate departmentalization, chains of command, and span of control. Minimize potential for conflict by having a rule or procedure for everything.	Is generally viewed as dysfunctional, but should be managed and confronted openly when it occurs.
Change (innovation)	Handle by means of rational accommodation and intervention, establishment of new rules and procedures.	Must be accommodated through changes in the informal structures of the organization as well as the formal structures.

Open system	
Rational Approaches	**Natural Approaches**
(Burns & Stalker, 1961; Woodward, 1965; Lawrence & Lorsch, 1967; Thompson, 1967; Perrow, 1967; Katz & Kahn, 1966; Becker & Gordon, 1966; Hage, 1965, 1980; Khandwalla, 1974; Shortell, 1977; Simon, 1965; Cyert & March, 1963; Alexis & Wilson, 1967)	(Hickson et al., 1971; March & Olson, 1976; Meyer & Rowan, 1977; Hannan & Freeman, 1977; Pfeffer & Salancik, 1978; Tushman & Nadler, 1978; Aldrich, 1979)
Contingency/Decision Theory Position May be attained in several ways depending on the nature of the tasks involved, the people involved, and external circumstances. Depends on the quality of the decisions made under uncertainty.	**Strategic Contingencies/Political Negotiation/Resource Dependence/Population Ecology Position** Overall objective is not efficiency per se but system survival. As such, political as well as economic transactions become important.
As above. In addition, one way that organizations survive is by expanding or changing their goals to meet new demands from the environment. Emphasis is on goal attainment.	As above. Emphasis is not on goal attainment but on obtaining resources and balancing internal political considerations of those vying for power in order to survive.
Not necessarily viewed as dysfunctional. Can promote creativity and innovation. The problem is to minimize disruptive conflict. Attending to different goals at different times may be helpful.	Viewed as a natural consequence of internal negotiations over power, given the strategic contingencies the organization faces.
Can occur either from within or without the organization. Again, depends on nature of tasks, people, and environment. Some evidence to indicate that more loosely structured organizations are more innovative in an "inventive" sense but that more tightly structured organizations may be better at implementing and diffusing the innovation. Ability to change or innovate is also a function of organizational learning over time.	Comes about both through external demands and internal political adjustments to those demands. Those who can most influence the type, pace, and direction of change at one point in time may not be most influential at another point in time as the organization's environment changes and its need for different kinds of expertise changes accordingly.

Table 4.1 — *continued*

Summary of theoretical perspectives on organizational issues.

Organizational Issues	Closed System	
	Rational Approaches	**Natural Approaches**
Social Integration/ Motivation	Can be attained through appropriate structural mechanisms (unity of command, span of control, etc.). Little attention given to the individual.	Achieved through the informal system of relationships among workers. Emphasis on nonpecuniary rewards, such as intrinsic job satisfaction and opportunities for personal expression and growth.
Coordination	A primary goal of the organization. May be achieved through appropriate departmentalization, hierarchy, and specification of rules and procedures.	Little attention given to it. Again, emphasis is on the informal work group as a coordinative mechanism.
Maintenance (adaptation to environment)	Essentially not considered.	Essentially not considered.
	Limitations 1. Incomplete motivational assumptions. 2. Little appreciation of nature or role of conflict. 3. No consideration of the limitations of individuals as information-processing beings. 4. Essentially no consideration of the environment in which organizations function. 5. A "one best way" approach: the "only way" to manage.	**Limitations** 1. Many of the studies upon which the theory is based have been poorly designed. 2. Limited view of human motivation—assumes all individuals want more participation and involvement. 3. Essentially no consideration of the environment. 4. A "one best way" approach.

Source: Table from *Health care management: A text in organizational theory and behavior* by Stephen Shortell and Arnold Kaluzny (New York: John Wiley & Sons, 1983), pp. 26-29. Reprinted by permission.

Open system

Rational Approaches	Natural Approaches
May be achieved in a variety of ways including both intrinsic and extrinsic factors contributing to job satisfaction. The emphasis is on role—getting people to function in their role and understanding each other's roles.	Is achieved through internal accommodation among competing groups that agree to go along with the dominant coalition at the time because it is in their best interest to do so.
The more specialized the organization and the greater the degree to which tasks are interdependent, the greater the need for coordination. May be achieved through committees and task forces as well as informal organization.	Primary reliance is placed on informal and emergent processes rather than on formal rules, procedures, or committees. Coordination is achieved through negotiation and bargaining.
Crucial to understanding organizational behavior. The organization must "negotiate" its environment by engaging in search procedures, dealing with uncertainty, and structuring itself to meet the demands of the environment.	Of primary importance. Those in leadership positions must manage the organization's environment as well as the internal structures and processes. Leaders must seek to "enact" their environments in addition to simply "reacting" to them.
Limitations A conceptually sound approach for the study of organizations, but requires much more research to replicate some of the early findings and define further the nature of the interaction between an organization and its environment. Problem of measuring the environment; perceptual versus nonperceptual measures.	**Limitations** There has been little empirical study to date of the open natural systems approach. The approach may also be somewhat of an overreaction to the rational contingency approaches. A middle ground would suggest that organizations survive in the long run through some degree of goal attainment in which certain kinds of organizational designs and processes provide a structural framework for channeling internal political negotiations. In brief, some degree of goal attainment would appear necessary in order for the organization to maintain sufficient credibility to continue to attract needed resources.

orientation. An organic style emphasizes flexibility, individual initiative, decentralization, and the encouragement of individual creativity. It tends to reflect many elements of the open system approach. Management approaches that are found at or near the midpoint of the continuum incorporate elements of both approaches and are described as ambidextrous.

Recognition of the open system concept and the organic/mechanistic concept marked a major turning point in the evolution of organization theory. A substantial amount of the research activity relating to organizational design since the early 1960s has been devoted to refining these concepts and making them more useful in daily management decision making. Six of the key ideas that have emerged are described below.

1.   History of the Organization and Personality of its Actors

Historical and personality factors are the first significant key factor to consider. Two important historical considerations are the size and life cycle of the organization. It is obvious that as an organization grows in size it will tend to develop more mechanistic characteristics in the form of rules, regulations, policies, impersonality, and so on. What is not quite so obvious is that organizations go through cycles of change depending on changes in the environment or on ways in which the organization undertakes to respond to environmental constraints and opportunities. For example, steady growth in the complexity and instability of the environment creates significant new challenges in maintaining an ambidextrous balance between mechanistic elements of management (which are necessary for effective coordination and control) and organic elements (which increase the speed with which the organization can adapt to a changing environment).

Changes in leadership and personality of managers can create a new cycle, because different individuals assess the environment, and respond to it, in different ways. Some managers are highly skilled in this regard, and some are not; some learn and improve with experience, some do not; and, finally, some are emotionally stable personalities who can deal with ambiguity in a mature fashion, and some are not.

2.   Definition of a System

One automatically thinks of the total organization as a "system," but it is made up of many smaller systems (work teams, units, departments, divisions, and so on) and it is only a small part of larger systems (for example, the acute care system or the health care system). A corollary of this is that organizational design theory can be used with regard to any level (subsystem) of the organization. Also, the nature of the environmental factors bearing upon each subsystem is likely to be different and may therefore require a different management solution. The technical, political, and cultural environments of importance to the manager of a pediatric ward, for example, are quite different from those relating to a geriatric ward, and both are different from the overall division of nursing. Accordingly, the best balance of organic and mechanistic styles of management will be quite different within and between different levels of the organization.

3. Describing the Environment

The third of the six key ideas concerns a way of summarizing the data about the nature of the environment. This is most commonly done in terms of two dimensions, each of which is a continuum: simplicity/complexity and stability/instability. Generally speaking, the more simple and stable the environment is the more mechanistic the organization can be because the need for adaptability is less. Conversely, the more complex and unstable the environment, the more organic the organization can and should be. In the past few years, for example, the environment of most health organizations has become dramatically more complex and unstable and managers have responded by trying to make the organization more organic in the hope that it can thereby adapt more quickly to change. One example of this is the widespread effort to decentralize authority for decision making and encourage more participation in the decision process.

4. Describing Technology

The fourth idea is a way of summarizing the data about technology. Technical variables involve relatively tangible and inanimate factors, such as money supply, number and types of workers, and the types of knowledge, material, and equipment. The nature of relevant technology is an unusually important environmental variable because it usually establishes quite rigid limitations on the options available to managers. Again, two subconcepts, complexity and interdependence, are basic. Technological complexity is defined by the number (variety) of exceptions to the "normal" case that are indicated by the technology and, given that technology, by how easy it is to define (analyze) an appropriate way to handle these exceptions. High variety (many exceptions) and low analyzability (difficult to define the best solution to the exceptions) are described as non-routine technology and tend to call for more organic forms of management. Low variety and high analyzability represent routine technologies and lend themselves to more mechanistic approaches. Looking only at this aspect of technology, for example, one might well expect a relatively organic management style to be used in a psychiatric ward because the knowledge (theory) underlying psychotherapy allows for many exceptions to the normal case and many variations on how to treat each individual case. Conversely, the style might be more mechanistic on a ward dealing with uncomplicated surgery.

The other subconcept has to do with the degree of interdependence that is created as a result of the technology, especially with other work groups, professions, departments, and so on. Interdependence can range from pooled (very low, as between a nursing unit and the accounting office), to sequential (the output of one unit is input for another, such as admitting and nursing), to reciprocal (where outputs flow back and forth, such as a surgical ward and the surgical suite).

Nursing technology, for example, creates high levels of interdependence with a wide variety of diagnostic, clinical, and support groups of units. The higher the level of interdependence, the greater the need for attention to communication and coordination. Accordingly, the need for good communication and coordination techniques within nursing subsystems, and between them and other subsystems, is greater than in many other components of the hospital, and this generally requires more organic styles of management so that rapid adaptability is possible. At the same time, many of the interdependencies of nursing are pooled or sequential, which means that relatively mechanistic as well as ambidextrous styles are also appropriate in several other situations.

5. Recognizing Dilemmas

The concept of organizational dilemmas is the fifth key idea. Many of the most important decisions in management involve balancing requirements that are in many ways incompatible but must be provided for if the organization is to survive. For example, both coordination and communication are essential for an organization to survive. Communication is usually improved if hierarchy is minimized because this reduces status barriers (which can be done by reducing the number of supervisors and decentralizing authority) but these measures will almost always make coordination more difficult, especially in larger organizations. Many other examples could be given, but they can be generally summarized in terms of an organic/mechanistic dilemma. Both styles have merit, and all organizations must have elements of each, so the challenge is to achieve and maintain an ambidextrous style that creates an appropriate balance between them. These dilemmas cannot be avoided; they can only be endured. As a result, they are one of the major challenges, and one of the major responsibilities, facing managers.

Health organizations face a number of unusual dilemmas. One of the more important is the need for high reliability in areas where the cost of error is so high that extraordinary means must be taken to minimize error. The degree to which an organization must require high reliability varies within the organization, and within each subsystem, along a continuum. When a nurse is assisting with transplant surgery or injecting intravenous chemotherapy, for example, there is a need for high reliability. With many other nursing functions, the need may be much lower. High reliability creates a dilemma for the organization because, on the one hand, an organic style of management may encourage the sense of individual responsibility that is needed to minimize errors but, on the other hand, a mechanistic style is more likely to ensure that controls are in place to prevent ill-informed or irresponsible behaviour.

The growing emphasis on patient expectations has created a similar dilemma. It is important to be attentive to the preferences and personal satisfaction of the patient and this is compatible with an organic style that allows the front-line worker more flexibility. On the other hand, the organization has both a legal and moral responsibility for the acts of its employees and agents, and this requires certain mechanistic elements in monitoring and controlling their behaviour.

6.   Ethical Accountability

A sixth key concept relating to organizational design theory concerns ethical implications of management decision making. It is unfortunate that this most important concept has yet to receive substantial and focussed attention from either organizational theorists or management practitioners. It is, however, fortunate that an open system/rational approach is well suited to deal with the complex problems presented by ethical issues in management. The open system orientation requires that the ethical milieu of the organization be considered by management in terms of both its impact on the organization and the impact the organization has on the environment. The rational approach requires that due and deliberate consideration be given to all relevant management variables, and there is no justification for arguing that ethical issues are not relevant in delivering health services. The organic/mechanistic concept facilitates analysis of the extremely important ethical issues related to determining how the organization can best fulfill its responsibility for the actions of its staff.

Two important ethical questions will be dealt with later in this chapter. The first is the responsibility of the health organization to rationalize existing patterns of physician decision making and interinstitutional competition, in the face of the evidence that, in their current form, both of these compromise the efficient and effective use of health resources. The second deals with the question of how organic health organizations can and should be given the moral and legal responsibility of senior management for the actions of their staff.

By the early 1980s, significant progress had been made in the sophistication and utility of management theory, but the price of this progress was complexity and ambiguity. An enormous number of environmental variables required assessment. There were also a large number of management options to consider. Furthermore, environmental variables kept changing, and this often changed the requirements and conditions of an effective management strategy. It became quite clear that good management decision making was much more complex, and had to be much more adaptable to changing circumstances, than had been recognized in the past. It was also clear that new insights were necessary so that this complexity and adaptability could be more easily understood and dealt with. These realizations led to a strategic management approach.

Strategic Management

The problem of designing and implementing an adaptable management approach was addressed in the 1980s and early 1990s with the idea of strategic management. This involves four steps:

- Assess the environment;
- Devise an overall management strategy based on this assessment;
- Make day-to-day decisions based on an overall management strategy as well as on immediate issues and problems; and
- Modify the management strategy on an ongoing basis in response to changes in the environment *and* feedback from the daily decision-making process.

This approach incorporates the open system perspective (step 1) as well as the contingency approach (steps 2 and 3), and recognizes the associated need for adaptability due either to a changing environment or to actual experience with implementing the strategy (step 4).

The remaining problem, how to grapple with the complexity of strategic management, has not yet resulted in a consensus among theorists but a framework developed by Noel Tichy (1983) is useful in addressing this problem. (See Table 4.2, p.76.) His TPC model, an acronym for *Technical, Political,* and *Cultural,* has been adapted for use in this chapter. In the following discussion, the nine cells in the TPC model will be referred to by number, from left to right, starting in the upper left hand corner. Thus, the technical system will include cells 1, 2, and 3; the political, cells 4, 5, and 6; and the cultural, cells 7, 8, and 9.

Tichy's framework incorporates four important assumptions. First, organizations are affected by three major categories of environmental variables: technical, political, and cultural (Tichy's ideas are sometimes described as TPC theory). Technical variables involve relatively tangible and inanimate factors, such as money supply, number and types of workers, and the types of knowledge, material, and equipment. Political variables basically involve the distribution of power in the environment, such as that held by government, professional associations, unions, pressure groups, and even influential individuals. Cultural variables include the values and beliefs of individuals and groups, such as attitudes regarding women's rights, professionalism, and commitment to a work ethic.

Second, in response to these environmental variables, organizations must develop three internal systems: technical, political, and cultural. The technical system deals with how managers plan for and organize the technical resources that are available from the environment (cells 1, 2, and 3 of Table 4.2). The political system deals with how they distribute power within the organization (cells 4, 5, and 6). The cultural system deals with how they manage attitudes and values, including both adjusting to the employee culture and attempting to change it (cells 7, 8, and 9).

Third, it is important that the three systems be in alignment or, put another way, be mutually supportive. For example, if the political system emphasizes staff involvement and decentralization of authority, the technical system should place relatively less emphasis on detailed position descriptions or rules and regulations about job performance. If this is not done, there is misalignment and, in this case, it could produce employee cynicism based on the discrepancy between how the work is actually done and how work roles are formally defined.

Table 4.2
Managerial tools for strategic management.

Managerial Areas	Mission and Strategy	Organizational Structure	Processes
Technical System	**(1)** • Assessing environmental threats and opportunities. • Assessing organizational strengths and weaknesses. • Defining mission and fitting resources to accomplish it.	**(2)** • Differentiation: organization of work into roles (production, marketing, etc.). • Integration: recombining roles into departments, divisions, regions, etc. • Aligning structure to strategy.	**(3)** • Fitting people into roles. • Specifying performance criteria for roles. • Measuring performance. • Staffing and development to fill roles (present and future). • Matching management style with technical tasks.
Political System	**(4)** • Who gets to influence the mission and strategy. • Managing coalitional behaviour around strategic decisions.	**(5)** • Distribution of power across the role structure. • Balancing power across groups of roles (e.g., sales vs. marketing, production vs. research and development, etc.).	**(6)** • Managing succession politics (who gets ahead, how do they get ahead). • Decision and administration of reward system (who gets what and how). • Managing the politics of appraisal (who is appraised by whom and how). • Managing the politics of information control and the planning process.
Cultural System	**(7)** • Managing influence of values and philosophy on mission and strategy. • Developing culture aligned with mission and strategy.	**(8)** • Developing managerial style aligned with technical and political structure. • Development of subcultures to support roles (production culture, R&D culture, etc.). • Integration of subcultures to create company culture.	**(9)** • Selection of people to build or reinforce culture. • Development (socialization) to mould organizational culture. • Management of rewards to shape and reinforce the culture. • Management of information and planning systems to shape and reinforce the culture.

Source: Adapted, with the permission of the author, from Noel M. Tichy, *Managing strategic change: Technical, political and cultural dynamics* (New York: John Wiley & Sons, 1983), p. 119.

Fourth, managers have three basic tools they can use to ensure alignment occurs: mission and strategy (cells 1, 4, and 7), structure (cells 2, 5, and 8), and human resource management, which is referred to in Table 4.2 as "process" (cells 3, 6, and 9). Each of these tools can be modified with regard to one or more of the three systems.

The following brief example will demonstrate how misalignment can occur and how the management tools can be used to correct it. Many health organizations have reduced the number of supervisors (a change in cell 2 of the technical system, in this case a change in the organizational chart). Many of these organizations have also moved to change the cultural system by modifying the mission and strategy (cell 7) in such a way that staff are encouraged to exercise their own values, attitudes, and judgement regarding their work (in other words, decentralizing authority). These two changes can be described as a shift to a more organic and less mechanistic management process.

Unfortunately, the above changes often result in a misalignment with the political system. Encouraging staff autonomy tends to compromise the power of middle managers and this is exaggerated by the extra work demands imposed on supervisors as a result of a reduction in their numbers. This type of misalignment can create many problems but one of the most dangerous is the blurring of accountability, particularly with regard to high reliability functions. One way to rectify the problem is to modify the policies and procedures (cell 2 of the technical system) in such a way that the parameters of supervisory authority are more clearly defined and there is less ambiguity about when participatory management techniques for planning, coordination, and quality control are acceptable and when they are not. In other words, the solution involves moving the balance point toward the mechanistic side of the organic/mechanistic continuum.

Tichy's model can be used to reduce substantially the complexity of strategic management because it provides a relatively uncomplicated set of guidelines regarding what variables should be examined and how the interaction effects between them can be planned for. The steps in strategic management now become:

•   Assess the environment in terms of technical, political, and cultural variables;

•   Devise an overall management strategy that includes:

   —   the planning and design of technical, political, and cultural systems that are appropriate in terms of the environmental variables; and

— the planning and implementing of management strategies involving goals, structure, and process that will
establish and maintain alignment;

• Establish a process whereby day-to-day management decision making is based on the above overall management
strategy; and

• Establish a process whereby the management strategy can
be modified on an ongoing basis in response to changes in
the environment and feedback from the daily decision-making experiences.

These steps can be used to describe or to assess an existing organization and, as well, to develop a strategy for change.

Management of Nursing Services: A Case Study

To illustrate how strategic management theory is used, I will
describe and critically assess the management changes in a hypothetical nursing department during the 1980s and early 1990s.
The example will be based in a hypothetical tertiary care hospital
because this type of organization is among the most complex in
modern society and it therefore offers a larger variety and magnitude of strategic management problems than most other health
organizations.

Although the following example is entirely hypothetical, it is
based on the type of environmental and management circumstances experienced by many acute care nursing departments in
Canada during the 1980s and early 1990s. Readers are encouraged to modify the following discussion in the context of their own
personal experience, their own knowledge of other management
theory and research, and the environmental and institutional
realities of their own organization.

Step 1: Environmental Assessment

The first step in strategic management is to assess the environment. The focus in this section is on the nursing division as the
"system" and the "environment" therefore includes all relevant
external variables, whether they exist within or outside of the
hospital. The analysis will show that the environment had become
increasingly complex and unstable in all three of the technical,
political, and cultural dimensions.

In the technical arena of this hypothetical hospital, there had been rapid and continuing growth in the variety and complexity of the knowledge, skills, and equipment that related to hospital operations and especially to medical and nursing practice. The changes in nursing were particularly significant because they reflected a rapid growth in the research-based knowledge underpinning the profession. The overall impact of these changes had been to increase costs but external funding agencies had steadily become more determined to reduce the rate of increase in hospital funding: technological change had in effect created a severe cost-revenue crisis. The crisis was particularly acute in nursing for two interconnected reasons. First, senior management (that is, chief executive officer and the board, who are ultimately responsible for all management policy and decisions) had not developed techniques for rationally planning and controlling the acquisition and use of technology by physicians, which had a substantial impact on nursing budgets. Second, even though nursing workload and output measurement technology provided valuable information, it was largely ignored by senior management because it indicated the nursing budget was increasingly inadequate and senior management did not wish to divert the necessary funds away from medical technology.

In the political environment, there had been rapid growth in the influence of nursing unions, a parallel growth in the technical sophistication as well as the professional self-esteem of nurses, and a slow but steady erosion of traditional medical dominance. Nevertheless, nurses continued to have relatively low political credibility, inside or outside the hospital, in great part because of the disunity caused by major differences in their education, work assignments, and career expectations and the much greater social prestige of physicians. This credibility was improving as the profession gained more experience in pressure group tactics and became more highly educated. But a major constraint on this progress was the continuing strength of chauvinistic attitudes directed at nurses, the stubborn myth that nurses are physicians' handmaidens, the fact that most nurses were female, and the mistaken belief that the nurturing elements of the nursing role are a low-skill activity based more on maternal instinct than on professional expertise. A further constraint was the aforementioned rejection of the information system as a means for providing objective data about workload, output, and productivity.

The cultural environment was dominated by the changes in the attitudes of nurses toward work and the nature of their organizational commitment. The advent of the "me generation," feminism, single parenting, unionization, research-based professionalization, different patterns of entry-level education, two-income families, and extensive experience with staff cutbacks had dramatically reduced the traditional willingness of many nurses to accept an authoritarian work environment or to invest a strong personal commitment in a specific organization. These changes were further exaggerated by the changing expectations of patients, who tended to be more demanding and skeptical, and the growing militancy of the union leaders, who were frustrated by the amount of effort required to move toward equity in pay and conditions of work.

The overall degree of environmental instability and complexity (turbulence) had increased rapidly during the decade and the rate of increase was continuing. The single most significant outcome was a growing cost-revenue crisis, to which nursing was particularly vulnerable because the main cause of the crisis within nursing was utilization decisions made by physicians, and nursing had little influence upon these decisions.

Steps 2 and 3: Development and Implementation of a Management Strategy in the 1980s

The second step is to describe and assess the management strategy of this hypothetical nursing department in terms of its technical, political, and cultural systems.

Although the department did have a formal statement of mission and strategy (Table 4.2, cell 1), this had been approved but never accepted by senior management. The most important part of the real mission was to respond to changes driven by the new technologies requested by physicians and approved by senior management in a relatively ad hoc decision-making process. The strategy for implementing this mission was heavily dependent on the resourcefulness of nursing middle managers in nourishing the individual and collective commitment of the nursing staff to the needs of patients and quality of care. This lack of comprehensive planning by senior management had precipitated a long series of "add-on" services by the nursing department, most notably in the area of intensive care programs, such as transplant services and trauma units, which had dramatically increased its operating costs and management complexity as well as the workload and stress at all levels of the department.

The technical structure of the department (Table 4.2, cell 2) reflected the foregoing pattern. A traditional hierarchy mainly based on clinical service units had been expanded over the years as new services were added. Absolute numbers of middle and

senior managers and support staff (including educators and clinical specialists) had increased significantly in response to increasing environmental turbulence, exponential growth in research
findings relevant to nursing practice, ad hoc expansion of services,
and the myriad of problems associated with growing pressures on
the budget. Although the department was well integrated internally, with extensive formal and informal mechanisms for planning and coordination, the efficiency of its cross-departmental
linkages had not kept pace with its growing interdependence with
other departments, particularly medicine. This was due partly to
preoccupation with cost-revenue problems on the part of nursing
but, most importantly, it was due to a lack of initiative and support from senior management, who did not understand the clinical
realities.

The technical aspect of process (Table 4.2, cell 3) was relatively ambidextrous but was under steady pressure to become
more mechanistic. The selection criteria for middle managers
emphasized leadership ability, teamwork skills, and commitment
to quality care. There had been a tradition of extensive consultation with staff nurses but, in response to the cost-revenue pressures, the process was becoming increasingly centralized. The
rapid rate of change and growth in technology, for example, had
required the development of policy and procedure manuals, orientation programs, and in-service education activities; the sheer volume of this workload meant that the process had become more
centralized. In response to the growing competition for funds, a
nursing information system had been implemented in an effort to
develop objective workload and output data. It included patient
classification, quality assurance, various aspects of cost analysis,
and, in an effort to reduce costs, a variable staffing component
that required some nurses to "float" between wards and services
depending on the workload of the unit. These measures also had
increased the centralization of staffing decisions, as well as the
time spent on data collection activities at the unit level, which
caused some morale problems among staff nurses and criticism
from the union.

The political and cultural systems of the nursing department
had been in reasonably good alignment with the technical system,
but this was beginning to show signs of breakdown. Politically,
there had been a tradition of wide involvement within the department in formulating strategy and these dialogues resulted in
effective coalition management and minimum conflict over the
distribution and balancing of power within and between the nursing subsystems. The associated cohesive spirit within the nursing
department, which had served in the past to enhance its credibili-

ty, was rapidly deteriorating due to unhappiness with the
increased centralization, staff disenchantment with the growing
demands placed on them by middle managers (who had been pre-
occupied for years with the dilemma of responding to ad hoc
expansion of services without the provision of adequate funding),
and the consequent growth in the militancy of the union.
Succession politics, appraisal, and reward systems were still
strongly based on teamwork skills and commitment to quality
care, but it was necessary for managers to put more and more
emphasis on the formal union contract as a framework for relationships with their staff. The most important emerging misalignment, however, was the growing gap between the high technical
need and the low political feasibility of a coalition with medicine
for the planning of cost and quality control mechanisms.

Surmounting the challenges imposed by the requirements of
the technical system had traditionally been heavily dependent on
the professional commitments that derived from the occupational
socialization experiences of nurses and a cultural structure and
process that supplemented and sustained these commitments. This
too had begun to degenerate as the differences in the type of educational background, work assignment, and career expectations of
nurses increased and the values of unionism became more influential. The relationships between nursing managers and staff nurses
were steadily becoming more difficult at the very time when cohesion and commonality of purpose was of increasing importance.

Step 4: Modifying the Strategy

Although the problems facing nursing were the result of a normal
evolution in the face of a turbulent and hostile environment, by
the late 1980s they had reached a point where corrective action
was required. In general theoretical terms the department had
been using an open system, rational approach to management but
the general style of management, which had been highly ambidextrous, had slowly moved under the pressure of rapid change
toward the mechanistic side of the continuum. In terms of the
strategic management process, the department had been forced
into a reactive posture by its limited influence over the acquisition
and use of new medical technology. The department needed to
move from this reactive strategy, which had been necessary during the period of rapid growth, to a proactive strategy, in close
cooperation with the medical department, oriented to restraint
and cutbacks. It also needed to move back to a somewhat more
organic style of management and to reinvigorate the commitment
of staff nurses to the professional values of nursing.

Based on the case evidence presented here, the necessary changes were quite clear. At least three were needed in the technical system. The first was the need for the nursing department to develop a strong strategic management program, with a major emphasis on mission definition and strategy formulation, and to do this in close cooperation with a comparable program in medicine, at all levels of the two departmental structures. This was the most important priority because as soon as this rationalization of the management process was underway the remaining two priorities could be accomplished more easily. The second priority was to streamline the structure of middle management and support personnel, which would allow some reductions in their number as a result of the rationalized strategy process. The third was to reduce the labor intensity of the information system, improve its reliability and validity, and better integrate it with operating cost data, because this data would become especially important as the hospital moved toward more rational planning and increased budgetary restraint.

The highest priority changes in the political and cultural systems related to the top and middle managers in the nursing department. The remarkable complexity and turbulence of the environment, and of the organization itself, had vastly increased their importance as technical experts, political actors, and cultural leaders. Politically, the most important issue was the need to strengthen their prestige and influence in the eyes of both their staff and the physicians. In terms of the cultural system, it was becoming increasingly urgent to re-emphasize their leadership role in demonstrating the validity of professional nursing values, reconciling these values with the complementary aspects of the union priorities, and establishing constructive ways of reconciling the differences.

Implementing these changes would have required substantial initiative and support from senior management. In particular, changing the pattern of medical decision making and renewing the prestige and flexibility of middle managers, while simultaneously reducing their numbers, would require a great deal of creativity, courage, and skill on the part of the chief executive officer and the board.

What Was Done

The cost-revenue problem reached crisis proportions for the hospital in the late 1980s and senior management was impelled to implement massive reductions in costs. Given the magnitude and the persistence of the growth in government deficits, and in the costs of medical technology, it had become quite clear that the two most important elements of a solution lay outside of the nursing department: rationalization of physician utilization decisions and of interinstitutional competition for services and programs. This would require a major redefinition of the mission and goals of the hospital and would result in major cost reductions and improved quality. Senior management were unwilling to confront directly either of these issues and chose to focus change on structure and process in other services and programs.

Nursing was poorly positioned for the ensuing interdepartmental competition for funds. The nursing department was accountable for the largest single component of the total hospital budget and it was an area of rapid and continuing growth in costs. Because neither its strategic plan nor its information system had credibility at the senior levels of management, the perception had been created that nursing had little objective policy or data with which to justify its priorities and little ability to rectify this problem. Nursing lacked sufficient inherent political power to overcome these deficits and its weakness was compounded by the cultural divisions within the department, particularly the growing split between nursing management and the union, as well as the lack of active support from medicine.

In the above context, senior management undertook to assume direct control of nursing. Massive changes were imposed on the department by the chief executive officer within the space of two or three years. The head of the nursing department was replaced by an incumbent willing to represent senior management to nursing, rather than nursing to senior management, so that control of mission and strategy decisions for nursing could be controlled at the most senior level. (In many Canadian hospitals at this time, the senior executive nursing position was simply eliminated.) The staff responsible for the information system were disbanded and variable staffing was terminated. Many middle management and support staff positions (including evening and night supervisors, the specialized intravenous team, and most nursing researchers and educators) were eliminated and a policy of decentralizing responsibility to the staff nurse level was instituted, which compromised the authority and stature of the remaining managers so severely that many began to question the relevance of their role. Management dismissals were focussed particularly on those who questioned or even failed to actively support these changes, most of whom were among the most experienced and professionally committed managers, and the implicit meaning of this was clearly understood by those who remained. Large reductions were also made in the staff nurse complement and this, in conjunction with the decentralization of responsibility for a good deal of day-to-day decision making to the staff nurse level, substantially increased nursing workload. Senior management also undertook to introduce a "new" corporate culture, and established a separate group of staff to initiate and maintain its acceptance.

Decisions relating to the technical system were now controlled by lay administrators who were unencumbered by objective data regarding quality or workload. Politically, the nursing department had been purged of its management leadership: the illusion of nursing power was created through decentralization but, in the absence of an effective nursing hierarchy, it meant that staff nurses and their immediate supervisors now had substantial accountability with little authority or influence, that the union was now the main voice for nursing as a collectivity, and that the power for all major policy decisions regarding nursing was vested with senior management. By introducing a new corporate culture, senior management had also undertaken to define what was considered appropriate in terms of values and philosophy. The litany of popular management buzz words that were introduced, such as empowerment, shared governance, coaching, customer (for patient), and total quality management, created the illusion that the new management strategy was more organic and that a new and better "vision" of institutional values had been created. In reality, the policy decision process for the department was more centralized and arbitrary than it ever had been before. In addition, by discounting the inherent dependency of patients, the complex moral and legal issues involved in determining how the organization and the individual professional should share their joint responsibility for each patient had been trivialized.

Critique

None of the general priorities needed to modify a strategy, which is the fourth step of strategic management described earlier in this chapter, had been fulfilled in this hypothetical situation. The nursing department had been precluded from developing a proactive strategy. Close cooperation in strategic management between medicine and nursing had not been facilitated. The nursing information system had been abandoned. The move to a more organic style of management, through an exaggerated form of decentralization, had seriously compromised the remaining prestige and influence of middle managers. The new vision of cultural values was based more on popular interpretations of management in Japanese automobile factories than it was on a science based assessment of the complex professional realities of nursing in

North American high tech/high touch health care organizations. In addition, the formal responsibility for cultural leadership had been removed from the middle managers in nursing, which further reduced their prestige and influence.

Senior management had misdiagnosed what was appropriate for both the hospital and for nursing, and had failed to anticipate the negative consequences of the decisions that they made.

A serious error was committed when senior management failed to focus on rationalizing physician decision making and interinstitutional competition. Part of the reason was their failure to understand that this hospital had entered a new phase in its life cycle—one in which the environmental changes were so great that the basic mission and strategy of the organization had to be drastically changed if it were to cope adequately with its current and future cost-revenue problems. Part of the reason was a failure to recognize the ethical implications of not understanding the issues; senior management did not fulfill their moral obligation to know and to act on readily available information that traditional patterns of resource utilization by physicians, and of institutional autonomy, resulted in a grossly inefficient use of social resources and unnecessary levels of ineffective service.

Senior management had failed to recognize that rapid advances in the technology of nursing, especially in the educational levels and research base, had created a need for a stronger, not weaker, administrative presence on the part of the nursing department. They had failed to understand that a proactive nursing management strategy, not subordinated to but in cooperation with the medical department, was essential if the hospital were to be assured that the benefits of the burgeoning professional expertise of nursing would be delivered to the patients. They had also dismissed the importance of an information system, at a time of drastic restraint and cutback when objective data regarding nursing workload and output had reached a new level of importance.

In the political and cultural arenas, senior management had seriously underestimated the need to support strong professional and administrative leadership at the senior and middle levels of nursing management. As a result, they had overreacted to the need for a more organic style of management and had reduced the number and the power of nursing managers and support staff to the point where they were dangerously limited in their ability to fulfill their responsibilities for political and cultural leadership.

At a more general level, senior management had failed to understand the concept of organizational dilemmas and the negative potentials associated with them. In many important ways, they had subscribed to the disadvantages inherent in a "one best way" approach to management. In their rush to enhance communication by massive decentralization and management dismissals they had seriously hampered coordination. In an effort to reduce traditionalism by introducing a "new" corporate culture, they had undermined professional values and norms. In an effort to stimulate individual initiative by staff empowerment, they had damaged the ability of the organization to properly fulfill its responsibility for the acts of its employees and agents in delivering high-reliability services.

An additional important oversight was in the area of managerial ethics. Even though the clinical professions had been active in the definition and resolution of ethical issues involving patients, the senior management of this hypothetical hospital had failed to grapple with the ethical issues surrounding the development and implementation of management policy regarding budget restraint and cutback. Termination of life, the right to information, and the right to respect, for example, were now recognized as important issues that required careful assessment regarding patients, but the same standards were not applied to employees. Careers were terminated with impunity, planning information was withheld, and little respect was shown for the integrity, judgment, or experience of middle managers when the time came for planning and implementing how budget reductions would be effected. Senior management had repeatedly ignored their ethical duty to know the relevant facts of the situation, to be objective in the analysis of these facts, and to be fair in responding to these facts.

It is unlikely that the management strategy described in this case study will persist because it creates too many problems. Inadequate utilization of nursing technology will result in increased patient complaints, more lawsuits, and lowered staff morale. The reduced number of middle managers and the increased degree of decentralization will lower administrative efficiency to unacceptable levels. The organization will be under great pressure to modify its approach in the direction of a more mechanistic style and to place more emphasis on professional values and norms.

Unfortunately, there are two major constraints on the degree and rate of change. First, until the mission of the institution is rationalized, there will be insufficient funds available for more than minor improvements. In nursing, as in other sectors of the health care system, optimizing the range and quality of service will depend on much more progress in rationalizing physician decision making and interinstitutional competition. Second, change will depend heavily on the skill and vigor with which nurses pursue efforts to increase their power within the institution. Power is not a sufficient cause of sound management, but it is a necessary cause and, in the final analysis, inadequate intraorganizational power is the root cause of the problems facing this nursing department.

Postscript

In this chapter, I have tried to present a hypothetical case that is representative of acute care nursing management problems in many Canadian hospitals in the last decade and to analyze it in the context of organizational design theory. Insofar as this interpretation is valid, the public has not been well served by those assigned stewardship for these hospitals; the vitally important contribution of nursing to efficient and effective care has been diminished, not enhanced.

Acute care nurses are engaged in one of the most complex and difficult professional roles in society. Their relationship with the patient is intimate, intense, and continuous. They must be skilled in dealing with the physical, social, emotional, and spiritual needs of the patient and, often, of relatives and friends as well. They are responsible for a knowledge base that is growing rapidly in all of these areas. They routinely deal with profound ethical problems. They function in a technical, political, and cultural environment that is one of the most complex in society and one often hostile to both their personal and their professional needs and potentials.

It is not possible for nursing to fulfill its immense potential for improving the efficiency and effectiveness of hospital services without support; nursing must and should enjoy superior leadership from senior management. Nurses must also accept and vigorously pursue new responsibilities. Nursing has made substantial progress in enhancing the research foundation that underpins its professional status and in establishing a powerful union movement that protects the wages and conditions of work of its members. The benefits of this progress to both the patient and the individual nurse will continue to be threatened, however, if nurses do not recognize the importance of the nursing administrator's role and undertake to support it vigorously.

In the final analysis, the value of a case study is not in the interpretation of the outcome, but in the analytic framework that is presented, the issues that are raised, and the intellectual stimulus that is provided to those who have a responsibility to deal with similar situations. If this framework and case study helps the reader to be a better manager, or contribute to better management, even by stimulating and guiding an analysis that refutes the propositions and conclusions that have been presented, it will have served its purpose.

Acknowledgements

Although the content of this chapter is solely my responsibility, I wish to thank several people who provided invaluable assistance: Bruce Finkel, Felicity Hey, Don Juzwishin, Dave Reynolds, Ginette Rodger, and Janet Storch. A special thanks to my three favourite nurses: Beth, Dorothy, and Jacqueline.

References

Shortell, S.M., & Kaluzny, A.D. (1983). *Health care management: A text in organizational theory and behaviour.* Toronto: John Wiley & Sons.

Tichy, N.M. (1983). *Managing strategic change: Technical, political and cultural dynamics.* New York: John Wiley & Sons.

Annotated Bibliography

The following dozen readings represent a significant list for nurse managers in Canada. Some of them are old, but all are classics related to understanding problems in the management of health care agencies in Canada in the 1990s.

Angus, D.E. (1991). *Review of significant health care commissions and task forces in Canada since 1983-84.* Ottawa: Canadian Hospital Association, Canadian Medical Association, Canadian Nurses Association. A thoughtful and accurate summary of recommendations from major studies done during this time period.

Blau, P.M., & Scott, W.R. (1962). *Formal organizations.* San Francisco: Chandler. This is "an oldie but a goldie." Blau and Scott synthesized a good deal of the contemporary research and contributed a number of valuable interpretations and insights, including the concept of organizational dilemmas.

Daft, R.L. (1992). *Organization theory and design* (4th ed.). St. Paul, MN: West. There are many excellent introductory textbooks in organizational design and this is one of them. It provides much more detail on theory and research than was possible in this chapter.

Growe, S.J. (1991). *Who cares: The crisis in Canadian nursing.* Toronto: McClelland & Stewart. A brilliant analysis of the problems and the promise facing Canadian nurses. This is essential reading for anyone with an obligation to understand the nursing profession.

Juzwishin, D.W.M. (1993). Ethical issues in health services administration. *Canadian Health Care Management* (pp. 12.1-12.12). Toronto: MPL Communication. Juzwishin was one of the first to recognize and write about ethical issues in management. An excellent overview of the existing literature and the major issues.

Perrow, C. (1973, Summer). The short and glorious history of organizational theory. *Organizational Dynamics.* Written 20 years ago, this short article is still one of the best available critiques of modern organizational theory. The annotated bibliography is also useful.

Rachlis, M., & Kushner, C. (1989). *Second opinion: What's wrong with Canada's health care system and how to fix it.* Toronto: Collins. A research-based critique of the Canadian health care system that exposes a wide variety of its fundamental problems.

Shortell, S.M., & Kaluzny, A.D. (1983). *Health care management: A text in organizational theory and behaviour.* Toronto: John Wiley & Sons. A collection of commissioned articles of core topics in both organizational behaviour and design as applied to health organization. Unusually high quality but designed for expert readers.

Spirn, S., & Benfer, D.W. (1982). *Issues in health care management.* Rockville, MD: Aspen Systems Corporation. An invaluable collection of classical articles tailored for the use of health services managers.

Storch, J.L. (1982). *Patients rights: Ethical and legal issues in health care and nursing.* Toronto: McGraw-Hill Ryerson. Storch was a pioneer in the area of ethical issues in health care and this is still one of the best overviews of the topic that is available. The bibliography is also excellent.

Tichy, N.M. (1983). *Managing strategic change: Technical, political, and cultural dynamics.* New York: John Wiley & Sons. A detailed exposition about the origins and substance of TPC Theory. Recommended only for the advanced reader.

Tichy, N.M., & Devanna, M.A. (1986). *The transformational leader.* New York: John Wiley & Sons. The authors use the TPC framework to discuss the planning and implementation of organizational change. Examples and cases from American business management are used extensively to provide practical and realistic insights.

C H A P T E R 5

Cost Containment: Doing More with Less

Jan Dick and Sharon Bruce

Jan Dick, RN, is former Vice-President, Nursing, at St. Boniface General Hospital, Winnipeg, and Assistant Professor, Faculty of Nursing, University of Manitoba. She is founder of the Academy of Chief Executive Nurses (ACEN). She is also a founder and former editor of *The Canadian Journal of Nursing Administration* and has been active in nursing administration organizations at the provincial and national levels.

Sharon Bruce, RN, BSN, MA (Manitoba), is a doctoral student in the Department of Anthropology, University of Manitoba, and a research assistant in the Faculties of Nursing and Medicine, University of Manitoba.

The Canadian health care system is considered by many to be one of the finest systems in the developed world. Notwithstanding this praise, the system is at a crossroads whereby the demand for high quality patient care is continuously compromised by a rapidly declining resource base. Added to this is the demand by provincial governments (as primary funders of the system) for even greater efficiencies and effectiveness within this current resource base.

How can this be accomplished? One response has been to adopt industrial programs, such as total quality management, that endeavour to improve efficiency and effectiveness. Another response has been to incorporate programs such as staff mix, organizational restructuring, and managed care. Finally, governments have chosen to limit and reduce resources to health institutions and agencies and explore alternative models of care delivery. The result of the latter has been bed closures, staff layoffs, program cancellations, reduction of management staff, and restructuring of the work force.

Nurses have an important role to play in the many changes occurring in health care. Consequently, knowledge of both the history of the health care system and the funding formulas currently in use are necessary if nursing managers are to make effective decisions and use resources efficiently. This chapter will include a review of the historical development of health care funding and current models of funding. Contemporary actions for cost reduction will be highlighted along with their impact on nursing. Finally, three approaches for cost reduction currently in use at the St. Boniface Hospital in Winnipeg, Manitoba, will be examined.

Terminology

The terms "efficient" and "effective" are prevalent in the literature regarding the Canadian health care system. Effectiveness refers to the extent to which output meets predetermined objectives, while efficiency refers to the ratio of inputs to outputs. Inefficiency and ineffectiveness translate into increased costs. The effectiveness and efficiency of health care are inextricably tied to the concept of quality because the determination of effectiveness and efficiency is dependent upon a definition of quality care (which includes measurable components of quality) (Ehrat, 1987). In other words, to determine if a process is efficient or effective, one must first have a predetermined quality standard against which comparisons can be made. The challenge for providers of health care is to ensure effective and efficient care without compromising quality.

Financing Health Care in Canada

Anyone seeking to understand the way health care is financed in Canada needs to be aware of four basic pieces of legislation that affect health care and hospital services. As well, this opening section offers a brief introduction to the current shift by funding agencies (mainly provincial governments) from a flexible budgetary system based on demand by the institution to a system in which the institution must adapt to a predetermined fixed budget.

The Hospital Insurance and Diagnostic Services Act

Prior to 1957, planning and construction grants were provided by the federal government to the provinces for the construction of hospitals (Vayda, 1986). Subsequently, extensive construction occurred. However, funding for the operating costs of these facilities fast became an issue and provinces began requesting financial support from the federal government. It was at this time that Saskatchewan introduced publicly funded hospital insurance. Under the terms of the plan, all residents received coverage for the costs of care received in a hospital. Other provinces soon followed Saskatchewan's lead and after much public pressure the federal government, in 1957, enacted the Hospital Insurance and Diagnostic Services Act (HIDSA), which was to provide financial assistance to provincial hospital insurance plans on a cost-shared basis. This act enabled prepaid coverage to be universally available to everyone. The federal government agreed to share with the provinces the costs of hospital services under a specific funding formula. If they wished to participate in the plan, provinces had to agree to several conditions, including: (1) a minimum but broad range of inpatient services to be insured (outpatient services were optional); (2) standardized national reporting; (3) services to be available on equal terms and conditions; and (4) adherence to basic standards (Sutherland & Fulton, 1988). If these requirements were met, the federal government was responsible for contributing half the hospital operating costs as well and an equalization component that offered subsidies greater than 50% of actual costs for the poorer provinces and less than 50% for the wealthier provinces (Vayda, 1986).

The Medical Care Act

The introduction of hospital insurance made the need for medical insurance obvious because hospitals were overburdened with providing services that could have been performed in physicians' offices. The introduction of medical insurance was received with considerable opposition by physicians. In an effort to resolve the impasse, the federal government appointed a commission under the chairmanship of Justice Emmett Hall to study the matter. Following the release of the Hall Commission report in 1964 and extensive federal/provincial negotiation, the Medical Care Act passed in 1967. This act also introduced a cost-sharing program between the two levels of government for hospital and medical fees. The program was conditional upon the following criteria: (1) coverage would be comprehensive (i.e., coverage would be inclusive of all insured services provided by hospitals, physicians, or other health professionals); (2) coverage would be universal (i.e., all residents of the province would be insured under uniform conditions and terms; (3) benefits would be portable from province to province; and (4) the plan would be administered by a public organization accountable to government. The funding formula was different from the hospital insurance program but the federal government was still responsible for 50% of the costs. The plan was again designed with the intention of providing poorer provinces with more assistance (Sutherland & Fulton, 1988).

Established Programs Financing Act

Within a short time it became obvious to the federal government that such sharing arrangements were costly and provided no incentive to the provinces to control costs. In 1969, a task force was appointed by the federal government to study the cost of health services. A new formula for federal contributions was enacted in 1977 under the Established Programs Financing Act (EPF); over the years, this particular legislation has changed names (e.g., to the Federal-Provincial Fiscal Arrangements Act) but the intent has remained intact. Federal contributions, rather than being dependent on actual costs, were tied to growth of the gross national product (GNP). Along with this change, federal income and corporate taxes were reduced and provinces allowed to increase their tax rates to balance federal reductions. It was now the sole responsibility of the provincial governments to supply any additional moneys required to meet cost increases that exceeded the growth of the GNP (Vayda, 1986). In other words, the federal government would provide block funding to the provinces, thus eliminating the cost-shared agreements of earlier years. The provinces could use the payments provided under the EPF at their own discretion (i.e., they could choose to spend it on health care or on other priorities) (Dick, 1988).

In 1982, a review of the EPF resulted in capping of federal contributions. In 1992, several changes were made to the act effectively to remove health services funding by the federal government by 1995 (Bill C-20). This change has initiated a process of intense study by the provinces to determine the actions required over the next few years to manage health care funding.

The Canada Health Act

Under the terms of the medical insurance agreement and the EPF any actions that restricted access to health services were considered violations of the four fundamental conditions required for federal funding. The federal government interpreted hospital user fees and extra billing by physicians to be such actions. In 1984, under the Canada Health Act, the federal government enacted legislation designed to eliminate extra charges (Vayda, 1986). Conditions for federal contributions to health care now included coverage of 100% of the population and limited application of extra charges to insured services. User fees and extra physician billing were penalized by the loss of one dollar of EPF payment for every dollar of user fees or extra billing (Sutherland & Fulton, 1988).

Many provincial governments have large deficits and stagnant economies, and therefore claim that there is a fixed amount of money with which to operate each hospital. Hospitals then must provide programs of care and services within a fixed budget which reflects the change from flexible to fixed funding (Dick, 1988).

Shift from Flexible to Fixed Funding

An institution's organization, policies, procedures, information systems, and attitudes are highly influenced by the manner in which money is generated. With respect to a tertiary teaching hospital, these elements are integrated with patient care, teaching, research, and the hospital's overall mission.

A dramatic change in the generation of revenue therefore affects the hospital. For example, in Manitoba two such major changes have occurred. The first occurred in 1958, with the advent of government-sponsored health insurance, and the second with the transition to fixed funding. Similar decisions have been made by other provincial departments of health across Canada. The dynamics can best be depicted by the schemata shown in Figure 5.1 (p. 96).

The dynamics of change depicted in the schemata markedly influence hospital management, especially nursing management, across Canada. Hospitals now must develop techniques whereby standards and volumes correspond to pre-established revenues. The hospitals operate in an environment where revenues are determined by a funding agency and costs are mainly generated by independent contractors (physicians). Such pressures require new and innovative management techniques and systems that respond to the new financial climate as well as fulfil hospitals' obligations to provide quality care.

Figure 5.1
Influence of funding models on patient care.

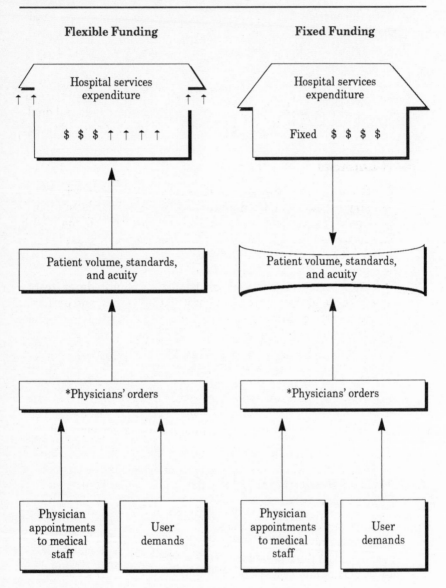

*Unpredictable, since related to individual patient need

Source: Based on Dick, J. (1988), Can we afford the care we give? In Besel, L. and R.G. Stock (Eds.), *Benchmarks I. A sourcebook for Canadian nursing management.* Toronto: Carswell, p. 328.

Quality of Care and Cost Reduction

With the current fiscal environment, nursing administrators and their counterparts have had to strike a delicate balance between cost control and the effective and efficient delivery of quality patient care. The fiscal pressures are such that mechanisms are required that will allow application of quality standards within the boundaries of cost compliance (Ehrat, 1987). Three such mechanisms include cost standards, medical utilization, and total quality management. Each of these is discussed in more detail below.

Cost Standards

The development of cost standards is most advanced in private industry in both the United States and Canada. Less common in both countries has been application of cost standards in the health care sector. As fiscal pressures have increased over the past decade, the development of cost standards in health care has advanced.

Cost standards are predetermined costs of procedures, tests, or services, and they serve as the basis for budgeting and performance reporting. Cost standards are composed of two factors: the quality or amount of resources required and their individual costs. The determination of the resource requirement for a given standard is dependent on a number of variables, including use of historical information, teaching affiliations, severity of illness, case mix, equipment and supplies cost, and geographic treatment patterns (Chandler, 1986). Many believe that cost standards can be used as the means for measuring productivity, efficiency, and effectiveness.

Utilization Management

Utilization management (sometimes referred to as UM) is a comprehensive plan used to increase the efficiency and effectiveness of services provided. Utilization management consists of two components: (1) comparison of actual performance to established standards of care and (2) development of measures to correct identified problems (Harrison, Juzwishin, & Roger, 1989; Sheps, Anderson, & Cardiff, 1991). The first component of utilization management is also referred to as utilization review and it consists of application of defined criteria, expert opinion, or both to the actual process of care in order to evaluate the efficiency of the process and determine the appropriateness of the decision-making processes. The second component occurs in response to deficiencies encountered in the review process and consists of identifying and employing techniques to modify behaviours of providers, patients, and administrators. The objective of utilization management is to achieve both cost containment and quality of care. In this respect utilization management is related to quality assurance, but the former focusses primarily on the process of medical care while quality assurance focusses on both structure and process in relation to the outcome of care (Sheps, Anderson, & Cardiff, 1991).

One significant aspect of utilization management is the examination of the necessity for care and the appropriateness of the care provided. This is often difficult because variation in treatment practice has been viewed as the privilege of physicians. The development of criteria to use as a yardstick for measurement is also difficult because treatment modalities often are not based on scientific research but on patterns of routine. Therefore, to be effective, utilization management programs must involve clinical leaders in both the development of standard criteria and analysis of observed practice (Harrison, Juzwishin, & Roger, 1989).

Total Quality Management

Total quality management (TQM) originated in the United States and was first tried successfully in the industrial sector of Japan following World War II. Total quality management is a "top-down" management philosophy that requires commitment to the continuous improvement of quality (Masters & Schmele, 1991) or product and service (Arikian, 1991). According to McLaughlin and Kaluzny (1990), total quality management calls for continuous improvement in the total process of providing care. Improvement is therefore based on both outcome and process.

Perhaps the best definition of TQM is "to do the right thing right the first time, on time, all the time, and to strive always for improvement and customer satisfaction" (Masters & Schmele, 1991, p. 8). One of the basic tenets of total quality management is that most problems in an organization are related to structure and process and not to employee errors (McLaughlin & Kaluzny, 1990). Total quality management differs from most quality assurance methods with which nurses are familiar in that a key feature is prevention. Rather than discovering errors or instances of poor service after they occur, total quality management deals with problems before they arise. Its application has increased productivity, improved and maintained quality, and reduced costs. It is obvious that if systems can be improved so that processes are always completed correctly the first time, costs will be reduced (Masters & Schmele, 1991).

As was the case for cost standards, TQM has primarily been applied in the industrial sector but many believe the methods can be successfully applied to nursing and health care (Casalou, 1991; McCabe, 1992; Williams & Howe, 1992).

Approaches to Cost Reductions

It is evident then that the economy of the country has a significant effect on the delivery of health care. The shift from flexible to fixed funding, along with significant revenue reductions, has demanded innovative techniques to ensure the delivery of quality and cost-efficient care. Examples of cost-cutting measures currently employed include preventive maintenance, group purchasing, product evaluation, and infection control. More recent strategies aimed at cost reduction include comprehensive operational reviews, zero-based budgeting, capping activities, downsizing (bed closures), envelope funding, consolidation of hospitals, and restructuring and work redesign. Each of these latter strategies will be briefly reviewed.

Comprehensive Operational Review

Comprehensive review involves establishment of operating standards for each area of activity and comparison of actual performance and productivity measures against those predetermined standards. In turn, areas for cost and operational improvement are identified.

Zero-Based Budgeting

In zero-based budgeting, a budget analysis is prepared for every expenditure decision centre, cost centre, and/or service centre in the hospital. Cost estimates are prepared for a variety of activity levels or service levels above and below those currently provided. Particular emphasis is paid to non-service costs, such as overhead or administrative support costs. During such a review, opportunities for cost reduction are identified and the consequences of not continuing with particular programs or services are evaluated.

Capping Activities

In agencies that propose capping activities, an activity level is determined for a particular clinical program; this usually considers both acuity and volume. For example, a determination will be made that a hospital will perform 500 open-heart surgical cases annually. The types of surgeries performed will be somewhat flexible but must remain within the dollars allocated to the program. Consideration is given to reduced length of hospitalization and to newer, more efficient surgical technology. Capping may lead to increased waiting time for surgery and to the economic notion of scarcity.

Downsizing

In hospital and nursing management, downsizing usually means bed closures, staff layoffs, and redesign of remaining activities. Reduction in average length of stay, medical utilization management, increased day surgery, and same-day admission for surgery have contributed to combating the effect of scarcity of services.

Envelope Funding

Envelope funding is a new approach to cost reduction being undertaken in Manitoba. It involves the establishment of a provincial program with a physician appointed as head (e.g., obstetrics, cancer care, pediatrics). A budget envelope is allocated for the complete program, including hospital care, community care, and so on. Allotments are then made to the various agencies involved in the program. Program standards and activity levels are to be determined by the program head. Understandably, many questions have been raised regarding this system, and details and guidelines are being developed.

Consolidation of Activities

The best examples of consolidation of activities in hospital management in the early 1990s are found in New Brunswick and Saskatchewan, although many differences exist in the process in the two provinces. In general, boards of hospitals merge into one larger regional board (in which community agencies may be included as well). Executive management is also merged, which may increase layers of management resulting in additional bureaucracy. The status and role of medicine and nursing in the new organizational structure seem to be downgraded. However, such consolidation may provide a better mechanism for consumer input. Data regarding the cost savings to be realized, if any, have not yet been provided.

Restructuring and Work Redesign

Savings may be realized when work processes are examined and changed. One example of change involves a reduction in levels of management. In this scenario, management becomes "leaner," resulting in changes to roles and responsibilities. The span of control for management personnel becomes larger (i.e., more individuals reporting to them), and the role becomes less supervisory. The expectation with such a change is that individuals within an organization (nurses) are professionals who are able to act in an autonomous role and therefore do not require complete supervision.

Some current models of workplace restructuring include as a central philosophy the concept of patient-focussed care. One such strategy is the managed care approach. According to Lamb, Deber, Naylor, and Hastings (1991), "managed care involves planning, organizing and implementing a system in which the goals of health care can be realized" (p. 4). Two common goals are cost containment and quality care. Managed care involves changes to the traditional fee-for-service health care system because this system encourages expensive overservice. A change to alternative methods of health care delivery is believed to result in containment of costs through the elimination of unnecessary care, the reduction in length of hospital stay, the use of preventive and health promoting strategies, and the efficient use of resources. These strategies will also result in an improved quality of care (Lamb, Deber, Naylor, & Hastings, 1991).

Other examples of change include staff mix (using the partner/helper concept in nursing), nursing without walls, and a patient-centred hospital that uses cross-training techniques, consolidation of departments, and other strategies to achieve the patient-centred goal. Approaches in restructuring and redesign hold much promise for nursing and will be reviewed more completely later in the chapter.

Impact on Nursing

The above approaches to cost reduction require careful planning and implementation time. The precipitous actions of some provincial governments to reduce costs has created a chaotic and unsettling environment for nurse managers. In such difficult economic times two important questions must be addressed: How can quality of care be maintained and improved? and, How can the nursing profession best provide care to those in need? Some solutions can be found by examining nursing information systems, patient outcomes, and work redesign.

Staffing Systems and Quality Care Indicators

The development of valid and reliable quality care indicators and productivity measures appropriate for nursing is crucial if nursing is to demonstrate the basis for the demand for nursing care in the health care system. Further research in this area is necessary if there are to be meaningful criteria for measurement, and it is the responsibility of the profession to establish acceptable standards for these measures (Cleland, 1990).

Hospital nurse staffing systems provide both nurse productivity information and a method for classifying patients based upon dependency on nursing care. Therefore, the nursing resources required do not generally correspond to medical severity indicators or the DRG (diagnostic related groups) groupings. In other words, a patient within a DRG group and a medical severity indicator may rate low in medical resource requirement but high in nursing care requirement (O'Brien-Pallas, 1988). If provinces are considering using DRGs as a method of payment without considering the nursing resources required, then there could be serious issues regarding the funding of true nursing costs. Reliable and valid information must therefore be provided to nursing managers in order that funding may meet true nursing costs.

Patient Outcomes

Patient outcomes from nursing care received are still not well described or designed. However, if appropriate grouping of production factors in nursing care delivery combine to provide production processes that create efficacious, efficient, and safe nursing care services at reasonable costs, then much has been accomplished. Those who pay for health services expect them to be given at reasonable, if not minimal, costs. Nursing can affect such production processes while achieving improvements (Cleland, 1990). For example, in hospitals nurses can establish pre-admission clinics in which patients are assessed for surgical procedures. All admission "work-ups" would be completed and same-day admission (same-day surgery) would be possible. Length of hospitalization would be affected without compromising quality. In the community, a specialized child and maternal health nursing service could be developed whereby mothers and newborns could be discharged within six to thirty-six hours after delivery. Length of stay is decreased and quality outcomes exist. Many more creative and innovative approaches are possible.

Further work in describing patient outcomes is required so changes and shifts from inpatient to outpatient care may be evaluated. If hospital nursing care is well planned to fit patients' needs so that the organization of the processes are smooth, and the patient returns home in a good physical and mental state, then the impact that nursing has on costs of outcome is obvious.

Work Redesign

Work redesign and work restructuring hold the greatest promise and opportunities for nursing in the 1990s. The idea that nursing work can be redesigned so that greater efficiencies are realized and quality care is delivered is being explored in both the United States and Canada.

Nursing work design must be reevaluated in response to economic realities. The downsizing occurring in most provinces is having a profound impact on the number of nurses employed, with the result that a surplus of nurses is available for employment. However, many options are available to nurses in different fields of practice. By acquiring appropriate additional education and relevant experience, nurses can prepare for the future health care system. Areas of employment in advanced clinical practice, such as community nurse managed centres, primary care, nursing case management, and professor-clinician appointments in a reformed nursing education model, should expand if the principles expressed by provincial governments are realized (i.e., greater emphasis on prevention, increased care delivered in the home).

St. Boniface General Hospital's Experience

Redesigning nursing care or nursing care delivery while maintaining quality and achieving more effective care can be successful in today's world of dwindling resources. At St. Boniface General Hospital in Winnipeg, three initiatives are being developed within a nursing model; these integrate practice, education, and research and prepare for nursing as a continuum of care.

The first initiative is the change to a new staff mix system. Many professional nurses commented during the 1980s that, increasingly, non-nursing tasks or low-level functions have crept into nursing work. Documentation began to be more time consuming, and computerized hospital information systems added to nursing work (Hughes et al., 1993). Primary nursing and total patient care nursing systems have to some degree added to these difficulties. Primary nursing and total patient care systems now require the professional nurse to have assistance with non-nursing or lower-level tasks. The systems are based on partnerships between a registered nurse and a helper; together they provide daily patient care. Care is focussed at the bedside and schedules are determined by patient needs. The registered nurse manages the partnership, and helpers are responsible for such activities as assisting patients to bathe and eat, taking vital signs, and positioning.

Helpers are trained in a special educational program that includes hands-on experience and is administered by the hospital. Licensed Practical Nurses (LPNs) or Certified Nursing Assistants could be used. However, in Manitoba the salary gap between registered nurses and licensed practical nurses has become so close that it is not financially sound to hire LPNs into this helper role. Further, provincial legislation introduced in 1981 presumes increased standards of practice so that LPN expectations and aspirations do not include a helper role. The approach taken at St. Boniface Hospital was to provide two options. The first option was that of further education—90 out of 120 LPNs opted for further education and up-graded to registered nurses. The second option was for LPNs to apply for the helper positions. The role of ward clerks will also be enhanced so that the clerical work on the nursing unit will be included in their job description. This system will save nursing salary dollars, allow for the provision of quality care, and permit the registered nurse the time to practise nursing.

The second system is known as integrated nursing practice groups. Although not yet fully developed, this system is based on the idea that nurses work naturally in groups and value group practice (Attridge & Callahan, 1990; Nuttal, 1991). The group of practising nurses consists of novice to expert specialized staff, professor-clinicians who practise as well as teach, students at both undergraduate and graduate levels, and nurse scientists. The group cares for a homogeneous set of patients (e.g., oncology patients). As well, in-hospital patient care, outreach, and community services are provided.

Nursing case management is being further developed in this model. Nurses maintain accountability for cost-effectiveness and quality of care. Nurses working in a variety of settings (e.g., acute care, ambulatory care, outreach) provide care across a continuum, reducing fragmentation and improving comprehensiveness. Because research and education are also integrated, the model constantly upgrades itself (i.e., new knowledge is gained in research and translated into education). The model is practice based and patient centred and is cost efficient in several areas. For example, costs are reduced because fragmentation and duplication of care are reduced. Education costs are reduced because professors also practise and education is more relevant (students are part of the nursing milieu). Graduates are less likely to require extensive continuing education in specialties if they complete a nursing major in their senior year.

The third system is a patient-focussed system that maximizes the amount of time the registered nurse spends on patient care. Care activities are being moved to the bedside, cross-training is being used, and more facilities will be situated at the unit level (e.g., housekeeping, satellite lab).

Conclusion

During the remainder of the 1990s, economic growth is predicted to be slow and governments are expected to continue their attempts at deficit reductions. Consequently, revenues to supply the health care system will continue to be reduced. Professional nursing wishes to serve efficiently and effectively and care for those in need while maintaining the quality of the care provided. Nurse managers can contribute and lead in the drive to efficiency and effectiveness through good business practices, good nursing management information systems, and creative approaches to work redesign.

This chapter has given an historical overview of the Canadian health care system in order to provide some insight into current funding systems and economic realities. The authors have outlined approaches to cost reductions and discussed the resulting impact on nursing. Although the St. Boniface General Hospital experience is just beginning, it provides some examples of work redesign that are underway in other jurisdictions as well.

The area of nursing economics, as it further develops in Canada, will become invaluable in supplying information from research. In turn, this will provide rationale for actions taken by nurse managers. Further research into nurse staffing systems, case mix management, nursing labour economics, and quality of work life for nurses will provide the "grist for the mill." Governments, leaders, and administrators require such information on which to base decisions affecting health care. Nurse managers can translate much of the nursing economics information into practice; a highly motivated, productive, and effective nursing work force can be the outcome.

References

Arikian, V.L. (1991). Total quality management. Applications to nursing service. *Journal of Nursing Administration, 21*(6), 46-50.

Attridge, C., & Callahan, M. (1990). Nurses' perspectives of quality work environments. *Canadian Journal of Nursing Administration, 3*(2), 18-24.

Casalou, R.F. (1991). Total quality management in health care. *Hospital and Health Services Administration, 36*(1), 134-145.

Chandler, A. (1986, September). Integrating standard cost information into operating budgets. *Health Care Financial Management,* pp. 127-128.

Cleland, V.S. (1990). *The economics of nursing.* Norwalk, CT: Appleton & Lange.

Dick, J. (1988). Can we afford the care we give? In L. Besel & R.G. Stock (Eds.), *Benchmarks I. A sourcebook for Canadian nursing management* (pp. 324-336). Toronto: Carswell.

Ehrat, K.S. (1987). The cost-quality balance: An analysis of quality, effectiveness, efficiency, and cost. *Journal of Nursing Administration, 17*(5), 6-13.

Harrison, F.P., Juzwishin, D., & Roger, R. (1989). Quality of care and utilization management: Contemporary tools and strategies. *Healthcare Management Forum, 2* (2), 18-23.

Hughes, L., Adaskin, E., Dreidger, M., Kennedy, L., McLean, M., McMorris, D., McMullan, P., Rapko, H., Rowluk, J., & Sinha, L. (1993). Impact of computerization on nursing: Automated order entry, care planning, and implications for recruitment. *Canadian Journal of Nursing Administration, 6*(2), 14-18.

Lamb, M., Deber, R., Naylor, C.D., & Hastings, J.E.F. (1991). *Managed care in Canada.* Ottawa: Canadian Hospital Association Press.

Masters, F., & Schmele, J.A. (1991). Total quality management: An idea whose time has come. *Journal of Nursing Quality Assurance, 5*(4), 7-16.

McCabe, W.J. (1992). Total quality management in a hospital. *Quarterly Review Bulletin, 18,* 134-140.

McLaughlin, C.P., & Kaluzny, A.D. (1990, Summer). Total quality management in health: Making it work. *Health Care Management Review, 15,* 7-14.

Nuttal, G. (1991). Unpublished internal document on cultural research project. University of Manitoba Faculty of Management, Manitoba.

O'Brien-Pallas, L. (1988). An analysis of the multiple approaches to measuring nursing workload. *Canadian Journal of Nursing Administration, 1*(2), 8-11.

Sheps, S.B., Anderson, G., & Cardiff, K. (1991). Utilization management: A literature review for Canadian health care administrators. *Healthcare Management Forum, 4* (1), 34-39.

Sutherland, R.W., & Fulton, M.J. (1988). *Health care in Canada.* Ottawa: M.O.M. Printing.

Vayda, E. (1986). The Canadian health care system: An overview. *Journal of Public Health Policy, 7,* 205-210.

Williams, T., & Howe, R. (1992). W. Edwards Deming and total quality management: An interpretation for nursing practice. *Journal of Healthcare Quarterly, 14*(1), 36-39.

C   H   A   P   T   E   R   6

Intraorganizational Politics

Ginette Lemire Rodger

Ginette Lemire Rodger, RN, BScN (Ottawa), MAdmN (Montréal), is a candidate toward a doctoral degree in nursing at the University of Alberta. From 1981-89 she was Executive Director of the Canadian Nurses Association, the Canadian Nurses Foundation, and the Canadian Nurses Protective Society. From 1974-81, she was Director of Nursing at Notre-Dame Hospital in Montréal. She has diversified experience in clinical nursing, management, education, and research and has been widely recognized for her contribution to nursing administration.

Intraorganizational politics is an important concept for nurse managers. It plays a significant role in every aspect of the professional (and social) life of nurse managers. The important questions, such as which health goals are pursued, who receives what care and when, which health care programs are maintained or deleted, which resources are allocated to these programs, which organizational models will be implemented and by whom, are all political issues. This topic of intraorganizational politics is directly related to nursing's ultimate goal—the consumer's health.

A Time of Change

The need for political knowledge and skills is now recognized more than ever by nurse managers who find themselves in an unprecedented time of change as the whole Canadian health care system is being overhauled and nurses find their role, their values, and their place in the system being questioned. This, however, is the nature of change. In 1963, Erikson predicted that the rate of change would continue to accelerate, that humans and institutions would face multiple simultaneous changes, and that the limits of human and institutional adaptability were not yet known. That was more than 30 years ago, when it was difficult to conceptualize that reality; today, change is still accelerating and intensifying.

Kurt Lewin (1951), a well-known theorist of change, would call the period of change that the Canadian health care system is experiencing "the unfrozen state." Change, according to his theory, has three stages: the unfreezing stage, a cognitive phase in which the individual is exposed to the idea of the need for change; the moving stage, a cognitive redefinition in which the change is planned and initiated; and the refreezing stage, in which the change is integrated and stabilized. During the unfreezing and moving phases, the next direction is initiated and movement begins. This is usually a time of insecurity, repositioning, challenges, and no clear answers. But it is also a time of opportunity. During this time, effective politics can make a great difference in setting the course of action of a project, a department, or an organization.

Need for Manager Awareness

As Starke and Rempel (1988) observe, "Because politics is so common, managers in all kinds of organizations must understand what it is and why it occurs. They must also learn to cope with its manifestations if they wish to be successful in their careers" (p. 12). Nurse managers must be knowledgeable about politics and related concepts, such as power, influence, and the political process. Theoretical knowledge is important, but not sufficient. Managers must develop abilities and skills in using these concepts if they are to influence decisions to support nursing goals. It is one thing to know about politics and another to be political.

The term "intraorganizational" in this chapter means within a health care agency. "Politics," as used in this chapter, can be defined broadly as influence. Pffeffer (1981) defines organizational politics as the behaviours of individuals as they attempt "to acquire, develop, and use power and other resources to obtain their preferred outcomes in a situation where there is uncertainty . . . about choices" (p. 7). Several other definitions are also relevant to this chapter.

Laswell (1936), for example, defined politics as "the study of influence and the influential" (p. 13) and said that to comprehend politics one must look not only at who draws power but also at the relationship the person has with those affected by the actions. The same notion of politics is echoed in the work of Stevens (1980b) as "a process by which one influences the decisions of others and exerts control over situations and events" (p. 208). If politics is defined in terms of influence and control, so is power. Shiflett and McFarland (1978) define power as "one person's degree of influence over others, to the extent that obedience or conformity are assumed to follow" (p. 19).

The definition for the actions required to bring about the concepts of politics and power is also important. Political action or process can be defined as a systematic series of actions directed toward influencing others into conformity with a pursued goal. It is interesting to note that the definitions of politics, power, influence, and the political process have similar roots. They all entail the notion of producing an effect by altering or modifying ideas, behaviours, or things. In other words, the mechanism central to politics and power is the process of planned change. The terms "planned change" and "political process" are used interchangeably in this chapter.

For more than a decade, I have used a political process framework (see Table 6.1) to show how nurses can successfully bring about organizational and social change. This framework highlights some of the elements of intraorganizational politics and, at the same time, can serve as a guide for nurse managers who want to use a political process to bring about change. The same five-step process is followed whether a manager wants to bring about a change, guide a change in a different direction, or prevent a change from taking place that could be detrimental to client care. A more detailed analysis of the five steps of the process follows.

Table 6.1

Political process framework.

1. Establish the goal and objectives

2. Assess positive and negative factors
   a. Social values and trends
   b. Key individuals or groups
   c. Sources of power
   d. Resources
   e. Timing

3. Plan the strategy

4. Implement the strategy

5. Evaluate and readjust the strategy

Establishment of Goal and Objectives

Since change is multifaceted and constant, the setting of goal and objectives is an important step in the political process. First of all, there is a need to set priorities among the competing issues. Which issues are essential to be dealt with and in what way? Some issues play a pivotal role in an organization because they control other secondary or dependent issues. Therefore, dealing with essential issues will in fact influence resolution of other issues.

Setting priorities means making choices. Choice implies being able to let go of some issues to concentrate the efforts of the group on the pivotal issues and then establishing specific objectives for each of these pivotal issues.

The political process is most effectively exercised when the purpose is clear. The process of clarifying objectives can take time and involve much thought, consultation, and research, depending on the scope of the issue being addressed. One may begin with a general idea of the desirable results or the goal, but there is also a need to refine the objectives, including what needs to be done, when, and where. The products of the establishment of the goal and objectives are (1) a clear goal, (2) a set of objectives, (3) target individual(s) or group(s), and (4) a message that conveys the value of the endeavour.

Barbara Stevens (1980a) reminds us that unity is a prerequisite for effectiveness in such endeavours and therefore must be considered in this first step of the political process framework. She urges nurses to debate their policies (goals and objectives) internally, make decisions, and then present a united face to the public or the organization that they are trying to influence.

For example, two goals are important for nurse managers to keep in mind in the present health care reform taking place in Canada because they are pivotal issues. These are: allocation of health care resources, and the leadership position of nursing in the health care system. Specific objectives are currently being developed by some nurse managers to address these issues in their milieu.

Health Care Resources

The allocation of scarce resources is often the most vital of issues in any organization and is reflected in power plays (political struggles). Del Bueno (1986) noted that "in times of economic scarcity, political activity increases as individuals compete for those declining resources. A power holder must not only have control of valued resources, but must be willing to use them to influence others. When power is hoarded it atrophies and blocks achievement" (pp. 125-126).

In an ideal world where nursing care would be as valued as other types of care, the allocation of resources would be a non-issue because objective data about the effects of such care would guide the allocation. However, this is a naive view of the allocation of health care resources in the real world. In fact, whoever controls resources influences and moulds the delivery of client care and determines who receives what care. For example, the way a hospital allocates its material resources, such as supplies and equipment, usually reflects the power and influence of physicians (Mason & McCarthy, 1985).

There is ample research evidence that nurses can deliver many health care services in a better and more cost-effective way, whether in hospitals or in the community (Canadian Nurses Association, 1993b; Denton, Gafni, Spencer, & Stoddart, 1982; Kassakian, Bailey, Rinker, Stewart, & Yates, 1979; Wilkins, 1993). In spite of the need for cost reduction in health care, there have been major roadblocks to the introduction of changes for more than 15 years, because the resources are controlled by stakeholders who favour the medical and hospital models.

Nursing has responsibility for an important part of the health care resources and should use this fact as part of a political process. Stevens (1984) suggests that a resource-driven model of practice for nursing is more in line with the reality of a society that is becoming increasingly aware of its limited resources than a goal-driven nursing practice: "In a resource-driven model, the planner asks what goals can be achieved with the available resources" (p. 184). Nursing's alternative mode of delivery of care is one creative solution that can be used in a resource-driven model where resources allocated for nursing care are in part transferred to delivery of nursing services in the community and in part reorganized within the agency to be more in line with a primary health care model. The ability to influence decisions and gain support for the efficient use of health care resources will be enhanced by developing political alliances within multidisciplinary teams. (This idea will be discussed further under the heading Sources of Power.)

Leadership Position of Nursing

Another example of a pivotal issue that should be considered in the establishment of goals and objectives is the leadership role that nurses must play in a time of transition. Prescott (1993) says that "registered nurses are one of the hospital's most important resources for achieving and maintaining a competitive advantage because they contribute in important ways both to cost savings and to delivering high-quality care" (p. 192). Prescott documents nursing utility and assets with outcomes research, such as the impact of nurses on hospital mortality rates, lengths of stay, costs, and morbidity outcomes. She concludes that nursing is an important component of hospital survival under a reformed health care system.

However, several organizational models introduced in the present wave of organizational change eliminate nursing positions at the policy and senior management levels. Some administrators have hired nurses as incumbents for the new management positions at this level because these managers recognize the need for nurses' knowledge and skills. However, the job description makes no reference to the nursing knowledge required. As a result, these actions make nursing invisible and disposable. Would any other industry wipe out its senior production managers or put them in advisory positions to the production line? Of course not!

In light of this disconcerting state of affairs, the Canadian Nurses Association (1993a) has reiterated its position that a chief executive nurse, at the senior management level, is essential. As well, the Canadian Nurses Association has identified key concepts to guide nurse managers in their quest for strong nursing leadership in their agencies (see Table 6.2). This is a pivotal issue for nurses and nurse managers. Nursing leadership positions at the policy and senior levels of management are a principal means to attain power in an organization and to be able to influence decisions related to client care and, in particular, nursing care (Stuart, 1986).

Health care resources and leadership positions are two examples of goals to be attained through intraorganizational politics. Once the goal is set and the objectives clarified, the second important step of the process is the assessment of the positive and negative factors that will help or hinder the attainment of the goal.

Table 6.2
CNA's key concepts for policy statement.

The Position of the Chief Executive Nurse

Clients have a right to high quality, efficient, effective nursing services.

Direction by a chief executive nurse with advanced educational preparation optimizes the quality of nursing services.

The chief executive nurse provides visionary leadership for the organization and for nursing to attain the organizational mission.

The chief executive nurse promotes collaborative and interdisciplinary management and care processes.

The chief executive nurse creates and maintains a nursing practice environment that fosters satisfying professional practice and promotes positive patient outcome.

The chief executive nurse reports directly to the CEO and participates in an advisory capacity at meetings of the governing body.

The chief executive nurse is an equal member of the senior management team.

The chief executive nurse is responsible for nursing service and has the required authority and resource base to ensure that standards are met.

The chief executive nurse collaborates with educational institutions.

The chief executive nurse participates and provides leadership for the profession in health care, professional and political arenas.

Source: Policy statement reprinted, with permission, from the Canadian Nurses Association, Ottawa.

Assessment of Positive and Negative Factors

The political process, or the exercise of power, requires that consideration be given to what will help achieve the objectives and what will impede progress. These elements are what Kurt Lewin (1951) calls "driving forces" and "resisting forces." Each has to be assessed in order to develop an effective strategy. The effects of the driving forces are used and maximized while the effects of resisting forces should be minimized. When negative factors are encountered, whether related to values or trends in the environment or to key players, resources, or timing, there are ways to deal with them appropriately and thereby increase chances of success. These options include avoiding, minimizing, or confronting. To marshal these options, thus maximizing the positive forces and dealing with the negative forces, nurse managers need to recognize prevailing values and trends within the organization.

Values and Trends

Prevailing social values, trends, and beliefs are important considerations because if reaching a goal means going against these factors, it will be difficult, if not impossible, to accomplish it. These values and trends in an organization are often referred to as the "organizational culture." Edgar Schein (1985) defines organizational culture as "a pattern of basic assumptions—invented, discovered, or developed by a given group as it learns to cope with its problems of external adaptation and internal integration—that has worked well enough to be considered valid and, therefore, to be taught to new members as the correct way to perceive, think, and feel in relation to those problems" (p. 9). Each organization has its own culture but within a large organization, subcultures also develop within specialized groups, departments, or units (Sovie, 1993). As Drucker (1992) reminds us, culture does not change; behaviour does. Therefore, if a nurse manager wishes to influence decisions, it is vital in intraorganizational politics to analyze the climate, the values, and the trends of the work environment.

How can a nurse manager assess organizational culture? Fleeger (1993) identifies two types of clues: the explicit clues, which include formal contracts, written mission statements, policies and procedures, organizational charts, and job descriptions; and implicit clues, which include the informal, unwritten rules and expectations, for example, regarding dress, communications, and behaviours. Both formal and informal clues must be used as indicators of values and trends in the organization.

Key Players

In planning or coping with change, there is also a need to look at which individuals or groups will affect and be affected by the plans, and to evaluate who might support the goal and who might oppose it. These might be termed the key players in the process of change. It is necessary to assess their strengths and what their particular goals might be. It may not be possible to identify all the forces for and against the change, but an effort must be made to gather as much useful information as possible in order to plan the nursing strategy.

Key players who support the goal can be considered a resource for the project, while key players who oppose the goal are likely to create conflict. Unfortunately, many nurses are not skillful at dealing with conflict. The choices are fairly limited when dealing with conflictual key players to the three ways mentioned above: the negative key players can be deliberately avoided; their impact can be minimized by identifying the specific area they oppose and trying to convince them either to support the goal or, at least, to be neutral; they can be confronted by developing arguments for the target group(s) on the reasons why the nursing goal is superior to the opposing view.

Del Bueno (1986) discussed these interfaces between individuals at different levels or from different departments or with different values. She states that it requires considerable managerial skill and tactics to resolve such conflicts and offers suggestions that have a high probability of success. Some of her suggestions include: build your team; choose your second-in-command carefully; establish alliances with both superiors and peers; maintain a flexible position and maneuverability; and project an image of status, power, and material success (pp. 127-128).

Sources of Power

What kinds of power will the key individuals or groups use to support or oppose the goal that was set? Does a group have different types of power than individuals? What are some effective strategies to ensure that the nurse manager has the capacity to influence each situation? What are the key variables that affect attainment of power?

There are various ways of describing types of power. With regard to the power of individuals, French and Raven (1959) describe five sources of power:

- **Legitimate power,** based on authority vested in a role or position that is accepted and recognized by others in the organization, such as a nurse manager position;

- **Reward power,** based on a person's use of positive sanctions such as money, positive evaluation, or other forms of gain;

- **Coercive power,** based on the use of negative sanctions such as threats or punishment;

- **Expert power,** based on valid knowledge or information in a given domain, such as nursing knowledge and skills; and
- **Referent power,** based on positive personal appeal to which others respond, often identified as charisma.

Davidhizar (1993) also identifies charisma as a source of power or political strength and recognizes that charismatic power is an emerging paradigm for modern managers.

Wieland and Ullrich (1976) discuss two derivative forms of power, which usually are not mentioned in the nursing literature. They identify *associative power,* which comes from an association with others who are perceived as powerful, and *lower participant power,* which is a form of power that those lower in a hierarchy hold over their managers.

Fergusson (1985) also describes a form of associative power, but refers to this as power through interdependence.

Similar types of power can be attributed to a group or an organization. In assessing the power of a group, however, the relative influence or potential influence should be considered by looking at a combination of factors. Versteeg (1979) identifies five factors that need to be considered:

1. **Size.** In terms of political power, the number of members and the percentage they represent of the total capacity of the group is an important factor. For example, nurses usually form the largest number of professionals in the agencies.

2. **Information base.** An informed membership, especially when it knows about the goal and about relevant professional and social issues.

3. **Expertise.** Similar to the idea of expert power of individuals, this refers to the knowledge base or the special expertise that the group offers.

4. **Physical resources.** Time and money provide a group with the ability to participate in the exercise of power.

5. **Personal attributes.** Similar to the referent power or charismatic power of individuals, this relates to the personal appeal of the group collectively and of its spokespersons.

What are some of the tactics that nurse managers can use with these types of power?

The power of an individual is relative to that of others in influencing the behaviour of others—or, in the context of this discussion, in influencing decisions. For example, in an organization such as a hospital or a community health centre, a nurse manager would have legitimate power due to his or her position. As well, this individual may have various degrees of the other forms of power, such as expertise and charisma.

It is useful for a nurse manager to determine the sources of power of key participants in relation to the objective and to use these to the maximum benefit. The nurse manager needs to weigh whether positional power would be a key to the decision or whether expert power would be most influential. To use the source of power of key individuals and groups to plan the strategy is known as a power strategy.

The literature discusses several tactics that are used to acquire and keep the derivative forms of power (i.e., associative power and lower participant power). For associative power, some of the tactics recommended include forming coalitions, negotiating or making trade-offs, lobbying, sitting on key committees, and taking part in social activities. In other words, the nurse manager needs to be in the right place at the right time with the right people.

As an example, forming a coalition can be defined as a temporary alliance between individuals or groups with a common goal in order to be more effective in influencing others into conformity with the goal. Caplow (1969) studied traditional coalitions in organizations and distribution of power among organizational triads. Sills (1976) later discussed Caplow's theory in light of relative power between the three parts of the triad and, in particular, the relationships in a hospital management triad formed by administrator, physician, and nurse.

Even though the size and the complexity of hospitals have changed in recent years, the basic mechanisms of the organizational triads are still valid today. Figure 6.1, which is adapted from the work of Caplow, shows the relationship between a hospital administrator (A), the medical director (B), and the senior nurse manager (C). In the triad, one must keep in mind that the positions are imbedded in the status order of the organization represented by the size of the circles. In fact, the power distribution is largely determined by the actual behaviour of the incumbent in the position. Furthermore, socialization of roles in adult life is often the result of primary and secondary socialization.

In this context, using Caplow's theoretical discussions, one sees that hospital administrators often share with physicians their primary socialization as men and their secondary socialization as university-educated. Physicians and nurses share their secondary socialization in the "laying on of the hands" and being educated in closed, caste-like professions with specific codes, entrance requirements, and rituals. So, in health care, when a coalition takes place between A and B it is considered a "conservative coalition" because it respects the primary and secondary

Figure 6.1
Organizational triad in hospital.

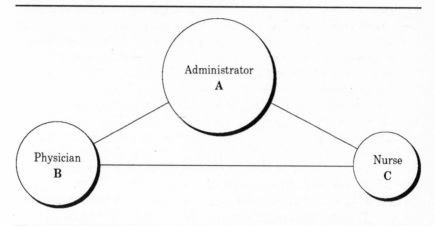

Source: Adapted, with permission, from T. Caplow (1969), *Two against one: Coalitions in triads* (Engelwood Cliffs, NJ: Prentice-Hall, p. 55).

socialization. When A and C enter into a coalition it is considered an "improper coalition" because it negates the primary and secondary socializations. And when B and C form a coalition it is considered a "revolutionary coalition," which is a winning coalition that has the potential to dominate the more powerful member of the organizational triad.

This theory can be applied to a debate over the need for bed closures. For example, a conservative coalition would be when the administrators, in coalition with physicians, have decided which beds to close and how many, and presented their recommendation to the board or the executive committee; such a recommendation would be accepted. An improper coalition exists when the administrators, in coalition with nurses, present a bed-closure plan despite opposition from physicians; such a recommendation also would likely be accepted. However, if the administrators recommend bed closures, but nurses and physicians, in a revolutionary coalition, oppose that recommendation, the administrators, the board, or the executive committee would be hard pressed to accept the recommendation.

Sills concludes that the system is kept in balance through rapid, intermittent coalitions between administrators and physicians or administrators and nurses which, in fact, prevent "revolutionary coalitions" from taking place. An understanding of patterns such as these is helpful for nurse managers so that they may analyze some of the ways in which decision making is carried out in organizations.

On a regular basis, nurses discuss and negotiate issues with other nurses and physicians, but they are not as skilful at influencing the interdisciplinary politics or the team process. Political alliances with the multidisciplinary team members is an important asset for nurse managers today. Devereux and Dirschel (1985) offer some guidelines on how to become proficient in the application of interdisciplinary politics:

1. *Know the situation—know the patient and the problem the team must handle.*

2. *Know the resources available from nursing and, in general, from the institution and/or community.*

3. *Listen to your colleagues' concerns and plans for action.*

4. *Emphasize mutuality of goals shared among members of the multidisciplinary team.*

5. *Reinforce what is legal practice of nursing. Work to ensure that all nurses are competent in their areas of practice and be alert to casual encroachment from other disciplines.*

6. *Expand the nursing goals to include those of the other disciplines that will help to build alliances in future interactions.* (p. 249)

Nurse managers can also use tactics of lower participant power, whereby those lower in the hierarchy can have power and influence. For example, Shiflett and McFarland (1978) noted that the nursing administrator may have power over the hospital administrators through: "(1) control of resources upon which the person is dependent; (2) control of the access of others to that person; (3) control of techniques, procedures or knowledge vital to the administrator; and (4) personality attributes such as charm, likeableness, or charisma recognized by the administrator as desirable in subordinates" (p. 20). Shiflett and McFarland also noted that this same type of power can be used by staff members against the nurse manager. One should also remember that derivative forms of power are more uncertain than other forms and that some forms are more likely to be considered legitimate than others, depending on the circumstances.

What are the key variables that affect the attainment of power? Instead of focussing on individual or group sources of power, Hickson, Hinnings, Lee, Schneck, and Pennings (1971) emphasize horizontal power, or relationships between groups and subunits within an organization.

Stuart (1986) also highlights the importance of interdisciplinary alliances within an organization and refers to this as the strategic-contingencies model.

> *Such an approach views intraorganizational conflict and negotiation as ongoing processes with the balance of power to effect change distributed dynamically among the various subunits. . . . The division of labor among these subunits is then the source of intraorganizational power, and each subunit's tasks, functioning, and links with the activities of other subunits are crucial power variables.* (p. 69)

In Stuart's model, three variables govern a subunit's power within the organization (nursing being a subunit or a department being a subunit): *centrality*—the degree of the subunit's interdependence with other subunits; *substitutability*—the possibility of replacement by others; and *coping with uncertainty*—the ability to handle, through a variety of mechanisms, inevitable but unpredictable occurrences.

In light of these variables, Stuart (1986) recommends four principles to help the nursing profession achieve its goal of quality patient care and control over the practice of nursing: increase connections with other subunits and maintain centrality; become irreplaceable (make nurses difficult to replace); demonstrate nursing assets, as Prescott (1993) does in focussing on research showing the positive impact of nursing care for clients and for the administration; and participate in high-level decision making where determinations are made about goals, resources, and activities desirable for the organization.

Resources and Timing

In assessing strengths and weaknesses in relation to previous factors, such as trends and values, key players, and sources of power, the same must then be done for resources. How much money and time might be required and what kind of people and what mix of each different element will be needed? Do you need consultants or staff with special skills? Often, the value of the time and energy of the people committed to the goal is underestimated. Belief and dedication to a cause is a resource of great value. The weaknesses identified in this area can be compensated for when the strategy is planned. For example, if the time available to attain the goal is limited, an increased number of volunteers can offset this shortcoming; or, if some special skills are needed, enlisting the help of an expert or a student in that specialty may be an alternative.

The timing of an issue is another critical factor to assess. Timing is often so critical that it may be necessary to wait to implement a plan until conditions are more favourable. Or, you may have to be ready to move when opportunities present themselves. Favourable and unfavourable times should be identified early in the process and then possible deadlines set for the accomplishment of the goal established to guide the plan.

The two first steps—establishing the goal and assessing the positive and negative forces—require the longest time and are the most important. Once these are done, the next step is to plan the strategy.

Plan the Strategy

Robbins (1986) has noted that, whereas passion and belief provide the fuel for achieving power, intelligence and logical strategies — in other words, a sound plan—provide the road maps by which success is eventually achieved. Once the goal and objectives are clear and consideration has been given to the positive and negative factors that will influence change, it is time to use all that knowledge in developing a strategy. The strategy is the action plan or the defined approach to reaching the goal. It is the framework within which the necessary activities are carried out.

A strategy may be developed for each targeted individual or group identified in the first step and, then, an overall or global strategy may be developed. At this point, all pieces of the puzzle must be brought together. The choice of activities used in the strategy should be congruent with the assessment of the positive and negative factors identified in the second step of the process. The strategy may include such tactics as establishing a core group to work on the issue, informing others, seeking expressions of support, active lobbying, and making trade-offs.

Implement and Evaluate the Strategy

Once the plan is completed, the implementation starts. An ongoing evaluation of the effectiveness of the tactics selected and the strategy as a whole must be conducted. In the worst-case scenario, some activities or tactics may not be effective and should be replaced by others.

There is always a need to monitor the political process and adapt strategies in the light of progress and changing conditions. Successful approaches can be duplicated and shared with other groups involved in the political process and unsuccessful approaches modified.

The Challenge for the Manager

Intraorganizational politics and utilization of the political process is a challenging area. Most studies on the topic, even in the recent literature, identify that nurses in general and nursing administrators in particular are ill prepared and tend to be apathetic political spectators (Byers, 1990; Cronkhite, 1991; Small, 1989). In light of the serious consequences of this state of affairs in time of reform, the situation creates important challenges for the nurse manager.

The first challenge comes from a bias that can be traced back to the Western philosophical view that men are rational and thus responsible for affairs of state, while women are emotional and therefore responsible for the affairs of the family—and for supporting men (Lloyd, 1984). Professions that are predominantly female, like nursing, are affected by these stereotypes. Although much progress has been recorded, these ingrained cultural views explain why such topics as politics and power begin to appear in the nursing literature only in the late 1970s and why many nurses are uncomfortable with these concepts even in the 1990s.

The second challenge is to provide positive role models for other nurses by using the political process, encouraging educational programs, and rewarding political participation and behaviour among colleagues.

The third challenge is to provide the climate that encourages nurses to promote unity and consolidate their political power by using the four principles for attaining power: increasing connections, becoming irreplaceable, demonstrating nursing assets, and ensuring that nurses participate in high-level decision making (Stuart, 1986).

Knowledge and skills related to intraorganizational politics are essential tools in the arsenal of an effective nurse manager of the 1990s. Nursing can be part of the solution in restructuring health care within current resources, but involvement depends on a nurse manager's knowledge of intraorganizational politics and on his or her political abilities.

An effective strategy to reach the goal can be planned and implemented through the judicious choice of priorities and the use of a political process drawing on multiple sources of power. With these ingredients and the determination of the nurse manager, success in influencing decisions that support the goals of nursing is assured.

References

Byers, S.R. (1990). *Relationship among staff nurses' beliefs, nursing practice and unit ethos.* Unpublished doctoral dissertation, Ohio State University, Columbus (from CIHNAL 1983-1993, Abstract No. 142524).

Canadian Nurses Association. (1993a). *Key concepts for policy statement on the position of the chief executive nurse.* Ottawa: Author.

Canadian Nurses Association. (1993b). *New directions in health care: Cost effective nursing alternatives.* Ottawa: Author.

Caplow, T. (1969). *Two against one: Coalitions in triads.* Engelwood Cliffs, NJ: Prentice-Hall.

Cronkhite, L.M. (1991). *The role of the hospital nurse administrator in a changing health care environment: A study of values and conflicts.* Unpublished doctoral dissertation, University of Wisconsin, Milwaukee (from CIHNAL 1983-1993, Abstract No. 161175).

Davidhizar, R. (1993). Leading with charisma. *Journal of Advanced Nursing, 18*(4), 675-679.

Del Bueno, D.J. (1986). Power and politics in organizations. *Nursing Outlook, 34*(3), 124-128.

Denton, F.T., Gafni, A., Spencer, B.G., & Stoddart, G.L. (1982). *Potential savings from the adoption of nurses practitioner technology in the Canadian health care system* (Report #45—Quantitative Studies in Economics and Population). Hamilton, Ontario: McMaster University.

Devereux, P.M., & Dirschel, K.M. (1985). Interdisciplinary politics. In D.J. Mason & S.W. Talbot (Eds.), *Political action handbook for nurses* (pp. 240-250). Menlo Park, CA: Addison-Wesley.

Drucker, P. (1992). *Managing for the future: The 1990s and beyond.* New York: Truman Tally Books/Dutton.

Erikson, E.H. (1963). *The challenge of youth.* Garden City, NJ: Doubleday.

Fergusson, V.D. (1985). Two perspectives on power. In D.J. Mason & S.W. Talbot (Eds.), *Political action handbook for nurses* (pp. 88-93). Menlo Park, CA: Addison-Wesley.

Fleeger, M.E. (1993). Assessing organizational culture: A planning strategy. *Nursing Management, 24*(2), 39-41.

French, J.R.P., & Raven, B. (1959). The bases of social power. In D. Cartwright (Ed.), *Studies in social power* (pp. 150-167). Ann Arbor, MI: University Press.

Hickson, D., Hinings, C., Lee, C., Schneck, R., & Pennings, J. (1971). A strategic contingencies' theory of organizational power. *Administrative Science Quarterly, 16*(2), 216-229.

Kassakian, M.G., Bailey, L.R., Rinker, M., Stewart, C., & Yates, J.W. (1979). The cost and quality of dying: A comparison of home and hospital. *Nurse Practitioner, 4*(1), 18-23.

Laswell, H.D. (1936). *Politics: Who gets what, when, how.* New York: World Publishing.

Lewin, K. (1951). *The nature of field theory.* New York: Macmillan.

Lloyd, G. (1984). *The man of reason.* London: Methuen.

Mason, D.J., & McCarthy, A.M. (1985). The politics of patient care. In D.J. Mason & S.W. Talbot (Eds.), *Political action handbook for nurses* (pp. 38-52). Menlo Park, CA: Addison-Wesley.

Pffeffer, J. (1981). *Power in organizations.* Boston: Pitman.

Prescott, P. (1993). Nursing: An important component of hospital survival under a reformed health care system. *Nursing Economics, 11*(4), 192-199.

Robbins, A. (1986). *Unlimited power.* New York: Simon & Schuster.

Schein, E. (1985). *Organizational culture and leadership: A dynamic view.* San Francisco: Jossey-Bass.

Shiflett, N., & McFarland, D.E. (1978). Power and the nursing administrator. *Journal of Nursing Administration, 7*(3), 19- 23.

Sills, G.M. (1976). Nursing, medicine, and hospital administrator. *American Journal of Nursing, 76*(9), 1432-1434.

Small, E.B. (1989). *Factors associated with political participation.* Unpublished doctoral dissertation, North Carolina State University, Chapel Hill (from CIHNAL 1983-1993, Abstract No. 119031).

Sovie, M.D. (1993). Hospital culture—Why create one? *Nursing Economics, 11*(2), 69-75.

Starke, A., & Rempel, E. (1988). Organizational politics and nursing administration. *Canadian Journal of Nursing Administration, 1*(4), 11-14.

Stevens, B.J. (1980a) Development and use of power in nursing. In National League for Nursing, *Assuring a goal-directed future for nursing* (Publication 52-1814). New York: Author.

Stevens, B.J. (1980b). Power and politics for the nurse executive. *Nursing and Health Care, 1*(4), 208-210.

Stevens, B.J. (1984). But it shouldn't be that way. *Nursing Outlook, 32*(3), 184.

Stuart, G.W. (1986). An organizational strategy for empowering nursing. *Nursing Economics, 4*(2), 69-73.

Versteeg, D.F. (1979). The political process. Or the power and glory. *Nursing Dimensions, 7*(2), 20-27.

Wieland, G.F., & Ullrich, R.A. (1976). *Organizations: Behavior, design, and change.* Homewood, IL: Richard D. Irwin.

Wilkins, V.C. (1993). Meeting community needs while conserving health-care dollars. *Journal of Nursing Administration, 23*(3), 26-28.

C   H   A   P   T   E   R   7

Medical Staff Organization

Louise Lemieux-Charles

Louise Lemieux-Charles, RN, BSN (Ottawa), MScN, PhD (Toronto), is Director of the Hospital Management Research Unit, Department of Health Administration, Faculty of Medicine, University of Toronto. She served as Member-at-Large, Nursing Administration for the Canadian Nurses Association (1984-1988) and has written many articles on administration and administrative issues.

Case 1

As a nurse on surgery, you are concerned that Dr. Jones' practice is different from her colleagues' in that her patients stay in hospital longer, receive more antibiotics, and at times do not seem to recover as quickly. You wonder to whom she is responsible for her practice.

Case 2

You have noted that Dr. Smith, a family practitioner, always has to wait for the obstetrician before he can proceed with a difficult delivery. You're unsure where those rules are written down.

Case 3

Your hospital recently instituted a Do Not Resuscitate policy, which is supposed to be adhered to by all staff physicians. In discussion with some of the physicians, they tell you that the medical staff assembly are concerned that any physician who follows the policy may risk a malpractice suit. Since the medical advisory committee approved the policy, you wonder what is the relationship between these two groups on this matter.

The above examples illustrate the confusion that may exist when nurse managers try to understand what regulates physician practice in hospitals and why those policies are different from those that influence the practice of other professionals in the organization. The author of this chapter reviews the organization of medical staff in hospitals and describes trends that potentially will redefine the relationship of the medical staff to hospitals.

Background

The current structure of the medical staff has evolved through the 20th century from non-organization (i.e., each physician using own set of standards) to a structure that is more formal and is increasingly part of the hospital's overall structure. Historically, physicians were reluctant to practise in hospitals partly because the care provided was custodial in nature. Patients usually were treated in their homes; they generally contracted with physicians and, in many cases, with nurses to deliver the required treatment and care. Some physicians owned and/or managed hospitals. This was possible partly because the technologies required were minimal and the overall care requirements were less complex than today's. However, as advances in diagnosis and treatment emerged, coupled with the growth of government financed care, physicians found themselves with more patients and an ability to do more for those patients. As a result, they turned over many of the administrative activities to nonclinically trained administrators while maintaining control by organizing themselves as "medical staff," with defined rights and privileges as well as responsibilities. The real power of the formally organized medical staff was in the ability of its individual members to admit patients (Shortell, 1991, p. 7). Hospitals were also better able to provide operating rooms, laboratory services, and professional staff, such as nurses and others, to deliver the care necessary for recovery.

Lacking an employer-employee relationship with the hospital, physicians found they needed to formalize their relationship to the hospital. Because physicians were not hospital employees and generally were reimbursed on a fee-for-service system, a parallel structure of authority and influence emerged (Alexander, Morrisey, & Shortell, 1986). This parallel structure was best illustrated on organizational charts where the medical staff reported directly to the board for their activities and the executive director of the hospital reported to the board for the activities of all other staff. There was little overlap in activity. This dual authority model was first described by Smith (1958) and further developed by Pauly and Redisch (1973) and Harris (1977). Though the hospital has traditionally been defined as the "doctor's workshop"

(Roemer & Friedman, 1971), it has recently been suggested that this metaphor may no longer describe the transitions occurring in hospital-physician relationships. On the one hand, hospitals are increasingly dependent on physicians to deal with complex clinical, bioethical, and administrative issues, yet physicians are more dependent on hospitals to provide them with expensive technology and support services (Alexander, Morrisey, & Shortell, 1986; Leatt, Vayda, & Williams, 1987; Shortell, 1985). This increasing interdependency may lead to difficulties in relationships if the medical staffs continue to be organized as voluntary groups with considerable autonomy regarding the use of hospital resources.

Provincial Hospital Acts and Accreditation

The most important predictors of how hospital medical staff are organized are, first, provincial legislation, specifically the provincial acts governing public hospitals and their regulations, and, second, subordinate legislation in the form of hospital bylaws (Leatt, O'Rourke, Fried, & Deber, 1992). These acts and regulations vary in specificity in terms of the manner in which they allow hospitals to function and the types of guidelines they provide, particularly for the organization and roles of medical staff. For example, in some western provinces, such as Alberta, physicians are not allowed to be members of their own hospital's governing board because of potential conflicts of interest, whereas in Ontario and Québec certain physicians are required by law to be full voting members of the board (Leatt et al., 1992). In a national survey of medical staff organization in Canadian hospitals (Leatt et al., 1992), it was found that in provinces with relatively high regulatory intensity, physicians were more closely involved with the governance and management of the hospitals. In provinces where the legislation was more loose or vague, hospitals would likely have more autonomy or discretion to organize their medical staff as they please. Consequently, there would be fewer external pressures to change the medical staff structures in hospitals in these provinces. The Canadian Council on Health Facilities Accreditation (1991) states that the medical staff "shall develop and recommend for adoption rules, regulations, policies and procedures to establish a framework for self-governance and a means of accountability to the governing body" (p. 5).

Medical Staff Organization

The primary functions of the medical staff organization are to: (1) provide the medical staff with a mechanism for self-governance; (2) provide a means for monitoring the quality of patient care and the performance of the medical staff; and (3) provide a mechanism for the review of applications to the medical staff and the assignment of medical staff categories.

Medical Staff Bylaws

The medical staff bylaws and the rules related to them are an attempt to codify and describe the complex relationship between a group of more or less independent professionals and an organization responsible for the delivery of high-quality care to the community it serves (Scott, 1992). The bylaws specify: the process for appointment and reappointment of medical staff; organizational structure of the medical staff, including provisions for the organization of departments and services; selection of department chiefs and division heads; responsibilities of officers; composition and terms of references of committees; procedures for delineating privileges; and the mechanism by which the medical staff consults with and reports to the governing board.

Medical Staff Structure

In most hospitals in Canada, medical staff report directly to the board of directors on medical issues, though this practice is changing as physicians become more involved in hospital matters. Medical issues may pertain to either physician interests or practice issues. Staff physicians' views are communicated to the board through a medical staff assembly structure whereas their conduct and practice are monitored through the medical staff organization. Figure 7.1 (see page 130) describes in more detail the specific relationships of the medical staff structure to the overall hospital structure. Until recently, the role of the chief executive officer (CEO) in this reporting relationship has often not been clear. For example, the medical staff might choose to deal with policy issues at the board level without first consulting with the chief executive officer. This practice is no longer common; most boards have clarified how they expect communication on different issues to take place.

Figure 7.1
Typical medical staff committee structure.

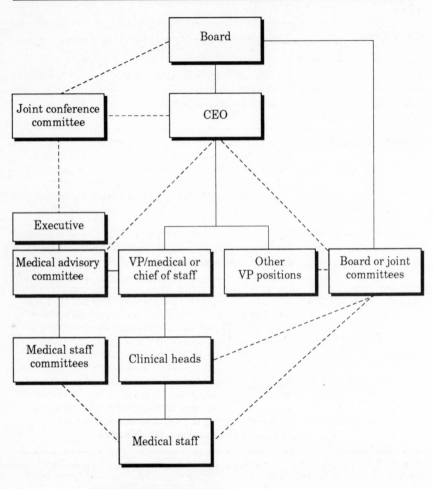

——————— formal reporting relations
- - - - - - - - communication relationships

Although many organizational structures show the chair of the medical advisory committee as reporting to the vice-president/medical or chief of staff and through that position to the chief executive officer, at present it is more common for the chair of the medical advisory committee to report *directly* to the board through its chief executive officer.

Source: Diagram from John G. Reid, Medical committee structure (p. C3.4), in D. Gellerman (Ed.), *Medical administration in Canadian hospitals* (pp. C3.1-C3.9). Ottawa: Canadian Medical Association, 1992. Used with permission.

Table 7.1
Officers of the medical staff.

Title	Definition
Chief of Staff	Appointed by the hospital board, is responsible for ensuring that the medical staff carry out their assigned functions. May or may not be chair of the medical advisory committee (MAC).
Chair/Medical Advisory Committee	Coordinates activities and chairs meetings of the MAC.
Department Head	May also be known as Chief of Service or Chief of Department. Accountable through the medical staff organization for the competence of and the quality of care given by members of the departments. Also responsible to administration for such functions as utilization review, budgeting, staff recruitment, education, and research.
President/Medical Staff	Represents and defends the interests of the medical staff as a whole and speaks on behalf of individual members.
Vice-President/Medical	May also be known as the Medical Director. As a hospital employee, is responsible for ensuring that the medical staff carry out responsibilities as outlined in the bylaws. Interprets hospital policy to the medical staff and conveys to the administration and hospital board a professional understanding of issues that concern the medical staff. Where this position exists, a chief of staff may not be required because responsibilities for the day-to-day operation of the hospital may be divided among department chiefs, chair of the MAC, and the Vice-President/Medical.

Source: Table compiled from information in various chapters of D. Gellerman (Ed.), *Medical administration in Canadian hospitals*. Ottawa: Canadian Medical Association, 1992.

Within the medical staff structure, leadership of the medical staff is provided through different positions. Table 7.1 describes each of the roles pertaining to the formal medical staff organization. These roles reflect very different responsibilities and generally, though not necessarily, are assumed by different individuals. For example, in smaller hospitals the chair of the medical advisory committee (frequently referred to as the MAC, but in some hospitals called the medical advisory board) and the chief of staff may be the same individual. Though the positions of chief of staff and president of the medical staff assembly may be assumed by the same person, this practice is discouraged as their responsibilities are in direct conflict. The president of the medical staff is an elected position. In all cases, except for the medical director position (also referred to as vice-president/medical in some hospital organizational charts), the physicians occupying these leadership positions maintain an active clinical practice.

The medical staff is usually organized according to medical departments. The most common departments reflect the major medical disciplines of medicine, surgery, obstetrics and gynecology, family practice, pediatrics, psychiatry, laboratory medicine, and radiology. In some larger centres, especially those affiliated with a university medical centre, other specialties, such as oncology, trauma, and emergency medicine, may also be part of the departmental structure. Formation of departments depends on the size of the medical staff, its level of specialization, and its relationships to other hospitals and the university. The role of the department chief has evolved to include both clinical and administrative responsibilities. In larger centres, the selection of the individual has been formalized to include input from both the medical staff and senior management. The term is usually three to five years, renewable on a one-time basis. Past practice included department chiefs being selected yearly on a rotational basis reflecting a practice of "it's your turn." The complexities inherent in managing health care institutions necessitated a change in this practice. However, because department chiefs continue to manage their own medical practice as well as ensuring the quality of practice of their colleagues and supporting hospital policies, they experience conflict in the role. Difficulty in recruiting department chiefs is not uncommon. Barriers to physician involvement can include: size of the department; physicians' concern about the impact of the role on peer relationships and referral networks; physicians' willingness to devote the time necessary to meet administrative requirements; and conflicts over administrative decisions directly affecting their practice (Lemieux-Charles, 1989).

Table 7.2 gives an example of the committee structure one is likely to encounter in a hospital. The medical staff committees required to be in effect in each institution are usually outlined in the provincial legislation and in accreditation standards. The parallel structure referred to earlier is evident in Table 7.2. Though many medical staff committees have hospital representatives as members, the integration between hospital activities and medical staff activities may not occur until they reach a board committee such as the Quality Assurance Committee (in many institutions

Table 7.2
Example of hospital and medical staff committee structure.

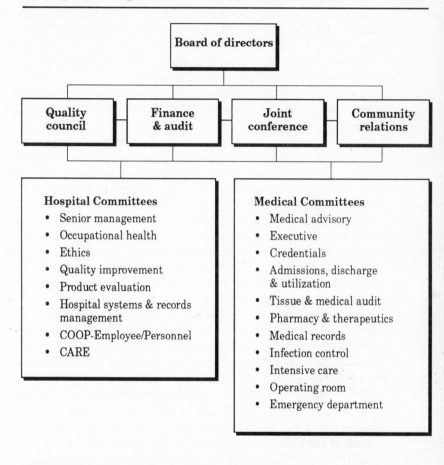

this committee has been renamed Quality Council to reflect better the quality improvement direction). In recent years, communication between the medical advisory committee and the senior management committee has been formalized in the majority of hospitals.

The medical advisory committee is the senior "cabinet" of the medical staff, consisting of department chiefs and elected officers (president and vice-president of the medical staff) (Reid, 1992). Its prime role is ensuring quality of medical care through its committee structure though, in many instances, it becomes involved with the board and administration in hospital strategic planning and operational issues through its responsibility for resource utilization. For example, issues surrounding numbers of beds available for care delivery, including decisions related to bed closures, are often vetted through the medical advisory committee because of the impact on delivery of medical care. The chair of the medical advisory committee is usually a member of select board committees.

The joint conference committee of the board consists of representatives of the board, administration, and medical staff. Its purpose is to act as a forum for conflicts that may arise between parties.

Credentialing

"Credentialing" is the process by which the qualifications, training, performance, and attributes of a health care professional who has applied for admitting and practice privileges (or for the continuation of those privileges) in a health care facility are verified and assessed (CHA, 1990). The process delineates clinical privileges, may place limits on practice based on training and experience, and provides for review under a quality assurance program. The decision to renew privileges is made on a yearly basis for all physicians. Every appointment is reviewed yearly by the medical advisory committee, which then recommends to the board continuation of the same privileges, modification of privileges, or cancellation of privileges. The assessment is based on the department chief's evaluation of the physicians' performance. There are different staff categories and each category has privileges. The majority of staff are generally in the "active" category when they hold their primary appointment in the institution. A physician may be placed in the "temporary" category if he or she is visiting an institution. Privileges define the scope of practice of the individual physician in the institution.

How can the above information be applied to the illustrations presented at the beginning of this chapter? In the case of Dr. Jones (Case 1), there would be an expectation that the chief of surgery would address the variations inherent in Dr. Jones' practice. The issue for nurses is the way in which the chief would become aware of this problem. The utilization committee and/or the pharmacy committee might, in its review of drugs used, highlight the problem and bring it to the chief's attention. On the other hand, the nurse could report the observation to the nurse manager who might speak to the chief, or it might be discussed at rounds held on the patient unit. Addressing performance issues is not easy, yet the nurse needs to understand that there is a method by which the issue can be examined. In the case of Dr. Smith (Case 2), the credentialing process is the mechanism by which physicians are given privileges to practise in particular ways. He did not have privileges that allowed him to work independently when faced with a complex obstetrical case. In this situation he would be required to seek the assistance of an obstetrician. The relationship of the medical advisory committee to the medical staff assembly, as illustrated in Case 3, is an interesting organizational issue. It would appear that communication between the groups was not adequate. In this case, the medical director (or vice-president/medical) would be called upon to interpret the policy and deal with the physicians' concerns that should have been anticipated prior to the final approval. The medical advisory committee is responsible for ensuring quality of care while the medical staff assembly addresses individual physician concerns.

The above examples illustrate how the medical staff relationship to the hospital has evolved from their being totally separate, when physicians used the hospital for their own purposes, to a situation in which physicians are being asked to be more accountable for their practice and involved in the management of the institutions in which they practise. As the 21st century nears, other external forces will influence the way in which medical staff are organized. Some of these forces and their potential impact on medical staff organization are explored in the following section of this chapter.

Medical Staff Organization in a Changing Health Care Environment

The traditional hospital structure has focussed on services provided by individual departments, such as medicine, nursing, nutrition, pharmacy, and so on. As governments have become increasingly interested in the costs associated with specific patient groups, the concepts of case mix groups, case costing, and program management have emerged. In addition, because physicians are seen to "drive" approximately 70% of all costs generated in a hospital, there have been attempts to involve them more closely in management of critical resources (e.g., budget and staff allocation). Support for such involvement was evidenced when Health and Welfare Canada hosted a meeting on the physician's role in management and invited representatives from key stakeholder national associations (e.g., Canadian Medical Association, Canadian College of Health Services Executives). It was accepted that physician involvement in the decision-making process of hospitals was important. The report of the meeting (Adams, 1986) identified the following points:

1. *Physicians are unwilling to assume greater management roles without being compensated.*

2. *They face ethical conflicts when they assume management roles and, therefore, are reluctant to do so.*

3. *Their involvement is essential because they are the only ones who can equate quality and quantity within the hospital.*

4. *They do not feel part of the hospital because in many cases they do not have offices or administrative staff within the institution* (p. 158).

There are differing views on whether inclusion of physicians in management is appropriate. It has been argued that such responsibilities force them to choose between clinical and financial considerations, which choice inevitably compromises the traditional doctor/patient relationship of trust (Chant, 1989; Fried, 1975). On the other hand, Veatch (1991) has argued that "rationing of health care is an inevitable correlate of living in a world of finite resources" and is "morally necessary" (p. 3).

The context in which physicians practise will affect both their formal structures (e.g., medical staff organization) as well as their way of dealing with issues. As noted above, the environment in which health organizations find themselves is more complex and less stable than it was a decade ago. Funding arrangements are changing, the work force includes a variety of professionals increasingly concerned about their work environment, and those who pay for care (governments and taxpayers) are concerned with varying patterns of medical care and subsequent outcomes of care. Ministers of health are concerned that the system is undermanaged. These pressures have led to a major reevaluation of the manner in which hospitals are designed, how budgets are formulated and allocated, and how hospital services and programs are managed.

To accommodate these new realities, the structure of the medical staff organization in hospitals is changing. The model of medical staff organization whereby one finds a parallel authority structure, as described earlier in this chapter, seems obsolete in the advent of hospital structures and/or organizations that increase physicians' involvement in policy development and management processes. Hence, increasing responsibility and accountability likely will be expected of chiefs and division heads for the practice of medicine within their respective departments and they increasingly will be involved in organizational decision making at the strategic level.

As noted earlier, the appointment of chiefs has been formalized in many hospitals through the use of selection committees made up of medical staff and administration. These committees identify suitable candidates, interview them, and recommend a candidate to the hospital board. Such an approach emphasizes the department chief's accountability to the organization. The issue of compensation for assuming management responsibilities remains contentious. Because physicians are paid on a fee-for-service basis, they view time involved in managerial activities, which includes attendance at meetings, as directly affecting their income. Though physicians are compensated for their time, the amounts vary significantly both between hospitals and within hospitals. For example, the chief of surgery is likely to receive greater compensation than the chief of family practice. The chief of staff generally receives a significant stipend.

It is unclear how far medical staff organization models will evolve. However, the province of Ontario's recent review of its Public Hospitals' Act gives a glimpse of a possible future (Ontario Public Hospitals Act Review, 1992). The recommendations, now in the public domain and awaiting response from key stakeholders, are based on six principles, which will guide the ways hospitals are to be managed in the future. They are:

- *accessible and equitable patient-centered treatment and care;*
- *responsiveness to community, regional, and provincial needs;*
- *accountability to the patient and the public;*
- *commitment to quality;*
- *management effectiveness; and*
- *respect for the values and traditions of the individual hospital* (1992).

These six principles are based on a belief that the distinction that currently exists between clinical and management issues has become largely artificial and that it serves to isolate medical and other clinical staff from structured involvement in management decisions. The report recommends that current arrangements be replaced by a system in which both clinical and operational decisions are made within unified management processes operating within a unified management structure directed by the chief executive officer. It is recommended that there be multidisciplinary advisory committees to deal with such matters as quality improvement, pharmacy and therapeutics, ethics, clinical records, resource allocation, and clinical human resource planning. In addition, discipline-specific committees advisory to management are to be established for each regulated health profession within the hospital to deal with credentialing, quality of care, peer review, rules and regulations, and discipline.

These recommendations acknowledge that many other disciplines are involved in the delivery of patient care and that the board needs to assume equal responsibility for activities of all regulated health professionals. Of note is the recommendation that the hospital develop a clinical human resource plan specifying the mix, number, and types of regulated health professionals required and the staging of their appointments or employment. This approach will affect not only the way physicians interact with the board, senior management, and other professional groups but also the structures presently in place to address medical issues. It will be important that physicians, given the new reality, examine ways and means of contributing to the management of the organization to ensure that the environment is conducive to the delivery of quality care.

For many physicians, the proposed changes are seen as a devaluation of the medical profession. In a sense, physicians will lose their privileged position of influence at the board level. Many are confused when on the one hand they are being asked to become more involved in management decisions and yet on the other hand they are no longer being treated as special. Few physicians appreciate that other professional groups may have as much right to be involved in clinical and management decision making as they do. As the legislation is being formulated, each group will have an opportunity to present its case to the legislators.

It would appear that the traditional balance of power is shifting but it is not yet clear what the new order will be. There is no question that physicians will be expected to assume broader management roles. However, it is unclear what the major channels for physician input in management decision making will be. The key forum until recently has been the medical staff organization. As new structures are instituted, they will affect other management forums, such as the senior management committee and program management committee. Physicians will need to learn how to use these new avenues for information and decision making.

Implications for the Nurse Manager's Role

The settings in which nurses practise are complex. Because they work in an interdisciplinary team and often rely on other members to ensure that the patient and family receive the best possible care, they need to understand the standards and practices that govern their colleagues' practice. Nurse managers are often in a position of interpreting the medical staff bylaws not only to the nurses but also to interns and residents. They need to be aware of the credentialing process and know which physicians have been credentialed and which have conditions placed upon their practice.

As noted above, the medical advisory committee established policies for the practice of medicine. For example, a Do Not Resuscitate policy would have been approved through the medical advisory committee. However, it is not always clear how the policy will be implemented once it has been approved. Nurses may find themselves expecting that all physicians will immediately change their practice as a result of the introduction of a new policy and become frustrated when they note inconsistencies in the implementation. In these situations, nurse managers should be discussing the issue with the department chief responsible for practice standards. If this approach fails, nurse managers need to find out what the next steps should be. Where a nursing department exists, concerns might be expressed to the vice-president/medical through the vice-president/nursing. In a programmatic structure, the issue may need to be raised with the medical director.

Conclusion

An understanding of how medical staff organizations have evolved can help nurses clarify roles and responsibilities assumed by members of the medical staff. The examples given at the beginning of the chapter illustrate how nurses and nurse managers can use this information to determine the most appropriate response to issues that affect the medical staff and, in many cases, the whole health care team.

References

Adams, O. (1986). Getting physicians involved in hospital management. *Canadian Medical Association Journal, 134,* 157-159.

Alexander, J.A., Morrisey, M.A., & Shortell, S.M. (1986, Fall). Hospital-physician integration and hospital costs. *Inquiry, 25,* 388-401.

Canadian Council on Health Facilities Accreditation (1991). *Standards for accreditation.* Ottawa: Author.

Canadian Hospital Association. (1990). *Guidelines for the appointment/reappointment process.* Ottawa: Author.

Chant, A.D.B. (1989). Practicing doctors, resource allocation and ethics. *Journal of Applied Philosophy, 6*(1), 71-75.

Fried, C. (1975). Rights and health care—Beyond equity and efficiency. *New England Journal of Medicine, 293,* 241-245.

Harris, J.E. (1977). The internal organization of hospitals: Some economic implications. *Bell Journal of Economics, 8,* 467-482.

Leatt, P., O'Rourke, K., Fried, B., & Deber, R. (1992). Regulatory intensity, hospital size and the formalization of medical staff organization in hospitals. *Health Services Management Research, 5*(2), 123-136.

Leatt, P., Vayda, E., & Williams, J. (1987). *Medical staff organization: An annotated bibliography.* Ottawa: Canadian Hospital Association.

Lemieux-Charles, L. (1989). *Hospital-physician integration: The influence of individual and organizational factors.* Unpublished doctoral dissertation, University of Toronto, Toronto.

Lemieux-Charles, L., & Leatt, P. (1992). Hospital-physician integration: Case studies of community hospitals. *Health Services Management Research, 5*(2), 82-98.

Ontario Public Hospitals Act Review: Steering Committee. (1992). *Into the 21st century: Ontario public hospitals: Report of the steering committee.* Toronto: Queen's Printer.

Pauly, M.V., & Redisch, M. (1973). The not-for-profit hospital as a physician's cooperative. *American Economic Review, 63,* 87-99.

Reid, J.G. (1992). Medical staff committee structure. In D. Gellerman (Ed.), *Medical administration in Canadian hospitals* (pp. C3.1-C3.9). Ottawa: Canadian Medical Association.

Roemer, M., & Friedman, J. (1971). *Doctors in hospitals: Medical staff organization and hospital performance.* Baltimore: Johns Hopkins University Press.

Scott, A.A. (1992) Medical staff bylaws. In D. Gellerman (Ed.), *Medical administration in Canadian hospitals* (pp. E1.1-E1.8). Ottawa: Canadian Medical Association.

Shortell, S.M. (1985). The medical staff of the future: Replanting the garden. *Frontiers Health Services Management, 1*(3), 3-48.

Shortell, S.M. (1991). *Effective hospital-physician relationships.* Ann Arbor, MI: Hospital Administration Press Perspective.

Shortell, S.M., Morrisey, M.A., & Conrad, D.A. (1985). Economic regulation and hospital behavior: The effects of medical staff organization and hospital-physician relationships. *Health Services Research, 20*(5), 597-628.

Smith, H.L. (1958). Two lines of authority: The hospital's dilemma. In G. Jaco (Ed.), *Patients, physicians and illness* (pp. 468-477). Glencoe, IL: The Free Press.

Veatch, R.M. (1991, Fall). Allocating health resources ethically: New roles for administrators and clinicians. *Frontiers of Health Services Administration, 8,* 3-29.

C H A P T E R   8

Ethical Dimensions of Nursing Management

Janet L. Storch

Janet L. Storch, RN, BScN, MHSA, PhD (Alberta), is Dean, Faculty of Nursing, University of Calgary, and author of a text and numerous articles on patients' rights and ethical issues in nursing. Prior to becoming Dean, she was Director of the Master's in Health Services Administration program where she pioneered work in health administration ethics.

Let who ever is in charge keep this simple question in her head (not, how can I always do this right thing myself, but) how can I provide for this right thing to be always done? (Florence Nightingale, quoted in Ulrich, 1992, p. 38).

There has been a reticence on the part of many administrators/ managers to recognize their ethical obligations in health care. Generally, those involved in direct client care are able to see the ethical dimensions of their care more clearly than managers, whose role is to facilitate rather than to provide care. However, during the 1980s, managerial ethics in health care began to be articulated with greater recognition of the ubiquitous nature of moral responsibility involved in nursing management. The directive given by Nightingale, cited above, speaks to the nurse manager's responsibility in facilitating ethical nursing practice as clearly as it does to responsibility in all other matters.

Nursing managers' ethical considerations include administration and management ethics (largely gleaned from business ethics), health care ethics, and nursing ethics. Until recently, ethical guidance has been in the form of professional codes, with a major focus on nursing practice. Ethical principles that also have significant application to nursing management have been widely used in nursing practice ethics.

Table 8.1
Ethical dimensions of management: Schematic design.

Principles	Macro-level	Meso-level	Micro-level
Justice	• Commit to systems that provide care for all with health needs • Affirm nurses as a critical resource	• Act as conscience on management team • Avoid compromises that decrease standards • Understand value biases in management	• Attend to client needs • Provide enabling experiences • Create healthy environments
Bring Benefit & Minimize Harm	• Advocate law reform • Advocate client-centred government policies • Interpret impact of funding initiatives	• Interpret nursing • Support nursing research • Develop guidelines for ethical practice • Provide support for nurses facing ethical problems	• Support creativity • Encourage innovation • Foster caring and connectedness
Autonomy	• Ensure nurses' voices are heard • Ensure nursing's views are represented • Advocate with confidence and conviction, even in the face of conflict	• Create policies to honour patient autonomy • Encourage supportive institutional structures to address ethical problems	• Meet client needs • Meet staff needs • Provide regular feedback on performance • Encourage meaningful participation in decision making • Avoid de-skilling/displacement

In this chapter, ethical principles will be applied to nursing management issues and tasks and major ethical dimensions of nursing management will be identified. First of all, four long-standing ethical principles will be identified. These then will be analyzed within a framework of macro-, meso-, and micro-level issues in nursing management and nursing management tasks (see Table 8.1). Macro-level issues are those involving community values, meso-level issues involve agency values, and micro-level issues involve personal and professional values (Hiller, 1984). Implications of these dimensions for nurse managers will be discussed and suggestions will be offered for managerial preparation and direction in dealing with ethical problems and issues.

The Place of Ethical Principles

In the late 1970s, bioethicists (notably Beauchamp and Childress, 1989) began identifying ethical principles pertinent to health care. Much of the literature in bioethics has used these principles to structure discussion about rights and responsibilities in health care. But since the late 1980s, this approach has been seriously questioned by many bioethicists and by feminists (Baier, 1989) suggesting that it may be narrow and misleading, that it may trivialize ethics, that the use of principles cannot satisfactorily address those many instances in which principles are in conflict, and that use of principles only may lead to a disregard for the context of the ethical problem. These criticisms must be taken seriously, and it must be understood that a broader perspective on ethics is critical in more systematic ethical analyses. Yet ethical principles remain as valuable tools in clarifying the array of ethical issues confronting health professionals. It is to this end these principles will be utilized here.

Among the ethical principles relevant to health care ethics, four have been most commonly utilized. These four are the principles of autonomy, beneficence, non-maleficence, and justice.

For many, *autonomy* is construed as the overriding principle in decision making since it involves respect for an individual's right to be self-governing, that is, to be "in charge" of his or her body and life. Autonomy (self-rule) forms the foundation for the legal doctrine of informed consent. Based in the writings of John Stuart Mill (1859), the individualism represented in this principle has been an underpinning of health care practice in North America.

Embodied in the principle of *beneficence* is the duty owed by professionals to those they serve. It is a duty to help, to confer benefit to others, and to prevent or minimize harm.

Non-maleficence is a principle of long standing, based on an ancient precept tied to the Hippocratic Oath of the medical professional and captured in the Latin phrase "primum non nocere," which translates "first, do no harm." Although this dictum was developed at a time when medical and ethical knowledge was still rather primitive, the dictum is relevant in the 1990s. The adverse effects of many medical technologies are serious or yet unknown. Non-maleficence is closely related to the principle of beneficence, but underscores the need to be conscious of weighing the benefits and the risks of each intervention. (These two principles, because of this close relationship, are shown together in the Table 8.1.)

The principle of *justice* requires that there be fairness in the distribution of resources. Complicating the application of this principle to health care practice are the competing ways in which fairness might be determined.

Justice and Nursing Management

The very essence of all good organisation is that every body should do her (or his) work in such a way as to help and not hinder every one else's work. (Florence Nightingale [1872], quoted in Ulrich [1992], p. 20)

One theoretical perspective on justice is that the greatest good of the greatest number of individuals should be served regardless of how resources are distributed. The development of this perspective is mainly attributed to philosophers such as Mill (1859), who held that the collective good should predominate in decision making. Competing with this approach is the one proposed by Rawls (1976), who advocated that when resources are insufficient to meet demands or needs, those who are least advantaged should receive preference in distribution. As various approaches to justice have been articulated, the positions taken to determine fairness are roughly the following:

- To each according to individual need
- To each according to social worth
- To each according to individual contribution
- Favour the least advantaged
- First come, first served
- Random selection
- An all-or-none approach

Since a primary role of management is to secure resources to enable tasks to be accomplished, a nurse manager's work involves major attention to resource allocation. In a time of shrinking resources and serious cost constraint in the delivery of health services, including nursing care and services, this task becomes an increasing challenge. At least one point of departure in this exercise for any nurse manager must be a clarification of personal values and beliefs about justice and how those values and beliefs are in harmony or dissonant with others' perspectives.

Macro-Allocation Ethics Pertinent to Justice

Primary responsibilities of the nursing manager with respect to a global distribution of resources (macro-allocation matters) are twofold. First, the nurse manager must commit to developing systems that will improve the fair distribution of resources for all individuals with health care needs. Second, the nurse manager must affirm nurses as critical human resources for enhanced health outcomes for clients.

Affirming the critical contribution of registered nurses to health outcomes for clients is a pressing agenda for nurse managers. The ability of registered nurses to provide holistic health care is one of the most significant contributions nursing can make to enhanced health outcomes. Except in isolated circumstances, the full contribution nursing can offer is often seriously restricted by legislation, regulation, agency policy, or personal preferences of other health care workers involved in programs of health service delivery. The feminist movement has been instrumental in assisting nurses to understand the many ways in which nurses (predominantly females) might be restricted in exercising their full potential for practice. Other health professions, with the exception of medicine, seem to have recognized this under-utilization of nurses for some time.

As the nursing role has changed from that of handmaiden to the physician (most evident in the Nightingale Pledge statement "With loyalty will I endeavour to aid the physician in his work") to a more interdependent and independent role, health care organizations have not kept pace with the potential human resource represented in nursing. Nurse managers must interpret nursing's critical role in health care to non-nursing managers/administrators, to other health professionals (particularly physicians), and to the general public.

On a broader scale, the nurse manager is in a critical position to influence health care reform to effect fairer distribution of programs and services, and to ensure that human resources in health care are maximized. The Barer and Stoddart (1991) report on medical human resources in Canada identified the number of ways in which nursing resources could be better utilized in health care. The initiative by the Alberta Association of Registered Nurses, for example, to develop strategies whereby nurses can be recognized as the point of direct client access to care also highlights the value of this human resource. Nursing's contribution is documented in various studies and evidenced in many settings across Canada, including areas geographically isolated or with specific population groups. Promoting these approaches to meeting clients' needs should be seen as an important agenda for the nurse manager, even within her or his own organization.

Meso-Level Allocation Ethics Pertinent to Justice

At the organizational level (the meso-level or intermediate level), the nurse manager's task might be conceived as being the "conscience" of the managerial team. As reductions in programs or services are planned, nurse managers must seek to ensure the welfare of clients and nurses. "When competent care is threatened due to inadequate resources or for some other reason, the nurse manager should act to minimize the present danger and to prevent future harm" (CNA Code, 1991, pp. 11-12).

Although it is both appropriate and necessary that the nurse manager develop loyalty to the management team overall, it may be that nurse managers too easily concede to the demands of others at the executive table. The proclivity of many nurse managers to reduce the numbers of registered nurses on staff while hiring auxiliary workers and personal care aides is often viewed as both short sighted and detrimental to nursing care. And although registered nurses may grieve over the loss of jobs and the apparent devaluing of their knowledge and skills, these actions raise broader questions about the ethics of compromise and, most importantly, the ethics of the potential decrease in the standard of care for the client without his or her knowledge or agreement.

One particularly troubling aspect of managerial decision making in health care organizations, and a problem of meso-level managerial ethics, is the rather pervasive, albeit unstated, belief in administrative science as value free (Astley, 1985). This belief leads to an unquestioning acceptance by many health administrators of the techniques of consulting firms which, under the guise of scientific management, market packages that redefine client problems. New words arise in administrative lingo; these are not always compatible with health care and may mislead health professionals in the appropriate direction of care. For example, only a few years ago, programs of "guest relations" and "therapeutic pampering" were heralded as the way to ensure clients received the attention they required during their health care episode. Therapeutic pampering (MacStravic, 1986) included attention to the client's gourmet dining desires and care of their pets. Although the fad was relatively short-lived (at least in the health administration journals), the definition of client need and health provider responsibility conveyed an uncomfortable acceptance of a materialistic definition of health need, raising the potential of leaving unaddressed other more pressing and less obvious health care needs.

Another troubling aspect of the acceptance of value-free management theory and method is the increasing reliance on numerical data and formulas for decisions about health service needs and priorities. In most provinces, some type of "formula" now dominates thinking about the budget to be assigned to a given health agency. Assumptions underlying the formula are not always made explicit and, as this formula gets translated within the particular agency, overreliance on mainly numerical data can also be misleading. The types of data used as indicators, as well as how those data might be interpreted, are not always made clear. It must be recognized that "our definition of problems and our search for alternatives becomes confined by our world view" (Storch, 1988, p. 271). In other words, choice of data is a value choice.

Micro-Level Allocation Ethics Pertinent to Justice

Within the nursing department (at the micro-level), direct concern for the clients' needs compels the nurse manager to ensure that clients' physiological needs and safety and security needs are met. In addition, responsibility for addressing the clients' needs for belonging, for self-esteem, and for self-actualization must also be viewed as a priority (Maslow, 1964; Storch, 1990). While the fiscal climate of health care mitigates against giving these needs sufficient attention, the competing emphasis on the clients' responsibility and control of their own health care situations stresses the need to view each health encounter as an enabling experience from which a client can grow and be better prepared to cope with and manage his or her own care (Antonovsky, 1979). Therefore, even though resources are constrained, preparing each client for future illness episodes or for better personal health management addresses future resource allocation, reinforces client autonomy and responsibility, and constitutes an ethical posture for the nurse manager.

Bringing Benefit and Minimizing Harm

It may seem a strange principle to enunciate as the very first requirement in a hospital that it should do the sick no harm. (Florence Nightingale [1863], quoted in Ulrich, 1975, p. 24)

Although the applications of the principle of beneficence and the principle of non-maleficence are more easily recognized at the level of client-caregiver interaction, these principles are equally significant to ethics in nursing management.

Macro-Level Activities Pertinent to Beneficence and Non-Maleficence

At the broadest level of influence, the nurse manager is in a critical position to work with professional associations and agency associations, usually in concert with the management team, for example to advocate for law reforms for client benefit and to press for government policies and practices in funding and approval of programs that promote the welfare of clients. This often means that nurses must develop political strategies (independently or with the team) to reach desired goals.

Given that the Criminal Code of Canada was written in the late 1800s (at a time when there was no knowledge of today's technological possibilities and limited understandings of human physiology), it is not surprising that many of its sections serve to restrict rather than to facilitate appropriate care of clients. This has been particularly true in matters of life support and termination of treatments.

The Criminal Code states that "Every one who undertakes to do an act is under a legal duty to do it if an omission to do the act is or may be dangerous to life" (quoted in Rodrigues, 1990, p. 128). This statement has been interpreted by many practitioners as compelling them to ensure that, once started, resuscitative actions (or any other treatments, for that matter) must be continued. Only through the efforts of nurses, supported by their nursing managers, was one Canadian hospital able to take leadership in developing a multiorganizational statement to set a different standard of practice. This standard allowed health professionals to set limits on resuscitative attempts where such attempts were considered medically useless treatment and not in the best interests of the client (McPhail, Moore, O'Connor, & Woodward, 1981). These actions, supported by parallel activities by the Law Reform Commission of Canada (1982), have been helpful in moving toward a more client-oriented approach to care. But limit-setting activities are still modest, since the Criminal Code has not yet been changed and since many physicians and hospitals still practise defensive medicine. The voice of nursing administrators is needed to move these policies toward legislative change. In doing so, the nurse manager will represent nurses who are often caught in the dilemma of unsigned orders or uncertain practices regarding their role in calling for resuscitation. New national, multiassociation policies are in process to address the vacuum of guidelines related to two pressing matters: improvements in do-not-resuscitate policies and advance treatment directives.

Involvement in setting and responding to government policies and practices that dictate levels of funding to agencies is also a critical role for nurse managers. Since only at this level can the needs of clients be represented to government, the responsibility rests heavily with the nurse manager to represent patients well and to interpret the consequences of funding decisions. This is not always a comfortable position for nurses, who may find that assessment of patient benefit is difficult to interpret to other managers. Clearly, the nurse manager cannot be engaged in self-serving defence of the nursing department. However, he or she must be well versed on client needs to advocate for them.

Meso-Level Activities Pertinent to Beneficence and Non-Maleficence

Since the nurse manager serves as spokesperson for the needs of the nursing department, or for nurses within the organization when there is no separate nursing department, he or she is the interpreter of nursing and nursing's potential to bring benefit to patients. Therefore, the nurse manager must:

- *Support outcome measurement with a knowledge of how research can contribute toward understanding those nursing practices that benefit and those that may be harmful or of questionable benefit;*

- *Support and initiate development of guidelines and policies that minimize harms and maximize health for patients and families;*

- *Ensure that mechanisms / structures are in place to prevent and address ethical violations; and*

- *Support nurses who are dealing with ethical dilemmas and those experiencing ethical distress* (CNA Code, 1991).

Bringing benefits to clients and reducing risk of harm involve vigilant attention to nursing practices, including both process and outcome. Only through systematic study of nursing practices can nurses know the effects of their care. With the added impetus of a recent focus on nursing care outcomes, as well as on the requirement that the ethical practice of nursing demands accountability, the need for nursing research to measure and determine improved approaches to cost-effective care has never been more pressing.

Guidelines for care must also be developed and updated to keep abreast of ethical issues confronting nurses in practice. Directives regarding the forgoing of medical treatment have been discussed in the previous section. Other notable needs are for guidelines for determining level of client competence, guidelines for informed consent and the process for obtaining consent, policies on client confidentiality, and guidelines for nurse-physician collaboration. The development of these types of guidelines normally requires negotiation, particularly since professional loyalties and beliefs about the relevance of such guidelines may cloud the issues. Nurse managers must ensure that the voices of nurses are not silenced in these discussions and that nurses' views are reflected in any policies or procedures developed.

Finally, mechanisms must be established to assist nurses in dealing with ethical problems. Under the CNA *Code of Ethics* (1991) those problems have been defined as falling into three types: ethical violations, ethical dilemmas, and ethical distress. While there is no practical defence for *ethical violations,* nurses may be placed in a position where the temptation to violate the standard expected is great (e.g., where team work and support of physician practices is difficult and appropriate channels to address these issues are not known or not available). Nurses may also find themselves involved in serious dilemmas of practice that require discussion to effect reasonable resolution. Agency ethics committees can be helpful but may also have inherent constraints, which require a higher level of intervention so that open dialogue can occur. The nurse manager can foster a more responsive ethics committee by bringing issues of inequitable power relationships to the senior management table for discussion and action.

Ethical distress has only recently been isolated from the quagmire of ethical problems (Rodney, 1988). Such distress largely (but not exclusively) arises from the dependent role of the nurse when nurses may be required "to provide particular types of care despite their personal disagreement or discomfort with the course of treatment prescribed" (CNA Code, 1991, p. iii). Such distress is increased when the nurse feels that his or her position has not been considered and does not feel the support of the team or of colleagues in the difficult tasks he or she is required to undertake. Nursing managers must be sensitive to these types of dilemmas and provide mechanisms to support nurses. Since these types of situations are more likely to arise when communication between physicians and nurses is poor, the nurse manager's role in addressing the root cause of the issue is critical.

Micro-Level Ethics Pertinent to Beneficence and Non-Maleficence

Openness to nursing practices that enhance client care and well-being is one of the ways nursing managers can remain sensitive to and supportive of nurses' creativity in addressing clients' responses to illness. Music therapy, therapeutic touch, massage therapy, and other less traditional approaches to pain control and to healing are practices that are becoming more commonly used by nurses. Nurse managers can do much to foster a climate for innovation and attention to individual client needs by supporting nurses in their practice, and occasionally, by removing organizational barriers to enable them to practise these alternative approaches to care. When the nurse manager is seen to value the individual nurse's knowledge, skills, and creativity, nurses are better able to concentrate on client needs. Such a climate also fosters an atmosphere in which caring and connectedness in nurse-client relationships can flourish.

Autonomy and Nursing Management

A charge nurse must exercise authority without appearing to exercise it. She must have a quieter, more impartial mind. She must be just and candid, looking at both sides, not moved by entreaties or by likes and dislikes but only by justice and reason. (Florence Nightingale, quoted in Barritt & Hill, 1975, p. 16).

The application of the principle of autonomy to nursing management is based upon the premise that the client's autonomy is to be protected, and that the nurse manager can often best ensure client autonomy by maximizing the autonomy and respect of nursing staff.

Macro-Level Activities Pertinent to Autonomy

Because nurses constitute the largest single component of health human resources, and because they (more than most other health professionals) are more constant attendants at the client's bedside or during the client's ambulatory care episode, they have important information about clients, about the workability of systems designed to serve clients, and about caregiver-client interactions that may be facilitating or interfering with client healing and

wholeness. For these reasons, nurses' voices need to be heard publicly in support of clients' needs and in support of health care
reforms, the better to meet the needs of groups of clients as well
as individual clients. Because nursing administrators/managers
are in more prestigious and powerful positions than staff nurses,
they attend meetings at which appropriate input from nursing
has the potential to make a difference in system reform to meet
clients' needs better.

Nurse managers must see their role as presenting and advocating for the views and positions of the nursing staff they serve,
particularly as those views support enhanced care for clients and
greater attention to client needs. From long traditions of sub-
servience and silence, nurse managers may tend to avoid raising
publicly nursing views that may conflict with predominant views
in health care. In many settings, nurse managers who attempt to
advocate for nurses and clients still encounter a hostile or reluctant management team skilled at disregarding the voice of nursing. The support of other nurse managers is critical in advocating
effectively with such a team.

Meso-Level Activities Pertinent to Autonomy

Initiating, developing, and refining policies that honour patient
autonomy are vital tasks of the nurse manager. Indications for
new policy or revised policy commonly arise from those nurses
providing direct care to clients/patients. Encouraging an open
invitation for all nursing staff to identify policy needs should be
seen as a nurse manager's ethical responsibility to his or her
nursing staff.

Nurse managers can also be instrumental in ensuring that
viable committees and other support structures (through which
ethical concerns can be raised and reviewed) are in place. Ethics
consultation committees are one common committee structure
designed to facilitate discussion of ethical problems, including perceived violations, dilemmas, and distress. But these committees
are not always accessible to nurses, and may not be providing the
interdisciplinary dialogue envisioned. If the findings of a pilot
study on ethics committees in Canada are reflective of other
agency processes, it would seem that the voices of nurses are still
muted by procedural issues and by power bases that nurse managers seem either unable or unwilling to rectify (Storch &
Griener, 1992). Greater access to ethics committees is necessary,
and possible, so that the independent voice of nursing can better
be heard and respected in decisions that belong to an entire
health care team, not an individual practitioner.

Apart from the work required to improve ethics committees or patient care committees, in many health agencies there appears to be a need to develop better ways in which nurses and physicians communicate, including ways to resolve misunderstandings and disputes. Nurse managers have a vital role in promoting respect for the autonomy of nurses by facilitating mechanisms that will provide a forum for open and constructive physician-nurse dialogue and conflict resolution.

Micro-Level Activities Pertinent to Autonomy

The nurse manager respects nursing staff and staff autonomy by recognizing the importance of meeting the needs of staff so that they may meet and serve the needs of patients and clients. An obligation stated in the CNA Code (1991) is that "Nurse managers must seek to foster environments and conditions of employment that promote excellent care for clients and a good worklife for nurses" (p. 17). Needs for safety, security, sense of belonging, self-esteem, and self-actualization (Maslow, 1964) are as real for nurses as they are for clients. It is important for nurse managers to recognize that neglecting to attend to nursing staff needs can be directly correlated with nurses' failure to meet client needs.

With renewed threats of communicable diseases (e.g., AIDS, hepatitis-B) and increasing cost constraint causing instability in health agencies, nurses' personal and job security is increasingly at risk. Also, with increasing use of part-time and casual staff, and with unit closures in hospitals displacing nurses from their collegial work groups, nurses' basic human needs for a sense of belonging are seriously threatened. As nurses attempt to adapt rapidly to new units and new services where well-known and comfortable knowledge and skills may no longer apply, their self-esteem is seriously compromised and self-actualization is made impossible. Are these ethical concerns? They are insofar as the nurse manager is committed to quality patient care and respect for nursing staff.

Attending to nursing staff needs will mean that nurse managers recognize and respond to the plight of nurses as systems change. Finding meaningful ways in which nurses can participate in decision making is one necessity; providing regular feedback on performance and on implications of change is another. One concern felt by many nurses is the trend towards de-skilling of nursing tasks and displacement of nurses. De-skilling is based on the premise that labour power should be purchased as cheaply as possible and that the manager should dictate to the worker the precise manner in which the work is to be done. The "labour process then becomes dissociated from the actual skills of the worker, and the conception of the task becomes divorced from the execution of the task" (Storch & Stinson, 1988, pp. 35-36). Measurement of nursing workload, patient acuity levels, and so on, while not necessarily problematic, may be misused and lead to a climate of de-skilling. Of greater concern, however, is the tendency to displace nurses with cheaper, often untrained or marginally trained workers, leading to a sense of devaluation of nursing by managerial preoccupation with tasks to be done rather than with holistic care and care that provides enabling experiences for clients. It is not surprising that nurses would feel betrayed by their nurse manager's agreement to de-skilling and to the displacement process.

Conclusions and Implications for Nurse Managers

Nursing needs to be more and more of a moral calling. (Florence Nightingale, quoted in Barritt & Hill, 1975, p. 19).

Ethical dimensions for nursing management are wide ranging, touching every aspect of the nurse manager's work. Macro-level dimensions demand that the nurse manager be courageous as spokesperson, political strategist, and advocate for health care reform, for maximizing the utilization of nurses as a valuable human resource, advocating client-centred attention in government policy and in law reform, and ensuring that nurses' voices are heard and their views well represented.

Meso-level ethical dimensions require that the nurse manager have considerable commitment, fortitude, and tenacity in seven main areas:

- In serving as the conscience of the health care team;
- In avoiding compromises that neutralize nursing contributions and lead to decreased standards of care;
- In recognizing that value judgements colour all managerial decision making;
- In interpreting nursing clearly;
- In supporting nursing research;
- In developing guidelines for client care; and
- In supporting nurses in dealing with ethical problems.

To do these things effectively, nurse managers must value nursing and be able to articulate nursing roles and contributions credibly and forcefully. A solid foundation in nursing philosophy and nursing conceptual frameworks is vital to such interpretation. Meso-level nursing management activities also necessitate attention to honouring client autonomy through the development and refinement of client-centred policies and through encouraging supportive structures in which meaningful dialogue can occur on ethical concerns.

At the micro-level of ethical dimensions of nursing management, attention to the needs of the whole person is critical. This will ensure that clients in health care are enabled through their health care encounters. Attention to fostering healthy environments for nurses and other care providers are equally important goals and activities of nurse managers. Supporting nursing innovation and creating a climate that fosters caring and connectedness are also critical responsibilities of nurse managers. Recognizing the importance of meeting nurses' needs in order to meet client needs and providing mechanisms for regular performance evaluation and for meaningful participation in decision making are additional ethical responsibilities.

The expectations raised but not fulfilled by many shared governance manoeuvres constitute a breach in commitment to ethical practice. Also, to de-skill and to displace is to devalue. Nurse managers must examine their motive for supporting these endeavours, and if they truly believe these positions to be justifiable, assist nurses and clients to understand their reasons.

The ethical dimensions of nursing management are exacting, and require serious self-examination and a high degree of accountability. Only with a strong belief in nursing's contribution to client care and an in-depth understanding of nursing (as well as a serious commitment to ethical behaviour) can the nurse manager feel comfortable and competent in meeting these demands.

Although the quote at the beginning of this chapter focusses on ensuring that the "right things are done" by staff nurses, the nurse manager's own ethical posture is critical. Role modeling ethical management practice is one of the most forceful ways to promote ethics in practice.

References

Antonovsky, A. (1979). *Health, stress and coping*. San Francisco: Jossey Bass.

Astley, W.G. (1985). Administrative science as socially constructed truth. *Administrative Science Quarterly, 30*, 497-513.

Baier, A.C. (1989). The need for more than justice. *Canadian Journal of Philosophy, 13*(Suppl.), 41-55.

Barer, M.L., & Stoddart, G.L. (1991). *Towards integrated medical resource policies in Canada*. Winnipeg: Manitoba Health.

Barritt, E.R,. & Hill, J. (1975). *Florence Nightingale: Her wit and wisdom*. Mount Vernon, NY: Peter Pauper Press.

Beauchamp, T., & Childress, J. (1989). *Principles of biomedical ethics* (3rd ed.). New York: Oxford University Press.

Canadian Nurses Association (1991). *Code of ethics for nursing* Ottawa: Author.

Hiller, M. (1984). Ethics in health care administration: Issues in education and practice. *Journal of Health Administration Education, 2*(2), 148-192.

Kant, I. (1976). From "Fundamental principles of the metaphysics of morals." In S. Gorovitz et al. (Eds.), *Moral problems in medicine* (pp. 23-25). Englewood Cliffs, NJ: Prentice-Hall. (Original work published in 1898.)

Law Reform Commission of Canada. (1982). *Euthanasia, aiding suicide and cessation of treatment*. Ottawa: Minister of Supply & Services.

MacPhail, A., Moore, S., O'Conner, J., & Woodward, C. (1981). One hospital's experience with a "Do not resuscitate" policy. *Canadian Medical Association Journal, 125*, 830-836.

MacStravic, R.S. (1986). Therapeutic pampering. *Hospitals and Health Services Administration, 31*(3), 59-69.

Maslow, A.H. (1964). A therapy of motivation. In H.J. Leavitt & L.R. Pondy (Eds.), *Readings in managerial psychology* (pp. 6-24). Chicago: University of Chicago Press.

Mill, J.S. (1859). *On liberty*. Harmondsworth: Penguin Books.

Rawls, J. (1976). Justice as fairness. In T. Beauchamp & L. Walters (Eds.), *Contemporary issues in bioethics* (pp. 44-46). Belmont, CA: Wadsworth Publishing.

Rodney, P. (1988). Moral distress in critical care nursing. *Canadian Critical Care Nursing Journal, 5*(2), 9-11.

Rodrigues, G.P. (Ed.). (1990). *Pocket Criminal Code*. Toronto: Carswell.

Storch, J.L. (1982). *Patient rights: Ethical and legal issues in health care and nursing*. Toronto: McGraw-Hill.

Storch, J.L. (1988). Major substantive ethical issues facing Canadian health care policymakers and implementers. *Journal of Health Administration Education, 6*(2), 263-271.

Storch, J.L. (1990). Caring for the caregiver. *Hospital Trustee, 14*(3), 10-11.

Storch, J.L., & Griener, G.G. (1992). Ethics committees in Canadian hospitals: Report of the 1990 pilot study. *Healthcare Management Forum, 5*(1), 19-26.

Storch, J.L., & Stinson, S.M. (1988). Concepts of deprofessionalization with applications to nursing. In R. White (Ed.), *Political issues in nursing: Past, present and future* (Vol. 3) (pp. 33-44). Toronto: John Wiley & Sons.

Ulrich, B.T. (1992). *Leadership and management according to Florence Nightingale.* Norwalk, CT: Appleton at Large.

C H A P T E R 9

Workplace Design

Mary Pat Skene

Mary Pat Skene, RN, BScN (Saskatchewan), MEd (Alberta), is Senior Vice-President, Caritas Health Group, Edmonton. She has been involved in the planning and commissioning of both the Walter C. MacKenzie Health Sciences Centre and the Grey Nuns Hospital, both in Edmonton. She maintains a keen interest in planning and commissioning and has travelled widely to observe recent design approaches that assist in good nursing care. As a representative of the Canadian Nurses Association, she participated in the 1990 Hospital Design Conference in Monza, Italy, presenting a paper on Canadian Hospital Unit Design.

"Bad sanitary, bad architectural, and bad administrative arrangements often make it impossible to nurse. But the art of nursing ought to include such arrangements as alone make what I understand by Nursing possible." (Florence Nightingale, 1859, p. 6).

Workplace design is important to all nurses, particularly nurse managers. It is critical that the workplace, whether in institutions or in the community, be designed to support the care needs of clients, but also to make it easier to nurse.

Nurse managers are critically positioned when it comes to determining the most appropriate design for an individual workplace, whether it be a newly constructed workplace or one being renovated. Because of the unique role of nurses in assessing and meeting care needs, nurse managers are in a position to articulate these needs clearly and ensure a design that will most efficiently and effectively meet them. The workplace must also support the nurse through appropriate adaptations to nursing practice.

Workplace design in the 1980s was predicated on a belief that the environment needs to promote health of mind as well as of body for clients, family members, and staff. According to well-known architect Eberhard H. Zeidler (1978), "We must create hospitals which not only heal the body but also heal the mind" (p. 28). This directive could be broadened to include all workplaces where care is available. Zeidler, who designed the Eaton Centre in Toronto and the Walter C. MacKenzie Health Sciences Centre in Edmonton, further states, "Health care today strives to improve the quality of life... [and] the emotional responses that we incorporate into our facilities [will] survive the technological changes that may take place in the future" (Zeidler, 1983, p. 11). The workplace design that occurred as a result of these beliefs was aesthetically pleasing but often costly from an operational standpoint. In the 1990s, hospital planners are being called upon to combine quality with cost consciousness, and design must reflect this in meeting the needs of clients, families, and staff.

This chapter will focus on the importance of nurse managers to the process of workplace design within a health-focussed environment. After a brief opening discussion of ergonomics, the roles of the nurse manager in the process of the five interrelated phases of workplace design—functional programming, operations planning, commissioning, occupancy, and postoccupancy evaluation—will be discussed. The chapter will close with some predictions that could affect design in nursing workplaces throughout the 1990s and beyond.

Ergonomics

Ergonomics is the study of the relationship between individuals and the demands of their working environment, especially with regard to fitting jobs to the needs and abilities of workers, thereby preventing injuries and maximizing productivity. Ergonomics involves three basic components of work design: the worker, the work method or procedure, and the workplace or work station.

For nursing, the worker is the nurse, and consideration must be given to the impact of the nurse on the environment and vice versa. In design of nursing workplaces, some changing characteristics of the nurse must be addressed. For example, in recent years nurses are remaining in the workplace for a longer career; thus, the increasing age of the nursing population indicates a need for some environmental changes, such as built-in supports for lifting patients and easier availability of supplies and equipment. The many procedures performed by nurses in the provision of care, the work method, also can be supported by the environment. For example, nurses would benefit from appropriate heights for bathing equipment, adjustable bed heights for care provision, and decreased distances between care support and care delivery. The design of the work station must include such considerations as ease of access, adaptability, and environmental support. In addition, an aesthetically pleasing work station is positive for nurses.

Ergonomics is a key concept relative to workplace design, as

Table 9.1
Definition of terms specific to workplace design.

Several terms specific to workplace design must be considered. These include:

• **Programming**	Identifying and documenting operational determinants and specific physical requirements to accomplish the defined objectives.
• **Functional programming**	The process of outlining the operational functions and determining space and facilities requirements for accomplishing these functions.
• **Operational programming**	The process of putting into action the functional programming.
• **Commissioning**	The transformation of a completed workplace into a functioning care unit or units.
• **Operational readiness**	A state of preparedness for planned functions.
• **Operational readiness exercises**	A series of simulated experiences designed to test training, systems, procedures, and equipment within a new or renovated environment.

the design must support the health of nurses. A well-designed workplace supports quality care, boosts staff morale, and increases efficiency and effectiveness of care delivery. Table 9.1 provides an overview of definitions of some of the terms used in ergonomics and in workplace design. Knowledge of these terms will assist nurse managers to participate in the planning processes with other professionals and be better able to interpret nursing needs.

Functional Programming

The process of outlining operational functions and determining space and facilities for realizing these functions is the first step in workplace design. This must be driven by a strategic vision. The opportunity at this point for creative input from nurse managers is significant.

Knowledge of historical trends in nursing care is important. From historical information, nurse managers have knowledge of what the demands have been. Based on this, and on knowledge of current research in areas such as demographics, it is possible to formulate predictions. In addition, leadership necessitates consideration of current, emerging, and predictive trends and issues about nursing and health care. In the quality-driven, cost-conscious, health-focussed environments of today, nurse managers must respond to real needs. Once the demand is determined and the needs identified, architects and planners, driven by nursing's strategic vision, can be creative in meeting the needs.

Basically, functional programming involves mapping out what must be done in the new or renovated workplace and determining how best to do it, what equipment is necessary, and what space is required. Developing computer simulation models of the projected demand can assist in the analysis of many factors. These factors include: changing demographics affecting both clients and workers, technological changes, changing practices of nurses and other health care professionals, changing expectations/needs of clients, and changes in administration of health care. Currently, nursing managers must address such major changes as an aging population, increasing technology, and clients with more education and knowledge about health as well as specific agency initiatives such as, for example, shortened lengths of stay for patients in acute care environments, preassessment clinics for surgical patients, and increased emphasis on partnership of nurses with other professionals in care delivery.

Establishing space requirements is tied to equipment and technology needs as well as to care models. However, space planning must include reference to the vision of the organization and the vision of care. This may mean that nurse managers will be asked to prepare detailed lists and diagrams of all proposed areas, with documentation about physical organizational concepts. The physical, psychological, emotional, social, cultural, and spiritual needs of the clients, families, and staff are part of this documentation. In addition, the systems to support the meeting of these needs must be defined (i.e., "clinical support systems" such as radiology, laboratory, respiratory therapy, dietary, rehabilitation, pharmacy, and pastoral care and "environmental support systems" such as supply distribution, housekeeping, and physical plant). The models for care delivery will affect the space requirements and require definition.

The first focus of functional programming for client care areas is the client and family. For example, many hospitals have outside windows for all clients and this has been found to have a positive outcome for client orientation and for general well-being. Locations of space and equipment for activities of daily living are important; there needs to be appropriate bathroom facilities, eating facilities, and recreational facilities. Family support areas or quiet spaces for reflection are also recommended. Two-dimensional diagrams will assist in assessing the adequacy of spaces but often, three-dimensional mock-ups are required for an appropriate assessment to be made.

A second focus is the caregiver. This requires an assessment of the spaces to support the caregiver in meeting the care requirements in the newly built or newly renovated spaces. This includes space for such things as supplies, medications, computers, clerical support, teaching spaces for client, family, and staff, and equipment storage. Office spaces are required but should be kept to a minimum. The need for staff relaxation space is becoming increasingly more important because of the intense and relentless change both in the workplace and in the home environment.

Operational Planning

The definition of operational (or operations) planning refers to a process of putting the functional program into action. In this phase, the question "Will it work?" must be answered. This does not mean "Will it work?" from the perspective of individual departments but as a coordinated whole.

An operations planner or a team of planners is assigned the responsibility for this phase. It is important to have a nurse planner involved in this phase either as team leader or as an integral member of the team. Often a senior-level nurse manager is involved at the operations level, but first-level nurse managers frequently are asked to assist, as part of the team, in the planning for each individual department. In this phase, as in the functional programming phase, holistic knowledge of care requirements, such as first-level nurse managers usually have, is invaluable.

The role of this team of professionals is as follows:

- To assist each program or department in determining the format and scope of the operations plan;

- To coordinate each operations plan with those of other programs or departments to ensure that the sum of all operations provides for the safe and efficient occupancy and operation of the workplace;

- To ensure that operations plans are developed within a time frame in keeping with the master schedule; and

- To ensure that issues identified in the planning process are documented through an appropriate mechanism for resolution.

Development of Operations Plans

A thorough and well-documented plan for the operation of all programs or services will be developed and adopted well in advance of the actual occupancy. These plans should include:

- A document describing the final operations of the departments, identifying changes in policies and procedures, changes in relationships with other departments, staffing needs, and the impact of new technology on the functioning of the department.

- A documented interim operations plan, which will describe the functioning of the department during both the move of other departments and the move of the department in question; this is particularly important when occupancy is phased in over a prolonged period of time.

- A decanting plan for the department or for a portion of the department when the department is required to move more than once or to move in stages.

- An occupancy plan, which will identify clients for transfer as well as equipment and furniture that will be moved. This will include details of a department's phasing-in of clients, staff, and services and of any special needs for equipment movers or consultants.

- A documented schedule of events and identification of a critical path for the move and for operations.

- A budget identifying commissioning costs and operating costs.

- A testing and evaluation mechanism.

- A staff orientation and development plan; commitment to staff orientation and development is the primary way that occupancy of a new or newly renovated space can be optimized and maximum benefits achieved.

Equipment Planning

Equipment planning includes inventory, tender, and purchase. Depending on the scope of the project, one or more individuals will need to be assigned to this function. From the nursing perspective, all direct care equipment requires assessment by the nurse planner in consultation with nurses who will be working directly with the equipment. This assessment may necessitate on-site visits to facilities that have this equipment in operation.

Actual tender and purchase will be left to the appropriate support personnel in the facility. The assessment of equipment once received is another area of nurse involvement.

Commissioning

The transformation of a completed building into a functioning workplace has been given the term "commissioning." This term is of British derivation and had its origins within the British Naval Services where it was used in reference to "putting into service a ship of war." When this term is used in relation to a new or renovated workplace, it refers to putting the new or renovated workplace into service. In its broadest context, commissioning is a method of change carried to completion.

In searching for a model of planned change, that developed by Havelock (1979) proves useful. This process approach emphasizes the solution of problems through analysis as well as by direct involvement of those affected by the solution. The four stages in this problem-solving model for planned change are appropriate to the commissioning process. These are: (1) diagnosing the problem, (2) selecting the solution, (3) implementing the solution, and (4) stabilizing the change.

The definition or diagnosis of the problem is the most critical step in the commissioning process. Problems can arise in a number of areas, such as redundancy, amalgamation of services, organizational structure, environmental design, new equipment, new and revised procedures, and the possible interface with existing operations, to name just a few. For an accurate diagnosis to be made, there must be involvement from as many staff as possible. This not only promotes a positive attitude toward the new workplace but also permits creativity when determining solutions.

The next step is selection of the solution. In this stage, a number of strategies can be used, especially the generation and analysis of alternatives. In analyzing the alternatives, such factors as benefit, workability, and diffusibility must be considered. In essence, this means asking: Will the potential solution do any good? Will it work? and, Will it be accepted as a viable solution? In addition to selecting the appropriate course of action, critical path diagrams and/or bar charts, along with appropriate programs or strategies, will assist in implementing the solution.

If the first two phases have been well carried out, the implementation phase will proceed relatively smoothly; if not, problems occur. Conflict resolution is a significant factor to be considered in this phase. Resistance to change is a natural part of human behaviour; coping with this resistance is a key component of commissioning. In this phase, the following activities are carried out: orientation of staff, preparation and resolution of deficiency lists, simulated operations (operational readiness exercises), scheduling for staff and client movement, contribution of public relations strategies, and, finally, occupancy.

Follow-up evaluation with a feedback mechanism is necessary if the change is to be a stable one. With a successful commissioning process, the change is implemented so skilfully that the transition is a pleasant experience. In the not-so-successful process, results can vary from slightly unpleasant to nightmarish. As stated by Drodge (1982), "no amount of extra staff or public relations can prevent the horror of seeing a new hospital that doesn't work" (p. 26).

Five of the more important parts of this model as they apply to commissioning, especially as these apply to first-level nurse managers, now are described in more detail.

Development of Policies and Procedures

A new, expanded, or renovated workplace necessitates development of new or revised policies and procedures. It is important to have a committee, with appropriate representation, charged with this task. Under the auspices of this committee, new equipment and procedures can be tried first within the existing workplace. This will reduce some of the apprehension generated by the change, because the new equipment and procedures will be clearly understood prior to the move.

Human Resources

Human resources planning involves activity analysis, position specifications, position descriptions, and the actual process of recruitment. It is important to ascertain the specific job-related functions for each type of position within the new, expanded, or renovated workplace. Hughes (1981, p. 28), in describing a major move at a large urban hospital, estimated that 90% of the jobs involved would change in some fashion, that 20% of the jobs would be totally changed, and that the planning would take six months. The reasons for such changes in nursing include such factors as changes in patient care delivery and an increase in computerization.

The human resources planning process also assists in identifying overlapping responsibilities. Job descriptions, based on the expected needs in the new areas, then must be developed.

Once the position descriptions are completed, the process of recruitment commences. Recruitment can be internal or external. Internal recruitment will be required when there is a substantial change in staffing patterns (e.g., an increase or decrease in the number of nursing managers or in the patient count for the nursing unit). The positions usually should be advertised internally, and nurse managers should follow the entire recruitment process and use the agency resources. It is important to consider the various union contracts when planning the recruitment. As well, the question of experienced practitioner versus inexperienced practitioner must be considered.

When internal recruitment does not provide the required numbers or the required experience, external recruitment must be pursued. Nurse managers need to be aware that if nursing staff is obtained externally, it is necessary to orient them to the accepted routines in care of patients as well as to the new environment. This requires additional time.

The next step to be considered is staff rotation. The first consideration is the care needs of the client. It is then necessary to consider the individual union contracts and the experience requirements in the individual departments on each shift. The rotation should be planned well in advance of the move, giving particular consideration to the day of the move.

Orientation Program

The orientation of all levels of staff to function within the new or renovated environment is crucial to the success of the commissioning process. Orientation is often one of the most significant means of allaying apprehension. Fear of the unknown can be a critical negative factor in the commissioning process.

An orientation program should enhance a positive attitude toward impending change. Presented within the framework of known skills and competencies, the program should be designed to:

- Provide staff with an overview of the philosophical perspective;

- Familiarize staff with the spatial organization, its special features and functions; and

- Prepare staff to implement specific procedural and equipment changes related to the new or renovated environment.

In my experience in commissioning a large acute care teaching hospital, each nursing staff member required three days of orientation. Orientation time for staff in other departments increased or decreased relative to the changes in the individual departments. "Core" content was identified as being required for all departments in relation to the building, its special features and functions, and to specific building systems (e.g., communications, fire, and security system).

Orientation puts those affected by the change in touch with the information required to function within the boundaries of the defined change. It does not stop once the move is completed. It should be continuous and supported by the appropriate education materials, and these must be accurate and consistent.

A variety of manuals can be developed to provide the required information and to permit early and easy access. An orientation manual should contain key information points on the material presented during orientation. There is also a need for a procedure manual, a policy manual, and specific departmental manuals. Once developed, they must be readily available to staff. Use of computers in preparation of manuals will help to maintain, enhance, and replace material in a timely manner.

Operational Readiness Exercises

Operational readiness exercises encompass a series of simulated experiences designed to test training, procedures, systems, and equipment within the new environment. Games and simulations have frequently been used in adult education. Operational readiness exercises have long played a significant role in military operations and their usefulness in the commissioning process is widely recognized.

The readiness of the staff and the readiness of the environment for safe client care can be accurately assessed through these exercises, and such a strategy is invaluable. It is generally agreed that the most significant learning takes place during the exercises. They provide a time to reinforce the learning points in relation to the new systems, new equipment, and procedural adaptations. In addition, these activities bring new teams of personnel together and promote an esprit de corps prior to client occupancy.

Client care scenarios test care delivery, training, procedures, systems, and equipment. Relationships with other departments are a major focus. With volunteers or staff acting as clients, these scenarios are enacted. The staff respond spontaneously to client needs, calling on their understanding of adaptations in care delivery and in new procedures, systems, and equipment. Both the staff response and the environment are evaluated. Suggested criteria for evaluation are:

- Functions appropriately; prepared to handle client needs independently;
- Requires minor adjustment or minimal additional training;
- Requires major adjustment or major additional training; or
- Inappropriate in present framework.

Based on this evaluation, planning for the actual move can be initiated. The prior identification and resolution of potential problems is extraordinarily valuable. The operational readiness process serves to identify problems and allow solutions to be worked out. An issues sheet can be used to record problems requiring resolution or areas where additional training is necessary.

Occupancy

Move day! The day or days of occupancy of the newly constructed or newly renovated space represent transformation of unoccupied space into a functioning workplace. The importance of the long hours of careful planning is appreciated as this transformation occurs. It is at once challenging, frustrating, and gratifying. The pinnacle of success is the actual move. Executing a move is, according to Lloyd (1983) "rather like going into the first grade in school—the unknown is challenging and uncertain, but embarking with confidence and with a positive attitude can make it a worthwhile experience" (p. 64).

Client Considerations

The effects of a new workplace on clients require consideration. The public relations function in communicating with clients and families, both in the agency and outside, about the move is a vital one and must be stressed. Health care facilities have tried a variety of ways to inform clients of an upcoming move. These include written pamphlets or brochures, newsletters, maps, information cards on dinner trays, visits by volunteers, and involvement of the staff. Even when all are used they can prove insufficient. The important principle is that clients and their relatives and friends are aware of and reassured about the upcoming change.

Postoccupancy
Evaluation

Evaluation and feedback activities are required for the stabilization of planned change. During the period immediately following change, all those involved are in a vulnerable state and need support and nurturing. Departments can and should use such tools as deficiency lists, issues lists, and checklists to identify areas that need solutions. Nurse managers must ensure that nursing staff have opportunities to comment and communicate about needs related to the move. As well, staff frequently can contribute to possible solutions or progress toward solutions.

Workplace Design
of the Future

Community-based, client-centred health care will be the principle behind workplace design in the future. Whether the facility be newly constructed or newly renovated, the focus will be on client, family, and staff as members of the community. The intent of this section is to leave the reader with a few points to ponder because they may affect workplace design for the future.

- Approximately 90% of medical admissions now enter the hospital through emergency departments; there are fewer elective admissions. This may be caused by the decrease in numbers of available acute care beds and a concomitant increase in outpatient services. Whatever the cause, one result is an increase of patients in the emergency department requiring admission but with no inpatient beds available. This means extended waiting periods in Emergency. Will this mean, in future, that hospitals will require planning for more meal service, for example, for the emergency department or perhaps for an "admissions area" where patients can have routine inpatient care within the department? Such a change could significantly affect nurses who chose the work area because they wished to provide emergency levels rather than routine levels of care.

- Day surgery units are increasingly common, with a shift to day procedures. The target of many hospitals is to have 60% to 70% of all surgery done on an outpatient basis. If this happens, space for this program will have to increase, and workplace design to accommodate the flow of this unit could change the face of the overall hospital design.

- Outpatient clinics also are increasing, and there will be a need to increase space available for this service. With the move to decrease numbers of inpatient beds, inpatient spaces may be renovated for outpatient programming.

- In the future, there will be a need to create environments more attuned to the acuity of the patient. This may mean a design move to larger rooms (i.e., for four to eight patients) so that nurses can deliver the care required and observe more patients at any given time. In some areas, the shower in each patient room is being used less frequently because more of the admissions are older and more acutely ill. Special bathing rooms may need to be designed to accommodate this change in demographics.

- If the trend is to these larger patient rooms, there will be a need for more patient lounges and "quiet rooms" where patients and family can be moved for private moments and where interdisciplinary interactions (e.g., nurse-physician or nursing team discussions) can take place.

- Having private rooms within a critical care unit is aesthetically pleasing for the patient and family but it definitely results in staffing inefficiencies. This is particulary so in planning for staff meal and rest breaks. I anticipate that critical care units of the future will once again be units without walls, because the need for direct patient observation and ease of access will override the need for privacy.

- At one time, it was believed that mobile medication carts, with patient-specific cassettes or drawers in a large cassette, was the answer to medication delivery. Hospital unit design in the 1980s accommodated this trend with a small alcove in which to park and, in some cases, to lock medications in the medication cart. This was appropriate when medications were delivered to a large group of patients by one medication nurse. However, with the advent of primary nursing, the case method of patient assignment, total patient care, or modular nursing, all nurses are responsible for administering medications to their own groups of patients. The result is that the nurses cannot all have access to one cart at the standard medication times. Medication carts have been moved out of their alcove into the hallways, and there is congestion at the site of medication preparation. In the future, the trend may be to wall-mounted individual patient cassettes or computerized patient dispensing.

- The obstetrical unit will continue to be designed for family-centred care. Within the delivery suite, birthing rooms are now equipped with a birthing bed where predelivery and delivery care occur in the same environment. This space will continue to be used, but the concept of the proposed "birthing centres" away from hospitals will also affect workplace design and agency planning.

- Psychiatric units will be designed with health of mind as a major focus. Units will be bright and spacious, and have large activity areas with easy access to the outdoors. Emphasis will be on outpatient programming, and bridging programs to allow patients to move from inpatient to outpatient status will increase.

- Pediatrics is shifting to a true community program with inpatient units complemented with extensive outpatient programs in keeping with the community-focussed care that this group of patients requires. Care-by-parent units will be more commonly used.

- The move toward patient-focussed care is promoting agency design that brings all programs and services within the same geographic space for a defined patient population.

- The growing focus on wellness, health promotion, and health teaching will affect design. Health resources centres (or "wellness centres") now provide programs and information to clients and families to assist them to attain and maintain an optimum level of wellness. These centres also provide an outreach into the community.

- Community health centres are now being designed in new or renovated spaces to meet health needs of the community. This trend will increase.

- Long term care facilities will continue to be designed to provide home-like environments for residents, and there will be an increased focus on outreach programming and respite care.

- The need for spaces to promote staff wellness will increase and may include on-site fitness centres and on-site facilities for child and elder care.

- Flexibility of design in all workplaces will be a definite asset because health care, health care requirements, and health care delivery are changing so rapidly.

Conclusion

The involvement of nurse managers in workplace design, within their individual areas of practice, is of paramount importance. In collaboration with the community and a variety of professionals, nurse managers are well positioned to articulate the needs of clients and to participate, in partnership with other health professionals, in articulating the needs of nursing staff. It is imperative that the workplace support both client and provider needs.

The design of the modern health care workplace is driven by a creative vision of health for all. A vision carries with it responsibility. In the words of the poet William Butler Yeats, "In dreams begins responsibility" (cited in Kanter, 1989, p. 17). I urge nurse managers to accept and welcome this responsibility.

References

Drodge, W. (1982). Successful commissioning of hospital construction. *Dimensions in Health Service, 59*(6), 25-26.

Havelock, R. (1982). *The change agent's guide to innovation on education.* Englewood Cliffs, NJ: Educational Technology Publications.

Hughes, M. (1981). Moving the hospital: Planning the manpower. *Dimensions in Health Service, 58*(8), 28-29.

Kanter, R.M. (1989). *When giants learn to dance.* New York: Touchstone.

Lloyd, D. (1983). Moving, ain't it great? *Medical Group Management, 30*(4), 58-65.

Nightingale, F. (1860). *Notes on nursing.* Boston: William Carter.

Zeidler, E. (1978). Build hospitals for future change. *Hospital Administration in Canada, 2,* 26-38.

Zeidler, E. (1983). Designing facilities: Trends for the future. *Hospital Trustee, 11,* 8-11.

P A R T   3

The Professional Dimension of the Nurse Manager's Role

C H A P T E R   1 0

Leadership Theory and Practice

Dorothy M. Wylie

Dorothy M. Wylie, RN, BScN (New York), MA (Columbia), MSc(HRD) (American University), is Associate Professor (part-time), Faculty of Nursing, University of Toronto, and a consultant in organization and management development. She is also Editor of the *Canadian Journal of Nursing Administration.*

The health care environment of today is complex and chaotic and, to master that environment, professional nurses need to renew and revitalize their leadership skills. Most organizational structures are now decentralized and there is a trend emerging toward programmatic structures. Program structures require a new brand of leadership behaviour and skills for nurses at all levels of the organization, and most particularly for the nurse manager. Barker (1991) states, "A new paradigm is emerging. This paradigm is characterized by the following: mutuality and affiliation, acknowledging complexity and ambiguity, cooperation versus competition, an emphasis on human relations, process versus task, acceptance of feelings, networking versus hierarchy, and recognition of the value of intuition" (p. 204). This shift requires nurses and nurse managers to learn new behaviours and new leadership skills; traditional and autocratic styles must be replaced, as they are now outmoded.

Kouzes and Posner (1987) describe leaders as pioneers who venture into unexplored territory, and who guide their followers to new and often unfamiliar destinations. The destination now is toward empowerment; the goal for the nurse manager is empowerment of self and empowerment of the staff. A new set of leadership behaviours is required to accomplish this goal.

The author of this chapter will examine leadership and leadership theory, including the recent concepts of transactional and transformational leadership, and superleadership. Implications for nurse managers will be explored and ways identified for first-level managers to develop or refine their leadership styles.

What Is Leadership?

Leadership is described and defined in many ways. Tannenbaum, Weschler, and Massarik (1961) describe it as "interpersonal influence, exercised in situation and directed, through the communication process, toward the attainment of a specified goal or goals" (p. 24). Burns (1978) states, "Leadership over human beings is exercised when persons with certain motives and purposes mobilize, in competition or conflict with others, institutional, political, psychological, and other resources so as to arouse, engage, and satisfy the motives of followers" (p. 18). Leaders are characterized by Nanus (1992) as those who "take charge, make things happen, dream dreams and then translate them into reality" (p.10).

Regardless of the definition one might choose, essential to leadership is a process of involving people, gaining their commitment, and energizing them to participate in the tasks related to achieving mutual goals.

Managers versus Leaders

A manager's position is a designated organizational role carrying formal power within the hierarchy of the organization. A leader's role can be assumed by anyone and does not require formal power or status. Therefore, managers and leaders are not one and the same. The effective manager is usually one who exercises effective leadership behaviour. Warren Bennis (1989) identifies 12 major differences between managers and leaders:

- The manager administers; the leader innovates.
- The manager is a copy; the leader is an original.
- The manager maintains; the leader develops.
- The manager focusses on systems and structure; the leader focusses on people.
- The manager relies on control; the leader inspires trust.
- The manager has a short-range view; the leader has a long-range perspective.
- The manager asks how and when; the leader asks what and why.
- The manager has an eye always on the bottom line; the leader has an eye on the horizon.
- The manager imitates; the leader originates.
- The manager accepts the status quo; the leader challenges it.

- The manager is the classic good soldier; the leader is his or her own person.

- The manager does things right; the leader does the right thing. (p. 45)

Implicit within the role of leader is the idea of change; the leader constantly seeks change, challenge, and opportunities. The leader creates a learning environment for self and others. Senge (1990) describes leaders as "designers, stewards and teachers" (p. 340).

Leadership/Followership

Followers are essential to the leadership process; gaining commitment and involvement of others is vital to an effective leadership role. Burns (1978) believes leaders "induce" followers to act where the wants, needs, and expectations of both are similar.

Leadership occurs between people and is a reciprocal process. In fact, it is the followers who determine whether the leader is effective or not. Kouzes and Posner (1989) found that followers want leaders who are honest, competent, forward-looking, and credible. Followership becomes more important in the examination of different leadership styles. Transformational leadership and superleadership recognize the importance of followers and the need to develop their potential. The leader needs to establish a style and a climate that permits all members of the group to contribute to the achievement of the group goals as well as the maintenance and growth of the individual and group. Followers flourish and develop in a supportive climate of trust and respect. Leaders with high expectations of their followers, those who coach and assist people to achieve these standards, are more successful in influencing the group. The type of leadership behaviour required to support and empower followers will be described later in this chapter.

Overview of Leadership Theories

Early examinations of leaders and research into leadership identified four theoretical ways that were used to identify characteristics or behaviours associated with leaders. Each of these four is examined further.

Personality Trait Theories

Early leadership theory focussed on personal characteristics of the leader, often looking at persons who were prominent in an historical or political sense. The idea was that leaders were born, not made, and such factors as height, weight, intelligence, and energy levels were thought to be significant. The social elite and the monarchy were described as the natural leaders, although in time this was found to be not entirely true.

Such characteristics as self-confidence, emotional control, dominance, and independence were thought to be related to leadership. Charisma and public image were also important. Eventually it was concluded that thinking in terms of personality characteristics and assuming all leaders were born that way was not useful. Researchers then began to look toward examining the behaviours that leaders displayed.

Behavioural Theories

In the 1940s, studies at Ohio State University and the University of Michigan strongly influenced the development of leadership theory. The Ohio study identified two dimensions of leadership behaviour and called them "initiating structure" and "consideration." The Michigan study identified similar concepts and labeled them "employee orientation" and "production orientation." Consideration (employee orientation) dealt with the extent to which a leader showed concern about the employee's welfare and job satisfaction. Initiating structure (production orientation) dealt with the tasks of the group and how the leader organized and defined the work roles to achieve goals. One other significant finding was that leader effectiveness did not depend solely on the style of the leader but was dependent upon the situation in which the style was used.

A classic study by Lewin, Lippitt, and White (1939) used a group of young boys to examine the differences of three different types of leadership styles on group productivity. The styles tested were democratic, autocratic, and laissez-faire. Democratic leaders gave information, encouraged group participation in decisions, and were flexible about how things were done. Autocratic leaders made all the decisions and supervised closely, giving more precise direction about how and what to do. Laissez-faire leaders gave no direction and were extremely flexible about how and what to do. The style of leadership did affect the productivity of the group. Productivity was highest in the autocratic-led group, but only when the leader was present. The democratic group showed greater cohesiveness and satisfaction than the other two groups, and had the least absenteeism. The study suggests there is a continuum of leadership behaviours ranging from autocratic through democratic to laissez-faire. Each style of behaviour has a different effect on group members' performance and level of satisfaction.

Tannenbaum, Weschler, and Massarik (1961) describe a range of patterns of leadership behaviour across a continuum from autocratic to democratic in relation to task orientation and relationship orientation. Actions taken by the leader are related to the degree of authority used by the leader and the amount of freedom that is then available for followers to make decisions. The behaviours on one end of the continuum are those of a leader who wishes to *maintain* a high degree of control. Behaviours on the opposite end of the continuum are those of a leader who *releases* a high degree of control to the followers. Whichever style is chosen along the continuum, it is important that the leader communicate clearly to the group the style being used. Both parties need to understand and be clear about the degree of authority the leader wishes to keep and the degree of authority being given to the followers. Lack of understanding of these two parameters frequently results in conflict. The authors concluded that the type of leadership chosen is based on three factors: the leader, the followers, and the situation. The leader's behaviour is influenced by: a value system; the degree of confidence in the followers; the comfort with the style chosen; and the level of security in an uncertain situation or tolerance of ambiguity. The followers also have a value system; each has expectations of the leader, and each may wish for varying degrees of independence and readiness to make decisions. The forces in the situation include the values and traditions of the organization; the nature and urgency of the problem; and the overall effectiveness of the group in its ability to make decisions. The successful leader knows his or her own self, understands the individuals in the group, knows the context of the environment in which they operate, and clearly states any expectations of followers.

Contingency Theory

A contingency approach to leadership matches the style of the leader to fit the situation. Fiedler (1967) believed that leadership styles are relatively inflexible. He found that certain types of leaders succeed in particular organizations, and that this could be related to interests, personality, and the nature of the situation. A leader may succeed in one situation and not in another. The leader seeks to satisfy personal goals as well as those of the organization. The ability to do so depends upon the leader's control and influence in the situation.

Fiedler identified three factors that lead to effective leadership. The most important factor is leader-member relations. Where there are good relationships of mutual trust, respect, and admiration, there is little need to use formal authority. The second factor is task structure. How rigidly the task of the group's work is structured affects the power of the leader. In high task structure, people are clear about what they have to do. In low task structure, group and member roles are unclear and the power of the leader is ambiguous. The final factor, position power, is the perceived authority of the leader. Where there is high position power, it is simple for the leader to influence followers. In situations where there is low position power, it is more difficult for the leader to influence.

Fiedler contrasts leadership styles on the two dimensions of task-oriented and relationship-oriented style. He measures leadership style on the least preferred co-worker (LPC) scale. The leader identifies the person whom he or she would be the least able to work with well. Those leaders with a high LPC rating are more people- and relationship-oriented; those with a low LPC rating are more task-oriented and less concerned with human relations.

Effective leadership is exercised when the leader's style, whether task-oriented or relationship-oriented, fits "favourably" in the situation.

Tri-Dimensional Leader Effectiveness Model

Hersey and Blanchard (1982) developed a leadership model based on the Ohio State studies using the concepts of "consideration" and "initiating structure." They describe leadership style as the behaviour pattern of the individual, as perceived by others, when the person is attempting to influence the group.

The leader's own perception of his or her behaviour (self-perception) may be very different from that of the follower. Leadership style is determined by the combination of two factors— task behaviours and relationship behaviours. Task behaviours are defined as the extent to which the leader organizes the group, and establishes channels of communication and ways of getting the task done. Relationship behaviours are those that facilitate relationships between the leader and the group members, open up communication, and provide socioemotional support. Based on work by Reddin (1970), an effectiveness dimension was added to the Ohio State model. This third dimension integrates the style of the leader with the specific needs of the situation, and is called the environment. The effectiveness of the leadership style is determined by the appropriateness of that style to the environment where it takes place.

Situational Leadership

The Situational Leadership® model (Figure 10.1) arose from the development of the tri-dimensional leadership effectiveness model. This model emphasizes the behaviour of the leader in relation to the followers and is based on the interaction of three factors: (1) the amount of guidance and direction a leader gives; (2) the amount of socioemotional support the leader provides; and (3) the readiness of the followers to perform a task.

Figure 10.1
The Situational Leadership® model.*

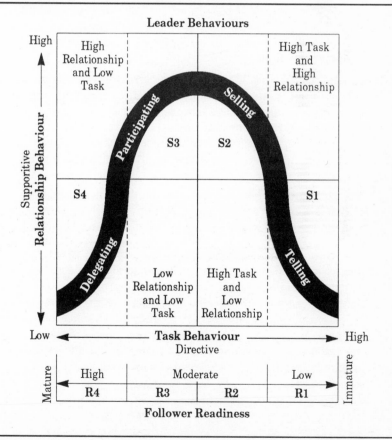

Source: Abstracted from P. Hersey & K. Blanchard (1988), Situational Leadership® handout (San Diego: University). Used with permission of Leadership Studies, Inc., Escondido, CA.

*Situational Leadership is a registered trademark of the Center for Leadership Studies. All rights reserved. Used with permission.

The model depicts the styles of leadership on a bell-shaped curve passing through four quadrants related to task and relationship behaviours of the leader. The concept of readiness is portrayed on a continuum of low readiness (R1) to high readiness (R4). The four styles of leadership are indicated by the abbreviations S1 to S4 and are described as:

S1—Telling. High task and low relationship style to be used where followers exhibit low readiness. This is a directive style for followers who are insecure or inexperienced in their task or function.

S2—Selling. High task and high relationship style to be used with followers with low to moderate readiness. This style provides for directive behaviour accompanied by supportive behaviour to give encouragement and reinforce the willingness of the follower. People classified as R2 are considered to be willing but not able (or confident) to take responsibility for their skills.

S3—Participating. Low task and high relationship style is used for individuals who display moderate to high readiness. At this readiness level (R3) the person is able but unwilling to perform. He or she may be competent at the task, but unwilling owing to lack of confidence (insecurity). A supportive, nondirective style is used to give positive reinforcement and to facilitate the person using his or her personal ability.

S4—Delegating. Low task and low relationship is used where followers are at a high level of readiness (R4) and are able and willing to take responsibility for their own efforts.

Situational Leadership theory indicates that there is no one best style to influence followers. The leadership style chosen depends upon the maturity level or readiness of the followers. That level is determined by the ability and willingness of people to take responsibility for their own behaviour in relation to a specific task or function. Maturity level is not related to age, but to the individual followers in terms of their abilities and experiences in relation to the task. The definitions for readiness levels are described as:

R1 = Unable and unwilling or insecure

R2 = Unable but willing and confident

R3 = Able but unwilling or insecure

R4 = Able/competent and willing/confident.

Both the readiness level of an individual and readiness level of a group can be considered. Groups that come together frequently and interact to achieve tasks can reach a high level of maturity in their group function. The leader may then choose to deal with the group in a style that matches the maturity level of the entire group. However, the leader also has to understand that there are differing levels of maturity among the individuals who make up the group. Therefore, different styles may be chosen when interacting with the various individual members of the group.

Later Theoretical Concepts

The early concepts of leadership behaviour have been developed extensively in recent years and lead to different ways of describing leaders. All build on the previous notions of initiating structure and consideration. Later theories such as transactional, transformational, and superleadership strongly emphasize the consideration or relationship aspect between leader and follower.

Transactional/Transformational Leadership

Transactional leadership is based on an exchange or transaction between the leader and the follower. Burns (1978) noted that "such leadership occurs when one person takes the initiative in making contact with others for the purpose of an exchange of valued things" (p. 19). The purposes of the exchange for each person are related and each is aware of the power of the other. However, there is not a binding relationship, and each individual may go his or her own way after the transaction. Burns likens the transactional leadership style to that used by the traditional manager who concentrates on daily operational activities, just to keep things going. Such a manager may institute first-level change at the operational level, but is not as concerned with second-level change at the system level.

In contrast, transformational leadership occurs "when one or more persons *engage* with others in such a way that leaders and followers raise one another to higher levels of motivation and morality" (Burns, 1978, p. 20). The leader takes the initiative to develop the connection with the follower and the dynamics of the relationship have a transforming effect. Burns cites the example of Gandhi, who elevated the hopes and expectations of the Indian population and personally enhanced the lives of millions.

Leadership is seen by Burns as a process of morality, as the engagement between leader and follower is based on shared motives, values, and goals. The leader's first task is to develop an awareness in the followers of their own needs, values, and purposes, and an ability to recognize their own self-identities. The leader arouses a sense of dissatisfaction for the follower, which can then become a source of energy to undergo change which the leader can influence.

Tichy and Devanna (1986) describe transformational leadership in organizations as a three-act play. The first act is recognizing the need for revitalization; the second act is creating a vision; and the third is institutionalizing change. Characteristically, transformational leaders:

- Identify themselves clearly as agents of change who want to make a difference;
- Are courageous, but take prudent risks;
- Believe in people and work toward empowerment of the individual;
- Are able to describe their values and demonstrate them in their behaviours;
- Are life-long learners;
- Have the ability to cope well with complexity, ambiguity, and uncertainty; and
- Are visionaries who can translate dreams and images to others.

SuperLeadership

Manz and Sims (1989) theorize that "to be effective a leader must successfully influence the way people influence themselves" (p. 7). Their "SuperLeader," then, "is one who leads others to lead themselves" (p. 5). This concept suggests that people are self-motivating and want to do a good job, and are therefore effective followers. Manz and Sims believe in a reciprocal view of influence; people and their world influence each other. Each person helps to create the world as it appears to him or her; on the other hand, who each person is and what he or she does is influenced by the world. Therefore, as the leader is part of the follower's world, he or she can be influential in a positive way, and vice versa. Through reciprocal influence, leaders and followers both can be successful.

The process of learning self-leadership is aided by role modeling, encouraging followers to set their own goals, guided participation, reward, and reinforcement. Manz and Sims distinguish between two types of rewards: externally administered rewards and natural rewards. Externally administered rewards are provided by the organization (or leader) and may be material in nature, such as a salary increase, improved fringe benefits, or more flexible scheduling. Natural rewards are built into the task itself and provide internal satisfaction for the person. Three elements that motivate people and provide natural rewards are: a sense of competence, self-control, and purpose. Leaders need to provide others with opportunities to take on tasks and challenges and develop these three elements. The role of the SuperLeader is to guide, coach, and support the follower in the development of self-leadership skills. Self-leadership has to be learned, as people usually do not come prepared with all the skills required for self-leadership. Promoting self-leadership in the individual results in greater self-esteem and independence for that person. This mode of leadership is in keeping with the new paradigm and directions identified by Barker (1991).

Research on Nursing Leadership

Yura, Ozimek, and Walsh (1976) were among the first nurse researchers to examine the leadership process in relation to nursing. In their study, nursing leadership was defined as "a process whereby a person who is a nurse affects the actions of others in goal determination and achievement" (p. 93).

Four key terms were found to be relevant to the leadership process: deciding, relating, influencing, and facilitating. These four terms were found to be essential to put into operation the leadership process. A revised definition was then produced to incorporate the four elements. "The nursing leadership process is a process through which determined goals are achieved through the four components of deciding, relating, influencing, and facilitating. Permeating all components is the act of communication" (p. 95). A taxonomy of behaviours related to the nursing leadership process was developed for each component. The exhaustive list defines the knowledge required for each element and the corresponding behavioural skills needed. Even though this study was carried out some years ago, the behaviours identified are similar to those set out in current leadership theories.

There is little research in the literature related to leadership and the nurse manager role. There has been limited research on leadership and the nurse executive role. Adams (1990) looked at the leadership style of chief executive nurses in 66 hospitals in the San Francisco Bay area, using the situational leadership model. She found that the CNEs used "selling" and "participating" almost entirely, and that "delegating" was not the first or second choice of behaviour. She notes that generally nurses do not delegate well, and, therefore, this is a significant point to consider. Current theory indicates a need to empower others, and nurse executives may well have difficulty releasing control to others.

Dunham and Klahfen (1990) studied a convenience sample of 80 nurse executives to identify transformational leadership characteristics. The group studied had previously been identified as excellent nurse leaders by their peers. Findings indicated that these excellent nurse executives did display both transactional and transformational leadership behaviours, and had a predominantly transformational leadership style.

McDaniel and Wolf (1992) tested transformational leadership theory in a nursing department consisting of an executive, 11 midlevel administrators, and 77 staff nurses. The transformational leadership qualities of individual consideration, charisma, and intellectual stimulation were examined. A hypothesis was that the transformational scores of the top echelon would be higher than those of the midlevel administrators, and this was supported in their findings. A second hypothesis, that leader self-assessment scores would be higher than the followers' assessment of the leader, was also supported.

McNeese-Smith (1993) studied 41 department managers and 471 staff members (a mix of nursing and non-nursing, with approximately one-half nursing) in two acute care hospitals. She used the framework developed by Kouzes and Posner (1987) to describe five behaviours practised by leaders: (1) challenging the process; (2) inspiring a shared vision; (3) enabling others to act; (4) modeling the way; and (5) encouraging the heart. The behaviour most related to employee productivity was "modeling the way." "Enabling others to act" was used most frequently and "inspiring a shared vision" least frequently. This study emphasizes the importance of effective role models who hold clear values and demonstrate them consistently in their behaviour.

The concepts of mentoring and role modeling appear frequently in the literature and are important to consider in the development of leadership.

There is obviously a need for significantly more research on leadership in nursing, particularly at the first-line manager level, as this position is critical to the development of staff nurses as leaders.

Standards for Nursing Administration

The Canadian Nurses Association standards (1988) indicate eight expectations of behaviour for nurse administrators. Standard VI (Table 10.1) identifies the criteria for leadership.

Table 10.1

Standard VI: Nursing administration provides leadership that is visible and proactive.

Criteria
The nurse administrator:

1. Seeks out new options and approaches to problems despite possible risks;
2. Seeks out new opportunities to improve program quality and productivity;
3. Inspires others to cooperate in achievement of professional and organizational goals;
4. Provides staff with stimulating opportunities for their creativity;
5. Encourages initiative by giving responsibility, resources and authority;
6. Rewards achievement and success appropriately;
7. Manages change effectively;
8. Identifies potential leaders and acts as a mentor to these individuals to further their career development;
9. Represents the nursing perspective within the organization;
10. Represents the organization and/or the nursing department before community, government agencies, and professional organizations;
11. Participates in activities of the professional organization;
12. Promotes nursing involvement in public policy-making bodies.

Source: Reprinted, with permission, from The Canadian Nurses Association/Association des Infirmières et Infirmiers du Canada, *The role of the nurse administrator and standards for nursing administration* (Ottawa: Author, 1988).

The behaviours described in the standard support the concepts of transformational leadership and superleadership for the nurse administrator. Nurse managers who demonstrate these behaviours provide the leadership qualities that are necessary to create an environment conducive to job satisfaction and productivity of the staff nurse.

Implications for Nurse Managers

Bennis and Nanus (1985) describe the leadership environments under three major headings: commitment, complexity, and credibility. They believe leaders have failed to empower followers, therefore the followers lack commitment. Distorted information and lack of communication are compounded by the complexity of organizations; traditional ways of communicating are no longer adequate because of the complexity. Poor communication, ambiguity, and lack of tolerance for uncertainty lead to a credibility gap between leaders and followers. Leaders in the 1990s are under deep scrutiny, and all forms of authority are challenged. Under these circumstances there is a shortage of leaders, and followers tend to be reluctant to accept leadership.

The dearth of leadership that Bennis and Nanus describe aptly applies to the nursing profession, especially relative to the complexity of the health care environment. Revitalizing nursing leadership and revamping the health care system are priorities for the profession.

Porter-O'Grady (1992) says that the leader of tomorrow must be comfortable with complexity and actually use it to advantage. Leaders will constantly struggle to adapt to change and chaos and will be forever adjusting and learning. As well, the leader will always need to be helping others with the same process.

Bass (1990) characterizes transformational leaders as using charisma, inspiration, intellectual stimulation, and individualized consideration. Charismatic leaders have a high degree of influence and can inspire and excite followers to accomplish great efforts. They have a vision of where they want to go and can articulate that image. Leaders who consider the individual characteristics of their followers and give recognition to those differences provide mentorship that helps each follower grow and develop. Followers are intellectually stimulated when leaders are creative and innovative and can show new ways of looking at situations and problems.

Given the importance of mentorship, it is essential that potential nurse leaders be identified early and groomed for the role. Bass believes that a management trainee's first supervisor makes a big difference in the individual's career success. It is important, then, that senior nurse leaders portray the qualities of transformational leadership and model them for novice leaders.

Senior nurse leaders also must create an organizational climate conducive to innovation and initiative and recognize the need to attract bright, knowledgeable individuals.

Young (1992) examined the types of leadership development activities identified by hospital nurse leaders to promote transformational leadership qualities. Nurses who scored high on transformational leadership scores: had a baccalaureate degree or higher; had five years of leadership experience; promoted staff nurse empowerment; believed they made a difference in the work environment; perceived previous informal education as important; and rated mentoring as the most important informal education experience. Stronger leadership development in undergraduate and graduate programs, better selection and assessment of those with leadership potential, and specific leadership training for first-line managers could enhance the achievement of transformational leadership skills for nurses in Canada.

Specifically, nurse managers need to be knowledgeable, be articulate, possess self-esteem, have an image of where the profession and the situation are heading, and inspire, challenge, support, and enable others. Bennis and Nanus (1985) say there is no simple formula for successful leadership, but that "it is a deeply human process, full of trial and error, victories and defeats, timing and happenstance, intuition and insight." (p. 223).

References

Adams, C. (1990). Leadership behavior of chief executive nurses. *Nursing Management, 21*(8), 36-39.

Barker, A.M. (1991). An emerging leadership paradigm: Transformational leadership. *Nursing & Health Care, 12*(4), 204-207.

Bass, B. (1990). From transactional to transformational leadership: Learning to share the vision. *Organizational Dynamics, 18*(3), 19-31.

Bennis, W. (1989). *On becoming a leader.* Reading, MA: Addison-Wesley.

Bennis W., & Nanus, B. (1985). *Leaders: The strategies for taking charge.* New York: Harper & Row.

Burns, J.M. (1978). *Leadership.* New York: Harper & Row.

Canadian Nurses Association. (1988). *The role of the nurse administrator and standards for nursing administration.* Ottawa: Author.

Dunham, J., & Klafehn, K.A. (1990). Transformational leadership and the nurse executive. *Journal of Nursing Administration, 20*(4), 28-34.

Fiedler, F.E. (1967). *A theory of leadership effectiveness.* New York: McGraw-Hill.

Fiedler, F.E., & Chemers, M. (1974). *Leadership and effective management.* Glenview, IL: Scott, Foresman.

Hersey, P., & Blanchard, K. H. (1982). *Management of organizational behavior: Utilizing human resources* (4th ed.). Englewood Cliffs, NJ: Prentice-Hall.

Kouzes, J.M. & Posner, B.Z. (1987). *The leadership challenge: How to get extraordinary things done in organizations.* San Francisco: Jossey-Bass.

Kouzes, J.M., & Posner, B.Z. (1989). Leadership is in the eye of the follower. In J. William Pfeiffer (Ed.), *The 1989 annual: Developing human resources* (pp. 233-239). San Diego: University Associates.

Lewin, K., Lippitt, R., & White R. (1939). Patterns of aggressive behavior in experimentally created social climates. *Journal of Social Psychology, 10,* 271-299.

Manz, C.C., & Sims, H.P., Jr. (1989). *SuperLeadership: Leading others to lead themselves.* New York: Prentice-Hall.

Marriner-Tomey, A. (1993). *Transformational leadership in nursing.* St. Louis: Mosby.

McDaniel, C., & Wolf, G.A. (1992). Transformational leadership in nursing service: A test of theory. *Journal of Nursing Administration, 22*(2), 60-65.

McNeese-Smith, D. (1993). Leadership behavior and employee effectiveness. *Nursing Management, 24*(5), 38-39.

Nanus, B. (1992). *Visionary leadership.* San Francisco: Jossey-Bass.

Porter-O'Grady, T. (1992). Transformational leadership in an age of chaos. *Nursing Administration Quarterly, 17*(1), 17-24.

Reddin, W. J. (1970). *Managerial effectiveness.* New York: McGraw-Hill.

Senge, P. (1990). *The fifth discipline: The art and practice of the learning organization.* New York: Doubleday/Currency.

Tannenbaum, R., Weschler, I.R., & Massarik, F. (1961). *Leadership and organization: A behavioral science approach.* New York: McGraw-Hill.

Tichy, N.M., & Devanna M.A. (1986). *The transformational leader.* New York: Wiley & Sons.

Young, S.W. (1992). Educational experiences of transformational nurse leaders. *Nursing Administration Quarterly, 17*(1), 25-33.

Yura H., Ozimek, D., & Walsh, M. (1976). *Nursing leadership: Theory and process.* New York: Appleton-Century-Crofts.

CHAPTER 11

Nursing Governance

Marilyn Monk

Marilyn Monk, RN, BSc (Mount Allison), MSc(A) (McGill), is Associate Executive Director (Nursing) at the Sir Mortimer B. Davis Jewish General Hospital, Montréal, and Assistant Professor, School of Nursing, McGill University. Her hospital has begun to implement a shared governance model.

Circumstances are now once again ... combining in curious ways. The status quo will no longer be the best way forward. The best way will be less comfortable and less easy but, no doubt, more interesting ... a word we often use to signal an uncertain mix of danger and opportunity. (Handy, 1990, p. 4)

Charles Handy's observations of change and opportunity seem particularly applicable to the complex business of health care delivery. Governments and leaders in Canadian and American health care agencies are actively and urgently seeking to design and establish innovative systems for the management and delivery of this vital and costly service. Traditional bureaucratic structures are necessarily being replaced by contemporary models that nurture professionalism and recognize the systemic nature of hospital operations. As management scholar Rosabeth Moss Kanter observed, "The years ahead should be a good time for dreamers and visionaries, for the barriers to innovation, the roadblocks to inspiration and imagination, are being knocked down, one by one" (Kanter, 1989, p. 17).

Historically, nurses have worked in hospital bureaucracies where constrictive hierarchy fostered dependent and obedient behaviour. These highly centralized and autocratic organizations function in a reactive mode, which conflicts with the proactive requirements of this decade. Frustration with these systems increased as the professional role of nurses matured and as the need became critical for a paradigm shift in the way organizations are structured.

Shared governance, which was inspired by the principles of empowerment, is an innovative, contemporary model for professionals. It is a structure and a way of behaving that requires profound changes in the role, responsibilities, and authority of administrators, managers, and clinicians. The potential to enhance patient outcomes is clear, and the preliminary research on its implementation indicates positive outcomes for nurses and nursing. As a system, it truly eliminates barriers to innovation and rewards creativity.

Traditional Organizational Design

The organizational model in a health care setting reflects power and authority, and helps to put the agency's philosophy into operation. Traditionally, nursing services, like other hospital departments, have been organized by a well-defined and unwieldy chain of command that tends to be deficient in flexibility and initiative. This structure is referred to as a bureaucracy, whose multitiered hierarchy reflects differences in power and authority. Departmental activities are vertically controlled and coordinated with downward and predominantly authoritarian communication. This line model is often complemented by the addition of staff or consultant positions in areas like quality assurance and education. However, decision-making responsibility rests with the chief nursing officer or carefully selected delegates.

This structure originated around the turn of the century when modern hospitals were first organized and bureaucracies were highly valued (Nyberg, 1991, p. 245). Originally, bureaucracies were created to manage and maximize the physical skills of an industrial work force, rather than the knowledge or thinking skills of professionals. In hospitals, they were supported by nurses and nursing supervisors who frequently were educated in religious orders or had served in the military.

Dual Roles of Nurses

Historically, the primary role of nurses in bureaucracies has been that of employee and this dates to the time when almost all nurses in a hospital were student nurses working under a matron and one or two supervisors. Obedience, discipline, adherence to rules and regulations, loyalty, and efficiency were the hallmarks of this role and the source of reward. Consequently, in traditional institutions nurse-employees had little opportunity to participate in decisions that affected their practice, their working environment, or the mission of the hospital.

The numerous limitations of this role are considered unacceptable by contemporary management thinkers. Manz and Sims (1989), in their book entitled *SuperLeadership,* point out that, in many organizations, hierarchical dependency produces task-focussed conformists who are good at following orders. Therefore, short term task performance rather than long term effectiveness is the focus of work, and institutional and individual creativity is markedly absent. This approach fails to bring out employee talent and, as a result, the organization and the employees are prevented from realizing their potential, and may not succeed in today's competitive reality (Manz & Sims, 1989, p. 142).

In contrast, the professional role of nurses has been rapidly evolving and challenging the constraints of the employee role. The characteristics of a profession include education at institutions of higher learning, a specialized research body of knowledge, and the autonomous formulation and control of standards of practice. A profession includes the responsibility for learning and development and for the maintenance of standards of competence and codes of ethics. Since the early 1980s, the professional role has been promoted and enhanced through increases in research-generated knowledge, development and growth in nursing education programs, increased societal recognition of and demand for nursing services, and increasingly complex and nurse-dependent treatment modalities.

However, although nurses began to enjoy professional autonomy and responsibility, they continued to work predominantly in environments that promoted and rewarded dependent behaviour. Unfortunately, as Tim Porter-O'Grady (1987) points out,

> the traditional organization, through its managers has constructed a whole range of strategies that limit the risk inherent in its trust of the nurse. Strong hierarchies, clear authority structures, solid approval formats, extensive policies and procedures ..., and task list job descriptions are excellent examples. All are designed to constrain those very behaviours inherent to professional practice. (p. 282)

The nursing literature identifies the failure of organizations to include nurses in decisions that affect their professional practice as a major source of conflict and unhappiness. Bureaucratic power structures led nurses to experience great dissonance between their ideal of professional practice and the reality of powerlessness to control the practice setting (Shidler, Pencak, & McFolling, 1989, p. 1). Conflicting and competing expectations from professional leaders, physicians, and administrators created role ambiguity and conflict. An institutional lack of awareness of the nature and value of nurses' work and its relationship to care outcomes contributed to nurses' low job satisfaction. Furthermore, nurses were rarely invited to influence hospital or departmental policy making, and therefore tended to ignore organizational needs. Handy (1990) refers to this organizational phenomenon as "theft of purpose" and suggests that the "apathy and disillusion-ment of many people in organizations ... is often due to the fact that there is no room for their purposes or goals in our scheme of things—left goalless, they comply, drift or rebel" (pp. 74-75). Consequently, nurses were considered by many to be poor corpo-rate citizens who tended the sick while others tended to the finances (Nyberg, 1991, p. 245).

Joan Trofino (1992) summarizes the issues thus: "They [nurses] have been limited, however, in their ability to fully par-ticipate in meaningful ways in many organizations, due to a morass of legal and historical precedents, outdated management systems, and traditional leadership values" (Trofino, 1992, p. 21).

The Restructuring Imperative

Nurses are in the difficult position of being professionals who want to provide excellent patient care and employees who are members of fiscally challenged organizations. However, neither the professional role nor the employee role of nurses can be inte-grated or maximized within the predominantly bureaucratic structures that characterize health care facilities. Yet, as Monk and Edgar (1991) point out, "each day in our hospitals, doctors, administrators, patients and families rely on nurses' clinical judgement and knowledgeable teaching, expect their expert deci-sion-making and efficient technical skills and depend on their car-ing" (p. 22). Clearly, nurses make contributions that affect the health of individuals and organizations and, because their effec-tiveness in this effort is fundamental to a hospital's ability to real-ize its mission and mandate, nurses must become included as key partners in the health care business.

The acute nursing shortage of the 1980s highlighted the piv-otal contributions and indispensable role of professional nurses. Moreover, studies on the shortage identified nurses' dissatisfaction with their working conditions and their powerlessness to control their practice, and helped to reveal the recent and significant transformation in the nature of nurses' work from handmaiden to highly skilled professional.

Furthermore, work attitudes and values have changed; professional employees desire work that is challenging and rewarding, and work relationships that are characterized by respect and recognition. As Handy (1990) points out:

> *[Professionals] get most of their identity and purpose from their work. They are the organization and are likely to be both committed to it and dependent upon it. They will work long and hard, but in return they want not only proper rewards in the present but some guarantee for their future. They think in terms of careers, of advancement, and of investing in the future. These, then, are not people to be ordered around. These are the new professionals who want their names to be known as well as their roles, who want to be asked, not told to do something, who see themselves in some sense as partners in the enterprise and want to be recognized as colleagues, not subordinates." (pp. 94-95)*

As a result, the nursing literature suggests that it is imperative to cultivate environments in which the nurse is supported as a professional and in which power is shared and independence promoted. However, the urgent fiscal requirement of the 1990s— to do more with less—has energized the industry actively to seek new and innovative ways of organizing hospitals and delivering health care.

Prescription for the Future

Many scholars echo the prescription of Rosabeth Moss Kanter (1989) for organizations of the future:

> *The new game of business requires faster action, more creative maneuvering, more flexibility, and closer partnerships with employees. It requires more agile, limber management that pursues opportunity without being bogged down by cumbersome structures or weighty procedures that impede action. Corporate elephants, in short, must learn how to dance.* (p. 20)

Table 11.1 (see page 196) summarizes the characteristics of bureaucracies and those required of successful organizations of the future.

Table 11.1
Organizational characteristics.

Bureaucracies	The New Organizations
Seek to preserve the status quo	Seek opportunities
Position-centred—derive authority from position	People-centred—authority derives from expertise and knowledge
Repetition-oriented to enhance efficiency	Seek innovation and creativity
Rules-oriented—reward adherence to procedure	Results-oriented—reward outcome
Pay for hierarchical position	Pay for value and contribution
Operate through formal structures	Maximize communication links and information sharing
Have specific mandates and well-defined territory	Seek experimentation and encourage relationships across territories

Source: Table compiled from information in R. Kanter (1989), *When giants learn to dance* (New York: Simon & Schuster, pp. 353-354).

Contemporary Management Theory and Organizational Models

Contemporary theorists (Bennis, 1989; Handy, 1990; Kanter, 1989) have written about the necessities of weakening and flattening the hierarchy, working with employees as partners, and creating and delegating to autonomous work units. In recent years nursing authors have advocated decentralization and participation in decision making as a means of tapping the potential of nurses, encouraging job satisfaction, and reducing turnover. Nursing research findings (Allen, Calkin, & Peterson, 1988; Volk & Lucas, 1991) indicate that staff nurses want to participate fully in decision making. As the profession has matured, practitioners who experience satisfaction and reward from increased clinical accountability and responsibility also desire and require increased responsibility and accountability for governance of their practice.

Since 1980, several organizational models have been tried and successfully replaced strict bureaucracies. Among them are participatory management structures and models of shared governance. Each of these is described briefly and, as well, the one particularly popular model of shared governance is reviewed in more depth. The new role of bylaws and changes in the role of nurse managers in a shared governance structure is also addressed.

Participatory Management

Participatory management is a specific contemporary organizational design and has been advocated and adopted by many nursing organizations. As Barker (1990) notes, "The basic principle of participatory management, regardless of its form, is that employees who will be affected by a decision have some formal way to contribute to the decision. This input is seriously considered and becomes part of the final decision" (p. 110). The process for obtaining this input is formalized structurally through the work of committees and task forces. Quality circles and decentralized nursing services are two forms of participatory management, both of which enhance employee involvement in governance. Nevertheless, in these management forms managers retain authority and accountability for decision making (Barker, 1990).

Participatory management has been an important step in the evolution of organizations that support nurses as professional employees. However, it has proven inadequate because it is not truly a professional practice model. As Porter-O'Grady (1987) points out, "If professional practice means accountability with control, authority and autonomy over factors relating to the professional's work then management benevolence will not address the issue" (p. 281). Nursing leaders who are implementing creative governance models all agree that professionals in organizations need to feel and experience ownership over the clinical and administrative issues that affect their practice. Leaders in organizations need to recognize and act upon the reality that "in this service-intensive, information-intensive age, every organization's primary resource is its people" (Bennis, 1989, p. 178). These leaders will need to structure work environments that reflect that reality.

Empowerment

As a means of capitalizing upon human resources, there has been a growing and widespread interest, by management scholars and leaders, in the concept of empowerment. Conger and Kanungo

(1988) have studied the phenomenon extensively and have articulated three fundamental principles:

- Empowering employees is a principal component of organizational effectiveness;
- Productive forms of organizational power and effectiveness grow when power and control is shared with employees; and
- Empowerment techniques markedly influence group development and team building.

However, they caution that (1) empowerment is not a well understood construct and frequently is simply and erroneously equated with employee participation and that (2) delegation as a process is of itself too constrictive to accommodate the complex nature of empowerment. They define empowerment as a "process of enhancing feelings of self-efficacy among organizational members through identification of conditions that foster powerlessness and through their removal by both formal organizational practices and informal techniques of providing efficacy information" (Conger & Kanungo, 1988, p. 473).

Table 11.2

Management practices that empower staff.

A. Organizational-level practices

1. Selection and training processes are designed to ensure requisite technical, linguistic, and social influence skills.

2. Organizations' policies and culture emphasize self-determination, collaboration, and high performance standards.

3. Loosely committed resources are available at decentralized or local levels.

4. Open communication systems are structured.

B. Leadership practices

1. The expression of confidence in subordinates accompanied by high performance expectations.

2. The fostering of opportunities for subordinates to participate in decision making.

3. The provision of autonomy and removal of bureaucratic constraint.

4. The setting of inspirational and/or meaningful goals.

5. The selection of leaders who are inclined to use power in a positive manner.

Source: Table compiled from information in J. Conger and R. Kanungo, "An Analytical Treatment of the Empowerment Construct," *Academy of Management Review, 13*(3), 471-482.

Conger and Kanungo report that, in contrast to employees in authoritarian systems, empowered employees develop "can do" attitudes that positively affect employee competence and innovative job behaviour and lead to positive work outcomes. Clearly, empowering nurses would help maximize their contribution to patients and strengthen hospitals. The essential empowering management practices described by Conger and Kanungo are listed in Table 11.2.

Shared Governance: An Innovative Professional Practice Model

A critical step in the process of empowering nurses is to develop innovative structures that permit nurses to influence their practice and practice environments. Consequently, in the late 1980s, forward-thinking nursing departments began to replace the bureaucratic model with professional models of organization.

Shared governance and self-governance models are currently being designed and implemented to enhance nurses' responsibility and authority over their work environments and clinical practice. A core attribute of the models is that they offer nurses not just participation but ownership in the organization. Table 11.3 lists six assumptions fundamental to the concept of shared governance.

Shared governance empowers nurses by giving them opportunities to play a significant role in decisions that affect them and by systematically sharing authority and accountability. Common features of professional practice models are listed in Table 11.4.

Table 11.3

Six assumptions fundamental to the shared governance concept.

1. Quality of care and nursing practice issues are concerns of staff nurses.
2. Nurses are responsible and accountable for professional competence and continuing development.
3. Nurses have the right to express their views and participate in decision making.
4. Each nurse has the right and need to be provided with the information necessary to participate in decision making.
5. Each nurse has the right to practise in a learning environment that supports the open exchange of ideas.
6. Nurses can and need to have collegial and collaborative relationships with nurses and other professionals.

Table 11.4
Common features of professional practice models.

- Staff nurses are the focus of shared governance structures.

- Clinical nursing functions are the heart of professional nursing and form the basis upon which governance is shared.

- Within nursing, other positions operate to support the work of the professional staff nurse.

- Professional collaboration replaces a chain of command; clear authority is transferred to individual nurses and groups.

- Standards are monitored by professional nurses.

- The manager's role is to facilitate, integrate, and coordinate the system and resources it requires and to mentor, develop and help educate the professional employee.

It is significant to note that, because of the flattened hierarchy that shared governance demands, the vertical dimension is less important; the horizontal dimension, the process whereby divisions and departments work together, becomes the key focus for an organization's success. As Kanter puts it, "the new organization is a triumph of process over structure" (Kanter, 1989, p. 116).

Councilar Model

Although the literature describes several models of shared governance, the councilar model is the most widely implemented configuration. This model advocates that staff and management councils govern at the departmental level in three domains—practice, quality assurance, and education—and in addition advocates an executive council and a management council (Figure 11.1). The practice, quality assurance, and education councils are composed mainly of staff nurses elected from each unit. Nursing bylaws describe the functional components and processes and outline the composition and method of appointment to councils. It is critical, as McDonagh (1989) states, that "the councils collaborate to provide continuity and to facilitate decision-making at the level of the whole system" (p. 18).

Similar committees can function to govern practice at the nursing unit level in the self-governance model. A brief description of the various councils and the bylaws illustrates how these interact.

Figure 11.1
Shared governance structure in the councilar model.

Source: Figure reprinted from K.J. McDonagh, B. Rhodes, K. Sharkey, and J.H. Goodroe, "Shared Governance at St. Joseph's Hospital of Atlanta: A Mature Professional Practice Model," *Nursing Administration Quarterly*, *13*(4), p. 19. Used with permission of Aspen Publisher, Inc. © 1989.

- **Nursing Management Council.** The nursing managers elect a council, whose role is often constructed to provide the human and material resources that staff nurses need to carry out their responsibilities and to facilitate system operations. Usually, staff nurses are represented in small numbers.

- **Executive Council.** The voting membership of the Executive Council is usually composed of the council chairpersons and the chief nursing officer. The bylaws could stipulate that other administrators or staff serve as nonvoting members. This council coordinates and integrates the work of all councils and addresses the whole nursing service. The council is usually responsible for strategic planning and development and review of the bylaws. The members of this council play important roles in leadership development and the process of empowerment.

- **Nursing Education Council.** In general, this council identifies and addresses the learning and development needs of the professional staff and is responsible for the ongoing development of orientation and preceptor-type programs.

- **Nursing Quality Assurance Council.** The primary mandate of this council is to monitor the care provided by professional nurses through assessment of compliance with established standards and identification of areas of weakness. This council works closely with unit-based staff and managers who actually do the monitoring, analysis, and corrective action interventions. This council also manages the credentialing process and initiates interdisciplinary problem solving.

- **Nursing Practice Council.** This council defines, implements, and maintains the standards of clinical nursing practice consistent with community, provincial, and federal standards. In this regard, the council reviews and approves all policies, procedures, issues, and practice standards that relate to or affect nursing practice. Often, the mandate includes job descriptions, peer evaluation processes, clinical ladder programs, adoption of a model of nursing, expanded role issues, and staffing issues that affect quality of care. In addition to the Quality Assurance Council, the Practice Council is in a position to determine needed practice changes.

Bylaws

Nursing bylaws are central to development of professional practice models. These bylaws are highly significant because they provide the governing structure for nurses, just as the medical staff bylaws currently do for physicians in Canadian institutions. Because the bylaws must be approved by the hospital's board of directors, they legitimize a professional nursing structure and thereby transform the role of nurses within the hospital corporation. The bylaws delineate the organization of shared governance, and provide a framework for the direction and priorities of the model.

The bylaws are based upon a careful consideration of the work to be done and create mechanisms that support that work (Jones & Ortiz, 1989; McDonagh, Rhodes, Sharkey, & Goodroe, 1989). For example, they establish councils and committees and define their purpose and membership. Due to rapid and ongoing organizational, professional, and societal development, bylaws need to be reviewed at least annually to ensure their congruence with the needs of nurses, patients, and institutions.

In summary, the bylaws describe the entire range of activities for which nursing staff is responsible and accountable. These include the provision of care, quality assurance activities, continuing education of professionals, development of standards of practice, peer review, and credentialing. In addition, the bylaws include a description of the philosophy and mission of the nursing department.

New Role of Managers in Shared Governance Structures

In shared governance structures, such as those described above, it is obvious that traditional managerial behaviour is no longer effective or required. As nursing staff become empowered, a new and important role of their leaders is to support and develop their decision-making skills.

Leaders in shared governance systems must be secure professionals who do not see empowering staff as an erosion of power or responsibility (McDonagh et al., 1989). Kathryn McDonagh and her team at St. Joseph's Hospital in Atlanta have a mature professional practice model in place. Their experience over eight years led them to believe that the new role must be learned. Initially, managers must understand and adopt the revolutionary concept of developing professional practice through staff nurse decision making. Secondly, to transform nursing organizations from bureaucracies to professional practice environments, nurse managers need to learn and acquire the leadership skills that empower others.

These skills fit with Manz and Sims's (1989) concept of superleaders, who lead others to lead themselves. SuperLeaders, characterized by their trust in subordinates and their tendency to see mistakes as opportunities, replace disempowering behaviours of commanding, controlling, and inspecting with supporting, coaching, and teaching activities. These leaders encourage self-observation and self-evaluation, and are liberal in their use of questions and verbal rewards. Consequently, they create unprecedented climates of openness, which further fosters proactive problem solving (Manz & Sims, 1989).

In his inspirational book on change and organizations, Charles Handy (1990) refers to this revolutionary organizational culture as "the culture of consent" (p. 143). In this culture, leadership is endemic, intelligent individuals are governed by consent, and a collegiate culture of colleagues and shared understandings drives progress. In terms of responsibility, the practitioner has authority over issues related to the role and work of the professional, such as practice, policy, quality of care, competence, education, peer review and relations, and credentialing; the manager maintains authority over issues of finance, resource use, interdepartmental conflict, and delivery system failures (Porter-O'Grady, 1991, p. 466).

Interestingly, the literature reports that, although managers remain crucial to effective organizations, fewer of them are required when professionals lead their practice (Trofino, 1992). Similarly, Barker (1990) suggests that role change, coupled with electronic technology, supports the reduction in the number of middle managers.

Managerial Losses and Anxieties in Cultures of Consent

Implementation of shared governance is an emotional experience because it involves a major change of perspective (Pinkerton et al., 1989). In this regard, Sullivan and Guntzelman (1991) have identified three areas of potential loss for managers:

- **Loss of power and control.** As staff nurses assume greater and more complex decisions, managers may feel a threat to their self-esteem. Anger and anxiety can result.

- **Loss of prestige.** As staff nurses become the new business team and become increasingly successful at engineering change, middle managers can feel a loss of prestige. The team becomes the heroine rather than the manager.

- **Loss of security and comfort.** This feeling of loss arises from the reality that old and familiar ways of doing work are no longer effective. New procedures, systems, and demands all promote feelings of discomfort. (Sullivan & Guntzelman, 1991, p. 30-31)

Middle managers, even those committed to shared governance, are vulnerable to these feelings of loss and may experience them as their health care environments are radically altered. Furthermore, in the early phases of implementation, ambiguity over professional and managerial sharing of decisions, and intolerance about inevitable mistakes and lengthy time lines that occur when novices begin to make decisions, can lead to great anxiety on the part of managers. In addition, charting unknown territory and the resulting demands of increased time and energy also contribute to managerial stresses.

Nevertheless, Kerfoot found that, in this more rewarding and complex role of colleague and peer, the manager's work becomes more enjoyable (Kerfoot, 1991).

Effects on Professional Nurses

Nursing authors who have implemented shared governance report that staff nurses experience increased self-esteem, self-confidence, and job satisfaction (McDonagh et al., 1989, p. 23). Through their participation on governing councils and as a result of leadership coaching and mentoring, nurses learn to present themselves and their ideas publicly, to chair meetings, to solve problems effectively, and to participate in the implementation of peer group decisions. These activities facilitate development of nursing leaders who can lead themselves and the profession (McDonagh et al., 1989, p. 23).

Education and mentoring are required to achieve this level of self-leadership. Barker (1990) maintains that formal instruction for staff in such topics as decision making, change, creativity, and innovation are needed to facilitate thoughtful and wise deliberations. Trofino (1992), for example, instituted a required course in basic management theory for all staff nurses, which included sessions on delegation, communication, and interviewing skills, among other essential leadership skills. An optional second-level course includes ethical issues, time management, and medical-legal concerns.

In concert with the hypotheses of Porter-O'Grady, Kerfoot has found that staff nurses feel greater satisfaction and commitment because of a sense of ownership and feel more fulfilled because of job enrichment and enlargement (Kerfoot, 1991).

Nevertheless, the process of developing professional practice behaviours is challenging for many staff nurses who bring to shared governance a history of dependent employee behaviour. Feelings of fear, often due to lack of self-esteem and self-confidence, sometimes cause resistance. Therefore, full and effective participation in governance occurs over time as education and coaching facilitate the process of empowerment.

Chief Nursing Officer and Administrative Roles

As in any organizational model, the chief nursing officer in an agency using a shared governance model interacts with medical, administrative, and board colleagues to promote quality patient care and to plan the strategic directions of the institution. Decisions concerning hospital mission and mandate remain within the administrative jurisdiction but do benefit from a participatory management approach. Moreover, implementing senior-level decisions through a shared governance approach will capitalize upon the knowledge and skills of both administrators and professional employees.

It is a particular challenge for nursing administrators to establish effective shared governance models within traditional bureaucratic institutions. In this environment, a major responsibility of the chief nursing officer is to lead an autonomous professional group to work cooperatively and collaboratively with the rest of the organization. This nurse will have to articulate clearly and champion fully a vision that views nurses as professionals in pivotal positions to influence the health of both individuals and organizations.

It is crucial that the chief nursing officer craft a futuristic statement that reflects a vision of professional nursing within the institution, a vision of patient care, and a vision of relationships between nurses, other professionals, the organization, and the community. Once articulated, the primary responsibility then will be focussed on the challenging task of communicating, selling, and realizing the vision.

Obstacles to Shared Governance

Shared governance, like empowerment, is a way of being, a way of thinking and behaving. It needs to be supported by profound structural change and significantly altered leadership behaviour. In addition to the implementation challenges, the literature identifies obstacles that can limit or prevent the realization of shared governance. Firstly, token attempts at sharing governance through simple delegation or minor structural changes indicate that an institution is fundamentally uncommitted to empowerment and serves to frustrate professionals. Secondly, beliefs of power-lessness and unworthiness, accompanied by feelings of victimiza-tion, are prevalent in nursing and combine to form major attitudi-nal obstacles to empowerment that can strongly entrench the sta-tus quo (Clifford, 1992).

Another important challenge to the success of shared gover-nance models are the demands of information sharing in informa-tion-intensive settings. If they are to be successfully empowered and share governance, staff and leaders alike need easy and rapid access to vast amounts of data, and decisions and plans need to be communicated clearly and quickly to many nurses and groups. The challenge of effective communication currently exists in less complex structures and is amplified in the newer models. Attention, at the planning phase, to communication issues is vital to the success of shared governance. Therefore, Wilson (1989) sug-gests that the early development of systems that plan, direct, and track information flow will help get shared governance models off to the right start. Seriously addressing potential obstacles is a fundamental requirement if professional practice environments are to evolve.

A Pioneering Law in Québec

The province of Québec is unique in its pioneering move to estab-lish shared governance in health care agencies through legisla-tion. In August 1991, Bill 120 was passed in the Québec National Assembly. The act based on this bill is intended to reform the health and social service system by focussing the legislation on the health care consumer. In accordance with the act, a Council of Nurses must be established for every public institution employing at least five nurses. The Council of Nurses is composed of all employed nurses and is accountable to the board of directors for:

- Assessing, generally, the quality of the nursing acts per-formed in the centre;
- Making recommendations on the rules of nursing care applicable to their members in the centre;
- Making recommendations on the proper distribution of care dispensed by their members in the centre;
- Assuming any other function entrusted to it by the board of directors (Province of Québec, 1991).

Furthermore, the council is required to give its opinion, in a manner determined by the bylaws, to the agency's executive director on:

- The scientific and technical organization of the centre;
- The means to be used to assess and maintain the professional standards of nurses;
- Any other question brought to its attention by the executive director.

The mandate of the council is exercised by an Executive Committee composed of four elected nurses, the chairperson of the Nursing Assistant Committee, the executive director, the chief nursing officer, and, ex officio, the nurse elected to the agency's board of directors. The functions of the Executive Committee, and any committee it forms to assist it to meet its objectives, are determined by bylaws approved by the board. In addition, the law stipulates that the council must form a Nursing Assistants Committee.

In Québec, the Council of Nurses provides a balance to the Council of Physicians, Dentists, and Pharmacists. Health care establishments had until April 1993 to establish their Executive Committees, and so little data are available on implementation. However, this bold and innovative step needs to be carefully monitored.

Research Findings on Shared Governance

The limited research findings on the outcomes of shared governance are positive. However, the findings are tentative because of the extreme difficulty of researching such a complex phenomenon and the paucity of conducted studies.

In Marlene Kramer's (1989) follow-up study of 16 hospitals, she noted a "debureaucratization" of their nursing departments through a flattening of the hierarchy and the development of shared governance in 12 of the hospitals. Staff nurse empowerment was clinically concentrated but also evident in financial and personnel areas. It is noteworthy that in these institutions, which she termed "magnet hospitals" because they attract nursing staff, a culture of excellence predominates and there is little or no nursing shortage (Kramer, 1990, p. 35).

Ludemann and Brown (1989) studied the outcomes of one shared governance model two years after implementation, using before and after assessments. They found that staff held more positive perceptions of their work environment, especially on items related to personal power and authority and on a climate for innovation. A similar study by Zelauskas and Howes (1992) found positive changes in nurses' perception of pay, promotional opportunities, authority, and the job in general. In addition, they found lower turnover rates and a decline in sick leave.

Similarly, a study of critical care nurses revealed that nurses desire a more participative approach and that this approach is positively associated with reductions in nurse turnover (Volk & Lucas, 1991). Kerfoot also reported a remarkable reduction in turnover and nursing vacancies in her hospital as the shared governance model matured (Curran, 1991).

The Way Forward

As Porter-O'Grady (1992) observed, "As with all systems, ... shared governance is not the end of a transition, rather it is simply a beginning.... Shared governance is a vehicle—no more, no less. It provides an organizational framework for behavioural and systems changes" (p. 283). And, as Handy (1990) observed in the quote at the beginning of this chapter, the best way forward will be less comfortable, less easy, and mixed with danger and opportunity (p. 4).

Innovation and creativity are the hallmarks of excellent organizations. Accountability to patients and communities demands that nursing leaders summon the courage to take the risks that challenge traditional hospital structures and to support environments that provide opportunities for professionals to share governance.

References

Allen, D., Calkin, J., & Peterson, M. (1988). Making shared governance
    work: A conceptual model. *Journal of Nursing Administration,
    18*(1), 37-43.
Barker, A.M. (1990). *Transformational nursing leadership*. Baltimore:
    Williams & Wilkins.
Bennis, W. (1989). *On becoming a leader*. Reading, MA: Addison-Wesley.
Bennis, W., & Nanus, B. (1985). *Leaders: The strategies for taking charge*.
    New York: Harper & Row.
Clifford, P. (1992). The myth of empowerment. *Nursing Administration
    Quarterly, 16*(3), 1-5.
Conger, J., & Kanungo, R. (1988). An analytical treatment of the empow-
    erment construct. *Academy of Management Review, 13*(3), 471-482.
Curran, C.R. (1991). An interview with Karlene Kerfoot. *Nursing
    Economics, 9*(3), 141-147.
Handy, C. (1990). *The age of unreason*. Boston: Harvard Business School
    Press.
Jones, L.S., & Ortiz, M.E. (1989). Increasing nursing autonomy and
    recognition through shared governance. *Nursing Administration
    Quarterly, 13*(4), 11-16.
Kanter, R. (1989). *When giants learn to dance*. New York: Simon &
    Schuster.
Kerfoot, K.M. (1991). Developing self-governed teams: The nurse manag-
    er's goal in shared governance. *Nursing Economics, 9*(2), 121-125.
Kramer, M. (1990). Magnet hospitals: Excellence revisited. *Journal of
    Nursing Administration, 20*(9), 35-44.
Ludemann, R.S., & Brown, C. (1989). Staff perceptions of shared gover-
    nance. *Nursing Administration Quarterly, 13*(4), 49-56.
Manz, C.C., & Sims, H.P., Jr. (1989). *SuperLeadership: Leading others to
    lead themselves*. New York: Prentice-Hall.
McDonagh, K.J., Rhodes, B., Sharkey, K., & Goodroe, J.H. (1989). Shared
    governance at Saint Joseph's Hospital of Atlanta—A mature pro-
    fessional practice model. *Nursing Administration Quarterly, 13*(4),
    17-28.
Monk, M., & Edgar, L. (1991, Summer). Restructuring to create a climate
    for clinical excellence in nursing. *Forum*, pp. 22-27.
Nyberg, J. (1991). The nurse as a professnocrat. *Nursing Economics, 9*(4),
    244-280.
Pinkerton, S.E., Eckes, A., Marrouiller, M., McNichols, M.B., Krejci, J., &
    Malin, S. (1989). St. Michael Hospital: A shared governance model.
    Nursing Administration Quarterly, 13(4), 35-47.
Porter-O'Grady, T. (1987). Shared governance and new organizational
    models. *Nursing Economics, 5*(6), 281-282.
Porter-O'Grady, T. (1991). Shared governance for nursing Part I:
    Creating the new organization. *Association of Operating Room
    Nurses Journal, 53*(2), 458-466.

Porter-O'Grady, T. (1992). *Implementing shared governance: Creating a professional organization.* St. Louis: Mosby-Year Book.

Province of Québec. (1991). *An Act respecting Health Services and Social Services and amending various legislation.* Bill 120, Chapter 42.

Shidler, H., Pencak, M., & McFolling, S. (1989). Professional nursing staff: A model of self-governance for nursing. *Nursing Administration Quarterly, 13*(4), 1-9.

Sullivan, M.F., & Guntzelman, J. (1991). The grieving process in cultural change. *Health Care Supervisor, 10*(2), 28-33.

Trofino, J. (1992). Nurse empowerment for the 21st century. *Nursing Administration Quarterly, 16*(3), 20-42.

Volk, M.C., & Lucas, M.D. (1991). Relationship of management style and anticipated turnover. *Dimensions of Critical Care Nursing, 10*(1), 35-40.

Wilson, C.K. (1989). Shared governance: The challenge of change in the early phases of implementation. *Nursing Administration Quarterly, 13*(4), 29-33.

Zelauskas, B., & Howes, D.G. (1992). The effects of implementing a professional practice model. *Journal of Nursing Administration, 22*(7/8), 18-23.

C H A P T E R   1 2

Theories and Conceptual Models: A Base for Nursing Practice

Mavis E. Kyle and Glenn Donnelly

Mavis E. Kyle, BSN (Saskatchewan), MHSA (Alberta), is Professor at the College of Nursing, University of Saskatchewan, where she teaches nursing management and nursing theory. She has held offices in the Saskatchewan Registered Nurses Association, the Canadian Nurses Association, the Canadian Association of University Schools of Nursing, and the Provincial Task Force on Nursing Informatics (Saskatchewan). She has developed a staffing and workload computer software program and presents numerous workshops.

Glenn W. Donnelly, BScN (Alberta), MN (Calgary), PhD (Columbia Pacific), is Executive Director of the Regina Branch of the Victorian Order of Nurses. He is a part-time member of the College of Nursing faculty, University of Saskatchewan, and is a clinical nurse specialist in adult health and illness. Dr. Donnelly has been active on a number of committees of the Saskatchewan Registered Nurses Association.

During the last 40 years, professional nursing has increasingly recognized that development of theories and conceptual models to direct the practice of nursing is essential if nursing is to maintain professional status and strengthen its contribution to the health care system. Nursing practice based on research must replace trial and error as a basis for practice, and all nurses must have an understanding of the underlying theory used in their discipline if they are to practise effectively. As well, they must be able to artic-ulate what nursing is to those in other health disciplines, to health policy makers, and to the general public.

Nurse managers must foster the spirit of inquiry and the use of theory and conceptual models. They must also be prepared to use these in their own practice as well as to encourage their use by the staff with whom they work. As noted by Henry and Arndt (1989), "People search for knowledge to help make sense of what occurs. Theory is an important form of knowledge: good theories help make important choices and undertake critical tasks to help individuals and organizations grow and succeed" (p. 1).

Some authors do not differentiate between theories and conceptual models, but in this chapter these will be discussed as separate entities. Conceptual models provide a way for nurses to organize events and activities and relate this organization to everyday nursing practice. Theories are proposals, as yet unproven, that give reasonable explanation to an event. Although both theories and conceptual models are made up of concepts and propositions, theories usually address specific and concrete phenomena, more so than conceptual models. Theories are not proved absolutely, however, and knowledgeable judgements can be made by people who accept them. Theories incorporate such concepts as stress, pain, and social support. The use of theories in practice is valuable, but provides a narrower focus than the use of conceptual models.

The purpose of this chapter is to provide an introduction to theories and conceptual models for use in practice. The role of the nurse manager in implementing and monitoring their use will be covered. A number of nursing theories, models, and major concepts will be identified and guidelines for implementation in a nursing care setting, along with the relationship to nursing care standards, will be explored.

Historical Highlights

Florence Nightingale was the first nursing theorist in that she documented the central concepts of nursing and emphasized the importance of the environment in promoting wellness. Following her work, little theory development took place until the last four decades. In the 1950s and 1960s, the major focus of theory development was in nursing education and in research at the graduate level. Today, courses in nursing models and theories are introduced in diploma, baccalaureate, and post-diploma certificate programs. As a result, more nurses are familiar with models and theories and, therefore, are able to use them in clinical settings.

The Canadian Nurses Association (CNA) recommended the use of conceptual models as a standard of practice in 1980 (CNA, 1980). Provincial nursing associations have followed suit during the 1980s. Little research has been done, however, on attitudes of nurses toward the use of models and theories in nursing practice. Laschinger and Duff (1991) reported on an Ontario study to determine attitudes of practising nurses toward theory-based nursing practice. Attitudes were significantly more positive among nurses working in agencies that had implemented theory-based practice. As reported by these authors, "nurses believed that theory-based practice would help them collect useful data, plan comprehensive care, would result in better care, should not be left to nurse scholars, and was important to the development of the nursing profession" (p. 6).

Many working nurses graduated before courses on nursing models and theories were included in their educational programs, and this may create a problem for nurse managers who wish to implement these into their agencies. This deficit can be dealt with by inservice education about models and by providing nursing literature that gives comprehensive coverage of the work of the individual theorists and reports of successful implementation of models in a variety of clinical settings.

Theory

The word "theory" is used every day in a variety of forms. "I have a theory why Mrs. Jones's wound is not healing" reflects an impression or hunch that might explain a happening. The following definition reflects a more scientific point of view: A theory is a "set of concepts, definitions, and propositions that project a systematic view of phenomena by designing specific interrelationships among concepts for the purpose of describing, explaining, predicting, and/or controlling phenomena" (Chinn & Jacobs, 1983, p. 70).

Nursing theorists have drawn from their knowledge of nursing, basic sciences, humanities, and social sciences to apply concepts to the study and practice of nursing. This scholarly approach has enhanced the opportunity to define nursing from a scientific point of view, as well as to clarify the "art" of nursing, which together reflect the theorists' point of view of professional nursing.

It should be noted that theories are tentative. They are not laws; rather, they are developed for the purpose defined above, or to solve problems. The range of subject material can be very broad or very limited. Three levels of theory are usually discussed in the literature:

Grand theories are broad in scope and complex. As noted by Kim (1983), they require further specification before they can be tested or verified. Grand theories use a general level of abstraction and are often difficult to link to reality. They have as their goal explicating a world view useful in understanding key concepts and principles within a nursing perspective (Walker & Avant, 1988). An example of a grand theory is found in the work of Jean Watson and reported in *Nursing: Human Science and Human Care* (Watson, 1985). The framework of her theory is seven assumptions about the science of caring and 10 "primary carative factors" that are derived from a humanistic perspective and a strong scientific knowledge base (Talento, 1990). Because of its broad scope and interdisciplinary dimensions, it is considered to be a grand theory.

Midrange theories are relatively broad in focus, but do not cover all the components of a phenomenon. They address a more limited number of variables in particular situations, yet are empirically grounded and focus on practical problems (Nolan & Grant, 1991). Chinn and Kramer (1991) give examples of midrange theories, including social support, prenatal maternal attachment, chronic fatigue, stress, coping, and pain control.

Micro theories are the least complex and deal with a narrow range of reality. They can be statements or hypotheses generated to answer questions. An example is the effect of preparatory sensory information on postoperative pain.

Another method of classification of nursing theory is described by Chinn and Kramer (1991). Their four levels are as follows:

- **Descriptive.** Describes a specific image or impression of a factor.
- **Explanatory.** Explains the relationship of a concept to other factors.
- **Predictive.** Provides information about predicted outcomes associated with a given situation.
- **Prescriptive.** Gives information about the impact that prescribed interventions will have on situational outcomes.

Capers (1986) provides an example to illustrate the levels of theory. She chose the concept of "pain." A descriptive theory would characterize the behavioural parameters that manifest pain.

Explanatory theory would define the relationship between behavioural manifestations of pain and other factors such as type of surgery, previous pain levels, and age of the patient. The predictive theory would focus on the likely pain-related behaviours of a teenage patient following abdominal surgery. Prescriptive theory would state specific nursing actions that would reduce the school-aged child's experience of pain following surgery as measured by the degree of behavioural manifestations associated with pain. The levels of complexity of theory move from descriptive at the beginning level, to predictive theory at the advanced level.

Theories are based on specific models and their beliefs. They provide tools that can guide practice and research. Theory, practice, and research are integrally related. The primary use of theory is to guide research; theory interacts with and guides practice; research validates and modifies theory and changes practice (Christensen & Kenny, 1990, p. 4). Nursing science has moved beyond establishment of frameworks to a focus on identification and study of phenomena that make up a body of knowledge for practice (Allan, Kerr, & Jenson, 1991, p. 87).

In summary, nursing theories are creative and rigorous structuring of ideas that project a tentative, purposeful, and systematic view of phenomena (Chinn & Kramer, 1991). They are testable and verifiable.

Conceptual Models

The term conceptual model (and synonymous terms such as conceptual framework, conceptual system, paradigm, and disciplinary matrix) refers to global ideas about individuals, groups, situations, and events that are of interest to a discipline (Fawcett, 1989). Specifically, a conceptual model is a set of concepts and the propositions that integrate them into a meaningful configuration (Lippitt, 1991). Concepts are abstract ideas that provide a mental image. Nursing itself may be seen as an enormous collection of concepts: all those things individuals consider important to nursing; all those things nurses need to know about and to develop theories about (Pearson & Vaughan, 1986, pp. 9-10). Propositions can be broad definitions of concepts or they can state the relationship between concepts in a conceptual model. Chinn and Kramer (1991) define propositions as "statements of relationship between two or more variables" (p. 202).

Most nursing authors agree that the four central concepts of conceptual models for nursing include health, environment, person, and the nature of nursing. The relationships among these concepts are useful in describing the nature and scope of nursing practice. Nurse theorists view these four concepts from a variety of perspectives so that they may delineate questions and propositions central to the nursing profession (Flaskerud & Halloran, 1980; Jennings, 1987).

Why should nurses use conceptual models as a basis for clinical practice? Jacqueline Fawcett (1989) identifies six major reasons for their use. They:

- Provide a distinctive frame of reference for nurses, telling us what to look at and what to speculate about;
- Allow nurses to focus on the relevant components of practice and rule out other components that are of less importance;
- Provide for thinking, for observation, and for interpretation of what is seen;
- Provide a systematic structure and a rationale for activities;
- Give direction to the search for relevant questions about a phenomenon;
- Point out solutions to practical problems.

Conceptual models have been in existence for centuries, but their use in the profession of nursing has been fairly recent. All models have evolved in two ways: first, they have evolved *inductively* from observations and intuitive insights that move from the specific to the general; second, they have evolved *deductively* from reasoning that moves from the general to the specific. Nurses who are providing care to patients may develop a conceptual model by constructing a framework of the key concepts and identifying the salient interrelationships among these concepts based on their knowledge and experience in a particular setting. This would be an inductive model. An example of deductive development would be when nursing scholars formulate a conceptual model that combines ideas from a number of fields of inquiry including nursing, then apply it to practice and research situations.

A model cannot reflect a total picture of reality. Rather, it is a simplification of reality, a representation of the world that includes only those concepts that the model builder considers relevant to the situation and aids to understanding (Lippitt, 1973; Reilly, 1975). Examples are the Neuman Systems Model, the Roy Adaptation Model, and the Orem Self-Care Model. Each model has a unique way of describing the major conceptual foci, as well as the interrelationships among the concepts. Nurse/patient relationships are analyzed in a unique manner within each model.

Table 12.1
Major themes of nurse theorists.

Problem-Oriented	Caring-Oriented	Interaction	Energy Field	Systems
Client-Centred	Humanistic/ Existential	Symbolic Interaction	Person/ Environment	Dynamic, Open
• Nightingale 1860	• Leininger 1970s	• Peplau 1950s	• Levine 1970s	• Neuman 1970s/'80s
• Abdullah 1960s	• Watson 1980s	• Orlando 1960s	• Rogers 1970s/'80s	• Roy 1970s/'80s
• Weidenbach 1960s	• Benner 1980s	• Orem 1970s/'80s	• Newman 1970s/'80s	• Johnson
• Hall 1960s	• King 1970s/'80s		• Parse 1980s	• CNA 1970s/'80s
• Henderson 1960s				• University of British Columbia 1980s
• NISS 1980s				

Source: Adapted from Moody, L.E. (1990), *Advancing nursing science through research* (Vol. 1). Newbury Park, CA: Sage Publications. Adapted and used with permission.

Nursing models can be classified in a number of ways. As early as 1974, Dorothy Johnson recognized the need to have a number of categories of nursing models because there are "different classes of approaches to understanding the person who is the patient" (p. 376). Johnson adds that not only do patients require "differing forms of practice toward different objectives, but also point to different kinds of phenomena, suggest different kinds of questions, and lead eventually to dissimilar bodies of knowledge" (p. 376).

For the purpose of this chapter, the classifications supported by Moody (1990) will be used. These include the following themes: (1) problem-oriented; (2) caring-oriented; (3) interaction; (4) energy field; and (5) systems. Table 12.1 documents the theorists whose work is reflected under this classification system.

Several conceptual models have been developed in Canada, three of which are listed here. In 1981, the Canadian Nurses Association Testing Service (CNA, 1981) published a model of nursing that described the context of nursing and provided "the framework for the examination blueprint which in turn would become the basis for the construction of the examination itself" (p. ix). Several educational institutions chose to use the model as a framework for their curricula. Another model was developed by the University of British Columbia for their curriculum (Campbell, 1987). In Saskatchewan, the Nursing Information System Saskatchewan (NISS) was developed in the early 1980s to provide an organized method of gathering and using nursing information; this currently is being computerized. In its manual form it is used by 95% of the hospitals in the province, and has been exported to agencies in most provinces. A group of nurses on the Provincial Task Force on Nursing Informatics recognized the underlying conceptual model and made it explicit through inductive development. The conceptual model reflects the components of NISS, the nursing process, and primary, secondary, and tertiary interventions (Kyle, Laing, Lee, & Gammel, 1990). The model has been well accepted by nurses who recognize it as a "picture" of what they do in their practice. It has been accepted as a viable model by nurse accreditors from the Canadian Council on Health Facilities Accreditation, and it meets the requirements of the provincial and national standards of practice.

Nursing Conceptual Models

Historically, nursing practice has been influenced by a so-called medical model whose major focus is the treatment and cure of disease. Professional nurses now see the need to implement a conceptual model of nursing to guide nursing practice. Capers and her colleagues (1985) have identified several reasons for this:

- *To promote quality nursing care for all patients;*
- *To facilitate a unified, goal-directed, nursing care approach;*
- *To increase professionalism of nursing practice by enhancing responsibility, autonomy, and accountability of registered nurses;*
- *To provide a practice environment that is professionally rewarding to registered nurses, thereby increasing job satisfaction and retention; and*
- *To give purpose, direction and organization to the nursing department* (Capers, O'Brien, Quinn, Kelly, & Fenerty, 1985, p. 29).

Some nurses base their practice on an unwritten model that they have developed for themselves as an outcome of their education and experience. An ethnographic study by Field (1983) described four nurses' perspectives of nursing over a five-month period. "A perspective is a combination of beliefs and behaviours composed of: (1) a definition of various situations; (2) actions; and (3) criteria for judgement" (Field, 1983, p. 4). Field's study found that the observed nurses all used their own models of nursing to guide their practice. Other nurses use models developed by nurse theorists; some choose components of several theories or models that are meaningful to their practice.

To promote consistency in an agency, a nursing manager and staff may decide to work together to implement or develop a model of nursing that will meet the requirement of providing quality care. The decision on which model to use will be based on the decision-making style used in the agency. If a shared governance model is in use, one would assume that the nursing staff would have significant input. It is essential that nurses and their managers recognize the complexity of implementing a conceptual model. Several years may be required to develop, refine, and validate the model. Evaluation strategies are required at every step of the process.

The project of choosing and implementing a conceptual model may be a component of the strategic plan for the department (see Chapter 23). Recognition of the need to implement a recording system that is consistent with the model should be included in the plan. The model must also be congruent with the system of patient care in use. For example, if a holistic concept of care is incorporated in the model, a primary, case, or total patient care system would be more useful than team nursing (see Chapter 17).

The Saskatchewan Registered Nurses Association (1989) identified a number of criteria to use when choosing a conceptual model of nursing practice. Table 12.2, which is based on the SRNA criteria, shows 16 points that nurse managers need to consider if the agency chooses a conceptual model to guide nursing practice.

Fawcett (1989) has identified four requirements that are inherent in a well-developed conceptual model:

- The model enables identification of a patient's clinical problems and the goal to be achieved as a result of the nursing intervention.

- The model identifies the environment within which care is to be given and the characteristics of the patient who will be receiving the nursing care.

Table 12.2
Criteria for choosing a conceptual model for nursing practice.

1. It fits with the nursing department philosophy.
2. It fits with the overall philosophy of the agency.
3. It fits with the long term and short term goals of the agency.
4. It provides direction for nursing practice.
5. It provides direction for specific nursing practice areas such as units or departments.
6. It has the potential to be supported by all nursing staff including administration.
7. It is logical and comprehensive.
8. It is relevant to the type of care given.
9. It is relevant to the type of client served.
10. The nursing process derived is easily adapted for recording and information systems that are in use in the agency.
11. It is able to be clearly understood and communicated to other disciplines.
12. It distinguishes nursing from other health care disciplines.
13. It has projected usefulness in direct care, nursing education, and nursing research.
14. It is useful for administration because it provides for outcome evaluation.
15. It fits with existing standards (e.g., Quality Assurance and/or Quality Improvement programs, Nursing Practice Standards).
16. Budget and resources are available to implement the model chosen.

Source: Adapted, with permission, from Saskatchewan Registered Nurses Association (1989), *Conceptual models for nursing*. Regina: Author.

- The model enables the use of the nursing process by identifying assessment format, specific category and labeling of diagnosis, mode of intervention and technologies used, and method of evaluation.
- The model specifies the nature of contributions of nursing intervention to the health and welfare of the patient/ client.

Huckabay (1991) has made the following observations:

A conceptual model that meets the above criteria will then be able to guide the clinician in terms of what to observe, how to interpret the observation and make a diagnosis, how to plan interventions, and how to provide outcome measures to evaluate the nursing care. Fawcett (1989) also points out that even

> *though the conceptual model provides the framework to carry through the steps of the nursing process, the specifics of the nursing assessment, diagnosis, intervention, and evaluation come from other theories. For example, if the patient is manifesting problems in the adaptation to illness, theories of adaptation are needed to describe, explain, predict, or control the actual or potential patient problems in specific situations. Also, these theories guide the nursing intervention necessary in the specific situations. (p. 22)*

Single versus Multiple Conceptual Models of Nursing

A major issue that is being discussed by nursing theorists is whether the discipline of nursing should have one or a number of conceptual models. Fawcett (1989) noted that those who advocate several different conceptual models do so because most disciplines have several conceptual models that present diverse views of their paradigm phenomena. This allows members of the discipline to explore phenomena in a variety of ways and avoids a restrictive viewpoint. Feldman (1980) noted that the use of several conceptual models permits "the profession to view nursing from many perspectives, thereby increasing understanding of its nature and scope" (p. 87). Barnum (1981) noted that use of multiple conceptual models avoids the problem of "premature closure on options of the discipline" and fosters development of the "full scope to the inherent potential of the discipline" (pp. 38, 43).

Several authors who initially supported the idea that there should be one conceptual model for the profession of nursing have revised their position with the recognition that nursing activities are highly complex and carried out in a number of situations meeting a variety of needs of clients/patients. Fawcett (1989) concluded that "it is unlikely that there ever will be one unified conceptual model of nursing" (p. 358).

Managers in each agency must decide whether there should be one or more models in use in the agency. It has been suggested that if the agency provides service to one category of patients, or encompasses just one specialty, there should be no difficulty in using one conceptual model to guide practice activities. However, there must be the recognition that not only individual patients, but individual nurses have unique ways of viewing the world, which may make it difficult to use a single model. On the other hand, agencies that provide a wide spectrum of services to a broad variety of clients may find it difficult to use one model to guide all nursing practice. It must be noted that use of more than one model in an agency can bring about problems for nurses who move from one department to another, and for patients who move from one specialty area to another as their health status changes.

Cost implications should also be taken into consideration. No guidelines have evolved regarding the number of conceptual models that can be used in an agency. Several of the conceptual models listed in Table 12.1 are appropriate for use in a number of specialties and for many categories of patients. The central criteria are that the model(s) chosen should fit the type of nursing practice and be based on the needs of the clients/ patients.

A comprehensive review of the literature should be done as part of the preparation for any project to introduce models. This will assist the managers and staff nurses to upgrade their knowledge about the work of various theorists and review examples of applications strategies that have been used in a variety of settings. Some useful references include George (1990), Marriner-Tomey (1989), Wesley (1992), McIvor (1987), Kristjanson, Tamblyn, and Koypers (1987), and Quiquero, Knights, and Meo (1991).

Managing the Implementation

A management process of planning, organizing, implementing, and evaluating can be used as a framework for incorporation of a conceptual model into the nursing unit or department.

Planning

Approval of the project by the senior administration and support from all nurse managers who will be involved in the process is critical to the success of the project. Involvement of general duty nurses, clinical nurse specialists, and nurse educators, in addition to the managers, will strengthen not only the planning phase, but also the implementation and evaluation phases.

Adequate resources must be in place. These include: a project coordinator who may be an expert from within the agency or an expert brought in for the project; committee members with relief time for committee activities; secretarial support; and a budget adequate to meet the needs for all aspects of the process. In particular, there must be recognition of the costs related to orientation of the nursing staff to the new focus of nursing practice. Will the total agency implement the conceptual model or will there be a pilot unit to initiate the project? Once this decision is made, the second step of the management process can be started.

Organizing

The committee struck to implement the project should develop terms of reference that are approved by management, develop procedures for implementing and evaluating the project, and determine how the resources will be distributed. To be consistent with the conceptual model, assessment of the need to change the system of patient care and the nursing information system in place should be reviewed. If changes are required, subcommittees may have to be struck and a longer timeline provided for success-ful completion of the project. Information dissemination strategies on the changes in the form of bulletins, seminars, and guest appearances at staff meetings should be developed for all health professionals. Awareness and cooperation will foster a positive attitude in the clinical setting. Information exchanged should con-tinue throughout the total project, including feedback from the users as implementation progresses.

Implementation

Education sessions will be necessary for all nursing staff. The number of classes and the content will be determined by aware-ness of the learning needs of the staff. The principles of adult learning should be incorporated to foster enthusiasm for the new knowledge and awareness of how it will affect the day-to-day prac-tice of each nurse. Change theory will be useful as the project pro-gresses. As the nurses begin practising, based on the conceptual model, they may have anxiety related to a change in the way they deliver nursing services. A caring atmosphere, with continuing support by the nurse manager, will help everyone focus on the goal of improved patient care and job satisfaction based on enhanced professional practice.

Evaluation

The evaluation process should be built in from the planning phase. Input from patients, their families, nursing staff and man-agers, other health professionals, and agency administrative per-sonnel, based on predetermined criteria, will point to the success or to the need for revisions in the project. Standards of nursing administration and nursing practice provided by professional nursing associations, as well as quality improvement criteria, can also be used for evaluation.

Conclusion

The goal of this chapter is to introduce the nursing management student, as well as the new nursing manager, to the use of theories and conceptual models. The role of nurse managers has been integrated throughout to clarify their responsibilities. Successful implementation will depend on the manager's knowledge, skills, and enthusiasm for carrying out nursing based on scientific principles while still fostering the art of nursing that is reflected in a caring attitude toward clients, patients, families, fellow nurses, and other colleagues in the health care delivery system.

References

Allan, M., Kerr, J., & Jenson, L. (1991). Nursing knowledge: A foundation for nursing practice. In J. Kerr & J. McPhail (Eds.), *Canadian nursing: Issues and perspectives* (2nd ed.). Toronto: C.V. Mosby.

Campbell, M.A. (1987). *The UBC model for nursing. Directions for practice*. Vancouver: University of British Columbia.

Canadian Nurses Association. (1980). *A definition of nursing practice: Standards of nursing practice*. Ottawa: Author.

Canadian Nurses Association. (1981). *A model for nursing* (CNA Testing Service). Ottawa: Author.

Capers, C.F. (1986). Some basic facts about models, nursing conceptualizations and nursing theories. *Journal of Continuing Education in Nursing, 16*(5), 149-154.

Capers, C.F., O'Brien, C., Quinn, R., Kelly, R., & Fenerty, A. (1985). The Neuman systems model in practice. Planning phase. *Journal of Nursing Administration, 15*(5), 29-38.

Chinn, P.L., & Jacobs, M.K. (1983). *Theory and nursing: A systematic approach*. St.Louis: C.V. Mosby.

Chinn, P.L., & Kramer, M.K. (1991). *Theory and nursing: A systematic approach* (3rd ed.). St. Louis: C. V. Mosby.

Christensen, P.J., & Kenny, J.W. (1990). *Nursing process, application of conceptual models* (3rd ed.). St. Louis: C.V. Mosby.

Fawcett, J. (1989). *Analysis and evaluation of conceptual models of nursing* (2nd ed.). Philadelphia: F.A. Davis.

Feldman, H.R. (1980). Nursing research in the 80's: Issues and implications. *Advances in Nursing Science, 3*(1), 85-92.

Field, P.A. (1983). An ethnography: Four public health nurses' perspectives of nursing. *Journal of Advanced Nursing, 8,* 3-12.

Flaskerud, J.H., & Halloran, E.J. (1980). Areas of agreement in nursing theory development. *Advances in Nursing Science, 3,* 1-7.

George, J.B. (1990). *Nursing theories* (3rd ed.). Norwalk, CT: Appleton & Lange.

Henry, B., & Arndt, C. (1989). Introduction: Nursing theory for nursing administration. In B. Henry (Ed.), *Dimensions of nursing administration.* Boston: Blackwell.

Huckabay, L.M.D. (1991). The role of conceptual frameworks in nursing practice, administration, education, and research. *Nursing Administration Quarterly, 15*(3), 17-28.

Jennings, B. (1987). Nursing theory development: Successes and challenges. *Journal of Advanced Nursing, 12,* 63-69.

Johnson, D.E. (1974). Development of theory: A requisite for nursing as a primary health profession. *Nursing Research, 23,* 372-377.

Kim, H.S. (1983). *The nature of theoretical thinking in nursing.* Norwalk, CT: Appleton-Century-Crofts.

Kristjanson, L.J., Tamblyn, R., & Koypers, J.A. (1987). A model to guide development and application of multiple nursing theories. *Journal of Advanced Nursing, 12,* 523-529.

Kyle, M.E., Laing, G., Lee, W., & Gammel, M. (1990). *NISS conceptual model of nursing.* Saskatoon: Health Systems Support Group.

Laschinger, H.K., & Duff, V. (1991). Attitudes of practicing nurses towards theory-based nursing practice. *Canadian Journal of Nursing Administration, 4*(1), 6-10.

Lippitt, G.L. (1973). *Visualizing change: Model building and the change process.* Fairfax, VA: NTL Learning Resources.

Marriner-Tomey, A. (1989). *Nursing theorists and their work* (2nd ed.). St. Louis: C.V. Mosby.

McIvor, M. (1987). Putting theory into practice. *The Canadian Nurse, 83*(10), 36-38.

Moody, L.E. (1990). *Advancing nursing science through research* (Vol. 1). Newbury Park, CA: Sage Publications.

Nolan, M., & Grant, G. (1991). Mid-range theory building and nursing theory-practice gap: A respite care case. *Journal of Advanced Nursing, 17,* 217-223.

Pearson, A., & Vaughan, B. (1986). *Nursing models for practice.* London: Heinemann.

Quiquero, A., Knights, D., & Meo, C.O. (1991). Theory as a guide to practice: Staff nurses choose Parse's theory. *Canadian Journal of Nursing Administration, 4*(1), 14-16.

Reilly, D. (1975). Why a conceptual framework? *Nursing Outlook, 23,* 566-569.

Saskatchewan Registered Nurses Association. (1989). *Conceptual models for nursing.* Regina: Author.

Stevens, B.J. (1981). Nursing theories: One or many? In J.J. McClosky & H.K. Grace, *Current issues in nursing* (pp. 35-43). Boston: Blackwell Scientific Publications.

Stevens Barnum, B.J. (1990). *Nursing theory analysis, application, evaluation* (3rd ed.). Glenview, IL: Scott, Foresman/Little, Brown Higher Education.

Talento, B. (1990). Jean Watson. In J. George (Ed.), *Nursing theories: The base for professional nursing practice* (pp. 293-309). Norwalk, CT: Appleton & Lange.

Walker, L.O., & Avant, K.C. (1988). *Strategies for theory construction in nursing* (2nd ed.). Norwalk, CT: Appleton & Lange.

Watson, J. (1985). *Nursing human science and human care.* Norwalk, CT: Appleton-Century-Crofts.

Wesley, R.L. (1992). *Nursing theories and models: A study and learning tool.* Springhouse, PA: Springhouse Corp.

C   H   A   P   T   E   R   1   3

Research as the Basis of Practice

Carolyn J. Pepler

Carolyn J. Pepler, N, BNSc (Queen's), MScN (Wayne State), PhD (Michigan), is Consultant for Nursing Research at the Royal Victoria Hospital, Montréal, and Associate Professor, School of Nursing, McGill University. Her primary focus at the hospital is the development of a climate of inquiry and the promotion of clinical research. She teaches a successful research utilization course for nursing staff at all local hospitals. In 1992, she received the Canadian Nurses Foundation/Ross Laboratories Award for Nursing Leadership.

"And nothing but observation and experience will teach us ways to maintain or to bring back the state of health." (Florence Nightingale, 1859, p. 74)

Research first served as the basis for practice in the nursing care advocated by Florence Nightingale. She used detailed observation, measurement, and statistical analysis to reach conclusions about nursing care during in the Crimean War. She pointed out that this was how nurses would learn about ways to nurse. Nursing knowledge and research skills have grown considerably, but the links among research, knowledge, and practice are not always clear.

Links among Research, Knowledge, and Practice

Research is a process of systematic examination of phenomena to increase knowledge of these phenomena, their characteristics, occurrence, and relationships with other variables. Knowledge may be acquired in many ways, but it is useful to think of conventional wisdom attained by thoughtful analysis of experience and scientific knowledge gained through research.

Much of the knowledge in any practice discipline is that of conventional wisdom. But, as the knowledge base expands and becomes more complex, it becomes increasingly important to build practice on scientific knowledge. The rigour involved in a scientific process provides for a systematic examination of variables, reduces bias in data collection and analysis, and allows for critique and testing by clinicians and researchers. Clinicians are able to explain and predict outcomes of their practice at a given point in time and to reexamine their practice as new knowledge becomes available.

To build practice on research, four interdependent components are needed: (1) meaningful research questions that are relevant to practice; (2) sound research to answer the questions; (3) knowledgeable nurses with skills in using research findings; and (4) clinical environments open to inquiry and change. Figure 13.1 illustrates the cyclical nature of the relationships among these components. Weaknesses in any one of the elements can constitute obstacles or barriers to research-based practice.

Nursing is a complex process. Specific techniques and procedures may have a scientific basis, but much of nursing practice is poorly understood. Answers to many questions have yet to be found, such as why do certain clients respond differently to interventions? or, how do clients' perceptions of their experiences affect their health?

The Canadian Nurses Association established three goals within its *Research Imperative for Nursing in Canada: The Next Five Years 1990-1995* (Canadian Nurses Association, 1990). The first is to develop nurse researchers; the second, to develop nursing research; and the third, to develop a research reality. A

Figure 13.1

Interdependency of components for research-based nursing practice.

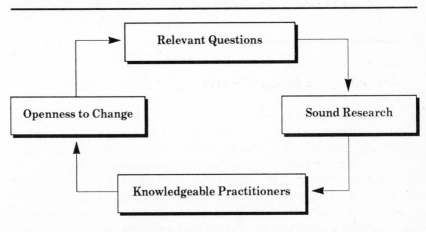

research reality is a world of nursing in which research is part of the substance of practice in all fields. Decisions are based on sound research: decisions that nurses make in relation to their clients and health care; decisions that administrators make in relation to staff and policies; and decisions that educators make in relation to students and learning. The Canadian Nurses Association is working with three other national nursing associations, the Canadian Association of University Schools of Nursing, the Canadian Nurses Foundation, and the Canadian Nursing Research Group, to build nursing research for the health of Canadians.

Advantages of a research base for practice include increased clarity in articulating the role of nursing, improved quality of care, increased cost effectiveness of health care, and increased nurses' satisfaction. This chapter contains a discussion of research activities, departmental strategies to promote these activities, the role of the nurse manager in developing research-based practice, and the economics of research.

Conduct and Utilization of Research in Nursing

Research activities include those involved in both the conduct and the use of research. The conduct of research is the planning and implementation of a research project for the purpose of generating knowledge. It may be carried out by researchers, clinicians, or a team involving both. The utilization of research has two major components: interpretation and use in practice of other people's research findings and use of rigorous research methods in practice (Crane, 1989; Horsley, 1985; Stetler, 1985). Research utilization is an integral part of sound clinical, administrative, and educational nursing practice and is essential for quality management. Similarities in the processes are outlined in Table 13.1.

The level and type of nurses' involvement in research activities requires different knowledge and skills, so it is not expected that all nurses will participate in the same ways. However, it is possible for all nurses to participate to some extent. For example, nurses from a 42-bed rural hospital in the United States have had an international impact on research utilization through the activities of their research committee and the production of an award-winning videotape on the topic (Horn Video Productions, 1987).

Understanding the value of research is the responsibility of all nurses. Fostering research is the responsibility of all nursing leaders.

Table 13.1

Research activities involved in the conduct and utilization of research in nursing.

The Conduct of Research	Research Utilization	
	Using Research Findings in Practice	**Using Research Methods in Practice**
• Identification of the problem or question	• Identification of the problem or question	• Identification of the problem or question
• Review and critique of the literature	• Review and critique of the literature	• Review and critique of the literature
• Clarification of hypotheses or research questions	• Evaluation of the scientific merit of findings	• Generation of clinical hypotheses or solutions to problems
• Design of the study	• Assessment of the clinical merit, fit, and feasibility of findings	• Baseline data collection
• Specification of the sample and methods		• Systematic testing of hypotheses
• Data collection	• Testing the use of findings	• Follow-up data collection
• Data analysis	• Decision making about utilization	• Comparative analysis
• Interpretation of findings		• Conclusions
• Conclusions	• Implementing a change in practice: cognitive or action application	• Implementation of solution to problem
• Dissemination of findings		

Knowledge Generation, Transformation, and Dissemination

New knowledge for nursing practice comes through nursing research, the study of phenomena that matter to nursing and over which nursing has control, and through research in related disciplines.

To be useful, research findings must be transformed into language meaningful to the user. For example, following a study of the effect of a particular approach to preoperative preparation, the researcher may write about the statistical analysis in detail to allow other researchers to assess its appropriateness. For practising nurses, details about the actual preparation for surgery are needed. This may be described in a second article, or the information may be obtained from the researchers. Clear information about the ways in which the patients' responses were measured is

important for researchers and clinicians because both groups need
to assess the reliability and validity of the measures, and nurses
need to use rigorous methods of measurement to assess the outcomes of their nursing strategies.

Models of Nursing Research Utilization

There are several models, or frameworks, for the steps needed to
use research findings in nursing practice. In their project, the
Conduct and Utilization of Research in Nursing (CURN), Horsley
and her associates teamed researchers and clinicians, who worked
together to critique research reports of tested interventions
addressing relevant clinical problems (Horsley, Crane, Crabtree,
& Wood, 1983). The information was transformed into a clinical
plan that could be readily understood and implemented. The
teams also developed a procedure to test the intervention on a
small scale. This process was used in decision making about
saline versus heparin locks for patients with intermittent intravenous medications (Donaldson, 1991). There is considerable evidence that saline is safe and cost effective; clinicians, working
with a multidisciplinary team, tested the technique in their own
hospital and developed new policies on the basis of the trial
(Goode, Titler, Rakel, Ones, Klieber, Small, & Triolo, 1991).

Another process was developed by Stetler and Marram
(1976) from a clinical perspective. It includes three phases: validation of the findings, comparative evaluation, and decision making.
One advantage of this model is that it allows for cognitive application of findings from descriptive studies. For example, a qualitative study on the impact of cancer pain on the family (Ferrell,
Rhiner, Cohen, & Grant, 1991) provides a vivid description of the
families' perspectives of living with a family member who is experiencing pain. Nurses can relate the experiences of the families in
the study to those of the clients with whom they work, thereby
using a richer knowledge base in their own practice. This is a cognitive application of research findings.

In 1991, the Registered Nurses Association of British
Columbia launched a province-wide program to help nurses
understand and use research findings in their practice. The
framework developed is similar to the Stetler/Marram model, but
it also provides direction for decision making about when to abandon or continue a project (RNABC, 1991).

Research utilization may progress through several phases.
One group of nurses in an immunodeficiency clinic had been using
knowledge of social support research cognitively. The nurses knew
that people with HIV infection have complex social support

networks that influence their ability to cope with the illness. So that they could use a more systematic measure of social support to track changes over time, they adapted a sociogram (Maxwell, 1982) and a social support measure (Norbeck, Lindsey, & Carrieri, 1983) for their own clinical use. Clients reported that the measurement process itself helped them become more aware of their resources, and the nurses are now planning an experimental study to test the effects of the measurement process. These nurses work in an environment that promotes research activities.

Nursing Department Strategies to Promote Clinical Research Activities

The paramount requirement for the successful development of research-based practice within a department of nursing is a spirit of inquiry and openness to change—a *philosophy of inquiry*. Without willingness to question and to challenge rituals and traditions, clinical agencies will not develop practice with a sound scientific base (Walsh & Ford, 1989). An open organization can develop policies and procedures that have a strong foundation in current research (van Koot & Laverty, 1992), and creating a research climate is a key responsibility of the nurse executive (Simms, Price, & Pfoutz, 1987).

The working environment is a major factor supporting or obstructing research-based practice. Barriers to research use are found in four categories: those related to the setting, the nurse, the research, and the presentation (Funk, Champagne, Wiese, & Tornquist, 1991a). In an American survey, Funk and her colleagues (1991b) found that eight of the 10 most frequently reported barriers were related to the setting (see Table 13.2, page 234).

To overcome these barriers, a commitment to encourage and support nurses' pursuit of questions is needed. This commitment is shown, first of all, in the philosophy and policies of the agency and the nursing department, then in the substantive support of an infrastructure for research and in staff development.

An Infrastructure for Research

The infrastructure for research in clinical agencies will depend on resources as well as on philosophy, and can vary from a nursing research committee to a full department. Resources include an

Table 13.2

Rank ordering of barriers to research utilization, showing type of barrier.

Rank Order	Barrier	Type of Barrier†
1	The nurse does not feel she/he has enough authority to change patient care procedures.	S
2	There is insufficient time on the job to implement new ideas.	S
3	The nurse is unaware of the research.	N
4	Physicians will not cooperate with implementation.	S
5	Administration will not allow implementation.	S
6	Other staff are not supportive of implementation.	S
7	The nurse feels results are not generalizable to own setting.	S
8	The facilities are inadequate for implementation.	S
9	Statistical analyses are not understandable.	P
10	The nurse does not have time to read research.	S
11	The nurse is isolated from knowledgeable colleagues with whom to discuss the research.	N
12	The relevant literature is not compiled in one place.	P
13	Implications for practice are not made clear.	P
14	The nurse does not feel capable of evaluating the quality of the research.	N
15	Research reports/articles are not readily available.	P
16	The research has not been replicated.	R
17	The research is not reported clearly and readably.	P
18	The research is not relevant to the nurse's practice.	P
19	The nurse feels the benefits of changing practice will be minimal.	N
20	The nurse sees little benefit for self.	N
21	The nurse is uncertain whether to believe the results of the research.	R
22	The nurse is unwilling to change/try new ideas.	N
23	The literature reports conflicting results.	R
24	The research has methodological inadequacies.	R
25	There is not a documented need to change practice.	N
26	The nurse does not see the value of research for practice.	N
27	Research reports/articles are not published fast enough.	R
28	The conclusions drawn from the research are not justified.	R

†S = Setting; N = Nurse; P = Presentation; R = Research

Source: Adapted from Sandra G. Funk, Mary T. Champagne, Ruth A. Wiese and Elizabeth M. Tornquist (1991), Barriers to using research findings in practice: The clinician's perspective, *Applied Nursing Research*, 4(2), 92. Used with permission.

administrative structure to foster research, personnel with research training, access to literature, time, support staff, space, and equipment.

An essential component is a committee structure. The stimulation of ideas and mutual support from a group process is advantageous, and, because of the many different research activities involved, the workload can be shared. A nursing research committee can review literature and disseminate findings, facilitate research utilization, provide information about research activities and resources, develop a research agenda, and review proposals for research (Vessey & Campos, 1992). Depending on the size and clinical scope of an agency, research may be best advanced by an agency-wide committee (Henderson & Brouse, 1992), unit-based committees (Hoare & Earenfight, 1986), or thematic interest groups, such as a pain management group (Belair, 1992).

Nurses with research training are those prepared at the graduate level. They may be full-time or part-time staff, or available only on consultation. Two positions that have been shown to be effective are the clinical nurse researcher, who is usually prepared at the doctoral level, and the clinical nurse specialist, who has master's preparation. The clinical nurse researcher may conduct research, foster a research climate, provide consultation to nursing staff on research projects, advise administrators on research-based decisions, review research proposals, and coordinate a research program. The title and responsibilities vary, but the ability to develop the role and relate to staff nurses and clinical issues is crucial (Knafl, Hagle, Bevis, & Kirchhoff, 1987).

The clinical nurse specialist, whose role is usually directly related to patient care, also contributes to research (Cronenwett, 1986; Fitch, 1992; Hamilton et al., 1990; Hickey, 1990). The clinical nurse specialist may conduct research, particularly in team projects, identify researchable clinical questions, interpret research findings for application in practice, and implement research-based innovations.

If it is not feasible to find agency staff with research training, arrangements can be made with consultants from academic settings or other agencies (Goode, Lovett, Hayes, & Butcher, 1987). Consultants with particular expertise may be sought for specific projects, or a consultant may meet with staff regularly to discuss a variety of clinical questions.

Access to literature may also depend on outside resources, and arrangements with interlibrary loan systems may be needed. Other aspects of seeking literature are discussed in relation to the role of the nurse manager, but time to seek consultation or use library resources is essential in any agency with a commitment to research-based practice.

Other structural resources such as space, support staff, and equipment demonstrate the commitment of the department of nursing (Fitch, 1992; Pepler, 1988). These not only provide tangible evidence of support, but can greatly enhance the productivity of researchers.

Demystifying Research

Research activities are often perceived by nurses as "something that somebody else does." The idea of research involvement may be threatening for nurses without background preparation, and staff development programs for nurses at all levels will help to demystify research. Whether nurses have had an introductory course in a baccalaureate program or not, knowledge and skills in using research concepts in practice need to be developed.

The department of nursing may facilitate nurses' participation in courses outside the agency, or programs may be offered within the department. A series of workshops for different groups of nurses may be expedient for introducing staff to ideas and strategies. It is appropriate to start with managers and senior nurses who will be leaders in an agency-wide program. A course, rather than a workshop, has the advantage of allowing nurses to use the new knowledge over time in their practice between sessions (Pepler, 1992).

Involvement of nursing staff in research activities is a powerful learning process as well (Hoare & Earenfight, 1986; Parker, Gordon, & Brannon, 1992). Links with schools of nursing provide an opportunity for students and staff alike to raise relevant questions and gain practical experience in integrating research and practice (Janken, Dufault, & Yeaw, 1988).

The Nurse Manager as Facilitator of Research Activities

A spirit of inquiry within the nursing department and the structural components of a research commitment will support the nurse manager in efforts to develop research-mindedness in the staff. The manager at the unit level still has a key role in helping staff raise questions, find answers, participate in research, conduct studies, and use findings in practice. The nurse manager at the unit level also must play a role in protecting the rights of patients and of staff in relation to research and must understand the differences between research and quality management.

Raising Questions

The nurse manager is the pivotal person in creating an environment open to questions. The questions may arise from any source: staff nurses, other nurse managers, senior nursing administrators, or members of other disciplines. The progress from "I wonder if..." or "How come...?" to research activities and improved practice can be determined by the initial response of front-line managers. Productive responses come from managers who are at ease with not knowing. Otherwise, the initial response may be "We tried that before" or "We can't because..." The manager who is secure without an answer will be comfortable in facilitating a search for one.

To find an answer, it is essential to clarify the question. The first question raised is often either vague or too specific. Through clarification, the nurse manager can not only show support, but help either to focus or to expand the question and to identify parameters that will assist in finding an answer. For instance, if the question is related to one patient, it may be helpful to identify broader characteristics or commonalities across several patients to develop a meaningful question with greater relevancy. If a question is vague or ambiguous, it will be useful to clarify specific circumstances or particular variables that are of interest.

Finding Valid Answers

In any research process, the first activity is searching the literature. This takes time. Nurse managers can facilitate the process by providing time to go to accessible libraries and read or bring material to the unit.

Computer searching is a relatively simple process, readily learned, and invaluable in providing a comprehensive search and saving time. It also facilitates browsing and stimulates curiosity. Browsing is an important component of literature review because ideas are triggered and answers may be found before the questions are articulated. Librarians may be able to send tables of contents from relevant journals to the units, so that staff can browse for articles more readily. It is helpful to encourage subscriptions to journals on the unit. While access to a few journals is not sufficient for a comprehensive review, it is useful for keeping up to date. The staff might be willing to share a subscription, costs could be negotiated with the administrator, or gifts could be directed toward a subscription.

Nurse managers can encourage staff to read research reports and think about the value and usability of findings. A journal club could be initiated in response to a staff member's question. It is best when reading is triggered by genuine interest in the topic, and it is most effective when a series of articles on the same topic are discussed over time. The issue can be explored in depth, and the similarities and differences in research methods and findings can be examined. A review article is a good beginning because it will give an overall critique and a comprehensive reference list (e.g., Atkins, 1991 on children's coping; Macriorowski et al., 1988 on falls; Shaver & Giblin, 1989 on sleep; VanCott, Tittle, Moody, & Wilson, 1991 on critical care nursing).

In the nursing research literature, there are reports of three broad categories of research: (1) descriptive studies of clinical phenomena, client characteristics, or clinical problems; (2) tests of measures or instruments; and (3) experimental studies of nursing interventions. The first type increases the reader's knowledge base and can be extremely useful in working with patients and families in similar circumstances, but these studies do not give directions for care. Those in the second category can be used by clinicians to measure clinical phenomena more accurately. The third type includes reports of interventions which, if found to be effective, can be implemented.

The process of finding relevant literature is the first step. It is then critiqued to determine the potential usability of the information. Nurse managers can help staff read critically by encouraging participation in courses and staff development programs, and by providing opportunities for discussion with a nurse with a knowledge of research. This may be a staff nurse, the manager, a clinical nurse specialist, or a faculty member. A number of questions need to be asked:

- Is the purpose of the study clearly explained?
- Is other relevant research reviewed adequately?
- Is the study design suitable to answer the research question?
- Is the sample adequate in terms of size and representativeness?
- Are variables clearly explained, if appropriate?
- Are data collection methods and measures valid and reliable?

- Are analyses appropriate and sufficiently comprehensive?
- Are findings reported clearly?
- Are findings discussed in relation to the theory and other research?
- Are conclusions and implications for practice derived from valid findings?

All these questions are important, but the last is critical. Clinicians sometimes have problems because the researcher may make a quantum leap from tentative findings to recommendations for practice. Some knowledge of research terminology, design, and methods is needed.

The nurse manager needs to be supportive and creative when immediate answers are not found. In some situations, the search may be redirected. For example, there is limited literature on family involvement in the care of hospitalized elders, but two related areas from which knowledge can be gained are quite well developed: literature on family involvement in nursing homes and family participation in the care of hospitalized children. Other times, the nurse manager may support the staff in seeking help to conduct a study to find an answer to their question.

Participating in Research

Answers generated through unit-based research are meaningful to informed nursing staff and usually relevant to their practice. Nurses may help to plan a project, such as discussing the question, methods, and feasibility with a researcher at an early stage. Having input to the research design increases the nurses' sense of involvement and commitment to the project.

Nurses' participation in a continuing study could include: (1) identifying potential subjects through a designated screening process, (2) asking patients if they are willing to speak to a researcher, (3) carrying out an intervention according to a protocol, (4) obtaining data (such as recording observations or collecting specimens), or (5) participating as a subject.

Nurse managers have many responsibilities related to the unit involvement in research conducted by nurses and other disciplines (See Table 13.3). These include both facilitating participation and limiting involvement as necessary. Both require a high level of awareness of potential projects, a clear understanding of the meaning and ramifications of involvement, and skill in facilitating approved projects. The nurse manager should be knowledgeable about all proposed research, regardless of the

Table 13.3
Nurse managers' responsibilities related to unit involvement in projects conducted by researchers outside unit nursing staff.

* Identify opportunities for involvement
* Review proposals for feasibility, including
    Potential for access to subjects (patients, family, staff)
    Ongoing projects
    Nursing skills
    Nursing time
    Study time frame and unit activities
* Arrange information sessions for researcher and staff
* Ensure that staff on all shifts are aware of project
* Facilitate training sessions for staff if applicable
* Collaborate with researcher regarding procedures
* Facilitate access to resources if applicable (e.g., space, records)
* Maintain regular contact with researcher for mutual updates
* Keep staff informed of study progress
* Arrange for session for researcher to report findings to staff
* Encourage staff to attend other presentations and read publications on the project

researcher's discipline, and, if nurses are likely to be involved, the manager should review research projects in detail before they begin. Special responsibilities regarding patients' and staff rights are discussed later.

Conducting a Study

Nurses who are planning to conduct a study need the nurse manager's input and support. Research projects conducted alone are rare, so teams and consultation should be encouraged. Few staff nurses have research experience, but many projects are manageable within normal nursing practice, with consultation and shared workload (Hoare & Earenfight, 1986; Youngkins, 1991). Opportunities for discussions are essential throughout the process, from idea to question to proposal to findings (Parker, Gordon, & Brannon, 1992).

The nurse manager is a key person to respond to nurses' ideas for projects. It is important to be supportive, but realistic as to the demands of research. If the nurse manager does not have the experience or expertise, nurses can be referred to a consultant.

The details of conducting research are beyond the scope of this chapter and can be found in appropriate textbooks. Very similar steps may be used in the process of testing findings from previous studies on a small scale on one unit. This is one stage in the process of using research findings in practice.

Using Research Findings in Practice

While every nurse can be involved in using research findings in practice, it is unrealistic to expect all nurses to lead the way. This is an important component of the nurse manager's role, with support from the department of nursing and prepared staff, such as a clinical nurse specialist or senior staff nurses. The answers to specific questions and the ideas for practice from research reports are rarely found in a directly applicable form.

The first step to using research findings is a thorough critique of the research reports to determine the validity of the findings, as outlined above. The next phase, which Stetler and Marram (1976) identify as comparative evaluation, is a careful comparison between the situation reported in the research and the particular clinical situation of the reader. Again, a series of questions is useful to consider. At this point, clinical expertise is essential, as well as a sound knowledge of the clinical situation. The nurse manager may be the best person to help staff nurses make this assessment.

- What are the similarities and differences between the problem identified in the study and the situation in the unit?
- What are the similarities and differences between the setting in the study and the setting in question?
- What are the similarities and differences between the people (patients, family members, staff) studied and those in the unit?
- How does a possible innovation fit with the philosophy and policies in the agency?
- How feasible is it to carry out the innovation on the unit?
- How feasible is it to use the same measurement techniques to assess the effectiveness of the innovation? If identical measures are not feasible, what alternatives are there?

In the decision-making phase, the nurse manager can help staff decide whether to use the findings cognitively or whether to take action based on the findings (MacGuire, 1990). Even cognitive application does not happen automatically. Suppose a researcher reports on factors related to the well-being of a particular population, for instance, dyspneic patients (Gift, Plaut, & Jacox, 1986), psychiatric patients (Holdcraft & Williamson, 1991), or mothers of hospitalized children (Schepp, 1991). The nurse manager can arrange for a discussion of how the findings relate to the population in the setting and how the new knowledge might influence care.

If action is to be taken, the nurse manager may use the new information as evidence of the need for change. Many groups may resist change (see Chapter 24) and the stronger the evidence, the more effective the argument. The research findings may prompt the nurse manager and staff to evaluate their own situation. Are they collecting enough information about clients to determine a need for change? What are the actual outcomes of current practice? What are the costs, human and financial, of current practice?

The final decision is whether to use an innovation as a model for a change in practice. It is useful to plan a trial period with a comparison before and after or a control group for whom the innovation is not used. One effective way to conduct a trial is to replicate the original study as closely as possible. Several sources provide clear information on this process (Horsley et al., 1983; Haller, Reynolds, & Horsley, 1979). Also, the original researcher can be consulted.

Protecting Patient and Staff Rights in Relation to Research

The nurse manager has the responsibility to protect patient and staff rights in relation to any research. The first step, once the possibility of a research project is known, is to ensure that the project has been approved by an appropriate research ethical review board. This is essential regardless of the researcher's discipline or institutional affiliation. A staff physician, a nurse from a graduate program, a university professor, or a psychologist from a community agency all need approval for research projects. In teaching agencies, it is likely that there is an established procedure, which agency researchers know about. But, in any agency, the nurse manager is often the first contact that researchers make. It is imperative that approval be verified. A nursing administrator or nurse researcher should sit on the review board.

It is also important that the nurse manager have an under-standing of the research protocol, the purpose, the procedures, the involvement of patients, and so on. If it is medical research or a project that does not involve nursing, the manager may still be called upon to answer questions or refer patients or family members to the researcher. The manager may be the only person who knows which other projects are in process. Patients or staff may need to be protected from "research overload." It may simply be an issue of timing. Data for one study may be collected at one time, and those for another at a different time of day or day of the week. This may not make a difference to the research, but it can make a big difference to the running of the unit.

If the manager or nursing staff are involved in a screening process for research subjects, this should be part of the research protocol, that is, it should be planned in advance with the researcher. Any screening that is not built into the project can seriously jeopardize the validity of the results.

The nurse manager needs to be involved in the approval process if the study includes any nursing staff participation. Nurses need to be informed participants. They need to know why the study is being done, why specific data are being collected, what the risks and benefits are for patients, and so on. The manager may be doing a balancing act between encouraging and facilitating research on the one hand and limiting access to patients or staff on the other.

Differentiating Research and Quality Management

An important distinction needs to be made between research and quality management activities. The nurse manager is responsible for the quality of care in his or her jurisdiction, and quality management is addressed elsewhere in this text. The activities of identifying problems, collecting data, testing solutions, and analyzing results may be similar, and the long term goal of both is improved nursing practice. However, the purpose of research is to add to the knowledge base, rather than to promote a high quality of care in a specific area. Thurston and Best (1990) discuss methods for integration of the two programs to improve nursing care.

The Economics of Research

As with any other aspect of nursing, there are costs and benefits to nursing research. Knowledge of these economics in general, and in relation to particular studies, will help nurse managers in their research role.

Costs of Doing Research

Nurse managers need to be aware of the indirect costs of participating in research, whether nurses or researchers in other disciplines are conducting the study. Cronenwett (1987) outlines several questions for consideration in the review of proposed studies. These relate to space, changes in nursing practice, staff involvement and time, patient time, numbers of study patients at one time, and supplies or other costs. These costs should be built into the budget of research grants.

The primary costs for nursing research involve personnel. In general, nurses do not use expensive equipment or procedures, but many nursing studies are labour intensive. The same questions need to be considered, whether the study is a large funded project or a small in-house study by the nursing staff. Time for planning, time for data collection, time for data analysis, and time for writing the report are essential. Pringle (1989) noted that one of the realities of research is that it is a long term process. Benefits make the costs worthwhile, but it is also well worthwhile to consider outside funding for research.

Funding Resources

Obtaining funding is a challenge in this time of restraint, when resources available for nursing research are limited. However, a truism also pertains: Nurses will not get funding if they do not apply. Federal and provincial government agencies fund research, as do non-governmental organizations, such as the Canadian Heart Foundation or the Arthritis Society. The Canadian Nurses Foundation and some provincial nursing associations have funds for small projects. The Canadian Nurses Association regularly publishes a list of resources for research funding.

Although seeking funds adds to the overall time for research, having deadlines for submission can provide a major stimulus to planning. For nurses unfamiliar with the process, it is essential to involve a knowledgeable consultant, as grant applications are highly competitive.

Economic Benefits of Nursing Research

As health care costs soar and resources diminish, nursing research has demonstrated that it can make a difference. In broad-based studies of delivery systems, nursing care has been found to offer better care at less cost (Fagin, 1990). Fagin pointed out that nursing programs such as long term care or hospital follow-up home care have been "uniformly successful in reducing costs *if they have served as an alternative to other types of care*" (p. 29, emphasis in original).

At a more specific level, the study of nursing interventions has shown how costs can be reduced. For example, a program with advanced nurse clinicians in a respiratory intensive care unit reduced ventilator days and chest X-rays in relation to a comparison unit, thereby reducing costs despite new positions (Ahrens & Padwojski, 1990). Brooten and her colleagues (1986) demonstrated that an early discharge program for very-low-birth-weight infants with counseling and home care by a hospital-based nurse specialist yielded a net saving of US$18 560 per infant. A recent study of developmentally supportive nursing in a neonatal intensive care unit showed that study infants went home an average of two weeks earlier than the control group and were more optimally developed at the time, reducing immediate costs of the care on the neonatal intensive care unit and, potentially, reducing long term costs of continuing health care for these infants (Becker, Grunwald, Moorman, & Stuhr, 1991). An analysis of 17 studies of the use of a saline flush for peripheral intravenous locks rather than heparin showed that saline was safe and could produce annual savings of over US$100 000 000 in American health care costs (Goode et al., 1991).

It is important for nursing researchers to consider the benefits in patient outcomes in terms of both better health and reduced health care costs, and it is important for nursing leaders to take advantage of sound research to improve care at lower cost.

Summary

This chapter has focussed on research-based nursing practice and the role of the nurse manager in developing it. The four interdependent components that are needed are:

- Meaningful research questions that are relevant to practice;
- Sound research to answer the questions;
- Knowledgeable nurses with skills in using research findings; and
- Clinical environments open to inquiry and change.

Research activities include the conduct of research, the use of other researchers' findings, and the use of rigorous research techniques in daily practice. All nurses can participate in some of these activities with the help of their leaders. The working environment constitutes one of the major barriers to the use of research findings, and the nurse manager is the key person in creating a climate of openness and inquiry.

The nursing department can provide structural supports and continuing education to facilitate research-based practice. The nurse manager can help staff directly to raise questions, find answers, participate in research, conduct studies, and use findings in practice.

There are costs involved in conducting and participating in research, but the benefits for patients and health care costs are significant. Nurse managers have a particular responsibility to develop nursing practice in their areas that is based on sound economics and sound research.

References

Ahrens, T.S., & Podwojski, A. (1990). Economic effectiveness of an advanced nurse clinician model. *Nursing Management, 21*(11), 72J, 72N. 72P.

Atkins, F.D. (1991). Children's perspectives of stress and coping: An integrative review. *Issues of Mental Health Nursing, 12*(2), 171-178.

Becker, P.T., Grunwald, P.C., Moorman, J., & Stuhr, S. (1991). Outcomes of developmentally supportive nursing care for very low weight infants. *Nursing Research, 40*(30), 150-155.

Belair, J. (1992). Pain management interest group. *Nursing Horizons, 10*(2), 12.

Brooten, D., Kumar, S., Brown, L.P., Butts, P., Finkler, S.A., Bakewell-Sachs, S., Gibbons, A., & Delivoria-Papadopoulos, M. (1986). A randomized clinical trial of early hospital discharge and home follow-up of very-low-birth-weight infants. *New England Journal of Medicine, 315*(15), 934-939.

Canadian Nurses Association. (1990). *Research imperative for nursing in Canada: The next five years 1990-1995.* Ottawa, Canada: Author.

Crane, J. (1989). *Factors associated with the use of research-based knowledge in nursing.* Doctoral dissertation, University of Michigan, Ann Arbor: University Microfilms International.

Cronenwett, L.R. (1986). Research contributions of clinical nurse specialist. *Journal of Nursing Administration, 16*(6), 6-7.

Cronenwett, L. R. (1987). The indirect costs of nursing research. *Journal of Nursing Administration, 17*(9), 6-8.

Donaldson, N.E. (1991, Fall). Peripheral saline locks: An alternative to heparin flushes. *The ORCUN Oration.*

Fagin, C.M. (1990). Nursing's value proves itself. *American Journal of Nursing, 90*(10), 17-30.

Ferrell, B.R., Rhiner, M., Cohen, M.Z., & Grant, M. (1991). Pain as a metaphor for illness Part 1: Impact of cancer pain on family caregivers. *Oncology Nursing Forum, 18*(8), 1303-1309.

Fitch, M.I. (1992). Five years in the life of a nursing research and professional development division. *Canadian Journal of Nursing Administration, 5*(1), 21-27.

Funk, S.G., Champagne, M.T., Wiese, R.A., & Tornquist, E.M. (1991a). Barriers: The barriers to research utilization scale. *Applied Nursing Research, 4*(1), 39-45.

Funk, S.G., Champagne, M.T., Wiese, R.A., & Tornquist, E.M. (1991b). Barriers to using findings in practice: The clinician's perspective. *Applied Nursing Research, 4*(2), 90-95.

Gift, A.G., Plaut, S.M., & Jacox, A. (1986). Psychologic and physiologic factors related to dyspnea in subjects with chronic obstructive pulmonary disease. *Heart & Lung, 15*, 595-601.

Goode, C.J., Lovett, M.K., Hayes, J.E., & Butcher, A.L. (1987). Use of research based knowledge in clinical practice. *Journal of Nursing Administration, 17*(12), 11-18.

Goode, C.J., Titler, M., Rakel, B., Ones, D.S., Kleiber, C., Small, S., & Triolo, P.K. (1991). A meta-analysis of effects of heparin flush and saline flush: Quality and cost implications. *Nursing Research, 40*(6), 324-330.

Haller, K.B., Reynolds, M.A., & Horsley, J.A. (1979). Developing research-based innovation protocols: Process, criteria, and issues. *Research in Nursing & Health, 2*, 45-51.

Hamilton, L., Vincent, L., Goode, R., Moorhouse, A., Hawker Worden, R., Jones, H., Close, M., & Dufour, S. (1990). Organizational support of the clinical nurse specialist role. *Canadian Journal of Nursing Administration, 3*, 9-13.

Henderson, A., & Brouse, J. (1992). Development of a research committee in a community hospital. *Canadian Journal of Nursing Research*, 5(2), 17-19.

Hickey, M. (1990). The role of the clinical nurse specialist in the research utilization process. *Clinical Nurse Specialist, 4*(2), 93-96.

Hoare, K., & Earenfight, J. (1986). Unit-based research in a service setting. *Journal of Nursing Administration, 16*(4), 35-39.

Holdcraft, C., & Williamson, C. (1991). Assessment of hope in psychiatric and chemically dependent patients. *Applied Nursing Research, 4*(3), 129-134.

Horsley, J.A. (1985). Using research in practice: The current context. *Western Journal of Nursing Research, 7*(1), 135-139.

Horsley, J.A., Crane, J. Crabtree, K., & Wood, D.J. (1983). *Using research to improve nursing practice: A guide.* New York: Grune & Stratton.

Horn Video Productions. (1987). *Using research in clinical nursing practice.* Ida Grove, IA.

Janken, J.K., Dufault, M.A., & Yeaw, E.M.S. (1988). Research round tables: Increasing student/staff nurse awareness of the relevancy of research to practice. *Journal of Professional Nursing, 4*(3), 186-191.

Knafl, K.A., Hagle, M., Bevis, M., & Kirchhof, K. (1987). Clinical nurse researchers: Strategies for success. *Journal of Nursing Administration, 17*(10), 27-31.

MacGuire, J.M. (1990). Putting nursing research findings into practice: Research utilization as an aspect of the management of change. *Journal of Advanced Nursing, 15*(5), 614-620.

Maciorowski, L.F., Munro, B.H., Dietrick-Gallagher, M., McNew, C.D., Sheppard-Hinkel, E., Wanich, C., & Ragan, P. (1988). A review of the patient fall literature. *Journal of Nursing Quality Assurance, 3*(1), 18-27.

Maxwell, M.B. (1982). The use of social networks to help cancer patients maximize support. *Cancer Nursing, 5*(8), 275-281.

Nightingale, F. (1859). *Notes on nursing: What it is and what it is not.* London: Harrison.

Norbeck, J.S., Lindsey, A.M., & Carrieri, V.L. (1983). Further development of the Norbeck social support questionnaire: Normative data and validity testing. *Nursing Research, 32*, 4-9.

Parker, M.E., Gordon, S.C., & Brannon, P.T. (1992). Involving nursing staff in research: A non-traditional approach. *Journal of Nursing Administration, 22*(4), 58-63.

Pepler, C.J. (1988). The nurse researcher in the clinical setting. In L. Besel & R. Stock (Eds.), *Benchmarks: A Sourcebook for Canadian Nursing Management.* Toronto: Carswell.

Pepler, C.J. (1992). Fostering change through education. *Canadian Nurse, 88*(1), 25-27.

Pringle, D. (1989). Another twist on the double helix: Research and practice. *Canadian Journal of Nursing Research, 21*(1), 47-60.

Registered Nurses Association of British Columbia. (1991). *Making a difference: From ritual to research-based practice.* Vancouver: Author.

Rich, O.J. (1978). The sociogram: A tool for depicting support in pregnancy. *Maternal Child Nursing Journal, 7,* 1-9.

Schepp, K.G. (1991). Factors influencing the coping effort of mothers of hospitalized children. *Nursing Research, 40*(1), 42-46, 1991.

Shaver, J.L., & Giblin, E.C. (1989). Sleep. *Annual Review of Nursing Research, 7,* 71-93.

Simms, L.M., Price, S.A., & Pfoutz, S.K. (1987). Creating the research climate: A key responsibility for nurse executives. *Nursing Economics, 5*(4), 174-179.

Stetler, C.H. (1985). Research utilization: Defining the concept. *Image: The Journal of Nursing Scholarship, 17*(2), 40-44.

Stetler, C.H., & Marram, G. (1976). Evaluating research findings for applicability in practice. *Nursing Outlook, 24*(9), 559-563.

Thurston, N., & Best, M. (1990). Clinical nursing research and quality assurance: Integration for improved patient care. *Canadian Journal of Nursing Administration, 3*(2), 19-23.

VanCott, M.L., Tittle, M.B., & Wilson, M.E. (1991). Analysis of a decade of critical care nursing practice research: 1979 to 1988. *Heart & Lung, 20*(4), 394-397.

van Koot, B., & Laverty, P. (1992). A research foundation for policies and procedures. *Canadian Nurse, 88*(1), 39-41.

Vessey, J.A., & Campos, R.G. (1992). The role of nursing research committees. *Nursing Research, 41*(4), 247-249.

Walsh, M., & Ford, P. (1989). *Nursing rituals: Research and rational action.* Oxford: Heinemann Professional Publishing.

Youngkins, J.M. (1991). The impact of one staff nurse's research. *MCN, 16,* 133-137.

CHAPTER 14

Quality Management: From QA to TQM

Monique Boulerice

Monique Boulerice, RN, BScN, MHA (Ottawa), is Vice-President, Nursing and Patient Care, at the Beauséjour Hospital Corporation in Moncton, New Brunswick. Before that, she was Director of the Introduction to Nursing Management: Distance Education Program in Ottawa.

The patient had not been well. Symptoms were vague; close observation did not reveal the nature of the problem. Nevertheless the crisis came, a call was made, and the patient was taken to hospital. An employee greeted us warmly, immediately collected pertinent information, and directed us to a quiet and comfortable waiting area. Within five minutes the patient was whisked into an examination room, and the need for immediate surgery and overnight monitoring was identified. The time of surgery, the procedure to be carried out, the expected outcome, the possible alternative course of treatment, and the consent for surgery were thoroughly explained. I was encouraged to return home and assured that I would be kept informed. Within three hours, a telephone call indicated that the surgery was a success, the patient was recuperating well, that close monitoring would follow during the night, and that I could call early in the morning for a progress report. The morning call was initiated by the hospital, indicating that the patient was progressing well and that an afternoon discharge was possible; they would keep me posted. A satisfied customer picked up a complete set of discharge instructions and recuperating furry friend from the Animal Hospital that same afternoon.

Comparing the quality of care described in this situation to health care consumers' expectations may seem a little unorthodox. Yet, irrespective of the environment or the nature of the consumer, expectations remain the same. The consumer expects a timely intervention that successfully addresses the problem, explanations about the cause of the problem, a recommended intervention with its possible benefits and potential complications, regular progress reports, and supportive discharge teaching and emotional support. To respond to these expectations, the health care organization, and more specifically the nursing division, must be inspired by the values of quality care and must strive for excellence.

This chapter offers an historical review of quality improvement from its emergence as a commitment to a community to the implementation of quality assurance (QA) programs in health care organizations. Over the years, various instruments were developed to measure quality. The introduction of QA programs challenged many practices and encouraged change. Parallel programs were developed throughout health care organizations. Every discipline recognized the importance of measuring quality, and each developed tools appropriate for its own areas. Organizations recognized the importance of coordinating these programs and, today, a significant number have organization-wide quality assurance programs.

The total quality management (TQM) model is the most recent attempt to redefine quality as a system-wide effort to improve effectiveness and to meet customer needs. This chapter also introduces the principles of total quality management, and describes how it can be implemented within institutions. The role of organizational services and, more specifically, the role of the nursing division within a TQM model is discussed.

Historical Overview

Whenever nurse managers meet to discuss common areas of interest, quality of nursing services soon becomes the topic of discussion. Gardner (1992) describes quality as the degree of compliancy with recognized standards. In nursing, quality of nursing services is measured by establishing realistic standards of professional practices and monitoring compliancy to these standards. To understand the concept of quality as it is being proposed today, an overview of its evolution provides an appreciation of how it has influenced the services offered by organizations, changed their practices, and affected the contribution of employees to the improvement of services. The discussion of the concept of quality began before the industrial revolution, when goods were produced by artisans committed to their craft. During this period, customer satisfaction was critical to the economic survival of the artisan. The industrial revolution that followed was marked by the introduction of power-driven equipment. As a result, the nature of the contract between provider and consumer changed, as products were now offered on a much larger scale (Keenan Widtfeldt &

Widtfeldt, 1992). To ensure quality performance, standards, rules, and inspections were introduced.

About 1870, Frederick Taylor, the father of the school of scientific management, sought to simplify work into a series of smaller tasks that would facilitate mass production (Walton, 1986). He developed plans and corresponding procedures, which not only facilitated task accomplishment but also became the basis for the formulation of evaluation criteria for measurement of work performance. This approach became the first recorded quality measurement initiative.

World War II generated a need for massive production of reliable army supplies. This led to implementation of quality control procedures, which consisted mainly of inspections to verify reliability of equipment, and identification and correction of defects (Keenan Widtfeldt & Widtfeldt, 1992). By the end of the war, consumer goods of all types were in such great demand that every product was purchased, no questions asked. When defects were identified or rework proved to be necessary, the profit margin was significant enough to cover repairs of defective merchandise (Walton, 1986). In the frenzy to meet consumer demand, quality control measures were forgotten and replaced by quantity. Because of an absence of competition, businesses were free to determine what would be produced, deciding what was best for the consumer.

Following World War II, Japan set out to reconstruct its economy. The country's guiding principle became "find out what consumers want and surpass their expectations." Based on a quality management theory developed by W. Edwards Deming, the man who is said to be the architect of Japan's success, a country destroyed by war became, over a twenty-year period, a formidable economic power and the envy of the world. In the early 1980s, the rest of the world discovered Deming and his theory. Since then, many North American companies have adopted the quality principles implemented by Japan, and have put them to work in their own organizations. In the late 1980s, it became clear that Deming's principles of quality management were also applicable to the health industry. Before discussing Deming's management system, the author of this chapter presents a broad overview of the quality assurance programs that have been instituted in health care organizations, and in nursing.

Quality Assurance in
Health Care
Organizations

A quality assurance program is a management system that demonstrates administrative and professional accountability. It consists of a review of activities and practices, assessing these against predetermined standards, identifying deficiencies and communicating them to the appropriate individual or group, and finally, proposing and implementing solutions. Initially, quality assurance in health organizations meant inspecting services and products (Marszalek-Gaucher, 1992). These practices are still very much in use today and they still play a major role in improving quality of services.

Managers used and still use a number of control systems to measure quality. Dietary departments, laboratories, and X-ray departments, to name a few, use these methods to verify that the patients are getting the right diets, that equipment is in good working order, that techniques are faultless and results accurate. External reviews such as fire inspections, narcotic counts, and distribution system evaluations, are continuous. Internal reviews, such as equipment maintenance programs, performance evaluation processes, and incident reporting practices, have been in place for a long time. Only recently have these practices been recognized as components of a quality assurance program.

In health care, formal quality assurance programs originated in the early 1970s. These were departmental programs, and the nursing division became one of the first services to implement them. At that time, there was no central body to direct institution-wide quality assurance activities and no involvement, interest, or commitment on the part of the chief executive officer (Wilson, 1992). Quality assurance programs were initiated by individual departments and professional groups who attempted to define quality of care, and to devise and refine quality measuring tools. Today, many health care organizations have in place agency-wide quality assurance programs. Unfortunately, many do not have in place the infrastructure to support this initiative and, in some cases, quality assurance is still seen as an extra activity that is not part of the organizational culture (Evans & English, 1992). Therefore, quality assurance activities are often developed at a lower level in the organization, and this has contributed to the development of specialists who work in functional positions with no legitimate power to implement changes. Although corrective actions are identified, they are not necessarily implemented, because no one is held accountable for implementation. Therefore, problems that were solved yesterday will need to be solved again tomorrow, even if a quality assurance program has been in place for years.

In the mid-1980s, risk management (RM) programs were introduced to anticipate and limit risk to the organization. The purpose of this initiative is to identify threats that could jeopardize the reputation or financial integrity of the organization (CCHFA, 1991). In the late 1980s, utilization management (UM) programs were instituted to address concerns about costs and management of resources. Utilization management consists of maintaining and improving quality of care through the effective and efficient use of resources (CCHFA, 1992). Quality assurance, risk management, and utilization management strive to provide quality services, establish standards, identify strategies to meet the standards, receive reports from departments on a regular basis, and follow through on recommended corrective actions. In many organizations, these three quality-related programs are administered separately. Many would argue that the three programs are different, yet there is also an interrelationship that cannot be denied. It is becoming more evident that the three programs complement one another, and since all three activities fall under administrative control it is logical that they be incorporated within one seamless, integrated program.

Use of Standards to Measure Quality in Nursing

Quality measurement is not new to nursing; measures to evaluate quality date back to Florence Nightingale when she identified policies and procedures to be used in delivering nursing care to wounded soldiers (Gardner, 1992). Nurses have always compared their performances against pre-established criteria, whether these were procedures, job descriptions, or, in more recent years, standards of nursing practice. Since the early 1970s, formal quality assurance programs have concentrated on establishing standards, collecting information, measuring the collected information against pre-established standards, and taking corrective action when discrepancies occur.

Three different types of standards have been used in nursing to evaluate quality: structure, process, and outcome standards. *Structure standards* identify the rules that determine how the service will be delivered. They focus on service, facility, policies, procedures, equipment, communication processes, and other elements. Although structure standards are important for measurement of quality, they do not necessarily guarantee effective outcomes; as an example, the presence of a policy that promotes nonsmoking practices does not guarantee adherence to the policy. *Process standards* are used to measure the quality of an activity against a desired outcome. The desired outcome must first be identified, then the appropriate activity or process is selected. For example, when the desired outcome is to relieve pain, the appropriate process or activity selected may be implementation of comfort measures and administration of analgesics. The major criticism of process evaluation is that the process may not necessarily be related to the quality of the outcome. For example, an acceptable nursing practice may be carried out, but may have no impact on patient outcome. *Outcome standards* describe the results of care or the expected change in the status of the patient. These are concerned with ability to meet the identified objective or expected results. To use the analogy of patient education, teaching aids correspond to structure, actual patient teaching relates to process, and patient learning to outcome. Structure, process, and outcome standards are interrelated. Irrespective of the quality assurance program adopted, these three types of standards, whether expressed in qualitative or quantitative terms, are normally used to some degree to monitor the quality of services delivered.

Measurement Tools

Three different methods have been used to measure quality in nursing. The first method is the *retrospective audit,* which was introduced in the early 1960s. This tool focusses on the process of care and is used in conjunction with the client's record. This instrument evaluates patient care after its delivery, and in some cases, after the client's discharge. The retrospective audit may proceed as follows: members of an audit committee are assigned, through a random process, to review a predetermined number of client records. Results of the evaluations are then reviewed by the full committee for acknowledgement or recommendations to the nursing unit. The retrospective audit presents some major drawbacks. A significant time period may elapse between delivery of care and audit of the recorded care. Therefore, identified deficiencies and implementation of subsequent corrective action may not benefit the client involved. As well, during a retrospective audit, the auditor's conclusions are directly related to the quality and completeness of the documentation.

A second method to measure quality is the *concurrent audit,* which measures the quality of care through observation of the care delivered to a client at a single point in time. The quality patient care scale (QUALPACS) developed in the early 1970s is such an instrument (Gardner, 1992). Its main advantage is the accuracy of the information collected. This instrument measures the quality of the intervention, involves clients in the evaluation of their care, and allows the provider of care the opportunity to justify its intervention. Concurrent audits may also present significant drawbacks; they are costly because staff may be mobilized on a regular basis and for predetermined periods of time to evaluate, through observations, the quality of care being delivered. Also, concurrent audits tend to evaluate tasks and activities instead of measuring how the total episode of care influences the quality of the outcome.

A third evaluation method is *outcome measurement,* which evaluates the results of care. An example of outcome measurement is the patient satisfaction instrument, which measures the quality of care received from the client's perspective. This instrument attempts to measure the client's perception of nursing care received, the knowledge that the providers exhibited, and the quality of the information or teaching received.

The major concern in today's health care environment is to control costs while enhancing quality. One way to do this is through better management of patient outcomes (Jones, 1993). Outcome measurement studies the relationship between quality and costs and also allows the move from an evaluation of tasks to a broader perspective where nursing practice is evaluated based on client outcomes. However, different professional and support groups contribute to client outcome, and managerial, clinical, and support processes also influence the quality of client outcome. It is often difficult, therefore, to identify nursing-dependent outcomes, or those outcomes directly related to nursing interventions. Nurses should continue to identify desired patient outcomes and, when the expected outcome is not met, nurses must identify the process that must be improved, or the external group that must correct the deficiency (Jones, 1993).

In 1992, the Canadian Nurses Association sponsored a conference on Nursing Minimum Data Set as a first step to develop a data set for nursing. A Nursing Minimum Data Set is the minimum set of information concerning professional nursing. It includes nursing diagnosis, intervention, and outcome (CNA, 1993). Such data can be used to measure client outcomes and cost of nursing services.

Nurses have a major role to play in the identification of nurse-sensitive outcomes or those nursing interventions that directly affect client outcome (Curran, 1993). As organizations move closer to automation, large amounts of data will be readily available from nursing assessments, interventions, and workload measurement systems to identify trends and develop outcomes critical to effective quality care. Because of the complexity of the challenge, collaborative efforts with other members of the health care team facilitate the development of valid and reliable measurement methods.

Monitoring Quality in Health Care Organizations

Quality assurance programs may be administered centrally or at the unit level. Under a centralized structure, standard identification and data collection is the responsibility of a quality assurance committee. The main disadvantage is that quality assurance programs may be administered by individuals not involved in patient care. Also, recommendations are made by members of a committee who may not have the authority to implement corrective actions. Within a decentralized, unit-based quality assurance program, individuals involved in the care develop evaluation criteria, monitor performances, and implement corrective actions (Reiley, 1992). Staff members are involved in the process, commitment to quality is increased, and an opportunity to contribute positively to the work environment is valued.

The drawback of unit-based quality assurance programs is the absence of information sharing across units. To correct this deficiency, Reiley (1992) suggests the formation of a nursing-wide quality assurance committee, with representation from all unit-based committees. This committee identifies the standards of care for the nursing department, addresses common issues, and shares plans for corrective actions.

The complexity of health care requires the involvement of a number of health disciplines, and since the unifying goal for all health care professionals is quality care, there is no doubt that collaborative action should significantly contribute to the identification of achievements and deficiencies of all contributors. Therefore, creation of a hospital-wide quality assurance program, with multidisciplinary representation, provides an opportunity for nurses to work with other professionals and to solve important clinical problems. A three-tier program that includes a unit committee, a departmental committee, and an organization-wide committee addresses quality improvement at all levels of the organization. Involvement of members of the board of directors on the organizational committee makes it easier to monitor quality of services throughout the organization.

From an external perspective, the Canadian Council on Health Facilities Accreditation, an independent peer review agency, provides direction to health care facilities about the requirements of quality care and how to meet them (CCHFA, 1990). Evaluation of quality is based on a number of structural and procedural standards and assumes that the presence of structure and standards results in quality care (CCHFA, 1990). The Council recognizes the limitation of structural and procedural standards and is examining outcome measures for incorporation within the accreditation process. In 1989, Council initiated a project to assess outcome measures and their relationship to quality. The project consists of analyzing outcome elements for preadmission activity, intermediate outcome, final outcome, and discharge planning. This project is in its final stage and its results will be published. In 1991, Council revised its accreditation standards, and quality assurance was included as a separate standard. In 1992, the standards were further revised; the Quality Assurance Standards for Mental Health and Rehabilitation are now described as quality management standards. It is expected that the 1994 revision will incorporate within the existing quality assurance standards the principles of quality improvement or total quality management.

TQM: A New Approach to Quality

Quality assurance programs were developed in an era when bottom lines were healthy and when more meant better. During that period, health organizations often lost sight of consumer demands, professional expectations, and ability to pay. At the same time, quality assurance programs were perceived as generating excessive paperwork and having too little impact on the quality of care to justify their cost.

In the 1990s, pressured by both external and internal constraints, organizations are forced to review their practices. Spiraling costs are compelling them to identify more effective methods to provide the quality care that health care consumers are used to, and to respond to consumer demands for a wider range of services and better health outcomes. Organizations must evaluate the appropriateness and effectiveness of treatments and services and, to address these issues, they must re-evaluate their approach to quality.

After witnessing the success of industry in implementing total TQM programs, many health care organizations are adopting this management philosophy, and hope to bring innovation to the management of health care.

Principles of TQM

Organization-wide systems for the continuous improvement of processes to meet customer needs have been described under different names: quality improvement (QI), continuous quality improvement (CQI), and total quality management (TQM) (Wilson, 1992). These terms refer to the same process, but since total quality management has been the term predominantly adopted in North America, it will be used here. TQM represents a system's approach to quality, based on a set of principles identified by W. Edwards Deming, and strives to improve the effectiveness of operational services and reduce costs (Lopresti & Whetstone, 1993). This management philosophy redefines the role of the organization in an attempt to find constant sources of improvement, to provide employment, innovation, and research, and to enhance services continually to its external and internal customers (Walton, 1986).

Implementation of TQM requires a vision, that is, a sense of purpose conveyed by management and shared by every employee in the organization to commit the organization to continuous improvement and wise use of resources (Marszalek-Gaucher, 1992). TQM also demands leadership. Managers influence their employees to strive enthusiastically toward the realization of organizational goals. They provide the resources and information to accomplish the job, delegate the authority to act, and reward those who contribute to quality improvement.

TQM is more than a way to manage; it requires "top-down" commitment to quality. It involves a different way of thinking, a different way of doing; it is part of the organizational culture, one that requires total commitment from everyone in the organization. Its success depends on the commitment of management, physicians, and employees, and an environment that values and rewards improvements (Lopresti & Whetstone, 1993).

Its implementation requires a knowledge of organizational processes. Unlike quality assurance, which pursues problems vertically through lines of authority, TQM cuts across the organization, resolves problems horizontally, and evaluates processes (Labovitz, 1991). Employees of the organization need to become familiar with organizational processes, because everyone is involved in planning and evaluating its many activities to meet customer expectations.

TQM requires the development of standards and corresponding quality indicators. These are developed to measure both internal and external customer satisfaction. Each department develops its own standards and a set of quality indicators, and these are used to measure performance. This process enables problems to be identified, and determines whether a problem can be resolved at the departmental level or whether a cross-functional team must be activated.

Implementation of TQM also requires a philosophy that focusses on the "customer." Based on Deming's belief that organizations must meet the needs of both their external customers (the recipients of care) and internal customers (employees), quality must be defined from a customer's perspective. Meeting customer needs means providing the best possible service to the external customer at the least possible cost, and meeting employee needs by creating an environment conducive to commitment and productivity. TQM includes the customer as part of the production process.

From the external customer's perspective, the organization has the obligation to meet both the immediate needs of clients and to position itself to anticipate and respond to future needs. It means:

- Providing effective educational programs to facilitate informed decisions about risks, benefits, and services;
- Facilitating more active participation in evaluating services;
- Discovering which activities have the greatest impact on outcome; and
- Organizing its services around activities and processes that make a difference.

The implementation of TQM also requires that everyone in the organization focus on internal customer needs. Employees are given control over the various processes, are encouraged to participate in problem solving, and are delegated the authority to make decisions (Duncan, Fleming, & Gallati, 1991). Competition or incompatibility of goals between employees or services is discouraged, and a team approach to improving processes and meeting goals is an integral part of the process. Employees work in cross-functional teams to improve the quality of their work, their departments, and ultimately, the organization. To do so, there must be a willingness to ask questions, to volunteer opinions, to learn new skills and techniques.

TQM advocates employee empowerment. Traditionally, goal setting, problem solving, and decision making were considered the domain of management, and the employee's role was to make management's plans work. The premise of TQM is that program evaluation is everyone's responsibility. Failure to achieve desired performance is usually due to problems within the system rather than employee error (Lopresti & Whetstone, 1993). Every employee in the organization contributes to the identification and evaluation of processes and to the resolution of problems while ascertaining that every process or activity meets the identified standards of care. Based on top-down leadership efforts, key organizational processes such as management and clinical care, which cut across departments and disciplinary boundaries, are assessed by employees.

Implementation of TQM requires a commitment to education. A number of educational programs are required at different phases in the implementation process. To ensure commitment, employees are exposed initially to the philosophy of TQM. This initiative is followed by familiarization with the TQM process, its tools, and its techniques. Finally, employees are taught the roles and responsibilities of team members and how these are integrated within the rest of the organization (Marszalek-Gaucher, 1992). Education is a continuous process, and regular programs are offered to share new knowledge, to review existing practices, and to orient new employees to the TQM philosophy.

Communication is a major component of TQM, and management communicates its commitment to quality to its customers (Horovitz & Cudennec-Poon, 1991). All staff and service providers are informed of the organization's definition of quality and how, through the creation of a response system, the organization consistently strives to improve its quality (Haywood & Nollet, 1991). In the search for continuous improvement, employees communicate on issues to be resolved with peers, with other services, and with external clients. All groups identify needs and expectations, evaluate the degree of satisfaction, and seek participation in decisions that affect them.

Conditions for Adopting a TQM Program

The decision to adopt total quality management is based on three conditions. First, the price must be right. Implementation is costly and includes the costs of structuring the system, of staff education, and of staff involvement in attending committee meetings and researching problems. Once the program is in place, maintenance costs need to be continually addressed. In the long run, the organization should recoup its investment, because the review process eliminates redundant steps and "things get done right the first time and all the time" (Flower, 1990, p. 68). Through the review process, many diverse procedures may be streamlined, such as reducing the number of late surgeries or revamping outpatient billing.

Second, TQM must deliver what it promises at the end of the three- to five-year period that it takes the organization to reap the benefits (Wilson, 1992). It must be able to demonstrate greater effectiveness of outcomes and increased customer satisfaction. These goals may meet with skepticism at different levels in the organization. Departments or professionals may fail to collaborate because clinical care is viewed as being the domain of physicians and management's involvement is seen as interference. Also, fear of malpractice may become apparent as improvement teams uncover errors in clinical and support areas (Laffel, 1990).

Third, the contribution of other organizational or departmental quality assurance programs that are in place must be recognized and some of their elements integrated within the new structure. TQM programs should not be implemented in isolation from existing quality assurance programs; a duplication of resources is wasteful and unacceptable at all times, but this is especially true in difficult economic periods. An effective TQM program focusses not only on operational reviews, where processes and client satisfaction are reviewed, but also on the clinical and professional dimension through use of audits of risk management issues and other quality assurance methodologies already in place (Wilson, 1992).

Issues to Be Addressed

TQM is said to improve quality and employee satisfaction and decrease costs, but to put this system into operation a number of practical issues must be addressed. TQM is based on team problem solving. Constant changes in employee population due to employee turnover, shift work, or rotation of staff between units diminish the effectiveness of the team. Employers have to balance their needs against employees' rights to personal time off and additional compensation. As organizations downsize, employees feel the strain of the added responsibilities, and team work may add to an already heavy workload.

Members of cross-functional teams are expected to resolve problems beyond the confines of their work areas, and members of such teams require educational programs to broaden their knowledge of the workplace and its operation. As well, formation of cross-functional teams requires multidisciplinary collaboration (Andrews & Wensel, 1992). Cross-functional teams may, in some cases, be perceived as a threat to managers and as contributing to the erosion of the management role. Conversely, some managers may relinquish their responsibilities to the team, although no team can replace the original thinking and courageous decision making of a good manager (Goodall, 1993).

TQM focusses on consumer satisfaction. Consumers, in most cases, are able to evaluate the quality of service and the technical competencies of providers. But, because of the complexities of health care, educational programs are required to help consumers evaluate treatment modalities, and to assume responsibility and make rational decisions for their own care.

Organizing for TQM

The chief executive officer is the mobilizing force in organizing for TQM. Because of the significance of the change, and the need to allocate resources to effect the change, the chief administrator must share his or her vision with the governing board and the senior executive team. The senior executive team manages the transition, and the senior nurse executive and his or her peers articulate the vision to the staff. Client satisfaction is the driving force behind the philosophy of TQM, and the initial step in organizing for TQM is to identify the internal and external customers of the organization.

Based on this information, an implementation plan that integrates TQM principles, the needs of the customer, and the goals and priorities of the organization is developed. The organizational structure is reviewed and changes are made to facilitate decentralized decision making. The result will be a flatter organization, which allows staff to become autonomous practitioners with authority to make decisions for their area of practice (Dubnicki & Williams, 1992). Job descriptions of all employees are redesigned to emphasize expected performance outcomes as opposed to a description of functions. The mandate of existing committees is revised to eliminate duplication and to ensure cross-organizational representation and participation.

An organization-wide quality committee is created to manage the TQM process, and to provide educational programs to employee teams on TQM principles and methods and on problem solving and communication skills. These teams are referred to as cross-functional teams and consist of employees selected to represent their departments. The cross-functional teams resolve cross-departmental issues by reviewing, revising, and implementing changes to existing or new processes (Prevost & Carr, 1991). When the team's mandate is met, the cross-functional team's work is complete.

TQM Process at Work

TQM is initiated at the organizational level, but areas of improvement are usually identified by individual departments or by employees following a performance audit, or by a customer of the service. The TQM process may be put into operation as follows: a problem, or a process in need of resolution or improvement, is identified by an employee or voiced by a customer (Wilson, 1992). The problem is clearly identified and brought to the attention of the manager of the department, who informs the senior administrative team or the quality committee.

The problem is reviewed and, if indicated, the mandate of the team is established and the formation of a cross-functional team, representing all services affected by the problem, is authorized. The mandate may be, for example, to study the chronic shortage of equipment and review the cleaning, repair, and maintenance of equipment, or to review the admission procedure to determine the amount of duplication of activities. A facilitator is appointed to provide training and resources to the members of the cross-functional team. In working through its mandate, the team follows Deming's (1982) Plan-Do-Check-Act cycle, which resembles the scientific method or the nursing process (see Figure 14.1)

Figure 14.1

Deming's cycle (P-D-C-A).

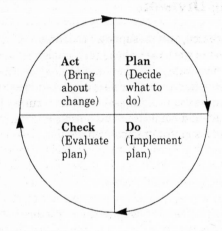

Source: Adapted with permission from E. Marszalek-Gaucher (1992), Total quality management in health care. In M. Johnson and J.C. McCloskey (Eds.), *The delivery of quality health care* (Vol. 3, Series on Nursing Administration). St. Louis: Mosby Year Book, p.112.

A problem or deficient process is examined and the issue is circumscribed. Information is collected and analyzed, and the root of the problem is identified. A number of potential strategies or solutions are suggested, the best alternative is selected, and a plan is drafted to implement the solution. Development of a plan is the first step of the Deming cycle (Plan). Then the plan is implemented (Do) and its effectiveness is tested (Check) against pre-established criteria. If the evaluation is satisfactory, action is taken to adopt the planned change (Act). More than one recommendation may be suggested for implementation, but only one is implemented and evaluated at any one time.

Under TQM, the problem or process is further evaluated for any other contributing factors. If others are identified, the process resumes with the resolution of the problem and resolution of a new plan. The review continues until all required improvements are addressed. Each subsequent evaluation of the same problem or process becomes less costly and time consuming, because the original collected data can be brought to the assessment of the new problem or process. It must be remembered that each subsequent change must support the previous changes. When the team completes its mandate, a report is submitted to the quality committee.

Implementation of TQM to the Nursing Division

As already discussed, TQM presupposes collaboration with the rest of the organization to work toward one goal: quality service. Past experiences have demonstrated that nursing's quality assurance programs were successful in addressing nursing issues but, frequently, interdepartmental issues remained unresolved. This occurred because the programs in place did not address cross-departmental issues, even when these had a significant impact on nursing. To prevent continued fragmentation, all energies need to be redirected to changing the system, and to adopting a model that cuts across all departments and which evaluates all service dimensions.

Katz and Green (1992) propose an evaluation of four main spheres of activity. They are the physical (structure), professional (staff), clinical (recipients of care), and administrative (governance) dimensions of services. The purpose of this division is to facilitate standard development, to "pinpoint problems or special opportunities for improvement" (p. 21) for each sphere of activity, and to create homogeneity between services. This approach facilitates a cross-departmental evaluation process, as each service identifies appropriate standards and corresponding criteria for each dimension. Figure 14.2 (see page 266) shows an example of a cross-functional quality model that can apply to the whole organization or to specific services such as the nursing division.

Commitment to the TQM philosophy is demonstrated when all systems and processes are evaluated and subsequent improvements are made, and each service or division within the organization develops a plan to implement it. To implement TQM within the nursing division, the following eight-step strategy is suggested.

Figure 14.2
Cross-functional quality model.

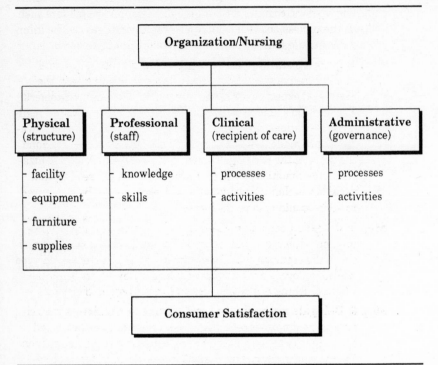

Step 1: Demonstrate leadership. TQM is top management-driven, and the chief nursing officer influences the values and beliefs of the division. The chief nursing officer initially carries out an assessment of the service, and shares her or his vision with all employees of the division. He or she allocates budgets, establishes a reward system, and acts as a coach and a facilitator. Authority is delegated to employees, allowing them to function as autonomous practitioners.

Step 2: Review the organizational structure of the division. The organizational structure is flattened, decision-making authority is delegated, job descriptions are reviewed, and committees are restructured with specific mandates to develop standards and resolve practice issues within the division.

Step 3: Define the customer. The internal and external customers of the nursing division are identified, along with their respective needs. External customers are other services, clients, families, visitors, community groups, suppliers, and regulators such as the professional bodies to which employees belong. The internal customers are employees within the nursing division.

Step 4: Develop standards. Professional, clinical, physical, and administrative standards are developed in keeping with the needs and expectations of the external and internal customers. The division's ability to meet these standards is evaluated regularly. Deviations from the standards are analyzed and improvements are made. When the resolution of the problem is beyond the scope of the nursing division, it is conveyed to the organization-wide committee. The committee reviews the request and decides whether a cross-functional team needs to be structured to address and resolve the issue.

Step 5: Provide education. Educational programs on the philosophy, principles, and operation of TQM are provided to all employees of the organization. Commitment to the program is achieved when employees are familiar with and believe in its benefits. Client teaching is also an integral function of the division.

Step 6: Delegate authority to staff members. Employees participate in the improvement of services when they are delegated the authority to solve problems, streamline processes, question the value of processes, and identify ways to improve or eliminate redundant steps or processes.

Step 7: Facilitate communication. Horizontal and vertical barriers to communication are eliminated. Staff members are regularly informed of individual and organizational performances. Communication between services is expected. Staff members communicate with peers and clients to identify needs and expectations and to seek their participation in decisions.

Step 8: Form teams. Nurses are used to working in teams and have always been aware of the interdependency that exists with other services. In TQM, cross-functional teams are set up to resolve problems or review processes with other individuals or services involved.

A Final Note

It may take up to five years from implementation for TQM to demonstrate its benefits fully. Yet, constant improvements are observed when everyone is committed to the philosophy of TQM and the goals of the organization or division. In nursing, the TQM process, through standard setting, facilitates development and evaluation of a model for professional practice, provides an opportunity for professional development and autonomy, and increases knowledge of operational issues in managing quality improvement projects. This system also enhances communication within and outside of the nursing division and increases the nurse's understanding of the working environment and its behaviours (Dixon, 1993).

Nurses are being asked to evaluate the quality of nursing interventions in terms of significant outcomes and cost savings. It is critical, at this time, that nursing divisions invest time and expertise to support organizational changes to control the use of resources. If nurses do not do so, employers will take it upon themselves to provide more cost-effective nursing care, even if it means pressuring regulators for changes in the practice of nursing.

References

Andrews, H., & Wensel, R. (1992). Promoting physician-nurse collaboration throughout the organization. *Healthcare Management Forum, 5*(2), 28-33.

Canadian Council on Health Facilities Accreditation (CCHFA). (1990). *Quality assurance—The future (outcomes measures project).* Ottawa: Author.

Canadian Council on Health Facilities Accreditation (CCHFA). (1991). *Risk management—A companion document to the CCHFA standards on risk management.* Ottawa: Author.

Canadian Council on Health Facilities Accreditation (CCHFA). (1992). *Utilization management—a companion document to the CCHFA standards on utilization management.* Ottawa: Author.

Canadian Nurses Association (CNA). (1993). *Papers from the nursing minimum data set conference.* Ottawa: Author.

Curran, C.R. (1993). Becoming the best: A case for best practice. *Nursing Economic$, 11*(1), 6.

Deming, W.E. (1982). *Quality, productivity and competitive position.* Cambridge, MA: MIT Press.

Dixon, I.L. (1993). Continuous quality improvement in shared leadership. *Nursing Management, 24*(1), 40-45.

Dubnicki, C., & Williams, J.B. (1992, September/October). The people side of TQM. *Healthcare Forum Journal, 35*(5), 55-61.

Duncan, R.P., Fleming, E.C., & Gallati, T.G. (1991, April). Implementing a continuous quality improvement program in a community hospital. *ORB,* pp. 106-112.

Evans, D., & English, G. (1992). Introducing total quality management. *Nursing Standard, 25*(6), 32-35.

Flower, J. (1990). You can discover the dimensions of quality that your customers most want or the ones that are not being well served by competitors. *Healthcare Forum Journal, 33*(5), 65-68.

Gardner, D.L. (1992). Measures of quality. In M. Johnson & J.C. McCloskey (Eds.), *The delivery of quality in health care* (Vol. 3) (pp. 42-58). St. Louis: Mosby Year Book.

Goodall, R. (1993, May/June). Continuous quality improvement revisited. *Leadership in Health Services, 2*(3), 6-11.

Haywood, F., & Nollet, J. (1991). *Managing service quality. Service plus—Effective service management.* Boucherville, PQ: G. Morin.

Horovitz, J., & Cudennec-Poon, C. (1991, January). Putting service quality into gear. *Quality Progress,* 54-58.

Jones, K.B. (1993). Outcomes analysis: Methods and issues. *Nursing Economic$, 11*(3), 145-151.

Katz, J., & Green, E. (1992). *Managing quality—A guide to monitoring and evaluating nursing services.* St. Louis: Mosby Year Book.

Keenan Widtfeldt, A., & Widtfeldt, J.R. (1992). Total quality management in American industry. *AAOHN Journal, 40*(7), 311-318.

Labovitz, G.H. (1991, March/April). Beyond the total quality management mystique. *Healthcare Executive,* 15-17.

Laffel, G. (1990, November). Implementing quality management in health care: The challenges ahead. *Quality Progress,* 29-31.

Lopresti, J., & Whetstone, W.R. (1993). Total quality management: Doing things right. *Nursing Management, 24*(1), 34-36.

Marszalek-Gaucher, E. (1992). Total quality management in health care. In M. Johnson & J.C. McCloskey (Eds.), *The delivery of quality health care* (Vol. 3) (pp. 71-85). St. Louis: Mosby Year Book.

Prevost, J.A., & Carr, M.P. (1991). Background information and transitional characteristics for surveyors. *Hospital transition to total quality management/continuous quality improvement.* Chicago: Joint Commission Accreditation of Health Care Organizations.

Reiley, P. (1992). Quality assurance programs. In M. Johnson & J.C. McCloskey (Eds.), *The delivery of quality health care* (Vol. 3) (pp. 71-85). St. Louis: Mosby Year Book.

Walton, M. (1986). *The Deming management method.* New York: Putman.

Wilson, C.R.M. (1992). *Strategies in health care quality.* Toronto: W.B. Saunders.

C H A P T E R   1 5

Clinical Advancement Models in Nursing Practice

Sharon Richardson

Sharon Richardson, RN, BScN, MEd, PhD (Alberta), is Associate Professor, Faculty of Nursing, University of Alberta, Edmonton. She is presently the recipient of a two-year postdoctoral award and spent the 1993-94 academic year at the Centre for the Study of the History of Nursing at the University of Pennsylvania, Philadelphia. Her previous experience includes nursing management in an urban hospital, direct patient care in hospital and northern community settings, and teaching in community college and university nursing programs.

Promoting and supporting excellence in clinical practice is one important responsibility of nurse managers. Many managerial activities are directed to this end; planning, organizing, staffing, directing, and controlling functions of nurse managers all relate to ensuring provision of quality client care. The restructuring of health care agencies affords an opportunity for innovation in quality patient care, while encouraging nurses whose primary role is direct patient care to progress in their careers. One mechanism for such restructuring may be the clinical advancement model, also known as the clinical ladder.

This chapter describes how clinical advancement models can foster excellence in clinical practice. It introduces the concept of excellence in clinical practice and reviews how staff nurses historically have been rewarded for their expertise. Then, the essential components of clinical advancement models are outlined, and the history of their development in the United States and Canada is traced. The chapter distinguishes between clinical ladders and career ladders, and concludes by identifying issues associated with clinical advancement models and their implications for nurse managers.

Excellence in Clinical Practice

Competence in clinical practice presupposes that established standards for nursing practice exist, that an individual's performance can be measured accurately, and that those who give direct care can correct deficiencies in the level of performance. To be deemed competent, a staff nurse must be seen to meet the nursing care needs of clients in whatever settings the nurse-client interaction occurs. Competence involves a match between the nursing care needs of clients and the ability of nurses to meet those needs. There is a sufficiency, but not a surfeit, of care delivered.

Excellence in clinical practice relates to superiority or preeminence of performance and implies exceeding others in some way when delivering direct patient care. Competence and excellence are not synonymous. Clinical advancement models are believed to foster excellence by stimulating increased achievement of highly motivated staff nurses and rewarding their expertise. As with competence, excellence in clinical practice also presupposes standards of nursing care and the ability to measure performance accurately. There are, however, no performance deficiencies.

Delivering quality patient care has generally been a priority in nursing. Hospitals, extended care centres, clinics, and community health agencies exist to meet the health care needs of citizens, including their need for nursing service. Matching a patient's level of nursing care need with the expertise of the nurse is an important function of first-line nurse managers. As Grantham and Ross (1988) observe, there has been increasing recognition during the past few years that nursing is practised at a variety of levels of competence. A descriptive assessment of nurses' development of clinical expertise is provided by Benner (1984), who identifies five levels of proficiency as the nurse progresses from novice to expert: novice, advanced beginner, competent, proficient, and expert. Benner defines these stages in terms of how a nurse perceives, assimilates, interprets, and acts in response to clinical situations. The stages are dependent on clinical experience, and Benner concludes that "Experience is therefore a requisite for expertise" (p. 3).

Cost containment as practised in health care agencies today intensifies the need to match clients with nursing personnel capable of meeting their needs. Accurate matching not only optimizes the abilities of individual nurses but also reduces the likelihood of errors or misjudgements in care that could compromise the patient's health status and that could predispose to litigation.

Rewarding Clinical Expertise

Historically, career progression in nursing has involved leaving direct patient care and moving into education or management streams. In part, this is because under the provisions of their collective agreements, most staff nurses reach their highest salary level after seven or eight years of clinical practice. Once this salary level is reached, there are no further monetary incentives for staff nurses to remain at the bedside. The talents of many clinically competent, and some clinically expert, nurses have been lost to patients because of this tendency for clinicians to migrate into nursing education or management to advance their nursing careers. Unfortunately, the skills and knowledge of competent practitioners have not always guaranteed them success in either nursing education or nursing management.

Recent Canadian nursing manpower surveys clearly identified limited rewards for clinical expertise as one of three major reasons why staff nurses expressed dissatisfaction with their jobs (Goldfarb Corporation, 1988; Government of Alberta, 1988; Government of British Columbia, 1988; Hospital Council of Metropolitan Toronto, 1988; Meltz, 1988). In the mid- and late 1980s, extreme job dissatisfaction was perceived as a significant factor in the shortage of nurses. Although changing economic conditions have mitigated this shortage, it is unlikely that staff nurses' dissatisfaction with their jobs is much less today than it was in 1988, since only a limited number of the solutions recommended in these manpower surveys have been implemented. Ways of rewarding clinical expertise recommended in these reports included merit pay, paid educational leave, and clinical advancement models.

Generally speaking, the terms clinical advancement model and clinical ladder are synonymous as these concepts are represented in North American nursing literature. Therefore, they may be used interchangeably. The tendency in Canada is to refer to clinical advancement models and in the United States to refer to clinical ladders. The reasons for this tendency are not known.

Background to Clinical Advancement Models

A clinical advancement model is a means of recognizing and rewarding nurses who choose to remain as caregivers in any setting where nursing is practised. It is also a mechanism for fostering career progression of caregivers so that they need not "leave the bedside." The elements or essential components of a clinical advancement model include: (1) a hierarchy of predetermined levels of practice; (2) criteria to define each performance level; (3) evaluation of nurses' performance for promotion from one level of practice to another; and (4) rewards associated with promotion.

Levels of Practice

Clinical advancement models with as few as two and as many as seven levels of practice have been described in the literature. The majority of models have four levels of practice, although three, five, and six levels of practice have also been described. With the exception of Bernal's (1978) description of a three-level model in a community health setting, all of the models have been implemented in hospitals. Table 15.1 (see page 274) identifies clinical advancement models described in nursing literature by levels of practice. This literature would prove useful to any nurse manager considering use of levels.

Most clinical advancement models are single-track, focussing only on clinical expertise, and are hierarchical in nature, with promotion being available from less expert to more expert levels of practice. A few models are characterized by parallel advancement pathways in administration and clinical practice (Hirsch, 1987; West, 1983) or administration, education, research, and clinical practice (Taylor & Salome, 1984; Weeks & Vestal, 1983). Still others have what Huey (1982) called a "Y-connector" (p. 1521) or branching structure part way up the hierarchical model, which facilitates lateral transfer into management (Gassert, Holt, & Pope, 1982) or, in the case of a hospital in New York, development of either the nurse clinician or the clinical nurse specialist roles (Wieczorek, Weissman, & Savino, 1983). These advancement models might more appropriately be called career models rather than clinical advancement models, since they do not focus solely on direct patient care activities of nurses.

Performance Criteria

Clearly stated and easily measured criteria for clinical performance are an essential element of any advancement model. This is easier said than done. Identifying a framework for organizing the required nursing behaviours of those who give direct care at each level of practice and then measuring these behaviours takes time and care. Huey (1982) notes that, historically, criteria have been based on education and years of experience rather than on behaviourally defined performance. In recent years, increased emphasis has been placed on developing performance criteria that reflect measurable behaviour, and there has been a concomitant decrease in criteria based on education or experience.

Table 15.1
Literature on clinical advancement models by levels of practice.

Two Levels
Jones (1988); Warren (1978)

Three Levels
Balasco & Black (1988); Bernal (1978); Davis (1987); Levine-Ariff (1987)

Four Levels
Aleksandrowicz & Dickau (1983); Bracken & Christman (1978); Broad & Derby (1981); Colavecchio, Tescher, & Scalzi (1974); Deckert, Oldenburg, Pattison, & Swartz (1984); Ebright, Malone, O'Connor, Callihan, Melhorn, Peirce, Taylor, & Wheatley (1984); Grantham, Ross, Mackay, Banfield, Brown, & Beanlands (1989); Kneedler, Collins, Galtas, & Lavery (1987); Knox (1980); Merker, Mariak, & Dwinnells (1985); Metcalf, Werner, & Richmond (1984); Taylor & Salome (1984); West (1983); Wine & Mapstone (1981)

Five Levels
Hirsch (1987); Kreman (1990); Lutz, Thomas, & Becker (1984); Mackinnon & Eriksen (1977)

Six Levels
Nelson & Arford (1977); Sossong, Benson, Ballesteros, Dauphinée, Dolley, Garrick, Gray, Couch, Miller, Pollard, & Smith (1987); Taylor, Watts, Amting, & Cavouras (1988); Vestal (1983); Weeks & Vestal (1983)

Seven Levels
Wieczorek, Weissman, & Savino (1983)

A popular organizing framework for criteria has been the nursing process (i.e., the knowledge and skills required to assess, plan, provide, and evaluate patient care). Another framework that has been used separately, as well as in conjunction with the nursing process, is role delineation. Roles can be related to clinical practice, leadership, research, and education, although various advancement models define these terms differently. For example, education sometimes refers to a nurse's personal participation in continuing professional education, and sometimes refers to patient teaching activity.

Evaluation of Performance

How a caregiver is evaluated and who is involved in the performance appraisal is as important as the criteria used in the assessment. Ideally, clinical performance should be assessed extensively by expert practising nurses. These nurses are peers. Many of the evaluation processes reviewed by Huey (1982) involved no clinical nurse input at all. Others involved minimal peer review. In these instances, evaluation was conducted by the first-line nurse manager, who made promotional decisions alone or in consultation with a supraordinate.

Clinical advancement models do not eliminate performance appraisals. Regularly scheduled evaluations should continue for caregivers, even if they are not moving up the clinical advancement model.

For those nurses wishing to advance to a higher level of practice, it is often necessary that they initiate the review process. This usually involves formally requesting an assessment of performance and collecting documentary evidence to support the claim of increased competency. A committee may be used to review applications for promotion from one level to another. The committee may have authority to decide whether or not to promote, or it may be permitted only to make recommendations to nursing administration, which has the final power to decide. In addition to documentation, the applicant may be interviewed and peers may be invited to make recommendations to the committee. In selected institutions in the United States, Huey (1982) found that nurses were also assessed in terms of competency to remain at their current level of practice, thus leading to the possibility of demotion or termination of nurses who failed to retain previously achieved levels of competency.

Promotional Rewards

A wide variety of rewards, both monetary and nonmonetary, have been associated with promotion in clinical advancement models. Although the National Commission for the Study of Nursing and Nursing Education (Lysaught, 1970) emphatically recommended salary increments both within and between levels of clinical practice to reward increased competence, American health care agencies have not always followed this advice. Some offer titles plus money. Others offer time off and financial assistance to attend professional continuing education. Few offer any authority to affect the clinical practice of less skilled nurses (Huey, 1982). Supporters of monetary reward for clinical advancement argue that level of earned income in North American society reflects success and ascribed status and that if clinical advancement models are to promote clinical excellence and increase bedside nurses' job satisfaction, salaries should be tied to performance rather than seniority.

There have been few clinical advancement projects in Canada, but a large number are reported in the American nursing literature since the early 1970s. What gave rise to the development of clinical advancement models in the United States? How have these models evolved over the years? What might Canadian nurses learn from a retrospective consideration of clinical laddering in American health care agencies? To answer these questions, a brief historical perspective on the development of clinical ladders in the United States and Canada follows.

Historical Perspective

In 1970, the National Commission for the Study of Nursing and Nursing Education in the United States examined and made recommendations about career opportunities and satisfaction of practising nurses (Lysaught, 1970). The Commission concluded that high levels of inactive or nonpractising nurses and high turnover and vacancy rates in hospitals were associated with nurse dissatisfaction in the work environment and were not just the consequence of the predominantly female composition of the profession. Nurses were not practising because they were dissatisfied with working conditions, not because as women this was a common employment pattern for their gender.

The Commission believed that nursing as a profession should develop a long term view of practice. It recommended replacement of the existing "undifferentiated approach" to clinical nursing skill by differentiated levels of practice reflective of increasing expertise and responsibility. The levels of staff nurse, clinical nurse, and master clinician (with appropriate intermediate grades) were recommended to reflect clinical competence. Promotion from one level of practice to another was recommended on the basis of demonstrable knowledge and skills, whether attained through experience, formal education, or self-directed study. Promotion was not recommended solely on the basis of years of experience or formal education. Further, the Commission recommended salary increments both within and between levels of practice to provide financial incentive and reward for increasing competence. Although neither the terms clinical ladder nor clinical advancement model appear in the Commission's report, clearly these were the concepts described. Two years following the publication of the Commission's report, the term clinical ladder first appeared in nursing literature.

American Clinical Ladders

Zimmer (1972) published the first proposal supporting the concept of the clinical ladder in direct patient care. The purpose of a clinical ladder as she conceptualized it was to "implement a system of clinical advancement that recognizes the performance of registered nurses who are concentrating on excellence in practice" (p. 18). Such recognition would "result in a higher rate of retention of nurses in careers in nursing and will secure a higher level of expertise in the delivery of nursing to patients and family" (p. 18). Zimmer cautioned that implementation of clinical ladders alone would not result in increased staff nurse retention, nor guarantee excellence in nursing practice. Concomitant strategies identified as equally important included adoption of the primary care method of patient assignment, unit-based work groups, unit-based clinically expert nurse managers, formalized support for continuing education activities, and other components of professional and administrative reward systems. Nonetheless, Zimmer asserted that recognition of excellence in practice via a clinical ladder was a significant and essential means of retaining bedside nurses and ensuring quality patient care.

The first clinical ladder discussed in literature was the model developed by the University of California Health Care Facilities (Colavecchio, Tescher, & Scalzi, 1974). Four levels of clinical practice, each characterized by behaviourally stated competencies, were described. The purpose of the clinical ladder was to reward clinical competence, knowledge, and performance "both extrinsically and intrinsically" (p. 54). A clear implication of the clinical ladder described by Colavecchio and colleagues was that a decentralized nursing service organizational revision would follow implementation. In such a structure, the traditional role of the nursing supervisor would become obsolete as the authority of the first-line manager and the competence of the caregiver became combined in a single clinician role. The need for nursing administrative services would remain but would be drastically redefined.

Zimmer's (1972) conceptualization of the clinical ladder and her rationale for adopting it served as the framework for the University of Wisconsin Center for Health Sciences system of clinical advancement, described by Anderson and Denyes (1975). Other clinical ladder programs developed rapidly in the United States during the 1970s. Many of these programs incorporated elements of Zimmer's original design (Sanford, 1987). A severe shortage of registered nurses in U.S. hospitals during the early 1980s is credited by French (1988) with stimulating interest in clinical ladders as a hiring and retention strategy. When the supply of registered nurses improved and the demand decreased, French noted that interest in clinical ladders waned.

Barhyte (1987) also acknowledged that an economic recession paralleled implementation of many clinical ladders, making it difficult to discern whether either or both influenced decreased turnover of staff nurses.

Canadian Clinical Advancement Models

The Clinical Promotion Project of the Victoria General Hospital in Halifax is, to date, the only Canadian clinical advancement model described in the literature (Grantham & Ross, 1988; Grantham, Ross, MacKay, Banfield, Brown, & Beanlands, 1989). Identified as part of an overall manpower planning strategy, the purpose of this career advancement program was to retain experienced nurses and recruit new nurses. Four levels of clinical practice derived from a competency-based performance appraisal system were identified.

> *The Clinical Nurse 1 is a beginning practitioner, or a re-entry nurse. The Clinical Nurse 2 is a skilled practitioner. The Clinical Nurse 3 is an advanced practitioner. The Clinical Nurse 4 is a specialist, acts in a consultative role and demonstrates excellence in providing comprehensive nursing care to patients and families with specialized health care needs.* (Grantham et al., 1989, p. 10)

These four levels of practice are hierarchical and reflect increasing clinical expertise. Promotion from a lower to a higher level is based on demonstrated competence. The reward system has not been detailed, although nurses receive no increase in salary as they move up the levels of practice (M. Grantham, personal communication, September 28, 1989).

In early 1989, a committee was established by the Vice-President, Nursing to investigate the feasibility of instituting a clinical advancement model at the University of Alberta Hospitals in Edmonton ("Everything you ever," 1990). A model was developed with three levels of clinical practice, although criteria for only the first two levels, i.e., safe, competent practice and advanced practice, were completed. As a result of hospital restructuring and layoffs of some committee members due to severe budget cutbacks imposed by the Alberta government, work on the clinical advancement model halted in late 1993. The status of the clinical advancement model and its possible implementation is part of the current nursing contract negotiations between the University of Alberta Hospital Board and its local collective bargaining unit of the Staff Nurses Associations of Alberta (H. Montgomery, personal communication, April 19, 1994).

What Is a Clinical Ladder?

The simplest answer to the question of what is a clinical ladder is the one put forward by Huey (1982): "Most nurses, if asked, would probably define a ladder as a means of career recognition and reward for nurses who chose to remain at the bedside" (p.1520). This answer implies increasing levels of demonstrated clinical expertise associated with tangible reward, such as salary increments. Del Bueno (1982) defines a clinical ladder as "a hierarchy of criteria intended to provide a means for evaluation and/or development of nurses providing direct nursing care to patients" (p. 19). She reiterates the perception reflected in most of the published American nursing literature that a clinical ladder system is intended to motivate new and experienced nursing employees, increase nurses' practical skills, and stimulate nurses to remain at the bedside where these skills can be rewarded.

Del Bueno (1982) distinguishes a clinical ladder from a career ladder. The latter is intended to allow people to advance into different job categories, as for example from licensed practical nurse to registered nurse. The Interim Report of the Premier's Commission on Future Health Care For Alberta (Government of Alberta, 1988) also makes this distinction. The Interim Report defines career ladder as "an educational process by which an individual in the nursing field can progress from being a nursing aide to becoming first a registered nursing assistant and then becoming a registered nurse by completing a series of prescribed post-secondary educational programs" (p. 32) and clinical ladder as "a system or path by which a nurse in professional nursing practice can advance in institutional settings through a series of levels or stages based on competencies" (p. 32). Thus, the terms clinical ladder and career ladder are not synonymous, although much confusion is evident in the literature about the distinction between them. This confusion is intensified by use of the terms "clinical career ladder" and "clinical career path," which most often describe variants on the career ladder theme.

Anticipated Outcomes

Two principal reasons are cited for clinical laddering: recruiting and retaining staff nurses and promoting clinical expertise. Various authors have identified a number of outcomes expected from implementation of clinical ladders. Balasco and Black (1988) and Colavecchio and colleagues (1974) identified recognition of highly qualified nurses, differentiation of levels of competence in clinical practice, and guides for evaluation of performance. Utilization of nurses in direct patient care based on their clinical competence, matching of salary levels with performance, and providing for increased levels of autonomy and independent decision making was emphasized by Bracken and Christman (1978). Knox (1980) perceived increased job satisfaction, increased retention of nurses involved in direct care, and motivation for new and experienced nurses to higher levels of practice as important. Del Bueno (1982) summarized rationale for clinical laddering thus:

> Most agencies considering a clinical ladder see it as a means to achieve one or more of the following objectives: increasing recruitment, reducing turnover, increasing job satisfaction, rewarding performance at the bedside, providing a mechanism for peer review, and motivating nurses to stay at the bedside. (pp. 19-20)

In a study designed to investigate the outcomes of clinical ladders in acute care hospitals in the United States, Strzelecki (1989) found that registered nurses identified important outcomes as: (1) differentiation of levels of nursing clinical competence; (2) reinforcement of responsibility and accountability in nursing practice; (3) guiding evaluation of clinical performance; (4) assuring opportunities for professional growth; and (5) providing for increased levels of autonomy and decision making. The 385 registered nurses from 24 hospitals who participated in this study (a response rate of 80%) expressed opinions that suggested they did not perceive clinical ladder programs as critical to their continued employment in the hospital. They also did not perceive that clinical ladders were effective in providing a reward and salary structure commensurate with levels of clinical practice. Findings of this study suggest that there may be some discrepancy between purported outcomes of clinical ladders as described in nursing literature and outcomes experienced by those who give direct care.

Issues Associated with Clinical Advancement Models

There are several issues associated with implementing clinical advancement models in Canadian health care agencies. These include: (1) effectiveness; (2) collective bargaining in nursing; (3) peer review; and (4) financial cost.

Effectiveness

There is a scarcity of research evaluating the effectiveness of clinical advancement models as a strategy to enhance job satisfaction of bedside nurses, reward clinical expertise, facilitate recruitment, and increase retention. Grantham and Ross (1988) were unable to locate any reports that objectively assessed the effectiveness and outcomes of a clinical ladder through a controlled study. Available evaluation research tends to be institution-specific and nongeneralizable to other settings (Sanford, 1987). Additionally, it has been difficult to factor out the effects of such variables as increased supply of registered nurses on reportedly significant findings endorsing use of clinical advancement models (Barhyte, 1987). Although Strzelecki (1989) designed and tested an instrument that could be used to measure the effectiveness of clinical ladder programs, no reports of subsequent studies employing it have been published. It appears that the situation described more than a decade ago by del Bueno (1982) continues today; that is, evaluation data have not yielded particularly impressive results.

Collective Bargaining

By definition, clinical advancement models provide recognition and rewards for individual staff nurses based on merit. This approach is very different from that evident in existing collective agreements, which specify formal employee recognition and salary increments according to number of hours worked. In most Canadian nursing collective agreements, yearly salary increments cease after seven or eight years of satisfactory work experience.

Peer Review

Related to the issue of collective bargaining is peer review. Clinical advancement models are recommended to involve monitoring and evaluating clinical performance by peers rather than by nurse managers. The rationale is that clinical expertise should be assessed by those most clinically competent. Peer review has been perceived as an effective means for a professional group such as nursing to increase its individual and collective autonomy and accountability. Nonetheless, individual nurses may experience difficulty associated with peer review because of limited previous experience with peer review, discomfort evaluating fellow nurses, the need for increased time to engage in peer review, and a possible tendency toward inflated evaluation associated with friendships with fellow employees. The first-line nurse manager may experience difficulty relinquishing control of subordinate performance appraisals and may find the review process and time frame cumbersome. Some nursing unions are clear in their opposition to peer review (United Nurses of Alberta, 1992, pp. 5-6).

Financial Cost

Appropriate rewards for caregivers as they progress through levels of clinical practice are an important issue. Increased status, monetary rewards, use of specific titles, granting of special privileges, increased autonomy, and special "perks" have all been identified as ways of rewarding nurses for improving clinical performance. Of these, monetary reward in the form of salary increments is often cited as the most satisfactory method. Selection of appropriate increment levels and justification of the nursing department budget to support these increments will be important to ensuring the success of clinical advancement models. If the increment levels are larger than those previously negotiated by the unions on the basis of years of nursing work experience, senior administrators will be concerned. If increments are less than previously negotiated under collective agreements, opposition from staff nurses and their unions can be expected. Levels of salary increases for nurses as they progress to higher levels of performance essentially the same as those previously associated with seniority increments may not be acceptable to staff nurses or unions or both. If a staff nurse now receives an almost automatic annual increment for "satisfactory" performance, why should that nurse endorse a clinical advancement model with comparable levels of performance based on measured nursing competencies?

The potential of restricted agency and departmental budgets to impede staff nurses' progression from lower to higher levels of clinical practice should also be considered. If the number of staff nurses who can be promoted in a given year is restricted by budget, the exercise of performance appraisal based on merit becomes meaningless. In identifying American hospitals with clinical ladder programs to participate in her research, Strzelecki (1989) found that nine hospitals had discontinued clinical ladders within the preceding two years because of inability to budget significant salary increases to compensate upper-level clinicians. Six other hospitals planned to discontinue their clinical ladder in the next year for the same reason. Four hospitals that had planned to implement clinical ladders were unable to budget the necessary dollars for upper-level clinicians because of a reduced budget for the nursing department. The cost effectiveness of clinical advancement models is especially relevant in a health care delivery environment characterized by cost containment and impending cost reduction. Vestal (1984) commented that nursing management should expect to "devote a considerable amount of energy to investigating and consolidating financial information that may influence the decision to implement a career ladder program" (p. 8) because the financial implications of clinical ladders may well be the deciding factor in their implementation.

Implications for Nurse Managers

Given the history of clinical ladders, their intended outcomes and the issues associated with implementing them in Canadian health care agencies, what advice might be offered to nurse managers seriously considering clinical advancement models as a way of promoting competence and facilitating excellence in clinical practice?

Why Implement a Clinical Advancement Model?

As a first step, nurse managers should ensure that they are clear in their reasons for thinking that a clinical advancement model would be advantageous. What is it, exactly, that a clinical advancement model is intended to achieve? If the goal is to promote clinical expertise of bedside nurses, what characteristics of the organization currently impede achievement of this goal? Does the health care agency truly value clinical expertise, and is it willing to reward excellence in direct patient care? The question of the purpose or objectives that a clinical ladder should achieve was first asked by del Bueno in 1982. It is still a valid and important question for nurse managers to answer.

What Kind of Clinical Advancement Model?

Once nurse managers have determined that a clinical advancement model will achieve some specified desirable outcome, such as promoting excellence in direct patient care, it becomes necessary to decide the nature and characteristics of the chosen model. How many levels of practice should there be—two, three, four, or more? What criteria will be used for measuring performance? Will performance alone be assessed, or will educational credentials also be considered? How will performance be assessed? Will there be more than a simple checklist of behaviours? Who will participate in the performance appraisal process—peers, nurse managers, others? What incentives and rewards will be offered to bedside nurses to advance in the hierarchy of performance levels? Is there a limit to the number of nurses who can be accommodated at each level of the model? Will there be provision for demoting as well as promoting bedside nurses?

How to Implement

It may be wise to pilot test a clinical advancement model on one or more selected nursing units before determining that implementation can proceed throughout a nursing division. In this way, benefits and limitations of the planned model can be assessed more accurately. Funding for pilot testing may be available from provincial government departments of health if it can be demonstrated that the activity may enhance the quality of nursing work life. Funding may also be available for development of specific components of the clinical advancement model, such as performance appraisal instruments and the process necessary to assess levels of an individual clinician's performance. For example, the Performance Based Development System, which comprises the mechanism for evaluating nursing competencies in the University of Alberta Hospitals' clinical advancement model, was purchased from Performance Management Services, Inc. in early 1991 with the assistance of a grant from the Alberta Department of Health's Nursing Job Enhancement Fund ("The performance," 1992).

When to Implement

Deciding whether nursing staff are ready for a clinical advancement model is a significant factor in successful implementation. As with any planned change, a variety of strategies may be employed both to assess readiness and to promote acceptance by staff nurses. Wicker and Stokes (1990) recommend appointment of a project director to coordinate the multiple decisions. They note that in addition to coordinating various committees, this director "tracks costs of the program, is available to the staff for questions and assistance, provides inservices to promote the program, and acts as a conduit between committees so that various aspects of the program are shared throughout the nursing department" (p. 1). A steering committee with staff nurse membership on its subcommittees is recommended by Wicker and Stokes for policy decisions.

Merker, Mariak, and Dwinnells (1985) perceive that developing and implementing a clinical ladder program involves six phases: convening a task force or ad hoc committee; writing the job descriptions; planning implementation; initiating educational programs and publicity; evaluating the staff and placement; and developing a process for promotion (p. 39). Although their estimated time frame for each phase seems rather ambitious—for example, four months to develop job descriptions and two months to plan implementation—the sequence of activities and behavioural benchmarks within each phase offer direction that may be useful to nurse managers.

Summary

Initially proposed as a strategy to recognize the performance of bedside nurses who are concentrating on excellence in direct patient care, clinical advancement models have since been promoted as a way of enhancing staff nurse satisfaction with their work life, thereby reducing staff turnover and facilitating staff retention. In times of economic constraint, attracting and retaining staff nurses becomes less of a problem; indeed, many hospitals in the early 1990s laid off nurses as a cost-cutting measure. In such an economic climate, turnover and retention become much less an issue.

What remains a significant issue, however, is how to promote clinical competence and foster clinical excellence of nurses engaged in direct patient care. Traditionally, excellence in clinical practice has been rewarded by promotion into nursing management or teaching. There have been no formalized mechanisms to foster and reward clinical competence of staff nurses. Clinical advancement models offer a way of acknowledging clinical expertise and operationalizing a "career" for clinicians at the bedside. More specifically, clinical advancement models enable clinicians to receive rewards equal to those received for moving into management or education, when increased levels of clinical expertise are demonstrated. It is for this reason that clinical advancement models should be considered by nurse managers as one strategy for promoting a more professional role for the bedside nurse.

References

Aleksandrowicz, L., & Dickau, S. (1983). A clinical ladder. *Nursing and Health Care, 4*(9), 510-514.

Anderson, M., & Denyes, M. (1975). A ladder for clinical advancement in nursing practice: Implementation. *Journal of Nursing Administration, 5*(2), 16-23.

Balasco, E., & Black, A. (1988). Advanced nursing practice: Description, recognition, and reward. *Nursing Administration Quarterly, 12*(2), 52-62.

Barhyte, D.Y. (1987). Levels of practice and retention of staff nurses. *Nursing Management, 18*(3), 70-72.

Benner, P. *From novice to expert: Excellence and power in clinical nursing practice.* Menlo Park, CA: Addison-Wesley.

Bernal, H. (1978). Levels of practice in a community health agency. *Nursing Outlook, 26*(6), 364-369.

Bracken, R., & Christman, L. (1978). An incentive program designed to develop and reward clinical competence. *Journal of Nursing Administration, 8*(10), 8-18.

Broad, J., & Derby, V. (1981). Development of a clinical nursing advancement system. *Nursing Administration Quarterly, 6*(1), 33-37.

Colavecchio, R., Tescher, B., & Scalzi, C. (1974). A clinical ladder for nursing practice. *Journal of Nursing Administration, 4*(5), 54-58.

Davis, S. E. (1987). A professional recognition system using peer review. *The Journal of Nursing Administration, 17*(11), 34-38.

Deckert, B., Oldenburg, C., Pattison, K., & Swartz, S. (1984). Clinical ladders. *Nursing Management, 15*(3), 54-55.

Del Bueno, D. (1982). A clinical ladder? Maybe! *Journal of Nursing Administration, 12*(9), 19-22.

Ebright, P., Malone, B., O'Connor, P., Callihan, J., Mehlhorn, P., Peirce, S., Taylor, W., & Wheatley, M. (1984). Clinical ladders? Yes! *Nursing Administration Quarterly, 9*(1), 65-71.

Everything you ever wanted to know about the clinical advancement model. (1990, October). *NUVO: The Nurses Voice*, pp. 6-7.

French, O. (1988). Clinical ladders for nurses: Expect a resurgence of interest but there will be changes. *Nursing Management, 19*(2), 52-55.

Gassert, C., Holt, C., & Pope, K. (1982). Building a ladder. *American Journal of Nursing, 82*(10), 1527-1530.

Goldfarb Corporation. (1988, March). *The nursing shortage in Ontario: A research report for the Ontario Nurses' Association*. Toronto: Author.

Government of Alberta. (1988). *Premier's Commission on Future Health Care for Albertans: Interim report—Caring and commitment: Concerns of nurses in the hospital and nursing home system*. Edmonton: Author.

Government of British Columbia. (1988, August). *Nurse manpower study* (Vol. 1-3). Victoria: Author.

Grantham, M., & Ross, S. (1988). Professional expectations: A career at the bedside. In L. Besel & R. Stock (Eds.), *Benchmarks 2: A sourcebook for Canadian nursing management* (pp. 53-61). Toronto: Carswell.

Grantham, M., Ross, S., MacKay, R., Banfield, V., Brown, J., & Beanlands, H. (1989). Recruiting and retaining competent clinical nurses: The Clinical Promotion Project, Victoria General Hospital, Halifax, Nova Scotia. *Canadian Journal of Nursing Administration, 2*(2), 8-10.

Hirsch, J. (1987). On the scene: Section II—University of California, San Francisco. *Nursing Administration Quarterly, 11*(4), 47-51.

Hospital Council of Metropolitan Toronto. (1988, November). *Report of the HCMT Nursing Manpower Task Force*. Toronto: Author.

Huey, F. (1982). Looking at ladders. *American Journal of Nursing, 82*(10), 1520-1526.

Kneedler, J., Collins, S., Gattas, M., & Lavery, S. (1987). Competency-based career ladders. *Nursing Management, 18*(7), 77-78.

Knox, S. (1980). A clinical advancement program. *The Journal of Nursing Administration, 10*(7), 29-33.

Kreman, M. (1990). Clinical ladders: A retention strategy. *Nursing Management, 21*(7), 23-25.

Levine-Ariff, J. (1987). A clinical ladder: The rungs of implementation.

Nursing Management, 18(12), 63-64.

Lutz, R., Thomas, L., & Becker, M. (1984). Responding to nursing as a dynamic workforce: The personnel perspective. *Nursing Administration Quarterly, 9*(1), 26-40.

Lysaught, J. (1970). *An abstract for action: The Report of the National Commission for the Study of Nursing and Nursing Education.* New York: McGraw-Hill.

MacKinnon, H., & Erikson, L. (1977). C.A.R.E.—A four-track professional nurse classification and performance evaluation system. *The Journal of Nursing Administration, 7*(4), 42-44.

Meltz, N. (1988, November). *The shortage of Registered Nurses: An analysis in a labour market context.* Toronto: The Registered Nurses Association of Ontario.

Merker, L., Mariak, K., & Dwinnells, D. (1985). *The clinical career ladder.* New York: Springer.

Metcalf, J., Werner, M., & Richmond, T. (1984). The clinical nurse specialist in a clinical career ladder. *Nursing Administration Quarterly, 9*(1), 9-19.

Nelson, C., & Arford, P. (1977). Strategy for clinical advancement. *The Journal of Nursing Administration, 7*(4), 46-51.

Sanford, R. (1987). Clinical ladders: Do they serve their purpose? *Journal of Nursing Administration, 17*(5), 34-37.

Sossong, A., Benson, M., Ballesteros, P., Dauphinée, S., Dolley, P., Garrick, E., Gray. P., Couch, D., Miller, P., Pollard, A., & Smith, C. (1987). An expanding universe: Professional career opportunities. *Nursing Management, 18*(2), 46-48.

Strzelecki, S. (1989). The development of an instrument to measure the perceived effectiveness of clinical ladder programs in nursing. *Dissertation Abstracts International,* DA 89-20312.

Taylor, B., & Salome, P. (1984). Mount Sinai's four-track career ladder program. *Nursing Administration Quarterly, 9*(1), 73-81.

Taylor, S., Walts, L., Amling, J., & Cavouras, C. (1988). Clinical ladders: Rewarding clinical excellence. *ANNA Journal, 15*(6), 331-334.

Ter Maat, M., & Werner, P. (1988). Clinical ladders and rehabilitation nurses. *Rehabilitation Nursing, 13*(6), 333, 336-337, 343.

The performance-based development system: Competency-based assessment and development in nursing. (1992, October). *NUVO: The Nurses Voice,* pp. 8-9.

United Nurses of Alberta. (1992, January). *Employers' shared governance programs.* (Available from the United Nurses of Alberta, Edmonton.)

Vestal, K. (1983). Nursing careerism—Challenges for the nursing administrator. *Nursing Clinics of North America, 18*(3), 473-479.

Vestal, K. (1984). Financial considerations for career ladder programs. *Nursing Administration Quarterly, 9*(1), 1-8.

Weeks, L., & Vestal, K. (1983). PACE: A unique career development program. *The Journal of Nursing Administration, 13*(12), 29-32.

West, E. (1983). Keeping talented RNs in hospital practice. *Nursing Management, 14*(8), 38-44.

Wicker, E., & Stokes, S. (1990). Critical decisions in developing a clinical-career ladder. *Recruitment and Retention Report, 3*(4), 1-3.

Wieczorek, R., Weissman, G., & Savino, A. (1983). A clinical career pathway: The Mount Sinai experience, Part 2. *Nursing and Health Care, 4*(6), 318-321.

Wine, J., & Mapstone, S. (1981). Clinical advancement. *Nursing Administration Quarterly, 6*(1), 65-68.

Zimmer, M. (1972). Rationale for a ladder for clinical advancement. *Journal of Nursing Administration, 2*(12), 18-24.

C H A P T E R   1 6

Performance Appraisal

Ardene Vollman and Heather Hartin-Avon

Ardene Vollman, RN, BScN (Saskatchewan), MA (Ed), PhD (Ottawa), is Director, Public Health Nursing, Mount View Health Unit, Calgary. A former nurse educator in Ontario and Québec, she holds adjunct appointments to the Faculties of Nursing and Medicine, Department of Community Health Sciences, University of Calgary. Her research interests include rural public health issues.

Heather Hartin-Avon, RN, BNSc (Queen's), MHA (Ottawa), has diverse clinical nursing experience and is past Member-at-Large, Nursing Practice, on the Board of Directors of the Registered Nurses Association of Ontario. Her primary area of interest within the field of health administration is human resource management. She is Pension Coordinator, National Human Resources, at the Canadian Red Cross Society, and is a casual staff nurse at the Ottawa General Hospital.

Health is a labour-intensive industry; 75% to 80% of total Canadian health care expenditures are allocated to human resources (Martin, 1990). Competition for funding in today's environment is intense, and organizations are faced with the challenge of getting the highest performance from every employee. To do this, managers must know where people can do better and where to focus valuable time, energy, and resources. A performance appraisal system can provide this information.

Performance appraisal is a process by which organizations evaluate employee job performance (Werther, Davis, Schwind, & Das, 1990). It is a process of gathering, analyzing, evaluating, and communicating information about how employees' job-related behaviours and their subsequent outcomes contribute to the achievement of corporate goals and compare to managerial expectations or some established standard to influence and develop performance. Appraisal can be formal or informal. An example of formal appraisal is the annual session that the nurse manager holds with each staff member to discuss his or her performance. Words of praise to commend a staff member for a task well done or to reprimand someone for failing to follow a policy or procedure are examples of informal appraisal.

The mere thought of a performance appraisal generates feelings of frustration and anxiety for both nurse managers and nurses. Nurse managers play a key role in ensuring optimal employee performance. In the words of the Canadian Nurses Association (1988), nurse managers provide for "the allocation, optimum use of, and evaluation of resources such that the standards of nursing practice can be met" (p. 10). Nurse managers must clearly understand the need for and purposes of performance evaluation as well as the relationship of performance evaluation to other human resource functions. In addition, nurse managers must also acquire and develop the skills necessary to evaluate performance and give feedback in a way that minimizes negative feelings, effectively promotes professional and organizational goals, develops people, and, in so doing, yields outcomes that benefit the client, the nurse, and the organization.

A Conceptual Framework for Performance Appraisal

Organizations today have published documents that outline their corporate vision, mission, values, goals, and objectives. As well, organizational structures in the form of charts and statements of departmental roles, functions, and responsibilities are widely circulated. Performance appraisal is not an isolated act; it is a continuous process that is inextricably linked to all organizational activities (Joiner, 1990). Within any organization, four resources (people, money, supplies, and knowledge) are managed and evaluated through standardized procedures appropriate to each resource and to each organization. This system is illustrated in Figure 16.1. A personnel management system is further illustrated to the right side of the model and will be used as a framework for further discussion.

Purposes for Performance Appraisal

Performance appraisals are used for three general purposes. First, they serve an evaluative function whereby information about employee performance is documented, communicated, and used to support administrative decisions. A second use is as a developmental function

Figure 16.1

The role of performance appraisal within an organization.

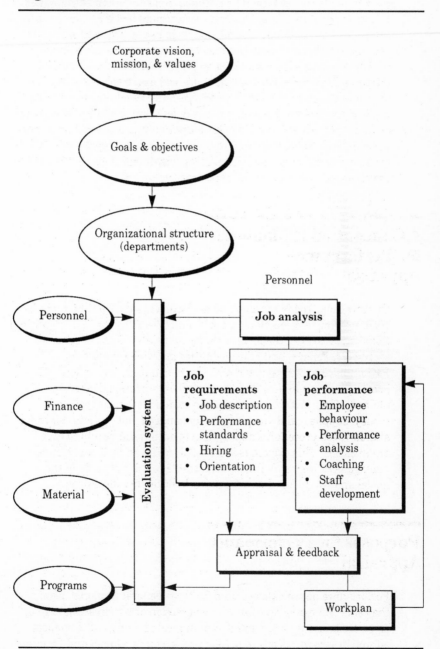

to identify areas for employee growth and to recommend ways of improving performance or enhancing the potential for performance. A third way an organization may use performance appraisals is to monitor the quality of the work force. Data are collected and analyzed to validate that selection procedures and training and development programs are maintaining acceptable standards of performance.

The purpose for which performance appraisal is used has significant implications for nurse managers. The evaluative and monitoring functions of performance appraisal are retrospective in nature. The nurse manager acts as a judge and assesses the value of the staff member's performance in light of previous behaviours and outcomes. Consequently, the role of the staff member in this process is passive or defensive. On the other hand, the developmental function of performance appraisal is prospective. The appraisal is no longer the sole territory of the manager; staff play an integral role to make the exercise interactive and meaningful.

Of the three purposes described above, it is mastery of the development aspect that should excite nurse managers if they aspire to excellence in employee performance. That philosophy is the focus of this chapter.

Restructuring is taking place in the health sector because of the prevailing climate of fiscal constraint. A developmental approach to performance appraisal will foster acceptance of change and a willingness or confidence to explore new practice options. Blitzer, Petersen, and Rogers (1993) have identified several benefits of a development-oriented appraisal system that help to improve individual and corporate performance. Such a system:

- Makes people feel uniquely valuable by creating an environment where staff members feel comfortable expressing their emotions and by rewarding ideas, efforts, and achievements;

- Makes people feel competent by helping to monitor progress toward achieving established goals and helping them to benefit from mistakes;

- Helps people feel secure by acknowledging what is happening in the organization;

- Helps people feel empowered when a nurse manager demonstrates awareness of and interest in their personal development goals and finds opportunities for them to expand their horizons; and

- Allows people to feel connected by the nurse manager's enhancing feelings of acceptance, appreciation, and respect among staff.

Planning the Appraisal Process

New managers and even experienced nurse managers are intimidated by the performance appraisal process. They do not like it because of the time it takes, the discomfort generated when one sits in judgement of another, the barriers that may be raised against rapport, and the fact that the appraisal system requires skills for which many managers feel ill prepared. Because of these very real emotions, managers may shortchange the process, then blame the system. Admittedly, no system is perfect, but careful planning according to the following four steps can reduce the stress on all parties and make the process effective.

Set the organizational context. Review organizational and departmental documents, economic and job forecasts, and trends in service delivery. Survey the literature regularly and maintain an active professional network to use in benchmarking and planning activities (Vaziri, 1992).

Analyze the job and determine its requirements. The foundation of performance appraisal is the job analysis, a description of what the work seeks to accomplish, necessary employee activities or behaviour required by the job, equipment used, factors in the work environment, and human requirements deemed essential for minimally acceptable job performance (Dolan & Schuler, 1987). It provides a framework for developing job-related evaluation criteria for performance. Collate and review job descriptions in light of the job analysis, provincial standards of practice, and special professional interest groups' recommended guidelines. Assess the efficacy of the systems internal to the organization that disseminate information and communicate expected standards.

Examine environmental influences. Policies, regulations, procedures, and standards of care should be reviewed regularly to ensure that they are current, relevant, realistic, and readily available to staff. Facilities, resources, and equipment must be inspected, maintained, and available if nurses are to fulfil their roles effectively. Staff must have opportunities to learn; staff development processes should be assessed.

Consider legal implications. Review and understand the employment contracts, labour code, and other relevant regulations. Ensure that the components of the performance appraisal system are written, job related, objective, easily understood, and up to date, and that they provide for staff input at all stages (Martin & Bartol, 1991).

At each phase of this preliminary preparation process, the nurse manager will be challenged to articulate his or her own philosophy and decide whether appraisal practices match that philosophy and the organizational values. Needless to say, if discrepancies come to light, the manager will need to resolve them by acting within the organizational structure to effect change (a lengthy process) or, after discussion with senior management colleagues and staff, work within the present system while acknowledging its shortcomings to bring a personal, more positive approach to bear on the performance appraisal process in the shorter term.

By reviewing and analyzing the components of the performance appraisal system, the nurse manager will have acquired background understanding of the organization's goals, values, structure, and personnel policies relevant to the appraisal process. This organizational knowledge and self-knowledge will assist in the next stages as appraisal data are collected, documented, and presented to each staff member.

Approaches to Performance Appraisal

To be effective, performance appraisal tools and strategies must address the complex nature of nursing work. A single task may entail many activities and have several outcomes. Ambiguous performance definitions and descriptions threaten the reliability and validity of measurement (Brown, 1988; Carroll & Schneier, 1982; Stone & Meltz, 1988); the key role of job analysis in performance appraisal cannot be stressed enough. Both manager and staff member must have knowledge of and agreement on what is to be done on the job. Clear objectives lead to satisfactory implementation, ease of subsequent measurement, and straightforward performance appraisal. Conflict and disagreement are an inevitable result when goals and tasks are ambiguous. In many cases, such factors as time lag between a nursing intervention and client outcome, multiple personnel, and social characteristics of the environment affect the certainty of cause-and-effect conclusions about performance. This lack of predictability may have an effect on performance measurement. Notwithstanding the difficulty, performance appraisal strategies can be devised that, along with appropriate data collection, documentation, and presentation to staff, meet the needs of the organization to evaluate performance, seek performance gaps, reward exemplary staff, and plan development strategies for individuals and the organization.

In general, managers need to assess two aspects of performance: behaviour and goals (Goodale, 1992). Considering that 85% of all problems in any organization are likely system-related, it is crucial for managers to distinguish between the two (Williams & Howe, 1992). Managers must be concerned not only with goals and objectives, but also with the context in which they were or were not achieved. This is important because, for reasons totally out of their control, staff may not achieve their agreed upon objectives even though their behaviour was appropriate and they tried to compensate for difficulties encountered. The nurse manager should ask not merely what took place, but what problems ensued and what actions the staff member took to try to overcome them (Burdett, 1988).

An employee may be measured or compared against other employees, herself, or some absolute standard (Dolan & Schuler, 1987). When a manager states "X is an excellent employee," it means X is being compared with others; "X has improved herself" means the nurse has done better on some criterion than had been achieved at her last performance appraisal; "X meets the job requirements" means that, compared to the standard set for that task or role, X meets the criteria. These statements contain different underlying conceptual or philosophical frameworks and require different methods of measurement.

To compare one employee to another, the following methods may be used:

- **Straight ranking.** Staff members are listed in order, from the best to worst.

- **Paired-comparison ranking.** Each staff member is compared with all other staff members in the work group.

- **Forced distribution.** This is a bell curve ranking system whereby the manager classifies a certain proportion of staff members in each of a number of categories with respect to performance criteria.

Depending on the appraisal tool, the relative performance comparison can be activity- or task-specific (most valid) or based on overall performance (least desirable).

These appraisal strategies can be time consuming and are most useful for small groups. Although performance ranking assists the manager in identifying strongest and weakest employees, it does not show the magnitude of the differences. Nor is it possible to compare individuals fairly across groups (e.g., nurses working in the public health program in a health unit cannot be compared to those nurses working in the home care program). As well, with forced distribution rankings, the manager is required to focus on how a staff member's performance compares to that of others rather than on how well he or she gets the job done.

To measure job performance against a standard, the nurse manager may employ the following methods:

- Weighted checklist;
- Forced-choice;
- Graphic rating;
- Critical incident;
- Behaviourally anchored rating scale (BARS);
- Behavioural observation scale (BOS); and
- Management by objectives (MBO).

One of the most popular methods is the graphic rating scale. When using a graphic rating scale, the manager indicates the degree to which a staff member demonstrates a particular trait, behaviour, and/or performance outcome. Each scale is a continuum of points from low to high. For example, the scale for measuring the teaching effectiveness of a public health nurse may range from one to five, one being very poor and five being very good. Although graphic rating scales are relatively easy to develop, permit comparisons across groups of nurses, and include several dimensions, there is potential for rater bias and room for interpretation by managers if measures and scale points are poorly defined. In addition, graphic rating scales are criticized because they fail to provide proper performance feedback to staff and are not useful for meeting development needs.

As an appraisal strategy, the behavioural observation scale (BOS) gives a descriptive picture of what the staff person does on the job. When using this method, the manager provides feedback in behavioural rather than personal terms that staff can use to improve job performance. Throughout the appraisal period, the manager records observations of critical incidents and behaviours that are particularly effective or ineffective in accomplishing the job or that are relevant to established criteria within each dimension of performance that is contained in a job analysis. When it comes time for the staff member's formal appraisal interview, the manager refers to his or her written record for the staff member and assigns a numerical score to each observation that reflects the degree to which this behaviour is exhibited. For instance, a sample BOS item used to evaluate competency in the area of nursing process for public health nurses is: "Independently conducts a needs assessment in the target client population on a regular basis to facilitate program revision and development"; the numerical values range from 1, "Almost Never," to 5, "Almost Always." The numerical values serve as a starting point for setting goals and objectives for performance improvement and/or development. BOS is based on a job analysis, its items and scale points are clearly defined, and it is useful for staff development purposes. However, it is time consuming and costly to develop a scale for each job activity within each dimension of performance.

To date, common appraisal methods used in practice have been past-oriented approaches. Even though staff cannot change past performance, feedback from the manager concerning its effect on the work group and the organization serves as an impetus for change in the future. Keeping in mind the developmental function of performance appraisal, strategies and tools should assist the manager to focus on future performance by evaluating staff potential or setting performance goals.

Management by objectives and work standards analysis are useful in determining progress toward goals and how the staff nurse works. Management by objectives is commonly used for developmental purposes. This approach appraises staff members on the basis of mutually agreed upon and objectively measurable performance goals for the future. In general, these goals focus on problem areas that have been identified or on special projects rather than on routine aspects of the job. The manager meets formally and/or informally with staff on a regular basis to measure progress toward the objectives and to provide performance feedback so that, when it is warranted, staff can change their behaviour to ensure attainment of the objectives. The work standards approach is a variation of management by objectives that is more commonly applied when appraising the performance of nonmanagerial employees. In this approach, the manager and employee do not jointly establish future performance goals. Instead, the organization determines these goals based on what has been done on the job in the past, how staff allocate their time among various job activities, and the length of time it takes to carry out a specific task under particular circumstances. Priority setting, decision making, and other processes can be illustrated using both methods.

In practice, both the management by objectives and work standards approaches have drawbacks. If objectives are too ambitious or too narrow, staff may become frustrated or dimensions of job performance may be overlooked. In addition, the essence of job performance may not be captured by established goals. A further disadvantage of the work standards approach is that the reliability and validity of the data suffer if staff are not willing to cooperate in setting the goals by articulating what they do in their job and the importance of the tasks.

In most organizations, a combination of the above methods is used. In health service settings, using a multifaceted approach will make it easier for the nurse manager to provide staff with a reliable and valid performance appraisal that addresses all dimensions of the complex and dynamic nature of nursing. The preceding discussion is intended to serve as a framework for the nurse manager to understand the approach to appraisal that the organization has taken, how to present and discuss the data during the appraisal interview, and how to assess and suggest to management which methods are most appropriate to his or her setting.

Gathering Performance Data

The nurse manager can gather performance data through three main methods: appraisal by the nurse manager or other supervisor delegated for the job; self-appraisal by the employee; or peer review. Each has positive aspects, but could have some limitations of which managers need to be aware.

Appraisal by Supervisor

Gathering information for performance appraisal is a continuous process. It does not preclude the immediate positive and negative feedback the nurse manager gives on a day-to-day basis throughout the appraisal period. It should illustrate performance behaviours and assist in bringing gaps to light and in planning for the future.

A file system of some sort should be put in place that allows the manager to record critical incidents and other anecdotal notes that illustrate staff behaviours relating to the tasks and activities inherent in the job. This may be an informal system for the satisfactory staff member, or might be more formal if specific documentation is required for disciplinary purposes. Nevertheless, both types of file systems can provide an effective paper trail in the event that a performance-related issue is disputed by a staff member (Scholtes, 1993).

Data from as many sources as possible should be collected. In many health institutions there are systems in place that track quantitative data on individuals, work units, and the department. As well, attendance information should be included in the data used for appraisal purposes. Getting input from multiple sources provides a larger database for decision making and enhances the reliability of job performance data. It also makes it possible to capture the essence of nursing work to a greater degree. Client satisfaction measures are occasionally used, and keeping track of unsolicited "beefs and bouquets" from professional colleagues within and external to the work group is also a helpful data source. There are tools available that can be considered for use by work groups and committees to measure effectiveness of performance and contribution to group outcomes.

Self-appraisal and peer review are also useful methods that, in conjunction with supervisor input, provide multiple sources of data to describe and measure the complex nature of nursing.

Self-Appraisal

Whether the appraisal technique is past- or future-oriented, requiring staff to conduct a self-appraisal can be beneficial if the performance appraisal process in the organization focusses on professional development and personal growth. Self-appraisal is becoming an increasingly common component of performance appraisal because it is part of the trend toward employee empowerment and participative management and enhances staff involvement in and commitment to the process of improving performance. As a form of performance evaluation, it has the following strengths:

- It is perceived by staff members as more satisfying than other methods and is more effective in reducing defensiveness when confronting problem areas or weaknesses (Northcraft & Neale, 1990);

- The supervisor has the opportunity to listen to how the staff member perceives the work environment and can then act upon this new information;

- Differences between the performance expectations of a supervisor and staff member can be clarified (Northcraft & Neale, 1990); and

- It can be a significant predictor of successful and speedy assimilation into a new role or setting (Ashford, 1990).

There are disadvantages associated with self-appraisal:

- Inexperienced employees may not have clearly established performance standards or professional goals by which to assess their performance and are likely to use a different frame of reference than the supervisor (Northcraft & Neale, 1990);

- Employees must balance the desire to analyze what they ought to be doing and how well they have performed their jobs with the ego threat of negative feedback. Immature or insecure employees may find this task a formidable challenge;

- Employees who frequently seek feedback and information about aspects of their job performance from the supervisor may be perceived as exhibiting weakness or insecurity (Ashford, 1990); and

- Unions may view self-appraisal as an abdication of management duties.

When employees underestimate their abilities, the organization loses the benefits of their efforts. In this instance, a staff member may not persist at a project even though the potential payoff is high. His or her aspirations may be reduced, precluding application for or acceptance of advanced roles that he or she may be capable of handling with some mentoring. In an alternative scenario, staff members may believe their performance is commendable, but they are expending their time and energy on activities that are directed toward goals in which the organization has no vested interest. For example, a community health nurse may have an interest in the impact of a hysterectomy on a woman's sexuality and bases her self-appraisal on all the things she is doing to assist this group of women. However, if the demographics of the population served by the health unit are such that few women would be candidates for a hysterectomy (e.g., a growing community with young families), the health unit has no vested interest in the nurse's goal to help this target group to the exclusion of services to higher-priority aggregates.

To take advantage of the benefits of self-appraisal and minimize negative consequences, the nurse manager is advised to:

- Maximize the amount of performance standard and feedback information given to staff members by holding more frequent informal appraisal sessions, including both positive and negative feedback;

- Foster an environment that affirms negative feedback as useful in terms of professional development and personal growth;

- Carefully balance the professional development and personal growth needs of employees with the organization's mission and corporate goals;

- Support self-appraisal by a mentoring or coaching system to instil an appropriate balance of realism into staff members' opinions of their skills, capabilities, and past performances;

- Consider using self-appraisal in conjunction with peer review to increase staff members' awareness of the impact of their behaviour on co-workers (Bader & Bloom, 1992); and

- Seek opportunities for professional development so that managers become comfortable with assuming mentoring and coaching roles.

As organizations continue to operate in an increasingly dynamic and complex environment, their internal control systems, such as performance appraisal, may also be in flux. In such situations, managers may become increasingly dependent on the self-management practices of their staff members.

Peer Review

Peer review is the process of having work performance evaluated by co-workers or colleagues of equal rank against established criteria or competencies. It is based on the principles of professional autonomy, accountability, and collegiality. McEvoy, Buller, and Roghaar (1988) outline the advantages of peer review:

- Peer ratings are reliable and valid judgements of employee behaviour;
- Peer ratings routinely have higher predictive validity than do supervisory ratings;
- Peer ratings are more stable over time than supervisory ratings and are more likely to focus on performance and results (outcomes) than effort expended (input);
- Peer review can foster more frequent and appropriate feedback that points out specific areas for improvement and is validated from several sources;
- Managers are provided with another option for input into employee performance evaluation; and
- Employee levels of professionalism and accountability to the work team can be enhanced through the peer review process.

Like self-appraisal, peer review is part of the management trend toward empowering staff (Spragins, 1991). As organizations have become flatter, managers are encouraging self-appraisal, personal and team goal setting, and team accountability. According to Gerstner, McAllister, Wagner, and Kraus (1988), peer review in nursing is a method of quality control and consumer protection that exemplifies a commitment to professional autonomy and the promotion of excellence in practice.

Concerns expressed about peer review programs include:

- Leniency or bias in ratings because of friendships, or fear of retaliation;
- Co-workers may not be fully aware of another's major job dimensions;
- The possibility of undermining the authority of a supervisor if control over ratings is relinquished;
- Difficulty maintaining confidentiality of ratings and anonymity of raters;
- It can be time consuming and resource intensive in terms of development and implementation;

- There may be tension created within work groups that interfere with cooperation; and

- Unions are generally against what they view as workers assuming management tasks.

Many of these concerns are not exclusive to peer review; the same criticisms are raised for other methods.

Peer review can be successfully introduced into a nursing workplace when there is support at all levels of administration and unit-level factors that can facilitate the process have been identified (Gerstner, McAllister, Wagner, & Kraus, 1988). Administrators must be willing to incur the direct and indirect costs associated with the time and effort invested in the implementation of a peer review process, not simply give lip service to it (Williams & Howe, 1992).

No one peer review process is appropriate for all organizations. A host of options concerning measurement tools and the range of performance to be assessed and participation options, procedures, training, and orientation need to be considered in the design phase. However, guidelines that will facilitate implementation and enhance acceptance of peer ratings include:

- Develop a performance management system that is derived from the organization's mission statement and corporate goals and is supported by written policies that clearly communicate objective criteria and competencies;

- Build on what is already working well in the organization's current performance management system;

- Develop the process cooperatively with administrators and staff members;

- Integrate peer input with some form of self- and supervisory appraisal;

- Assure the confidentiality and anonymity of peer ratings;

- Make peer feedback on a day-to-day basis a process goal;

- Recognize that building group process and interpersonal communication skills is critical to a constructive process;

- Market the potential benefit of multiple-rater systems;

- Address participants' concerns in a straightforward manner; and

- Be receptive to participants' suggestions for refining and improving the process.

The degree to which staff members are comfortable with the peer review process depends upon the history of the work unit, the extent to which it has developed as a team, and the level of trust that staff members have in each other and in their supervisor. Effective interpersonal communication is the foundation of a constructive peer review process; reciprocal responsibilities of team members and supervisors are key factors in achieving the ultimate goals of peer review. Although the potential advantages of peer ratings are well documented in the literature, peer review remains largely underutilized as a tool for responding to the performance pressures of the 1990s (Bader & Bloom, 1992; Buhalo, 1991).

For the nursing profession, the potential benefits extend beyond the organization. The profession will benefit from the heightened autonomy that is realized when nurses communicate more effectively with one another, assume increased personal and peer accountability for evaluation, and think more critically about their own and their peers' practice. In turn, the public will benefit from the profession's commitment to the promotion of excellence in practice.

Presenting the Data

The formal interview is the principal component of the performance appraisal process and it is the most challenging one for managers (McAlister, 1993). Nurse managers must carefully prepare for the interview. If it is not conducted properly, staff members will not know any more about where they stand after the session than they did before, and opportunities to promote or enhance professional development and personal growth will be missed.

The appraisal interview is the culmination of the impromptu meetings with and informal positive and negative feedback given to staff since their previous performance appraisal interview. There should be no surprises in this session! By the time the formal appraisal is held, both nurse manager and staff member should have a good idea of how things are going. Boissoneau, Gaulding, and Calvert (1989) describe three phases within the interview process:

Preview. Set the stage. Reiterate both the organizational philosophy of performance appraisal and the job-specific performance criteria. Give staff time to prepare a self-assessment. Set the time, place, and agenda for the interview. The interview should be on work time, not a day off, so plan how you will relieve the staff member from duties for the duration of the interview. Prior to the interview, take time to reflect on the communication style, likes and dislikes, interests, and motivations of each staff person and plan your approach accordingly.

Interview. Carry out the discussion. Hold the interview in private, free of interruptions. Defuse any anxiety; show empathy. Articulate your expectation of full participation, reiterate goals for the meeting, review the agenda. The staff nurse should present his or her self-appraisal first; then the manager provides feedback, starting with positive points and areas of agreement. Discuss and resolve areas of disagreement, using a problem-solving stance to reduce the emotional charge (Malinauskas & Clement, 1987). Conclude the session by working with the staff member to identify needs, establish goals and objectives, and devise a plan of action to facilitate professional development and personal growth. This work plan should outline the activities, tasks, or responsibilities on which the staff member will focus for a specified period of time, the steps that need to be undertaken to accomplish the items identified, and the expected results (Schwartz, 1993). After the interview, the nurse manager prepares a written summary of the session to be read and signed by the staff member and placed on the personnel file. There should be no surprises in the summary; no new job-performance feedback, positive or negative, should be included.

Review. Conduct regular feedback sessions. Performance feedback is a continuous process, not a periodic activity. The work plan provides the basis and focus for future planning and feedback sessions to discuss progress and make necessary adjustments. Staff development activities can be planned and outcomes evaluated during this phase. Use coaching and mentoring processes to foster achievement of the goals and objectives set in the interview.

The role of documentation during all phases is critical. The benefits to the organization of well-documented performance appraisals are great; the risks of poor documentation are high. Organizations use performance appraisals when making significant human resource decisions; this creates the potential for conflict and misunderstanding between the employer and staff and is a factor in the trend toward increasing litigation (Martin & Bartol, 1991). In general, the employer will be able to mount a more convincing argument for the legitimacy of its actions when performance appraisals are on file that document related performance issues. In addition, the potential for an employer to be sued for libel based on what nurse managers write in staff members' performance appraisals can be minimized if the statements are based on performance criteria that are concise, objective, and easily understood by all parties involved (Saxe, 1988).

The nurse manager's written comments must reflect a thorough, clear, and precise analysis of the reasons behind the staff member's job-performance strengths and weaknesses. Generalizations tend to take weaknesses out of context and overemphasize them; ambiguous wording can lead to an inaccurate and incomplete summary of performance. Cyr (1993) outlines a seven-step process that can guide the nurse manager in preparing written comments.

- Select and focus on a job activity, an individual, observable responsibility, or task;

- Indicate the degree to which this activity or task is performed or responsibility carried out;

- Describe when or where the observed performance happens, with whom it happens, under what circumstances, and during what type of activity or task;

- Suggest an influential factor that positively or negatively affects the activity, task, or responsibility in question. These factors may stem from the individual staff member, the organization, or the external environment. Be careful not to make inaccurate inferences or draw false conclusions;

- Point out trends in the improvement, decline, or maintenance of job performance levels. When a behaviour occurs once, it is an incident; twice is a coincidence; three times is a pattern (Smith, 1993). The activity, task, or responsibility under discussion should be part of an observed pattern, not an isolated incident or a one-time uncharacteristic behaviour (Ilgen & Feldman, 1990);

- Give an example, a "representative instance" of a situation, that involves the activity, task, or responsibility under discussion that is drawn from an observed trend in job performance; and

- Show consequences, the short- and long-term outcomes of the job activity, so that the nurse sees his or her work in terms of its effect on others and how it contributes to overall organizational success.

Current Developments

As management paradigms shift from control to democracy and empowerment, organizations are seeking ways to involve subordinates, clients, and others in performance assessment and quality management. The three most notable developments are: upward/reverse appraisal, 360-degree feedback, and total quality management (TQM). These processes each have strengths and limitations and require a major organizational commitment to change if they are to be implemented.

Upward/Reverse Appraisal

The attitudes and behaviours of managers ultimately affect overall corporate functioning (Ludeman, 1993). More organizations are recognizing that staff members are in the best position to provide information on management performance. As a result, greater attention is being given to staff participation in appraisal of their immediate supervisor's performance (Buhalo, 1991; Milne; 1993). This method is referred to as upward feedback or reverse appraisal.

In day-to-day interactions with the immediate supervisor, staff members are the recipients or consumers of managerial practice and are able to observe leadership behaviours (Tornow, 1993). Many managers may be unaware of how they are perceived by their staff members and, therefore, a performance appraisal system that elicits input from staff members enhances the managers' self-awareness of their strengths and weaknesses (Dolan & Schuler, 1987). Accepting this feedback provides guidance on the skills that need improvement for better management and leadership and in turn can enhance the working relationship between the manager and staff members so that the manager is able to contribute to overall organizational effectiveness (Ludeman, 1993; Milne, 1993; Northcraft & Neale, 1990; Tornow, 1993). An additional advantage to allowing employees to review their manager's performance formally is that the process serves as a strong motivator by demonstrating that staff opinions are valued (Milne, 1993). However, fear of reprisal, the nature of the relationship between staff members and their supervisor, lack of understanding of the principal responsibilities of their manager, and diverging ideas regarding the important performance criteria related to job success can impede the accurate appraisal of the leadership and management potential of the supervisor (Dolan & Schuler, 1987; Northcraft & Neale, 1990).

Upward feedback/reverse appraisal programs exist in various forms (Buhalo, 1991; Ludeman, 1993). The program may be voluntary in nature and used only as a development tool, with comments and recommendations not shared with anyone other than the manager being reviewed. In a second form, upward feedback/reverse appraisal can serve as part of the formal appraisal system, and as such, is mandatory. In organizations utilizing this approach, higher levels of management receive the final results. In some organizations, across-the-board standards comprise the upward feedback or reverse appraisal program; in others, managers are involved in and have ownership of the program and develop their own process with staff members.

The drive toward increased effectiveness is forcing organizations to develop a corporate culture characterized by a focus on quality and employee empowerment. Since managers' attitudes and behaviours ultimately affect organizational functioning, upward feedback/reverse appraisal provides guidance on the skills that need development for improved management and leadership and helps them to "walk their talk" (Ludeman, 1993).

Managers who opt into this process have an effective means of role modeling positive responses to the performance appraisal system—openness to feedback, acceptance of criticism and praise, nondefensive responses, and assertive seeking of important and relevant information related to job performance objectives and standards. Upward feedback/reverse appraisal also demonstrates a commitment to looking at both sides of the work environment and developing a more professional relationship with staff members (Milne, 1993), a commitment that will benefit the health service delivery sector, the individual organization, the staff member, and the client.

360-Degree Feedback

Organizations are becoming more consumer-driven and, therefore, staff need to receive performance feedback from external and internal consumers. Internal consumers, such as staff in other departments, will become important sources of performance feedback as restructuring creates flatter organizations where front-line staff work more independently and interact directly with others rather than using supervisory intermediaries.

The term 360-degree feedback is popularly used to refer to the practice of integrating objective performance feedback from an employee's supervisor(s), peers, direct reports, customers, and self-ratings to provide an accurate, comprehensive summary of his or her skills, abilities, styles, and job-related competencies (Nowack, 1993). This practice builds on the merits of multiple ratings. For example, the recipient of the feedback receives valuable information from diverse perspectives about how others view his or her performance and gains insight into strengths and weaknesses, both of which can guide plans for professional development. Edwards (1990) claims that this team approach to performance evaluation reduces two of the problems associated with top-down appraisals: the immediate supervisor who does not promote an employee whose performance at work makes the supervisor look good, and the supervisor who focusses on upper management's needs rather than those of the employee. The perceived disadvantages of 360-degree feedback are similar to those associated with peer review and upward feedback/reverse appraisal.

The 360-degree feedback method gives a holistic picture of one's performance at work. It is a powerful tool. It can assist staff to acknowledge and accept critical feedback and thus lead to better job performance. If an organization is to survive and thrive in these times of economic constraint, continuous quality improvement initiatives, and competitive challenges, all staff members must strive to make optimal contributions to the organization.

Total Quality Management

Total Quality Management (TQM), discussed in Chapter 14, has a number of implications for performance appraisal. Advocates of TQM suggest that this new approach is incompatible with the traditional performance appraisal system (Scholtes, 1993). TQM is built upon basic concepts and values that reflect a consumer focus, systems thinking, teamwork, and continuous improvement. Traditional performance appraisal goes against these requirements, given that it is primarily focussed on individual performance. Under TQM, managers will need to relinquish the old paradigm of the nature of work and the purpose of leadership. It is not realistic to abandon professional standards of practice, so nurse managers will be faced with ensuring that these are maintained in a TQM environment.

Role of the Professional Regulatory Body

Since nursing is a self-regulated profession governed by acts in each province and territory, the provincial regulating bodies share with the employers of nurses the responsibility for assessing competence and protecting the public. In most provinces, the relevant act defines professional misconduct and incompetence. The complaints procedure is generally outlined in the act and is well documented in the association (or college or order) bylaws. All nurse managers must be thoroughly familiar with these acts and refer to them regularly.

Associations also provide consultation services to all members, managers and nurses alike, through professional nursing consultant staff. Several also publish useful resource documents. The Registered Nurses Association of British Columbia (RNABC), for example, may, during the licensing process, request references or performance appraisals on applicants. The nurse manager is most often the source for completion of these documents. RNABC forms are based upon the standards of nursing practice, and a booklet outlining practice indicators for each standard is included in the request for information.

It is an unfortunate reality of corporate life that not all employees are exemplary performers. Complaints are received by professional regulatory bodies, and investigations may be conducted as warranted by the nature of the complaint. Complaints may come to the professional regulatory body from many sources: manager, colleague, physician, or member of the public. In Nova Scotia, 25% of complaints received are filed by the manager. In this case, the manager becomes a key witness to the professional discipline committee of the association. When complaints are filed from other sources, the manager may be witness for the association or the nurse. Managers may also be called to give information on policies, procedures, and generally accepted practice within a specific unit (see also Chapter 30). In terms of performance appraisals, nurse managers are often questioned on policies of their institutions with regard to these evaluations. In addition, they would be asked to speak to the content of the performance appraisals. The Registered Nurses Association of Nova Scotia further indicates that, many times, the appraisal does not reflect the problems that are before the discipline committee, even though verbal evidence supports the issues and often supports the fact that the problems have been of a continuing nature. It is extremely difficult to justify disciplinary actions legally under these circumstances.

Conclusion

Performance management processes include the recruitment, selection, and orientation of staff; performance appraisal; and employee communication, training, and development. Performance appraisal is linked between human resources and clinical managers to quality assurance and program evaluation processes. In the health sector, where the staffing costs can reach 70% to 80% of the total budget, it is vital that personnel perform optimally. It is also critical for managers to allocate dollars, time, and energy where they can have the most impact on organizational effectiveness and efficiency. A performance appraisal system that reflects the mission, vision, values, goals, and objectives as well as the shifting paradigms in management and organizational processes and structures is key to ensuring optimum outcomes for clients and effective utilization of all resources.

References

Ashford, S.J. (1990). Self-assessment in organizations: A literature review and integrative model. In L.L. Cummings & B.M. Staw (Eds.), *Evaluation and employment in organizations* (pp. 59-100). Greenwich, CT: JAI Press.

Bader, G.E., & Bloom, A.E. (1992). How to do peer review. *Training & Development, 46*(6), 61-2, 64-6.

Blitzer, R.J., Petersen, C., & Rogers, L. (1993). How to build self-esteem. *Training & Development, 47*(2), 58-60.

Boissoneau, R., Gaulding, D.J., & Calvert, D.N. (1989). Performance appraisal as a strategic choice for the health care manager. In A.S. Sethi & R.S. Schuler (Eds.), *Human resource management in the health care sector* (pp. 95-126). Westport, CT: Greenwood Press.

Brown, R.D. (1988). *Performance appraisal as a tool for staff development.* San Francisco: Jossey-Bass.

Buhalo, I.H. (1991). You sign my report card I'll sign yours. *Personnel, 68,* 23.

Burdett, J. (1988). Results driven performance appraisal. *The Human Resource, 5*(1), 19-21.

Canadian Nurses Association. (1988). *The role of the nurse administrator and standards for nursing administration.* Ottawa: Author.

Carroll, S.J., & Schneier, C.E. (1982). *Performance appraisal and review systems.* Glenview, IL: Scott Foresman.

Cyr, R. (1993). Seven steps to better performance appraisals. *Training & Development, 47*(1), 18-19.

Dolan, S.L., & Schuler, R.S. (1987). *Personnel and human resource management in Canada.* St. Paul: West.

Edwards. M.R. (1990). An alternative to traditional appraisal systems. *Supervisory Management, 35*(6), 3.

Gerstner, M., McAllister, L., Wagner, P.L., & Kraus, C. (1988). Peer review. In S.E. Pinkerton & P. Schroeder (Eds.), *Commitment to excellence: Developing a professional nursing staff* (pp. 199-209). Rockville, MD: Aspen Publishers.

Goodale, J.G. (1992). Improving performance appraisal. *Business Quarterly, 57*(2), 65-70.

Ilgen, D.R., & Feldman, J.M. (1990). Performance appraisal: A process focus. In L.L. Cummings & B.M. Staw (Eds.), *Evaluation and employment in organizations* (pp. 1-57). Greenwich, CT: JAI Press.

Joiner, C.L. (1990). Performance appraisal. In N. Metzger & E.A. Guggenheim (Eds.), *Handbook of health care human resources management* (2nd ed.) (pp. 199-214). Rockville, MD: Aspen Publishers.

Ludeman, K. (1993, May). Upward feedback helps manager walk the talk. *HRMagazine,* pp. 85-93.

Malinauskas, B.K., & Clement, R.W. (1987). Performance appraisal interviewing for tangible results. *Training & Development, 41*(2), 74-9.

Martin, D.C., & Bartol, K.M. (1991). The legal ramifications of performance appraisal: An update. *Employee Relations Law Journal, 17*(2), 257-286.

Martin, J.-C. (1990, October 10). Executive in Residence, Faculty of Administration, University of Ottawa. Personal communication.

McAlister, J. (1993). Appraisal interviews do's and don'ts. *Supervisory Management, 38*(4), 12.

McEvoy, G.M., Buller, P.F., & Roghaar, S.R. (1988). A jury of one's peers. *Personnel Administrator, 33,* 94-6, 98, 101.

Milne, J.L. (1993). Should employees review their supervisors? *Canadian Manager/Manager Canadien, 18*(1), 5.

Northcraft, G.B., & Neale, M.A. (1990). *Organizational behavior: A management challenge.* Toronto: Dryden Press.

Nowack, K.M. (1993). 360-degree feedback: The whole story. *Training & Development, 47*(1), 69-72.

Saxe, S.D. (1988). Do performance appraisals violate the Human Rights Code? *The Human Resource, 5*(2), 18-9.

Scholtes, P.R. (1993, Summer). Total quality or performance appraisal: Choose one. *National Productivity Review,* pp. 349-363.

Schwartz, A.E. (1993). A performance work plan and development plan. *Supervisory Management, 38*(1), 8-9.

Smith, M.L. (1993). Give feedback, not criticism. *Supervisory Management, 38*(2), 4.

Spragins, E.E. (1991). Measuring performance—Making peer review work. *Inc., 13*(10), 161, 163.

Stone, T.H., & Meltz, N.M. (1988). *Human resource management in Canada* (2nd ed.). Toronto: Holt, Rinehart & Winston.

Tornow, W.W. (1993). Editor's note: Introduction to special issue on 360-degree feedback. *Human Resource Management, 32*(2/3), 211-219.

Vaziri, H.K. (1992, October). Using competitive benchmarking to set goals. *Quality Progress,* pp. 81-85.

Werther, W., Davis, K., Schwind, H., & Das, H. (1990). *Canadian human resource management* (3rd ed.). Toronto: McGraw-Hill Ryerson.

Williams, T., & Howe, R. (1992). W. Edwards Deming and total quality management: An interpretation for nursing practice. *JHQ, 14*(1), 36-39.

C H A P T E R   1 7

Organization of Patient Care

Bonnie L. Lendrum

Bonnie L. Lendrum, RN, BScN, MScN (Toronto), has developed a breadth of management experience in both community and hospital nursing. She has practised in both Québec and Ontario, and is Director, Nursing Education and Professional Development at Chedoke-McMaster Hospitals, Hamilton, Ontario.

Nursing care can be provided successfully to patients in any one of four principal care delivery models. There is no "right" or "best" model in an absolute sense; the literature is equivocal about benefits and outcomes for patients, nurses, and organizations (Giovannetti, 1986; Irvine & Evans, 1992; MacDonald, 1988). Nursing care delivery models are structures that support specific beliefs about the work of nurses, about patient care, and about organizations. Such models can inspire the work of nurses but can just as easily dispirit nursing work. Although care delivery models are not philosophies of nursing, each represents certain philosophical leanings. Knowing and understanding the departmental and unit philosophy is an important step in the process of selecting a model.

The selection of a care delivery model that is right for the organization is a significant undertaking for the nurse manager. Extensive consultation with all stakeholders is an important phase of exploring current values and beliefs and gaining commitment to additional ones. Selecting one model over another is an implicit and explicit process of stating beliefs about people (patients, their families, and nurses) about work (autonomy, responsibility, decision making, and expertise), about relationships (therapeutic, hierarchical, collegial), and about professional practice. The selection of a care delivery model is one instance where the process is as important as the outcome.

In this chapter, four principal care delivery models—functional nursing, team nursing, primary nursing, and case management—will be reviewed briefly, and the assumptions underlying each model will then be identified and discussed in detail. The criteria and process for the selection of a single model will be identified and the selection process will be discussed.

Functional Nursing

Functional or task-centred nursing began in the 1950s. A combination of factors (chemotherapy revolution, World War II, and a societal acceptance of hospitals) created a shortage of registered nurses. Nurses' aides were trained on-site to provide nursing care. The belief system upon which functional nursing rests is rooted in classic scientific management circa 1920 (MacPhail, 1988). That system was useful when North America was shifting from an agrarian economy to a manufacturing base and when the average worker was semi-literate. The beliefs at that time about efficiency, division of labour, and rigid controls were explicit and were accepted by workers. The introduction of functional nursing 30 years later in the 1950s illustrates the acceptance of beliefs about people and work that had become implicit.

Functional nursing as it derived from scientific management emphasized efficiency, division of labour, and control. Efficiency and division of labour were present in such designations as "medication nurse" and "treatment nurse." These nurses would be assigned to administer all medications or treatments to a geographical cluster of patients during the shift; the entire shift could easily be spent administering and recording all medications or treatments.

Control was evident in the written procedures that guided the work of bedside nurses. Most of these nurses were in fact either student nurses or lay workers; because they were either unskilled or in the process of acquiring skill, their work was standardized, recorded in procedural format, and closely supervised by a head nurse.

Hierarchy, in the sense of division of labour and control, was evident in the work of the head nurse. Registered nurses in this position supervised the work of the medication, treatment, and bedside nurses. From this supervisory position, the head nurse exercised control over the work that was accomplished (what was done, who did it, and how it was done). Control was also exercised with communications. Head nurses accompanied physicians on rounds and communicated to the physicians on behalf of the bedside, treatment, and medication nurses, and then communicated back to those nurses from the physicians.

Discussion

People

There is an unspoken acknowledgement in functional nursing that tasks supersede individuals. In other words, the people (nurses) are interchangeable as long as the work is done efficiently and to standard. This assumption is likely the basis for the phrase "a nurse is a nurse is a nurse."

Functional nursing, by dividing the work of nurses into a sequence of tasks, carried with it the assumption that patients can be approached in an assembly-line method. This assumption may be the basis of the phrase "doing up patients." Functional nursing tends to take the form of reducing the patient to an object. Patients cannot be partners in care planning and decision making in this model. Other workers are the partners with whom the events of the shift must be choreographed.

Work

The autonomy of the caregiver is limited. The circumscription of work directs decisions about the timing and nature of nursing care. Clinical judgements about timing of treatments with a specific patient cannot be realized when the bedside caregiver is dependent upon the schedule of the treatment nurse. Nursing responsibility is reduced to responsibility for the tasks associated with patient care for that shift. Responsibility for the full process and content of patient care rests with the head nurse.

Relationships

There is no reason to predict a therapeutic nurse-patient relationship from this model. The professional nurses (registered) who have the skill are engaged in medications and treatments. The worker at the bedside is either unskilled or inexperienced. Patients are the recipients of scheduled tasks. Collegial relationships can develop well in this model (McMahon, 1990) because of the interdependency required to conduct the components of work. That choreography can be easily disrupted, however, by a worker whose work rhythm does not match that of colleagues.

Hierarchical relationships are established by the division of labour. Prestige is associated with distance from the bedside. Basic care, which is "at the heart of nursing," is not valued in this model as "challenging and important work" (Wilson-Barnett, 1988, p. 794).

Communication

Nurse-to-nurse communications are task related, with a time reference that is for the duration of the current shift and possibly the next one. Communications about the patient to other members of the health team are managed through the head nurse. Communications are received from the nurses and transmitted to the appropriate recipient. The return message about care implications for nursing is given by the head nurse to the caregiver.

Professional practice

The head nurse is the single individual who has the organizational opportunity to exercise professional practice fully. Although others may have the personal ability, that expression is limited by the division of labour. Continuity of care is managed through the head nurse as coordinated events (Shortell, 1976). Caregivers think in time frames associated with the tasks for their shift. This division of labour becomes a barrier to reflective analysis of the process and content of patient care. Functional nursing risks the de-skilling of nurses who have been educationally prepared to function in a professional manner.

Team Nursing

Team nursing was another response to the nursing shortage in the 1950s. The intent was to use the skills of professional nurses better and to supervise the increasing number of auxiliary staff. Team nursing carried with it an explicit commitment to achieving goals through group action (Lambertsen, 1953). There was also the expectation that it would improve patient care, and provide better education for student nurses (Jenkinson, 1958).

Shift schedules are commonly organized so that a team of nurses and aides routinely work together. One member of the team, often a senior and skilled clinician, is designated team leader. For purposes of work efficiency, the unit is arbitrarily split into two or more groups of patients (e.g., east hall/west hall or teams 1, 2, and 3). Nurses on each team communicate within the team about their patients.

The team leader is the principal communicator with the physician and other team members, and is often assigned the clinical responsibility of distributing all regularly scheduled drugs. Team members are assigned to work either as individuals or as dyads. When patients are assigned to the individual nurse that nurse has the total care of the patient; when the assignment is to a dyad the care is accomplished according to skill (RN-aide dyad) or interest (RN-RN dyad).

Discussion

People

Team nursing carries with it the explicit belief that members will work together to reach mutually agreed upon goals (Lambertsen, 1953). No one member has superiority over another; each has an important job to do in the course of caring for the patient (Lambertsen, 1953). Peterson (1973) noted that "team nursing was democracy at work" (p. 62). Patients are considered to be part of the team and have authority for their lives. They are consulted about their health responses and goals. However, the experience of participation may diminish as the number of caregivers increases. A dyad pattern versus an individual assignment pattern creates the risk that team nursing could become as task centred as functional nursing.

Work

The nurse at the bedside is autonomous for decisions about nursing care for that shift and can make recommendations for the next shift based on the health response of the patient. The team leader is vested with the responsibility to coordinate the decisions of the other health professionals with the practice of nursing and to make nursing decisions beyond the immediate shift. The decentralization of decision making from the head nurse to the team leader and the bedside caregiver represents a push to encourage staff nurses to think in larger time frames. The head nurse in this model still carries significant clinical responsibility for continuity of events, but less so than with functional nursing.

Relationships

The concept of team nursing emphasizes the participation of all team members in planning care for the patient. There is the expectation that members will come to know and understand the patient's perspective. This process represents the first steps in developing a therapeutic relationship. Because the nursing future with the patient is focussed only on the current shift and perhaps the next one, there is no push for the individual nurse to engage in a long term therapeutic relationship. If this happened, it would be short-lived and would be a positive comment on the skill of the particular nurse who had been taking care.

Relationships between colleagues have the potential to develop well within team nursing. The word "team" carries with it expectations of participation and cooperation. The structure of the team meeting provides not only for communication about patients, but exchanges that can support the learning and professional development of team members.

Communication

The process of communicating about the patient is a design feature of team nursing. Intraprofessional team meetings (nursing) and inter-professional team conferences (nursing and other health disciplines) support the sharing of information and questioning about progress toward health goals. The intraprofessional team meeting is a daily event in which the progress of that day is discussed. It is in effect a change-of-shift report to the team leader, but is done in group. The interprofessional team conference occurs with a frequency that matches acuity and turnover of the patients. The focus of the team conference is progress toward goals that facilitate discharge from hospital.

The bedside caregiver is not necessarily included in interprofessional team conferences. The team leader may represent all bedside caregivers. Consequently, the structure of interprofessional conferences can limit the time reference of the bedside nurse. The team leader, through that participation, is exposed to a larger time frame than bedside colleagues. That exposure offers opportunities to reflect upon the trajectory of the patient's illness and ultimate recovery. The nurse is moved to think beyond daily events. Systematic reflection is an essential activity in beginning to evaluate both the process and content of nursing care.

The care plan or kardex is the recorded means of communicating events that are to occur in the course of the patient's care. It is maintained by the team leader and reviewed and revised at intraprofessional team meetings and interprofessional team conferences. The process of using the care plan contributes to continuity of care through coordination of events. Since bedside caregivers usually do not record directly on the kardex it may not be an up-to-date method of communicating care (Kron & Gray, 1987).

Professional practice

Development of team nursing coincided with a shortage of registered nurses and was considered to be an improvement upon functional nursing. Professional practice in functional nursing was the domain of the head nurse. Team nursing extended the participation in professional practice to other nurses, the team leaders. The structural feature of team leaders was considered a strength during a time of unskilled or semi-skilled co-workers. It can in fact be a weakness with a different skill mix. When the majority of staff are registered nurses, the bedside nurse is left to perform in a less capable manner than one would expect given professional preparation.

The communication structures support continuity of events, and the delivery system supports continuity of person (Fletcher et al., 1983). The latter is still dependent upon the team leader, however, as the patient assignment is developed over the week. The team leader, through participation in conferences, is the nurse most likely to develop an extended nursing time frame and to engage in reflective practice analysis. Team nursing, like functional nursing, may contribute to failure to use the skills of professionally prepared nurses.

Primary Nursing

Primary nursing was a response in the early 1970s to the increased acuity of hospitalized patients, the demand for more registered nurses in acute care hospitals, and the availability of registered nurses with baccalaureate degrees. It paralleled the development of clinically focussed nursing research.

Primary nursing is premised on decentralized decision making, case assignment, caregiver-to-caregiver communication, and 24-hour accountability (Manthey, 1980). Primary nurses are assigned when patients are admitted to a unit and maintain that assignment for the duration of stay. When the primary nurse is not on duty, the care is managed by an associate (Manthey, 1980).

Community health nursing agencies (e.g., the Victorian Order of Nurses and public health agencies) operate within a primary nursing model. The term "team" may be used, but it is in the context of describing a geographically bounded cluster of nursing districts. "Team members" act as each other's associate nurses because of geographical proximity.

Discussion

People

Decision making about patient care is decentralized to the bedside caregiver. That decentralization is a positive statement about the capability of the bedside caregiver to assess, plan, participate in, and evaluate the nursing care of patients. The design features of limited numbers at the bedside and decentralized decision making create the expectation that the nurse will engage the patient in decisions about care. Primary nursing, unlike functional nursing, engages the whole person (the patient) in the course of care, not just body parts that require nursing work. Family members are likely to be included in care discussions and decisions. The level of that involvement, however, would depend upon the skills of the nurse and the supports within the workplace for family nursing practice.

The patient's experience of continuity of care is through continuity of person and events. The primary nurse and the designated coterie of associate nurses provide the patient with a limited group of nurses (continuity of person) with whom to interact. Continuity of events in the patient's illness and recovery is managed through the development and maintenance of a nursing care plan. Nurse-to-nurse communications at change of shift are at the level of caregiver to caregiver.

Work

The adjective "primary" in primary nursing refers to the vesting of primary authority and primary responsibility for decisions about care in one nurse, the primary nurse. The staff nurse is the nurse most authoritative about and responsible for a particular patient's care. Decision making about nursing events with the patient is decentralized to the level of the bedside caregiver. The primary nurse carries that authority and responsibility over a 24-hour period seven days a week. As such, the primary nurse would be available on a day off for consultation about a patient. The primary nurse is both the caregiver and care planner. Associate nurses provide the care according to the care plan in the absence of the primary nurse. Associates may make slight modifications to the plan, but substantive modifications would be made in consultation with the primary nurse.

Relationships

The structure of the primary nurse's work provides for the development of therapeutic nurse-patient relationships. Patients with recurring hospitalizations to manage chronic disease may particularly benefit from such a relationship with their primary nurses. Collegial relationships may suffer in a primary nursing model if primary nursing is equated with absolutely independent work. The reality of nursing work is that patients need coverage during breaks, and that nurses need physical help caring for some patients. If supportive relationships (Coeling & Wilcox, 1990) are not structured into the work day, then abandonment and frustration may be the consequence.

Primary nursing leads to a flat versus a hierarchical organization at the unit level. The head nurse's role is to maintain standards of practice and to coordinate patient assignments and staff nurse shift schedules. Because nurses' work is at the bedside, there is not the same hierarchy that is associated with functional nursing. When it does exist, the hierarchy is more likely to be clinically than administratively based.

Professional practice

Primary nursing, unlike functional and team nursing, provides the caregiver, regardless of professional preparation, with the opportunity to engage fully in professional practice. Primary nursing has been equated by some institutions with an all-RN staff. Manthey (1988) disputes this practice. She maintains that the caregiver would operate within the scope of practice defined by the professional registering body (Manthey, Ciske, Robertson, & Harris, 1970). Where a procedure is beyond the caregiver's scope of practice, it would be assigned to an appropriate colleague. The caregiver would, however, be responsible for ensuring that the procedure was done.

The role of the head nurse is markedly different in primary nursing from the role in either team or functional nursing. The head nurse is more involved with managing the care delivery structure and interpersonal relationships than in managing the clinical events for each patient (MaGuire, 1986). That management includes:

- Developing schedules to provide for matching of primary and associate nurses across shifts;
- Assigning primary nurses to newly admitted patients;
- Balancing the workload on any given day; and
- Making it possible for primary nurses to attend patient conferences.

The structural maintenance work does not preclude clinical involvement. In fact, there is perhaps greater opportunity to influence practice development on a primary nursing unit than on other units. The head nurse will always be held accountable for the standard of care given by staff. On a primary nursing unit there is more time to focus not only on development of standards but also on the development of staff to meet those standards reliably. Two activities that the head nurse can pursue are:

- Matching new admissions with actual or developing skills of primary nurses; and
- Engaging the bedside caregiver in a reflective analysis (evaluation) of the progress of the patient's care from admission to discharge (see MacGuire, 1989a, 1989b, for principles of primary nursing and operational terms).

Head nurses will engage in role transition when a unit shifts from functional or team nursing to primary nursing. The role changes from a supervisory relationship to a mentoring relationship. During this time, they need support. Without it, the new care delivery model may falter and return to the original model.

Case Management

Case management as an approach to care originated in community mental health (Baker & Visch, 1989; Fisher, 1987; Kanter, 1989; Maurin, 1990). In that setting, case management is practised by all members of the health care team. The term was subsequently adopted by third-party payors and hospitals.

Case management has specific meaning for nurses, largely as a result of work done by the New England Medical Center Department of Nursing (Zander, 1988; Zander, Etheridge, & Bower, 1987). The model is designed to manage health care costs and simultaneously derive benefits for patients and staff. Case management is built on a foundation of managed care.

Managed care is a method of matching the care of individuals within a diagnostic related group (DRG) to a plan of care that has been designed for the typical patient within that group. That plan is called a care map or critical path. It specifies, for each day of the hospital stay, the health outcomes to be reached, the work to be done by the various professionals, and the professional responsible for meeting each outcome. The critical path can be considered a work plan for the professional. For the patient, it creates a structure for continuity of events. Managed care contains health care costs by specifying the type, the amount, and the frequency of care to be received by the typical patient within that diagnostic related group. For the professional, there may be a feeling of participating in a lock-step approach to care. The patient, however, should have the experience of choreographed, evenly paced care.

Patients with atypical responses to the course of treatment show up as variances on the critical path. Variances "flag patient care issues that could alter the anticipated date or quality of patient outcomes" (King, 1992, p. 16). Individualized approaches are developed to get the patient back on track.

Managed care can be employed for the majority of hospitalized patients. The development of critical paths involves collaborative and time-consuming work by all disciplines (Guadalupe, DelTogno-Armanasco, Erickson, & Hartner,1989; Mckenzie, Torkelson, & Holt, 1989). Care activities and outcomes for all involved disciplines are made explicit for each day of a patient's hospitalization.

Case management takes managed care two steps further by formalizing continuity of person within the role of case manager, and introducing the concept of "episode of illness." A primary caregiver, the case manager, is identified for patients within a diagnostic related group. He or she is involved with those patients from the admission to the last outpatient department visit. The case manager has the privilege of experiencing the patient's trajectory of illness and recovery (episode of illness), and participating in care on every unit to which the patient may be admitted. Not only does the case manager become expert in the clinical care of a specific population of patients; there is the unprecedented opportunity to evaluate fully the effects of nursing care across the episode of illness from prehospitalization to postdischarge. In all other care delivery models, nurses are limited to evaluating the effects of nursing care on their unit for the amount of time they are involved with a patient.

Case management is unlike all other care delivery models in that it spans the organization and prescribes the care to be provided to the patient by all disciplines. Case management could conceivably be adopted within a hospital that has a variety of care delivery models (Sandhu, Duquette, & Kerouac, 1992; Zander, 1988) at the unit level.

Case management combines elements of primary and team nursing. The case manager is analogous to the primary nurse, but may or may not be involved in bedside care. The case manager follows the patient's care throughout the hospitalization. For a surgical patient, that would involve seeing the patient before admission, on the surgical unit, in the ICU, in the step-down unit, and back on the surgical unit. Nurses who give bedside care in the absence of the case manager are analogous to associate nurses in primary nursing.

Case management is similar to team nursing in the structured team approach to communications. Case conferences are a means of assessing not only the progress of a particular patient but of the cluster of patients within that diagnostic related group.

Discussion

People

The development of critical paths directs the sequence and much of the content of the nursing care. The approach to that care, however, remains as individual as the nurse and the patient. The assignment of a nurse to be the case manager carries with it the tacit belief that patients and the organization benefit from continuity of person. The patient benefits from a nurse who experiences the episode of illness; the organization benefits from a nurse who helps colleagues be conscious of costs. Case management carries with it the assumption that nurses are capable of this expansion to their role. Newman (1990) depicted the case manager's role as that of a clinician prepared at the master's level. Etheridge and Lamb (1989) note that a baccalaureate degree is the minimum preparation to fulfil this role.

When patients are given copies of their critical paths they can appreciate the sequence of events that will happen in the course of the hospitalization. The sequence provides a framework within which approaches to care can be individualized by the nurse and the patient. Patients and family are "empowered through informed and participatory decision-making" (King, 1992, p. 15).

Work
The responsibility for the overall process and content of the nursing work lies with the case manager. The autonomy to make nursing decisions also rests with the case manager. When the case manager is not a caregiver, decision making is centralized; when the case manager is also the primary nurse, decisions are decentralized. Responsibility for work done during a shift rests with the bedside nurse, who can approach decisions about daily care within the constraints of the care delivery model on the unit.

Communication
The case manager functions as the communications centre. He or she attends to a patient's progress by following the care on all units to which that patient is admitted. In doing so, the case manager has direct contact with all caregivers and can bring nurses from a variety of units and clinics together to help address both the current and anticipated needs of patients. Communications with other professionals are facilitated by the critical paths. With the work plan for each discipline specified, communications from nurses to other professionals can be directed toward understanding the patient's response rather than to reminding and requesting.

Professional practice
Case management provides an unprecedented scope of practice for staff nurse case managers. Because there are fewer case managers than staff nurses, the scope of practice for staff nurses is still determined by the unit care delivery model even when case management is in place in the hospital.

Variations on the Models

Variations to functional, team, and primary nursing have developed as a result of shortened length of stay and part-time labour (Kramer & Schmalenberg, 1987a, 1987b), twelve-hour shifts, nursing shortages, and nursing salaries. Total patient care is a variation on primary nursing that commits nurses to the central tenets but not the actual structure of primary nursing (Kramer, 1990). It derives from the case method of assignment (see Alfano, 1969). Continuity of person is provided by assigning nurses to the same patients for as many days as the nurse is scheduled to work. Continuity of events is managed by the head nurse or designate.

Modular nursing (Marriner, 1984; Young & Hayne, 1988) is a variation on team and primary nursing. It may involve the pairing of a registered nurse and an assistant to a module of patients. This pairing results in division of work through assignment of tasks to the appropriate practitioner. The model can be reduced to functional nursing, although that is not the intent of the design.

A model called "Pro-act" (Crabtree Tonges, 1989a, 1989b; Ritter, Fralic, Crabtree Tonges, & McCormac, 1992) is a variation on case management, functional, team, and primary nursing. The clinical care manager is equivalent to the case manager, but is not a caregiver. Unit-based primary nurses act as caregivers, and licensed practical nurses or certified nursing assistants function as associates in their absence. Nurses' aides are assigned tasks (functional nursing) by registered nurses. Team concepts of mutual goal setting and communication appear to be the glue that holds this model together. Continuity of person and events is provided by the clinical care manager and the primary nurse.

Selecting a Model:
Criteria and Process

The selection of a care delivery model is a process, not an event (Berry & Metcalf, 1986; Coeling & Wilcox, 1990; Fralic, 1992; Guadelupe et al., 1989; Wood, Bankston, Bickford, & Bogdan, 1990). Recognizing and understanding the assumptions underlying each model is an important first step. It is also important to recognize and understand the environment in which the care delivery model will operate. The environment includes the organization (internal) and the larger society (external). Factors to consider when assessing the environment are itemized in Table 17.1. No single factor will provide the nurse manager with clear direction for proceeding with a change in the care delivery structure. Each factor will need to be weighed for its relative importance.

The review of the environments will help to identify the supports and constraints to changing the care delivery model. That review may also help to identify the models that would be most acceptable within the organization. However, the review does not engage one in a deliberative comparison of the models against selected criteria. Those criteria should be developed to highlight values expressed in the nursing mission and philosophy (see Table 17.2, page 326). Discussion about change then will be based upon beliefs that members of the nursing department support.

Table 17.1

Environmental factors to consider when selecting a care delivery model.

Internal Environment

The organization:

1. How do the values in the organization's mission statement address patients, communication, work, and professionalism?
2. Which goals in the five-year plan support change?
3. Which disciplines will need to be included in discussions about a change in care delivery? What concerns will they express?

The nursing department:

1. What is the tenure, skill mix, educational preparation, and professional orientation of nursing staff and managers?

   1.1 How will each of the above influence the selection of a care delivery model?

2. How do the values in the nursing mission and philosophy address patients, communication, work, and professionalism?

Patients:

1. What are the major patient populations supported by the hospital or unit?

   1.1 How would each population be served by each care delivery model?

External Environment

Economic:

1. What will be the influence of the latest or upcoming contract settlement?
2. How will a new care delivery model be interpreted in light of the current fiscal climate?

Health trends:

1. How will the model match consumer expectations for inclusion in care?

Political:

1. Which models and their variations have been profiled over the last three years in professional publications?

   1.1. Will there be pressure to adopt one of those models? Which one?

   1.2 Where will the pressure come from and how will it be expressed?

Regulatory:

1. How is scope of practice being interpreted by the professional and regulatory bodies?

   1.1 How will that interpretation influence the selection of a care delivery model?

Table 17.2
Criteria for the selection of a care delivery model.

---

1. What is good for patients? Does the model:
   1.1 have the patient as a central focus?
   1.2 support continuity of care?
   1.3 highlight patient outcomes?

2. What is good for nursing? Does the model:
   2.1 fit with the nursing mission and philosophy?
   2.2 maximize professional practice?
   2.3 maintain control of nursing practice within nursing?
   2.4 minimize non-nursing tasks?
   2.5 promote job satisfaction?

3. What is good for the organization? Does the model:
   3.1 fit with the hospital mission and role?
   3.2 maintain or improve quality of care?
   3.3 promote optimum utilization of beds and other resources?
   3.4 promote collaborative practice?

Source: These questions were developed by S.D. Smith, Vice-President, Nursing Services, Chedoke-McMaster Hospitals, 1992. Used with permission.

The nursing department in one Canadian hospital recently went through the process of selecting a care delivery model. Survey questions developed by Thomas and Bond (1990) were modified and given to nursing unit managers representing 32 units. Twenty-three of the nursing unit managers could identify the model to which their unit ascribed. However, each of these units in fact had blended models, such as functional and team nursing, team and primary nursing, and total patient care with team and primary nursing. It was evident that a consultative process was needed to bring about a consistent model throughout the hospital.

The consultative process involved hosting a day-long think tank for staff nurses from the nursing practice steering committee, clinical nurse specialists, clinical educators, nursing unit managers, and directors of nursing. The agenda included an historical perspective on care delivery, a review of the survey results, the organizational and social context for change, and evaluation of practice models. Small groups were organized to evaluate each practice model against selected criteria (see Table 17.2). The grading was done on a three-point scale. Each grade had to be accompanied with a justification for the answer; the process encouraged considerable discussion.

The think tank was successful. There was consensus for one model by the end of the day. That success, however, came on the heels of a year-long consultative process that had been completed six months earlier. The nursing department had engaged all nursing staff in the development of a mission and philosophy for nursing. By the time the think tank was organized there was considerable staff nurse appreciation for the values and beliefs (see Mark, 1992) stated in the mission and philosophy. Without that base of commitment, discussion about changing care delivery models might have faltered.

Conclusion

This review of care delivery models has addressed underlying assumptions. Understanding the inherent beliefs and values is an important step in selecting a care delivery model. The best model is the one that inspires your nurses to care and provides them with a vision of their profession.

Staff nurses need to be included in the selection process. Both they and the organization will benefit from a review of the values and beliefs that join them. Making the process explicit helps nurses to understand not only why they have selected one model but why they have rejected other models. The care delivery model that you and your staff ultimately select will then reflect your mission and philosophy and support daily nursing practice.

Acknowledgements

Grateful acknowledgement is given to Gloria Harrison and Susan Smith, who critiqued the manuscript for this chapter, and to Lois Wyndham and Lois Cottrell, the best librarians an author could have.

References

Alfano, G.J. (1969). The Loeb Center for Nursing and Rehabilitation, a professional approach to nursing practice. *Nursing Clinics of North America, 4,* 487-493.

Baker, F., & Visch, T. (1989). Continuity of care and the control of costs: Can case management assure both? *Journal of Public Health Policy,* Summer, 205-213.

Berry, A.J., & Metcalf, C.L. (1986). Paradigms and practices: The organization of the delivery of nursing care. *Journal of Advanced Nursing, 11,* 589-597.

Coeling, H.V.E., & Wilcox, J.R. (1990). Using organizational culture to facilitate the change process. *American Nephrology Nurses' Association, 17*(3), 231-236.

Crabtree Tonges, M. (1989a). Redesigning hospital nursing practice: The professionally advanced care team (ProAct) model, part 1. *Journal of Nursing Administration, 19*(7), 31-38.

Crabtree Tonges, M. (1989b). Redesigning hospital nursing practice: The professionally advanced care team (ProAct) model, part 2. *Journal of Nursing Administration, 19*(9), 19-22.

Etheridge, P., & Lamb, G.S. (1989). Professional nursing case management improves quality, access and costs. *Nursing Management, 20*(3), 30-35.

Fisher, K. (1987). Case management. *Quality Review Bulletin, 13*(8), 287-290.

Fletcher, R.H., O'Malley, M.S., Earp, J., Littleton, T.A., Fletcher, S.W., Greganti, M.A., Davidson, R.A., & Taylor, J. (1983). Patients' priorities for medical care. *Medical Care, 21*(2), 234-242.

Fralic, M.F. (1992). Creating new practice models and designing new roles, reflections and recommendations. *Journal of Nursing Administration, 22*(6), 7-8.

Giovannetti, P. (1986). Evaluation of primary nursing. *Annual Review of Nursing Research, 4,* 127-151.

Guadalupe, S.O., Del Togno-Armanasco, V., Erickson, J.R., & Harter, S. (1989). Case management— A bottom-line care delivery model. Part II: Adaptation of the model. *Journal of Nursing Administration, 19*(12), 12-17.

Irvine, D., & Evans, M. (1992). *Job satisfaction and turnover among nurses: A review and meta-analysis.* (Quality of Nursing Worklife Research Unit Monograph Series, Monograph No. 1). Toronto: University of Toronto Faculty of Nursing.

Jenkinson, V. (1958). Group or team nursing: Report on a 5 year experiment at St. Georges Hospital, London. *Nursing Times, 54,* 62-64, 92-93.

Kanter, J. (1989). Clinical case management: Definition, principles, components. *Hospital and Community Psychiatry, 40*(4), 361-368.

King, M.L., (1992). Case management. *Canadian Nurse, 88*(4), 15-17.

Kramer, M. (1990). The magnet hospitals: Excellence revisited. *Journal of Nursing Administration, 20*(9), 35-44.

Kramer, M., & Schmalenberg, C. (1987a). Magnet hospitals talk about the impact of DRG's on nursing care—Part 1. *Nursing Management, 15*(9), 38-42.

Kramer, M., & Schmalenberg, C. (1987b). Magnet hospitals talk about the impact of DRG's on nursing care—Part 2. *Nursing Management, 15*(10), 33-40.

Kron, T., & Gray, A. (1987). *The management of patient care: Putting leadership skills to work* (6th ed.). Toronto: W. B. Saunders.

Lambertsen, E.C. (1953). *Nursing team organization and functioning: Results of a study of the division of Nursing Education, Teachers College, Columbia University.* New York: Bureau of Publications, Teachers College, Columbia University.

Macdonald, M. (1988). Primary nursing: Is it worth it? *Journal of Advanced Nursing, 13,* 797-806.

MacGuire, J. (1989a). An approach to evaluating the introduction of primary nursing in an acute medical unit for the elderly—I. Principles and practice. *International Journal of Nursing studies, 26*(3), 243-251.

MacGuire, J. (1989b). An approach to evaluating the introduction of primary nursing in an acute medical unit for the elderly—II. Operationalizing the principles. *International Journal of Nursing studies, 26*(3), 253-260.

MacPhail, J. (1988). Organizing for nursing care: Primary nursing, traditional approaches, or both? In J. Kerr & J. MacPhail (Eds.), *Canadian nursing issues and perspectives.* Toronto: McGraw-Hill Ryerson.

Maguire, P. (1986). Staff nurses' perceptions of head nurses' leadership styles. *Nursing Administration Quarterly, 11*(1), 34-38.

Manthey, M. (1980). *The practice of primary nursing.* Boston: Blackwell Scientific.

Manthey, M. (1988). Myths that threaten. *Nursing Management, 19*(6), 54-55.

Manthey M., Ciske, K., Robertson, P., and Harris, I. (1970). Primary nursing. *Nursing Forum, 9*(1), 65-83.

Mark, B. (1992). Characteristics of nursing practice models. *Journal of Nursing Administration, 22*(11), 1992.

Marriner, A. (1984). *Guide to nursing management* (2nd ed.). Toronto: C.V. Mosby.

Maurin, J.T. (1990). Case management: Caring for psychiatric clients. *Journal of Psychosocial Nursing and Mental Health Services, 28,* 7-12.

Mckenzie, C.B., Torkelson, N.G., & Holt, M.A. (1989). Care and cost: Nursing case management improves both. *Nursing Management, 20*(10), 30-34.

McMahon, R. (1990). Power and collegial relations among nurses on wards adopting primary nursing and hierarchical ward management structures. *Journal of Advanced Nursing, 15,* 232-239.

Newman, M.A. (1990). Toward an integrative model of professional practice. *Journal of Professional Nursing, 6*(3), 167-173.

Peterson, G. (1973). *Working with others for patient care.* Dubuque, IA: Wm. C. Brown.

Ritter, J., Fralic, M.F., Crabtree Tonges, M., & McCormac, M. (1992). Redesigned nursing practice: A case management model for critical care. *Nursing Clinics of North America, 27*(1), 119-128.

Sandhu, B.K., Duquette, A., & Kerouac, S. (1992). Care delivery models. *Canadian Nurse, 88*(4), 18-20.

Shortell, S.M. (1976). Continuity of medical care: Conceptualization and measurement. *Medical Care, 14,* 377-391.

Thomas L.H., & Bond, S. (1990). Towards defining the organization of nursing care in hospital wards: An empirical study. *Journal of Advanced Nursing, 15,* 1106-1112.

Wilson-Barnett, J. (1988). Nursing values: Exploring the clichés. *Journal of Advanced Nursing, 13,* 790-796.

Wood, J., Bankston, K., Bickford, B., & Bogdan, B. (1990). An effort to identify the optimum method of patient care delivery. *Critical Care Nursing Quarterly, 12*(4), 5-9.

Young, L.C., & Hayne, A.N. (1988). *Nursing administration: From concepts to practice.* Toronto: W.B. Saunders.

Zander, K. (1988). Nursing case management, resolving the DRG paradox. *Nursing Clinics of North America, 23*(3), 503-520.

Zander K., Etheridge, M.L., & Bower, K.A. (Eds.). (1987). *Nursing case management: Blueprints for transformation.* Boston: New England Medical Center Hospitals.

CHAPTER 18

Measurement of Nursing Workload

Phyllis Giovannetti

Phyllis Giovannetti, RN, BN (McGill), ScD (Johns Hopkins), is Professor and Associate Dean, Graduate Education, Faculty of Nursing, University of Alberta. She is internationally recognized for her work in the area of the development and evaluation of nursing workload measurement and costing systems.

Determining the appropriate number and mix of nursing personnel required to meet nursing care demands of patients/clients, commonly referred to as nursing resource management, is a complex and multidimensional endeavour. A number of interrelated factors are involved, such as: the extent and variability of patient requirements for care; availability of nursing and other health care related personnel and their scopes of practice; recruitment, retention, and scheduling policies; institutional policies, standards of practice, and philosophies of care; methods and procedures for estimating costs, productivity, efficiency, effectiveness, and the quality of care; union contracts and labour standards; technology, availability of support personnel and services; and physician practices. Compounding the impact of these variables are the multiple and variable objectives of government, governing boards, administrators, physicians, nurses, other health care professionals, and the public. Given that labour costs represent the largest single item of a hospital budget and that nursing personnel are the most significant component of the labour budget, it is not surprising that the topic is passionately discussed among nurses, extensively written about in health care journals, and frequently debated by health care managers.

This chapter does not try to provide the solution to nursing resource management—if indeed there is one. Although other complex multidimensional challenges, such as sending men and women to the moon, have been overcome, nurse staffing has not. What the reader will uncover in this chapter are some of the common techniques available for the measurement of nursing workload in hospital settings, a discussion of the limitations of the systems, and possible future directions. But first, a review of the past.

Historical Perspectives

Attention to the question of the number and kinds of nursing personnel required to meet the care demands of different publics is not new to the discipline. Anyone who suggests that nursing resource management represents a new and recent focus is seriously uninformed. There is ample evidence that Florence Nightingale addressed not only the question of how many nurses were required for each of her many exploits, but gave serious thought to the larger question of human resource planning. The processes that she used to arrive at each decision are not well documented, although it seems clear that her decisions went largely unchallenged. Her personal power and influence in this regard were really quite remarkable.

Using a broad approach, it is possible to view the development of nursing resource management in three stages. First, decisions were made primarily on the basis of the perceived requirements of recognized leaders in the field, giving rise to the notion of power derived from personal and professional sources. This approach remained predominant until about the mid-1930s. Possibly driven by rapid growth in both the size and complexity of institutional care, the search for a more scientific approach began, resulting in what came to be known as the period of global staffing standards. Fixed staff-to-patient ratios in terms of hours per patient-day became the norm for the determination and allocation of nursing personnel resources. This approach assumed that the basis for staffing was the number of occupied beds. For example, a hospital with an average census of 500, employing a fixed ratio of 3.5 hours per patient-day, would require 1750 nursing hours per day or 24-hour period (500 x 3.5).

This approach to staffing levels was prevalent within health care institutions until about the mid-1960s. In most cases, the average hours of care per day (the fixed ratio) were derived from the dual forces of precedent and pressure: historical budget allocations served as the precedents and existing budget constraints and market conditions exerted the pressure. The number of nurses assigned to each shift was generally based on a further assumption about the distribution of workload, such as 40% on day shift, 30% on evening shift, and 30% on night shift. The difficulties inherent in measuring the quality of care effectively limited any estimate of the effects of staffing levels based on such global averages. This is not to suggest that the quality of nursing care was not considered. Rather, quality was largely judged to be the outcome of well-managed institutions employing well-qualified nurses.

As evident from the above, the notion of fixed hours per patient-day is based on the assumption that all patients are equal in terms of nursing care requirements. Florence Nightingale knew that assumption was incorrect and so do today's managers. Although percentage of occupied beds may provide a useful unit of analysis for financial accounting, it is of limited value to nurse managers who must ensure that patients' varying requirements for care are adequately met on a shift-by-shift basis.

The work of Connor, conducted at the Johns Hopkins Hospital in Baltimore, was instrumental in bringing about a shift in focus from occupied beds to the unique needs of the patients who occupy the beds. This was the beginning of the third stage, the development of nursing workload measurement systems (Connor, 1961; Connor, Flagle, Hsieh, Preston, & Singer, 1961). As part of a study on the optimal organization of nursing staff, Connor developed a three-category patient classification scheme using criteria that, through observational studies of direct nursing care, were deemed to reflect a significant proportion of nurses' time. The criteria for assigning patients to categories included physical needs, emotional support requirements, and specific patient states. The physical criteria, frequently referred to as activities of daily living (ADL), included ambulating, bathing, and feeding. The remaining criteria considered in the classification scheme were defined as the patients' needs for emotional support (slight or marked), the need for treatments such as suctioning and oxygen, and physical states such as unconsciousness or impaired vision. The classification scheme was easy to apply and the criteria offered little opportunity for variability in interpretation among nurses.

Subsequently, a direct nursing care workload index was computed on the basis of the average direct care times revealed through continuous observational studies. The number of patients in each category was multiplied by the average care time associated with each class, and the products added to provide an estimate of total hours of direct nursing care required for the following day. Further study at the same hospital by Wolfe and Young (1965a, 1965b) produced the concept of controlled variable staffing. Using the direct care index developed by Connor and adding a constant for indirect care, the total workload for the next 24-hour period could be determined. It was suggested that nurse managers maintain a basic or fixed staff on each unit to satisfy the daily minimum demand and add, from a float pool, additional staff as needed on the basis of the relative peaks in demand.

Although controlled variable staffing was related to the total workload required and to the total nursing hours available, professional nursing judgement was considered to be significant in the final staffing determinations. The investigators recognized that the computations from the patient classification scheme reflected averages, and that at any one time there could be patients whose care needs departed significantly from the assigned averages. For this reason, it was recommended that the assignment of personnel to high workload units and the removal of personnel from the low workload units should continue to be based to some extent on the experience and judgement of the nursing supervisor. (It should be noted that centralized staffing was the most prevalent modus operandi at this time). The investigators also postulated that the complexity of the nursing tasks involved and the levels of nursing personnel available were important variables to be considered in staffing decisions. They did not, however, derive decision criteria that included these variables. Later in this chapter, the consequences of not attending to the issues of professional judgement, complexity of nursing tasks, and levels of nursing personnel are more fully disclosed.

In summary, a number of significant findings were revealed in the early Johns Hopkins studies. First, the demand for patient care was not a function of census alone (i.e., occupied beds), but rather the number of patients in each category of care present on the unit. Second, a wide variation in total nursing workload existed from day to day and shift to shift. Third, the variation in nursing workload was independent from unit to unit. Fourth, the main determinant of total nursing workload was the number of Category 3 or intensive care patients on the unit at any one time.

In the more than three decades that have passed since the landmark work of Connor and colleagues, similar findings have been reported in hundreds of studies in Canada, the United States, Great Britain, and Europe. The results have led to a proliferation of staffing schemes, many of which are remarkably similar to the one developed by Connor. The reasons why the staffing systems continue to be widely used are not surprising: they represent for the most part a comprehensive approach to resolving a complex question. The next section of this chapter explores the various nursing workload measurement systems.

Approaches to the Measurement of Nursing Workload

The precise number of different nursing workload measurement systems (NWMSs) available or in use throughout North America is not known, and no single document exists cataloguing all of the systems. Their endorsement by both Canadian and United States hospital accreditation bodies, as evidence of a planned approach to staffing based upon the assessed needs of patients, has led to their wide application. A Canadian survey conducted in 1988 revealed that 53% of a random sample of 218 hospitals reported having a workload measurement system in place in one or more clinical settings. The percentage was considerably higher for teaching hospitals than for nonteaching hospitals with greater than 300 beds (O'Brien-Pallas & Cockerill, 1990; Cockerill & O'Brien-Pallas, 1990). The newly revised Canadian Management Information System (MIS) Guidelines recommend that the systems be used as proxies for the costing of nursing care, which will no doubt lead to even greater application in Canada (The MIS Group, 1993).

Edwardson and Giovannetti (1994) note that many systems have been developed by vendors and consequently are not fully described in the published literature. Still more have been developed and/or substantially modified by institutions and also not published. The interested reader may wish to consult an earlier publication by Giovannetti (1978) or the more recent manual by Lewis (1989), both of which contain numerous examples of widely used systems. While it is sometimes difficult to clarify the distinctions between the systems, three major approaches to the assessment of staffing are commonly identified: (1) patient profiles or prototype evaluations; (2) critical indicators or factor evaluations; and (3) tasking documents. Most systems use only one approach, although some employ a combination of approaches (Giovannetti & Johnson, 1990). The first two approaches, prototype and factor evaluation systems, employ the concept of grouping or patient classification. The term patient classification, however, is not precise enough to describe all nurse staffing methods and is gradually being replaced by the more descriptive label nursing workload measurement system. Another reason to avoid the use of the generic term "patient classification" is the propensity for confusion with other patient classification schemes such as case mix groups (CMGs) and diagnostic related groups (DRGs), both of which refer to medical resource allocation systems. Other terms such as "severity"

and "acuity" have also been used to describe nursing workload measurement systems. These terms, too, are misleading, for they suggest
an intent beyond the measurement of nursing care time. A patient's
degree of illness, as depicted in the common usage of severity or acuity, does not necessarily reflect the intensity of the demand for nursing care. Further, these terms are typically used for medical schemes
which, like DRGs, are considered to be inappropriate for the measurement of patients' requirements for nursing care.

Prototype Systems

Prototype systems are characterized by broad descriptions of the
characteristics of a typical patient in each of the defined categories.
For example, a prototype system might contain the following description of a patient whose nursing needs are considered to be "moderate":

- Able to assume little, if any, responsibility for his/her own activ-
  ities of daily living (ADL);
- Activity is partially controlled; patient may not be able to deter-
  mine or communicate his/her wants or needs;
- Requires some treatments, observations, and medications as
  frequently as every 2 hours or more often;
- Manifests some overt behaviour, anxiety, depression, distur-
  bances in sensory perception;
- Requires some instruction, demonstration, and support;
- Requires isolation care.

The actual characteristics of the patient are compared with
those described in the profile, and the patient is then assigned to the
category that most closely matches the profile or prototype description. Such systems are easily modified for speciality units (e.g., pediatrics, surgery, oncology) by the inclusion of unit-specific terminology
such as "under two years of age," "immediate post-op," or "receiving
chemotherapy." Many of the earliest workload measurement systems
were of this type. Clearly, professional judgement is required in placing the patient in the most appropriate category. The more general
the descriptors, such as "needs assistance in ADL," the more judgement required. It is of interest to note that current medical case mix
systems such as diagnostic related groups and the Canadian equivalent, case mix groups, are of this type, although the descriptors for
these medical systems are considered to be more precise and thus
requiring less judgement on the part of the rater.

Factor Evaluation Systems

Factor evaluation systems are possibly the most common approach to the measurement of nursing workload and employ the selection of specific elements or indicators of care representing either unique care activities or clusters of care activities. As with the prototype systems, the care activities listed are those considered to correlate most highly with varying amounts of nursing care time. Indicators such as the level of assistance required with feeding, bathing, and ambulation have, through time, demonstrated their usefulness in distinguishing between patients who require extensive nursing care time from those requiring minimal nursing care time. For this reason, such indicators are almost always included in nursing workload measurement systems in one form or another. Other indicators, such as patient condition (e.g., unconsciousness), patient state (e.g., blindness), and specific nursing activities (e.g., complex dressing change), and indicators reflecting the emotional and teaching needs of patients, are prevalent.

By definition, the indicators represent care requirements that demand a significant portion of nurses' time. They do not represent all that nurses do, or even what may be viewed as most important. Nonetheless, the number of indicators and their labels differ widely among the available systems and indicators are frequently added, deleted, or modified to reflect different clinical specialities—in many cases, for no other apparent reason than to provide the user with a "unique" system. The major criteria are: their contribution to statistical validity of the classification scheme; user acceptability; and face validity (Hanson, 1979).

The distinguishing feature between prototype and factor evaluation systems is that in the former the rater must select the most appropriate *category* whereas in the latter, the selection process is restricted to the selection of the most appropriate *indicators*.

The designation of patient category in the factor evaluation systems involves a second stage, which is based on a set of decision rules. For many systems, the decision rules are quickly learned and the task of classifying patients takes very little time. Less than 15 minutes for a unit of 35 patients is considered reasonable. A distinguishing feature between many of the systems is their degree of sophistication at this level, and many of them make use of computer software for the calculation of category and, ultimately, the staffing standards.

Another feature that distinguishes the many factor evaluation systems is the manner in which the weights for each indicator are developed and recorded. Some systems use alpha codes, such as A, B, or C, to represent an ordinal scale. For example, a weight of C for complete bath, and a weight of B for a partial bath, means nothing more than the common-sense notion that complete baths take more time than partial baths. Some systems use integers, such as 1, 2, and 3, to convey the same information. To the uninformed, however, the interpretation might be that a "3" for complete bath means that it takes 3 times as long to provide a complete bath than to do what needs to be done for the patient who is able to "self-bath or tub." A second misinterpretation of the weight in this example is that it takes three minutes to do a complete bath and two minutes to "assist" with a bath. Thus, it is critical that the user understand the nature of the weights. It is also critical that the user understand what is included in the indicators. Most, if not all, factor evaluation systems include extensive background materials regarding what is and what is not included or meant by the brief descriptor that is named on the classification form.

Tasking Documents

The third approach to the measurement of nursing workload is distinguished from the previous types in that it does not rely on the categorization or grouping of patients. Systems of this type employ an extensive listing of nursing care tasks or activities. In most instances, each task or activity is associated with a value representing the actual time required to complete the task or, more commonly, a coefficient representing the relative value of each activity. For example, the activities associated with the need for assistance with diet might include a weight of 1 for "self-feed," 8 for "assistance," 12 for "tube feed," and 16 for "total feed." In this instance, a correct interpretation would be that patients requiring tube feeding take 12 times longer in relation to diet activities than do those patients who can feed themselves. Patients are independently assessed on the basis of their need for each task or activity and the outcome of the assessment yields a unique value for each patient. If the weights are based on real time, the sum of the activities required would represent the amount of nursing care time required. If the weights are proxies for real time, the nursing care time required would be determined by multiplying the total value of all relevant activities by some constant as specified by the developers of the system.

As is the case with the other approaches to workload measurement, tasking documents can be easily modified to speciality areas, and differ with respect to the number of tasks cited, their respective values, and their relevance to either a specific shift or a 24-hour period of time.

Establishing Hours of
Care and Staffing Levels

The establishment of staffing levels, or the number of nurses required, is an expected outcome of a nursing workload measurement system. As evident from the previous discussion of system types, the creation of groupings, as described in prototype and factor evaluation systems, or the listing of discrete nursing tasks or activities, as described in the tasking systems, does not yield precise staffing levels. A second step is required, and a variety of approaches have been used for establishing the *total* of nursing care hours and, thus, the number of staff required in a particular setting and for a given mix of patients. Some of the approaches are unique to the type of NWMS employed, while others can be applied to all types. For example, both prototype and factor evaluation type systems are designed to be represented by an average or mean care time for each category. The average care time per category may be derived from extensive observational timing studies of the care delivered to a representative sample of patients in each category, or may be established on the basis of professional judgement and consensus among expert nurse practitioners. The components of nursing that are included in the average care time may also vary among systems. Typically, the average care time per patient category includes the time for direct care activities only (i.e., those activities carried out in the presence of the patient, such as medication administration).

Clearly, not all nurses' time is spent on direct patient care. Three other components of work are frequently identified and necessarily included in the determination of staffing levels: indirect care time, personal time, and unit-related time. *Indirect care time* refers to those activities linked to particular patients but not carried out in their presence, such as preparing medications. *Personal time* takes into account such activities as staff meal time, coffee breaks, and normal fatigue and delay time that occur in any work setting. *Unit-related time* refers to time involved in maintaining a nursing unit and is considered largely independent of the number of patients or mix of patients (e.g., narcotic count and inservice education). Again, the percentage of time devoted to indirect care, personal time, and unit-related activities can be determined through observational timing studies or estimated on the basis of experience and judgement.

The following example illustrates the steps involved in linking a prototype or factor evaluation type system to specific staffing levels.

Suppose that the categorization process resulted in 3 category I patients, 7 category II patients, 15 category III patients, and 5 category IV patients. Further assume that from observational sampling studies, the average (mean) direct care time in minutes on the day shift for each of the four patient categories is 15, 40, 95, and 140, respectively.

Patient Category	Mean Direct Time (min)	x	No. Patients	=	Total Care Time (min)
I	15		3		45
II	40		7		280
III	95		15		1425
IV	140		5		700
			30		2450

Multiplying the number of patients in each category by the corresponding mean and totaling the products reveals, in this example, that a total of 2450 minutes or 40.83 hours of direct nursing care time is required on the day shift. If one assumed that nurses devoted 100% of their 8-hour shifts to deliver direct care, the total number of nurses required would be 40.83 ÷ 8 = 5.1 nurses. Of course, that assumption is not realistic. Indeed, it has been found that on the average, nurses spend somewhere from 25% to 50% of their time on direct care. Obviously, this figure would differ depending upon the shift considered as well as the structural and functional operations of each unit. Assume that, on the basis of an extensive work sampling observational study, it was determined that nurses were available for the delivery of direct care only 33% of their time on the day shift. Given that 40.83 hours of direct care are required and each nurse has available 33% of 8 hours (i.e., 2.7 hours), the staffing requirements would be 15.1 nurses (i.e., 40.83 ÷ 2.7).

The above example illustrates the process whereby a prototype or factor evaluation type NWMS can be transformed to yield staffing levels. A great many derivations of the above exist. For example, staffing may be determined for a 24-hour period rather than on a per-shift basis. Where the care demands of patients fluctuate widely throughout a 24-hour period, classification on each shift has frequently been advocated. Some institutions consider each nursing unit to be unique and insist upon separate timing coefficients for each unit. Others may average together the times for similar units, such as all medical units, pediatric units, or surgical units, while still others are content to use standard measures across all units. Some vendors or institutions combine direct and indirect care, and thus their coefficients or values for each category would likely be somewhat higher than in the previous example. Similarly, the percentage of nurses' time available to provide direct and indirect care would also be higher. All of these definitional variations coupled with the vagaries of sampling and methodological differences should serve to remind the reader that both intra- and interinstitutional comparisons about how nurses spend their time may be quite misleading. The findings of a variety of work sampling studies have been highlighted by Prescott, Phillips, Ryan, and Thompson (1991).

One final reflection from the above illustration is worthy of note in considering the number of nurses required. Recall that in the previous illustration, the "system" suggested that 15.1 nurses were required. As staffing coordinator, you might easily conclude that 15 nurses would be sufficient. If the "system" had recommended 15.5 nurses, you might have been inclined to raise some other questions before deciding to allocate 15 nurses or 16 nurses. For example, what are the competency levels and experiences of the available nurses? Are the 5 patients in category IV considered to be "light" or "heavy"? Are discharges or new admissions expected? Clearly, a variety of factors not amenable to the nature of the data collection must be considered in arriving at a decision. This is one of the "subjective" components or professional judgement areas that need to be acknowledged in all existing NWMSs. As systems become computerized, there appears to be an increasing tendency to rely solely on the output of the computer, ignoring the realities of the limited scope of measurement involved in estimating both the demand for care and nurses' response to that demand.

Deriving staffing levels from tasking documents is also relatively straightforward, although dependent upon the conceptual basis for development of the listing of tasks or activities. Each item is represented by a coefficient or value reflecting its real time, standard time, or relative time, derived from estimation procedures or extensive observational time studies. Some tasking documents include both direct and indirect care time in the value of the coefficient, while others distinguish between the two through specification of the task. As previously noted, tasking documents differ considerably in the precision used to define the discrete tasks and thus range from systems employing fewer than 50 items to those with more than 200 items. Generally, constants are used to reflect the additional time required for personal time, unit-related work, and, if not included in the tasks, indirect care time. The underlying assumption of tasking documents, and one that has been frequently challenged, is that the sum of the parts (discrete nursing tasks) is equal to the whole.

The same caveats mentioned with respect to the final determination of staffing levels for factor and prototype evaluation systems apply to tasking documents. The limits of measurement and the complexity of the patient care environment should serve to reduce dependency on the outputs of NWMSs. All of the systems available today were intended as guides to staffing levels; professional judgement always has been considered a necessary adjunct to the final decision on staffing levels. Unfortunately, many users forget that fact.

The references cited previously as sources for details of the various NWMSs also contain, to varying degrees, details regarding the approaches to quantification or the development of staffing levels. In addition to those cited earlier, the work of Thibeault (1990) is extremely useful for both vendor-supplied information and expert critique on the quantification procedures of three widely used systems.

Maintaining Credibility

As is the case for all instruments or measurement devices, questions of the consistency of the measures and their accuracy are of prime importance. Thus, the development and implementation of NWMSs have been closely linked to the measurement and demonstration of reliability and validity.

Reliability refers to repeatability, or the consistency with which the instrument yields the same or similar results. For example, you would expect that two nurses independently assessing the care requirements of the same group of patients/clients at the same time would yield the same or very similar results. Although there are several forms of reliability, the classic test for NWMSs is achieved through measurement of rater equivalence. This test of equivalence attempts to determine if the same results can be obtained using different observers at the same time, and is referred to as inter-rater reliability. A reliable instrument should produce the same results if all observers (or raters) are using it in the same way.

The traditional approach to measurement of inter-rater reliability has been calculation of the percentage of agreement between nurse raters. Error or disagreement in the measurement process can arise from a variety of sources (e.g., disagreement on definition of the assessment items, inadequate knowledge of or failure to follow the rules of assessment, disagreement in the use of clinical judgement, and differences in knowledge about the care needs of the patient/client). It follows, then, that sufficient training in the use of the NWMS, coupled with complete knowledge of the patient, is essential. It is for these reasons that the developers of NWMSs advocate extensive nursing inservice education programs at the time of implementation to achieve a high level of reliability and further advise continuous testing of inter-rater reliability to maintain acceptable levels of reliability. Alas, this advice has not always been heeded. Other

than during the implementation phase, reliability testing is often
ignored and in a relatively short period of time, the value of the system is eroded. Staff quickly lose confidence in the results, and misuse
of the system ensues. Recognizing the potential problems of unreliable
systems, the Canadian National Task Force on Nursing Workload
Measurement recommended a regular monitoring program with 85%
to 90% inter-rater reliability for tasking documents and 90% to 95%
inter-rater reliability for category systems (The MIS Group, 1993).

Validity refers to the extent to which the instrument measures
what it purports or seeks to measure. For example, if the NWMS designates Patient A as requiring 3 hours of care, evidence that Patient A
received 3 hours of care would attest to the validity of the system.
While there are many types of validity, the above example illustrates
predictive validity. Since the intent of NWMSs is to predict staffing
requirements for some future time period, such as the next shift or
subsequent 24-hour period, predictive validity is considered to be the
most appropriate type. Validity, like reliability, must be monitored
periodically. Changes in the scope of practice of nurses, physicians,
and other care providers can all affect the time that it takes to care
for patients and thus alter significantly the validity of the NWMS. As
noted at the beginning of this chapter, a wide range of variables
impinge on staffing levels. Thus, changes in any of them can render
staffing projections invalid.

The degree of satisfaction or agreement among professional
nurses as to the established hours of care represents a relatively
quick and easy method of estimating the validity of the system.
Although this form of evaluation is subjective, it has been found that
the judgement of the professional nurse usually reflects the situation
on the unit (Williams & Murphy, 1979). This should not be too surprising given that the original intent of the systems was to make
"consistently reproducible a process that experienced nurses do quickly and automatically in their heads" (Williams, 1988, p. 91).

As previously noted, development and implementation of a
NWMS generally involves some form of timing study to establish validity. Subsequent monitoring of validity may entail a repeat of such
studies to verify the original established hours of care or as the basis
for a new standard. The significant commitment of both time and
money necessary for monitoring validity has often been greater than
users are willing to commit. All too frequently, such monitoring is
ignored, and legitimate mistrust and misuse result. The potential for
easing the task of monitoring reliability and validity does exist with
computer technology. However, only one system makes use of this
capability (Giovannetti & Johnson, 1990).

In addition to evidence attesting to the reliability and validity of
NWMSs, a third consideration for maintaining credibility has to do

with the broader area of education. If NWMSs are to be useful in staffing decisions, including their impact on effective utilization of nursing resources as well as recruitment and retention, it follows that nurse users need to know the parameters of the systems. It is difficult to employ the necessary professional judgement if one is uninformed of the basic tenets of the system. Again, developers have advocated full understanding and training. Although training is common during the implementation phase, user orientation frequently falls by the wayside over time. Education regarding the basic development of the system also needs to be extended to non-nurse users, such as administrators, finance officers, and other care providers, especially physicians (De Groot, 1989a, 1989b; Giovannetti & Mayer, 1984).

Failing to maintain credibility among nurses in the NWMS has often had serious consequences. The following quote from a union newsletter provides some insight into the question of NWMS credibility.

> *The end result [of patient classification is]... chronic under-staffing, increased stress [nursing], reduced patient care, increased legal liability, and growing job dissatisfaction. So what can... [staff nurses] do to offset the results of patient classification systems? Basically, the answer is to outsmart the computer! ... outsmart the management minds that devised this sophisticated means of saving money.* (Richardson, 1987, p. 1)

The article concluded with a plea to union members "to join in a concerted action to stop the chronic understaffing that employers seem committed to in their undying need to balance their budgets" (Richardson, 1987, p. 1).

A few months following the preceding advice, patient classification systems were cited as one cause of serious staff nurse concerns in an illegal 19-day strike of nurses in Alberta. In a brief to the government on the topic of the issues that indirectly led to the strike, the unionized nurses stated their opposition to "the introduction of all administrative systems whose effect is to reduce staffing levels, to erode the quality of patient care, and to increase the legal liability under which nurses work" (United Nurses of Alberta, 1988, p. 51). Both striking and nonstriking nurses charged that patient classification systems led to dissatisfaction. They said that nursing hours designated to patients do not provide for individuality of patients' care; that variable staffing methods devalue nurses' skills and work; and that staffing becomes a game of numbers. Further, they charged that patient classification systems have resulted in the removal of control that nurses once had over their patient care; reliance on individual professional judgement has been replaced with objective criteria for establishing what patients need; and patient classification impinges upon the autonomy of a nurse and undermines the status of professional nursing judgement. The content of nursing work is controlled by management, rather than professional nurses (United Nurses of Alberta, 1988; Staff Nurses Association, 1988).

It is not my intention to suggest or imply that dissatisfaction among nurses is a consequence of nursing workload measurement systems. Nevertheless, the systems are frequently misunderstood and misused not only by nurses but by non-nurse managers and executives as well.

Conclusion

Effective management and utilization of nursing resources remains a critical and complex issue. Answers to the question of "how many nurses" depends upon answers to many other questions. Furthermore, the way that nursing resources are managed has a direct effect on the well-being of recipients of care and, many would argue, on those who provide the care. Poor management practices could have indirect long term effects on the preparation of and availability of adequately prepared nurses, on the roles and functions of other health care providers, and on the costs of care. Although resolution of nursing resource management issues is not easily forthcoming, they are no more or less intractable than those of other health care workers, including physicians. The fact that the largest proportion of nurses (well over 80% in Canada) are employees, compounded by the fact that these nurses are employed in what is viewed as the most costly component of the health care system (i.e., acute care institutions), has contributed to the scrutiny given to nursing management by policy makers.

The major aim of this chapter has been to acquaint the reader with the major types of nursing workload measurement systems used to determine staffing levels in acute care institutions. Although the systems have been useful, they are not without limitations and in some cases have been seen as contributing to bureaucratization of nursing and to technical alienation (Campbell, 1988). As suggested by Storch and Stinson (1988):

> *The techniques are commendable when they serve their intended purpose of enhancing the quality of care by improving decision-making. However, when these techniques become used as ends in themselves, or are used to effect cheaper and less effective levels of care, they become instruments of the deskilling [professional disintegration] of nurses because the craft and creativity of nursing is destroyed.* (p. 36)

Future Directions

As this book goes to press, the Canadian health care system and, indeed, all segments of Western society are undergoing profound changes. Predicting the form and structure of the health care system of the 21st century is difficult and risky. Futurists advise that the only certainty about the future is that it will be different. Nonetheless, there are realities with respect to nursing resource management and utilization that may serve to guide nurse managers in the difficult challenges ahead. The remainder of this chapter briefly outlines two of these.

Attention to Costs

First is greater attention to cost issues. It may seem surprising that effective utilization, not a new concept for nurses at least, has been duly discussed and debated in the absence of data reflecting the true costs of care. Attention to costs of care in relation to outcomes of care is long overdue and for nurses is a welcomed perspective. For too long, the real costs of nursing care have been meshed with unrelated costs such as hospital room and board, maintenance, supplies, and equipment. Measures of hospital output have been viewed largely in terms of mortality and morbidity statistics with no acknowledgement of the contribution of nursing care to improvements in these statistics.

In Canada, most provinces are committed to determining costs of care at both the departmental level (e.g., nursing, pharmacy, housekeeping) and the global (i.e., patient-specific) level , as advocated by The MIS Group (1993). Explication of these costs will assist in determining appropriate practices and the impact of policies and structures on such costs. It will also assist the public in determining appropriate responses to health care needs in terms of settings, providers, and priorities. Greater knowledge and involvement by users of health care services are unequivocally hallmarks of the coming changes.

Although explication of the costs of care are welcomed, nursing lacks tools and procedures for identifying costs. Nursing workload measurement systems were not designed to measure costs; they ignore the skill level of the nurse provider and ignore the severity of illness of the patients. They were designed to predict the volume of work (rather than to capture the volume of work done), and for the most part are not accompanied by procedures to capture or retain patient-specific data. Nonetheless, the systems have been used, sometimes with modifications, to obtain some assessment of the costs of nursing care. This practice has been more common in the United

States, where the opportunity to charge for nursing care is in keeping with the health care system.

The Canadian National Task Force on Nursing Workload Measurement has recommended that nursing workload measurement systems be used as proxies of nursing costs in keeping with the national plan to develop departmental and global costs (The MIS Group, 1993). The recommendation was made with full knowledge of the limitations of NWMSs with respect to costs but was seen as a practical alternative until such time as costing systems become available. Nevertheless, costing activities will lead to further evaluation of the effectiveness of medical case-costing systems, such as diagnostic related groups and case mix groups, and some indications of variations in the costs of nursing care. Since Canadian hospitals are moving quickly to implement funding systems based on case costing, similar to the U.S. Prospective Payment System, the consequences of such actions on resources for nursing care are urgently in need of evaluation.

Development of a Data Set

A second direction that is gaining momentum is the development of a data set unique to the needs of nursing. In the U.S., the elements of nursing data have been defined, although to date they are not mandated as essential data and thus are not part of a national or state hospital discharge data set (Werley & Lang, 1988). In 1992, the first national conference on this topic was held in Canada, and the essential nursing components of a National Health Data Set were proposed (CNA, 1993).

The identification and retention of patient-specific data that relate to the demand for care (including patient-specific characteristics), the provision of care (including interventions and resources), and the outcomes of care will do much to assist in evaluating the effectiveness of nursing care. The details of the health information mandate and its importance are covered well in Chapter 28. With this level of data available on-line, the assessment of nursing resources required will be a logical by-product of electronic and likely more integrated patient care systems. Separate systems to measure nursing workload for the purpose of staff determination and assignment will no longer be necessary.

Nurse managers must remain attuned to the tenets of health care in general and to nursing economics in particular. Nursing is not a special interest group within the health care system; nursing is a central and essential element. Profound changes will need to take place to ensure that nurses become partners with the public and with other providers to ensure the economic accountability that needs to accompany our existing professional accountability.

References

Baar, A., Moores, B., & Rhys-Hearn, C. (1973). A review of the various methods of measuring the dependency of patients on nursing staff. *International Journal of Nursing Studies, 10,* 195-203.

Buchan, I.M. (1979). *Nurse staffing methodology in Canada.* Ottawa: Canadian Nurses Association.

Campbell, M.L. (1988) Accounting for care: A framework for analysing change in Canadian nursing. In R. White (Ed.), *Political issues in nursing: Past, present, and future* (Vol.3) (pp. 45-70). Chichester: John Wiley & Sons.

Canadian Nurses Association. (1993). *Papers from the Nursing Minimum Data Set Conference.* Ottawa: Author.

Cockerill, R.W., & O'Brien-Pallas, L.L. (1990). Satisfaction with nursing workload systems: Report of a survey of Canadian hospitals, Part A. *Canadian Journal of Nursing Administration, 3*(2), 17-22.

Connor, R.J. (1961). A work sampling study of variations in nursing work load. *Hospitals, 35,* 40-41.

Connor, R.J., Flagle, C.D., Hsieh, R.K.C., Preston, R.A., & Singer, S. (1961). Effective use of nursing resources: A research report. *Hospitals, 35,* 30-39.

De Groot, H.A. (1989a). Patient classification system evaluation. Part 1: Essential system elements. *Journal of Nursing Administration, 19*(6), 30-35.

De Groot, H.A. (1989b). Patient classification system evaluating. Part 2: System selection and implementation. *Journal of Nursing Administration, 19*(7), 24-30.

Edwardson, S., & Giovannetti, P. (1994). Nursing workload measurement systems. In J.F. Fitzpatrick & J.S. Stevenson (Eds.), *Annual review of nursing research* (pp. 95-123). New York: Springer.

Giovannetti, P. (1978). *Patient classification systems in nursing: A description and analysis.* (DHEW publication No. HRA 78-22). Hyattsville, MD: U.S. Department of Health and Human Services.

Giovannetti, P. (1984). Staffing methods—Implications for quality. In L. Willis & M. Linwood (Eds.), *Measuring the quality of nursing care* (pp. 123-150). London: Churchill Livingstone.

Giovannetti, P., & Johnson, J.M. (1990). A new generation patient classification system. *Journal of Nursing Administration, 20*(5), 33-40.

Giovannetti, P., & Mayer, G. (1984). Building confidence in patient classification systems. *Nursing Management, 15*(8), 31-34.

Hanson, R.L. (1979). Issues and methodological problems in nurse staffing research. *Communicating Nursing Research, 12,* 51-56.

Lewis, E.N. (1989). *Manual of patient classification: Systems and techniques practical application.* Rockville, MD: Aspen.

O'Brien-Pallas, L.L., & Cockerill, R.W. (1990). Satisfaction with nursing workload systems: Report of a survey of Canadian hospitals, Part B. *Canadian Journal of Nursing Administration, 3*(2), 23-26.

Prescott, P.A., Phillips, C.Y., Ryan, J.W., & Thompson, K.O. (1991). Changing how nurses spend their time. *IMAGE: Journal of Nursing Scholarship, 23*(1), 23-28.

Richardson, T. (1987). Patient classification. *News Bulletin: United Nurses of Alberta, 11*(2), 1.

Soeken, K.L., & Prescott, P.A. (1986). Issues in the use of Kappa to estimate reliability. *Medical Care, 24,* 733-741.

Staff Nurses Association of Alberta. (1988). *Submission to the Premier's Commission on Future Health Care for Albertans* (Unpublished report). Edmonton: Author.

Storch, J.L., & Stinson, S.M. (1988). Concepts of deprofessionalization with applications to nursing. In R. White (Ed.), *Political issues in nursing: Past, present, and future* (Vol. 3) (pp. 33-44). Chichester: John Wiley & Sons.

The MIS Group. (1993). *National Task Force Report on nursing workload measurement.* Ottawa: Author.

Thibeault, C. (1990). *Workload measurement in nursing.* Montréal: Québec Hospital Association.

United Nurses of Alberta. (1988). *Brief to the Premier's Commission on the Future Health Care of Albertans* (Unpublished report). Edmonton: Author.

Werley, H.M., & Lang, N.M. (Eds.). (1988). *Identification of the nursing minimum data set.* New York: Springer.

Williams, M.A. (1988). When you don't develop your own: Validation methods for patient classification systems. *Nursing Management, 19*(3), 90-92, 94, 96.

Williams, M.A., & Murphy, L.N. (1979). Subjective and objective measures of staffing adequacy. *Journal of Nursing Administration, 9*(11), 21-29.

Wolfe, H., & Young, J.P. (1965A). Staffing the nursing unit: Part I, Controlled variable staffing. *Nursing Research, 14,* 236.

Wolfe, H., & Young, J.P. (1965B). Staffing the nursing unit: Part II, The multiple assignment technique. *Nursing Research, 14,* 299.

Young, J.P., Giovannetti, P., Lewison, D., & Thoms, M.L. (1981). *Factors affecting nurse staffing in acute care hospitals: A review and critique of the literature* (DHEW Publication No. HRA 81-10). Hyattsville, MD: U.S. Department of Health and Human Resources.

C   H   A   P   T   E   R   1   9

Staffing Trends and Issues

Janet M. Beed and Barbara Rigby

Janet M. Beed, RN, BN (Dalhousie), MScN (Toronto), CHE, is Vice-President, Patient Care at the Ontario Cancer Institute/Princess Margaret Hospital, Toronto. In both her current and her previous roles, she has been directly involved in budget preparation and variance analysis.

Barbara Rigby, RN, BScN (Queen's), MHSc (McMaster), is Director of Nursing and Ambulatory Care at Ontario Cancer Institute/Princess Margaret Hospital, Toronto, and a Lecturer at McMaster University, Hamilton, Ontario. Throughout her career as a Nurse Manager and Director of Nursing, she has prepared staffing schedules for units as large as 76 beds as well as ambulatory clinic schedules.

This chapter contains definitions of variables affecting staffing and scheduling and a description of how to work with these variables to prepare a schedule. The chapter will conclude with a discussion of some of the more current and developing staffing trends or philosophies. Whenever possible, examples will be given for illustrative purposes.

For nurse managers, matching patients' needs with appropriately skilled staff, in a cost-effective manner, will continue to be a challenge. The salary budget for nursing in most acute care facilities represents approximately one-third of the total operating budget. This large portion of an agency's resources must be managed, and staffing plans are a tool to assist with this key responsibility. Developing a method to staff a patient care unit, ambulatory clinic, operating theatre, community agency program, or any other setting where staff must be assigned on a rotating basis (henceforth referred to as the unit schedule) is a process, not a task. This process involves a clear understanding of the variables that influence staffing, and demands intimate knowledge of how to work with these variables to balance patients' needs with staff mix in a cost-effective way. It is advisable to view this process as a complex puzzle, to be approached with creativity and enthusiasm.

The importance of a task or responsibility is usually related to its perceived value or outcomes. Regrettably, it is difficult to confirm a direct relationship between staffing and nurse satisfaction or staffing and quality of patient care. The complex nature of the work units, the numerous variables that contribute to nurse satisfaction, and the ability to measure this satisfaction conclusively make a direct relationship difficult to quantify. Further, "the ability to capture the elusive nature of quality makes it difficult for hospitals to know at what level to staff a nursing unit to ensure that the quality of patient care rendered is appropriate" (Behner, Fogg, Fournier, Frankenbach, & Robertson, 1990, p. 70).

Understanding the Variables

It is essential for a nursing manager to understand the definitions of the variables involved in establishing and improving a schedule for the work unit. The manager must also comprehend the interdependence of each of the variables between and among themselves, so that manipulation of one variable can be associated with an expected outcome or outcomes. A description of five key variables—departmental philosophy, hours of operation, hours of work, workload variables, and staffing standards—follows.

Departmental Philosophy and Strategic Plan

The philosophy, goals, objectives, and strategic plan of the hospital and nursing department, described in Chapters 17 and 18, will directly affect the management philosophy, care delivery system, desired staffing levels, and staff mix of the work unit. A management philosophy that promotes continuing formal education, participation, delegation of non-nursing tasks, and decentralized decision making will encourage more flexible work schedules than a more hierarchical structure.

The choice of system for delivery of care will also influence the staff mix and division of workload. Primary nursing, team nursing, functional nursing, and patient-focussed care models will all influence the level of preparation required to meet the nursing care needs. When considering a model for the delivery of nursing care, patient risk must be considered at all times and balanced against cost containment.

Finally, although patient satisfaction is an important goal of all agencies, the degree of satisfaction is determined by the institution's mission and vision. When planning or reviewing the staffing for a unit, it is important to ask two questions. The first is: "What level of staff would provide care that will exceed the patient's expectations?" The second, which arises out of the first, given this level of care, is: "How far can I lower this level before I enter a situation of patient risk?" The selected level of care should reflect a balance between both these situations and an understanding of the institution's expectations.

Hours of Operation

One need only visit a busy unit to learn that staffing is an emotional topic. This can be appreciated when one views staffing as the mechanism through which work groups are determined—and recognizes the fact that these work groups frequently become an individual's social group because of common scheduled days off. Further, the staffing schedule determines who will enjoy a pattern of work that most reflects the "non-shift world" (e.g., Christmas days off, regular day shift).

Given the emotional nature of staffing, it is important to place this responsibility into a work context. Simply stated, staffing is the daily assignment of personnel to responsibilities or tasks on the unit. To determine how to match these two variables, a common measurement form is required. The common measurement most frequently used is the objective time variable, hours. The unit to be staffed can be assessed in terms of hours of operation and the staff to be scheduled can be assessed in terms of hours of work.

The first step a nurse manager must take is to determine the hours the unit is, or should be, open. Generally, a hospital inpatient unit requires 24 hours a day, seven days a week, while a short-stay unit may run only 18 hours a day, five days a week. Hours of operation best suited to your unit should be determined in consultation with the medical staff who admit to the unit on a regular basis. Key questions should explore the projected length of stay for the patients and the associated projected demand for care. Figure 19.1 shows the possible distribution of patient need across the length of stay for two patients, one admitted for a bone marrow transplant and one admitted for a hip replacement. Note, for example, that, for days 5 through 15 in the care of a patient with a bone marrow transplant, the nursing care is intensive, and staffing would need to be adjusted accordingly.

Each projection will be influenced by individual patient factors. The nurse manager must ascertain if there will be common patient factors, such as age or co-morbidity associated with a particular patient population. Co-morbidity, such as diabetes, spinal cord injury, and sensory impairment, can significantly influence a patient's need for nursing support above and beyond that associated with the admitting diagnosis.

Figure 19.1

Distribution of patient need: Two types of patient.

(a)   Patient with allogenic bone marrow transplant

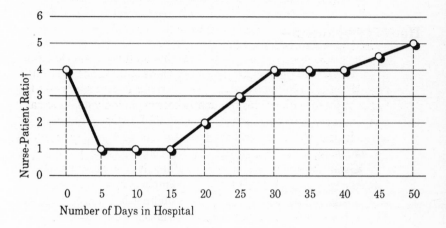

(b)   Patient with hip replacement

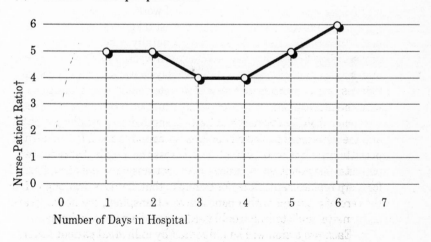

† Nurse-patient ratio = one nurse needed per indicated number of patients.

When establishing or reviewing the patient population, multidisciplinary discussion will also be of assistance. The hours of support provided by the physiotherapist will influence the hours of support provided by the nurse. Frequently, support staff will establish a plan of care that is implemented by them Monday to Friday, and assumed by the nurses on Saturday and Sunday. Through involvement of the members of the team at this phase of the scheduling process, the nurse manager establishes a communication pattern that promotes mutual problem solving of staffing issues. Such communication may thereby reduce the possibility of change in support services without consultation.

Hours of Work

The hours of work for the mix of staff included in the unit schedule are determined by the existing collective agreements of the bargaining units of the affected staff. In the absence of a collective agreement, the health care agency will have hours of work defined through approved personnel policies.

Most agencies address hours of work using two categories: paid hours and effective hours. Paid hours reflect the number of hours for which the nurse is remunerated and incorporates both worked hours, benefit hours, and local agreement activities that secure payment while away from the place of work. The importance of determining effective hours can be illustrated by answering the question "How many nurses would need to be hired if you wanted to have in attendance one nurse 24 hours per day, 365 days per year?" In most provinces, the collective agreements indicate that a full-time staff nurse will be paid for 1950 hours per year, which represents 7.5 hours of work per day. Clerical and administrative staff generally work 1820 hours per year, or 7 hours per day.

Effective hours reflect the number of hours during which the staff member will be present providing direct and indirect care to patients. Direct care is described as time spent with the patient (e.g., changing a dressing) and indirect time described as the time spent preparing for or following up on a direct activity (e.g., documentation of the wound being dressed). Effective hours are determined by subtracting the institution's benefit hours from the paid hours. Benefit hours include sick days, vacation days, statutory holidays, education days, and leaves with pay such as bereavement leave.

Benefit hours are determined through hospital policies and through historical patterns of use. For example, if you have an average sick time of six days per year per staff member, then this should be built into the calculation. If you are developing a new unit, you would be wise to speak with units of a similar nature to estimate the absenteeism on this new unit.

Table 19.1
Determining benefit hours.

Benefit hours	No. Days per Year	No. Hours per Day	Total Hours per Year
Vacation	15	7.5	112.5
Statutory holidays	9	7.5	67.5
Float days	3	7.5	22.5
Paid education days	3	7.5	22.5
Average paid sick days	6	7.5	45.0
Total benefit hours			270.0

The first problem-solving step is to determine how many hours there are in one year: 24 hours x 365 days = 8760 hours per year. The second step is to determine how many hours a nurse is actually present in a year. When one nurse is paid for 1950 hours per year, the actual presence of the nurse on that unit can be determined by subtracting the benefit hours as calculated by the institution from the paid hours (see Table 19.1). In this example, 1950 – 270 = 1680 effective hours. If there are 8760 hours per year requiring coverage and one nurse provides 1680 hours per year, by simple division of 8760 by 1680 you can determine that 5.2 nurses will need to be hired if you require one nurse to be available 24 hours a day, 365 days of the year.

To provide a second example, consider the staffing for an operating room that runs five days per week and is closed on statutory holidays. The number of hours of operation would be calculated as follows: 5 days x 52 weeks – 9 statutory holidays = 251 days x 7.5 hours = 1882.5 hours per year. As was the case in the previous scenario, one nurse is paid for 1950 hours per year. The effective hour calculation in this example is different, however, as the number of hours that the unit will be open and the nurse not in attendance will not include statutory holidays. The effective hours for a nurse employed in the operating room will be 1748 hours. Therefore, to provide attendance for one nurse in the operating room during its hours of operation in one year, 1.08 nurses would need to be hired.

The terms used to describe these totals (e.g., 4.7 nurses or 1.08 nurses) can be confusing in an environment where casual and part-time work is common. To minimize confusion, staff positions are usually expressed as full-time equivalents (FTE). A full-time equivalent, depending on the job category, can represent 1950 or 1820 hours of work. For example, to determine the 4.7 FTEs on a unit requiring 1950 hours, you would use the following: (4 staff x 1950 hours = 7800 hours) + (0.7 staff x 1950 hours = 1365 hours of work) = a total of 9165 hours of work.

The 4 FTEs could comprise four individuals each working full time; six individuals, two working full time and four working part time; eight individuals each working half time, or any combination of full- and part-time staff that you can conceive.

Workload Indicators

When hospitals first became interested in determining the costs of nursing care, rudimentary systems were used. Patient volumes and patient census were key data forms for the manager and the challenge was to assign staff based on these data, rather than on the extensive experiential body of knowledge of the senior leader.

In the 1960s, patient classification systems emerged. Throughout their evolution, they began to be referred to as nursing workload measurement systems (NWMSs). (See Chapter 18 for a detailed discussion.) Simply stated, patient classification is a systematic approach to determine the nursing care needs of the patients and the nursing resources required to meet this need. Frequently, this is referred to as patient acuity. "The acuity level is the result of identifying the direct nursing services provided to the individual patient and the patient's significant others" (Van Slyck, 1991, p. 30). In addition to acuity data, patient classification systems allow for activities that are unit related but not necessarily patient related. By capturing both these nursing role components, staffing decisions can be made on a daily basis and scheduling can be planned based on a retrospective analysis of the variance between actual staff use and the staff requirements predicted by the organization's specific patient classification tool.

Few hospitals rely on patient classification systems alone to generate their current or projected workload data. In a study of user satisfaction with nursing workload systems in Canadian hospitals, only 70% of the nursing respondents indicated that they used the information frequently or all the time (Cockerill & O'Brien-Pallas, 1990). In a later report, O'Brien-Pallas, Cockerill, and Leatt (1992) concluded that "Criticisms associated with the ability of systems to capture the complexity of nursing work may be justified" (p. 17).

Comparability of workload and, specifically, nursing workload associated with particular patient populations appears to be an increasing area of interest for government funding agencies. Patient classification systems generally cannot fulfil this mandate. A study of four different classification systems found that "all systems produced statistically and clinically significant differences in hours of care estimates for an average patient on an average day" (O'Brien-Pallas, Cockerill, & Leatt, 1992, p. 21).

Determining nursing workload costs associated with a particular patient population for the purposes of cross-institutional comparison is best done using a basic ratio formula, paid hours per patient-day. Paid hours were defined earlier in the chapter. Patient-days are the cumulative number of days that a patient stays in the hospital. For example, on a 20-bed unit that is open 365 days of the year, the maximum number of patient-days would be 20 x 365 = 7300. If the unit ran at 80% occupancy, the actual patient-days would be 7300 x 0.80 = 5840 patient-days. In a recent comparison of costs for intensive care units, using the formula paid hours per patient-day, variability from institution to institution was evident with a high of 36 paid hours per patient-day and a low of 24 paid hours per patient-day. A similar comparison of oncology units showed a range from 6.9 to 12.6 paid hours per patient-day. Key to any comparison is a clear definition of the staff included in the paid hour calculation, (e.g., unit secretaries, respiratory therapists, or simply front-line nursing staff).

Staffing Standards

The final variable to be addressed is that of staffing standards. There are certain standards of staffing that cannot be changed and patient acuity situations that cannot be captured through the patient workload data. These issues can be described as issues related to critical mass. This suggests that the volume of the need is not in synchrony with the resources assigned. Such a situation would occur when the census of a unit drops so that one nurse could adequately care for all the patients on the unit, but issues related to patient and staff risk indicate that a unit cannot be staffed by one person alone. It is the manager's responsibility to be attentive to these situations and look for opportunities to maximize the nurses' productivity. An example of this might be the merging of the unit with another unit to improve the utilization of the required staff.

Conversely, staff themselves sometimes compromise standards by providing care that is not considered basic to the unit. For example, nurses on a unit may change a burn dressing to accommodate an outpatient who does not wish to wait in the outpatient area. Such extra workload items are rarely captured by the workload system.

Frequently, the number of these extras increases, sometimes to a point where patients on the unit are placed in a situation of risk. The manager needs to be attentive to this unit activity and either capture the work in a manner that can be reflected in the staffing levels or persuade staff to avoid carrying out the extras.

Staffing standards cannot be developed for all situations that may occur, given the variable nature of the work. Rather, key situations that create poor use of resources and place patients at potential risk should be determined in consultation with the staff and reviewed frequently for relevance and occurrence.

So far, five key variables that can influence staffing and the unit scheduling system have been explored. The manager also should be aware that "in an environment of continually shrinking resources, we must create databases that enable us to question not only the effectiveness, but the appropriateness of the activities performed by the nursing staff" (Van Slyck, 1991, p. 30). Models to assist with staffing have been developed, but they have seen limited use because of their complexity and information-intensive nature (Sitompul & Randhawa, 1990). After analysis of these variables, the next step is the creation of a schedule.

Creating the Schedule

Creating a staffing plan, whether for an inpatient unit or an ambulatory care setting, is a challenge to every nurse manager. Drawing on an understanding of the variables involved in establishing or improving a unit schedule and the interdependence of these variables, a manager begins to develop a staffing plan. The plan must address needs of the patients, accommodate the variations in workload and skill mix required by the care delivery model, meet contractual obligations of all bargaining units, and ensure optimal quality of work life for staff.

To accomplish this, a complex process must be undertaken, including a staffing study, determination of the staffing complement, conceptualization of a basic staffing plan, and development of a schedule.

The Staffing Study

The staffing study begins with an examination of the 10 critical elements of staffing:

1. Type of clinical service (e.g., pediatrics, geriatrics, ICU, oncology);
2. Physical layout of the unit;
3. Volume indicators (census, number of visits);

4. Number of providers (staff physicians, residents);
5. Medical expectations;
6. Patient acuity;
7. Level of nursing care required (standards);
8. Support staff available (e.g., clerks, porters, nutrition aides);
9. Legal considerations (contracts, scope of practice);
10. Organizational staffing policies (vacations, statutory holidays, sick time).

The second step is the completion of an activity study, which determines:

*   Tasks undertaken, the frequency of those tasks, and the time taken to complete each task;
*   Ratio of direct and indirect care activities;
*   Level of appropriate personnel to undertake the tasks;
*   Appropriate allowance for fatigue, personal variation, unavoidable waiting, and personal time.

This information can be used to calculate: the paid hours per patient-day or the average time per patient visit; the percentage of time for direct and indirect care; and the percentage of time required for personal time (see also Chapter 18). Some professional organizations, such as the Oncology Nursing Society (Miaskowski, 1990; Miaskowski & Buchsel, 1992), have identified staffing standards (e.g., average paid hours per patient-day for specific populations).

The next step involves an examination of the past staffing history for the unit, using census for inpatients or activity records for ambulatory care. The patient classification data (e.g., Medicus, Grasp) plus information about sickness, holiday, and vacation times and about overtime are incorporated with this. The nurse manager then includes data on the required staffing mix. It is essential to remember that trends can change.

This step should be followed by a review of current staffing levels to determine whether they provide safe, comprehensive care to meet the patients' needs and complete the work of the unit while utilizing the most appropriate level of staff.

Finally, examination of the strategic directions of the organization, the department of nursing, and the unit must be undertaken. This process will enable the nurse manager to identify changes that will influence staffing. Changes in patient demographics, acuity, and length of stay, new drugs and treatments, and the economic environment can all alter staffing requirements.

Staffing plans that involve the nursing staff in their development are less apt to fail. The nurses will have more confidence in the plans, a factor that increases nurses' satisfaction in the workplace (Mueller, 1987; Ringl & Dotson, 1989).

The Staffing Complement

The staffing complement for a unit is determined by utilizing a formula to calculate the number of full-time equivalents (FTEs) required to care for all patients while the unit is open. For inpatient units this means 24 hours per day, 7 days per week, 365 days per year. In ambulatory care units, it may mean 8 hours per day, 5 days per week (productive days).

- **Staffing formula for inpatient units.** To determine staffing for a unit where the number of paid hours per patient-day and percentage occupancy are known and the number of effective hours can be calculated (as demonstrated previously in the section "Hours of Work"), the following formula can be used: (number of paid hours per patient-day x number of beds x % occupancy x 365 days per year) divided by (number of effective hours for 1 FTE). This will equal the number of FTEs required.

  E.g., $$\frac{6.37 \times 21 \times 0.85 \times 365}{1680} = 24.7 \text{ FTEs}$$

  To determine the paid hours per patient-day on an existing unit, for use in calculating the FTEs needed for a changed number of beds, this formula can be used: (current number of FTEs x effective hours) divided by (number of beds x % occupancy x 365 days).

  E.g., $$\frac{24.7 \times 1680}{21 \times 0.85 \times 365} = 6.37 \text{ paid hours per patient-day}$$

- **Staffing formula for ambulatory clinics.** To determine staffing for clinics where the paid time per visit and the number of visits and productive days per year are known and the effective hours can be calculated, the following formula can be used: (paid time per visit [including direct and indirect hours] x number of visits x number of productive days per year) divided by (number of effective hours per year for 1 FTE). This will equal the number of FTEs required.

E.g., $$\frac{1.0 \times 325 \times 252}{1680} = 48.75 \text{ FTEs}$$

The Basic Staffing Plan

The basic staffing plan for each unit should include the basic number of staff in each category required to staff the unit on each shift. The ratio of registered nurses (RNs) to other personnel, such as registered nursing assistants (RNAs) and clerical workers, must be determined. Staff may be all RNs with clerical assistance; RNs and RNAs and clerical; or RNs and RNAs in combination with other staff (porters, orderlies, clerks).

Warstler (1972) suggested the following proportions of staff needed for each shift: 47% for days, 35% for evenings, and 17% for nights. When workload measurement systems can be used, the need of patients for nursing care should be the basis for staffing. For example, numerous late surgeries or chemotherapy administrations may require higher evening staffing. An intensive care unit may require the same staffing level around the clock.

If required to meet the needs of patients, additional staff may be added to the basic numbers. They may be assigned as unit-based relief or as a casual departmental "float" pool. Relief staff provide the flexibility to meet unpredictable changes in workload due to patient acuity and supplement basic staff absences due to sickness, vacation, or statutory holiday time. They are not guaranteed a certain number of hours nor a permanent schedule. They may be prebooked or called to duty on an as-needed basis. Financial resources will control the total number of personnel used in both the basic and relief groups per unit on an annual basis.

Table 19.2 (see page 362) demonstrates a basic staffing plan for a 27-bed oncology unit with a paid hours per patient-day of 6.57; an occupancy of 85%; and a staff mix of RNs, RNAs, and unit clerks. Table 19.3 (see page 362) demonstrates a basic staffing plan for a medical oncology clinic.

The Schedule

Schedules are patterns of staffing that meet the requirements of the basic staffing plan and that demonstrate an equitable distribution of working hours and time off. Schedules must accommodate the language of collective agreements of bargaining units as well as hospital staffing policies and staff preferences.

Table 19.2
Basic staffing plan for a 27-bed oncology unit.

Category	Day	Evening	Night	Total
RN	6	3	2	11
RNA	1	1	2	4
Unit clerk	1	0.5	0	1.5
Totals	**8**	**4.5**	**4**	**16.5**

Table 19.3
Basic staffing plan for an oncology clinic.

Pts/3-h Session	RN†	RNA	Clinic Aide	Unit Clerk
10	2.0	0.75	0.5	0.5
20	4.5	1.0	0.5	0.5
30	7.0	1.2	0.5	0.5

† Based on an RN time per visit of 33 min

Cyclic Scheduling

Schedules are usually determined for a certain number of weeks (e.g., six weeks) and are repeated in cycles. Cyclic schedules can be developed to match the needs of each unit. Figure 19.2 shows an example of a simple cyclic schedule.

Certain advantages are associated with cyclic scheduling. Once the schedule is determined, it undergoes only minor changes to accommodate such things as statutory holidays and temporary unit closures. Nurses know what their schedule will be for many months in advance and may schedule personal plans with a reasonable degree of assurance that they can be kept. Requests for special time off can be kept to a minimum. As well, cyclic schedules can be designed to accommodate rotating, permanent, or mixed shifts as well as fixed days off (e.g., four-day or five-day weekends), and work periods that meet collective agreement language and staff preferences.

Figure 19.2
Example of a cyclic schedule.

Nursing Staff†		Week Day													
		S	M	T	W	Th	F	S	S	M	T	W	T	F	S
Head nurse	A				D8	D	D8	D	D			D	D8	D8	
RN	B	N	N	N						N	N	N			N8
RN (part-time)	C				N8	N8							N8	N8	
CNA	D		N8	N	N				N	N	N	N			
CNA	E	N			D	D	D8						D	N	N
RN	F	E			E	E	E8						E	E	E
RN (part-time)	G		E8	E8				E8	E8			E8	E8		
Hospital assistant	H				D	D	D	D8				D	D	D	
Rotation for 5 RNs	1	D	D	E						D	D	D8			D
	2	D			D	D						D	D8	D	D
	3			D8	E	E			E	E	E	E			
	4		D	D	D			D	D8	D	D				
	5		D	D			N	N	N				D	E8	
Rotation for 5 CNAs	1			D8	D	N	N				D	D			D
	2	D	E8			D	D						D	D	D
	3				D8	D	D	D			D	D	D		
	4		D8	D	D			D	D	D	D				
	5	N		D	D					D	D8	N	N		

† Every person from A to H repeats the same two-week
schedule continuously. Five RNs and five CNAs rotate
through all lines of their respective schedules in numerical
sequence, i.e., 1 to 2 to 3, etc.

Key: RN = Registered Nurse
    CNA = Certified Nursing Aide

N = 19:15 - 07:30 hours
N8 = 23:15 - 07:30   "
D = 07:15 - 19:30   "
D8 = 07:15 - 15:30   "
E = 11:15 - 23:30   "
E8 = 15:15 - 23:30   "

Source: Used, with permission, from J.M. Hibberd, *Compressed work week for nursing staff: A field experiment* (unpublished Master's Thesis, University of Alberta, 1972), p. 52.

The major disadvantage with cyclic scheduling is the inflexibility once the schedule is established. This disadvantage can be minimized through a system that allows staff to exchange shifts. It is the manager's responsibility to set the criteria for shift exchange. For example, similar experience and skill sets (e.g., the ability to assume charge) may be required. In addition, both parties involved in the switch must agree.

Schedules should be reviewed periodically to ensure that they match the strategic goals of the organization, department of nursing, and unit. They must be designed to meet patient acuity needs by encompassing the appropriate numbers and categories of staff. Staff satisfaction with the schedules must also be part of any review.

Self-Scheduling

Historically, the work schedule has been a major source of discontent among nurses and a problem for nurse managers. Because patients require around-the-clock care, nurses must be available to provide that care 24 hours a day, seven days a week. Self-scheduling as a staffing methodology was developed to provide nurses with a sense of control over both their professional and personal lives.

The lack of control over schedules has been described by many authors (Cooperrider, 1980; Miller, 1984; Ringl & Dotson, 1989; Tully, 1992) as a major factor in nurses' dissatisfaction with the workplace and in difficulties with staff recruitment and retention. High levels of staff turnover can be expensive for an organization in terms of recruitment, orientation costs, and lower productivity levels.

For self-scheduling to succeed, unit staff must either provide the impetus for, or display a high level of interest in, adopting this methodology. The organization of a staff committee to facilitate the process increases commitment (Tully, 1992).

The self-scheduling implementation process would include:

- Formulating short- and long-term goals;
- Establishing guidelines (see Table 19.4);
- Reviewing collective agreement scheduling language if required;
- Reviewing hospital staff policies;
- Reviewing staffing complement;
- Developing a scheduling form for staff to complete;
- Establishing the method for rotating the ranking of first choice; and

Table 19.4

Examples of guidelines for self-scheduling by registered nurses.

- Shift and weekend work must be shared equitably and in accordance with Article E in the collective agreement.
- There must be minimum of two nurses on each day shift and a minimum of one on each night shift.
- There must be at least one senior nurse on each 12-hour shift. A senior nurse is a full-time or part-time nurse capable of assuming charge.
- The nurse manager will approve the final schedule and post it in accordance with the collective agreement.
- A nurse wishing to make a change in the schedule after the finalization date must exchange time with another nurse.
- Shift exchanges shall be in accordance with Article E.3 of the collective agreement.
- Each nurse is expected to work 50% of paid holidays set out in the collective agreement.

- Having staff practise scheduling well in advance of the implementation of the new schedule, so that adjustments can be made, if necessary, to provide appropriate coverage or a fair and equitable rotation for each staff member.

One advantage to self-scheduling has been described as increased staff satisfaction (Miller, 1984; Ringl & Dotson, 1989). Kathleen Tully (1992) says that two years after implementation, surveys indicated a high level of satisfaction: "However, this was not always the case; rather, it is the result of many revisions to the original process and guidelines. It is also the consequence of personal and professional growth experienced by staff" (p. 72).

Self-scheduling also can promote collaborative and negotiation skills. It may promote an increased sense of responsibility for covering the unit appropriately and reduce absenteeism.

Nurse managers also benefit from self-scheduling. Time previously spent preparing schedules can be allocated to other unit-related activities. The nurse manager is the facilitator of the process, empowering the nurses to make effective choices that will improve their work schedule and still provide quality patient care.

Difficulties can also occur with self-scheduling. Staff may see scheduling as the manager's responsibility and not want to take added pressure on themselves (Alexander, Palladino, Evans, Harp, Marable, & Whitmer, 1993). Some nurses feel considerable stress related to the assertiveness required to ensure that they get a fair schedule and to discourage others from taking advantage of the system.

There is also less long term predictability with self-scheduling and, therefore, the possibility of more difficulty in scheduling special personal time.

Modified Staffing Schedules

In an effort to cope with a rapidly changing economic environment, wide variances in workload demands, and to improve employee satisfaction with work schedules, a number of innovative staffing methodologies are being attempted.

Modified work weeks have been described in the literature. Some of these modifications include: changing the start of the hospital work week (Lampat, Frederick, Young, & Dankbar, 1991); use of 10-hour work days (Hung, 1991; Velianoff, 1991); 12-hour shifts (Lant & Gregory, 1984); and weekend alternatives (Metcalf, 1982). Other approaches include: permanent shifts, cluster staffing (Maras, 1992), and flextime (Arnold & Mills, 1983; McGuire & Liro, 1986).

Evaluation of these modified approaches has demonstrated varying levels of success. Some have been overwhelmingly successful, saving time and money, improving morale, productivity, and staff satisfaction, and decreasing absenteeism and turnover. Others have been less successful, with quality of care decreasing (Vik & MacKay, 1982), primary nursing being threatened, and/or no noted change in medication errors, staff morale, or agency use (Imig, Powell, & Thorman, 1984).

Other Staffing Trends

Nurse managers should be aware of the advantages and disadvantages of two other staffing trends: the use of the "float pool" and the more recent trend to job sharing.

Float Pool

Float pools consist of staff, frequently known as casual or relief staff, who are employed by an agency to work on an as-needed basis but who have no hours committed to them. This arrangement allows the hospital to respond to variations in workloads and patient acuity in a flexible and cost-effective manner. Requirements of the float pool vary from organization to organization. Some institutions require the employee to make a commitment to work all shifts and a minimum number of weekends and holidays. Others do not. Often, the responsibilities of both management and staff may be defined in collective agreements. Float staff may be all registered nurses or a combination of both professional and nonprofessional staff. They may be managed by staffing coordinators or by nursing supervisors.

The issue of float pools is a long-debated topic among nurse managers. Some do not hire float personnel. Others question whether float personnel should be unit-based or in a departmental or agency pool. Kutash and Nelson (1993) described some of the difficulties with float pools: staff may fail to understand the policies and procedures of a variety of units; there may be inconsistencies in supervision and evaluation of these staff; and pool staff may have less commitment to the organization than full-time staff.

Unit-based casual relief staff have the advantages of a small number of flexible staff under the direct supervision of a nurse manager and a higher level of commitment to one unit. Their primary obligation is to their unit, and expectations of them are the same as of the full-time staff in terms of communication meetings, inservices, and performance standards. Some organizations permit unit-based relief to obtain additional hours of work through the float pool when their commitment to the unit is fulfilled and they desire extra work.

Another variation within float pools is to have specialty members within the pool who can provide coverage in complex care areas (e.g., OR, ICU, bone marrow transplant units). Specialty staff usually have worked full time in the area or have been thoroughly oriented to the unit.

Job Sharing

Job sharing is another staffing methodology frequently explored. Job sharing describes the process by which two part-time staff fill one full-time equivalent position. They contract to provide coverage on the shifts required for a full-time position and to cover for each other during absences, such as vacations or sick time. Advantages to the individual include permanent part-time scheduled work hours, often shared benefits, flexibility while belonging to one unit, and job satisfaction. The major disadvantage to the organization occurs when collective agreements require payment in lieu of benefits to part-time staff. Job sharing then doubles the benefit costs for the one full-time position.

Use of flexible staff in a variety of models can provide a mechanism for responding to staffing needs resulting from sporadic changes in patient volumes and patient needs. It is an essential component of efficient and effective management of nursing resources.

Cross-Utilization/Cross-Training

The terms cross-utilization and cross-training represent two completely different approaches to creative staff utilization.

Cross-utilization is an enhancement of the historical approach of "floating." Floating refers to a process where shift by shift, in response to patient need, nurses permanently assigned to a unit are reassigned to another unit or department with which they may not be familiar. Cross-utilization identifies groups or partnered units with similar patient populations requiring similar nursing skills (American Organization of Nurse Executives, 1993). As the individual units in the group experience variations in census and acuity, skilled staff move from one to the other. This process benefits patients and staff because patients receive care from personnel with the appropriate skill mix and nursing staff become familiar with colleagues in the group and feel more inclined to include these "floating" nurses in the unit activities or coffee and lunch breaks. The nurse manager considering cross-utilization maintains her responsibility to ensure that there are appropriate supports through policies and standards of care, and a clear accountability and decision-making structure.

Patient-focussed care, also known as patient-centred care, is a hospital care delivery philosophy that draws on the need for cross-training. Patient-focussed care is based on the belief that the health care system has become so specialized that it is difficult for the patient to receive timely, personalized care. In a traditional care delivery philosophy, it has been suggested that a patient in the process of being admitted might see 15 to 25 different staff. Each of these staff may perform his or her duties at an exemplary level, but the patient must travel to each of these individuals, wait to be seen, and then repeat much of the information already given in previous stops.

A patient-focussed hospital reduces the mixture of specialized people and places that a patient must experience throughout a hospital stay. This is done through cross-training, which is a system that requires a staff member with one skill set to learn and assume responsibility for an additional set of skills. Cross-training focusses on increasing customer satisfaction by decreasing the number of staff with whom the customer must interact and on increasing staff productivity through the elimination of "down time."

The patient-focussed care model frequently requires redesign of units. For example, each nursing unit might need to be equipped with an admitting area, diagnostic laboratory, satellite pharmacy, and rehabilitation room. The Lakeland Regional Medical Centre, where the Booz-Allen model of hospital "decompartmentalization" was first elaborated, had bedside care provided by teams of "multi-skilled practitioners" made up of a "care pair" of a registered nurse and a technician; this pair was backed by a unit-based pharmacist, unit clerk, and unit support aide (Weber, 1991).

The movement to patient-focussed care holds appeal because its design focusses on decreasing the number of personnel, the amount of waiting time, and the amount of travel time patients experience in the daily process of care. Most institutions in the Canadian health care systems would require redesign of their current patient care units to accommodate the increased number of functions in one geographic area that are required by this model. The impact of cross-training on professional standards of practice would also need to be resolved if implementation of this new staffing trend is more than a fad.

However, nurse managers can learn from the patient-focussed model within their divisions. If patients must meet with several different nurses in the course of a regular day, and wait for one nurse to respond to another for care to take place, then the application of the care concepts of patient-focussed care should be explored.

Conclusion

Nursing unit staffing and scheduling is no longer just a monthly task for the nurse manager. It is a complete process that involves a clear understanding of the variables that influence staffing, and an intimate knowledge of how to manipulate those variables to provide cost-effective care that meets the needs of the patient population.

The process uses a variety of tools such as staffing studies, workload measurement tools, and/or patient classification systems to accomplish the goal of cost-effective care. Innovative staffing approaches allow nurse managers to cope with a rapidly changing economic environment and wide variations in workload demands. Improved employee satisfaction, increased productivity, and decreased absenteeism have also been demonstrated in some evaluations.

Regardless of what tools or methodologies are used, the approach to unit staffing must be systematic and based on sound reasoning and a clear understanding of the variables involved. Only this, combined with attention to detail, will produce a schedule with the number and skill mix of personnel appropriate for the desired level of patient care.

References

Alexander, C., Palladino, M., Evans, B., Harp, K., Marable, K., & Whitmer, K. (1993). The art of the deal. *American Journal of Nursing, 93*(3), 70-74.

American Association of Nurse Executives. (1993). Cross-utilization of nursing staff. *Nursing Management, 24*(7), 38-39.

Arnold, B., & Mills, E. (1983). Care-12: Implementation of flexible scheduling. *Journal of Nursing Administration, 13*(7/8), 9-14.

Behner, K.G., Fogg, L.F., Fournier, L.C., Frankenbach, J.T., & Robertson, S.B. (1990). Nursing resource management: Analysing the relationship between costs and quality in staffing decisions. *Health Care Management Review, 15*(4), 63-71.

Cockerill, R.W., & O'Brien-Pallas, L.L. (1990). Satisfaction with nursing workload systems: Report of a survey of Canadian hospitals. Part A. *Canadian Journal of Nursing Administration, 3*(2), 17-22.

Cooperrider, F. (1980). Staff input in scheduling boosts morale. *Hospitals, 54*(15), 59-61.

Hibberd, J.M. (1972). *Compressed work week for nursing staff: A field experiment.* Unpublished Master's Thesis, University of Alberta.

Hung, R. (1991). A cyclical schedule of 10 hour, 4 day workweeks. *Nursing Management, 22*(9), 30-33.

Imig, S.I., Powell, J.A., & Thorman, K. (1984). Primary nursing and flexistaffing: Do they mix? *Nursing Management, 15*(8), 39-42.

Kutash, M.B., & Nelson, D. (1993). Optimizing the use of nursing pool resources. *Journal of Nursing Administration, 23*(1), 65-68.

Lampat, L., Frederick, B., Young, D., & Dankbar, G. (1991). Success stories. *Nursing Economic$, 9*(4), 263-265.

Lant, T.W., & Gregory, D. (1984). The impact of the 12-hour shift: An analysis. *Nursing Management, 34,* A-B, D-F, H.

Maras, V. (1992). Implementing cluster staffing—One manager's experience. *AORN Journal, 55*(4), 1074-1077, 1080.

McGuire, J.B., & Liro, J.R. (1986). Flexible work schedules, work attitudes, and perceptions of productivity. *Public Personnel Management, 15*(1), 65-73.

Metcalf, M.L. (1982). The 12-hour weekend plan—Does the nursing staff really like it? *Journal of Nursing Administration, 12*(10), 16-19.

Miaskowski, C. (1990). *The 1989 national survey of salary, staffing and professional practice patterns in oncology nursing.* Pittsburgh: Oncology Nursing Press.

Miaskowski, C., & Buchsel, P.C. (1992). *The national survey of salary, staffing, and professional practice patterns in ambulatory oncology clinics.* Pittsburgh: Oncology Nursing Press.

Miller, M.L. (1984). Implementing self-scheduling. *Journal of Nursing Administration, 14*(3), 33-36.

Mueller, J. (1981). A look ahead: What should hospitals do to attract nurses? *RN, 50*(10), 104.

O'Brien-Pallas, L.L., & Cockerill, R.W. (1990). Satisfaction with nursing
    workload systems: Report of a survey of Canadian hospitals. Part B.
    Canadian Journal of Nursing Administration, 3(2), 23-26.
O'Brien-Pallas, L.L., Cockerill, R., & Leatt, P. (1992). Different systems, dif-
    ferent costs? *Journal of Nursing Administration, 22*(12), 17-22.
Ringl, K.K., & Dotson, L.D. (1989). Self-scheduling for professional nurses.
    Nursing Management, 20(2), 42-44.
Sitompul, D., & Randhawa, S. (1990). Nursing scheduling models: A state-of-
    the-art review. *Journal of Society in Health Systems, 2*(1), 62-72.
Tully, K.C. (1992). Self-scheduling: A strategy for recruitment and retention.
    Focus on critical care. *AACN, 19*(1), 69-73.
Van Slyck, A. (1991). A systems approach to the management of nursing ser-
    vices. Part III: Staffing system. *Nursing Management, 22*(5), 30-34.
Velianoff, G.D. (1991). Establishing a 10-hour schedule. *Nursing
    Management, 22*(9), 36-38.
Vic, A.G., & MacKay, R.C. (1982). How does the 12-hour shift affect patient
    care? *Journal of Nursing Administration, 12*(6), 16-19.
Weber, D.O. (1991). Six models of patient-focused care. *Health Care Forum
    Journal, 34*(4), 23-31.
Warstler, M.E. (1972). Some management techniques for nursing service
    administrations. *Journal of Nursing Administration, 2*(6), 25-34.

C H A P T E R   2 0

A Female Profession: A Feminist Management Perspective

Patricia E.B. Valentine

Patricia E.B. Valentine, RN, BSN (British Columbia), MA (Calgary), PhD (Alberta), is interested in viewing nursing through a feminist lens. Her area of research involves the idea that women bring a different perspective to organizations and that this needs to be acknowledged in the administrative literature. She is Associate Professor, Faculty of Nursing, University of Alberta.

When you say feminist, there still is that impression of the lady standing on the pedestal burning her bra, and so when someone asks you, are you a feminist? that image comes to mind and you think no, I'm not, you know, the radical female liberated person. (Valentine, 1988a, p. 169)

This statement, by a Canadian nurse educator, typifies the response of many, if not most, nurses to the word feminist. Nurses often express this notion despite the fact that they have never belonged to any feminist groups or read any feminist literature. Discussion of nurses' "dis-ease" (Valentine, 1988b, p. 2.29) with feminism first appeared in the nursing literature in 1985 (Baumgart cited in Allen, 1985; Chinn & Wheeler, 1985; Vance, Talbot, McBride, & Mason, 1985) and continues to the present day (Miller, 1992). Part of the uneasiness with adopting a feminist philosophy relates to the fact that it forces women to reassess their relationships with men, a disconcerting task. For nurses, it means reflecting on their work relationships with male physicians and nurses.

The nursing literature suggests that, in the past, Canadian nurses generally have not embraced feminism (Miller, 1992; Valentine, 1988b). The first and, to date, only Canadian nursing conference on feminism was held in 1991. The nursing management literature reflects this same trend (Miller, 1988). Why might a feminist perspective be useful to nurse managers? The purpose of this chapter is to: (1) introduce nurse managers to feminism, (2) discuss gender issues relevant to managing a predominantly female work force, and (3) discuss implications of a feminist perspective for the management of health care organizations.

Feminism has many meanings. One publication listed 12 definitions of feminism (Miller, 1988, pp. 133-134), ranging from feminism as a "social awakening of women" (Gilman, 1916, p. 168), as a "political movement" (Mitchell, 1986, p. 4), as "a conceptualization of women's condition" (Oakley, 1986, p. 48), as "a set of principles for interpreting the status of women" (Ferree & Hess, 1985, p. 27), to feminism as a "world view" (Billington-Grieg, 1911, p. 693; Bunch, 1983, p. 250; Ruzek, 1986, p. 184). Chinn and Wheeler (1985), both nurses, defined feminism "as a world view that values women and that confronts systematic injustices based on gender" (p. 74). According to French (1985), "feminism is the only serious, coherent, and universal philosophy that offers an alternative to patriarchal thinking and structures" (p. 442).

Feminist Theories

Although there are many feminist perspectives, only three mainstream feminist theories will be discussed. These follow an historical pattern.

Liberal Feminism

Liberal feminism was the first to emerge and evolved from feminist roots of the 1800s. Liberal feminism includes equal opportunity for women and is critical of the inequitable distribution of wealth, position, and power based on family, race, and sex. Being a wife and mother is not considered oppressive in itself; rather, it is "the political, social and economic imperatives that channel women into these roles" (Chinn & Wheeler, 1985, p. 74). To overcome oppression, women must have the same rights as men. To accomplish this, women need improved educational opportunities to allow them to compete, a behaviour that often produces discomfort for women. Legislation that actively discriminates against women also needs to be changed (Adamson, Briskin, & McPhail, 1988, p. 10).

Social Feminism

Social feminism views women's oppression through four categories: gender, class, race, and sexual orientation (Adamson et al., 1988, p. 11). Social feminism analyzes cultural institutions that contribute to the oppression of women, such as the patriarchal family, motherhood, housework, and consumerism. In different classes, these institutions operate differently. Social feminists analyze the relationship that exists between the private sphere of the home and the public domain of productive work, suggesting that socioeconomic class oppression and oppression of women are "mutually reinforcing" (Chinn & Wheeler, 1985, p. 75). Unlike liberal feminists, who find the social and economic system acceptable, social feminists challenge the political system, arguing that equity will never be attained until fundamental changes are achieved in the distribution of power, wealth, and privilege.

Radical Feminism

Radical feminism is derived from a women-centred world perspective. Radical feminists view childbearing as pivotal to women's experience but also as the material basis of their oppression. Women's childbearing and childrearing roles are considered the major reason for male superiority and control over women's bodies. Men express this control through exploitive behaviour toward women, the culmination of which is violence against women (Adamson et al., 1988, p. 10). Radical feminism challenges the current concepts and vocabulary of patriarchal systems and aims to formulate concepts from a women's perspective. For women-defined thought, culture, and systems to develop, gender discrimination and sexually stereotyped roles must be eliminated. When male-defined concepts are not used as the norm, women's experience can be the focus of attention, with the result that differences between men and women are validated. Female values such as nurturance and creation are emphasized along with the aim to create a nonmilitaristic, nonhierarchical society.

In sum, while liberal and social feminism are based on women's relationship to men, radical feminism is not. Liberal feminism means equality with men while social feminism means equal to men without class distinctions (Chinn & Wheeler, 1985). Radical feminism means discovering, analyzing, and valuing women's experience without imposed male standards. Feminist theories, like nursing theories, are "action-oriented," are always in process, are used to explain phenomena, and are used as guides for research (Miller, 1988, p. 135). Although feminism is not a unified political ideology, there are at least three factors that all feminist theories have in common:

(1) all recognize the exploitation and the oppression of women, (2) all support equal rights and opportunities for women, and (3) all are oriented to initiating change (Adamson et al., 1988, p. 9).

Gender Issues and Management of Female Work Forces

Two specific gender issues affect female-dominated work forces, such as nursing. Nurse managers need to be especially aware of gender issues that have contributed to exploitation and oppression of women in general and of nurses in particular. Gender issues also contribute to "nurse abuse." Each of these has implications for nurse managers.

Exploitation and Oppression of Nurses

As indicated above, all feminist theories recognize the oppression and the exploitation of women. Feminism provides insight into patriarchy, which is a "system originating in the household wherein the father dominates [and]... the structure is then reproduced throughout the society in gender relations" (MacKinnon, 1982, pp. 528-529). Patriarchy plays a large role in the oppression of nurses.

Oppression results from the ability of dominant groups to impose their norms and values on society and have them accepted as the "right" ones, which are then readily enforced because of the power held by the dominant group. As a result, the values of the oppressed group remain invisible, trivialized, or devalued. To achieve power, the oppressed group assimilates the beliefs and values of the oppressors, believing that to mimic them will lead to power and control. Instead, such an action results in "marginalized" individuals, who become alienated from both groups and often develop characteristics of self-hatred and low self-esteem (Bush & Kjervik, 1979; Greenleaf, 1978; Grissum & Spengler, 1976) and submissive-aggressive behaviour. Since aggression cannot be expressed openly, it often results in "horizontal violence" (Freire, 1971, p.48), where there is persistent infighting among oppressed group members. This constant conflict is then used by the oppressors to criticize the oppressed for being unable to govern themselves. Thus the status quo is retained, based on fear of aggression against the oppressors, and becomes the basis for submitting to the oppressors. Along with this fear, the fear of change itself is assimilated (Roberts, 1983).

Because nurses are usually isolated from all vestiges of power, they often fail to recognize oppression because it is so complete

(Cleland, 1971). This is especially true in hospitals using a bureaucratic/ corporate model of administration where physicians and administrators (usually male) hold the power and nurses (usually female) are unaware of the oppressiveness of the environment. Nurses are made to feel inferior because the caring ideology of nursing is not valued in the same way as the curing ideology of medicine. As a result, nursing is viewed as "natural" to women and nurses are seen to require few skills and knowledge. This belief contributes to physicians' failure to support increased education for nurses.

Nurses exhibit oppressive behaviour in several ways. For example, nurses often practise submissive-aggressive behaviour by complaining about physicians but rarely confronting them. Horizontal violence results in nurses' being unsupportive of one another, and nurses' groups generally lack cohesiveness because of infighting (Grissum & Spengler, 1976). Some nursing leaders act as "queen bees," a term used to describe antifeminists who are successful women (Staines, Tavris, & Jayaratne, 1974). In this syndrome, some nursing leaders act as an elite who, in retrospect, acknowledge no barriers to the achievement of their senior positions. This type of leadership promotes divisiveness and competition among nurses and sabotages their efforts to work together to change the system.

Recognizing and understanding oppression is crucial for nurse managers who are responsible for facilitating quality patient care. Nurse managers need to recognize their dual role of advocating for staff nurses but accounting to administration for efficiency and effectiveness of the delivery of nursing care. Helping staff to appreciate their unique contributions to patient care is an important role for nurse managers. This role may also involve "consciousness raising" to increase nurses' awareness of their work in the context of women's work, not merely as health care workers, and pointing out to staff nurses the pattern of blaming themselves or others for their problems. Emphasizing nursing's knowledge, practices, and values in contrast to delegated medical (technical) procedures would result in general support for the notion that nursing is a major player in health care delivery rather than continuing to concede this control to physicians and administrators.

Recognition of and insight into the queen bee syndrome is important for understanding nursing elites and for avoiding this syndrome. For example, equitable treatment of various types of health care workers, such as nursing assistants, diploma-prepared nurses, and baccalaureate graduates, is crucial for collaboration and solidarity among women health care workers. Also, managers need to concentrate on developing the leadership role of bedside nurses (Roberts, 1983). This involves a restructuring and a shifting of priorities to staff nurses. The shared governance models being implemented by some hospitals are moving in this direction but need to be monitored carefully to guarantee this outcome.

Nurse Abuse

Although the "handmaiden mentality" may be disappearing, "the control, domination, intimidation and nullification of individual will implicit in a system of medical patriarchy generates many nurses... who do not recognize their abusive situation" (Lovell, 1981, p. 28). Abuse—whether physical, verbal, or sexual—was not spoken of much until the 1980s (Aggarwal, 1992, p. xii). Although the literature on nurse abuse is limited, it follows the same trend (Hadley, 1990). According to Hadley (1990), determining that nurse abuse exists in the workplace is not as problematical as estimating the extent of the problem. Perpetrators of nurse abuse include patients, family members, physicians, and other health care colleagues, including nurses.

Katzman (1985) suggested that medicine and nursing are probably the most sex-typed occupations in North America. This sex role stereotyping has led to an oppressive relationship between physicians and nurses where nurses are portrayed as subordinate and submissive while physicians are perceived as dominant and aggressive (Martin, 1985). This stereotyping often results in nurse abuse. "Every day, in some way, shape or form, nurses continue to be abused by physicians" (Leear & Odorisio, 1990, p. 77).

Friedman's (1982) survey of nurse-physician relationships found that nurses were the target of multiple abuses from physicians. Park (1979) described the nurse-physician relationship as "an authoritarian relationship masked by democratic forms and complemented by benevolent paternalism" (p. 16). Research results from a survey of the extent of physician abuse of nurses in a California county suggested that 64% of nurses reported experiencing some form of verbal abuse at least once every two or three months (Daiz & McMillin, 1991), while 30% of the respondents reported experiencing some type of sexual abuse at least once every two to three months. Sexual propositioning was the most frequent form of abuse (19%), followed by sexual insult (16%), and finally by suggestive touching (13%) (Diaz & McMillin, 1991). Nearly one-quarter of the nurses experienced a threat to their physical person by one or more physicians during their career (Diaz & McMillin, 1991). In the open-ended section of a Manitoba Association of Registered Nurses (MARN) survey of nurse abuse (10 000 nurses, 51% return rate), physicians were listed as verbal abusers in 11 out of 12 health care settings, a northern nursing station being the exception (MARN, 1989). However, there is no indication of the extent of the problem.

Results from several American studies provide some insight into nurse abuse by patients. An exploratory study of physical assaults by patients in a Massachusetts veterans' hospital revealed 91 assaults on 67 registered nurses (Lanza, 1983). In a follow-up study of 99 registered nurses in the same setting, Lanza (1985) found approximately 20% of the nurses had not been assaulted, while another 20% had been assaulted more than three times, and the remaining nurses had been assaulted from one to three times in their career. A survey of nursing staff in an Ohio veterans' medical centre indicated that 76% of the registered nurses encountered abusive behaviour from patients on a weekly basis (Basque & Merhige, 1980). Research findings from a study conducted at a Maryland state hospital revealed that only 203 of the 1108 assaults were formally reported (Lion, Snyder, & Merrill, 1981). A veterans' administration centre in Cincinnati reported 200 incidences of violent behaviour toward nurses over a period of 5.5 years (Jones, 1985).

The MARN (1989) study concluded that, in all the health care settings they studied, nurses were repeatedly the victims of abuse, most frequently carried out by patients and families (p. 4). Another survey of 3000 randomly selected Ontario nurses indicated that one in three registered nurses had been physically assaulted by a patient in the previous 12 months and more than 60% of the nurses had been assaulted during their nursing career ("Violence in nursing," 1992). The majority (98%) of the assaults were perpetrated by patients, and "males assaulted nurses twice as often as females" ("Violence in nursing," 1992, p. 20).

Nurse managers need to be sensitive to nurse abuse and clearly identify it as a workplace issue. When abuse is recognized, support should be given to the abused nurse by colleagues, especially the nurse manager. Since violence against women is generally an issue of male power, insisting on being treated as colleagues rather than handmaidens is a first step. Advocating for policies and procedures for dealing with nurse abuse that are strongly endorsed by senior administration is another step. An example of a procedure instituted by one hospital was a "code pink," where nurses who were experiencing abuse would page a code to a central area and the charge nurse, along with all available nurses, would congregate around that nurse (Bradley, 1992). In another hospital, operating room nurses banded together and wrote up every incident of nurse abuse by physicians, including direct quotes. In a short time, 30 reports were filed, which stimulated the chief executive officer of the hospital to call a meeting with administrative heads; the outcome was resolution of these issues through weekly meetings with the service's physicians (Patterson, 1991). Another effective tool is to publish, in the institution's newsletter, all instances (including quotes) of nurse abuse.

Equal Rights and Opportunities

Two areas where the feminist struggle for equal rights and opportunities for women applies in the nursing situation concern recognition of the comparable worth of women's work and recognition of the "second shift" phenomenon, because working women also routinely fulfil double roles as chief housekeepers and child care workers at home. These two feminist factors have implications for nurse managers of the 1990s.

Comparable Worth

Nurses' work, like other women's work, is not highly valued nor monetarily well compensated by society. Instead, the existing system defines women's (nurse's) work as marginal (Blum, 1991, p. 135) because it calls for qualities such as "caring" and "nimble fingers" (Walby, 1988, p. 30), characteristics associated with "ministering mothers" (O'Brien, 1987, p. 12). These skills are rarely acknowledged when professions are evaluated using traditional male-generated criteria (Parsons, 1986).

Constraints placed on women by childbearing responsibilities have resulted in making them a distinct form of paid labour power. Women workers are believed to differ from men workers through a preference for part-time work, a tendency to drop out and return to work as family needs dictate, and an inability to work overtime or move location. Because of these assumptions, women (nurses) often have been exploited by employers (Walby, 1988, pp. 30-31) even though evidence suggests that women remain in continuous employment over increasingly longer periods of time than in the past (Peitchinis, 1989, p. 164). According to a 1986 survey conducted by the Registered Nurses Association of Ontario (RNAO), turnover rates of nurses have declined appreciably in recent years (RNAO, 1988, p. 3).

Although some progress has been made toward equalizing women's and men's wages, "previous research suggests that, all else [being] equal, predominantly male occupations and integrated occupations pay more than predominantly female occupations" (Blau & Beller, 1988, p. 518). Also, much of the work on affirmative action and job integration has been concerned with male-dominated professions, while there has been a subtle bias against women's work (Blum, 1991, p. 142).

Because of glaring wage disparities between men and women, the Canadian government has attempted to bring economic redress to women by instituting "equal pay" initiatives. In Canada, equal pay legislation appeared in the 1950s and has evolved through four stages: (1) equal pay for equal work; (2) equal pay for similar or substantially similar work; (3) equal pay for work of equal value; and (4) pay equity (Neale, 1993, p. 2). The first two stages have been effective in dealing with direct discrimination where employers intentionally pay women less for performing the same job as men. One major problem in using the first two stages for nursing is the lack of male comparison groups in hospitals, where most nurses work and where most of the work force is female (RNAO, 1988, p. 2).

A more effective tool for eliminating the wage gap for nurses is legislation that pertains to stages three and four, and compares jobs according to their "value" or comparable worth. However, in stage three, a complainant, to receive equity in pay for work of equal value, must lodge a complaint before the legislation can be invoked. This procedure has not proved to be effective in the Canadian federal public service because of the lengthiness of the procedure. For example, in 1970, the Royal Commission on the Status of Women (1970) recommended that pay rates for nurses and workers in four other female-dominated professions "be set by comparing them with other predominantly male professions in terms of the value of work and the skills and training involved" (Royal Commission on the Status of Women, 1970, p. 80). After many years of negotiations, this dispute has yet to be settled (Morris, Bégin, & Harder, 1990, pp. 2-4).

On the other hand, pay equity is proactive in setting deadlines for developing and implementing pay equity plans and using the collective bargaining process (Neale, 1993). Although pay equity for Canadian nurses was not initiated until the late 1980s, Schreiber (1993) recently pointed out that most hospital administrators are not committed to the elimination of gender discrimination in nurses' wages.

Although most nurse managers probably support a liberal feminist perspective on equity in nurses' wages, they may be unaware of the history of Canadian pay equity legislation because women-dominated fields have generally been ignored. Feminist policy dilemmas result from whether to put the emphasis on difference or on equality. For nursing, the emphasis should focus on differences or on comparable-worth strategies that give value to women's work. In the 1990s, nurses do not have to sacrifice extrinsic rewards such as pay to work as nurses. By being aware of wage discrepancies between men and women (nurses), nurse managers can help to raise the consciousness of their colleagues about pay equity issues and support staff nurses in their activities to secure more equitable wages. This may involve waking staff nurses up from the lulling effects of paternalism, which manifests itself in nurses' belief that employers treat them equitably.

Second Shifts

Research on work culture tends to ignore the work experience of
women employees, especially as it pertains to leaving the workplace
and traveling home to start the "second shift" (Hochschild, 1989).
Hardy (1990) concurred, stating, "the impact of the work women do at
home, ... has not been studied systematically in nursing" (p. 23). Most
of the studies of work culture have been carried out on males using a
male perspective and using males as the research subjects.

Hochschild (1989) studied 145 Americans, 100 of whom were
two-career couples, with the remaining 45 being people who participated in these couples' daily lives, such as baby-sitters, school teachers,
and day-care workers. In-depth interviews were carried out with 10
families. The major finding was that women who worked both inside
and outside the home put in, annually, an extra month of 24-hour days
(Hochschild, 1989). This work schedule exhausted the women and
often made them resentful. In this study, 20% of the male participants
shared the housework and the child care equally, 70% carried out less
than one-half but more than one-third of these tasks, while 10% of the
men did less than one-third of the work (p. 8). Hochschild also noted
that there were distinct qualitative differences in the type of work
carried out by the men and by the women. Research by Jougla,
Bouvier-Colle, Manquin, Diaz-Valdez, and Minvielle (1983) on women
in Montpellier, France, concluded that the only significant differences
between housewives (n=2480) and working women (n=2160) were
"fatigue, overwork, and nervousness" (p. 70) in the working women.

Valentine's (1988a) case study of women nurse educators in a
Canadian hospital school of nursing found that the multiple expectations of the faculty had a major impact on their work lives. As one
nurse educator said, women feel compelled to be successful in so many
areas: in their jobs and as mothers, homemakers, and wives. Because
the nurse educators in the study were largely responsible for the child
care arrangements and the overall management of their households,
the dilemmas of child care were often played out at work. In the faculty lounge, conversations frequently revolved around such issues as
child care costs, competence of baby-sitters or day-care workers, and
problems of children's first day at school. During the course of the
study, two faculty members quit because of pressures associated with
trying to work and care for several young children at home.

For these working women, ill children posed dilemmas that resulted in taking time off work, or spending the day at work worrying, phon-
ing home frequently and trying to make arrangements to leave early.
The problems of making alternative child care arrangements also sur-
faced when they awoke to find a sick child or when the school phoned
them at work to inform them about an ill child (Valentine, 1988a).

The second-shift responsibilities also posed dilemmas in trying to fulfil employer expectations/career goals, such as pursuing further education. Several of the nurse educators indicated that they were unable to enrol in graduate work until their children were of a certain age. Convincing partners of the need for advanced education was another issue. Instructors who were single and/or single parents were concerned about the need to work full time to support themselves and their family and still be able to give the required attention to their studies. Education takes time, energy, and money. Although all the participants in this study had baccalaureate degrees, these statements apply to all nurses who are attempting to upgrade their education.

Being aware of the oppression of the patriarchal family and the way that motherhood and household responsibilities impinge on women's work lives is crucial for nurse managers who have input into policies that can support women workers. Being advocates for on-site day care, for flexible working hours for nurses with young children, and for allocation of days off that can be taken when nurses' family members are sick are examples of such policies. Nurse managers need to recognize and discuss the "superwoman syndrome" with staff members and support staff who are trying to negotiate more equitable household management and child care arrangements with their partners. Recognizing the special needs of single mothers and single women, who often have other family members to care for, are other examples of the adoption of a social feminist perspective. To attract and retain the best nurses, nurse managers practising liberal feminism would encourage staff members to upgrade their education. The managers should support this stance by lobbying senior administration and unions for assistance with tuition fees, by providing flexible hours, by supporting staff nurses when they become discouraged with their studies, and by rewarding them when they complete courses.

Female Management Style

Nurse managers need to be aware of the distinct culture of nursing (women's) organizations if they are to change nursing units and better accommodate the realities of the female world. For example, nurse managers need to recognize the overlap between home and work, accept this, and build in mechanisms to capitalize on it. Since caring is the major ideology underpinning nursing and family life, this behaviour needs to be role modeled by nurse managers.

Nurse managers can begin with a strong understanding of what sociologists describe as the "work culture," which has special meaning both for female-dominated work forces in general and for nursing in particular.

Women's Work Culture

The way women (nurses) work together is germane to nurse managers. Bernard (1981), a sociologist, has studied the "female world" for more than four decades. This world includes cultural elements, such as "rituals, roles, dress customs, gestures, communication patterns, reference groups... [and] visible properties and practices of sex roles as... reflected in everyday life" (Lee & Gropper, 1974, p. 371). The nursing world has developed in concert with this female world. However, since most management literature adopted by nursing comes from organizational and administrative literature based on the male world, nurse managers need to be aware of the management literature evolving from a female perspective.

In the 1950s, traditional management literature acknowledged gender differences, although in the 1960s few articles recognized gender differences and the instruments used in research remained gender biased. In the 1980s and 1990s, gender differences were again being taken into consideration in many management research studies (Hearn & Parkin, 1983; Mills, 1988; Mills & Tancred, 1992). Unfortunately, most of the literature concerned women who worked in male-dominated organizations rather than studies of women who worked in female-predominant milieus such as nursing.

Nursing, which is 96% female, provides fertile ground for studying women's work world. The case study of nurse educators in a Canadian hospital school of nursing revealed that the nursing school also had a distinct culture (Valentine, 1994). Childbearing, childrearing, and household management roles produced a blurring of the nurse educators' private lives with their work lives. Helgesen's study (1990) of four American women executives revealed the same phenomenon. The executives' childrearing/homemaking experiences provided them with a variety of management skills, such as "balancing conflicting demands" (p. 33) and developing effective organizational skills that produced holistic women with a form of psychological integration that contributed to the incredible energy they displayed.

Lamphere's (1985) study of women in several American blue-collar industries who "[brought] the family to work" (p. 520) through celebrations such as birthdays and baby and wedding showers found these rituals facilitated the creation and the maintenance of cohesion among the workers. These rituals helped to establish friendship bonds and to bridge age divisions within the organizations and contributed to the humanization of the workplace. Valentine's (1988a) case study of nurse educators and Acker's (1992) study of British elementary school teachers supported Lamphere's conclusion that "a strong sense of community was sustained by [women's celebratory] rituals" (p. 18).

For the nurse educators, satisfying relationships with other colleagues, nursing students, and support staff were a crucial part of their work activities (Valentine & McIntosh, 1990). Four constructs emanating from this study indicated a striving for connection in relationships through the use of food, social events, meetings, and supportive gestures. As Gilligan (1982) and several other researchers (Belenky, Clinchy, Goldberger, & Tarule, 1986; Berzoff, 1989; Chodorow, 1978; Helgesen, 1990; Loden, 1985; Lyons, 1983; Miller, 1984, 1986) have found, women tend to see the world through relationships, "a world that coheres through human connection rather than through systems of rules" (p. 29).

In recent times, feminist theories have praised women's empathic orientation to others and have seen this characteristic as an important aspect of adult development (Berzoff, 1989). Two American studies of men and women in a variety of organizations (Loden, 1985; Statham, 1987) found that "positive, satisfying relationships" correlate with productive individuals (Loden, 1985, p. 118).

Several studies have found that women prefer a nonhierarchical approach to work relationships. For example, Gilligan's (1982) research supported this conclusion and Neuse's (1978) study found that, to facilitate the participation of others, women willingly ignore formal hierarchy and minimize their personal power. Naisbitt and Aburdene (1986) concluded that hierarchical structures are becoming obsolete in organizations and are giving way to "an environment for nurturing personal growth" (p. 72) with a "networking style" (p. 72) of management that encompasses all workers as resources. In the study of a Canadian hospital school of nursing, Valentine (1988a) found that the hierarchy was minimal and the structure was purposely flattened to allow for increased participation of instructors. The result was a highly participatory environment with considerable input into decisions.

Although there is little research on decision making among women/nurses, the following studies provide some insight into this phenomenon. Shakeshaft (1987) pointed out that several researchers found that "women [were] perceived as being more democratic and participatory than [were] men" (p. 187). Studies by Charters and Jovick (1981), Fishel and Pottker (1975), and Meskin (1974) revealed that women principals put their emphasis on interpersonal relationships that produced a nonstructured, participatory style of decision making. Valentine (1992) reported that nurse educators in her study usually made decisions by consensus after considerable discussion and input from both instructors and students. A study of 16 American women health care executives described their management style as "consensus building [and] working as a team" (Muller & Cocotas, 1988, p. 74). According to Loden (1985), having input into decision making creates a feeling of ownership in the final decisions, even when the original ideas are not accepted. Cooperative discussion also tends to minimize the "win-lose element of voting" by directing the energy of the group toward "reaching decisions that every member can accept" (Loden, 1985, p. 125). All-female managerial groups that used consensus as the decision-making method reached the best technical decisions, according to research on 48 teams that developed decision-making exercises in wilderness survival for management development programs (Lafferty & Pond, 1974).

Initiating Change

Crucial lessons from the women's movement have been the development of a sense of community, a commitment to each other as women, and a valuing of female friendships. Nurses' traditional empathic orientation to others now needs to be directed to colleagues as well as to patients. Recognizing the importance of relationships to female development and experimenting with ways to facilitate the development of satisfying, supportive relationships in the workplace will result in less turnover and better patient care. Realizing that it is antagonistic to women's nature to work in rule-dominated environments, and minimizing this orientation, will help to reduce frustrations experienced on nursing units. Various celebratory occasions, such as births, birthdays, summer picnics, Christmas parties, and potluck meals, are important and need to be recognized, not merely as social occasions, but as integral aspects of work life that promote social solidarity.

Moving away from the hierarchical model that is predominant in most health care settings is another change that nurse managers could implement. Flattening the structure on nursing units by treating all workers in a collegial way and recognizing each worker's unique contributions is one way to accomplish this. Also, nurse managers can help by insisting that other health care colleagues, especially physicians, treat nurses as equals. Developing a nurturing, collegial environment both organizationally and physically is important for both patients and staff. It is interesting that most hospitals have doctors' lounges but few have nurses' lounges where nurses can congregate to discuss issues both domestic and professional.

Routine staff meetings should be held to encourage staff input into the important decisions that affect their work lives. Utilizing a consensual model of decision making facilitates the integration of staff, promotes a win-win atmosphere, and produces greater worker commitment to the implementation of decisions. It also allows for the best decisions to be made, because all workers' ideas are considered.

Mainstream feminist theories discussed in this chapter reveal the oppressive atmosphere in which nurses often work. A feminist perspective can be used to focus on gender issues in the workplace and on the female culture of nursing organizations. To view a female-dominated profession such as nursing through a feminist lens takes courage, but will provide nurse managers with a different perspective on quality of work life issues. Feminism provides insight into the distinctive nature of the nursing culture and an understanding of the implications this has for nursing management.

A feminist approach suggests that nurse managers need to be: advocates for staff nurses regarding their unique contributions, their worth, and their roles at home on the second shift; teachers who raise staff nurses' consciousness about oppression and its ramifications; and supportive colleagues who act as role models of appropriate feminist behaviour to patients and staff.

Above all, nurse managers need to be agents of change, because integrating feminism into nursing management involves initiating change and having the courage to sustain it.

References

Acker, S. (1992, April). *Gender, collegiality, and teachers' workplace culture in Britain: In search of the women's culture.* Paper presented at the annual meeting of the American Educational Research Association, San Francisco, California.

Adamson, N., Briskin, L., & McPhail, M. (1988). *Feminists organizing for change: The contemporary women's movement in Canada.* Toronto: Oxford University Press.

Aggarwal, A. (1992). *Sexual harassment: A guide for understanding and prevention.* Vancouver: Butterworths.

Allen, M. (1985). Women, nursing and feminism: An interview with Alice Baumgart, R.N., Ph.D. *The Canadian Nurse, 81*(1), 20-22.

Basque, L., & Merhige, J. (1980). Nurses' experience with dangerous behavior: Implications for training. *The Journal of Continuing Education in Nursing, 11*(5), 47-51.

Belenky, M., Clinchy, B., Goldberger, N., & Tarule, J. (1986). *Women's ways of knowing: The development of self, voice and mind.* New York: Basic Books.

Bernard, J. (1981). *The female world.* New York: The Free Press.

Berzoff, J. (1989). From separation to connection: Shifts in understanding women's development. *Affilia: Journal of Women and Social Work, 4*(1), 45-58.

Blau, F.D., & Beller, A.H. (1988). Trends in earnings differential by gender, 1971-1981. *Industrial and Labor Relations Review, 41*(4), 513-529.

Blum, L. (1991). *Between feminism and labor: The significance of the comparable worth movement.* Berkeley: University of California Press.

Billington-Grieg, T. (1911, November). Feminism and politics. *The Contemporary Review*, 693-703.

Bradley, V. (1992). Workplace abuse: Unrecognized emergency department violence. *Journal of Emergency Nursing, 18*(6), 489-490.

Bunch, C. (1983). *Learning our way: Essays in feminist education.* Trumanberg, NY: Crossing Press.

Bush, M., & Kjervik, D. (1979). The nurse's self-image. In D. Kjervik & I. Martinson (Eds.), *Women in stress: A nursing perspective* (pp. 46-58). New York: Appleton-Century-Crofts.

Charters, W.W. Jr., & Jovick, T.D. (1981). The gender of principals and principal/teacher relations in elementary schools. In P.A. Schmuck, W.E. Charters, Jr., & R.O. Carlson (Eds.), *Educational policy and management: Sex differentials* (pp. 307-331). New York: Academic Press.

Chinn, P., & Wheeler, C. (1985). Feminism and nursing. *Nursing Outlook, 33*(2), 74-77.

Chodorow, N. (1978). *The reproduction of mothering.* Berkeley: University of California Press.

Cleland, V. (1971). Sex discrimination: Nursing's most pervasive problem. *American Journal of Nursing, 71*(8), 1542-1547.

Diaz, A., & McMillin, D. (1991). A definition and description of nurse abuse. *Western Journal of Nursing Research, 13*(1), 97-109.

Ferree, M., & Hess, P. (1985). *Controversy and coalition: The new feminist movement.* Boston: Twayne.

Fishel, A., & Pottker, J. (1975, Spring). Performance of women principals: A review of behavioral and attitudinal studies. *Journal of the National Association for Women Deans, Administrators and Counselors,* 110-117.

Freire, P. (1971). *Pedagogy of the oppressed.* New York: The Seabury Press.

French, M. (1985). *Beyond power: On women, men and morals.* New York: Summit Books.

Friedman, F. (1982). A nurse's guide to the care and handling of MDs. *Registered Nurse, 3*(3), 39-43.

Gilligan, C. (1982). *In a different voice.* Cambridge: Harvard University Press.

Gilman, C. (1916). Femina: A magazine for thinking women. *The Forerunner, 7*(6), 168.

Greenleaf, N. (1978). The politics of self-esteem. *Nursing Digest, 3*(3), 1-16.

Grissum, M., & Spengler, C. (1976). *Womanpower and health care.* Boston: Little, Brown.

Hadley, M. (1990). Background paper regarding abuse of nurses in the workplace. *Alberta Association of Registered Nurses Newsletter, 46*(9), 6-9.

Hardy, L. (1990). Nursing work and the implications of "the second shift". *Canadian Journal of Nursing Administration, 3*(4), 23-26.

Hearn, J., & Parkin, W. (1983). Gender and organizations: A selective review and a critique of a neglected area. *Organization Studies, 4*(3), 219-242.

Helgesen, S. (1990). *The female influence.* Toronto: Doubleday.

Hemphill, J.K., Griffiths, D.E., & Fredericksen, N. (1962). *Administrative performance and personality.* New York: Bureau of Publications, Columbia University.

Hochschild, A. (1989). *The second shift: Working parents and the revolution at home.* New York: Viking.

Jones, M.K. (1985). Patient violence: Report of 200 incidents. *Journal of Psychosocial Nursing, 23*(6), 12-17.

Jougla, E., Bouvier-Colle, M.H., Manquin, P., Diaz-Valdez, R., & Minvielle, D. (1983). Health and employment of a female population in an urban area. *International Journal of Epidemiology, 12*(1), 67-76.

Katzman, E. (1985). *A study of the influence of stereotypical male-female attitudes and behaviors on role transition in nursing and on nurse-physician interprofessional relationships.* Unpublished doctoral dissertation, Syracuse University, Syracuse.

Lafferty, C., & Pond, A. (1974). *The desert survival station.* Plymouth, MI: Human Synergists.

Lamphere, L. (1985). Bringing the family to work: Women's culture on the shop floor. *Feminist Studies, 11*(3), 519-540.

Lanza, M.L. (1983). The reactions of nursing staff to physical assault by a patient. *Hospital and Community Psychiatry, 34*(1), 44-47.

Lanza, M.L. (1985). How nurses react to patient assault. *Journal of Psychosocial Nursing, 23*(6), 6-10.

Leear, D., & Odorisio, C. (1990). Forms of nurse abuse. In L. Gasparis & J. Swirsky (Eds.), *Nurse abuse: Impact and resolution* (pp. 65-109). New York: Power Publications.

Lee, P., & Gropper, N. (1974). Sex-role culture and educational practice. *Harvard Educational Review, 44*(3), 369-410.

Lion, J.R., Snyder, W., & Merrill, G.L. (1981). Underreporting of assaults on staff in a state hospital. *Hospital and Community Psychiatry, 32,* 497-498.

Loden, M. (1985). *Feminine leadership: Or how to succeed in business without being one of the boys.* New York: Times Books.

Lovell, M. (1981). Silent but perfect "partners": Medicine's use and abuse of women. *Advances in Nursing Science, 3*(2), 25-40.

Lyons, N. (1983). Two perspectives: On self, relationships, and morality. *Harvard Educational Review, 53*(2), 125-145.

MacKinnon, C. (1982). Feminism, Marxism, method and the state: An agenda for theory. *SIGNS: Journal of Women in Culture and Society, 7*(3), 515-544.

Manitoba Association of Registered Nurses (MARN). (1989). *Nurse abuse report.* Winnipeg: Author.

Martin, D. (1985). Domestic violence: A sociological perspective. In D.J. Sonkin, D. Martin, & L.E.A. Walker (Eds.), *The male batterer: A treatment approach* (pp. 1-32). New York: Springer.

Meskin, J.D. (1974). The performance of women school administrators—A review of the literature. *Administrator's Notebook, 23*(10), 1-4.

Miller, C. (1992, February). Feminism and nursing: The uneasy relationship. *Canadian Nursing Management Special Report #45,* 1-4.

Miller, J. (1984). The development of women's sense of self. *Work in Progress,* No. 12. Wellesley, MA: Stone Center Working Papers Series.

Miller, J. (1986). *Toward a new psychology of women* (2nd ed.). Boston: Beacon Press.

Miller, K. (1988). *Feminist ideology in nursing: A foundational inquiry.* Unpublished doctoral dissertation, University of Colorado, Denver.

Mills, A. (1988). Organization, gender and culture. *Organization Studies,* *9*(3), 351-369.

Mills, A.J., & Tancred, P. (1992). *Gendering organizational analysis.* Newbury Park: Sage.

Mitchell, J. (1986). Reflections on twenty years of feminism. In J. Mitchell & S. Oakley (Eds.), *What is feminism—A re-examination* (pp. 34-48). New York: Pantheon Books.

Morris, M., Bégin, P., & Harder, S. (1990). *20 years later: An assessment of the implementation of the recommendations of the Royal Commission on the Status of Women.* Ottawa: Research Branch, Library of Parliament.

Muller, H., & Cocotas, C. (1988). Women in power: New leadership in the health industry. *Health Care for Women International, 9*(2), 63-82.

Naisbitt, J., & Aburdene, P. (1986). *Reinventing the corporation.* New York: Warner Books.

Neale, D. (1993). *Women and work: Changing gender role attitudes in Alberta, Survey Highlights #12.* Edmonton: Population Branch Laboratory, Department of Sociology, University of Alberta.

Neuse, S. (1978). Professionalism and authority: Women in public service. *Public Administration Review, 38,* 436-441.

O'Brien, P. (1987). 'All a woman's life can bring': The domestic roots of nursing in Philadelphia, 1830-1885. *Nursing Research, 36*(1), 12-17.

Oakley, A. (1986). Feminism, motherhood and medicine—Who cares? In J. Mitchell & A. Oakley (Eds.), *What is feminism—A re-examination* (pp. 127-150). New York: Pantheon Books.

Park, J. (1979, November). Negotiating ambiguity: An aspect of the nurse-doctor relationship. *New Zealand Journal of Nursing, 72,* 14-16, 36.

Parsons, M. (1986). The profession in a class by itself. *Nursing Outlook, 34*(6), 270-275.

Patterson, P. (1991). Sexual harassment is more about power than sex. *OR Manager, 7*(12), 4.

Peitchinis, S. (1989). *Women at work: Discrimination and response.* Toronto: McClelland & Stewart.

Registered Nurses Association of Ontario (RNAO). (1988). *Brief to pay equity commission on gender discrimination in female dominated establishments with no male comparison groups.* Toronto: Author.

Roberts, S. (1983). Oppressed group behavior: Implications for nursing. *Advances in Nursing Science, 5*(4), 21-30.

Royal Commission on the Status of Women. (1970). *Report of the Royal Commission on the Status of Women.* Ottawa: Author.

Ruzek, S. (1986). Feminist visions of health: An international perspective. In J. Mitchell & A. Oakley (Eds.), *What is feminism—A re-examination* (pp. 184-207). New York: Pantheon.

Schreiber, R. (1993). Pay equity and North American nurses. *Nursing and Health Care, 14* (1), 28-33.

Shakeshaft, C. (1987). *Women in educational administration.* Beverly Hills: Sage Publications.

Staines, G., Tavris, C., & Jayaratne, T.E. (1974). The queen bee syndrome. *Psychology Today, 7*(8), 55-60.

Statham, A. (1987). The gender model revisited: Difference in the management styles of men and women. *Sex Roles, 16*(7/8), 409-429.

Valentine, P. (1988a). *A hospital school of nursing: A case study of a predominantly female organization.* Unpublished doctoral dissertation, University of Alberta, Edmonton.

Valentine, P. (1988b). Nursing and feminism: Confronting the 'dis-ease.' In *Proceedings of The Olive Anstey International Nursing Conference on "Professional Promiscuity,"* (pp. 2.29-2.32), Perth, Australia.

Valentine, P. (1992). Nurse educators and decision making: A female perspective. *Canadian Journal of Nursing Administration, 5*(3), 10-13.

Valentine, P. (1994). Women's working worlds: Case study of a female organization. In D. Duncan & P. Schmuck (Eds.), *Women in leadership in education: An agenda for a new century.* New York: SUNY Press.

Valentine, P., & McIntosh, G. (1990). Food for thought: Realities of a woman-dominated organization. *Alberta Journal of Educational Research, 36*(4), 353-369.

Vance, C., Talbot, S., McBride, A., & Mason, D. (1985). An uneasy alliance: Nursing and the women's movement. *Nursing Outlook, 33*(5), 282-285.

Violence in nursing: Study confirms what most nurses know. (1992). *Registered Nurse, 4*(3), 20-22.

Walby, S. (1988). *Gender segregation at work.* Philadelphia: Open University Press.

C H A P T E R 2 1

The Quality of Nursing Work Life

Linda-Lee O'Brien-Pallas, Andrea O. Baumann, and Michael J. Villeneuve

Linda-Lee O'Brien-Pallas, RN, BScN, MScN, PhD (Toronto), is Associate Professor and Career Scientist, Faculty of Nursing, University of Toronto.

Andrea O. Baumann, RN, BScN (Windsor), MScN (Western Ontario), PhD (Toronto), is Professor and Associate Dean, Faculty of Health Sciences (Nursing), McMaster University. Dr. O'Brien-Pallas and Dr. Baumann co-direct the Quality of Nursing Worklife Research Unit.

Michael J. Villeneuve, RN, BScN, MSc (Toronto), is Research Coordinator of the Quality of Nursing Worklife Research Unit at the Faculty of Nursing, University of Toronto.

The management of nursing services demands not only that patient care standards be maintained at cost levels organizations can bear, but also that attention be paid to the quality of the work life of those staff for whom the manager has direct responsibility. Understanding the complex interactions among the numerous variables and relationships that constitute a quality work environment presents a challenge for even the most seasoned nurse administrator. This chapter will focus on the following objectives:

*   Define quality of work life (sometimes referred to as QWL) and present a framework for its examination.
*   Present an overview of research related to quality of nursing work life, and discuss the factors that influence job satisfaction, stress, and burnout.
*   Suggest several approaches for promoting professionally rewarding work settings.
*   Discuss implications for nurse managers.

What Is a Quality Work Environment?

The definition of activities that constitute *work*, and the meaning ascribed to work, have interested social scientists for the past 30 years (Quintanilla & Wilpert, 1988). The nature of the environments in which work is performed has come under similar scrutiny. Any given work environment may be perceived as being high in quality by some individuals while it is considered stifling or chaotic by others. Because the meaning and nature of quality work environments are highly individual, it is impossible to define explicitly a *quality* work environment. In a general sense, a quality work environment is one where the goals of the organization are achieved in an atmosphere that allows the individual worker's goals and needs also to be met. From a nursing perspective, one could define a quality work environment as one in which the needs and goals of the individual nurse are met at the same time as the patient or client is assisted to reach his or her individual health goals—and where both outcomes are realized within the cost and quality framework mandated by the organization where the care is being provided. Quality of work life is a complex and multivariate phenomenon that has many interrelated parameters. Although a precise definition of the quality of work life is still emerging, the characteristics of quality work environments have been identified from a number of studies that have been completed.

Quality of Nursing Work Life: A Unifying Framework

Recognizing the complexity of nursing work life and building on the work of others (Leatt & Schneck, 1976; Vogt, Cox, Velthouse, & Thames, 1983), O'Brien-Pallas and Baumann (1992) developed a model for the examination of factors that influence nursing work life. Although the details of the model are presented elsewhere (O'Brien-Pallas & Baumann, 1992), a brief summary of the model is provided here as a guide for discussion in this chapter. A schematic of the elements of the model is presented in Figure 21.1.

Essentially, factors that influence the work life of nurses can be categorized as being either internal to the individual or environment in which the nurse is employed, or external to these elements. Outcome variables that can be measured include staff retention,

Figure 21.1
Factors influencing quality of nursing work life.

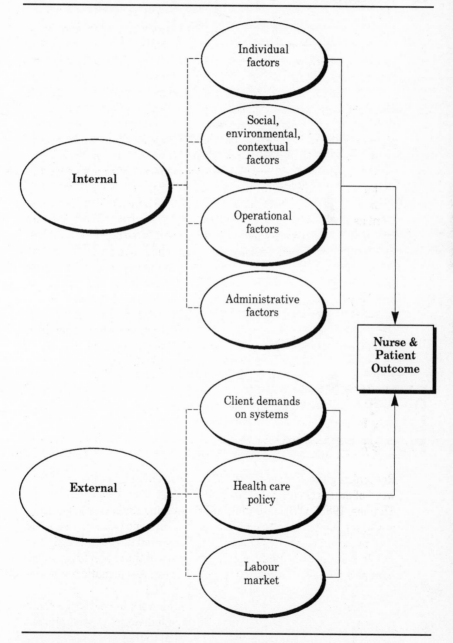

Source: Reprinted, with permission, from L. O'Brien-Pallas and A. Baumann (1992), Quality of nursing worklife—A unifying framework. *Canadian Journal of Nursing Administration*, 5(2), 12-16.

client and caregiver satisfaction, stress, group cohesion, organizational commitment, motivation, and quality of care. Individual characteristics that influence quality work environments have received the least amount of research attention. O'Brien-Pallas and Baumann (1992) classified individual factors into home life/work life interplay and individual needs. The home life/work life interplay reflects the factors that are characteristic of a largely female workforce—primarily, the need to balance demands at home with those in the work environment. Individual needs reflect the unique characteristics of the person, including such variables as the need for autonomy and for respect and recognition from others.

The quality of work life of any practising nurse is influenced by the characteristics of the environment (i.e., the work context) in which the individual is employed. Nurse managers must be aware of the sociocultural environments that exist within nursing units or teams, and in the broader organizations in which they work. The model would suggest that practices traditionally perceived as *good management* may influence both nurse and client outcomes. Strategies such as setting a comfortable climate, maintaining open and good communications, and encouraging good interprofessional relations are (among others) variables that exert an important influence on work life.

The model also identifies that the very nature of the work (i.e., the work design) in which the nurse is involved may influence outcomes. Issues such as the organization of day-to-day care delivery activities, the degree of technology on the unit, and the availability of equipment and materials are hypothesized to influence nursing work life. The administrative practices of the organization and unit or work team—including, in part, such issues as policies, benefits packages, and opportunity for advancement—are also considered to influence both nurse and patient outcomes.

Three external dimensions were hypothesized by O'Brien-Pallas and Baumann (1992) to influence nurses' quality of work life. Reflecting the unique world in which nurses work, these external dimensions are: client demands on the system, overall health care policy, and the labour market. Although the nurse manager may not be in a position to influence these dimensions directly, knowledge of their potential for influencing quality of work life outcomes is important. In concert with rapid changes in technology, shorter hospital stays and continuous changes in client acuity and demographics have resulted in clients' making demands on the system that are quite different than was the case even five years ago. The need to control overall health care costs has resulted in the downsizing of the hospital system, creating a reduction in the number of active treatment beds in many communities and an emphasis on more community-based health care services. Finally, the labour market for nursing and nursing-related work traditionally has been defined to include registered nurses, registered nursing assistants, and, increasingly during the past several years, health care aides. The recent introduction of the multiservice or multiskilled worker into the traditional model of health care delivery will have an eventual impact on quality of work life.

This brief review of O'Brien-Pallas and Baumann's model (1992) reinforces that the definition and development of quality work environments are highly complex, and involve a variety of interrelated factors that influence both nurse and patient outcomes. Nurse administrators need to be aware that there is more to creating and maintaining quality work environments than having moderately satisfied employees. A satisfied employee is only one of the many outcomes that must be considered as characteristic of a quality work environment.

Review of the Literature

A generally accepted thesis is that satisfied employees give better quality care as well as maintain a higher quality work environment. Nurse managers should be familiar with some of the recent literature related to the concept of satisfaction and to an important allied factor: stress.

Satisfaction

In 1992, Irvine and Evans conducted an extensive review of the nursing and allied health care literature and identified 70 studies in which the factors that contribute to enhanced job satisfaction and retention among nursing staff were identified. These researchers then conducted a meta-analysis on the studies to clarify knowledge in the area and to identify future research foci. They concluded that a plethora of correlates of job satisfaction existed (see Table 21.1, page 396).

Irvine and Evans's (1992) conclusions find support in the results of a second meta-analysis, completed recently by Blegen (1993). In Blegen's investigation of 48 satisfaction studies—involving over 15 000 nurses—job satisfaction was strongly associated with stress $(r = - .61)$, *organizational commitment* $(r =.53)$, *communication with supervisor* $(r = .45)$, *autonomy* $(r = .42)$, *recognition* $(r = .42)$, and *routinization* $(r =- .41)$. Other factors that correlated with job satisfaction, in descending order, were *fairness, locus of control, age, years of experience, education,* and *professionalism.*

Autonomy has been correlated consistently with nurse satisfaction in the literature but, to date, no standardized definition has

Table 21.1
Correlates of job satisfaction and ranges of r.

Concept	Number of Studies	Range of r
Autonomy	7	.15 to .50
Stress	7	$-.15$ to $-.43$
Head nurse leadership	5	.30 to .47
Supervisor relationships	4	.29 to .57
Role conflict	5	$-.22$ to $-.48$
Job feedback	3	.29 to .43
Opportunity for advancement	4	.22 to .37
Pay	4	.07 to .37
Age	5	.01 to .47
Job tenure	4	.04 to .35
Work overload	3	$-.13$ to $-.29$

Source: Compiled from information in D. Irvine and M. Evans, *Job satisfaction and turnover among nurses: A review and meta-analysis* (Toronto: University of Toronto Faculty of Nursing Monograph Series, 1992).

emerged. Seybolt (1986) associated autonomy in nursing with freedom to make decisions and to do work fairly independently. One of the difficulties for nurse managers is that *freedom to make individual decisions* and to structure work independently may not have the same meaning for different nurses. Nurses who work in institutions may have little or no control over the terms of their work, which may be defined by a series of policies and procedures (Bernhard & Walsh, 1990). Nurses do make independent clinical decisions about patient care in the context of the variety of settings where they work. Although Seybolt (1986) determined that the need for autonomy was greater for mid-career nurses than for new recruits, very little is known about how to operationalize autonomy in a practice setting.

Toft and Anderson (1989) concluded that one of the major psychological functions of supervision is the reduction of role conflict for staff. Although role conflict and ambiguity are inherent in the nursing role, leadership strategies, such as representation, consultation, and involvement of staff in decision making, can lead (directly and indirectly) to a significant reduction in role ambiguity among nursing staff. Supportive supervision also can result in reduced role ambiguity and more open, supportive relations among co-workers. Closely related to leadership and supervision is the feedback given to employees about the job itself. Feedback, or the extent to which employees receive clear information about the effectiveness of their performance, has been positively correlated with job satisfaction.

Generally, older nurses experience higher levels of job satisfaction than do beginning nurses. Seybolt (1986) identified that nurses have different needs throughout their career. While feedback was highly correlated with job satisfaction for all nurses, nurses in the advanced career group need to feel that the work they do is meaningful; relative to them, entry-level nurses have a greater need for a sense of autonomy in the work they do.

Stress and Burnout

Stress has been identified consistently by researchers as having a negative relationship with nurse job satisfaction and job performance. As the level of perceived stress increases, the level of job satisfaction generally decreases. Working in conditions of unrelenting and excessive stress can lead to a state known colloquially as burnout (Campbell, 1988). Characteristics of burnout in nursing include emotional exhaustion, depersonalization of patients or clients, and having little sense of personal accomplishment (Robinson, Roth, Keim, Levenson, Flentje, & Bashor, 1991).

Gray-Toft and Anderson (1981) reported that workload, feeling inadequately prepared to meet emotional demands of patients and their families, and dealing with death and dying are pervasive sources of stress for practising hospital nurses. Other factors contributing to nursing stress and burnout relate to specific work settings, and may include structural and environmental characteristics of the facilities in which nurses work (Gray-Toft & Anderson, 1981; Topf & Dillon, 1988), supervisory practices and leadership style (Cameron et al., 1992; Duxbury, Armstrong, Drew, & Henly, 1984; Toft & Anderson, 1989), relationships with co-workers and support from supervisors (Fong, 1990), fatigue (Scott, 1991), being pulled to work on other nursing units (Foxall, Zimmerman, Standley, & Bene, 1990), and shift work (Coffey, Skipper, & Jung, 1988; Milne & Watkins, 1986). Finally, because of the gender mix of the nursing work force, many nurses will experience stressors that challenge women who combine personal and professional caregiving careers (Ross, Rideout, Carson, & Danbrook, 1992). As noted by Attridge and Callahan (1989), the stress that female nurses experience is to some degree also a reflection of the stress faced by all women confronting inequities in society.

Stress also arises as a result of issues unique to the nursing role (e.g., staff nurse versus educator) or specific clinical area itself (Åström, Nilsson, Norberg, & Winblad, 1990; Bourbonnais & Baumann, 1985; Burke & Scalzi, 1988; Dewe, 1989; Foxall et al., 1990; Gallop, Lancee, & O'Brien-Pallas, 1991; Hare, Pratt, & Andrews, 1988; Hawley, 1992; Power & Sharp, 1988; Rosenthal, Schmid, & Black, 1989; Scott, 1991; Tyler, Carroll, & Cunningham, 1991). However, in at least one study, no significant difference in overall stress levels across groups was noted; rather, the only significant differences found were in the type(s) of stress perceived to be most significant for each group (Foxall et al., 1990).

Increasing attention to violence has provoked some researchers to study the phenomenon of abuse as a source of nurses' stress. Studying verbal and physical abuse, for example, Graydon, Kasta, and Khan (1992) found that 33% of the registered nurses they surveyed (*n*=603) had experienced some form of abuse *within the past five days*; although the rate of nurse abuse was consistent across the three settings used in the study, abuse rates were higher in certain clinical areas (e.g., extended care). Gallop, Lancee, and Shugar (1992) found that nurses also had difficulty in dealing with violence in the psychiatric setting.

The way nursing work is structured and the basic personality characteristics of the nurse are two important factors accounting for different perceptions of stress among hospital nursing staff. When work units are structured so as to reduce levels of role conflict and role ambiguity, stress levels may decline similarly (Gray-Toft & Anderson, 1981). Further, when units and policies are structured so that they capitalize on the motivating factors known to exist in nursing work (e.g., recognition, responsibility, advancement), satisfaction may also be improved (Simpson, 1985). Studies remain underway to determine the effect on nurses of experiencing a critical incident stress debriefing program immediately following specific stressful incidents in the job setting (Eagle, McCann, Campeau, Cooper, Mascarin, & Price, 1992).

Discussing "hardy" (or stress-tolerant) personalities, Kobasa (1979) suggested that hardiness encompasses the concepts of commitment, challenge, and control. Kobasa asserted that the person having these personality characteristics would be better able and more likely to fend off stress and disease. Hardy individuals have a higher sense of commitment and purpose, and a greater sense of control over their own destiny. Theoretically, nurses possessing such characteristics may be able to cope better with the pervasive, continuous stressors present in nursing. However, in a study of 100 intensive care unit (ICU) nurses, Topf (1989) found only partial support for the hypothesis that hardiness in nurses is associated with less stress or burnout, and she found further that greater stress was not linked with higher rates of burnout. Topf did observe that less commitment to work was more strongly linked to burnout than was stress. Other conditions and coping strategies that may buffer stress—used by nurses known to have decreased levels of burnout—include seeking social support and using planful problem solving and positive reappraisal in the work setting (Ceslowitz, 1989; Ogus, 1990).

Comparing ICU versus non-ICU nurses, Maloney and Bartz (1983) found that ICU nurses were significantly more alienated and sensed significantly more external control than their non-ICU counterparts—exactly the opposite of the traits associated with hardiness theorized by Kobasa (1979). At the same time, these ICU nurses were more adventurous, and sought significantly more challenge, than the non-ICU nurses with whom they were compared. The investigators suggested that alienation (or detachment) may serve as an effective strategy to buffer the stress and emotional strain of working with critically ill patients and their families (Maloney & Bartz, 1983). The non-ICU nurses, on the other hand, exhibited less resistance to becoming involved with patients, perhaps because of the greater likelihood that the patients would recover. They also seemed to have a decreased need for adventure, despite the fact that their other personality traits seemed to predict that they would be able to handle such risks.

Not all types of stress negatively influence nurses' work lives. Many nurses seek out stressful environments specifically, and they seem to thrive on the challenge of surviving the experience. Again studying ICU nurses, Levine, Wilson, and Guido (1988) noted that those nurses who enjoyed the notoriously stressful critical care setting the most had high levels of self-esteem, and were categorized as being the androgynous or masculine type. Further, they tended to be aggressive, headstrong, competitive, resourceful, and mechanical in nature. That this personality type suits the stressful critical care environment finds support in the results of a study by Bailey, Steffen, and Grout (1980), who noted that two of the three sources of greatest stress in the ICU—patient care and interpersonal relationships— were also two of the three leading sources of job satisfaction. These nurses were evidently able to manage the stress and/or to frame it as a (positive) challenge. The high level of nursing turnover noted among some ICUs cannot be denied, however. Since alienation from work has been linked with burnout (Topf, 1989), the greater sense of alienation exhibited by ICU nurses may be a contributing factor and should not be ignored.

The perception of stress, then—as with the definition of quality—is highly individual in nature. The published research contains many contradictions with respect to defining, measuring, and coping with stress; in some cases, it seems unclear whether stress should even be avoided. Solutions to the problems of managing stress require an equal variety of strategies, tailored to the realities and needs of individual settings.

Approaches to Promoting Professionally Rewarding Work Environments

While a significant and substantial body of research related to nursing job satisfaction has been accumulated, little empirical evidence exists with respect to the efficacy of managerial interventions on the overall satisfaction of nurses. However, common sense would suggest that certain interventions may be more meaningful than others, depending on the characteristics of the caregiving situation. Given the extensive knowledge base that does exist around the correlates of nurse satisfaction, a nurse manager should conduct an assessment of the nursing team to determine the extent to which any of these variables may be present—and may be influencing satisfaction and overall work life. Nurse managers are in the unique position of being able to interact with both patients and staff, and to practise a "management by walking around" philosophy as a data-gathering technique. The model for examining quality of nursing work life developed by O'Brien-Pallas and Baumann (1992) can serve as a guide to the areas that should be included in an assessment by the nurse manager.

Individual Characteristics

In examining the unique characteristics of the nurse as an individual, the nurse manager should look at the age range of his or her staff. If the staff complement includes nurses having a variety of ages and levels of experience, then the nurse manager must address the needs of the workers differently than if the group were more homogeneous in terms of age and work experience. Are many of the staff working full time as well as managing young families at home? Is there a need for job sharing and/or more flexible scheduling than is currently available? Do the staff, in general, have a positive self-image? Do they exhibit a positive attitude? Do they respect each other and share a common philosophy about the type of care that will be provided? Given the mix of staff on the unit, do staff have sufficient autonomy—and are there opportunities for recognition for a job well done?

Given the nature of the nursing team and the mix of staff, the

leader's management style must be consistent with the .
staff. Seybolt (1986) suggested that nurses at different sta&
careers seem to respond best to different management styles. ^
graduates and entry-level employees need clear, consistent expla..
tions about the expectations of the job. They need to be given room to
grow, yet be provided adequate positive feedback about their work. A
young nurse may have a strong need for clinical autonomy, but may
look to the organization to provide some structure with respect to routine policies and patient care procedures. While still "learning the
ropes," the new employee should not be given repetitive, tedious work;
rather, his or her assignment should allow for the execution of a variety of interesting and challenging caregiving situations under conditions that will allow the employee to feel relatively protected. Mid-
career nurses require more freedom overall to make decisions and
work fairly independently. Staff in this age group must understand
and share the expectations of the job in order to experience satisfaction in their work. Nurse managers working with workers at this
stage must strive continually to keep nurses committed to and planning the directions of the nursing team.

Advanced career nurses need a nurse manager who can help
them see the results of their efforts. Because of their experience,
these nurses are often put in the charge position, and can become so
burdened with paperwork that they lose sight of the results of their
work. A nurse at this level needs a manager who can instil a sense of
excitement in the work. Managers working with nurses in this age
group should also regularly point out the importance of the work
being done, and remind staff that patients and families do benefit as
a result of the contribution made by nurses.

The late career nurse needs a nurse manager who makes a
point of acknowledging the individual who has handled a situation
particularly well. Too often, the late career nurse does not receive
deserved praise because the manager assumes that the staff member
knows when he or she has done a good job. Nurses at this career stage
are expert in the day-to-day management of patient care and need to
be encouraged to participate in developing the vision for the future
growth of the care environment. A creative nurse manager will work
with the practitioner at this career stage to help the individual from
falling into the "we've always done it this way" trap.

The preceding examination of the career cycle of the nurse
makes clear that the leadership and management style needed by
staff nurses can differ solely as a result of the experience and age mix
of the individual workers. If the staff mix includes primarily beginning or entry-level practitioners, then a more directive, standards-
driven approach to management may be necessary. If most of the staff

have been on the unit for some time, then the challenge involves using a participative style that continually focusses on the goals of the unit and organization and encourages practitioners to be involved in setting that direction. The choice is influenced by the nature of the individuals that make up the group. Quality work environments are those where the manager adapts the style to meet the needs of the situation.

There are several styles of leadership that are seen as conducive to enhancing the quality of nursing work life. The participative or democratic style is one where the leader can receive input about decisions that affect aspects of the functioning of individual units (Bernhard & Walsh, 1990). This style enhances individual nurses' contributions to decisions that could potentially have an impact on delivery of care and quality of working life for the nurse. Several assumptions must be met for the participatory style to be effective. Nurses have to have adequate databases to make decisions, and be willing to take responsibility for the decisions. In addition, they have to be tolerant of the ambiguity and uncertainty that so often are coupled with organizational decisions where there may be rapidly shifting priorities. Participatory decision making requires a culture change from the rule-based algorithmic approach to one where individual approaches are encouraged and rewarded.

Kotter (1990) differentiated between the concepts of management and leadership. This delineation is important as it separates clearly two important aspects of the manager's role. A leader promotes change, sets directions and goals, tolerates ambiguity, and responds quickly to rapidly changing environments. The motivational aspect of leadership is one that has to be recognized, especially in times of great change of both structure and function in traditional public institutions. Encouragement by creating challenging opportunities at the unit level will result in a corporate culture that values the leadership potential of each individual employee (Kotter, 1990). The management function is more a coordinating one and can be bureaucratic in nature (e.g., human resource planning, budgetary planning). Organizations that encourage both leadership and management functions enhance the quality of input from individual nurses.

Organization of Work: The Work Design and Work Context

Examination of the ways in which nursing work is organized on a day-to-day basis is important. Are the jobs of the various categories of caregivers organized so that there is no overlap among different job classifications, and each group of workers can identify a piece of the work that is meaningfully its own? Is the workload on the unit manageable, given the number and mix of staff employed? Although the staff may demonstrate that they can manage heavier-than-acceptable workloads on occasion, this demand should be the exception rather than the rule. In examining workload, care should be given to ensure that workload and shift work are distributed equitably across the members of the work environment. Improving the measurement of nursing work and workload remains the object of significant research (O'Brien-Pallas, Cockerill, & Leatt, 1991; O'Brien-Pallas et al., 1992). Current systems are not very sensitive; research efforts are aimed at addressing the influence of the complexity of patient conditions, characteristics of nurse caregivers, and the environments in which nurses work on the amount of nursing resources consumed by patients.

Different systems of nursing care delivery (Grohar-Murray & DiCroce, 1992) can enhance the ability to plan and shape the direction of care. These systems are frameworks to structure and organize the work of nursing designed to the characteristics of the individual unit and/or agency where the care is provided. The systems that are most commonly in place in hospitals are *team nursing, primary care nursing,* and *modular nursing,* with the recent addition of *case management.* (Refer to Chapter 17.) The methods that have evolved have both advantages and disadvantages for delivery of care, staff satisfaction, and cost of services. However, the model of care on the unit should be periodically examined by the staff in the context of relevance to the current environment.

A nurse manager should observe staff as they provide care to observe for obstacles impeding its smooth delivery. Staff should be encouraged to provide feedback to the nurse manager about such issues as delays in receiving linen, physical layout of the unit, and all other barriers that impede smooth delivery of care. The infrastructure present on the nursing unit, or in the community health centre, or in the outpost nursing station, can exert an enormous influence on a worker's ability to achieve even the simplest objectives in any organization. Even as the 21st century nears, highly skilled, educated, and experienced hospital nurses still must frequently abandon direct patient care activities to act as porters, secretaries, floor cleaners, and couriers. Work sampling studies have consistently demonstrated that the least skilled workers spend the greatest amount of time providing direct nursing care. To use one of the most expensive and educated workers on any health care team—the mid-career staff nurse—to run errands that could be accomplished by lower-skilled workers, computers, telephones, or fax machines can have a devastating effect on job satisfaction. It is inappropriate and dehumanizing to ask registered nurses to carry out work that can and should be done by simple, cheap machines. The goal of finding the most basic supplies needed to provide nursing care—linens, patient gowns, incontinence pads, and medications—can become the main activity of caregivers in many workplaces. The low morale in nursing is no mystery to the nurses who work in these conditions every day; higher salaries and better vacation benefits are important, but they do little to compensate for the great frustrations that nurses face every day as they simply try to get the job done.

The types and levels of stress present in any work setting must be assessed on a continuing basis, and such assessment must include an examination of the effect(s) of stress on the various team members. Jobs should be designed so that there is variety in the types of tasks in which nurses are involved; routine, repetitive work consistently demonstrates a negative correlation with satisfaction. Unless checked early, these factors can go on to be sources of frustration to the nursing staff. However, there is no denying the fact that most institutional nursing is difficult, heavy, physical labour, involving repetitive tasks and requiring many levels of rapid decision making—much of it taking place at times that tax the human body and spirit.

To improve satisfaction and control stress, nurse managers would do well to keep two things clearly in mind. First, as noted by Kramer and Schmalenberg in their now classic study of American magnet hospitals, the manager should never lose sight of the fact that the nursing department has primary responsibility for producing "the product of the organization": patient care (1988a, p. 13). All efforts of the entire organization must support and encourage the workers (i.e., nurses) who produce the vast bulk of the company's product. This situation clearly does not exist in most institutions in 1993. Directly related to the first assertion, nurses have made clear that their levels of stress can be decreased, and their overall satisfaction improved, by way of some very simple interventions:

- Nurses need adequate supplies of the basic materials required to provide patient care (i.e., the product);

- Nurses need time to provide a reasonable quality of care to each patient;

- Nurses need the full support of the supervisor and the nursing department as they strive to "produce the product" of the organization: patient care; and

- Nurses need to feel that their work is valued, recognized, and rewarded by the organization.

When these conditions exist, many of the stressors that cause dissatisfaction and turnover disappear—as was clearly evidenced in the magnet hospitals study (Kramer & Schmalenberg, 1988a, 1988b).

Work World

Nurse managers also need to be cognizant of the impact of broader organizational imperatives on bedside staff. Unless clear communication patterns about the mandate of the organization and changes in organizational imperatives are routinely communicated, the strategic plans of the organization may filter down to staff in a manner other than was originally intended. In times of organizational restraint and cutbacks, nurse managers must assess the impact of such changes on staff morale and continue to provide staff with opportunities to talk about the issues that are relevant to them. These same communication strategies are necessary when dealing with changes to the health care system external to the organization in which the nurse is employed.

Implications for Nurse Managers

A review of the literature suggests that many of the factors that are influential in creating quality work environments are within the span of control of the nurse manager. Managers need to be aware of the evolving critical mass of knowledge about factors affecting quality work environments coming from such sources as the Quality of Nursing Worklife Research Unit, a collaborative venture of the University of Toronto and McMaster University in Ontario.

Based on evidence from the institutions that participated in the magnet hospital studies, the visibility and accessibility of the leader clearly was the cornerstone of success of those nursing departments (Kramer & Schmalenberg, 1988a, 1988b). The first-level manager, by being equally visible and accessible to staff, has a pivotal role in creating the culture and professional standards in the workplace. She or he must embody and translate the mission, core values, and strategic plans of the organization to the staff.

Nurse managers must be comfortable in their role as managers and leave staff to do nursing care. Nursing staff want the opportunity to work autonomously, make independent decisions, and be accountable for their actions. Nurse managers can assist staff to understand and expand their roles only if they are able to let go of some of the traditional caregiving activities in which managers have been involved. A shared vision of the outcomes of nursing and a clear understanding of roles will ensure that managers and practitioners are united in their actions.

A workplace culture that values the unique contribution and needs of the individual worker, and that champions shared values and clear role expectations, are prerequisites for quality work environments. Only once these conditions exist can a nurse manager reasonably expect a quality work environment to flourish. To achieve this goal, nurse managers should keep in mind several basic principles identified by researchers and nurses in practice:

- Nurses are generally happier when their personality traits and skills match the needs of the job and clinical area;
- Nurses need feedback, praise, and learning opportunities at *all* stages of their careers;
- Many work life concerns disappear when nurses are provided with the basic equipment and supplies required to do the job;
- Nurses place a high value on direct nursing care and are frustrated by the pervasiveness of non-nursing tasks that they are asked to carry out;
- Although nurses value direct nursing care, they continue to experience stress when dealing with dying patients and death, and meeting the emotional demands of patients and families;
- Consensus has been reached with respect to the factors having the greatest impact on job satisfaction across roles and settings, i.e., autonomy, levels of stress, head nurse leadership and communication, role conflict, feedback and recognition, opportunity for advancement, salary, and routinization of tasks; and
- Excellent clinical practice must be rewarded formally if institutions hope to keep experienced clinical nurses at the bedside.

Nurse managers have the ability to alter many of the factors discussed affecting quality of work life, and must take the initiative to do so. Quality work environments do not just happen—they are created. Although the task may be daunting, the challenge is clearly worthwhile in terms of benefits to the workers, to patients or clients, and to the organization itself.

References

Åström, S., Nilsson, M., Norberg, A., & Winblad, B. (1990). Empathy, experience of burnout and attitudes towards demented patients among nursing staff in geriatric care. *Journal of Advanced Nursing, 15,* 1236-1244.

Attridge, C., & Callahan, M. (1989). Women in women's work: Nurses' stress and power. *Recent Advances in Nursing, 25,* 41-69.

Bailey, J., Steffen, S., & Grout, J. (1980). The stress audit: Identifying the stressors of ICU nursing. *Journal of Nursing Education, 19,* 15-25.

Bernhard, L., & Walsh, M. (1990). *Leadership: The key to the professionalism of nursing* (2nd ed.). St. Louis: C.V. Mosby.

Blegen, M. (1993). Nurses' job satisfaction: A meta-analysis of related variables. *Nursing Research, 42,* 36-41.

Bourbonnais, F., & Baumann, A. (1985). Stress and rapid decision making in nursing: An administrative challenge. *Nursing Administration Quarterly, 9*(3), 85-91.

Burke, G., & Scalzi, C. (1988). Role stress in hospital executives and nursing executives. *Health Care Management Review, 13*(3), 67-72.

Cameron, S., Horsburgh, M., Drakich, J., Rieger, F., Pickard, D., Armstrong-Stassen, M., & Schneider, L. (1992) *Impact of hospital work environment on job satisfaction and retention of nurses.* Toronto: Ontario Ministry of Health Nursing Innovation Fund.

Campbell, M. (1988). The structure of stress in nurses' work. In B. Bolaria & H. Dickinson (Eds.), *Sociology of health care in Canada* (pp. 393-405.). Toronto: Harcourt Brace Jovanovich.

Ceslowitz, S. (1989). Burnout and coping strategies among hospital staff nurses. *Journal of Advanced Nursing, 14,* 553-557.

Coffey, L., Skipper, J., & Jung, F. (1988). Nurses and shift work: Effects on job performance and job-related stress. *Journal of Advanced Nursing, 13,* 245-254.

Dewe, P. (1989). Stressor frequency, tension, tiredness and coping: Some measurement issues and a comparison across nursing groups. *Journal of Advanced Nursing, 14,* 308-320.

Duxbury, M., Armstrong, G., Drew, D., & Henly, S. (1984). Head nurse leadership style with staff nurse burnout and job satisfaction in neonatal intensive care units. *Nursing Research, 33,* 97-101.

Eagle, J., McCann, C., Campeau, H., Cooper, G., Mascarin, C., & Price, P. (1992). *Evaluation of an intervention to reduce critical incident stress in hospital nursing staff.* Hamilton, ON: Quality of Nursing Worklife Research Unit/ McMaster University.

Fong, C. (1990). Role overload, social support, and burnout among nursing educators. *Journal of Nursing Education, 29,* 102-108.

Foxall, M., Zimmerman, L., Standley, R., & Bene, B. (1990). A comparison of frequency and sources of nursing job stress perceived by intensive care, hospice and medical-surgical nurses. *Journal of Advanced Nursing, 15,* 577-584.

Gallop, R., Lancee, W., & O'Brien-Pallas, L. (1991). *Nursing satisfaction and the difficult psychiatric patient.* Toronto: Ontario Ministry of Health Nursing Innovation Fund.

Gallop, R., Lancee, W., & Shugar, G. (1992). *A comparison of residents' and nurses' perceptions of the difficult short stay patient.* Toronto: Ontario Ministry of Health Nursing Innovation Fund.

Gray-Toft, P., & Anderson, J.G. (1981). Stress among hospital nursing staff: Its causes and effects. *Social Science and Medicine, 15A,* 639-647.

Graydon, J., Kasta, W., & Khan, P. (1992). *The personal and professional impact on the nurse of verbal and physical abuse.* Toronto: Ontario Ministry of Health Nursing Innovation Fund.

Grohar-Murray, M., & DiCroce, H. (1992). *Leadership and management in nursing.* Norwalk, CT: Appleton & Lange.

Hare, J., Pratt, C., & Andrews, D. (1988). Predictors of burnout in professional and paraprofessional nurses working in hospitals and nursing homes. *International Journal of Nursing Studies, 25,* 105-115.

Hawley, M.P. (1992). Sources of stress for emergency nurses in four urban Canadian emergency departments. *Journal of Emergency Nursing, 18,* 211-216.

Irvine, D., & Evans, M. (1992). *Job satisfaction and turnover among nurses: A review and meta-analysis.* Toronto: University of Toronto Faculty of Nursing Monograph Series.

Kobasa, S. (1979). Stressful life events, personality, and health: An inquiry into hardiness. *Journal of Personality and Social Psychology, 37,* 1-11.

Kotter, J. (1990). *A force for change—How leadership differs from management.* New York: Free Press.

Kramer, M., & Schmalenberg, C. (1988a). Magnet hospitals: Part I Institutions of excellence. *Journal of Nursing Administration, 18*(1), 13-24.

Kramer, M., & Schmalenberg, C. (1988b). Magnet hospitals: Part II Institutions of excellence. *Journal of Nursing Administration, 18*(2), 11-19.

Leatt, P., & Schneck, R. (1976). *An inquiry into the relationships among environment, technology, structure, process and behaviour within nursing subunits.* Unpublished proposal, University of Alberta, Edmonton, AB.

Levine, C., Wilson, S., & Guido, G. (1988). Personality factors of critical care nurses. *Heart & Lung, 17,* 392-398.

Lyons, T.F. (1971). Role clarity, need for clarity, satisfaction, tension, and withdrawal. *Organizational Behaviour and Human Performance, 6,* 99-110.

Maloney, J., & Bartz, C. (1983). Stress-tolerant people: Intensive care nurses compared with non-intensive care nurses. *Heart & Lung, 12,* 389-394.

Milne, D., & Watkins, F. (1986). An evaluation of the effects of shift rotation on nurses' stress, coping and strain. *International Journal of Nursing Studies, 23,* 139-146.

O'Brien-Pallas, L., & Baumann, A. (1992). Quality of nursing worklife issues—A unifying framework. *Canadian Journal of Nursing Administration, 5*(2), 12-16.

O'Brien-Pallas, L., Cockerill, R., & Leatt, P. (1991). *A comparison of the workload estimates of five patient classification systems in nursing.* Ottawa: NHRPD.

O'Brien-Pallas, L., Irvine, D., Peereboom, E., Murray, M., Ho, R., Beed, J., & Young, J. (1992). *Factors that influence variability in nursing workload at the Hospital for Sick Children.* Toronto: The Hospital for Sick Children Foundation.

Ogus, E.D. (1990). Burnout and social support systems among ward nurses. *Issues in Mental Health Nursing, 11*, 267-281.

Power, K.G., & Sharp, G.R. (1988). A comparison of sources of nursing stress and job satisfaction among mental handicap and hospice nursing staff. *Journal of Advanced Nursing, 13*, 726-732.

Quintanilla, S., & Wilpert, B. (1988). The meaning of working—Scientific status of a concept. In V. de Keyser, T. Qvale, B. Wilpert and S. Quintanilla, *The Meaning of Work and Technological Options* (pp. 3-14). New York: John Wiley & Sons.

Robinson, S., Roth, S., Keim, J., Levenson, M., Flentje, J., & Bashor, K. (1991). Nurse burnout: Work related and demographic factors as culprits. *Research in Nursing and Health, 14*, 223-228.

Rosenthal, S., Schmid, K., & Black, M. (1989). Stress and coping in a NICU. *Research in Nursing and Health, 12*, 257-265.

Ross, M., Rideout, E., Carson, M., & Danbrook, C. (1992). *Nurses' work: Combining personal and professional careers.* Toronto: Ontario Ministry of Health Nursing Innovation Fund.

Scott, K. (1991). Northern nurses and burn out. *The Canadian Nurse, 87*(10), 18-21.

Seybolt, J.W. (1986). Dealing with premature employee turnover. *Journal of Nursing Administration, 16*, 26-32.

Simpson, K. (1985). Job satisfaction or dissatisfaction reported by registered nurses. *Nursing Administration Quarterly, 9*, 64-73.

Toft, P.A., & Anderson, J.G. (1989). Organizational stress in the hospital: Development of a model for diagnosis and prediction. In G. DeFriese, T. Ricketts, & J. Stein (Eds.), *Methodological advances in health services research (pp. 119-140).* Ann Arbor, MI: Health Administration Press.

Topf, M. (1989). Personality hardiness, occupational stress, and burnout in critical care nurses. *Research in Nursing and Health, 12*, 179-186.

Topf, M., & Dillon, E. (1988). Noise-induced stress as a predictor of burnout in critical care nurses. *Heart & Lung, 17*, 567-574.

Tyler, P., Carroll, D., & Cunningham, S. (1991). Stress and well-being in nurses: A comparison of the public and private sectors. *International Journal of Nursing Studies, 28*, 125-130.

Vogt, J., Cox, J., Velthouse, B., & Thames, B. (1983). *Retraining professional nurses: A planned process.* St. Louis: C.V. Mosby.

C H A P T E R   2 2

The Nursing Unit as a Learning Environment

Jude A. Spiers

Jude A. Spiers, RN, BA (Nsg) (Massey, New Zealand), is a New Zealand nurse currently completing her Master's degree in Nursing at the University of Alberta. She worked
as a Staff Development Officer at Waikato Hospital, New Zealand, before coming to
Canada for her graduate studies.

Continuing personal and professional education is one of the greatest challenges facing nurses working in a dynamic health care environment. Nursing's body of knowledge and skill is constantly evolving
to adapt to changes in societal expectations resulting from shifting
patterns of health and illness, rapid innovations in technology, and
increases in scientific knowledge. The nurse manager as an educator
can be a facilitator of experiential learning, a collaborator in assessing learning needs and planning educational programs, and a role
model in promoting a spirit of inquiry and ceaseless learning. This
chapter is intended to provide an overview of managerial responsibilities in developing programs, coordinating resources, collaborating
with educational agencies, and assisting individual nurses to identify
learning strategies.

The nursing unit as a learning environment is a vast realm in
which there is potential to combine both formal education with collective learning through informal and incidental peer group interactions.
Professional and personal development are most likely to occur where
and when they are most effective in relation to the nurse and the
organization. A nurse's motivation to take advantage of all sources of
learning is closely related to her or his willingness to learn how to
learn. This desire to be self-directed in lifelong learning is influenced
by the opportunities and support found within the working milieu.
The nurse manager shares responsibility for creating an environment

Figure 22.1
Responsibilities in continuing education.

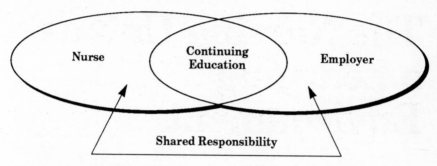

Shared Responsibility

- Assess own skills and knowledge
- Identify own learning needs
- Communicate learning needs
- Use educational resources
- Use new learning in practice
- Evaluate own learning
- Share knowledge and skills
- Maintain record of learning
- Support the learning of others
- Invest own time, energy, and money

- Develop a philosophy that supports education
- Incorporate continuing education values in all personnel decisions
- Base programs on identified learning needs and goals
- Inform staff of opportunities
- Pay costs of required programs, share costs of optional programs
- Adjust staffing assignments for attendance
- Provide educational leaves
- Support use of new learning in practice
- Provide opportunities for learning and sharing with others
- Promote the transferability of qualifications to other institutions

Source: Developed from the Canadian Nurses Association (1992), *Position statement on continuing education.* (Appendix). Permission to use material obtained from the Canadian Nurses Association.

in which learning is a consciously integrated, essential, and enjoyable aspect of work. Encouraging and supporting continued learning and development through both formal (such as orientation and preceptorship programs) and informal opportunities need to be founded on a philosophy of shared responsibility and respect for self-direction. The Canadian Nurses Association (1992) has specifically described the components of this shared venture as shown in Figure 22.1.

Principles of Adult Learning

Andragogy, the "art and science of helping adults learn" (Knowles, 1990, p. 54), is a philosophy oriented toward helping people learn not what they ought to know, but rather how to continue finding out so that they may meet the needs and goals of the individual, the institution, and society (Knowles, 1970). It is based upon four assumptions of the characteristics of adult learners and implications for learning:

*   As individuals mature, their self-concepts move from dependent to self-directed. Adults want to be self-reliant and need to know why they should learn something. Adults are more aware of their learning styles and can learn about how they learn.

*   Adults accumulate experiences that provide a rich resource for learning. Experiential learning, which values a learner's knowledge and skills, is effective because it demonstrates respect for the person.

*   Adults are ready to learn when they see a need to be able to do something effectively. Using these "teachable moments" enhances the perception of learning's applicability to the individual's development and performance.

*   An adult is more task-, life-, or problem-centred than subject-centred.

Self-directed learners are those who take the initiative in "diagnosing their learning needs, formulating learning goals, identifying human and material resources for learning, choosing and implementing appropriate learning strategies, and evaluating learning outcomes" (Knowles, 1985, p. 81). This does not imply that learning occurs in isolation, but that it usually occurs best in association with various kinds of helpers. The role of the nurse manager as an educator, therefore, is that of a resource, consultant, and co-learner rather than provider of education. That is not to suggest that there is no place for directive education and learning. In fact, in Knowles's (1985) revised view of andragogy, he suggests that the characteristics of directed and self-directed learning should be viewed on a continuum. There are times and situations in which people are indeed dependent on others for direction because their experience is inadequate, inappropriate, or entirely lacking. In a nurse's first attempts at carrying out a clinical technique, approaching a particular client situation, or dealing with a medical crisis such as a cardiac arrest, her or his focus will be on understanding the procedure or problem, and will depend on colleagues' support and direction. As she or he becomes more confident in practice, efforts to extend abilities may not concentrate on the subject content as such, but on the interpersonal and leadership aspects of nursing practice. Within the multitude of situations in a working day, a nurse may be a novice in one situation, depending on external resources for direction, yet a leader and consultant in another.

"Situational leadership" is a theory that is useful in helping a manager to identify the degree of readiness, or maturity, a person exhibits in performing a specific task, function, or objective, and to choose the most appropriate leadership style or behaviour to meet the demands of the situation (Hersey & Blanchard, 1982). In this theory, maturity refers to the ability and willingness to be self-directing in behaviour, and the degree of confidence in assuming responsibility in a specific situation. So, in a totally unfamiliar situation, a nurse may not have the knowledge, skills, or confidence to act. The nurse manager may need to be very directive in explaining the situation, actions, and roles. For example, many nurses recall their first involvement in a cardiac arrest as being able to follow specific directions but otherwise feeling "frozen" with anxiety. Yet, in another situation, the same nurse will be highly competent and confident and seek opportunities to share her or his knowledge and skills.

Figure 22.2 shows how a nurse manager's educational leadership approach depends on the demands of the situation as well as on

Figure 22.2

Learner styles and manager responses.

Participating	Selling
Learner Able; not willing/confident	**Learner** Not able; willing/confident
Manager Low task; high relationship	**Manager** High task; high relationship
Delegating	**Telling**
Learner Able; willing/confident	**Learner** Not able; not willing/confident
Manager Low task; low relationship	**Manager** High task; low relationship

Source: Adapted, with permission, from J. Zurlinden and B. Bongard (1991), Situational leadership. *AORN Journal*, 54(5), 969.

the needs and abilities of the nurse. There are two central types of leadership behaviour—task behaviour (i.e., organizing and defining roles, and providing specific directions as to how, when, why, and where tasks are to be accomplished) and relationship behaviour (i.e., maintaining personal relationships, listening, and providing emotional support and reassurance). The manager's assessment of the nurse's degree of willingness and ability determines which mix of leadership behaviours will be most helpful (Irurita, 1988; Pavlish, 1987; Zurlinden & Bongard, 1991).

Creating a Learning Climate

An ideal working climate is one in which learning is regarded as an integral aspect of work, and work is regarded as continued learning. Nurse managers can be highly influential in moulding the philosophical atmosphere that establishes learning as a valued priority and a collective responsibility. The atmosphere is important because many successful learning opportunities occur through interactions with others in daily work. A substantial amount of learning is informal and experiential, occurring through networking and coaching. Incidental learning, another aspect of experiential learning, is unintentional, a byproduct of another activity, and largely "buried" in the context of other tasks (Marsick & Watkins, 1990).

It is important for nurse managers to support staff development directly and indirectly by integrating the formal aspects of education into the opportunities inherent in daily practice. Working with a novice nurse is an ideal opportunity not only to teach technique, but also to model expert professional behaviours. Delegating responsibilities for committee work or preceptorship programs extends an expert nurse's leadership and managerial skills. In this manner, every individual is regarded as a resource for discovering the knowledge embedded in practice.

Nurse managers need a sophisticated level of knowledge and skills to maintain the workplace as a learning environment. A 1991 study by Adams (1991) found that managers perceived learning needs in a wide variety of managerial skills, including organizational and political systems, personnel management, interpersonal relations, and resource allocation. Clearly, the workplace is as much a learning environment for the nurse manager as it is for the staff nurse. Recognizing one's own need for continuous learning, and acting on those needs, is the most powerful modeling tool in creating a learning environment.

Needs Assessment

Accurately identifying individual or group learning needs is the first step toward planning strategies to support personal and professional development. Although there are various definitions of learning needs, basically these constitute the gap between the present level of competency and a higher level required for the effective performance to meet individual or organizational goals, either as perceived by the individual or observed by someone else (Knowles, 1970). Approaches to needs assessment range from formal, systematically planned processes to informal activities, depending on the context and purpose. Whichever approach is chosen, it is vital to promote active involvement between the nurse manager, other group leaders (such as preceptors or nurse educators), and the individual or group whose needs are being assessed.

Methods of assessing needs may be clustered within various models (Puetz, 1987). The two models most commonly used in identifying unit-specific or individual needs are the discrepancy and competency models. *Discrepancy model approaches* seek to identify the difference between current practice and desired practice in a system. Discrepancies (which are not necessarily negative) are gaps in knowledge or skill related to individual or group performance or the intention to implement a change that, if present, would solve or eliminate a problem in the system (Puetz, 1987; Simpson, 1992). *Competency model strategies* are those that identify individual learning needs in relation to specific standards of performance. Individuals' current abilities are compared to these standards, and any gaps are considered to be a learning need. Competency-based systems are often integrated with performance appraisal systems to define performance expectations, assess performance, and identify strengths and needs. The Vancouver General Hospital, for example, has developed a competency evaluation system based on unit-specific competency criteria for four levels of development (orienting/dependent practice; independent practice; leadership and ability to assist others in practice; and advanced practitioner with resource and consultative roles). Change in job performance as the nurse gains expertise in practice identifies strategies to help the nurse progress to the next developmental level (Beetstra, 1992).

The Performance Based Development System (PBDS) is another competency-based approach and is used at the Foothills Hospital, Calgary, and the University of Alberta Hospitals, Edmonton. This system involves a diverse set of simulation techniques to measure performance abilities in clinical practice in acute care areas, and has also been adapted to assess performance in areas such as nursing unit management or clinical supervision, and preceptoring. The system enables educators and managers to: assess the level of competency and identify the learning or development needs of novices; diagnose problems in continuing performance; validate the achievement of expected levels of competency; and identify cross-training needs according to specific unit-based practice standards (del Bueno, 1990; Montgomerie, 1993).

Assessment in the Performance Based Development System focusses on the level of knowledge and skills in the areas of: critical thinking, including clinical decision making, care planning, priority setting, and problem solving; interpersonal relationships, such as communication and conflict management; and technical skills and procedures (Henderson, 1992). In this system, the criteria and methods for assessment are developed by clinical experts within specific clinical areas, based on the most common patient conditions, the most frequently required skills, and the nursing practice policies. The assessment techniques include multimedia presentations, including videotapes and audio tapes of realistic, clinically based, simulated patient clinical problems or unit situations, games, small group exercises, and skill labs.

The Performance Based Development System assessor develops action plans recommending learning options based on the patterns and trends of competencies and needs identified during the assessment process (which may take up to ten hours for a new graduate nurse). These recommendations, which may include formal classes, preceptorship activities, or clinical assignments, are used by the nurse manager and nurse to create an individualized orientation or development plan (Montgomerie, 1993). Although the Performance Based Development System is time- and labour-intensive to initiate and adapt to the organization's specific needs, the benefits are considered to be cost effective by reducing the need for block orientation programs (Weeks, Tsubai, Gleason, & Cavouras, 1988).

Continuing Nursing Education Programs

Continuing nursing education refers to a multitude of activities and programs from orientation to the work setting to certification in a nursing specialty. It should be a frequent and integral part of any nurse's personal and professional career. Nurses can make many choices about how they will continue to learn: deciding to read one particular journal and not another; attending certain types of professional or educational meetings; or choosing to learn through specific problem-solving situations. The choice indicates a personal perception of their direction in continuing development. Failure to find programs that adequately fulfil perceived needs is one of the most common reasons cited by nurses for not engaging in regular continuing education activities (Yuen, 1991).

There is a wealth of literature on the description, development, and evaluation of continuing nursing education programs that cannot be addressed here. Readers interested in this area are advised to refer to the wide range of staff development/training and continuing education texts and journals. The purpose of this section is to provide the reader with a brief overview of the essential features of the purposes and elements of orientation, inservice, continuing education, and certification programs.

Orientation

Orientation is the process through which staff are introduced to all aspects of their work setting when they commence employment, or when changes occur in their existing roles. Orientation provides a transition to a new setting by establishing a formal process to facilitate socialization into the work team; it is a means of helping a nurse align the expectations of the role with actual job responsibilities and gain assistance in developing required competencies (Abruzzese & Quinn-O'Neal, 1992). Although orientation combines both formal and informal processes, the actual structure is determined by the organization's philosophy. For reasons of efficiency, however, many programs are divided into a generic induction into the organization (usually provided by a centralized training department), followed by a unit-specific orientation. Induction programs provide a general welcome and overview of the organization's philosophy, mission, and structure, including client populations served, personnel and employment policies and paperwork, and mandatory education (such as fire, safety, cardiopulmonary resuscitation, and universal precautions for infectious diseases). Unit-based orientation usually follows to clarify job responsibilities and unit-specific policies/procedures, and to validate and develop practice and knowledge competencies.

Effective orientation programs specifically address individual needs rather than providing a standardized plan regardless of the nurse's existing competencies (O'Grady & O'Brien, 1992). Developing individualized programs entails a dedication of time and effort by both the nurse manager and the new staff member, as well as by others who may be involved (for example, preceptors, clinical educators or specialists, and senior staff nurses), but the result is more cost effective than involving the nurse in a lengthy process of reviewing material that is already well understood. The importance of accurate and complete needs assessments cannot be stressed enough as the foundation of effective orientation programs.

Socialization into the unit's culture, norms, and values is a crucial and subtle process, but the ability to adjust to a complex work environment is critical to the formation of positive attitudes and to job satisfaction. It is estimated by Welch and Stull (1991) that the informal social structure—the unwritten rules and norms—constitutes some 90% of the knowledge learned in orientation. Since informal rules are often more powerful than formal or public ones, it is essential that staff orienting new members are those who are able to actualize the unit's mission and who are knowledgeable about, and able to articulate, the culture of the unit.

Preceptorship

Preceptorship is an adaptation of the mentor concept traditionally used in industry and business. It assists the social and professional integration of a nurse into a new role by establishing a time-bound relationship with a competent peer practitioner (Modic, 1989). Preceptors facilitate socialization through a consistent one-to-one relationship; this supports the new nurse's growth, development, and increasing independence because the preceptor provides a role model and guide who is able to counsel, coach, and inspire. For the new staff member it is a valuable way of reducing anxiety and developing self-confidence in client care and patient management expertise. Some research suggests that the cooperative nature of the relationship results in a higher level of patient care and a readiness on the part of the new staff member to assume full responsibilities sooner than with traditional orientation methods (Giles & Moran, 1989; McGrath & Princeton, 1987).

Readiness to become a preceptor requires a thorough understanding of the varied and demanding expectations placed upon an expert role model. Careful preceptor selection and preparation is an essential aspect of managerial support for a preceptor program. Initial preceptor preparation generally occurs through workshops that address principles and issues of preceptorship, adult learning processes, interpersonal communication, and skills in needs assessment and performance evaluation. However, to prevent preceptor burnout, recognizing and addressing a preceptor's need for ongoing learning and support must be a continuing concern to the nurse manger (Roberson, 1992). Staffing schedules should allow for maximum contact between the new staff member and the preceptor, as well as time for preceptors to plan and develop orientation programs. During the work day, an appropriate environment for coaching and teaching means that the preceptors' normal client care workload should be reassessed. It is important to remember that the assignment of two nurses to a case load does not necessarily halve, but will probably increase, the preceptor's workload and responsibilities.

This mode of orientation primarily focusses on the close preceptor relationship, so it is essential to match preceptor and orientee learning styles, a significant but often ignored aspect of preceptor relationships (Carroll, 1992). Complementary ways of teaching and learning, of perceiving and processing information, and of expressing ideas help build a constructive relationship. Involving staff in the initial meeting with the new staff member may provide indications of the most suitable preceptor match. In the same way, inviting staff opinion in preceptor selection is profitable, as the candidate's colleagues often have a clear idea about teaching styles.

The role of preceptor augments and does not eliminate the involvement of the nurse manager (or others) in orientation. Preceptorship allows the nurse manager to acknowledge expert practitioners in a way that is professionally satisfying (without significantly affecting the unit budget), as well as allowing the nurse manager to focus personally on specific areas of the new staff member's performance. Close communication with both the preceptor and new staff member should be maintained so that the effectiveness of the relationship may be periodically evaluated.

Inservice Education

Inservice refers to the education activities provided by the institution, within the work day, that seek to develop or improve the knowledge (including attitudes and values), skills, and abilities required to meet organizational performance expectations. Inservice activities are based on the policies and procedures particular to the institution and have the objective of assisting employees to adapt to changes related to new technology, knowledge, procedures, or products. Potential educational methods depend on the type of change and desired outcome. Multimedia and self-directed approaches, such as audiovisual and computer-assisted learning packages, skill labs, case studies, simulations, and brief seminars or demonstrations, are all often sufficiently flexible to be used within the unit setting. The inservice approach will be influenced by variables such as the availability of required resources and by the nature of the working environment. Any constraints within the work setting must be weighed against the difficulties of scheduling staff to attend block sessions off the unit.

The success of inservice is intrinsically related to whether or not nurses perceive that it is relevant to actual practice. Interest and commitment is likely to diminish if nurse managers or educators develop programs without validating that the nurses share a common perception of a learning need. Although this seems to be an obvious fact, manager-driven courses continue to be a primary concern reported by nurses (Yuen, 1991). Establishing a unit-based education committee, whose members identify learning needs and inservice strategies, is one way of reducing this possibility. This committee has the added benefits of involving all stakeholders in the inservice process, as well as creating a climate of shared responsibility, motivation, and diversity of perspectives.

Continuing Nursing Education

Continuing nursing education is the lifelong process of ordered, directed, and ongoing learning experiences intended to enhance nursing practice and the fulfilment of the nurse's professional goals. It is broader in scope than inservice in that the learning may be organizationally desirable but is not regarded as essential to meet job performance expectations. However, the potential for continuing nursing education to have a positive impact on nursing practice often depends on the degree of receptivity to innovation in practice within the work context (Waddell, 1991). The nurse manager's willingness to assist nurses who are seeking to extend their academic credentials may be a major determining factor in nurses' decisions to continue their education. Support can be offered in a variety of ways, from acting as a referee in scholarship or bursary applications to negotiating alternative working schedules (such as part-time work, job sharing, summer employment, or providing educational leave). A positive and supportive attitude toward education and the opportunity to use and share enhanced knowledge and skills is fundamental to helping nurses maintain their motivation. Combining work, study, and a personal life often seems manageable—until the end of the term when papers and exams are due! In today's health care environment, continuing education is a necessity, not a luxury (if it ever was). It is a central responsibility of the nurse manager as an educator not only to expect and support staff to pursue continuing education, but also to energize their staff's endeavours. Every nurse's needs can be met in some way because the range of topics and forums of activity is infinite, encompassing the entire spectrum of current interests and concerns in nursing, health care, and beyond.

Certification

Certification, as defined by the Canadian Nurses Association, is the "voluntary and periodic (re-certification) process by which an organized professional body confirms that a registered nurse has demonstrated competence in a nursing specialty by having met predetermined standards of that specialty" (CNA, 1989, p. 3). CNA certification is aimed at promoting excellence in nursing care by recognizing the increasing knowledge and skill required for expert practice in specialized areas. Nurses with certification are an asset because of their increased breadth of practice and responsibility in clinical decision making. However, although there is increasing appreciation of nurses with specialized expertise, there is as yet little recognition in terms of clinical career ladders or remuneration (Calkin, 1992; Reimer, Wyness, Courtney, & Conrad, 1992).

Canadian nurse specialist Margaret Wood (1992) suggests that the actual process of one nurse's applying for certification has a positive impact on the entire work group. The application procedure (which readers may obtain from their nursing association) requires peer performance appraisal and extensive preparation for the certification examination. Colleague involvement and support, for example in reviewing the literature or consulting expert resources, kindle a learning atmosphere, and questions, discussions, and debates are stimulated (Wood, 1992). The number of certified nursing specialties is limited, but growing, in Canada; some nurses have sought American certification until their specialty achieves similar recognition by the Canadian Nurses Association.

Physical Resources

The affective and cognitive aspects of a learning environment emanate from the staff. However, motivation and energy to engage in learning opportunities is mediated by fatigue and stresses from shift work and demanding workloads. Maintaining a collection of learning resources, such as videos, poster displays, and journals that can be perused during short lull periods in the working day is extremely useful to complement other forms of continuing education.

Audiovisual resources, such as videos and films, may be rented or purchased from commercial vendors, libraries, or professional organizations. Texts and journals, always an important resource for keeping abreast of current knowledge, are more likely to be read if they are easily accessible, so a library of essential materials is a valuable investment. Access to some references of broader professional interest can be arranged in conjunction with the nurse educator/specialist or the agency's librarian who may be able to photocopy the indexes of journals (naturally, keeping within copyright provisions) or prepare summaries of articles for reference in the work setting. One popular and cost-effective variation is the preparation of "journal tidbits" in which excerpts of important information gleaned from a variety of journals are recorded onto a tape and distributed to each unit with accompanying written materials (Morton, 1990).

Self-paced learning using self-instructional learning modules or self-contained packages of materials are an increasingly viable option for a range of topics in practice, from orientation to medication administration. These can be developed within the unit or agency, or borrowed from distance learning centres or other library sources. Another self-paced learning mode, notice boards, is a notoriously underused learning resource, although poster displays are a popular visual learning medium (Rosier, Wall, & Discoe, 1989). There are an infinite number of innovative ways to present information, and their development can be as much a learning experience as their scrutiny. The most recent development in self-instruction techniques is computer-assisted instruction programs (CAI), which have numerous advantages for adult learners, including individualized interactive dialogue and multiple learning modes There are various modes of computer-assisted instruction, including tutorials, instructional games, and simulations, which may be purchased or developed on the unit (using special software that requires little or no skill in programming) for a wide range of educational topics (Alessi & Trollip, 1991). Several journals, such as *Computers in Nursing*, *Nurse Educator*, and *Journal of Continuing Education*, contain information about new software, including the source, author, price, and necessary hardware.

The capital outlay for educational resources is a major consideration, although the expense should be balanced with the length of expected use and the benefits of enhancing staff's learning potential. Rapid advances in hardware and software are making multimedia more sophisticated, affordable, and accessible. Costs can be shared between units or agencies, or the staff (within or beyond the unit) as a whole can make a commitment to raise funds for educational equipment.

Clients and Student Education

Client education is a significant part of professional nursing practice. The nurse manager has a key role in ensuring that clients' learning needs are met—from both the clients' and nurses' perspective. Nurses, although believing that their teaching is based on the learning needs of their clients, still too often derive the identification of client needs from their own perspective, with the client's views remaining virtually unexplored and undocumented (Sullivan, 1993).

The net result is that clients do not receive the type of coaching they need as adult learners. The nurse manager's role in communicating client education expectations and standards during orientation, in performance appraisals, and in daily work with nurses must be complemented with administrative strategies to ensure that teaching has an equal priority with other clinical responsibilities. It is also important to remember that the increasingly popular use of self-directed educational packages, such as programmed instruction booklets, multimedia, and computer-assisted learning in client education, should never replace, only enhance, personal coaching interactions.

Accommodating both clients' care requirements and the educational needs of nursing students can be a challenge in a busy working environment, as client care is a priority over student educational activities. However, today's students are the nurses of the future, so clinical experiences should combine high-calibre client care and educational opportunities. Nursing students who are welcomed, oriented, and integrated into a working environment will work and learn to their maximum capacity, especially if time has been invested in determining mutual student and unit expectations, and identifying student abilities and learning needs. The nurse manager has pivotal responsibilities in successfully balancing service and education needs, starting with the determination that the number of students in the unit will not adversely affect normal functioning. Negotiating appropriate student placements with educational agencies must be based on the characteristics of the clinical area, which will define the expectations and roles of students, preceptors, and faculty or clinical instructors. The type of clients will influence levels of student supervision or independence, which in turn further clarifies these roles and responsibilities. Preceptors, for instance, assume a different role with students than do staff nurses in a setting where the instructor is constantly available. Preceptorship of students is growing in popularity in Canada as a means of acknowledging the wealth of professional nursing knowledge to be found in practising with an expert nurse (Myrick & Barrett, 1992). However, whether students are supervised by their own instructor or are preceptored, the nurse manager's role is essentially one of coordination and facilitation between the needs of the nursing clients, unit staff, and nursing students. Maintaining communication links with educational agencies is the foundation for a supportive learning and working milieu that meets both nursing care and nursing educational objectives.

Supporting students from other health disciplines, such as physiotherapy, social work, and medicine, is an additional aspect of the nurse manager's role. The goal of effective client care and efficient unit functioning depends on having *all* students integrated and supported. The time expended in working with other disciplines will result not only in the quality of client care being maintained, but will expand other disciplines' ability to work with nursing's contribution to client care.

Formal modes of collaboration between service and educational agencies is one way of enhancing cooperation between nursing education and practice. Collaboration may take many forms, including shared appointments, in which a faculty member shares a position with a service staff member, and joint appointments, in which the appointee holds a position with associated responsibilities in each institution (Acorn, 1990). Collaboration provides opportunities for faculty to become involved in and responsive to the realities of clinical practice and for service personnel to keep abreast with advances in nursing research. Cooperation between service and education promotes identification of clinical research problems as nurse educators and clinicians combine their theoretical and practical knowledge (Hawkin & Hillestad, 1990; Reilly & Oermann, 1985). In terms of broader continuing nursing education, joint sponsorship of programs (such as conference, specialty courses, and distance education programs) can serve the needs of the larger nursing community by pooling the resources and skills of the range of local nursing experts.

Conclusion

The nurse manager has a primary role in developing a working environment in which learning is valued as an integral aspect of work and work is regarded as continuous learning. The nurse manager as an educator, whether as a facilitator, coordinator, or coach, should always strive to recognize and integrate formal and informal learning opportunities. Nurses, when supported in their quest to discover the knowledge and competencies to carry out their jobs effectively, will in the process use their professional and personal potential to the full.

Acknowledgement

The author acknowledges the advice and support of Shirley Stinson, RN, EdD, Faculty of Nursing, University of Alberta, and Daniel Scott, RN, BA, BN, in the preparation of this chapter.

References

Abruzzese, R. & Quinn-O'Neal, B. (1992). *Nursing staff development.* Toronto: Mosby Year Book.

Acorn, S. (1990). Joint appointments: Perspectives of nurse executives. *Canadian Journal of Nursing Administration, 3*(4), 6-9.

Adams, D. (1991). Management needs of head nurses and supervisors: Designing a continuing education course. *Journal of Continuing Education in Nursing, 22*(1), 16-20.

Alessi, S., & Trollip, S. (1991). *Computer-based instruction: Methods and development.* Englewood Cliffs, NJ: Prentice-Hall.

Beetstra, J. (1992). Evaluating competence. *The Canadian Nurse, 88*(5), 32-34.

Calkin, J. (1992). Specialization issues. In A. Baumgart & J. Larsen (Eds.), *Canadian nursing faces the future* (2nd ed.), (pp. 327-342). Toronto: Mosby Year Book.

Canadian Nurses Association. (1989). *CNA's certification program: An information booklet.* Ottawa: Author.

Canadian Nurses Association. (1992). *Position statement on continuing nursing education.* Ottawa: Author.

Carroll, P. (1992). Using personality styles to enhance preceptor programs. *Dimensions of Critical Care Nursing, 11*(2), 114-119.

Del Bueno, D. (1990). Experience, education and nurse's ability to make clinical judgments. *Nursing and Health Care, 11*(6), 290-294.

Giles, P.F., & Moran, V. (1989). Preceptor program evaluation demonstrates improved orientation. *Journal of Nursing Staff Development, 5*(1), 17-24.

Hawkin, P.L., & Hillestad, A. (1990). Promoting nursing's health care agenda through collaboration. *Nursing and Health Care, 11*(1), 17-19.

Henderson, E. (1992). Performance based development systems. *AARN Newsletter, 48*(1), 10-11.

Hersey, P., & Blanchard, K.H. (1982). *Management of organizational behavior: Utilizing human resources* (4th ed.). Englewood Cliffs, NJ: Prentice-Hall.

Irurita, V. (1988). A study of nurse leadership. *The Australian Journal of Advanced Nursing, 6*(1), 43-51.

Knowles, M. (1970). *The modern practice of adult education.* New York: Association Press.

Knowles, M. (1985). Applications in continuing education for the health professions. *Mobius, 5*(2), 80-100.

Knowles, M. (1990). *The adult learner: A neglected species.* Houston: Gulf Publishing.

Marsick, V.J., & Watkins, K.E. (1990) *Informal and incidental learning in the workplace.* London: Routledge.

McGrath, B.J., & Princeton, J.C. (1987). Evaluation of a clinical preceptor program for new graduates—Eight years later. *The Journal of Continuing Education in Nursing, 18*(4), 133-136.

Modic, M.B. (1989). Developing a preceptorship program: What are the ingredients? *Journal of Nursing Staff Development, 16*(2), 20-23.

Montgomerie, H. (1993). *The performance based development system: Competency based assessment and development in nursing.* (Unpublished report.) Division of Nursing, University of Alberta Hospitals: Author.

Morton, P. (1990). Providing CE to evening and night staff. *The Journal of Continuing Education in Nursing, 21*(5), 230.

Myrick, F., & Barrett, C. (1992). Preceptor selection criteria in Canadian basic baccalaureate schools of nursing—A survey. *The Canadian Journal of Nursing Research, 24*(3), 53-68.

O'Grady, T., & O'Brien, A. (1992). A guide to competency-based orientation. *Journal of Nursing Staff Development, 8*(3), 128-133.

Pavlish, C. (1987). A model for situational patient teaching. *The Journal of Continuing Education in Nursing, 18*(5), 163-167.

Puetz, B.E. (1987).*Contemporary strategies for continuing education in nursing.* Rockville, MD: Aspen Publishers.

Reilly, D.E., & Oermann, M. (1985). *The clinical field: Its use in nursing education.* Norwalk, CT: Appleton-Century-Crofts.

Reimer, M., Wyness, A., Courtney, P., & Conrad, J. (1992). Seeking certification. *The Canadian Nurse, 88*(9), 23-25.

Reynalds, A. (1983). An introduction to computer based learning. In L.S. Baird, C.E. Schneier, & D. Laird (Eds.), *The training and development sourcebook.* Amherst, MA: Human Resource Development Press.

Roberson, J.E. (1992). Providing support for preceptors in a community hospital. *Journal of Staff Development, 8*(1), 11-13.

Rosier, P., Wall, B., & Discoe, A. (1989). Posters: Valuable education tool. *Journal of Continuing Education in Nursing, 20*(5), 238.

Simpson, M.C. (1992). Nursing staff development: An emerging field of nursing practice. In K.C. Kelly, (Ed.), *Nursing staff development: Current competence, future focus* (pp. 203-226). Philadelphia: J.B. Lippincott.

Sullivan, P. (1993). Felt learning needs of pregnant women. *The Canadian Nurse, 89*(1), 42-45.

Waddell, D. (1991). The effects of continuing education on nursing practice: A meta-analysis. *The Journal of Continuing Education in Nursing, 22*(3), 113-118.

Weeks, L., Tsubai, E., Gleason, V., & Cavouras, C. (1988). Hospitals and agencies: Allies or adversaries? *Nursing Economics, 6*(5), 234-240.

Welch, L.G., & Stull, M.K. (1991). Energizing professional orientation. *Journal of Nursing Staff Development, 7*(5), 220-224.

Wood, M.R. (1992). Obstetric certification. *The Canadian Nurse, 88*(9), 26-27.

Yuen, F. (1991). Continuing education: Some issues. *Journal of Advanced Nursing, 16,* 1233-1237.

Zurlinden, J., & Bongard, B. (1991). Situational leadership. *AORN Journal, 54*(5), 967-980.

PART 4

The Corporate Dimension of the Nurse Manager's Role

C H A P T E R   2 3

Strategic Planning: A Blueprint for Orderly Goal Attainment

Edna McHutchion

Edna McHutchion, RN, BScN, MEd, PhD (Alberta), is an Associate Professor in the Faculty of Nursing, University of Calgary. A certified psychologist, she also has served in administrative roles in several agencies, including most recently as Associate Dean, Graduate Program, at the University.

The health care system and all other social support systems that provide Canadians with a sense of security are currently under intense scrutiny. Escalating costs and shrinking resources are pervasive, and Canadians are no longer exempt from effects of the rapidly changing global economy (Regush, 1987). The impact of these economic forces on health care agencies is giving rise to many changes in organizational structures and processes, but too often "band-aid" solutions are applied to the surface of problems. The potential for erosion of services to patients requires nurses working at all points in the health care system to take action based on clearly identified needs of patients and families. The likelihood of being heard and supported by key stakeholders is enhanced by choosing carefully selected corporate language and tactics. Strategic planning is one corporate process that can facilitate and secure orderly goal attainment.

Strategic planning, as the term is used in this chapter, is defined and operationalized as a systematic process for reaching and securing a preferred future goal. The process may be used and modified for long term or short term planning and goal setting. The purpose of this chapter is to provide a blueprint to guide nurse managers through the strategic planning process. The blueprint encompasses steps that can be employed to incorporate individual, professional, and organizational realities. Specific tactics and examples are included to develop and explain the blueprint in more detail.

The Mandate

Although they know that taking time for systematic planning and long-range goal setting would be ideal, today's nurse managers are hard pressed to meet the daily demands of increased workloads. Shrinking resources create confusion and a scramble for market share throughout the health care system. Even in organizations where participatory management and shared governance are stated goals, too often directives come from the top down without sufficient consultation or follow-up evaluation of results (Boeglin, 1993). The notion of participatory management and shared responsibility for organizational planning, if only partially applied, is, in fact, counterproductive. Furthermore, to suggest that nurse managers take on one more administrative task, such as strategic planning, may be perceived by already overburdened managers as senior administrators' defaulting on their responsibility. Relegating responsibility for strategic planning to staff at the unit or program level may be resisted.

Nightingale's words, however, speak to today's nurse managers and staff as cogently as they did to nurse pioneers in 1859. Nightingale wrote of the "art of multiplying oneself." Nightingale puts the essentials of care planning into perspective in the following statement: "Let who ever is in charge keep this simple question in her head (*not*, how can I always do this right thing myself, but) how can I provide for this right thing to be always done?" (1969, p. 41).

It is worthwhile to reflect on the constant bombardments of band-aid ideas for instant problem solving and to ask Nightingale's question, "How can I provide for this right thing to be always done?" Strategic planning is one process that merits consideration as a blueprint for reaching and securing a preferred future on behalf of patients and families.

Evolution of Strategic Planning

It is apt that a method borrowed from the military be used to put Nightingale's advice into current practice. Strategic planning (like nursing) has a fascinating historical foundation in the military that is beyond the scope of this chapter. Since the 1950s, the idea and tactics of strategic planning have been borrowed from the military by the corporate world and have been interpreted to mean a disciplined method of moving an organization toward a shared vision or preferred future.

Corporate image and market share are now prime concerns of health care providers. The pressure is on to deliver cost-effective health care services (Strasen 1988). Even in Canada, where universal health care is, at least for the moment, a valued precept, nursing managers are pressed to prove that they are allocating scarce resources efficiently in order to provide the consumer of health care with cost-effective and compassionate service. At the unit or program level, it is necessary to be proactive even to maintain the status quo (Miller, 1989; Thomas, 1993; Toohey, Shillinger, & Baranswski, 1985).

An essential component of the nurse manager's role is that of long-range planning (Canadian Nurses Association, 1988). Taking time out to plan forestalls crisis management and provides management and staff with a clear and shared sense of direction. Strategic planning offers a comprehensive frame of reference for budgeting human and material resources, facilitates healthy communication, and provides a blueprint for continuity of multistage projects even during periods of rapid staff turnover (Strasen, 1988).

Based on history and on current realities, there is strong momentum, if not an irreversible force, that makes proaction an essential part of the nurse manager's mandate. Strategic planning is a blueprint for frugal and sensitive use of human and material resources to address current health care demands and dilemmas. The Canadian Nurses Association standards for nursing administrators underline the point: "Nurse executives are singularly qualified to participate in strategic organizational planning... [and] they have the ability to analyze client information and interpret the potential of corporate activities on client care" (CNA, 1988, p. 5).

A Blueprint for Strategic Planning

Strategic planning, as defined in this chapter, is a systematic approach to reach and secure a preferred future. The process may be modified to achieve short term as well as long term goals.

The blueprint is a seven-step process (see Figure 23.1, page 432) and is presented as a way for an individual nurse manager to lead a group through strategic planning. The plan includes realities of personal, professional, and organizational strengths and limitations that need to be recognized if a successful outcome is to be achieved. A rationale and suggested tactics are described for each of the seven steps in the strategic planning process. A hypothetical planned change is included as an example to explicate the steps in the blueprint. In the example, eight beds in a treatment-oriented 24-bed acute care unit are to be changed to palliative care beds.

Figure 23.1
The strategic planning steps: An overview.

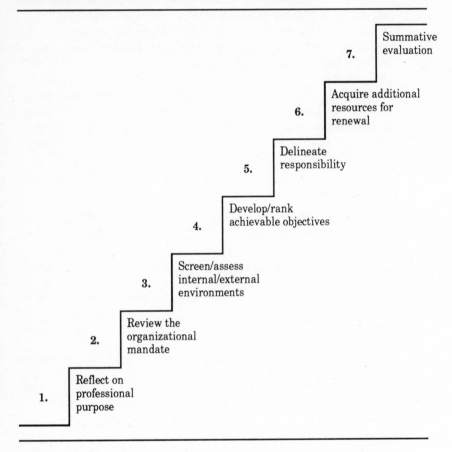

Step 1: Reflect on Professional Purpose

A front-line manager seldom finds time on a regular basis for self-reflection or for expression of opinions about professional standards or organizational goals. To refer to the military analogy, a nurse manager, like a battle-weary soldier, may focus solely on the unit's survival and feel removed not only from administrative headquarters but also from one's own personal and professional attributes and purpose. If motivation and energy are to be renewable resources in the planning process, reflection on personal goals and a frank assessment of one's own abilities to facilitate the change are necessary parts of the first step.

Equally important is reflection on the Canadian Nurses Association philosophical statement about nursing administration: "Nurse leaders should be able to coordinate and guide, enabling those around them to expand their capabilities while achieving goals" (CNA, 1988, p. 3). From personal and professional perspectives, strategic planning points the way to "effective and efficient delivery of organized nursing services" (CNA, 1988, p. 3).

Chenoy (1984) outlines essential characteristics of a successful strategic planner, and these may serve as guidelines for reflection on personal and professional standards and attributes. Chenoy's characteristics of the successful strategic planner include the following two main points:

- The ability to see the whole picture and to be able to translate abstractions such as vision and philosophy into clear, understandable pictures, and

- The willingness to be future oriented and to formulate plans based on society's needs in order to free the organization from the status quo or imposed order and to improve service, even though less than perfect information is available.

For example, this one question is fundamental to the proposed hypothetical change: Is there the personal and professional will and the resource potential to develop the palliative care component in this acute care setting?

A further premise on which this process is based is that one person cannot develop or reach the preferred goal alone. Before starting, negotiate for additional resources. The steps from here are taken with a group representative of the organization (Fox & Fox, 1983). If an external consultant is available, so much the better. However, the process can be undertaken within the unit, program, or agency without external assistance. Key stakeholders need to be included and supportive of the planning process and outcomes. Members of the formal and informal power structure in your portfolio need to feel included even if it is not feasible to have everyone involved equally. It is important for the planning group not to be perceived as an exclusive enclave. Authority and resources to match the responsibility must be secured. It is essential that senior administration be involved, supportive, and informed of progress. It is important to note that, for this and further steps, it is necessary to build in both formative and summative evaluation (e.g., evaluation of the process and outcomes of strategic planning both during and at the end of the project).

The strategic planning process is not a linear process. The process is separated into artificial steps only for purposes of explanation. Each step needs to be revisited, reviewed, and evaluated on an

Figure 23.2
Organizational management components.

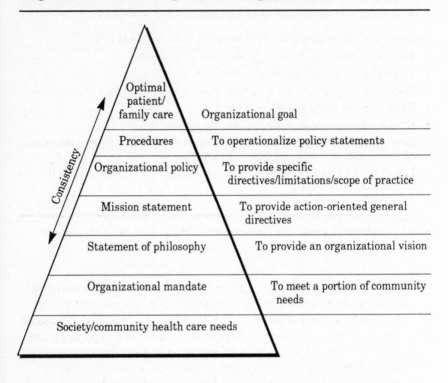

ongoing basis to measure continuing fit and value. In this way, strategic planning reflects the nursing process. For example, assessment takes place continuously throughout all phases of the nursing process. In a similar fashion, continuous assessment is necessary throughout strategic planning (Thomas, 1993).

Step 2: Review the Organizational Mandate

In times of turbulence and entrenchment, reviewing and reworking organizational philosophy and mission statements may seem to be a time-consuming and useless exercise. Statements of philosophy and organizational mission statements too often sit on shelves gathering dust until the next accreditation process. However, authors such as Thomas (1993) believe that reviewing and assessing these documents is fundamental if the nurse manager is to develop a successful strategic planning process. After the review, the strategic planning team

Table 23.1
Nursing management philosophy.

As nurse managers at the Cross Cancer Institute, we believe in:
* Facilitating excellence in patient care as our primary goal
* Respecting the dignity, uniqueness, and autonomy of each individual
* Promoting the importance of quality of life for the patient and for the caregiver
* Maximizing potential and encouraging growth
* Utilizing available resources creatively and responsibly
* Developing our management style as a dynamic process that requires consistency, open communication, and active participation
* Exceeding the standards established by our professional associations and the Cross Cancer Institute.

Source: Used with the permission of Nursing Management, Cross Cancer Institute, Edmonton, Alberta.

may have an opportunity to influence the reshaping and revitalizing of these pivotal statements of organizational philosophy and mission. For example, the palliative care philosophy that inspired the proposed change at the unit level may influence change in the larger organizational context. Times of crisis do open opportunities for influencing the direction of the larger system that are not possible in times of complacency. However, it is essential that before unit plans are developed, consistency and fit with the overall organizational mission statement are assessed. Consistency of the interrelated parts of the organizational structure and process are depicted in Figure 23.2.

As you review Figure 23.2, it is helpful to remember that in general, a desirable organizational statement of philosophy precedes the development of a mission statement. The mission statement, in turn, shapes organizational policies and procedures. Although frequently visionary and abstract, a statement of philosophy should be focussed on the beliefs and values that shape the work of the organization and provide the impetus for positioning your organization for success by addressing the question of how you wish to be perceived (Graham et al., 1987). An example of a statement of philosophy is included as Table 23.1. By then shaping the visionary statement into concrete, action-oriented directives, a clearly articulated mission statement greatly affects patients and families as well as professional and personal futures. The mission statement may in fact be considered the raison d'être for the organization. Organizational policies and procedures are essentially ways and means to achieve the organizational mission.

Figure 23.2 reminds nurse managers of the need to monitor and on occasion to speak forcefully concerning the pivotal nature of optimal patient/family care as it relates to the organizational mandate. It is tempting to use corporate strategies inappropriately in the race for market share. Figure 23.2 is in fact a reminder of the nurse manager's mandate to "interpret the potential impact of corporate activities on client care" (CNA, 1988, p. 5).

It is useful to have a common understanding of terminology when reviewing the organizational mandate. Words such as goals and objectives tend to be used interchangeably and create confusion during a planning exercise. Because objectives differ from goals, it is useful to differentiate the terms. According to Fox and Fox (1983), "A goal is a general description of an aspiration or a desired state of affairs" (p. 11), such as optimal patient/family care. However, goals must be broken down into concrete elements called objectives. Fox and Fox continue:

Objectives are defined as specific end points or targets, achievement of which brings about the reality of the goal. Each of the objectives must be stated in clear, concise, and measurable terms. Precision in operationalizing objectives requires prime consideration because they direct the concentration of resources. Objectives also serve as standards for evaluation. (p. 11)

An example of an objective related to the organizational goal of optimal patient/family care and specific to the proposed goal for the hypothetical unit would be: "By June 15, 1995, on Unit 57, four beds will be designated exclusively for palliative care patients." This objective meets the criteria of consistency with the organizational goal of optimal patient/family care as well as consistency with the statement of philosophy given in Table 23.1. Further, the objective is concrete, clear, concise, and measurable and may be used as a variable for evaluation of a larger initiative.

All of the foregoing components for organizational management are meant to be working guidelines to enhance organizational effectiveness. With this thought in mind, a review of the organization's documents (e.g., statement of philosophy, mission statement, policy and procedures manual) may breathe new life into planning throughout the organization, and become valuable tools for strategic planning beyond the unit.

There are two measures to keep in mind when reviewing the documents. The first measure is the fit of the documents with external and internal realities of community needs. Realities change rapidly in a turbulent society and require constant attention and flexibility in rethinking and reworking organizational documents. The second measure that cannot be overemphasized is the need for internal consistency throughout the organization. Policy and procedures should reflect the mission and philosophy statements or be reworked.

The components mentioned in Figure 23.2 should be used on a continuing basis to serve as a template or model of the larger institutional mandate for the strategic planning group's direction and for purposes of comparison and consistency. For example, the proposed change in incorporating palliative care on an acute treatment unit is consistent with the nursing philosophy as described in Table 23.1. Palliative care and this process are congruent with all seven of the beliefs presented in the nursing management philosophy statement.

Step 3: Scan and Assess Internal/External Environments

It could be argued that step 3 should precede step 2. However, in a similar fashion to the process of brainstorming, too much critical analysis can bring a visioning process to a halt. At this point, pragmatic assessment of internal human and material resources is essential to developing reasonable and achievable objectives (step 4). Leavitt and Bahrami (1988) noted that "strategy is about how we can plot the best route to move toward where we already know we want to go, given the rocky world out there" (p. 274).

Scanning the internal and external environments is related to reconnoitring the internal and external rocky world. Frequently, this step of the process requires assessment and creative interpretation of internal and external realities. As part of the assessment process, the successful strategic planner has a vast array of materials at hand. Databases include governmental annual reports, population laboratory data, Statistics Canada annually updated information, and financial reports from community agencies, as well as other local community assessment data. As is the case with reviewing or reshaping organizational philosophy, mission, and goals, key players must be involved at least tangentially. Because palliative care is interdisciplinary in scope, representation from staff and management across disciplines should be considered. In any case, linkages with external bodies, such as government and other community agencies, are often as useful and more readily accessible than internal contacts, although scanning both environments is important. Nurse managers from other internal and external environments are valuable sources of information and support. For example, home care nurses or, in this instance, other palliative care coordinators, may be helpful. Part of the environmental assessment process is to project potential opportunities and threats/impediments that may influence reaching the preferred future. These projections should not be given more weight than they deserve, as conditions are constantly in flux. For the same reason, environmental scanning and assessment are ongoing concerns and plans may have to be adjusted. However, by developing links across systems, extensive and current information is more readily available and will provide a realistic basis for planning.

Step 4: Develop and Rank Time-Sequenced Achievable Options

As mentioned previously, there is much discussion about the differences between goals and objectives. The important point for strategic planning is to have the team agree on a definition of terms. As noted earlier, the choice for this chapter is to describe goals as descriptive and not necessarily quantifiable whereas objectives are targets to aim for and are definitive, concrete, and measurable. As Gray (1986) noted, having only generalizations to work with makes implementation very difficult.

Gray further noted that "targets don't mean much if no one maps out the pathways leading to them" (1986, p. 94). The important point for consensus is that an action plan is needed to reach the preferred future. To evaluate for the team's satisfaction as well as to justify outcomes to external critics, refinement and definition are necessary. To keep the team morale high and to have a sense of continuing momentum, the action plan should include: specific objectives; date for completion of each objective; and the designated person responsible for each objective (see Table 23.2).

Table 23.2
Sample action plan.

Objective	Proposed Completion Date	Designate	Completed
Report prepared on: 1. Literature related to palliative care philosophy	June 1, 1994	M. Jones	May 26, 1994 *M.J.*
Report prepared on: 2. Review of organizational documents	June 15, 1994	S. Rogers D. Roberts	June 5, 1994 *S.R.* *D.R.*
3. _____ etc.			

Another important point is that the time-sequenced objectives be achievable and ranked. This step is a critical point of the process because visionaries in the group may feel constrained and frustrated by the required attention to detail and measurement potential.

Another important concern is time phasing. Bartlett (1988) stated in an editorial on this process that "the most important attitudinal requirement for strategic planning is to take a long term perspective. Whereas patient care activities seldom require thinking beyond the next few hours, effective program development necessitates charting growth during the next 2-3 years" (p. 1). It is useful to post an overview of the plan for easy reference. In this way, the team is encouraged and motivated by reaching objectives along the way to attaining the final goal.

It is not necessary to let the group stall on behavioural language to define the selected objectives. The essential idea is to filter the objectives for clarity. Do not have more than one expected outcome per objective. The objective and time sequence need to be achievable and renegotiable given constraints of team members' other duties.

As never before in the process, it is necessary to weigh the objectives in relation to preferred outcomes and the team's visionary goals. Are they congruent with the organization's overall philosophy and mission statement? If not, the balance must be achieved by reworking one component or the other.

As a preface to taking step 4, ranking the objectives is necessary. However, build in contingency strategies to allow flexibility in the event of unforeseen events and outcomes.

Step 5: Delineate Responsibility

It is essential to separate step 5 from step 4. A division of labour must be achieved. However, delegation of tasks implies a top-down process that should be avoided. Up to this point, group members have had the opportunity to work, think, and plan together. Mutually deciding which member of the group has the interest and ability to achieve individual objectives is more in keeping with a spirit of cooperation. Therefore, delineating agreed upon responsibility rather than delegating tasks is more congruent with healthy group process and the need to achieve positive outcomes.

One way to secure the ideal person for the task is to outline clearly the objectives and the agreed upon timelines. It may be helpful, at this point, to describe how the objectives fit within the preferred goals of the strategic planning process and to request the group to assess whether and how the process fits within the organizational mission. For example, a review of the philosophy statement (see Table 23.1, page 435) with a view to evaluating consistency of philosophy to the unit plan would be useful. Although the timelines are somewhat negotiable, it is best to have had them developed during step 4 so that an objective, organized whole is maintained. The other useful tactic is to use a flip chart or blackboard to present the individual tasks and commitments. Usually, when healthy group process has been maintained, volunteers for tasks are forthcoming. It is important to have everyone on the team take an active part and be kept informed. Circulate action-oriented minutes to the team and other key players shortly after the meeting. Built-in reporting mechanisms and status reports encourage mutual support and evaluation of progress.

Based on a belief that persons work better when encouraged than when punished or threatened, the leader should not personally take on many of the tasks; this allows the leader to be available to provide support and help in difficult situations. Memos of progress and notes of encouragement are helpful to keep up esprit de corps.

Step 6: Acquire Additional Resources for Renewal

It is likely that by this time, through continuous evaluation, the team will know whether or not the goals are likely to be reached and secured. Even before the final evaluation, it is useful to reflect on the past, present, and future of the group and the strategic planning process.

"Know thyself" is sage advice. Questions may guide your reflection. What is your usual style of work? Are you an innovator but not so useful at maintenance tasks? What are your personal and professional needs at this time? Who would be best to carry the program or project through to the next phase of development? If you continue as leader, are you standing in the way of others' growth and development as strategic planners? It is important to see the process through to step 7, which is evaluation. However, reflect again on Nightingale's words, "Let who ever is in charge keep this simple question in her head (*not*, how can I always do this right thing by myself, but) how can I provide for this right thing to be always done?"

Part of the renewal phase may be grooming another nurse manager or staff nurse to see the project, program, or designated change systematically through this or another cycle of the strategic planning process. As Thomas (1993) noted, by using an established strategic planning cycle as a guide, a continuous process can be implemented to provide direction and communicate expectations. The steps of the strategic planning process described in this chapter may be thought of in a cyclical fashion. For example, when the four designated palliative care beds are in use, the nurse manager may wish to be more involved in the evaluation process, and another colleague may choose to spearhead the opening of the other four designated beds.

Step 7: Summative Evaluation

There are two necessary levels of summative evaluation required to complete a successful cycle of strategic planning. Both microsummative evaluation and macrosummative evaluation are important. The microevaluation is focussed on the strategic planning process itself (i.e., how well did the group function?). The macroevaluation is based on overall outcomes of the goals and objectives developed by the planning group (i.e., was the goal achieved?).

Microsummative evaluation may be overlooked or considered self-serving. However, celebration of successful outcomes and analysis of different-from-planned outcomes are essential to a healthy group and organizational renewal. Macrosummative evaluation is essential for making a realistic assessment of the achievement or nonachievement of the defined objectives. Macroevaluation further includes an assessment of the project's fit with the team's and organization's declaration of the preferred future of the organization, as well as with other strategic plans that are under way in the organization.

Micro-level tactics. Rituals are often in short supply, but they serve important functions at both personal and professional levels. The simple notion of going out for lunch or implementing some other symbolic ritual that fits for the group may pay dividends in the future. Closure is important for the team. Formal and/or informal letters of appreciation are in order and will be another vehicle for reflection and personal closure. For example, in the instance of the successful launching of the eight-bed palliative care unit, a ceremony with invited participants and community dignitaries would be in order.

Macro-level tactics. If future strategic planning exercises are to be enhanced as a result of current strategic planning, formal evaluation and debriefing of the process and outcomes are necessary. It is useful to preface a team meeting with a short historical overview of the context, process, and outcomes. Each participant needs input and an opportunity to speak and be heard about the outcomes of the strategic planning process. Each participant needs to have input and access to the final report of the project. It is important that each team member receive recognition as well as take responsibility for the project outcomes. A written report must be developed and circulated to key constituents. Include substantive data in the report and appendices to support the group's findings and recommendations for future action by senior administrators. There are likely to be implications for policy and procedural changes, and these implications should be well documented and structural changes facilitated in order to secure the preferred goal. Obtain sufficient resources to have the report organized and presented in a professional style. Include a succinct executive summary so that the report will compare well with the multitude of reports and papers crossing busy senior administrators' desks every day.

It is useful at this point to reflect on all of the steps of the strategic planning process cycle as a vehicle for review and critique of the process and outcomes so that future endeavours based on this experience will be refined and will benefit from the lessons learned (see Figure 23.3).

Figure 23.3
The strategic planning process cycle.

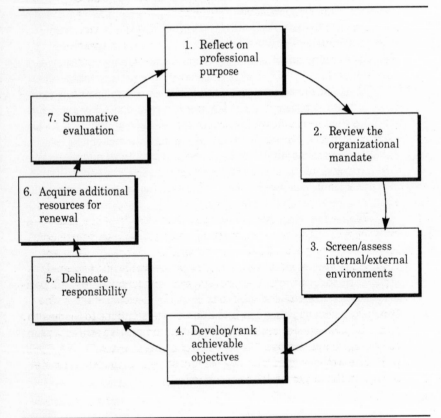

If this blueprint is used in an actual strategic planning process, then reflect, from the perspective of the catalyst and leader for the process, on what worked and what did not work. If the chapter is being used from the perspective of a prospective strategic planner, review the process, mentally applying the steps to a familiar situation or problem, and evaluate the potential of the blueprint for use in actual practice.

Concluding Thoughts about Strategic Planning

Canadian nurse managers are key players in moving their corner of the health care system toward a preferred future. By taking a systematic approach to planning at the unit or program level, the nurse manager influences positive changes in the larger organizational goals, philosophy, and mission, which in turn influence larger systems changes.

Strategic planning is described as having seven discrete steps. However, the strategic planner who uses the steps as a blueprint for reaching a preferred future knows that "hard reality" and formative evaluation create overlap. Strategic planning is continuous; it is a cyclical process that applies to any long- or short-term planning exercise. Strategic planning is a safeguard against the tendency in times of crisis to apply the latest "quick fix" to chronic problems (Drucker, 1991).

The health care system is in flux. Turbulent times become nursing's opportunity to move the system in a direction that is more compatible with the needs of patients and families. Although there are constraints and impediments, using corporate skills and essential experience with patients and families, the nurse manager is well positioned to act, to speak out, and to be heard by decision makers who currently are hard pressed to find appropriate solutions to the health care crisis. Successful implementation of an innovative strategic plan can energize and promote "change in a positive direction" (CNA, 1988, p. 3). The well-designed plan may in fact serve as a model for pivotal change in the larger health care community.

References

Bartlett, E.E. (1988). Preparing for strategic planning. *Patient Education and Counseling, 11*, 1-2.

Boeglin, M.J. (1993). Shared governance. In A. Marriner-Tomey (Ed.), *Transformational leadership in nursing* (pp. 89-100). St. Louis: Mosby Year Book.

Canadian Nurses Association. (1988). *The role of the nurse administrator and standards for nursing administration*. Ottawa: Author.

Chenoy, N.C. (1984, Summer). Strategic planning—Understanding and responding to a rapidly changing world. *Health Management Forum*, pp. 3-19.

Drucker, P.F. (1991). The discipline of innovation. In M.J. Ward & S.A. Price (Eds.), *Issues in nursing administration* (pp. 171-176). St. Louis: Mosby Year Book.

Fox, D.H., & Fox, R.T. (1983). Strategic planning for nursing. *Journal of Nursing Administration, 12*(5), 11-17.

Graham, P., Constantini, S., Balik, B., Bedore, B., Hooke, M.C.M., Papin, D., Quamme, M., & Rivard, R. (1987). Operationalizing a nursing philosophy. *Journal of Nursing Administration, 17*(3), 13-18.

Gray, D.H. (1986). Uses and misuses of strategic planning. *Harvard Business Review, 64*(1), 89-97.

Leavitt, H.J., & Bahrami, H. (1988). *Managerial psychology; Managing behavior in organizations* (5th ed.). Chicago: University of Chicago Press.

Miller, K.L. (1989). Nurse executive leadership: A corporate perspective. *Nursing Administration Quarterly, 13*(2), 12-18.

Nightingale, F. (1969). *Notes on nursing*. New York: Dover.

Regush, N. (1987). *Canada's health care system: Condition critical*. Toronto: Macmillan.

Strasen, L. (1988). Strategic planning: An effective management tool for nursing. *Nursing Management, 19*(5), 80B-80D.

Toohey, E.M., Shillinger, F.L., & Baranowski, S.L. (1985). Planning alternate delivery systems: An organizational assessment. *Journal of Nursing Administration, 15*(12), 9-15.

Thomas, A. (1993). Strategic planing: A practical approach. *Nursing Management, 24*(2), 34-38.

CHAPTER 24

Managing Change

Brenda M. Mongomery

Brenda M. Montgomery, RN, BScN (Mount St. Vincent), MHSA (Dalhousie), has broad experience in senior nursing administration in both hospital and university settings and was President of the Registered Nurses Association of Nova Scotia from 1990 to 1992. She has made extensive use of change models to facilitate change within organizations, agencies, and groups of stakeholders. She is a lecturer at Dalhousie University School of Nursing.

Change in today's health care organizations is an everyday occurrence, driven by increased rates of technological inventions, new treatment modalities, decreased resources, emergent delivery patterns, and consumer demands. As Porter-O'Grady stated in his 1992 address to a Canadian Hospital Association conference, "chaos is the norm." Nurse managers have a responsibility to incorporate changes into their department, and to do so successfully, along with their normal day-to-day activities. These changes must be made while minimizing the chaos and confusion for an already pressured staff.

This chapter will focus on the process of change. The use of three different types of models will be discussed, as well as common reactions to change and possible leadership roles that managers can adopt. Other chapters will deal with specific activities, such as quality improvement and organizing patient care, that may indicate the need for change and the actual process of deciding what change is desired.

Change Defined

The *Concise Oxford English Dictionary* defines change as "alteration; substitution of one for another," or "make or become different," or even "to get rid of." These definitions imply that the outcome is the change; however, anyone who has tried to make a change will likely agree with Belasco (1990) that "Change is a process, not a destination. It never ends."

Successful implementation of a change is usually far more dependent on the process used to bring it about than the specific end goal. A successful nurse manager must have a selection of tools to help bring about change and a knowledge of which tool to use when.

Definitions and discussions of change frequently convey that change is always a result of rational decision making and within the control of the organization's planners; however, this is not so. Change can result from one of three different activities. These are developmental activities, spontaneous reactions or responses to activities, and consciously planned activities. The manager can prepare for potential results from developmental or spontaneous change, but not in a systematically controlled manner as in planned change; the following discussion will explain why.

Developmental Change

Developmental change occurs as an organism or organization grows and becomes more complex. All nurses are familiar with the development of a human embryo and fetus, a development that is characterized by increasing size and complexity based on the organism's need. The first system to develop is the cardiovascular system, allowing for provision of nutrients and oxygen and removal of waste; the respiratory system does not begin primitive activities until eight weeks later. Immediately at birth these two systems begin working in a very different, more complex, and interactive way to sustain each other and the newborn.

Organizations also grow and develop, often in highly predictable ways. An example of this might be when a small community clinic is opened in a rural community. The clinic is open for eight hours a day and is staffed by one full-time registered nurse, a physician two days a week, and a full-time receptionist/secretary. The staff are all enthusiastic about the role the clinic can play in the community to improve health by emphasizing health promotion activities. Staff communication is simple, usually one to one, and general problems are discussed over lunch and solved in a collaborative manner. The clinic is highly successful; as a result of community-identified needs, a mental health counselor, a nutritionist, and four persons to deliver home care are added to the staff. As well, specialized physicians provide support on a periodic basis for "well-women" clinics, "seeing all you should" clinics, and "elder assessment" clinics. Staff communication patterns are now complex and often break down, turf-protection activities begin, the receptionist feels overworked and angry at being "everybody's servant," and community input indicates clients feel "the place is less user-friendly."

These unwanted changes are the result of the evolution of a

larger and, therefore, more complex organization. It has grown with little or no planning for the new required interactions and task changes. The unwanted changes are a result of developments that were necessary to meet defined needs, so could not be avoided, but the manager could anticipate some of the changes and plan to minimize negative outcomes wherever possible. Job descriptions may require revision, regular formal staff meetings are required, and some clear organizational charts need to be developed to prevent further deterioration. What cannot be controlled is the fundamental fact that change will occur.

Spontaneous Change

Spontaneous change is the type of change that is often called a reaction. The human organism reacts to the invasion of a virus, and, although the actual process is the same for all, the impact may differ from time to time within one individual or at the same time in different individuals. A cold may cause major disruption to the health of one person and may even lead to a life-threatening illness, while in another a similar cold is a minor inconvenience for a few days. The impact of the reaction to the virus causing the cold is largely dependent on the total condition, both physical and psychological, of the host.

Organizations also may be invaded by an unexpected virus in the form of totally or partially unanticipated events occurring in the environment. Examples of these include short term events, such as a major air crash near a small regional hospital, an unexpected wildcat strike that virtually closes all tertiary care hospitals, or an unusually heavy and prolonged snow storm in a widespread rural community serviced by the Victorian Order of Nurses. Long term events can also create reactive change. A recent common one is the dramatic impact of HIV on policies and practices of health care agencies. Another one, less widespread but becoming increasingly common, is the hazard of staff's developing environmental illness due to current building design.

The defining factor about spontaneous change is that the organization could not have either fully anticipated or avoided the event and, therefore, have little or no time to plan response strategies. Managers can reduce reactive impact by general planning, using such mechanisms as disaster plans. A major factor in successfully responding to the need to make spontaneous change is the flexibility, cohesiveness, and levels of trust within the organization. Just as the healthy individual responds quickly and effectively to minimize the impact resulting from the invasion of a cold virus, the healthy organization is able to minimize the impact of an unexpected event and call on its resources to manage the required changes.

Planned Change

Planned change assumes a future altered state that is brought about
as a result of determining deficiencies within what exists, deciding on
one or more possible desired states, and enacting a plan to achieve
these. An example of individual planned change is your reading this
book to gain new knowledge or insights, and perhaps taking courses
to develop your management ability further. Another example is a
person's deciding to improve his or her health status and planning
and carrying through an exercise and nutrition program.

Organizations are constantly involved in planned changes. These
can be department specific, such as a unit in a long term care facility's
moving to a "no restraint" policy. Planned change can also be long
range, overall changes, such as those identified as part of the strategic
plan of a provincial Victorian Order of Nurses. Success in bringing
about planned change is a major part of any nurse manager's role.

The remainder of t⠀'s chapter will be devoted to a discussion of
strategies to help bring about change and to identifying potential
problems with the change process.

Change Models and Strategies

Change, by its very definition, assumes that there are existing structures and/or processes that need revision and that strategies must be
developed to bring this about. Ohmar (1982) writes that strategy
involves a clear understanding of the elements of the situation,
restructuring the elements in the most advantageous way, and finding the best possible solution to the problem at hand. If this sounds a
lot like nursing process, it should, because both are problem-solving
processes. Sound problem solving is often aided by the use of a model
that can provide a framework or blueprint for planning action, checking progress, and evaluating results.

Three change models will be described, each one of which is best
suited for use in differing situations. Bennis, Benne, and Chinn
(1969) examined a number of previously developed change models
and suggest that all models fall into one of three categories: *rational-
empirical, normative-reeducative,* and *power-coercive.*

Table 24.1 summarizes the characteristics and assumptions
that underlie the development of each group of models. Each group of
models has distinctive characteristics and work best when the
assumptions underlying their development apply. The nurse manager

Table 24.1

Change models: Comparative analysis.

Model	Characteristics	Assumptions
Rational-empirical	• Communication is focus of model • Target group will rationally assess pros and cons • Model is noncoercive • Model is fully participative/democratic	• Target system is natural • Target group has the choice of adopting or rejecting change • Initiator chooses not to or cannot use power to make change • New knowledge will result in change
Normative-reeducative	• Model recognizes that change will have to deal with needs, feelings, values • Not all responses to change are rationally based • Communication of new knowledge will not necessarily result in change • Model is partially participative/democratic	• Target system will have restraining and driving forces within it • Leader/manager has decided change must occur • Initiator may use and has some power to create change
Power-coercive	• Power is focus of model, to defeat resisting forces • Feelings, values, needs of opposing forces are not a factor • Vested interest will outweigh knowledge • Model is nonparticipative and nondemocratic	• Target system is hostile and resistant to change • Leader/manager is willing to risk win-lose outcome • Initiator has or can create a significant power base • Potential total loss is better than not taking action

who is familiar with the assumptions and characteristics will be able to select the change model most appropriate to the situation.

Each category of change models has a number of possible models that a nurse manager could utilize; however, for clarity, one example of each category will be described and applied to a nursing situation.

Rational-Empirical Change Models

Rational-empirical models for change focus on the goal and on the communication of this to all concerned. The best-known model in this category is one described by Rogers and Shoemaker (1971). The model was refined from earlier work Rogers carried out with Dutton and Jun; it utilizes the construct of three phases: (1) *invention* of the change, (2) communication of information regarding change, or *diffusion*, and (3) adoption or rejection of change, or *consequence*.

For example, a nurse manager has been exposed through the nursing literature to the concept of a primary nurse patient care delivery system and wonders if this may be better for the unit and staff than the existing team nursing method. She is concerned that change is needed because some staff and some patients have expressed a level of dissatisfaction with the current system. The following shows how the three phases of the Rogers and Shoemaker Model apply.

Phase 1: Invention

The manager needs additional information to be able to "invent" the possible change for her unit. She searches out two institutions, of a similar size and range of services as her own, and arranges for site visits. After the visits, she examines data such as staffing requirements, the professional/nonprofessional staff mix, policies, contracts, and patient demographics. Based on her data analysis, she decides that it is highly possible that primary nursing would work well for patients and staff.

Phase 2: Communication, Diffusion

This phase will move through three overlapping stages: awareness, interest, and education. The staff need to be made *aware* of what the concept of primary nursing involves and that the manager believes it might be a useful approach for this unit. Further *interest* could be sparked by providing articles or having presentations by staff who are using primary nursing in their work areas. Once there is a reasonable level of interest, true *education* would begin. This would include all details of how primary nursing could be used by the unit. The education would include at least known positive and negative features, changes that might be required in policies, procedures, or routines, staffing patterns, and role expectations.

Phase 3: Consequence—Adoption or Rejection

At this point, the staff may decide to run a trial of the method to add to their knowledge prior to making a decision. Alternatively, the choice may be made at this point. The staff, using the normal unit decision-making process (see Chapter 25 for methods), will decide either to adopt or to reject primary nursing.

It is critical for the manager to realize that if this change model is utilized, the target group, the staff, have the full right and responsibility to adopt or reject the proposed change. If the change is adopted, it will become the norm over time and be *institutionalized*.

The use of a rational-empirical model works well if the target group is discontented with the current situation or has a history of being open to change (or both). It can also be used when there are clear advantages and few disadvantages to its adoption by the target group. It is also a useful model if the manager is unclear whether the change would be advantageous. If none of the situations described above apply, then a model from one of the other two categories should be used.

Normative-Reeducative Change Models

The change model from the normative-reeducative category that is best known is one developed by Lewin (1951), generally recognized as the earliest pioneer in change theory. Lewin's model focusses on process and on the total system, including all the potential players or stakeholders who may be affected by the change. Other models in this category, such as those of Havelock (1973) and Lippitt (1973), focus on the role of the leader in the process, often termed the change agent. Many nurses leaders are already familiar with the change agent role as described by Lancaster and Lancaster (1982).

Lewin's model for change identifies three phases: *unfreezing*, *moving to a new level* (change), and *refreezing*. A key part of the Lewin model is the initial development, subsequent updating, and use of a force field analysis throughout phases 1 and 2. The concept of a force field assumes that, within any system, large or small, there will be forces for (driving forces) and against (restraining forces) the proposed change. These forces may be structures or processes (e.g., procedures and people with their values, feelings, attitudes, and habits). The forces can be mapped to provide a force field which is then analyzed. The model suggests that when the existing or arising restraining forces are reduced to a strength below that of the driving forces, the change will occur.

To illustrate these steps, the example used above can also be used here. The nurse manager wishes to incorporate change to primary nursing. She has examined the climate of the unit and found that the assumptions suggest she should use a normative reeducative model. She chooses to use Lewin's model as her blueprint. In this example, the nurse manager becomes a change agent.

Phase 1: Unfreezing

Step 1 in unfreezing is for the leader of this change to develop a comprehensive force field map (see Table 24.2). Not all the driving or restraining forces will be identified at the beginning; some will arise during the process. For example, if it is discovered that it would be useful to have people who have frequent readmissions placed on this unit to improve continuity of care, the admitting department may perceive the planning of this as an extra burden and may need to be added as a restraining force.

The nurse manager can employ a number of strategies to "unfreeze" the system and increase the climate of readiness for change. For example, she could increase the level of discomfort and frustration with the current team nursing by providing information about the benefits of primary care nursing. Reducing the resisting forces would also allow for movement; for example, she could meet with the night and evening supervisors and explore and address their concerns. Providing a supportive climate for change by highlighting successful changes achieved by the unit in the past will reduce the need for security and emphasize the driving force of being "leaders."

Phase 2: Moving to a New Level (Change)

Once the system is sufficiently unfrozen, the leader can begin to direct the efforts of staff to produce the desired change. The manager can do this by:

- Providing information in a variety of formats;
- Providing forums for discussion of the change and the feelings and problems it creates;
- Promoting trial runs of primary nursing;
- Encouraging new patterns of care and allowing for and supporting people when mistakes occur;
- Keeping focussed on the desired goal and giving frequent feedback on positive progress;
- Anticipating normal differences in people's willingness to adopt change and giving continued support;

Table 24.2

Force field analysis of change in nursing care delivery system.

Driving Forces	Target System	Restraining Forces
Some staff frustrated with current team system ➤	**Nursing Staff** ◀	Security of staff used to providing care using team nursing
Administrative support for change ➤		
Some staff have worked with and like primary nursing ➤		◀ Fear that primary nursing means more work/responsibility with no more support for RNs
Unit has reputation as "leader unit" in hospital ➤	**Goal: To Inplement Primary Nursing** ◀	Physicians have expressed dislike of primary nursing as "poor for communication"
Unit has successfully managed innovative change before ➤		◀ Other health care team members concerned about role changes
Latest patient survey expressed concern regarding "too many different nurses giving me care" ➤		◀ Night/evening supervisors not sure system can work
Unit physical layout is not conducive to team nursing ➤		◀ Staff like the socializing aspect of team reports and team meetings

Note: Forces may not always be evenly balanced.

Source: Derived from Lewin, K. (1951), *Field theory in social sciences: Selected theoretical papers.* New York: Harper & Row.

- Revisiting force field map, updating it with new information, and acting on resultant analysis;
- Maintaining a trusting, supportive work climate.

Phase 3: Refreezing

The refreezing phase is reached when primary nursing is the pattern of care delivery but is not yet fully entrenched. During this phase, the target system continues to need reinforcement of and support for the new behaviours, or old habits will return. For example, it would be easy for staff on the night shift to slip back to team nursing, especially when admissions occur on their shift. During this phase, other staff can begin to accept responsibility for maintaining the change.

The normative-reeducative model works well if the manager clearly sees a need for change, such as patient concerns or dissatisfaction with the kind of nursing given. However, the change cannot be achieved without staff support, and the change may well involve a number of others within the system but not under the direct supervision of the manager. As with all planned change, it must be based on a clearly defined need to change, not simply a desire to try something new.

Nurse managers should recognize that a normative-reeducative model requires more effort on their part (as change leaders) than a rational-empirical model would require. The nurse manager, therefore, selects this model based on the underlying assumptions of the situation. If a review of the assumptions shows that neither rational-empirical nor normative-reeducative models are suitable, the manager should consider the use of the final category of model.

Power-Coercive Change Models

Power-coercive models focus on people's declared or reasonably anticipated refusal to accept a change when those same people have, or appear to have, the power to prevent the change. Power-coercive models are described in texts by Haley (1969) and Alinsky (1972), and have been enacted by such human rights activists as Gandhi and Martin Luther King. These models generally arise in the political arena. In the past, nurses have not utilized this type of model much, except in the formalized context of labour negotiations, probably because of a perceived lack of power. However, an examination of the model's roots shows it was developed for use by people who could be considered as lacking power within the system.

The models used by both Haley (1969) and Alinsky (1972) identify eight steps. How these steps are used can be illustrated using an extension of the earlier example in which the unit wished to implement primary nursing instead of the previously used team nursing. The nursing staff used the rational-empirical change model and decided to adopt the primary nursing care delivery system. The physicians working on the unit do not like the change, as they feel it is not as convenient for them. At a meeting of the medical advisory committee, they pass a motion that physicians must not support any change in nursing care delivery, and they do not support the change to primary nursing on any unit in the hospital. The motion is taken to the next meeting of the executive committee of the hospital and, despite the senior nurse administrator's opposition, it is supported. The unit is notified that it must revert to team nursing. The nurses on the unit are upset and decide to use a power-coercive model to try to change the executive committee's acceptance of the physicians' motion.

Step 1: Define Issue and Desired Outcome

A small, nominated group of nurses, along with the unit manager, define the issue as "control of nursing practice," and the desired outcome is recognition of nurses' responsibility and right to control how nursing is practised within an interdisciplinary patient care approach.

Step 2: Identify Opponent(s)

The executive committee members are the primary target, as it is they who have the final decisional power and they who accepted the view that physicians could demand the right to control nursing practice. The medical staff are secondary targets, as they exert control through the executive committee.

Step 3: Organize a Following

Initially, the nurse manager would discuss the concern and its ramifications with other nurse managers and develop a core support group. The nurse managers have to recognize that they have the obligation to review the ethics of further action as they have an implied obligation to support administrative decisions of the agency. The decision may be that they have an overriding ethical obligation to the professional practice of nursing. If this decision is reached, nurse managers could continue to be involved in the action. The core support group would discuss the matter with the nurses on other units and gather support for action as required.

Step 4: Build a Power Base

Once nurses are fairly substantially behind the group, they would be wise to approach other departments who could potentially be affected by similar rulings from physicians, such as physiotherapy, nutrition services, pharmacy, and social work. The effort is concentrated on developing as large, diverse, and powerful a following as possible.

Step 5: Begin Action

With a solid power base, a core group, preferably of nurses and other disciplines, would develop an action plan that steadily escalates pressure. It may begin by sending a "letter of concern" to the executive committee stating the issue, desired outcome, and supportive rationale. A reasonable date and time for response would be included in the letter. If there is no response or a negative one, the group moves to the next step.

Step 6: Continue Action with Increasing Pressure

The core group previously will have mapped out future moves. These may include such activities as having all involved departmental staff refusing to attend all hospital committees, working in strict adherence to policies and procedures, or not attending educational sessions after having fully booked them. As the battle escalates, increasingly obstructive (power demonstration) actions may need to occur, such as refusing to record such nondirect care data as patient census, workload data, or quality assurance data. Other actions could include refusing to do normally assumed tasks, such as deciding on patient transfers from ICUs. The purpose is to demonstrate clearly to the persons with decisional power that there is a large amount of operational power within the groups affected.

Step 7: Final Struggle

The battle is now fully joined and is moving to a finale. Efforts of the group must now escalate and all possible pressure be brought to bear. For example, nursing might suggest that, if physicians are to decide on nursing care, then a physician on each unit would be required to approve, in writing, a nurse's floating from one unit to another before she or he does so. Activities should be designed to create maximum disruption to the key opponents while allowing the nurses to fulfil their duty to provide safe, effective nursing care. The actions, if possible, should demonstrate the inherent problems with the proposed system if physician control were allowed to continue.

Step 8: Recognize Outcome

All those involved when the power-coercion change model is brought into play must be prepared to win or lose if this model is used. If the outcome is a reversal of support for the physicians' motion, there will be a period of hostility by the physicians (the "losers") toward other staff. The "winners" must be prepared to weather this period with no recriminations. If, however, the motion is not revoked, the nurses' group will have lost some credibility with senior staff and this, too, may have repercussions that will have to be lived through.

The power-coercive model should not be used frequently nor over minor changes, as there is clearly potential to lose even more than the desired change. The senior nurse administrator will have to be sure that the actions of the nursing staff do not convey to others that the nursing staff are either out of control or engaging in collective insubordination. All nurse managers, and particularly the senior managers, have to be sure that they are not viewed as being in collusion with staff to defy an executive decision. Senior hospital administration could view actions such as those described as evidence of a refusal to support corporate team decisions and, therefore, a matter for dismissal or demotion. Although careful thought must be given to using the power-coercive model, nurses should not hesitate to use it over matters of serious consequence. Leaders who utilize this model have a responsibility to prepare and support staff through either a win or lose outcome. In addition, it must be realized that once this model of change is adopted, the target group will also use the model against the initiators.

Change Models in Health Care Today

Other chapters in this book have discussed the changes in today's health care organizations and the increased awareness and application of feminist thinking, models, and practice. There is no single feminist model of change, although feminist principles can govern the use of models. For example: First, nurse leaders can follow a feminist principle and begin to refuse to make change based on decisions made purely on scientific evidence when this is not supported by common sense and practical experience. As Hagell (1989) points out, "Nursing has a distinct knowledge base which is not grounded in empirico-analytic science and its methodology, but which stems from the lived experiences of nurses." Second, when choosing to consider change and selecting a model, the nurse manager must recognize that most nurses are women and that evidence supports the idea that women work best using consensus rather than confrontation. Third, nurse managers need to recognize that nurses have been socialized to avoid conflict and not use overt power; this socialization need not control the choice of model, which should be based on the assumptions and situation.

Hersey and Weaver-Duldt (1989) explore the idea that selection of a change model should also be based on the group's level of motivation and task maturity. The more motivated and more independent the staff are, the more likely they are to respond to consultative methods, and the converse is also held to apply. Many nurses have significant task experience (maturity) but have not been allowed to develop independence. The nurse manager must foster the required independence.

A number of researchers and authors have explored and continue to explore both individual and group reaction to change. Reactions are especially unpredictable when, as Tappen (1989) points out, the system responses are multifactorial and based on many individuals' experience, values, needs, attitudes, and coping abilities. There is no foolproof way of predicting how any one individual will respond to a specific change, but some general reactions can be noted. When change is introduced, people can be expected to move through three phases of concern: (1) self-concern—what does this mean to me, my status, my role?, (2) skill concern—what new skills will I need, where will I get them, can I learn them?, (3) outcome concern—who will judge the outcome of change, will I have input? Few people can move to the second or third phases of concern until the questions raised in the prior phase have been answered.

Rogers and Shoemaker (1971) described six categories of responses to change. These range from innovators, who seek out and love change, to rejectors, who actively resist any change. Nurse managers must recognize that, as any change involves personnel, people's reactions to change are critical to success, and allow for differing rates of acceptance.

Evaluation of Change

The final phase of a change in any organization is evaluation, which should include both process and outcome evaluation. The manager could well use the four foci proposed by Gordon (1983):

- **Affective reactions.** Did staff like process, are outcomes pleasing (e.g., do they like primary nursing)?

- **Learning.** Has change resulted in personal or collective growth (e.g., did staff learn to deal with conflicting ideas)?

- **Behavioural changes.** Are there new desired or undesired behaviours evidenced in staff (e.g., the nursing assistants are less willing to learn new skills)?

- **Performance changes.** Are there hard data that change is beneficial (e.g., increased patient satisfaction, decreases in nursing staff absenteeism)?

Successful nurse managers will be those who recognize that change can be more of an opportunity than a threat. They have a range of strategies to help them implement change, and they create a trusting, risk-taking environment in which nurses are ready to be active participants in change. In essence, the manager becomes a transformational leader who, as Tichy and Devanna (1990) say, "moves from the vision to a viable set of blueprints so that a long-term, enduring set of behaviours can be made part of the organization."

References

Alinsky, S.D. (1972). *Rules for radicals: A practical primer for realistic radicals*. New York: Vintage.

Belasco, J. (1990). *Teaching the elephant to dance*. New York: Crown.

Bennis, W., Benne, K., & Chinn, R. (1969). *The planning of change*. (2nd ed.). New York: Holt, Rinehart & Winston.

Gordon, J. (1983). *A diagnostic approach to organizational behaviour*. Toronto: Allyn & Bacon.

Hagell, E. (1989). Nursing knowledge: A women's knowledge, a sociological perspective. *Journal of Advanced Nursing, 14*, 226-223.

Haley, J. (1969). *The power tactics of Jesus Christ and other essays*. New York: Avon.

Havelock, R.G. (1973). *The change agent's guide to innovation in education*. New Jersey: Educational Technology Publishing.

Hersey, P., & Weaver-Duldt, B. (1989). *Situational leadership in nursing*. Toronto: Prentice-Hall.

Lancaster, J., & Lancaster, W. (Eds.). (1982). *The nurse as a change agent*. St. Louis: C.V. Mosby.

Legge, K. (1984). *Evaluating planned organizational change*. Toronto: Academic Press.

Lewin, K. (1951). *Field theory in social sciences: Selected theoretical papers*. New York: Harper & Row.

Lippitt, G.L. (1973). *Visualizing change: Model building and the change process*. La Jolla, CA: California University Associations.

Ohmar, K. (1982). *The mind of the strategist*. New York: McGraw-Hill.

Porter-O'Grady, T. (1992). Unpublished keynote address to Canadian Hospital Association Conference. Ottawa: Canadian Hospital Association.

Rogers, E., & Shoemaker, S. (1971). *Communication of innovations*. Glencoe, NY: Free Press of Glencoe.

Tappen, R. (1989). *Nursing leadership and management: Concepts and practice* (2nd ed.). Philadelphia: F.A. Davis.

Tichy, N., & Devanna, M.A. (1990). *The transformational leader*. Toronto: John Wiley & Sons.

C   H   A   P   T   E   R   2   5

Decision Making and Problem Solving

Karran Thorpe

Karran Thorpe, RN, BScN, MN, PhD (Alberta), is Assistant Professor in the School of Nursing, University of Lethbridge. She has experience in intensive care nursing, hospital planning, management, and education.

The challenges in health care delivery seem almost insurmountable in an era of unprecedented change. Nurses, regardless of position, situation, or setting, can influence nursing education as well as nursing and health care practice through systematic problem solving and defensible decision making. If nursing management is decision making, then effective decision making is one cornerstone by which nursing expertise is judged.

This chapter gives an introduction to decision making, problem solving, and critical thinking; it defines and differentiates among the terms and shows how they relate to the work of nurses. Two models of decision making are presented and applied to nursing situations. Finally, there is an overview of implications for nurse managers relative to policies and procedures, ethical practice, staff satisfaction, and participative decision-making practices.

Clarification of Major Terms

The terms "decision making," "problem solving," and "critical thinking" are used frequently in nursing and often used interchangeably without consideration of the accuracy of the phrase when it is applied. These three terms will be defined briefly; a discussion on their use in nursing follows.

Decision Making

Often, decision making is viewed simply as the activity of selecting from among alternative solutions to a problem. Lancaster and Lancaster (1982) note that the decision-making process includes "the problem, the decision maker, the process, and the decision itself" (p. 23). However, Bernhard and Walsh (1990) expand this definition and suggest that decision making is "a systematic process that begins with a need or problem, and ends when an evaluation of the choice is completed" (p. 130). Both definitions imply the notion of numerous steps in the decision-making process, including the important, and sometimes overlooked, step of evaluation. Drucker (1974) acknowledges the key role of the decision maker when he writes that decision making is a risk-taking and judgemental activity that ideally focusses upon the understanding of the problem rather than on a right answer. Further, the role of other participants in this process serves to mobilize managers, workers, and resources of the organization for effective action. In reality, then, decision making is a complex, systematic, sequential, and time-consuming process.

Problem Solving

Problem solving has been defined as "a process used when a gap is perceived between an existing state (what is going on) and a desired state (what should be going on)" (Strader, 1992, p. 228). This process involves a search for information to clarify a problem (i.e., process) and to suggest potential alternatives as solutions (i.e., product). Tappen (1989) combines both the *process* and the *product* by defining problem solving as "a series of steps designed to help... organize information available in order to come up with the best possible solution to a problem" (p. 135). The problem-solving process, therefore, can be said to entail deliberate and thoughtful action to overcome some kind of difficulty for which there is no apparent, ready-made resolution, and the product sought is the best solution.

Critical Thinking

Although there is much discussion in the literature about critical thinking, there is little consensus about its exact meaning. For instance, in a 1964 manual, Watson and Glaser (1964, cited in Miller, 1992) perceived critical thinking as the composite of attitudes, knowledge, and skills as follows:

> *(1) attitudes of inquiry that involve an ability to recognize the existence of problems and an acceptance of the general need for evidence in support of what is asserted to be true; (2) knowledge*

of the nature of valid inferences, abstractions, and generaliza-
tions in which the weight or accuracy of different kinds of evi-
dence are logically determined; and (3) skills in employing and
applying the above attitudes and knowledge. (p. 1402)

However, Bandman and Bandman (1988) describe critical thinking as
a multidimensional cognitive undertaking that is creative and encompasses "rational examination of ideas, inferences, assumptions, principles, arguments, conclusions, issues, statements, beliefs, and
actions" (p. 5). Thus, critical thinking entails a creative and innovative, yet rational, approach to the application of sound analytical
skills to all circumstances of inquiry.

Relationship of Major Terms

There is widespread agreement that decision making and problem
solving are allied but distinct processes. Although the steps may vary
from one model to another, many writers describe several steps common to each process (e.g., Bergeron, 1987). As shown in Figure 25.1,
critical-thinking skills (a) are prerequisite to sound decision-making
and problem-solving activities. At this stage, critical-thinking skills
enhance the manager's ability to separate the real problem from various symptoms. But critical-thinking skills also permeate each of the
nine steps. The decision-making process (c) involves a number of
steps but is said to be complete once a choice is made (b). In contrast,
the problem-solving process (d) goes on to include implementing and
evaluating the decision. While these three processes appear to share a
common sequence of steps, it is important to understand clearly that
the processes are not just different labels for the same activity but
truly separate, albeit compatible, undertakings.

Being a successful problem solver necessitates being able to
match the solution correctly to the problem. Moreover, problem solving
typically depends more on an individual philosophy than on any scientific or technical abilities. One may interpret this comment to mean
that decision making is an integral component of problem solving.
Since successful decision making depends upon selecting the best alternative to solve the actual problem, the decision maker's own perspective is as important as any scientific ability applied in decision making.

Central to successful problem resolution and decision making is
the ability to address each situation with the critical-thinking perspective of sound analytical skills, innovation, and a variety of view-
points. Bandman and Bandman (1988) concur that decision making,
problem solving, and scientific reasoning require critical-thinking
skills to be effective. Nevertheless, scientific reasoning, problem-
solving, and decision-making processes are enhanced when nurse managers possess and utilize sound analytical skills. It is also important

Figure 25.1

Relationships among critical thinking, decision, decision-making process, and problem-solving process.

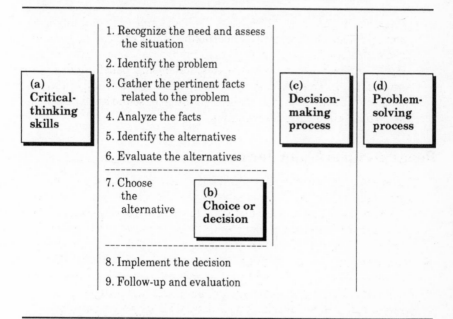

1. Recognize the need and assess the situation

2. Identify the problem

(a) Critical-thinking skills

3. Gather the pertinent facts related to the problem

4. Analyze the facts

5. Identify the alternatives

6. Evaluate the alternatives

7. Choose the alternative

(b) Choice or decision

(c) Decision-making process

(d) Problem-solving process

8. Implement the decision

9. Follow-up and evaluation

Source: Adapted, with permission, from Methuen, Inc., Toronto. From Bergeron, P.G. (1987), *Modern management in Canada: Concepts and practices.* Toronto: Methuen, p. 189.

to be innovative, open to all ideas, and as creative as possible in approaching the tasks of problem solving and decision making.

When managers and administrators are not directly involved in decision making, they are often directing and controlling the decision-making process of others. For example, participative decision making reflects the involvement of subordinates in the decision-making process. Various levels or types of involvement are demonstrated in nursing organizations. Some subordinates may wish more opportunities to participate in budgetary decisions than other subordinates. This need or desire to participate in decision making may depend upon the issue being resolved, or it may depend upon the subordinates' personal make-up or perception of autonomy in the workplace (e.g., Fralic, 1989).

Clearly, the interrelated but separate processes of decision making and problem solving are enhanced by employing critical-thinking abilities to clarify the problem statement in the initial stages and also throughout each step of the decision-making and problem-solving processes, as demonstrated in Figure 25.1.

Models of Decision Making

There are numerous decision-making models available. For instance, the Kepner-Tregoe (1976, 1981) model provides a systematic problem-solving and decision-making framework used in private and public industry worldwide; the Program Evaluation and Review Technique (PERT) employs a chart to illustrate the sequencing of, and relationships among, the key activities; and a decisional grid enhances the comparison and contrasting of alternatives based upon specific criteria. However, few models are used on a daily basis, despite the fact that they facilitate decision making by fostering objectivity and impartiality.

Two models of decision making are discussed in this section: the Claus-Bailey model (Bailey & Claus, 1975; Claus & Bailey, 1979) and the Vroom-Yetton model (Vroom, 1973, 1982; Vroom & Yetton, 1973).

Figure 25.2

The Claus-Bailey systems model for problem solution.

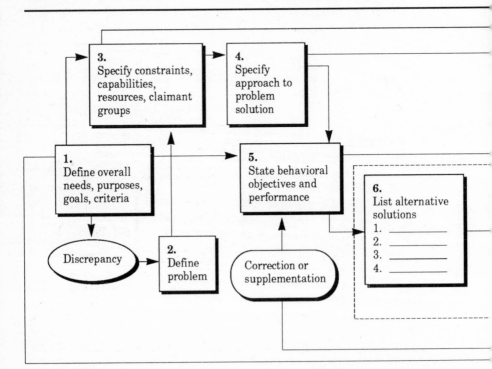

Source: Reprinted with permission of the authors. From K.E. Claus & J.T. Bailey (1975), *Decision making in nursing: Tools for change.* St. Louis: C.V. Mosby, p. 19.

Claus-Bailey Model

Bailey and Claus (1975; see also Claus & Bailey, 1979) developed a systematic process for problem solving and decision making. There are ten steps in their model (see Figure 25.2).

The first step of this model provides the framework for the decision by requiring identification of the overall needs, purposes, and goals. Although these elements may have been initially identified for a program or activity before the problem arose, they should be specified once the problem arises. The second step requires identification of the actual problem, called the *discrepancy* in this model (Bailey & Claus, 1975, p. 20). In other words, there must be a difference between the existing circumstances and what is desired, or between what is and what should be. (Put another way, step 1 is the statement of what should be and step 2 is the statement of what is.) During step 3, the manager compares those factors that will help and those that will hinder the making of the decision. Further, the manager identifies all the stakeholders who will be affected by the decision.

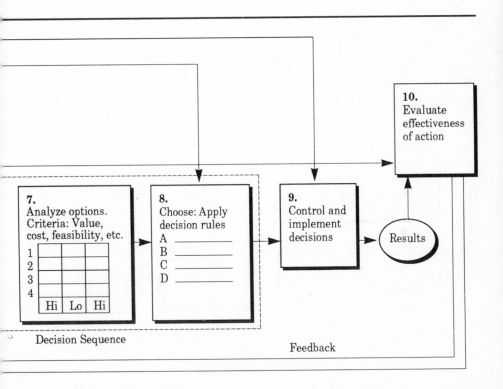

Step 4 entails stating the approach or framework to be used by the manager. The approach reflects the underlying assumptions the manager holds about decision making and the factors to be treated as more or less important in the process. During step 5, behavioural objectives for the decision are written. Stated as expected outcomes, it is important to differentiate between the critical (must be satisfied) objectives and the noncritical (desirable, but not essential) objectives.

The *decision sequence* of this model encompasses the next three steps (6, 7, and 8). Step 6 is often referred to as the search step, since it involves the preparation of potential solutions. It is necessary to seek as many solutions as possible, since the greater number of alternatives suggested in this step, the greater the likelihood of making a sound decision. Step 7 pertains to the analysis of the various proposed alternatives. In this step, the manager compares each of the alternatives with the objectives and with other noted criteria, for instance, cost effectiveness and risk involvement. On the basis of decisional rules (related to step 4), the manager then selects the best problem-solving alternative, thus completing step 8.

The exercise of control and the implementation of the decision constitute step 9. The manager endeavours to do everything possible to ensure a positive acceptance of the decision among those individuals involved in its implementation. Finally, an evaluation of the effectiveness of the decision is undertaken to assess whether or not any revisions are necessary and to determine the success of the decision's implementation (step 10).

The Claus-Bailey model is based upon "systems theory, operations research procedures, and design engineering" (Claus & Bailey, 1979, p. 34), downplays the role of individuals in contributing ideas, and, therefore, depersonalizes any negative responses to a chosen alternative. A major advantage is the abbreviated, but effective, three-step decision sequence that staff nurses can use daily. Although using the ten-step model shown in Figure 25.2 may be time consuming, managers are able to retrace their steps to explain exactly how a decision was made.

Application of the Claus-Bailey (1975) Model

The model is applicable to all nursing settings. For example, ethical dilemmas occur regularly in nursing and are likely to increase in the future. The increase in ethical dilemmas may be explained in part due to advances in technology used to maintain life, demands of consumers to gain access to that technology, and the diminishing resources (e.g., human and economic) available to provide this technology.

Ethical decision making is influenced by the health care professional's own values and beliefs and guided by a number of ethical principles. As one example, the Alberta Association of Registered Nurses (AARN, 1987) describes six principles: autonomy, beneficence, nonmaleficence, fidelity, veracity, and justice. These principles have a theoretical base and typically differentiate between right and wrong behavioural responses. To foster sound ethical decision making, nursing managers need to understand clearly not only the situation but also the principles pertinent to the dilemma.

Imagine a situation where Mrs. Ashley, a 36-year-old mother of three young children, has recently been diagnosed with lung cancer. Aware of the diagnosis and prognosis, her husband has decided to withhold the information from his wife and children. Her physician concurs with this decision. Since Mrs. Ashley is hospitalized for chemotherapy, the physician has directed the nurses to provide no information to the client about her diagnosis and treatment. The nurses have developed a friendly relationship with her and she now asks many questions about her condition and treatment. The nurses, who are obliged to follow the physician's directions, are concerned for the client and frustrated in providing nursing care.

Three principles especially relevant to this case study are autonomy, veracity, and fidelity. Autonomy embodies the individual's right to make an independent choice regarding health care. As long as the individual's choice does not negatively affect others, the individual—in this case, Mrs. Ashley—is free to select a course of action and, further, to expect others—such as health care professionals—to respect that choice. Veracity refers to truthfulness, that is, the responsibility of health care professionals is to be honest (not deceitful) in providing information (e.g., about a diagnosis) to the client. Fidelity pertains to faithfulness—maintaining confidentiality and functioning as a client-advocate. Obviously, the principle of fidelity relates directly to the relationship between any health care professional and the client.

The first step in the Claus-Bailey model is to define the overall purposes, needs, and goals. The major purpose of nursing, universally, is to provide safe, competent, and ethical nursing care to each client. Other more specific purposes are to assist the client to meet any health care deficits, to regain an optimal level of health, and to function independently. All of these purposes are relevant to the ethical problem described in the case study.

Maslow's (1954) theory of motivation based on hierarchy of needs supports a comprehensive assessment of the client's needs. This theory suggests a hierarchical arrangement of needs such that lower-level needs (e.g., physical, safety, and belonging) must be met before higher-level needs (e.g., self-esteem and self-actualization) can be met. In this case, basic physiological needs for Mrs. Ashley encompass a need to understand the disease process as well as treatment modalities, in addition to appropriate nutrition, rest, and exercise. Moreover, self-esteem needs for Mrs. Ashley may be defined in terms of remaining independent, fulfilling her roles as wife and mother, and participating in decision making.

Several goals are important for Mrs. Ashley, including being able to cope with current treatment and to regain independence as demonstrated by actively participating in decisions regarding her health care.

Identifying the discrepancy (step 2) is possible after a thorough assessment of needs. The disease process is affecting Mrs. Ashley's physiological and safety needs, and the lack of information about her diagnosis and treatment is compromising her ability to meet belonging, self-esteem, and self-actualization needs. Thus, the discrepancy lies in her lack of knowledge about her health status.

Here the problem is an ethical dilemma affecting Mrs. Ashley, her husband, the nurses, and the physician; Mr. Ashley has decided to withhold information and his request is granted at the expense of the client. Mrs. Ashley is denied the right to make an independent choice regarding her health care because of a lack of information, and the nurses are compromised in providing holistic nursing care. Indeed, the nurses are expected to provide nursing care without being respectful, truthful, or faithful to the client.

Thus, the positive and negative forces that affect the situation begin to become apparent. Step 3 is to identify the constraints and resources, which are the forces that oppose each other. In this example, there are three forces with their opposing resources. The first constraint is that the husband and physician wish to withhold information. The opposing force is that the client requests information about her diagnosis and treatment from nurses; nursing's principles support the client's right to be informed about diagnosis, treatment, and prognosis so that she can make independent decisions (veracity). A second force is that the husband and physician expect the nurses to provide nursing without providing information; because both only "visit" the patient in the hospital, they are less troubled about this withholding of information. The opposing force is that nurses are involved throughout the 24-hour period in providing nursing care to the client and are routinely confronted by a client who wishes to be treated fairly, humanely, and with dignity (fidelity). A third force is that the husband and physician, believing they are acting in the best interest of the client, have usurped her right to participate in decision making. The opposing force is that nurses believe the client has a right to know about her diagnosis and treatment and to participate in the decision-making process (autonomy).

In step 4, the underlying assumptions deemed important need to be identified. A client-centred, holistic approach integral to nursing (e.g., based upon Orem's [1990] theory of self-care) assumes that clients are capable of caring for themselves, that they want to be involved in the decision-making process, and that they act responsibly when adequately informed. One underlying assumption, then, is that providing current knowledge about the disease process is necessary. It is further assumed that the client is a rational being who has a right to choose freely from among health care options and that nurses have a responsibility to be honest and to assist the client in the decision-making process.

Step 5 is to state behavioural objectives and performance criteria essential to a good solution. One specific behavioural objective for Mrs. Ashley is for her to participate in making health care decisions. She needs to be fully informed about her diagnosis and treatment options to fulfil this objective. Thus, her husband and physician need to reconsider their positions regarding withholding information. Appropriate performance criteria include the attainment of independent physical and psychosocial functioning for the client. A positive self-concept can be measured by the extent to which Mrs. Ashley actively participates in determining when and how specific nursing care will be provided. Moreover, by confiding in the nurses a personal response to her diagnosis, Mrs. Ashley demonstrates not only an acceptance and willingness to work with her diagnosis but also an ability to attain self-actualization.

It is important to list all possible alternative solutions to this ethical dilemma (step 6). For instance, the following alternatives are suggested:

- Maintain the status quo; respect her husband's decision to withhold information and follow the physician's directions.

- Answer the client's questions honestly, thereby informing her about her diagnosis and treatment, regardless of her husband's request and her physician's directions.

- Initiate a conference with the physician and husband to advocate on the client's behalf regarding her right to participate in decision making and to be informed honestly about her diagnosis, treatment, and prognosis. Further, discuss the nurses' ethical responsibility—to be truthful and faithful—to the client.

Next, in step 7, it is necessary to establish specific criteria against which to analyze the various alternatives. In Mrs. Ashley's situation, the criteria for analyzing the alternatives are based upon the relevant ethical principles as well as the needs of, and risks to, the client. The criteria are also linked to the behavioural objectives and performance criteria. These criteria include: the ethical principles of autonomy, veracity, and fidelity, as well as the basic needs of physical

Figure 25.3
Analysis of alternatives.

Criteria	Ideal	Alternatives		
		1	2	3
Autonomy	**Hi**	**Lo**	**Mod**	**Hi**
Veracity	Hi	Lo	Mod	**Hi**
Fidelity	Hi	Lo	Mod	**Hi**
Risk to client	Lo	Hi	Mod	**Lo**
Physical comfort	Hi	**Hi**	**Hi**	**Hi**
Safety	Hi	**Hi**	**Hi**	**Hi**
Belonging	Hi	Mod	Lo/Mod	**Hi**
Self-esteem	Hi	**Lo/Mod**	Mod	**Hi**
Self-actualization	Hi	Lo	Mod	**Hi**
Score		2	2	9

Note: Alternatives shown in bold type match the ideal. A match = 1 point in the scoring.

comfort, safety, belonging, self-esteem, and self-actualization. An analysis of the alternatives is presented in Figure 25.3. Each alternative is scored according to the criteria, using a simple rating scale of high (Hi), moderate (Mod), or low (Lo).

Decisional rules can now assist in selecting the best alternative. The first decisional rule pertains to the ethical dilemma in Mrs. Ashley's case. As shown in Figure 25.3, alternative 3 best addresses the ethical principles of autonomy, veracity, and fidelity. Alternative 2 may cause a negative response from her husband and may also interfere with the client-physician relationship. A second decisional rule addresses the risk to the client. Assuming that risk is reflected in knowledge and ability to participate in decision making, alternative 3 provides the best solution. Further, in meeting the client's needs, all three alternatives appear to meet the basic needs of physical comfort and safety. However, only alternative 3 provides the potential of meeting the remaining needs of belonging, self-esteem, and self-actu-alization. Thus, alternative 3 provides the best solution in meeting the client's basic needs with the least risk while applying the three ethical principles relevant to Mrs. Ashley's case.

After applying the decisional rules, the nurses select alternative 3, as step 8 in the process. To implement the decision as step 9, the nurses invite her husband and physician to attend a client-centred conference to present their perspectives and concerns. The nursing unit manager is invited to lend support to the nurses' role in client advocacy and to assist in clarifying the ethical dilemma faced by the nurses. The process concludes with step 10, the evaluation of the out-comes of meeting with her husband and physician. It should be noted that resolving the problem with her husband and physician has, in turn, repercussions about providing care to Mrs. Ashley. And so the problem-solving cycle continues.

Vroom-Yetton Model

The Vroom and Yetton (1973) normative (prescriptive) model (see Figure 25.4, pages 472-473) is well known in management and leader-ship circles. This model focusses on how managers determine that a problem is to be solved—using autocratic or participative approaches — rather than on the actual solution. There are three processes, labeled autocratic, consultative, and group (symbolically represented as A, C, and G, respectively). Each process is further identified with a Roman numeral (I or II), indicating the variants on the process (Vroom, 1973, p. 67). For example, the decisional styles include AI, whereby the manager solves the problem alone with whatever information is avail-able at the time, and AII, whereby the manager solves the problem alone but obtains necessary information from subordinates, who may or may not know why the information is being collected or how it is used. In CI, the manager shares the problem with relevant subordi-nates individually, collecting ideas and suggestions before making a decision. In CII, the problem is shared with subordinates in a group setting; the group collectively gives ideas and suggestions, but the manager makes the decision, which may or may not reflect the subor-dinates' influence. The GI model is omitted from the discussion here because it applies to comprehensive models outside the scope of this chapter; it involves a sharing of the problem with a subordinate and analyzing the problem together to obtain a mutually acceptable solu-tion. In GII, the manager acts as a chairperson of a group meeting that is directed toward reaching a consensus in the decision-making process; the manager does not influence the group and accepts and implements the group's solution even if he or she does not support it.

Figure 25.4
The Vroom-Yetton decision model.

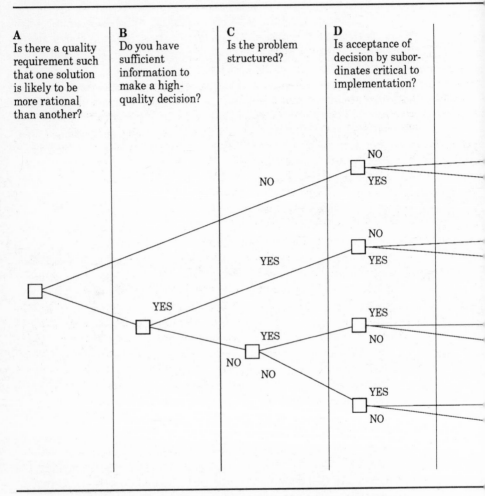

A	B	C	D
Is there a quality requirement such that one solution is likely to be more rational than another?	Do you have sufficient information to make a high-quality decision?	Is the problem structured?	Is acceptance of decision by subordinates critical to implementation?

Source: Reprinted with permission from AMACOM, A Division of American Management Association. From V.H. Vroom (1973), A new look at managerial decision making. *Organizational Dynamics, 1,* 70.

The effectiveness of decisions depends upon the quality or rationality of the decision, the commitment of subordinates to implement a decision, and the time required to make a decision. These components relate to seven situational properties that Vroom and Yetton (1973) call problem attributes:

E
If you were to make this decision by yourself, is it reasonably certain that it would be accepted by your subordinates?

F
Do subordinates share the organizational goals to be attained in solving this problem?

G
Is conflict among subordinates likely in preferred solutions?

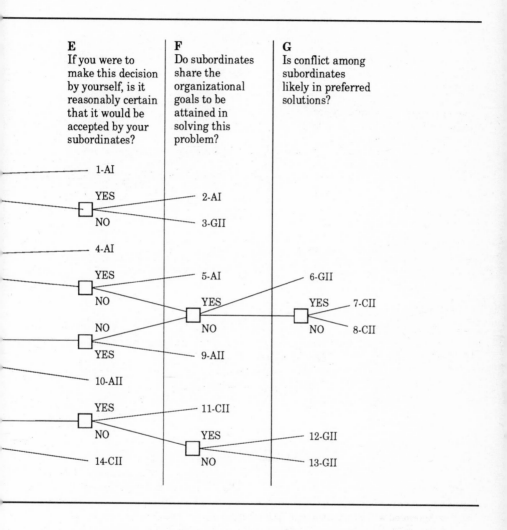

A.   The importance of the quality of the decision;

B.   The extent to which the leader possesses sufficient information to make a high-quality decision by himself or herself;

C.   The extent to which the problem is structured;

D.   The extent to which acceptance or commitment on the part of subordinates is critical to effective implementation of the decision;

E.   *The prior probability that the leader's autocratic decision will receive acceptance by subordinates;*

F.   *The extent to which subordinates are motivated to attain the organizational goals as represented in the objectives explicit in the statement of the problem;*

G.   *The extent to which subordinates are likely to be in conflict over preferred solutions.* (Vroom, 1973, p. 69)

Managers can quickly and correctly assess the problematic situation by answering seven diagnostic questions and developing a decision tree (see Figure 25.4).

Starting at the left-hand margin, managers answer the appropriate questions and move to the next box according to the Yes or No response. A number, indicating the problem type and one of the decision-making processes (see Table 25.1), is noted at the terminal box of the various paths. When more than one alternative is available within the feasible set, the option closest to the left is the one considered to be the most time efficient (Vroom, 1973).

Table 25.1

Problem types and the feasible set of decision processes.

Problem Type	Acceptable Methods
1.	AI, AII, CI, CII, GII
2.	AI, AII, CI, CII, GII
3.	GII
4.	AI, AII, CI, CII, GII*
5.	AI, AII, CI, CII, GII*
6.	GII
7.	CII
8.	CI, CII
9.	AII, CI, CII, GII*
10.	AII, CI, CII, GII*
11.	CII, GII*
12.	GII
13.	CII
14.	CII, GII*

* Within the feasible set only when the answer to question F is yes.

Source: Reprinted with permission from AMACOM, A Division of American Management Association. From V.H. Vroom (1973), A new look at managerial decision making. *Organizational Dynamics*, 1, 71.

This model encompasses four major steps: selection of an organizational problem or decision to be made; identification of diagnostic questions; identification of the path to be followed in the model; and determination of the problem type. The model is a tool that can specify one or more decisional processes deemed appropriate to solve a problem.

If this model is used, there also are seven "rules" that protect the quality of the decision and clarify the level of acceptance and participation by subordinates. Nurse managers are referred to the original article (Vroom, 1973) for a complete review of the model.

Several advantages of the Vroom-Yetton model have been described. For example, this model tends "to stimulate people to think differently about problem solving and decision making, to increase their flexibility, to consider their own behavior, [and] to provide a vehicle for contemplating behavior changes" (LaMonica & Finch, 1977, p. 26). LaMonica and Finch (1977) also note a number of limitations concerning the model. For example, since all of its aspects are open to multiple interpretations, the model requires flexibility in application; delegation, a significant function of managers today, is omitted as an option; and the model does not require managers to communicate to subordinates the decisional style (e.g., autocratic, consultative, or group) being used (LaMonica & Finch, 1977).

Application of the Vroom-Yetton Model

Consider this scenario: Ms. Marple, vice-president of patient care services of a large urban hospital, is implementing a new organizational structure that has implications throughout the nursing department. Recently, in keeping with the current economic climate, the president requested all senior administrators to submit their proposals demonstrating significant cost-cutting measures. Ms. Marple wishes to maintain quality nursing practice while addressing the need to trim the nursing budget. The problem is for Ms. Marple to determine the best decisional style to use in preparing the proposal for the nursing department.

In using the Vroom-Yetton model, the first step is to state the organizational problem clearly. For Ms. Marple, the problem is to document, in proposal format, the various cost-cutting strategies that would reduce the nursing budget while simultaneously supporting the provision of quality nursing care.

It is not necessary to address each of the seven diagnostic questions in order to resolve every problem. Therefore, step 2 requires the identification of the diagnostic questions relevant to this problem. Ms. Marple realizes the potential impact that budgetary restrictions have on subordinates, but she accepts the responsibility of writing and submitting a proposal representative of the nursing department. She concludes that the first six questions are important to this problem and subsequently follows the path (step 3) from A to F by answering Yes or No to each question (see Figure 25.4, pages 472-473). The path leads to the determination of the problem type (step 4) and the following analysis:

Questions:
- A. Quality?—Yes
- B. Manager's information?—No
- C. Structured?—No
- D. Acceptance?—Yes
- E. Prior probability of acceptance?—No
- F. Goal congruence?—No

Problem type—13

Feasible set—CII

Minimum person-hours solution—CII

In this instance, the decision tree led to only one useful solution: CII. The CII decisional style provides an opportunity for Ms. Marple to involve various subordinates in the problem-solving process even though she retains the prerogative to make the decision. These factors help her decide to use the CII method.

Implications for Nurse Managers

The process and skills of sound decision making and problem solving are critical to nurse managers. Moreover, nurse managers need to understand their own and their subordinates' roles in decision making and problem solving. A few implications for nurse managers regarding policies and procedures, ethical practice, staff satisfaction, and participative management are discussed.

Development of Policy and Procedures

Policies and procedures govern the practice of nursing in any organization. Policies are general statements that assist all personnel in their decision-making activities whereas procedures are guides to action. Moreover, policies allow the separation of decision makers into two general levels—senior administrators, who initiate policy, and nurse managers, who make decisions within the parameters established by policy. Since policies tend to set limits, they provide direction for managers as decision makers, foster uniformity throughout the organization, and thereby facilitate the work of nurse managers.

Nagelkerk and Henry (1990) differentiate between two types of decisions: (1) routine or operational, and (2) nonroutine or strategic. Routine decisions involve day-to-day problems and activities, a limited number of resources, and minimal to moderate risks. Typically, nurse managers make numerous routine decisions in the daily operations of their units, such as deciding to purchase more supplies because of an increased demand. Nurse managers are further guided by the policy that stipulates the need to remain within a certain percentage of an operational budget. Nagelkerk and Henry (1990) point out that "nonroutine, strategic decisions involve novel situations, complex problems, and usually a considerable amount of personal anxiety. Substantial amounts of scarce resources are involved; so are high degrees of risk" (p. 18). An example of an issue requiring a strategic decision is whether or not to implement case management or program management of care in a hospital setting. Senior administrators are usually involved in resolving this kind of problem since there is no policy established to guide the decision-making process.

In providing nursing care, staff nurses follow the procedural guidelines unique to each institution. These guidelines accommodate some flexibility among individual nurses; that is, there is room for independent decision making among the nursing staff. Nevertheless, procedures are established to restrict the amount of freedom in decision making among the staff members to ensure the safe and uniform implementation of care.

Ethical Practice

The environment today for nursing administrators and managers is complex, fast-paced, and continually changing. Whereas ethical dilemmas are not new to nursing, staff nurses and nurse managers alike face ethical controversies as a result of the changes in health care practices. Objective and rational decisions derive from reasoning based upon social, economic, and ethical dimensions of issues. Nurse managers need to present themselves as moral role models; they also need to be committed to meeting positional and organizational as well as professional expectations. Ultimately, the real test of any just decision is reflected in the implementation of those judgements followed by an evaluation of the decision or action.

Among the ethical norms that guide nurse managers and staff nurses in their decision making are the various codes of ethics (e.g., AARN, 1987; Canadian Nurses Association [CNA], 1991), provincial standards of nursing practice (e.g., AARN, 1991), and personal and organizational philosophies. The AARN (1987) guidelines include nursing beliefs, ethical principles, a generic decision-making model, and several exemplary case studies. In the CNA document, ethical guidelines pertain to such practices as nurses' treating clients with respect, providing competent nursing care, being client advocates, maintaining confidentiality of client information, and fostering collegial relationships with other nurses. Once again, managers must not only demonstrate sound ethical practice on their own behalf but also ensure an environment that enables, indeed, ensures, that staff nurses practise according to professional guidelines.

Staff Satisfaction

Decision-making autonomy is often linked directly to nursing professionalism and job satisfaction. Nevertheless, some research findings demonstrate little support that decision-making autonomy in nursing increases job satisfaction or performance, or decreases turnover among nurses (e.g., Hinshaw, Smeltzer, & Atwood, 1987).

Dwyer, Schwartz, and Fox (1992) investigated the preference for decision-making autonomy among 151 registered nurses, working full-time in a medium-sized, private hospital. Their results indicated that "nurses may differ considerably in this preference [for decision-making autonomy] and that these differences have important implications for programs designed to enhance nurse autonomy" (p. 22). One solution may be to socialize nurses, through education, regarding the value of decision-making autonomy in nursing practice. Another approach may be for nurse managers to recognize, and take advantage of, the individual differences among nursing staff. Nurses with a lower desire for autonomy may derive job satisfaction when working under the guidance of a clinical nurse specialist, whereas those nurses who have a high desire for decision-making autonomy may gain greater satisfaction working in a primary care milieu or in a shared governance environment (Dwyer, Schwartz, & Fox, 1992; Porter-O'Grady, 1992).

Fostering Participative Management

Participative management ensures that nurses are involved in decisions that affect their practice. This process generally necessitates changes in roles for all nursing personnel, organizational structures, and communication. As facilitators, rather than directors, nursing managers gain satisfaction from fostering successful and satisfied nurse practitioners. Demonstrating increased accountability, nursing managers have time to concentrate on planning and organizing their work. Similarly, staff nurses benefit from working independently, but cooperatively, with individuals in other departments. With an increased efficiency of nurse-patient ratio, there is better utilization of professional nurses, who have opportunities to develop and demonstrate their skills and abilities. Thus, there is less overtime, resulting in lower costs for the agency, decreased absenteeism, and increased job satisfaction.

Valentine (1992) discovered "that women nurse educators used a cooperative, collaborative, highly participatory style of decision making that resulted in decisions based on consensus" (p. 10). Several significant implications emerge from this study. One implication pertains to the lack of fit between the nurse educators' democratic style of decision making and the hierarchical and autocratic style of decision making typically employed by senior hospital administrators (often male). Perhaps the dissatisfaction expressed by nurses in hospital settings stems in part from the differences in gender perspectives regarding decision-making practices. Interestingly, Schwartz (1990) observes a discrepancy in the literature, whereby nursing journals espouse "the virtues of autonomous and participative decision-making [for staff nurses]" (p. 38) and hospital publications promote the status quo. These differences may be congruent with the varied stances of nursing and hospital administrators regarding the role of nurses in decision making. Valentine (1992) correctly recommends that more research is needed to examine nursing organizations in general and to assess whether or not the collaborative style of decision making is preferred by most nurses.

Summary

Decision making is integral to the work of nurse managers and administrators. This chapter has provided an introduction to the concepts of decision making, problem solving, and critical thinking, providing definitions of each of the concepts and demonstrating the relationships among them. Two decision-making models have been briefly described—the Claus-Bailey model and the Vroom-Yetton model. A few implications for nurse managers pertaining to the development of policies and procedures, ethical practice, staff satisfaction, and fostering participative management have been delineated.

References

Alberta Association of Registered Nurses. (1991). *Nursing practice standards and competencies for nurses beginning to practice in Alberta.* Edmonton: Author.

Alberta Association of Registered Nurses. (1987). *Guidelines for bioethical decision-making in nursing.* Edmonton: Author.

Bailey, J.T., & Claus, K.E. (1975). *Decision making in nursing: Tools for change.* St. Louis: C.V. Mosby.

Bandman, E.L., & Bandman, B. (1988). *Critical thinking in nursing.* Norwalk, CT: Appleton & Lange.

Bergeron, P.G. (1987). *Modern management in Canada: Concepts and practices.* Toronto: Methuen.

Bernhard, L.A., & Walsh, M. (1990). *Leadership: The key to the professionalization of nursing* (2nd ed.). Toronto: C.V. Mosby.

Canadian Nurses Association. (1991). *Code of ethics for nursing.* Ottawa: Author.

Claus, K.E., & Bailey, J.T. (1979). Facilitating change: A problem-solving/decision-making tool. *Nursing Leadership, 2*(2), 32-39.

Drucker, P.F. (1974). *Management tasks, responsibilities, practices.* New York: Harper & Row.

Dwyer, D.J., Schwartz, R.H., & Fox, M.L. (1992). Decision-making autonomy in nursing. *Journal of Nursing Administration, 22*(2), 17-23.

Fralic, M.F. (1989). Decision support systems: Essential for quality administrative decisions. *Nursing Administration Quarterly, 14*(1), 1-8.

Hinshaw, A.S., Smeltzer, C.H., & Atwood, J.R. (1987). Innovative retention strategies of nursing staff. *Journal of Nursing Administration, 17*(6), 8-16.

Kepner, C.H., & Tregoe, B.B. (1981). *The rational manager: A systematic approach to problem solving and decision making* (2nd ed.). Montréal: Kepner-Tregoe.

LaMonica, E., & Finch, F.E. (1977). Managerial decision making. *Journal of Nursing Administration, 1*(3), 20-28.

Lancaster, W., & Lancaster, J. (1982). Rational decision making: Managing uncertainty. *Journal of Nursing Administration, 12*(9), 23-28.

Maslow, A.H. (1954). *Motivation and personality.* New York: Harper.

Miller, M.A. (1992). Outcomes evaluation: Measuring critical thinking. *Journal of Advanced Nursing, 17*(12), 1401-1407.

Nagelkerk, J.M., & Henry, B.M. (1990). Strategic decision making. *Journal of Nursing Administration, 20*(7/8), 18-23.

Orem, D. (1990). *Nursing concepts of practice* (4th ed.). New York: McGraw-Hill.

Porter-O'Grady, T. (1992). *Implementing shared governance: Creating a professional organization.* Toronto: Mosby Year Book.

Schwartz, R.H. (1990). Nurse decision-making influence: A discrepancy between the nursing and hospital literatures. *Journal of Nursing Administration, 20*(6), 35-39.

Strader, M. (1992). Critical thinking. In E.J. Sullivan & P.J. Decker (Eds.), *Effective management in nursing* (3rd ed.), (pp. 225-248). Toronto: Addison-Wesley.

Tappen, R.M. (1989). *Nursing leadership and management: Concepts and practice* (2nd ed.). Philadelphia: F.A. Davis.

Valentine, P.E.B. (1992). Nurse educators and decision making: A female perspective. *Canadian Journal of Nursing Administration, 5*(3), 10-13.

Vroom, V.H. (1973). A new look at managerial decision making. *Organizational Dynamics, 1*(4), 66-80.

Vroom, V.H. (1982). Can leaders learn how to lead? In D.R. Hampton, C.E. Summer, & R.A. Webber (Eds.), *Organizational behavior and the practice of management* (4th ed.) (pp. 597-607). Glenview, IL: Scott, Foresman.

Vroom, V.H., & Yetton, P.W. (1973). *Leadership and decision-making.* Pittsburgh: University of Pittsburgh Press.

Watson, G., & Glaser, E.M. (1964). *Critical thinking appraisal manual.* New York: Harcourt, Brace & World.

CHAPTER 26

Human Resources— Human Management

Sonia Acorn and Janet Walker

Sonia Acorn, RN, BN (McGill), MScN (Boston), PhD (Utah), is Associate Professor, School of Nursing, University of British Columbia, where she teaches nursing administration and nursing research. She has extensive experience in nursing administration.

Janet Walker, RN, BSN, MSN (UBC), is Nurse Manager, British Columbia Cancer Agency. She is Adjunct Professor, School of Nursing, University of British Columbia, where she teaches nursing administration and nursing research.

It is easy to think of organizations merely as the glass and concrete that give them shape. However, organizations are more correctly viewed as human beings who freely gather to achieve an agreed upon goal. That people *are* the entity is an appreciation critical to managers who hope to succeed in the area of human resources management.

This chapter is introduced with a background of present realities and future predictions within the Canadian work force and the health care industry. Against this background, a general overview of human resource management is outlined so that the reader will have a sense of the whole field. For those aspects where there are comprehensive discussions that are readily available either in other chapters of this text or elsewhere, the reader will be so directed. Specific focus is placed on those ideas and practices of human resource management that are either new or that require some explanation to be of significant benefit to the nurse manager. Staffing issues range from hiring to separation. Job issues include job analysis and job descriptions. Organizational issues revolve around change in size and the resulting impact on people. Addressed throughout are the implications for the nurse manager.

Key Factors Affecting
Nursing Resources

The following section focusses on key factors that will shape the
future human resource pool of nurses in Canada. They include demographics and psychographics, which directly affect the numbers and
nature of the available human resources.

Demographics

Changing trends among Canada's population are affecting the characteristics of its work force. One trend of significance is that of aging,
which was identified as far back as 1977 (Statistics Canada, 1977).
The other trend of significance is the changing cultural mix. Data
from Statistics Canada (1990) illustrate patterns of ethnic makeup
between 1901 and 1986. These trace a decline among the traditionally
predominant ethnic groups of British and French. In contrast, there
has been a consistent increase among other ethnic groups and they
now form 31% of Canada's population (Statistics Canada, 1993a).
Immigration patterns that directly affect cultural diversity reveal
dramatic changes. Of those people immigrating to Canada before
1961, most were from Europe (87%) or the United States (7%) with a
small number from Asia (3%) or the Caribbean and southern hemi-
sphere (3%). In contrast, of those people immigrating after 1981, most
were from Asia (43%), followed by those from Europe (29%), and the
Caribbean, Africa, and Oceana (20%) (Statistics Canada, 1990).

Canada's nursing work force is similar to the national work
force in that it continues to grow in age and increase in ethnic diversity (Statistics Canada, 1989, 1992). For example, of Canadian nurses
and nursing students, 17% report that they are immigrants to
Canada. This mirrors the national picture. With regard to ethnic origins, 46% of nurses report the single origin of British or French.
However, 34% report multiple ethnic origins.

Recent statistical information on nurses in Canada reveals several significant facts and trends. First, the pool of registered nurses is
larger than ever before, consisting of nearly double that in 1970
(Canadian Nurses Association, 1971; Statistics Canada, 1993b). Since
1986, Canada's population has grown by 7.9% (Statistics Canada,
1992b); its nurses by 11% (Statistics Canada, 1988; 1992a); and its
regularly employed nurses by 14% (Statistics Canada 1988; 1993b).
Second, participation rates in the labour force remain high and stable
at 88% (Statistics Canada, 1988; 1993b). Third, the median age of the
working nurse is rising. In 1986, the largest group of these nurses

was found in the 30- to 39-year age range. By 1992, the largest group occupied the 35- to 44-year age range (Statistics Canada, 1988; 1993b). By the mid-1990s, most of Canada's working nurses will be 40 years of age or older. The last trend of significance is the continued increase in part-time employment, with the result that 38% of hospital nurses and 34% of community nurses work part time (Statistics Canada, 1992a).

Psychographics

While demographics offers information such as age and occupation, the newer study of psychographics offers additional information on personal values, perspectives, and behaviour. Personal values can be defined as those beliefs that the individual considers right, fair, just, or desirable (Posner & Munson, 1979), and can be expected to shape individual and organizational behaviour directly. These values are changing. A national survey in the United States that drew on demographics and psychographics revealed rising levels of cynicism about society in general and the workplace in particular. That cynicism was evidenced by, among other things, a mistrust of management and a frustration over the lack of meaningful participation in worklife (Mirvis & Kanter, 1991).

In Canada, the management consultant group of Towers Perrin (1992) studied recent changes involving demographics, organizational culture, and the marketplace. Applying this knowledge to health care, the consultant group developed a profile of future health care workers. The profile includes older workers who will be looking for early retirement, a smaller pool of new workers to join the work force, a greater cultural diversity, people who expect to share in the decision making about their work and organization, and a group of people whose work energy and goals must be balanced with personal lifestyle goals.

Nursing Staff of the 1990s

Based on the identified factors affecting health care workers, it is possible to project what a typical hospital or health unit staff might look like. Most will be registered nurses since the increasingly sophisticated needs of health care consumers will require equally sophisticated practitioners. However, the focus on matching skills to the required work will mean greater use of support personnel, from clerks to nurse assistants. Tools such as job analysis can be useful to managers, as they bring about the necessary redistributions of skills. Overall, the work group will represent a duality between the traditional worker and the "New Age" worker. Two-thirds will be more than 40 years of age and will prefer traditional work practices that typically involve the use of rules to shape the work processes. A smaller group will be under age 40, and this group will be more comfortable with few rules and little structure.

There will be present many different cultures and the different personal lifestyles that go with them. Whatever the age or culture, all staff members will expect to be closely involved in the organizational direction and decision making that affect their work lives.

Implications for the Nurse Manager

The central challenge will be to work effectively with the two realities of old and new. The manager will need to assist older staff in becoming comfortable with constant change as the prevailing environment. Support will be necessary so that staff can let go of rigid rules and work comfortably instead with the ambiguity of many systems. A helpful approach will be to promote actively the participation of all staff members, since this will underscore the respect and value of each person. This respect for the individual will meet one of the key needs for workers as the 1990s come to a close.

Managers will need to be aware of the importance that staff will place on the balance between their work and private lives. The stress of balancing work and family life, and the conflicts with respect to this balance, must also be recognized. Nollen (1989) points out that the two major types of conflict involve the general lack of time for work or family and the burden of assuming and managing very different roles within work and within the family. Effective managers will work to achieve an organizational culture that is family-friendly. This will involve such things as employee participation in work schedules that are consistent with child care and elder care needs. Increased requests for reduced or part-time work by employees can be anticipated. Managers will have to be both flexible and innovative in meeting the individual needs and requests of their staff while at the same time finding ways to maintain patient and client continuity.

For aging staff who will be considering retirement, managers can be helpful by developing individualized programs of decreasing work hours over time. Although most collective agreements do not provide for such programs, it will be up to the manager to persuade both the organization and the unions of the need for them.

Increased cultural diversity in health care presents managerial challenges from both clients and staff. The report of Alberta's "Building Cultural Communities" project provides front-line scenarios that illustrate the need for multicultural sensitivity in health care (Urbanowski, 1992). With respect to human resource management, health care managers will need to become familiar with various cultures, and particularly with those aspects of a culture that shape work values and expectations. Employment practices that facilitate multicultural staffing include attention to nondiscrimination in recruitment, hiring, and performance appraisals; the inclusion of multiculturalism in the vision and mission of the organization; and the development of cultural awareness through programs of orientation and education (Canadian Council on Multicultural Health, 1992).

Process of Human Resource Management

Managers are charged with being completely familiar with all matters within their scope of responsibility. In particular, they need to understand the values and key purposes within that scope of responsibility, since these shape the manager's behaviour with respect to human resources. Whether that scope involves the smallest unit of the organization or the entire organization, there must be a logical and comprehensive process that effectively addresses the human resource needs. Table 26.1 illustrates such a process for the nurse manager.

Looking at the Person/Job Fit

Achieving a successful person/job fit begins with the job, and it involves a complete understanding of all requirements of the job. These requirements are determined through job analysis. One of the results of such an analysis is the job description, which sets out both the job functions and job obligations. Based on the job description, then, applicants are selected for their matching knowledge, skills, and abilities.

Most managers oversee existing jobs with existing job descriptions. However, as health care providers struggle to meet client needs in more progressive and efficient ways, new and different jobs will be evolving. Job analysis can be a valuable tool for the manager in examining existing jobs as well as designing new ones. Traditionally, job analysis has consisted of observing an existing job as it is being performed, interviewing the performer of the job, and completing various checklists of tasks or requirements. The time and expertise required is substantial, and many organizations opt for a consultant to perform the analysis. For jobs in the design stage, or jobs that require revision for the future, Schneider and Konz (1989) offer what they call "strategic job analysis." This approach begins with an assessment of predicted changes in the environment, such as changes in societal values,

Table 26.1
Overview of human resource management.

1. Understanding what is to be accomplished
 Mission of the organization
 Philosophy, goals, and objectives of the department/unit

2. Looking at the person/job fit
 Assessment of individuals' skills and needs
 Assessment of work group
 * Job analysis
 * Job descriptions

3. Choosing the best person for the job
 * Recruitment
 * Interviewing process
 Selection

4. Assuring a successful work experience
 Support
 Mentoring
 Performance appraisal
 Training and development

5. Maximizing the person/job effectiveness
 * Promotions, transfers, separation

6. Making the necessary changes
 * Downsizing
 * Bumping
 * Merging
 * Managing the impact on staff

7. The critical element: People skills
 Caring environment
 Supportive communication
 Healthy work relationships

* As some of these dimensions are addressed in other chapters, the focus in this chapter is only on the items marked with an asterisk.

economic markets, and technological growth. Based on this information, people within the organization who are knowledgeable about the job collaborate to develop or revise job tasks and to document the knowledge, skills, and abilities necessary to perform the new job. For a detailed overview of job analysis, readers are directed to the *Canadian Recruitment Management Handbook* by John Kelly (1986).

Job descriptions are precise listings of job components. They include the job purpose and required skills, including education and experience, responsibilities, and duties. The description should be developed with care since it provides the foundation for compensation, hiring, training, and performance appraisal (McKeown & Novak-Jandrey, 1991).

Managers who develop job descriptions should be aware of the *National Occupational Classification* (Employment and Immigration Canada, 1993) and its earlier versions, which are prepared by Employment and Immigration Canada. One especially useful version is the *Canadian Classification and Dictionary of Occupations* (Department of Manpower and Immigration, 1971; Employment and Immigration Canada, 1980) and its companion guide (Employment and Immigration Canada, 1989). For example, the 1980 publication, which is frequently referred to as the CCDO, sets out 12 different nursing titles, including such variations as graduate nurse, public health nurse, clinical nurse specialist, and outpost nurse. Then, for each specific occupational title, the 1980 edition presents 14 job components, which are described and rated. As illustrated in Figure 26.1, these include such items as general educational requirements, worker functions, aptitude factors, and temperament factors. For example, the job component of work functions is expressed in three functional relationships: data, people, and things. Taken together, these rated functions describe the required complexity of performance.

Choosing the Best Person: Recruitment and Interviewing

Recruitment. Recruitment refers to the process of attracting suitably qualified applicants to an organization so that vacant positions can be filled efficiently. Most agencies will have a human resources department whose responsibility it is to recruit employees. The responsibility of the nurse manager is to consult with the nurse recruiter and provide information about the employment needs of a specific unit or area. Guides are available for the development of specific nurse recruitment plans. For example, Pattan (1992) developed a six-step plan for nurse administrators that includes a detailed planning database.

Figure 26.1

Occupational description.

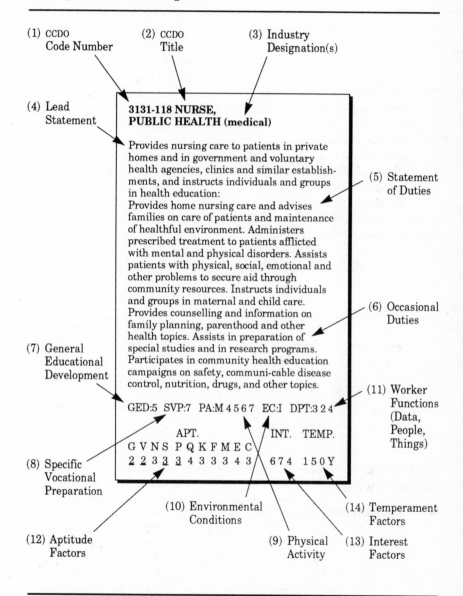

(1) CCDO Code Number

(2) CCDO Title

(3) Industry Designation(s)

(4) Lead Statement

3131-118 NURSE, PUBLIC HEALTH (medical)

Provides nursing care to patients in private homes and in government and voluntary health agencies, clinics and similar establishments, and instructs individuals and groups in health education:

(5) Statement of Duties

Provides home nursing care and advises families on care of patients and maintenance of healthful environment. Administers prescribed treatment to patients afflicted with mental and physical disorders. Assists patients with physical, social, emotional and other problems to secure aid through community resources. Instructs individuals and groups in maternal and child care. Provides counselling and information on family planning, parenthood and other health topics. Assists in preparation of

(6) Occasional Duties

(7) General Educational Development

special studies and in research programs. Participates in community health education campaigns on safety, communi-cable disease control, nutrition, drugs, and other topics.

GED:5 SVP:7 PA:M 4 5 6 7 EC:I DPT:3 2 4

(11) Worker Functions (Data, People, Things)

APT.
G V N S P Q K F M E C
2 2 3 3 3 4 3 3 3 4 3

INT. TEMP.

6 7 4   1 5 0 Y

(8) Specific Vocational Preparation

(10) Environmental Conditions

(14) Temperament Factors

(12) Aptitude Factors

(9) Physical Activity

(13) Interest Factors

Source: Reprinted with permission of the Minister of Supply and Services Canada, 1993. The illustration is from information from Employment and Immigration Canada (1989), *Canadian classification and dictionary of occupations* (p.4) (Ottawa: Minister of Supply and Services), and the text is from Employment and Immigration Canada (1980), *Canadian classification and dictionary of occupations: Major occupations in major groups* (p.53) (Ottawa: Minister of Supply and Services).

If the manager wishes to attract the same type of nurse who is already on the unit, one of the best recruiting strategies is to ask staff members to use their personal networks. Experience has shown that professional friendships reflect similar value and belief systems. Thus, the nurse who is a friend of the staff member will be very similar to the staff member. If the manager wishes to attract a different type of nurse, or one who is already practising within the specialty, the manager may direct the recruiter to advertise in the specialty journals in an effort to reach the specific population of nurses who work in that specialty. The manager needs to consider all these factors in her or his plan, and instruct the recruiter accordingly.

Interviewing process. Once a potential employee has been attracted to the agency, the interview is used as a mechanism to evaluate the applicant's fit with the vacant position. Interviewing practices vary. In some agencies, the nurse recruiter will interview a number of applicants and select the strongest candidates for a further interview by the manager. In other agencies, the recruiter and the manager will together interview selected candidates. However it is done, the manager makes the decision about selection, so it is particularly important for the manager to achieve the goals of the interview.

The purpose of the hiring interview is to exchange accurate and critical information between the applying nurse and those who represent the organization. Research has shown that one of the biggest contributors to new employee dissatisfaction and separation is the unrealistic information presented by interviewers who oversold the job and/or organization (Wanous, 1973, 1980). Accuracy of information is enhanced by creating a relaxed atmosphere of unconditional acceptance. In such an atmosphere, the applicant will be most likely to show her or his real self.

There is a great deal of literature with respect to the interviewing process. One of the most practical and concise treatments is that by Conlow (1991), who identifies four key steps for success:

- Prepare for the interview;
- Set a positive tone with the candidate;
- Conduct a businesslike interview;
- Evaluate all information objectively.

Conlow goes on to provide step-by-step direction, complete with sample tools and guides. A particularly helpful addition for the new manager is the distinction that is made between behavioural questions and informational questions. The former are aimed at assessing job skills; they should be open-ended questions that deal with priorities of the job duties. Examples include, "Tell me how you..." or "Describe a time...." The latter type of questions are designed to gather additional information about the candidate. Examples include, "What are your goals?" and "Why did you leave your last job?" For a literature review on the interviewing process and the development of a employment interview questionnaire within the Canadian nursing context, readers are referred to Heslin and Faux (1991a, 1991b).

Among other things, preparation for the interview includes choosing an interview guide (usually available from the human resources department) and deciding on the number of interviewers. Many managers routinely include a staff nurse in the interview process. The advantage for staff is the direct involvement in the selection of new team members. The advantage for the interviewee is that she or he hears the job requirements described by a person who is actually performing that job.

Immediately after the interview, it is vital that the manager take time to record her or his evaluation of the applicant promptly. In the normal course of events, the manager who is favourably impressed will ask the human resources department to proceed to obtain references on the applicant. Providing that the references are suitable, the manager then instructs the human resources department to make the formal job offer.

Maximizing Person/Job Effectiveness

Just as people have distinct personalities, so do organizations. The personality of an organization is referred to as organizational culture, and is composed of its unique history, traditions, and values. In hiring or promoting people, it is important to consider the fit between a person and an organization.

Promotions. When openings occur for a managerial position, the organization may decide to look only internally for a candidate or hold an external search. The collective agreement may mandate an internal search initially and, if no suitable candidate is found, the search is opened up to external candidates. Each organization needs to assess the internal versus external mix of staff, especially at the managerial level. Internal people assist in carrying through the history and culture of an organization, which is important to a sense of stability. Promotions from within the organization provide incentives and encouragement to others. If the organization has been diligent in its pursuit of excellence and committed to development of its people, there should be candidates with enthusiasm and commitment ready to move into higher positions. However, it is frequently argued that too many internal people will contribute to "staff inbreeding," a stifling of new ideas, and a desire for the status quo. The guiding principle should be the best "person/job fit" for the organization at the time.

Transfers. One means of maximizing the person/job effectiveness is through use of transfers within the organization. There are several ways in which transfers are appropriate. In some cases, when nurses are hired, there may not be an opening on the unit of preference and on which their skills might be best utilized. In other cases, nurses develop specific skills through experience and continuing education, and may wish to transfer to maximize the use of these new skills. Still other nurses may feel the need for a change after a certain length of time on a specific unit. Transfers between nursing units would permit the use of skills and knowledge and assist in prevention of burnout in cases where a nurse is in need of change. Such transfers should be voluntary, but the wise nurse manager will be aware of transfers as a developmental strategy as well as a contributing factor to job satisfaction and retention.

Separations. Nurses leave organizations for a variety of reasons— promotions or changes in clinical focus, family requirements such as a family member who has been transferred, or unhappiness with the current organization. Whatever the reason for the move, and whether the individual nurse is leaving on good terms or not, it is important for the organization to acquire information from the departing nurse on her or his impressions of the work climate.

The cost of nurse turnover is well documented in the literature (Bland Jones, 1990; Prescott & Bowen, 1987). Exit interviews and questionnaires are two means of obtaining information about the reasons for nurse turnover. The interview is a verbal exchange of information between the departing nurse and a hospital representative. The questionnaire is a written tool that the nurse is requested to complete. Although there is little literature on exit interviews/questionnaires, the issues appear to be the value of interviews versus questionnaires, who should conduct the interview (human resources personnel or nursing), and when the information should be gathered. Whitis and Whitis (1983) recommend the personal interview that is conducted by a member of the personnel department during the last two weeks of employment. There are, however, limitations to the exit interview as an accurate source of data. If an employee has negative feedback regarding the organization, there are several reasons why the employee may hesitate to be completely candid. The employee may fear poor future references or may think that negative comments will not be accepted and acted upon.

Information from 59 hospitals surveyed by Leahey and Henderson (1991) indicated that 53% use both exit interviews and questionnaires. Where exit interviews are used, the interview is most frequently conducted by the nurse recruiter or member of the human resources department, with only 17% conducted by the head nurse. These same authors also recommend the questionnaire method, using a short tool that is completed after the employee has left the institution. Tutton (1989) also believes that the written questionnaire mailed to the employee after he or she has left the organization is the best method of gathering reliable data on reasons for departure. However it is gathered, exit information is valuable to the nurse manager for purposes of evaluating the organization, improving employee relations, and lessening employee turnover.

Involuntary separation. Managing the involuntary separation of an employee from the organization is an infrequent but dreaded responsibility. Jesseph (1989) identifies four types of involuntary separation: dismissal for just cause, termination resulting from an employee's failure to fulfil job expectations, layoff (which means "subject to recall"), and elimination of a position resulting from an organizational restructure. Whatever the circumstances, the ending of a person's job means traumatic disturbances in personal identity and economic well-being. It is vital that the manager appreciate the many implications that are present for both the employee and the organization. These implications could have legal, organizational, or individual ramifications.

If a manager believes that involuntary separation may be in an employee's future, it is essential that the manager do two things. First, the manager must work closely with the human resources department. The nurse manager needs not only advice about personnel management, but guidance and interpretation on legislation governing human rights, employment standards, and collective agreements. Failing to understand or adhere to all such regulations could expose the organization to possible legal action by the employee. As well, there should be an array of support services for the employee, including outplacement counseling. Managers will want to be fully informed in all of these areas so that they can reduce, as much as possible, the trauma of involuntary separation, and to protect, as much as possible, other employees and the organization from unintended and negative consequences. The second "must" for a manager is to keep her or his superior fully informed. One's superior could have valuable advice and, depending on the organization's practice, the superior may need to be partially or wholly involved in the actual separation.

Rothman (1989) offers a four-step procedure for managers to facilitate the process of involuntary separation. The first step is analysis, wherein all factors and the context are reviewed for reasonableness, fairness, and consistency with the handling of other, similar situations within the organization. The second step involves preparation, including deciding who will perform the actual separation or termination, where and when the termination interview will take place, what information will actually be presented to the employee, and how anticipated reactions might be handled. The third step addresses the actual termination meeting. Important factors include a calm and non-blaming statement of the reason(s) leading to the termination, time to listen to the employee, clear information about any continuation of benefits, severance pay, outplacement services, and introduction to a human resources representative for further support. The final step is reflection on the entire matter to see if there is anything that the organization or its managers could do to prevent future involuntary separations.

Making the Necessary Changes

Continuing pressure to control costs and reallocate health care resources requires creative alternatives to traditional delivery systems. Terms such as merging, downsizing, resizing, and rightsizing are used to describe current strategies to improve health care efficiency.

Downsizing. Downsizing of hospitals is a reality of the 1990s. Pressures to reshape the health care industry include the drive by federal and provincial governments to bring deficits under control, increased consumer demand, and a focus on community care. In discussing the downsizing experience in the United States, Van Sumeren (1986) states that the downsizing trend in hospital utilization can be expected to continue for the foreseeable future. This trend can also be expected in Canada as governments struggle to control health care costs. Downsizing is disruptive to total hospital environment and traumatic to employees, particularly because the downsizing inevitably involves staff reductions.

When an organization is faced with budget constraint, the most common reactions are to incorporate across-the-board cuts, implement hiring freezes, and freeze capital expenditures. These remedies are successful on a short-term basis, but when major restraint is called for the organization must look to downsizing. Haywood (1990) defines downsizing as a specific reduction in personnel to achieve a predetermined cost reduction and overall restructuring effort. Another term in the current literature is rightsizing, which Haywood describes as a well-developed strategy that includes redefining the mission and goals of the organization, with long-range implementation planning involving close communication with employee groups and full understanding and support of management personnel at all levels.

Several authors have suggested downsizing processes (Bruce & Patterson, 1987; Kazemek & Channon, 1988a, 1988b; Tomasko, 1987). The common threads that run through these models are the need to start the downsizing process early. Decreasing budgets or underutilization of hospital beds are a clear indication that planning for downsizing should begin. These models suggest conducting a thorough organizational assessment, preparing downsizing plans, developing a communication plan, and conducting team-building sessions. Team building counteracts the anxiety and grief that often result from downsizing an organization. Also important is the need for management training to assist managers to become knowledgeable about the changes and strategies required in sustaining the streamlined organization. Of paramount importance is the need for management to work closely with the hospital's human resources department and union representatives at every stage of the downsizing.

Kazemek and Channon (1988a) discuss untargeted and targeted approaches to downsizing. The untargeted approach occurs when hospital management has refused to admit that the "patient is sick" and delays remedial action until time is a crucial factor and options are driven by the need for expediency. Untargeted approach options include across-the-board reductions, voluntary excused absences, and attrition or early retirement. Across-the-board cuts fail to reflect the strategic mission and goals of the hospital, penalize efficient departments, and fail to enforce changes in inefficient departments. With voluntary excused absences, management requests employees to volunteer not to work their scheduled hours. This works on a short term basis, but in the long term, employees become disgruntled about the loss of income. The attrition or early retirement approach results in staff reductions through voluntary decisions made by staff. A disadvantage of this option is that management is unable to select and retain employees who are the most productive and who will be most beneficial in a new, streamlined organization.

The targeted approach, according to Kazemek and Channon (1988a), is a proactive approach that will result in improvements in performance. They outline six steps in the process: (1) ensure that strategic decisions are current and within the mission of the organization; (2) conduct a productivity analysis to determine the actual amount of overstaffing that exists; (3) conduct an organizational analysis whereby functions and activities are examined to determine whether they are critical to the success of a new, streamlined organization; (4) analyze the management structure to determine whether excessive layers of management exist; (5) make the downsizing decisions; and (6) target specific employees. The information from the first four steps is used to make the decisions on which positions to eliminate. There is a tendency for hospitals to be overly conservative in the number of positions targeted for reduction. However painful it may be, it is recommended to make a deep, clean cut to prevent the need for multiple rounds of cuts and repeating this traumatic process (Kazemek & Channon, 1988a; Mullaney, 1989).

Bumping. Some collective agreements contain a clause that enables an employee, if his or her position is eliminated, to request the job of another employee with less seniority in service. This phenomenon is commonly referred to as "bumping." Although this clause provides for protection of more senior employees, it contributes to stress and tension in the workplace. This tension results when employees who have worked together, become friends, and shared much together in the workplace, are now in a situation where one can cause the other to move to a less desirable shift or work unit, or forfeit one's job to the more senior employee. Not only are individual lives disrupted, but the work environment is also disrupted. An employee having little or no experience in a particular area may "bump" someone less senior and move into their work unit. Therefore, the staff on the unit to which the more senior employee is transferring not only grieve the loss of the friend and colleague who has been bumped, but they must assist in the orientation a the new staff member.

Merging. Merging is the process of combining two or more organizations and their assets to form a new entity. It is used by hospitals to enhance the efficiency of service delivery (Fink, 1988). Merging may also involve the combining of two or more nursing units to form a new unit. Staff are frequently resistant to the plan to merge as it involves the breaking up of work groups, the need to change routines, or the threat, whether real or imagined, of staff layoffs.

Managing the Impact on Staff

The emotional impact of downsizing or merging must be recognized and addressed by management. The emotional toll is felt both by those who are laid off and those who remain (Fottler & Schuler, 1984). According to these same authors, the most important element in the implementation plan is to develop a timetable and to communicate it effectively. Once the final determination about numbers is complete, action needs to be swift. This helps prevent rumours and undue anxiety. Effective communication is of paramount importance at all stages of downsizing.

During the actual layoff process, managers must work closely with the human resources department. Information material needs to be prepared and discussed with employees identified for layoff. This material needs to include information on benefits, layoff pay, and outplacement services. Outplacement services provide a range of assistance to displaced employees. Common features of outplacement services include: assistance with résumé writing and completing job résumés, typing résumés at no cost, providing self-assessment exercises to identify strengths, weaknesses, and potential new careers, and posting of job opportunities. Counseling should be made available to those who identify an interest or need.

The process of rebuilding takes two forms—an actual restructuring of the workload to accomplish the same amount of work with fewer people and coping with the emotional dimensions of downsizing (Mullaney, 1989). Employees who survive the downsizing or merger will grieve over the loss of their co-workers. Management must devote time to rebuilding confidence and trust among those who remain. Time must be devoted to listening to employee concerns and maintaining open communication with all levels of the organization. Kazemek and Channon (1988a) recommend a series of open forums for employees on all shifts to assist with the rebuilding efforts.

Conclusion

The changes that herald the 21st century will have an impact on every part of work life. Managers who recognize these changes and address them with sensitivity will be promoting the interests of staff, protecting the interests of patients or clients, and advancing the efficient delivery of health care. As key players within the organizations of health care, nurse managers have the opportunity and the challenge to ensure that human resource management is informed, effective, and caring.

References

Bland Jones, C. (1990). Staff nurse turnover costs: Part II, measurements and results. *Journal of Nursing Administration, 20*(5), 27-32.

Bruce, A., & Patterson, D. (1987). Resizing hospital nursing organizations, an alternative to downsizing. *Nursing Management, 18*(11), 33-35.

Canadian Council on Multicultural Health. (1992). *Health care for Canadian pluralism: Towards equity in health.* Downsview, ON: Author.

Canadian Nurses Association. (1971). *Countdown 1971.* Ottawa: Author.

Conlow, R. (1991). *Excellence in management.* Los Altos, CA: Crisp Publications.

Department of Manpower and Immigration. (1971). *Canadian classification and dictionary of occupations* (Vol. 1-2). Ottawa: Minister of Manpower & Immigration.

Employment and Immigration Canada. (1980). *Canadian classification and dictionary of occupations: Major occupations in major groups* (Cat. No. MP53-1/23-1980E). Ottawa: Minister of Supply & Services.

Employment and Immigration Canada. (1989). *Canadian classification and dictionary of occupations: Guide* (Cat. No. MP53-8/1989E). Ottawa: Minister of Supply & Services.

Employment and Immigration Canada. (1993). *National occupational classification* (2 vols.) (Cat. No. MP53-25/1-1993E). Ottawa: Minister of Supply & Services.

Fink, C. A. (1988). The impact of mergers on employees. *Health Care Supervisor, 7*(1), 59-67.

Fottler, M. D., & Schuler, D. W. (1984). Reducing the economic and human costs of layoffs. *Business Horizons, 37*(4), 9-15.

Haywood, B. (1990). Job reduction: Downsizing or rightsizing. *Journal of Healthcare Material Management, 8*(6), 24-26.

Heslin, K.A., & Faux, S.A. (1991a). The staff nurse employment interview selection process: Judgement and decision errors and how to avoid them. Part I. *Canadian Journal of Nursing Administration, 4*(4), 25-29.

Heslin, K.A., & Faux, S.A. (1991b). The staff nurse employment interview: Predicting performance outcomes. Part II. *Canadian Journal of Nursing Administration, 4*(4), 30-36.

Jesseph, S.A. (1989). Employee termination, 2: Some do's and don'ts. *Personnel, 66*(2), 36-38.

Kazemek, E.A., & Channon, B.S. (1988a). Avoiding the trauma of organizational downsizing. *Healthcare Financial Management, 42*(5), 40-46.

Kazemek, E.A., & Channon, B.S. (1988b). Nine steps to hospital downsizing. *Healthcare Financial Management, 12*(12), 96,98.

Kelly, J. (1986). *Canadian recruitment management handbook.* Don Mills, ON: Commerce Clearing House Canadian Limited.

Leahey, M., & Henderson, G. (1991). When nurses terminate: The exit interview/questionnaire. *Nursing Economics, 9*(5), 336-342.

McKeown, A., & Novak-Jandrey, M.L. (Eds.). (1991). *Human resource management in the health care setting.* Chicago: American Hospital Association.

Mirvis, P.H., & Kanter, D.K. (1991). Beyond demography: A psychographic profile of the workforce. *Human Resource Management, 30*(1), 45-69.

Mullaney, A.D. (1989). Downsizing: How one hospital responded to decreasing demand. *Health Care Management Review, 14*(3), 41-48.

Nollen, S.D. (1989). The work-family dilemma: How HR managers can help. *Personnel, 66*(5), 25-30.

Pattan, J.E. (1992). Developing a nurse recruitment plan. *Journal of Nursing Administration, 22*(1), 33-39.

Posner, B.Z., & Munson, J.M. (1979). The importance of personal values in understanding organizational behaviour. *Journal of Human Resource Management, 18,* 9-14.

Prescott, P.A., & Bowen, S.A. (1987). Controlling nursing turnover. *Nursing Management, 18*(6), 60, 62-66.

Rothman, M. (1989). Employee termination, 1: A four step procedure. *Personnel, 66*(2), 31-35.

Schneider, B., & Konz, A. (1989). Strategic job analysis. *Human Resource Management, 28*(1), 51-63.

Statistics Canada. (1977). *Perspective Canada II* (Cat. No.11- 508E). Ottawa: Author.

Statistics Canada. (1988). *Nursing in Canada 1986* (Cat. No. 83-226). Ottawa: Author.

Statistics Canada. (1989). *Canadians and their occupations: A profile* (Cat. No. 93-157). Ottawa: Author.

Statistics Canada. (1990). *Ethnic diversity in Canada* (Cat. No. 98-132). Ottawa: Author.

Statistics Canada. (1992a). *Nursing in Canada 1991* (Cat. No. 82-003S22). Ottawa: Author.

Statistics Canada. (1992b). *A national overview* (Cat. No. 93-301). Ottawa Author.

Statistics Canada. (1993a). *Ethnic origin* (Cat. No. 93-315). Ottawa: Author.

Statistics Canada. (1993b). *Nursing in Canada 1992* (Cat. No. 83-243). Ottawa: Author.

Tomasko, R. (1987). *Downsizing: Reshaping the corporation of the future.* New York: American Management Association.

Towers Perrin. (1992). *Achieving employee commitment: The power of communication* (Teleconference, December 14, 1992, 90 Gerrard St. W.). Toronto: Telemedicine Canada.

Tutton, J. (1989). Evaluating exit interviews. *Nursing Times, 85*(49), 46-48.

Urbanowski, R. (1992). Excellence in diversity. *Leadership, 1*(6), 19-21.

Van Sumeren, M. (1986). Organizational downsizing: Streamlining the healthcare organization. *Health Care Management Review, 40*(1), 35-39.

Wanous, J.P. (1973). Effects of a realistic job preview on job acceptance, job attitudes, and job survival. *Journal of Applied Psychology, 58*(3), 327-332.

Wanous, J.P. (1980). *Organizational entry, recruitment selection and socialization of new comers.* Toronto: Addison-Wesley.

Whitis, R., & Whitis, G. (1983). The exit interview: A nursing management tool. *Journal of Nursing Administration, 13*(10), 13-16.

C H A P T E R 2 7

Interdisciplinary Teams and Group Process

Dorothy M. Wylie

Dorothy M. Wylie, RN, BScN (New York), MA (Columbia), MSc(HRD) (American University), is a consultant in organizational and management development and Associate Professor (part-time), Faculty of Nursing, University of Toronto. She also is editor of the *Canadian Journal of Nursing Administration*.

Health care settings of the 1990s are complex environments, serving clients with multiple and diverse health care needs. The aging population and the increasing number of persons with chronic illnesses demand a blend of services to meet medical, nursing, rehabilitative, psychosocial, and recreational needs. No single discipline has the expertise and capability to provide the necessary services. Interdisciplinary teams, who can work together in a collaborative manner, are an essential requirement to meet the current and future needs of the patient population.

The author of this chapter will describe the group process as a background to a discussion of interdisciplinary teams and the collaborative process. Models of group development are presented, along with the characteristics of an effective team. The role and function of the nurse manager as a team leader and team member are outlined.

Overview of Group Dynamics

Luft (1970) defines group dynamics as the "study of individuals interacting in small groups" (p. 1). A group can consist of two or more people who perceive themselves as a group; the key element in group dynamics is the interaction that occurs among individuals. Groups come together to achieve a purpose through communication and inter-action. An individual usually belongs to several groups, such as in the home, workplace, classroom, associations, and clubs.

People often join groups to meet their own needs for affiliation, self-esteem, or recognition, as well as to undertake a task. Membership in the group then becomes important in terms of fulfilling these needs and providing a source of satisfaction for the individual.

Group Structure

A group is a social system with its own boundaries, structure, and culture. Dimock (1987) points out that the structure and culture of the group become so firmly established that it is extremely difficult to change the usual ways of doing business once they have begun. In fact, it may be easier to start a new group than to get an existing group to change behaviours.

Group membership tends to become inclusive for the members and exclusive for those who are not members. Nonmembers then may be viewed as outsiders. Groups can be powerful forces that influence the individual within the group, as well as those outside the group.

Size of the group can be a significant factor. Group interaction tends to decrease as the number of persons in the group increases (Zander, 1986). As a result, persons who belong to large groups are often less satisfied with membership in the group, as there is less opportunity for participation and interaction. Large groups with lim-ited interaction allow the group member to feel anonymous, which often results in lack of cooperation.

Basic Functions of Group Process

Tasks, interaction, and self-orientation are the three basic functions that affect the group process (Boshear & Albrecht, 1977). Task behav-iours achieve the goals of the group and can be called the work of the group. They might include such activities as gathering facts, develop-ing goals, sharing information, clarifying issues, or reaching consen-sus in problem solving. Interactions form the group process, or how the group performs as a group. Communicating, expressing feelings, attempting to resolve disagreements, and establishing the norms of behaviour for the group make up these activities. Self-oriented behav-iours are those which group members use to meet their individual needs. They may not always be useful to achievement of group goals or to positive interaction. Members may dwell on personal concerns and issues, waste time, dominate the discussion, have side conversa-tions with others, not listen, or continually interrupt.

These three basic functions may be carried out in either a direct or an indirect way. Direct activities are open, and reasons for behaviour are shared with the group, resulting in open communication, open participation; they reveal personal needs and wishes, and lead to frank discussion of interpersonal issues. Indirect activities, often called "hidden agendas," are covert behaviours and not openly shared with the group. Undercover behaviours—such as undermining projects, making hidden agreements with other members, promoting personal needs above others, and suppressing or avoiding interpersonal issues—may be played out. Hidden agendas exist in most groups. All groups have both surface agendas and hidden agendas, and work at both at the same time (Bradford, 1978). Groups may work well superficially, when the hidden agenda is resting or has been settled. However, in the event of a crisis the hidden agendas will surface again. Hidden agendas may arise around the group task, group leadership, or the individual member, and can be anticipated in any group.

Groups often form norms of behaviour early in their development. Norms are the expectations of the group about how their members behave in achieving a task. Norms may be formalized into written statements of procedure or may be informal and unexpressed. Regardless of their format, norms can strongly influence an individual's behaviour in a group. When groups demand strict adherence to group norms, there is a high degree of conformity and cohesiveness. In some situations this is positive; in others, it may not be constructive and can lead to "groupthink." This term was coined by Janis (1983) and is defined as extreme concurrence; it may produce poor group decisions by limiting exploration of various alternative solutions to the problem.

Group Roles

Dimock (1985) outlines 14 roles that group members carry out to achieve the functions of the group (see Table 27.1, page 504). The task roles, and the group-building and maintenance roles, contain 11 functions, all of which are essential to development of the group. The self-orientation role is carried out through three individual functions. Group roles can be assessed through group observation and keeping a record of the roles that each member plays.

Group Leadership

Studies have shown that leadership styles can range from an autocratic, authoritarian style to a democratic, more participative style. Situational leadership theory (Hersey & Blanchard, 1982) presents the idea that leadership style needs to vary according to the situation and the readiness of followers to undertake the task. Readiness is defined as the person's ability and willingness to take on the task.

Table 27.1
Roles of group members.

Task Functions

1. Defines problems. Group problem is defined; overall purpose of group is defined.

2. Seeks information. Requests factual information about group problem, methods to be used, or clarifies a suggestion.

3. Gives information. Offers facts or general information about group problem, methods to be used, or clarifies a suggestion.

4. Seeks opinions. Asks for the opinions of others relevant to discussion.

5. Gives opinions. States beliefs or opinions relevant to discussion.

6. Tests feasibility. Questions reality, checks practicality of suggested solutions.

Group-Building and Maintenance Functions

7. Coordinating. A recent statement is clarified and related to another statement in such a way as to bring them together. Proposed alternatives are reviewed.

8. Mediating/harmonizing. Interceding in disputes or disagreements and attempting to reconcile them. Highlights similarities in views.

9. Orienting/facilitating. Keeps group on track, points out deviations from agreed upon procedures or from direction of group discussion. Helping group progress along, proposing other procedures to make group more effective.

10. Supporting/encouraging. Expressing approval of another's suggestion, praising others' ideas, being warm and responsive to ideas of others.

11. Following. Going along with the movement of the group, accepting ideas of others, expressing agreement.

Individual Functions

12. Blocking. Interfering with the progress of the group by arguing, resisting, or disagreeing beyond reason, or by coming back to same "dead" issue later.

13. Out of field. Withdrawing from discussion, daydreaming, doing something else, whispering to others, leaving room, etc.

14. Digressing. Getting off the subject, leading discussion in some personally oriented direction, or making a brief statement into a long, nebulous speech.

Source: Reprinted with permission from H.G. Dimock (1985), *How to observe your group* (2nd ed.). Guelph, ON: University of Guelph.

Building on this notion, Dimock (1987) suggests that the appropriate leadership style is determined by the followers and the situation. He advises group leaders to start groups off with a more structured and directive approach. At the same time, the leader should assess the abilities of the group members and then slowly move along the continuum to a more facilitative coaching style according to member readiness.

Models of Group Development

There are many models of group development (Bales, 1950; Bion, 1961; Jones, 1974; Lacoursiere, 1974; Schutz, 1958; Tuckman, 1965). It is commonly accepted that groups move through identifiable stages during their development. Basically, every group will proceed along a continuum of independence through dependence on to interdependence. Often groups become bogged down in the early stages of development and cannot proceed along the continuum to interdependence, where group members share roles and functions.

Each model describes the task and interpersonal behaviours that a group undergoes as it moves through the stages. The stages are categorized by different labels in each of the models. However, the basic premise is that every group does move from one stage to another, and that movement through the stages depends upon whether the concerns of the group in the present stage are dealt with and resolved. Each stage has concerns related to personal, interpersonal, and task issues. Where these concerns are not dealt with and resolved, they will continue to reappear each time the group comes together to deal with a problem or critical issue.

Jones's (1974) model depicts group growth along the two dimensions of personal relations and task functions (see Figure 27.1, page 506). Groups will move through the four stages of the two dimensions. Progress or setbacks at each stage of the personal or task dimension will influence group development. Orientation to the task is stage 1. This stage reflects a dependency on the leader to guide and direct members. At stage 2, members begin to organize their own approach to the task. Conflict may develop among members at stage 2 as differing ideas, methods, and behaviours begin to surface. In stage 3, as some level of trust begins to emerge and members get to know each other better, there is movement toward group cohesion. Information begins to flow as members share perceptions, feelings, and ideas at the task level as well as the personal level. Stage 4 indicates interdependence as members begin to feel more comfortable in working together, can openly share and communicate, and can work toward a higher level of problem solving.

Figure 27.1
Four stages of group development.

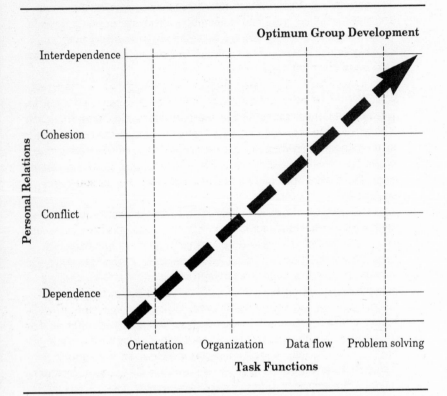

Source: Reprinted from J.W. Pfeiffer (Ed.) (1991), *Theories and models in applied behavioral science* (Vol. 2). San Diego: Pfeiffer & Company. Used with permission.

Schutz (1958) developed a three-stage model based on interpersonal relations and identified the stages as inclusion, control, and independence. Movement through the stages is perceived to occur in a cyclical manner rather than along a straightforward linear line.

Tuckman (1965) proposed a developmental model of group process. The model identified four stages, which were labeled forming, storming, norming, and performing. Later work (Tuckman & Jensen, 1977) added a fifth stage, adjourning. The forming stage is the orientation time when members seek guidance from the leader and direction on rules and functions and determine their commitment to the group. The storming stage is characterized by competition and conflict with resistance to other members' roles and ideas. Members experience discomfort in this stage; some become passive and others vocal and hostile. During the norming phase, a sense of cohesion starts to develop; team members buy into the group as trust and open communication emerge. There can be a sense of energy and creativity. The performing stage is one of interdependence, where group goals and roles are clear, yet flexible. Members are more confident, morale is good, and productivity related to task is high. The final stage of adjournment involves task completion and giving up of relationships developed among the group.

Lacoursiere (1974) identified four stages of group development, and categorized them as orientation (the group has fairly strong positive expectations accompanied by fears and anxieties); dissatisfaction (the group experiences increasing frustration, and a sense of depression and anger); production (a more realistic view of what the group might be able to accomplish is developed); and termination (where the group feels sadness at parting and attempts to carry out some self-evaluation).

Regardless of the model chosen to illustrate group development, specific elements must be in place for groups to be effective. The goals of the group need to be clear and will need to be clarified from time to time to keep the group on track. The necessary group roles and functions must be carried out to maintain the life of the group. Every group member has a responsibility to see that the functions are fulfilled. Open, two-way communication is essential and should provide opportunities for members to express perceptions and feelings as well as ideas. Positive norms need to be established to create a climate of trust and to allow for participation by each member of the group. There should be opportunities for leadership of the group to be spread among the members and to alternate according to the skill requirements needed, the functions to be fulfilled, and the abilities of the group members.

Health Care Teams

Larson and LaFasto (1989) define teams as consisting of two or more people with specific performance objectives or goals to be achieved. Teamwork or coordination of activity between or among members is required for the attainment of the objectives or goals. Teams may be intradisciplinary or interdisciplinary. An interdisciplinary team is made up of members of different professions (such as medicine, nursing, pharmacy, psychology, social work, or others). Ducanis and Golin (1979) describe the interdisciplinary team "as a functioning unit, composed of individuals with varied and specialized training, who coordinate their activities to provide services to a client or group of clients" (p. 3).

The interdisciplinary team has emerged over the past several decades to deal with clients' increasingly complex health and social needs that can no longer be met by an individual professional. Early beginnings of the team approach started in community and mental health and in child development and rehabilitation centres. Although the concept of interdisciplinary teams has been in place for many years, only recently have research and study been undertaken to examine the effectiveness and outcomes of the team approach.

Intradisciplinary teams are composed of members of the same profession, such as registered nurse and registered nursing assistant or licensed practical nurse. Team nursing, which began in the early 1950s, promoted the concept of teamwork among nursing staff members to provide care more efficiently and effectively to groups of patients during severe nursing shortages.

The team idea is now being revived as "nurse extenders" are being added to nursing teams to undertake non-nursing and routine nursing tasks to lighten the workload of the professional nurse.

Why Teams Don't Work

Common problems associated with interdisciplinary teamwork have been identified in the literature (Baggs et al., 1992; Briggs, 1991; Chavigny, 1988; Deber & Leatt, 1986; Ducanis & Golin, 1979; Fagin, 1992; Fried & Leatt, 1986; Fried, Leatt, Deber, & Wilson, 1988; Temkin-Greener, 1983). Such problems include: lack of clarity of roles; confusion over accountability; leadership issues; lack of clearly defined mutual goals; poor communication skills combined with inadequate problem-solving skills and inadequate decision-making methods; infringement of the disciplinary boundaries; and lack of conflict management skills. All these major issues contribute to the failure of teamwork. The group development models provide some insights into these issues. Many of these weaknesses of team function relate to lack of group process skills and poor management of the health care team function.

Ducanis and Golin (1979) use a team system model (Figure 27.2) to explore the various and complex dimensions of team interaction. The components are the team, the client, and the organizational setting (context). These three components affect the goals, activities, and outcomes of the team. The model is an open systems approach, which includes a feedback loop to provide information that will influence and change goals and activities.

Figure 27.2
The team system model.

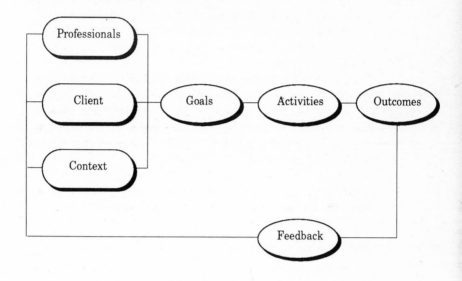

Source: Reprinted with permission from A.J. Ducanis and A.K. Golin (1979), *The interdisciplinary health care team: A handbook.* Germantown, MD: Aspen Systems.

The Professionals

The professionals who come together to make up an interdisciplinary team come to the table each bearing all the trademarks of their own professions. They have been educated and socialized into the professional norms and standards unique to their particular disciplines. Historically, rigid boundaries have existed around each professional discipline, and each member carries a personal perception of his or her own profession and of other professions. Distorted perceptions of others' roles, overlapping of roles, status issues, and varying points of view all contribute to interprofessional conflict and a poorly functioning team.

Traditional stereotypes colour interactions between professionals and can be illustrated by the "doctor-nurse game," described by Stein in 1967 (Stein, Watts, & Howell, 1990). Stein talked about the hierarchical relationship between doctors and nurses and interactions between the two that preserved a superior/subordinate relationship. Open disagreement between the two players was to be avoided at all costs. In communication and consultation, the nurse assumed a passive manner and made recommendations in a way that these appeared to be initiated by the physician rather than the nurse. Stein, Watts, and Howell (1990) describe the changing climate of organizations and of nurse-physician relationships. Nurses are now better educated, seek greater autonomy, and have a more equal relationship with physicians. The former hierarchical arrangements are beginning to crumble and dissolve—but at a rather slow pace.

Fagin (1992) promotes the need for greater collaboration between physicians and nurses and describes other barriers that contribute to tensions in the relationship. Elements that contribute to the complexity of the situation include: nursing's inability to describe, clearly, its role and scope of practice; differences in education level; sex-role stereotyping and gender differences; social differences; and status accorded to "hands-on" activities versus intellectual activities. The barriers outlined by Fagin are not unique to nurse-physician relationships. The same types of issues are played out between and among the other professional groups that make up the interdisciplinary team.

Deber and Leatt (1986) contrasted health care team members' perceptions of their ideal role in decision making with their perceptions of their actual role in decision making. Multidisciplinary renal teams across Canada and in Michigan were studied. The makeup of the teams consisted of nephrologists, physicians, surgeons, nurses, social workers, dietitians, and technicians. The findings showed that leadership of the team and the major responsibility and accountability for clinical decision making was assumed by the nephrologist. Others, mainly the semiprofessionals, submitted to the dominant profession, medicine. The ideal of a collaborative multidisciplinary renal team with equal representation and equal decision-making powers was maintained by the members. Despite this ideal, perceptions about the actual behaviour were quite different.

Where there are differences between perceptions of the ideal role and the actual role, role conflict and role ambiguity can occur. When the person who occupies the role cannot behave as he or she thinks appropriate, role deprivation results. Nurses have expressed feelings of role deprivation in numerous job satisfaction surveys. The result is burnout, frustration, and high turnover. Lack of role clarity among the group members contributes to dysfunction of the health care team.

Status differences among the professions tend to fuel issues around leadership of the team. Physicians often assume the leadership role because they are legally responsible for the patient. In terms of the goals of the health care team in relation to the needs of the patient, the physician may not always be the best person for the role.

In addition, the physician may lack the necessary group skills to ensure a well-functioning team.

In summary, the characteristics of the professional role accompanied by traditional hierarchical relationships among professions can produce conflict in the team and lead to a dysfunctional group in terms of meeting the goals of the client and the health care team.

The Client

Traditionally, the client has not been seen as part of the interdisciplinary team. As consumers become more vocal and knowledgeable, they wish to be actively involved in decisions affecting their own health and have begun to be included in team activities. Not only the client, but the family and significant others are now being included.

Spitzer and Roberts (1980) raised several questions as to whether people are better off being cared for by teams. Such questions include: Do teams further depersonalize medical care? Do patients prefer health teams? Do they have a choice?

Ducanis and Golin (1979) pointed out that the relationship between client and individual professional becomes diluted in the team approach. There is an impact on both patient and professional. Clients may feel less structure and support with the group approach, and a loss of a one-to-one relationship. There is the possibility that the client can receive conflicting information from various team members. The team conference with the client present is a more formalized approach to communication and may inhibit team interaction and openness. I have observed team conferences where communication seems stiff and formal, and each discipline tends to speak for its particular set of goals for the client, rather than a more holistic, goal-oriented approach. Some patients and families may feel intimidated by the size and professional composition of the group and, therefore, may not see the process as helpful or supportive to them.

Little study of client satisfaction with interdisciplinary teams has been carried out, and it would be useful to undertake such studies to determine the effectiveness of this approach, as well as the effectiveness of the health care team.

The Context

Organizations are defined social systems built on a mission statement and based on a philosophy or set of values. Each is, therefore, somewhat unique and displays its own culture and climate. Teams are developed within that particular culture to achieve the goals and objectives set by the organization to achieve its mission.

However, the reality of health care in the 1990s is the need to face rising costs and increasingly restrained resources. Hospitals are abandoning traditional hierarchical structures and functional departments and moving to more decentralized organizational approaches. Program management is emerging with organizational structures focussing on clinical programs (such as rehabilitation services, cardiovascular services, women's and children's health). A clinical and administrative team is set up to manage the programs and build on the concept of the interdisciplinary team. The result of the breakdown of functional departments (for example, nursing, pharmacy, social work) is a further blurring of roles and the boundaries between disciplines. Where functional departments remain in place, the individual team member assumes a dual reporting relationship to the program head and to the discipline head, and this can lead to conflicting values and goals. Each program has its own goals and objectives, which may or may not be synonymous with those of the total organization. Working in these newer organizational structures, which allow greater authority and accountability for the use of human and physical resources, places even greater pressure on the health care team and reinforces the need for each member to become proficient in group membership skills to ensure efficient and effective performance.

Organizations may not be structured to support team work. Hackman (1990) points out that groups cannot flourish where members have multiple tasks to perform, where staff assignments continually shift or group membership changes, and where organizational rewards are based on the individual rather than the team. Under these conditions, issues about quality of service arise and tension develops about how to work effectively and efficiently within limited time constraints.

Health care teams associated with teaching hospitals face another set of issues when team members are learners and move in and out of teams on a rotating basis. The learners not only may lack group skills, but also may be weak in the clinical expertise they bring to the group and therefore lack credibility in the group. Changing membership in the group contributes to the difficulty in moving on to a productive stage of group development.

Characteristics of Effective Teams

Regardless of the particular task or purpose of the group or team, Hackman (1990) suggests that there are three main dimensions to group effectiveness: productivity; the process of the work; and the personal well-being of the members. In terms of productivity, the results of the group's work need to conform to a standard of quality, quantity, and timeliness for the client; in other words, to the satisfaction of the client. The process of doing the work should contribute to the members' satisfaction with the way they interact and achieve the purpose of the group. A relationship is established whereby members enjoy the work and want to continue to work together. Individual group members want to feel that they personally have grown and developed throughout the process and have had learning opportunities that contribute to their well-being.

Groups are a social system and as such, will behave according to the climate they have created. Therefore, those who develop work groups need to focus on creating conditions that will support effective team work. Collaborative effort, or working well together, flourishes in a climate of trust. Trust occurs in an environment that contains: honesty and integrity; openness and willingness to share and receive information; consistency of responses and behaviour; and respect by treating each other with fairness and dignity (Larson & LaFasto, 1989).

Varney (1989) describes successful teams as having the following characteristics:

1. *Team member roles are clear to each person, as well as to others on the team, and individuals are committed to their jobs and accept and support the roles of others.*

2. *Individuals have goals (performance measures) that they have agreed to. The sum of individual goals adds up to the team goals.*

3. *Structure, practices, policies, and systems are understood and agreed to by all members.*

4. *Work relations are seen as an essential part of an effective work team; therefore, they are discussed, and interpersonal problems are solved and not left to fester.* (pp. 7-8)

Building Effective Work Teams

Nurse managers have multiple roles in connection with work teams. First and foremost, they are the leaders of the work group on the nursing unit. Unit team effectiveness, patient satisfaction and outcomes, and staff satisfaction are all major components of the role. Further to this, the manager and the unit staff participate in one or more interdisciplinary teams, as well as serving on numerous committees and task forces, both interdisciplinary and intradisciplinary in makeup. The manager may take a leadership role in some cases or membership role in others. Regardless of which, it is essential that the nurse manager develop knowledge, skill, and expertise related to the group process and group development.

Varney (1989) believes that the manager must know what constitutes effective team work, and must also develop the abilities to observe, diagnose, and problem-solve to promote effectiveness. As a team leader, the manager needs to know the abilities and readiness of team members to take on the responsibility of the task, as well as adjust his or her leadership style to fit the situation. As groups become empowered and self-managed, leaders need to know when to step aside and let go. The leader may then assume the follower role, being mindful that the test of good leadership is good followership.

Teams have a life of their own, as demonstrated in the various models of group development. Knowledge about stages of group development and awareness of strategies to shape the course of development are vital strengths that nurse managers need to acquire.

References

Baggs, J.G., Ryan, S.A., Phelps, C.E., Richeson, J.F., & Johnson, J. (1992). The association between interdisciplinary collaboration and patient outcomes. *Heart & Lung, 21*(1), 18-24.

Bales, R.F. (1950). *Interaction process analysis: A method for the study of small groups.* Reading, MA: Addison-Wesley.

Bion, R.W. (1961). *Experiences in groups.* New York: Basic Books.

Boshear, W.C., & Albrecht, K.G. (1977). *Understanding people: Models and concepts.* San Diego: University Associates.

Bradford, L.P. (1978). *Group development* (2nd ed.). San Diego: University Associates.

Briggs, M.H. (1991). Team development: Decision-making for early intervention. *Infant-Toddler Intervention: The Transdisciplinary Journal, 1*(1), 1-9.

Chavigny, K.H. (1988). Coalition building between medicine and nursing. *Nursing Economics, 6*(4), 179-184.

Deber, R., & Leatt, P. (1986). The multidisciplinary renal team: Who makes the decisions? *Health Matrix, 4*(3), 3-9.

Dimock, H.G. (1985). *How to observe your group* (2nd ed.). Guelph, ON: University of Guelph.

Dimock, H.G. (1987). Groups: *Leadership and group development* (rev. ed.). San Diego: University Associates.

Ducanis, A.J., & Golin, A.K. (1979). *Interdisciplinary health care team: A handbook.* Germantown, MD: Aspen Systems.

Fagin, C.M. (1992). Collaboration between nurses & physicians: No longer a choice. *Nursing & Health Care, 13*(7), 354-363.

Fried, B.J., & Leatt, P. (1986). Role perceptions among occupational groups in an ambulatory care setting. *Human Relations, 39*(12), 1155-1173.

Fried, B.J., Leatt, P., Deber, R., & Wilson, E. (1988). Multidisciplinary teams in health care: Lessons from oncology and renal teams. *Healthcare Management Forum, 1*(4), 28-34.

Hackman, J.R. (1990). *Groups that work (and those that don't): Creating conditions for effective teamwork.* San Francisco: Jossey-Bass.

Hersey, P., & Blanchard, K. (1982). *Management of organizational behavior: Utilizing human resources* (4th ed.). Englewood Cliffs, NJ: Prentice-Hall.

Janis, I.L. (1983). *Groupthink* (2nd ed.). Boston: Houghton Mifflin.

Jones, J.E. (1974). A model of group development. In J.W. Pfeiffer (Ed.) (1991), *Theories and models in applied behavioral science* (Vol.2). San Diego: University Associates.

Lacoursiere, R.B. (1974). A group method to facilitate learning during the stages of psychiatric affiliation. *International Journal of Group Psychotherapy, 24,* 342-351.

Lacoursiere, R.B. (1980). *The life cycle of groups: Group development stage theory.* New York: Human Science Press.

Larson, C.E., & LaFasto, F. (1989). *Teamwork: What must go right/what can go wrong.* Newbury Park, CA: Sage.

Luft, J. (1970). *Group processes: An introduction to group dynamics* (2nd ed.). Palo Alto, CA: Mayfield.

Ornstein, H. J. (1990). Collaborative practice between Ontario nurses and physicians: Is it possible? *Canadian Journal of Nursing Administration, 3*(4),10-14.

Schutz, W. (1958). *Firo: A three dimensional theory of interpersonal behavior.* New York: Holt, Rinehart & Winston.

Spitzer, W.O., & Roberts, R.F. (1980). Twelve questions about teams in health services. *Journal of Community Health, 6*(1), 1-5.

Stein, L.I., Watts, D.T., & Howell, T. (1990). The doctor-nurse game revisited. *The New England Journal of Medicine, 322*(8), 546-549.

Temkin-Greener, H. (1983). Interprofessional perspectives on teamwork in health care: A case study. *Milbank Memorial Fund Quarterly, 61*(4), 641-658.

Tuckman, B.W. (1965). Developmental sequence in small groups. *Psychological Bulletin, 63*(6), 384-399.

Tuckman, B.W., & Jensen, M.A. (1977). Stages of small group development revisited. *Group & Organization Studies, 2*(4), 419-427.

Varney, G.H. (1989). *Building productive teams.* San Francisco: Jossey-Bass.

Zander, A. (1986). *Making groups effective.* San Francisco: Jossey-Bass.

C   H   A   P   T   E   R   2   8

Management of Nursing Information

Kathryn J. Hannah and Betty J. Anderson

Kathryn J. Hannah, RN, BSN, MSN (Medical College of Georgia), PhD (Alberta), is Director, Information, Management Consulting Branch, Alberta Health, and Professor, Department of Community Health Sciences, Faculty of Medicine, University of Calgary.

Betty J. Anderson, RN, BScN, MN, is a Clinical Nurse Specialist in Critical Care at the Royal Alexandra Hospital, Edmonton.

The focus of this chapter is on nursing's role in managing information in health care facilities. It will focus on the *use* of information, *not* on information systems (i.e., the hardware, software, selection, or implementation). Detailed information and discussion of nursing responsibilities, roles, and contributions to selection and implementation of information systems in health care organizations are beyond the scope of this chapter. The issues for nurses no longer relate to computers or management information systems, but rather to information and information management. The computer and its associated software are merely tools to support nurses as they practise their profession.

Far too much attention has been directed to the technology rather than its content (i.e., the data and information requirements of nurses). Current hospital information systems do little to assist nurses in their real role, which is providing nursing care. Nurses must be able to manage and process nursing data, information, and knowledge to support patient care delivery in diverse care delivery settings (Graves & Corcoran, 1989). To accomplish this goal, nurses must attend to the content (the data) contained in information systems and stop being distracted by the glamour and romance of the technology.

The information management role for nursing is, of necessity, related to the role of nursing within the organization. In most hospitals, nurses manage both patient care and patient care units within the organization. Usually, nurse clinicians manage patient care, and nurse managers administer the patient care units. Therefore, for some time, nursing's role in management of information generally has been considered to include the information necessary to manage patient care using the nursing process *and* the information necessary for managing patient care units within the organization (e.g., resource allocation and utilization, personnel management, planning and policy making, and decision support).

Nursing practice is information intensive. Nurses constantly handle enormous volumes of patient care information. In fact, they constantly process information mentally, manually, and electronically. Nurses have long been recognized as the interface between the patient and the health care organization. They integrate information from many diverse sources throughout the organization to provide patient care and to coordinate the patient's contact with health care facilities. They manage patient care information for purposes of providing nursing care. There is also a long-standing tradition that nurses have the role of custodians of information on behalf of other caregivers and users of patient information. A classic study of three New York hospitals found that registered nurses spend from 36% to 64% of their time on information handling, with those in administrative positions spending the most time (Jydstrup & Gross, 1966).

A major factor that influences nursing's role in managing patient care environments is the patient assignment methodology in use in the hospital or on the individual patient care units (see Chapter 17). Each of these patient assignment methodologies requires a different nursing role in managing patient care information and, consequently, different information management skills for the nurses involved.

Similarly, nursing's role in managing information for purposes of administering patient care units is influenced by the role of the nurse managers within the organization. Variations in decision making, patient assignment, documentation protocols, and institutional governance style all affect nursing's role in information management for administrative purposes. However, the single most important element that determines nursing's role in information management for administrative purposes is the governance model in use in the hospital (see Chapter 11).

Obstacles to Effective Nursing Management of Information

In most hospitals, the three major obstacles to more effective nursing management of information are: the sheer volume of information, the lack of access to modern information handling techniques and equipment, and the inadequate information management infrastructure. The volume of information that nurses manage on a daily basis, either for patient care purposes or organizational management purposes, is enormous and continues to grow. Nurses continue to respond to this growth with great mental agility. However, human beings have limits, and one of the major sources of job dissatisfaction among nurses is information overload, resulting in information-induced job stress.

Antiquated manual information systems (e.g., hand writing the order, requisition, medication card, and kardex entry for each medication) and outdated information transfer facilities (e.g., nurses hand carrying requisitions and specimens for stat blood work to the lab on nights because the pneumatic tube system and the portering system are not available between the hours of 24:00 and 07:00) are information-redundant and labour-intensive processes, to say nothing of an inappropriate use of an expensive human resource. Modern information transfer and electronic communication systems allow rapid and accurate transfer of information along electronic communication networks.

Software and hardware for modern electronic communication networks are only two aspects of an information infrastructure. The other major lack in most hospitals is the absence of appropriate support staff to facilitate information management. These support staff require expertise both in information systems and in a solid understanding of their use in the health care system and its organizations and institutions. Similarly, financial and statistical support staff are necessary to help nursing managers analyze and interpret information appropriately.

Issues Related to Effective Nursing Management of Information

Primary among the nursing issues related to information management is the lack of adequate educational programs in information management techniques and strategies for nursing managers. At the time of writing, only a few preservice nursing education programs offer courses in modern information management techniques and strategies related to nursing. At a minimum, such a program must include advanced study of information management techniques and strategies, such as information flow analysis and use of spreadsheets, databases, and word processing packages. Ideally, such courses would also introduce concepts and provide hands-on experience related to use of patient care information systems.

Nursing involvement and participation in selection and installation of patient care information systems and financial management systems are imperative. Regrettably, many senior nurse managers fail to recognize the importance of such participation and opt out of the process. They then complain when the systems do not meet the needs of nursing. Senior nursing executives must recognize the importance of allocating staff and money to participation in the strategic planning process for information systems in their organizations. Other senior management personnel also must recognize the importance of including nursing input into the strategic planning process for information systems. In any hospital, nurses are the single largest group of professionals using a patient care system, and nursing represents the largest part of the budget requiring financial management. Nursing, therefore, represents the single largest stakeholder group related to either a patient care information system or a financial information system.

Nurses have been involved in management of nursing information since the initial systems for gathering minimum uniform health data, which can be traced back to systems devised by Florence Nightingale more than a century ago (Verley, 1970). This early role in management of nursing information began to change dramatically with the introduction of computers into health care and nursing environments. The role evolved as nurses became more involved in selection and use of information systems. These developments have been well documented elsewhere (Hannah, Ball, & Edwards, 1994).

Despite Nightingale's early attempts to develop a nursing database, nurses in Canada have yet to define the minimum set of data elements essential to the practice of nursing. In fact, at the time this chapter was written, in Canada there are absolutely no nursing data elements that are collected and stored provincially or nationally for use in decision making related to health policy or resource allocation. These data gaps have been recognized, and Canadian nurses have developed a heightened awareness of the importance of collection, storage, and retrieval of nursing data. Attention is now being directed at initiating the process by which the nursing profession in Canada will begin to address the essential data needs of nurses in all practice settings (Canadian Nurses Association [CNA], 1990).

The patient discharge abstracts prepared by medical records departments across Canada and the United States currently contain no nursing care delivery information. The abstracts therefore fail to acknowledge the contribution of nursing during the patient's stay in the hospital. This omission is important because the abstracts are used by many agencies for a variety of purposes, including funding allocation and policy making. Much information vital to determination of costs of hospitalization and effectiveness of nursing care in achieving appropriate patient outcomes is being lost.

At a time when considerable emphasis is being placed on the development of a national health database in Canada, it is important that a minimum number of essential nursing elements be included in that database. In Canada, these nursing data elements are beginning to be referred to as the *Nursing Components of Health Information*. Such a set of data elements would be similar to the uniquely nursing elements included in the Nursing Minimum Data Set currently being tested in the United States. The purposes of the Nursing Minimum Data Set are "to establish comparability of nursing data across clinical populations, settings, geographic areas, and time; to describe the nursing care of patients and their families in both inpatient and outpatient settings; to show or project trends regarding nursing care needs and allocation of nursing resources according to nursing diagnoses; and to stimulate nursing research" (Werley, Devine, & Zorn, 1988, p. 1652). Such data are essential because they allow description of the health status of populations with relation to nursing care needs, establish outcome measures for nursing care, and investigate the use and cost of nursing resources. The nursing profession must provide leadership in defining appropriate nursing data elements to be included in the national health database, specifically through the patient discharge abstract. In Canada, there is a need to extend the use of the concept of the Nursing Components of Health Information.

Thus, the salient issue in information management for nurses in Canada is that of identification of nursing data elements that are essential for collection and storage in a national health database. These data elements must reflect the data that nurses use to build information that is the foundation for clinical judgement and management decision making in any setting where nursing is practised.

The remainder of this chapter will focus on the issue of defining those data elements essential to the practice of nursing.

Contextual Factors Influencing Development of Health Information in Canada

Canadians have a unique health care system, one that is the envy of many countries. One thing that makes the Canadian health care system unique is the belief in health as a right—not a privilege or an economic commodity, but rather a right for Canadians. This philosophy is reflected in the principles on which the health system is based and legislated through the Canada Health Act. These principles include: universality, portability, accessibility, comprehensiveness, and public administration.

Unfortunately, the health system is presently in a box analogous to the room in which Alice in Wonderland finds herself when she begins to grow. Alice grows until the room becomes too small. One gets the same feeling about the health system right now. The system is under enormous pressures, as depicted in Figure 28.1 (see page 522). Provincial revenues have been decreased as a function of the worldwide economic recession. This decrease is contributing to the erosion of the tax base. Furthermore, the reduction in federal/provincial transfer payments is resulting in diminished provincial revenues across the country. In addition, there are expectations of new programs necessitated by the kinds of conditions and people using the provincial health systems.

New technologies are being developed, such as lithotripters, laser colposcopy, and major organ transplants (e.g., heart, lung, and kidney). New treatment modalities and new programs are being devised. These initiatives are enabling patients to survive who, 10 years ago, would have died. Consequently, patients in Canadian hospitals are much sicker than were those patients in hospital even five years ago. Simultaneously, profound demographic changes are occurring as baby boomers move through the aging process. The result of all of these factors will be an increase in the cost of health care for an increasingly aging population.

There is also a shifting paradigm in terms of the value and emphasis placed on community-based practice. The emphasis is moving away from acute care hospitals to community-based care and

Figure 28.1
Pressures affecting the health care system.

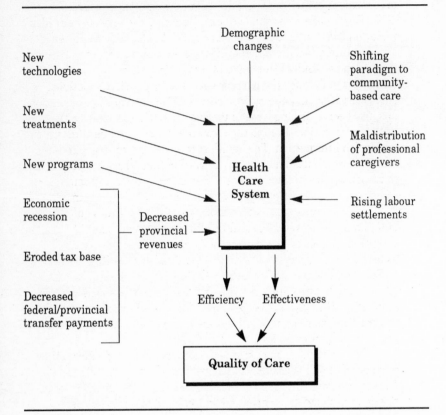

treatment, with a corresponding emphasis on health promotion and disease prevention. At the same time, Canada has a poor geographical distribution of caregivers, and also a poor distribution by specialty, whether it be nurses, physicians, dentists, or other health care providers. Accompanying all these issues are salary expectations. Until very recently, labour settlements have continued to include rising salaries despite erosions in health care budgets; now, labour unions in the health care sector are struggling to prevent erosion of past salary gains and to promote job security. There also are increased demands for services from a more knowledgeable public, and this places a further burden on the health care system. The overall picture is one in which the expenses and costs associated with health care are rising and the resources available to pay for health care in Canada are being reduced. Nurse managers need to find ways in which nurses can be more efficient and more effective and can maximize the quality of care that is available to patients within available resources. Nurse managers must identify strategies to provide enhanced information management to facilitate use of the ever diminishing resources.

These, then, are some factors influencing the drive toward identification of essential data needs of nurses. In Canada, the information revolution has prompted initiatives by health care organizations to develop or acquire automated information systems focussed on the utilization of data for the purposes of resource allocation, patient-specific costing, and outcomes of services. The information revolution has also been a driving force in the evolution of a national system for health information through the formation of the Canadian Institute for Health Information. The health care system is undergoing profound reform, initiated by action at the federal and provincial levels in response to recommendations of numerous reports and commissions (Angus, 1991). Roles of health care providers and organizations are being examined with a view to eliminating duplication of services and functions, as well as providing efficient delivery of quality health care. New models of care delivery are emerging, such as patient-focussed care, managed care, and hospitals without walls. These new models are directed at eliminating inefficiency in the structure and approach to health care. Care is being "de-institutionalized" and the scope of medical practice is changing. There is an increasing trend toward consumerism, in which self-help and other groups expect to be involved in their own care.

The inevitable conclusion is that information and information management will become increasingly important in the future. Nursing must ensure that information related to the nursing contribution to patient care is available in local and national data sets. Thus, the data elements from which this information is derived must be collected and stored in a retrievable format.

Background on Hospital and Health Minimum Data Sets

Background information about health data sets in the U.S., U.K., and Canada are detailed extensively in other sources (Anderson & Hannah, 1993; Hannah, 1993). The contents of these data sets are summarized in Table 28.1 (see pages 524-525). From this comparison of the data sets, it is evident that the Uniform Hospital Discharge Data Set (UHDDS) collected in the U.S., the Korner Minimum Data Set (MDS) collected in the U.K., and the Health Medical Record Institute

Table 28.1
Comparison of minimum data sets.

UHDDS[1]	Korner MDS[2]	NMDS[3]
Care Items	**Care Items**	**Care Items**
Medical diagnosis	Medical diagnosis	Nursing diagnosis
Procedure and dates	Operative procedure	Nursing intervention
		Nursing outcome
		Intensity—nursing care
Patient Demographics	**Patient Demographics**	**Patient Demographics**
Personal ID	Date of birth	Personal ID
Date of birth	Sex	Date of birth[6]
Sex	Residence	Sex
Race, ethnicity	Marital status	Race, ethnicity[6]
Residence		Residence[6]
Service Items	**Service Items**	**Service Items**
Facility/agency no.	Health district no.	Facility/agency no.[6]
Attending physician identification	Code of GP or consultant	Health record no.
Operating physician identification	Right of admission[5]	Principal nurse provider ID
Admission date	Nursing episode code[5]	Admission date[6]
Discharge date	Date of admission, consult, & beginning of stay	Discharge date[6]
Disposition of patient	Admission source	Disposition of patient[6]
Expected principal source of payment	Admission method	Expected principal source of payment[6]
	Date of discharge; end consultation	
	Intended management	
	Length of stay/bed use	
	Nursing home	
	Operational plan[5]	
	Destination of discharge/transfer	
	Method of discharge	
	Category of patient	

HMRI[4]	HI:NC[7,8]
Care Items	**Care Items**
Medical diagnosis (most responsible primary, secondary)	Client status (nursing diagnosis)
	Nursing intervention
	Nursing intensity
Procedure and dates	Client outcomes
Patient Demographics	**Patient Demographics**
Health care no.	Unique geographical location
Date of birth, age	Unique lifetime identifier
Sex	Language
Weight (newborn/infants <28 days)	Occupation
	Living arrangements
Postal code	Home environment, incl. physical structure
	Responsible caregiver upon discharge
	Functional health status
	Burden on care provider
	Education level
	Literacy level
	Work environment
	Lifestyle data (i.e., alcohol/tobacco use)
	Income level
Service Items	**Service Items**
Prov./institution no.	Unique nurse identifier
Chart no.	Principal nurse provider
Most responsible doctor	
Most responsible consultant	
Admission date, hour	
Institution from	
Admission category	
Admit by ambulance	
Discharge date, hour	
Length of stay, institution	
Live/death codes	
Responsibility of payment	
Main patient service	

[1]   1984 Revision of the Uniform Hospital Discharge Data Set, by the Department of Health & Human Services, 1985, *Federal Register, 50*(147), 31 038 - 31 040.

[2]   National Health Service (1982). *Steering group on health services information*. London: Author (p. 61).

[3]   H. Werley et al. (1991), The Nursing Minimum Data Set: Abstraction tool for standardized, comparable essential data. *American Journal of Public Health, 81*, 421-426.

[4]   Health Medical Records Institute (1991), HMRI *abstracting manual*. Toronto: Author (pp. 5.5-5.6).

[5]   M. Wheeler (1991), Nurses do count. *Nursing Times, 87*, 64-65.

[6]   Data items included in UHDDS.

[7]   Canadian Nurses Association (1993), Papers from the Nursing Minimum Data Set Conference. Ottawa: Author (pp. 153-154).

[8]   These data elements are in addition to those included in the HMRI data set.

(HMRI) abstract data collected in Canada all fall short on inclusion of nursing data elements. Both UHDDS and HMRI abstracts focus on physician-derived clinical data. Despite recent inclusion of two nursing data elements in the Korner MDS, this data set also focusses on physician-derived clinical data. Given the absence of nursing data elements, these data sets thus fail to provide a complete and accurate representation of all activity directed at patient care. Information derived from these data sets is, therefore, inadequate for use in decision making because of these nursing data gaps.

European nurses have recognized these data gaps and are currently undertaking research directed at addressing their data needs. European nurses recognize that their health systems need to include nursing data elements that are significant in the nursing decision-making process. A research initiative has recently been undertaken by the Danish Institute for Health and Nursing Research to develop a European classification of nursing practice compatible with and usable by the European information industry. The objective of this research program is to contribute to the development of a more comprehensive clinical record by specifying the minimum basic patient data relevant to nursing: nursing diagnoses of the patient's health problem, nursing interventions, patient outcome, and nurses' resource consumption. Inclusion of these data in clinical data sets is expected to enable nursing leaders to demonstrate the value of nursing services; calculate staffing needs, productivity and quality; and provide a database for research.

In response to the recognition of the information gap created by the exclusion of nursing data elements from the Uniform Hospital Discharge Data Set in the United States, Werley and colleagues developed the Nursing Minimum Data Set (NMDS) in 1985, building on initial work by Werley and colleagues in 1977 (Werley, 1988a). The NMDS, achieved through a consensus conference at the University of Wisconsin-Milwaukee School of Nursing, is defined as "a minimum set of items of information with uniform definitions and categories concerning the specific dimension of professional nursing, which meets the information needs of multiple data users in the health care system" (Werley, 1988a, p. 7). This nursing data set consists of nursing care elements, patient demographic elements, and service elements displayed in Table 28.1 (Werley & Lang, 1988). Through use of terms, criteria, and guidelines used for development of UHDDS, NMDS conferees achieved consensus on (1) the purposes of a NMDS and (2) identification and definition of data elements (Abdellah, 1988; Werley, Devine, Zorn, Ryan, & Westra, 1991; Werley & Lang, 1988).

In addition to the development of uniform definitions for the data elements, standard classification systems are being developed for each element to aid collection of uniform, accurate data. Werley and Lang report that the classification systems currently being tested for use in describing the nursing care elements include: the North American Nursing Diagnosis Association (NANDA) taxonomy (NANDA, 1989); a 16-item nursing intervention classification scheme and a 7-item nursing intervention classification scheme, both of which were developed by members of the NMDS task force; a nursing outcome classification scheme based on the resolution status of the nursing diagnosis; and a classification scheme for the intensity of nursing care based on the total hours and the staff mix of nursing personnel resources consumed by a patient (Werley & Lang, 1988). These nursing care element classification schemes remain in the testing and evaluation phase.

Research activity continues and is directed at development of nursing diagnoses (Jenny, 1989; Martin, 1982; McLane, 1987; NANDA, 1989), at intervention classification schemes (Bulechek & McClosky, 1990; Grobe, 1990; McClosky et al., 1990), and at outcomes (Lang & Marek; 1990). There is evidence of research directed at the use of the NMDS to validate the defining characteristics of nursing diagnostic labels (Rios, Delaney, Kruckeberg, Chung, & Mehmert, 1991).

Development of Nursing Components of Health Information

Prompted by the work on the NMDS in the U.S., and in response to contextual factors influencing nursing nationally, nurses in Canada have recognized the importance of collection and storage of essential data elements (CNA, 1990). Initiatives are currently underway directed at definition of these essential data elements. Among these initiatives are strategic plans for development of nursing components of health information.

In Canada, nurses are in the fortunate position of recognizing the need for nursing data elements at the time when the status of national health information is under review. Initiatives intended to promote the vision of a national health database are becoming a reality in Canada, such as the establishment of the Canadian Institute for Health Information in February 1994. The challenge for nurses is to capitalize on this timing and define those data elements required by nurses in Canada. To prevent nurses in Canada from losing control of nursing data, nurses must take a proactive stance and mobilize resources to ensure the development and implementation of a national health database that is congruent with the needs of nurses in all practice settings.

At the national level, the Canadian Nurses Association responded to a resolution (CNA, 1990) and convened the invitational Nursing Minimum Data Set Conference in Alberta in October 1992. This NMDS conference, an historic event, culminated in recommendations for a Canadian nursing minimum data set and for proposed data elements to be considered for inclusion as nursing components in a national health database. As well, a number of strategies were proposed that may be undertaken to achieve consensus on nursing data elements to be included in a national health database.

The data elements displayed in the column on the right in Table 28.1 were proposed for *addition* to the HMRI database as an initial step toward creating a cross-sectoral, multidisciplinary, longitudinal national health database in Canada (CNA, 1993). The nursing care items endorsed are comparable to those included in the American NMDS. However, considerable discussion ensued over the labeling of two of the nursing care elements. *Client status* was accepted as the label to represent the phenomena addressed by nurses that are commonly labeled nursing diagnosis. Client status is client focussed and conceptually broader, as it is situationally dictated and thus more representative of nursing settings and populations; as well, it reflects a wellness approach. *Client outcomes* was accepted as the label in lieu of nursing outcomes, again to emphasize the client focus and the unique multidisciplinary nature of the national health database. Several data elements besides those collected in the HMRI data set were suggested for consideration under patient demographics. Again, these proposed elements reflect the breadth in nursing practice settings and populations. One could question, however, the "essential" nature of each of these elements for inclusion in a "minimum" data set. Data elements proposed for inclusion in the service items category include those items in the HMRI data set with the addition of two nursing-specific items: unique nurse identifier and principal nurse provider. These nursing data elements will enable the unique nursing contributions to client well-being to be tracked.

The strategies proposed for the achievement of consensus among Canadian nurses on nursing data elements for inclusion in a Canadian data set for health information are well documented in the proceedings of the conference (CNA, 1993). Continued commitment from the CNA is integral to the success on this professional issue.

At a CNA meeting in 1993, a resolution was passed resulting in a change in the name from Nursing Minimum Set Data to *Health Information: Nursing Components* (HI:NC). This name is intended to reflect the importance of the nursing data elements being incorporated into a national health information data set rather than being created as a stand-alone data set. As well, this new name is congruent with the focus on a Canadian national health data set, a focus that emphasizes the client and the client's needs and outcomes as opposed to those of the individual health care professions.

As nurses in Canada embark on development of the nursing components of health information, several issues germane to the development of minimum data sets emerge. Giovannetti (1987) warned of the need to ensure that data are available, reliable, valid, and comparable. Murnaghan (1978) emphasized the importance of defining the scope of the data set to ensure that only those essential data elements are collected and to avoid proliferation of data.

Furthermore, attention must be directed to coordination and linkage of data. Three aspects of data linkage demand attention. First, the hardware must have the capability of supporting database linkage. Second, the content must be developed in a manner that lends itself to integration. Third, the ethics of data linkage with respect to patient information, including security, confidentiality, and privacy of data, must be addressed (Hannah, 1991).

Once the nursing components of health information are developed, three issues emerge: (1) promoting the concept to ensure widespread use; (2) educating users to ensure the quality of the data that are collected; and (3) establishing mechanisms for review and revision of the data elements (Murnaghan, 1978).

Implications of the Nursing Components of Health Information

In the absence of a system for collection, storage, and retrieval of nursing data elements, it is evident that much valuable information is being lost. This information is important to demonstrate the contribution nursing makes to the care of the patient and to demonstrate the cost effectiveness of nursing care (Werley, Devine, & Zorn, 1988; Werley et al., 1991). The trend is away from nursing-specific models of patient care delivery to patient-focussed models that emphasize collaboration of disciplines, multiskilling of health care providers, standardization of care, and streamlining of documentation through charting by exception. In this move, it is imperative that nurses be able to articulate what is and is not nursing's role. Furthermore, nurse administrators and nurse managers will be asked to demonstrate nursing's contribution to patient care in terms of outcome measures that are objective and measurable. Nurse administrators and nurse managers require nursing data to identify outcomes of nursing care, defend resource allocation to nursing, and justify new roles for nursing in the health care delivery system (Gallant, 1988; McPhillips,

1988; Werley et al., 1991). Similarly, nurse administrators need to understand and value nursing data so that, in the selection and implementation of information systems for their organizations, they can insist that they or their designates play a major role and that nursing data needs are incorporated into the selection and implementation criteria. (For greater detail on selection and implementation, see Hannah, Ball, and Edwards, 1994.)

Although, on the one hand, nursing must preserve its professional identity, this must be balanced against professional compartmentalization. Collection and storage of essential nursing data elements that are not integrated as components of a national data set will serve to ghettoize nursing. This is dangerous at a time when significant emphasis is being placed on multidisciplinary collaboration, patient-focussed care, and patient outcomes. In view of priorities such as these in health care, the need for integration of data elements could not be clearer.

Nurse clinicians need to know what nursing elements are essential for archival purposes so that nursing documentation includes these elements. With the move toward standardization of care through the use of care maps, it is essential that outcomes of nursing care are determined and included. As health care organizations embrace the concept of charting by exception in an effort to decrease the valuable hours spent by health care workers in documentation, nurses must be sure that the tools that outline the inherent patient care delivered are not devoid of nursing's contributions. If there are no data that reflect nursing activities, there will be no archival record of what nurses do, what difference nursing care makes, or why nurses are required. In times of fiscal restraint, such objective nursing data are necessary to substantiate the role of nurses and the nurse-patient ratios required in the clinical setting.

Nurse researchers need a database of essential data elements: first, to facilitate the identification of trends related to the data elements for specific patient groups, institutions, or regions and, second, to assess variables on multiple levels including institutional, local, regional, and national (Werley, Devine, & Zorn, 1988). Collection and storage of essential nursing data elements will facilitate the advancement of nursing as a research-based discipline (Werley & Zorn, 1988). Nurse educators need these essential nursing data elements to develop nursing knowledge for use in educating nurses and to facilitate the definition of the scope of nursing practice (McCloskey, 1988).

Finally, definitions of nursing components of health information are essential to influence health policy decision making. Historically, health policy has been created in the absence of nursing data. At a time of profound health care reform, it is essential that nurses demonstrate the central role of nursing services in the restructuring of the health care delivery system.

It is clear that a priority for nursing in Canada is the identification of the nursing components of health information—those essential nursing data elements that must be collected, stored, and retrieved from a national health information database. Nursing leaders must respond to the challenge to identify those data essential for the management of patient care and patient care units. As Werley (1988b) said so clearly, "Nurses cannot leave the decision making about nursing's essential retrievable data to vendors and other health care professionals; those decisions are part of the responsibilities that members of an autonomous profession must assume" (p. 431).

The nursing components of health information have the potential to provide nurses with the data required to build information for use in reshaping nursing as a profession prepared to respond to the health needs of Canadians in the 21st century. However, the window of opportunity to have nursing data elements included in a national data set is narrowing. Nurses must ensure that the vision of nursing components in the national health information system becomes a reality for nursing in Canada.

Acknowledgement

Parts of this chapter are based on material previously published in K.J. Hannah (1992), Nursing management of information, in M. Ogilvie & E. Sawyer (Eds.), *Managing information in Canadian health care facilities* (Ottawa: Canadian Hospital Association Press). This material is used with the permission of the publisher.

References

Abdellah, F.G. (1988). Future directions: Refining, implementing, testing, and evaluating the Nursing Minimum Data Set. In H.H. Werley & N.M. Lang (Eds.), *Identification of the Nursing Minimum Data Set* (pp. 416-426). New York: Springer.

Anderson, B.J. & Hannah, K.J. (1993) A Canadian Nursing Minimum Data Set: A major priority. *Canadian Journal of Nursing Administration,* 6(2), 7-13.

Angus, D.E. (1991). *Review of significant health care commissions and task forces in Canada since 1983-84*. Ottawa: Canadian Hospital Association.

Bulechek, G.M., & McCloskey, J.C. (1990). Nursing interventions: Taxonomy development. In J.C. McCloskey & H.K. Grace (Eds.), *Current issues in nursing* (3rd ed.) (pp. 23-28). St. Louis: Mosby.

Canadian Nurses Association. (1990, June). *Report of the resolutions committee.* Unpublished report available from the author, Ottawa.

Canadian Nurses Association. (1993). *Papers From the Nursing Minimum Data Set Conference.* Ottawa: Author.

Department of Health and Human Services. (1985). 1984 revision of the Uniform Hospital Discharge Data Set. *Federal Register, 50*(147), 31 038 - 31 040.

Gallant, B.J. (1988). Data requirements for the Nursing Minimum Data Set as seen by nurse administrators. In H.H. Werley & N.M. Lang (Eds.), *Identification of the Nursing Minimum Data Set* (pp. 165-176). New York: Springer.

Giovannetti, P. (1987). Implications of Nursing Minimum Data Set. In K.J. Hannah, M. Reimer, W.C. Mills, & S. Letourneau (Eds.), *Clinical judgment and decision making: The future with nursing diagnosis* (pp. 552-555). New York: John Wiley & Sons.

Graves, J.R., & Corcoran, S. (1989). The study of nursing informatics. *Image, 21,* 227-231.

Grobe, S.J. (1990). Nursing intervention lexicon and taxonomy study: Language and classification methods. *Advances in Nursing Science, 13,* 22-33.

Hannah, K.J. (1991). The need for health data linkage hospital/institutional needs a nursing statement. In Hospital Medical Records Institute, *Papers and recommendations from the national workshop on health care data linkage* (pp. 17-18). Don Mills, ON: Hospital Medical Records Institute.

Hannah, K.J. (1993). Development of a Nursing Minimum Data Set in the U.S., U.K. and Europe. In Canadian Nurses Association, *Papers from the Nursing Minimum Data Set Conference.* Ottawa: Author.

Hannah, K.J., Ball, M.J., & Edwards, M.J. (1993). *Introduction to nursing informatics.* New York: Springer-Verlog.

Hospital Medical Records Institute. (1991). *HMRI Abstracting Manual.* Toronto: Author.

Jenny, J. (1989). Classifying nursing diagnoses: A self care approach. *Nursing and Health Care, 10*(2), 82-88.

Jydstrup, R.A., & Gross, M.J. (1966). Cost of Information Handling in Hospitals: Rochester Region. *Health Services Research, 1,* 235-271.

Lang, N.M., & Marek, K.D. (1990). The classification of patient outcomes. *Journal of Professional Nursing, 6,* 158-163.

Martin, K. (1982). A client classification system adaptable for computerization. *Nursing Outlook, 30,* 515-517.

McCloskey, J.C. (1988). The Nursing Minimum Data Set: Benefits and implications for nurse educators. In National League for Nursing, *Perspectives in Nursing 1987-1989* (pp. 119-126). New York: National League for Nursing.

McCloskey, J.C., Bulechek, G.M., Cohen, M.Z., Craft, M.J., Crossley, J.D., Denehy, J.A., Glick, O.J., Kruckeberg, T., Mass, M., Prophet, C.M., & Tripp-Reimer, T. (1990). Classifications of nursing interventions. *Journal of Professional Nursing, 6,* 151-157.

McLane, A.M. (1987). Measurement and validation of diagnostic concepts: A decade of progress. *Heart & Lung, 16* (Pt. 1), 616-624.

McPhillips, R. (1988). Essential elements for the Nursing Minimum Data Set as seen by federal officials. In H.H. Werley & N.M. Lang (Eds.), *Identification of the Nursing Minimum Data Set* (pp. 233-238). New York: Springer.

Murnaghan, J.H. (1978). Uniform basic data sets for health statistical systems. *International Journal of Epidemiology, 7,* 263-269.

National Health Service/ Department of Health and Social Security Steering Group on Health Services Information. (1982). *Steering group on health services information: First report to the secretary of state.* London: Author.

National Health Service/ Department of Health and Social Security Steering Group on Health Services Information. (1984a). *Steering group on health services information: Second report to the secretary of state.* London: Author.

North American Nursing Diagnosis Association. (1989). *North American Nursing Diagnosis Association: Taxonomy I: Revised 1989.* St. Louis: Author.

Rios, H., Delaney, C., Kruckeberg, T., Chung, Y., & Mehmert, P.A. (1991). Validation of defining characteristics of four nursing diagnoses using a computerized data base. *Journal of Professional Nursing, 7,* 293-299.

Verley, H. (1970). *Florence Nightingale at Harley Street.* London: Dent & Sons.

Werley, H.H. (1988a). Introduction to the Nursing Minimum Data Set and its development. In H.H. Werley & N.M. Lang (Eds.), *Identification of the Nursing Minimum Data Set* (pp. 1-15). New York: Springer.

Werley, H.H. (1988b). Research directions. In H.H. Werley & N.M. Lang (Eds.), *Identification of the Nursing Minimum Data Set* (pp. 427-431). New York: Springer.

Werley, H.H., Devine, E.C., & Zorn, C.R. (1988). Nursing needs its own minimum data set. *American Journal of Nursing, 88,* 1651-1653.

Werley, H.H., Devine, E.C., Zorn, C.R., Ryan, P, & Westra, B.L. (1991). The Nursing Minimum Data Set: Abstraction tool for standardized, comparable, essential data. *American Journal of Public Health, 81,* 421-426.

Werley, H.H., & Lang, N.M. (1988). The consensually derived Nursing Minimum Data Set: Elements and definitions. In H.H. Werley & N.M. Lang (Eds.), *Identification of the Nursing Minimum Data Set* (pp. 402-411). New York: Springer.

Werley, H.H., & Zorn, C.R. (1988). The Nursing Minimum Data Set: Benefits and implications. In National League for Nursing, *Perspectives in Nursing—1987-1989* (pp. 105-114). New York: National League for Nursing.

Wheeler, M. (1991). Nurses do count. *Nursing Times, 87*(16), 64-65.

C H A P T E R   2 9

Financial Aspects of Nursing Management

Pamela Elliott

Pamela Elliott, RN, BN, MBA (Memorial), is Nursing Consultant—
Administration/Management with the Association of Registered Nurses of
Newfoundland. She is involved in management development of nurses throughout the
province, and has served as the nursing representative on several provincial committees addressing issues related to health care funding, restructuring, and resource management.

The Canadian health care system is facing challenging times. The
increasing economic pressures, in particular, are creating major challenges for even the most experienced health care administrators. The
impact of these pressures infiltrates the entire organization. Nursing,
which is often the largest department in any health care agency, is
undoubtedly affected. This means that nurse managers must develop
their financial management skills. They must become adept at managing resources in a cost-effective manner.

In this chapter, the nurse manager will be introduced to basic
concepts related to nursing budgets. The chapter will provide an
overview of sources of revenue, details about the budgeting process,
an introduction to cost containment, and a glossary of terms, strategies, and concepts. An illustrative example is provided to help readers
comprehend the budgeting process.

Speaking the Language

Nurses are comfortable with the complex jargon used in the health
care field. Terminology from medicine, pharmacology, and nursing is
integrated into basic nursing education programs. However, it is
often not until nurses become managers that they are exposed to the
jargon related to accounting and financial management.

Nurse managers are not expected to function as full-fledged professional accountants or financial managers. They are, however, expected to be able to speak the language. They must be able to communicate with other managers in the management of scarce resources. This means that they must have a basic understanding of the most commonly used terms. The Glossary at the end of this chapter (see pages 551-553) lists the terms most commonly used in the financial aspects of nursing management. Many of these terms will quickly become part of the nurse manager's vocabulary during the budgeting process.

In the budgeting process, nurse managers will most often be concerned with the expense aspects of budgeting rather than the revenue aspects. Consequently, the bulk of this chapter will focus on matters related to expenses. However, it is important for nurse managers to be aware of how much money their respective unit has been allocated and where that money comes from. Sources of revenue may vary with the agency and the province.

Sources of Revenue

The Canadian health care system is the envy of many countries. The elaborate technology, large physical structures, and the highly skilled health care professionals constitute a system that is both complex and expensive to operate. Most consumers do not pay directly for all the services they receive. So, where does all the money come from for day-to-day operations?

Typically, each nursing unit is allocated a portion of the total budget of the organization. The organization receives its revenue from a variety of sources, including provincial government funding, charitable fundraising, and, on a much lesser scale, certain user fees, such as for room rates, cosmetic surgery, or equipment rentals. The majority of its funding, however, does come directly from the government.

Provinces now spend $43.8 billion a year on health care, a 242% increase over the past decade (Kirby, 1992). Where do provinces get these extraordinary amounts of money? They receive funding from two main sources: taxes and federal government transfer payments. The major federal transfer programs are the Equalization Program, Established Programs Financing (EPF), and Canada Assistance Plan (CAP). The Equalization Program provides unconditional grants to the seven less affluent provinces. All provinces benefit from Established Programs Financing transfers in support of health and postsecondary education and from Canada Assistance Plan cost sharing of eligible social assistance and welfare expenditures (Government of Newfoundland and Labrador, 1992).

In recent years, the federal government has been implementing fiscal restraint policies and has cut contributions to health care under the Established Programs Financing. It is expected that cash transfers for health will disappear completely by the year 2009. This is happening at a time when health care costs are rising (Kirby, 1992). This trend has contributed to increasing fiscal hardships for the provinces and, consequently, the health care system is experiencing tremendous pressures.

Health care organizations are being urged to adopt a more businesslike orientation. There is a pressure to manage scarce resources more efficiently in attempts to meet increasing demands and needs. Efficient management requires a knowledge of the budgeting process.

The Budgeting Process

The nursing budget constitutes one of the largest department budgets in most hospitals and, in many cases, involves managing millions of dollars (Hodges & Poteet, 1991). The management of these resources often rests with nurse managers. The degree of their involvement in the budgeting process will depend on a number of factors, including the administrative style and policy (decentralized budgeting versus centralized budgeting), the type of budget, and the approach to budgeting.

There are several different approaches to budgeting. Two of the more common approaches are incremental budgeting and zero-based budgeting. Incremental budgeting is a traditional budgeting approach. The budget is developed annually, based on expenditures from the previous year. Expenditures from the previous year are analyzed and reasons for deviations from the budget allocations are evaluated. Projections are made based on factors of change, which may include inflation, salary raises, program expansion, and new programs. The new budget is determined as an incremental cost over last year's budget. Zero-based budgeting is a different approach in that expenditures for the previous year are irrelevant. Each year the budget begins at zero. This approach is based on the assumption that any expenditure must be justified as essential to the organization's function each year. It requires more precise planning and allows for more participation than incremental budgeting. It pressures managers to set priorities and justify resources. One drawback is that it can be very time consuming (Sullivan, 1990).

These are just two of the approaches found in the health care system. Regardless of the approach, there are advantages to nurse managers' being involved in the budgeting process. Such involvement:

- Aids in decision making;

- Helps to establish goals and set priorities;

- Stimulates cost consciousness;

- Helps to prevent waste;

- Helps to see the effects of policies implemented and in describing overall performance;

- Provides a continuous check on the volume and cost of hospital operations (Dorman, 1991);

- Provides opportunity to document beneficial patient outcomes and relate them to nursing actions and assist the nursing department in obtaining resources;

- Provides opportunity to make others aware of how nursing contributes to the success of the organization.

Many organizations are moving to a decentralized approach to budgeting. That means that more and more first-line managers are becoming involved in the actual development of budgets, as opposed to being handed a budget that was developed by senior management. Here, too, the steps used in the development of the budget will vary with the agency. Some common steps are: assess the environment; set objectives; determine and justify expenses; and evaluate.

The steps used are similar to those in the basic nursing process (assessment, planning, implementation, and evaluation). They take on a different look when they are applied to the financial aspect of management as opposed to the traditional clinical aspect. The nurse manager must master both if she or he is to be effective (Felteau, 1992).

The steps in the budgeting process often involve filling out forms and performing mathematical calculations at least on an annual basis. Although estimations and projections may be done only once a year, the budgeting process is an ongoing one.

The manager may have to develop the nursing budget from scratch. Most nursing budgets have two major components: labour costs and supplies.

Labour costs often constitute 75% or more of the budget. This part of the process requires that the nurse manager be familiar with the applicable collective agreements, evaluate the past year's financial performance, and make realistic projections for the coming year.

A number of factors must be considered and calculated into the labour expenses budget. Examples of these factors include:

- The staffing pattern;
- Actual salaries of current staff;
- Salary scales and increases;
- Shift differential;
- Holiday pay;
- Overtime;
- On-call pay;
- Experience differential;
- Educational differential;
- Turnover;
- Fringe benefits;
- Replacement costs;
- Anticipated program or volume changes; and
- Charge pay.

The other part of the budget, the supplies budget, usually covers everyday operating items, such as dressings, medications, syringes, and tubings. A good materiels management program assists in determining the amount of supplies that will be required. Large health care agencies usually have a materiels management department. In small facilities, nursing is often the department that oversees the purchasing and storage of supplies. Either way, nurse managers are involved in the management of supplies, given the fact that nurses are usually the biggest users of the more costly supplies.

After the budget has been developed and approved, and the resources allocated, the manager's job is not complete. The budgeting process requires monitoring and controlling of expenditures. Monitoring is usually done through regular review of periodic budget reports. Computerization has allowed many agencies to adopt a monthly review system. The reports usually provide data related to projected (or budgeted) costs, actual costs, and variances. Analysis of the variances provides opportunity for the nurse manager to intervene and/or alter plans if an excessive surplus or deficit exists. An example of such forms can be found in the following real situation. The intent of this example is to illustrate some of the budgeting concepts in use in one facility. The forms, processes, policies, and support services available to nurse managers will vary with the agency.

Illustrative Example:
The Waterford Hospital
Nursing Budget

Waterford Hospital is a provincial psychiatric teaching hospital in St. John's, Newfoundland. It provides inpatient care as well as extensive outpatient and community care. Total budget for the organization is approximately $37 million. Nursing is the largest department and in 1992 consumed approximately $14 million. The nursing department has 25 managers that are involved in the budgeting process.

Traditionally, Waterford Hospital had used a centralized approach to budgeting but in recent years has moved to a decentralized process. Nurse managers are involved in all aspects of budgeting. They develop their unit budgets from scratch. To assist with the "number crunching," projections, and monitoring, the hospital has several forms that must be completed by each unit manager.

The first form is a biweekly attendance record (see Figure 29.1, pages 540-541), which is completed every two weeks by the unit manager for each employee and forwarded to the payroll department. A copy is sent to the personnel department and another copy kept by the unit. The accumulated records are useful tools for assisting in projection for annual budgets. To complete this form, the nurse manager will need a copy of the collective agreements, the staffing schedule, and, of course, a calculator. A calculator will quickly become one of the instruments used regularly by a nurse manager throughout the budgeting process.

The next form to be completed is a form for estimating the annual total salary costs for the unit (see Table 29.1, page 542). This form can be developed for the agency by the finance department, working with a group of nurse managers so that the form will meet the needs of all units. To complete the form, the nurse manager will need a copy of each of the respective collective agreements, staffing schedules, employment data about each employee (e.g., pay scale and date of hire), and information about past and projected salary expenditures.

Examples of how some of the calculations may be made are as follows:

Overtime budget for staff nurses

1. Estimate the number of shifts that may require overtime (e.g., four 8-h shifts = 32 h)
2. Multiply the number of hours by the overtime salary rate (e.g., 32 x 1.5 [basic hourly salary rate])

Figure 29.1
Example of a biweekly attendance record.

SUNDAY —

MONDAY —

TUESDAY —

WEDNESDAY —

THURSDAY —

TOTAL

OTHER HOURS

REG. HOURS	VAC. HOURS	PD.SICK HOURS	WORKERS' COMP.	FAMILY LEAVE		TOTAL REGULAR HOURS
10	20	30	400	90		

DEPARTMENTAL ALLOCATION DEPT.#

OTHER

WORKED STAT. PREMIUM 0.5

O/T 1.5	O/T 2.0	PAID STAT. DAY	SHIFT DIFF.	WEEK END/DIFF.	IN CHARGE	CALL BACK		TOTAL OTHER EARNINGS
60	70	85	95	40	110	120	130	

60	70	85	95	40	110	120	130

COMMENTS

Source: Reprinted, with permission, from Waterford Hospital, St. John's, Newfoundland (1992).

Table 29.1
Example of form to determine total annual salary costs.

Waterford Hospital
Departmental Budget
For the Year Ending _____

Dept.: Nursing — (Name of Unit)

Posts	Position	Pay Group	Pay Scale	Contract Date	Budgeted
1	Nursing Sup I	Manager will need to		n/a	$ 49 500
7	Psy Nurse I	know the pay group, pay		July 1	$286 629
8	Nurse I	scale, date of hire for		April 30	$241 256
2	Psy Nsg Asst III	each employee		April 30	$ 59 752

Total Regular Salary Costs   **$637 137**

Account Detail	Budgeted
Stat Premium	$ 5 400
Vacation Relief	$38 800
Overtime Relief	$25 000
Shift Differential	$ 5 000
In Charge	$ 3 700
Uniform Allowance	$ 3 496
Education Differential	$ 3 000
	$84 396

Total Salary Costs   **$721 533**

Source: Reprinted, in part, with the permission of Waterford Hospital, St. John's, Newfoundland (1992). The actual form used in the hospital has 16 account detail categories listed. The figures in this table are fictitious and are used only for illustration.

Shift differential for staff nurses

1. Estimate the number of nurses that will be required for each shift. The manager will have to consider the staff pattern for 365 days per year, the number of nurses on 12-hour night shifts, the number on 12-hour day shifts, and those doing only part-time shifts.

2. Multiply the number of nurses on each shift by the appropriate hourly shift differential.

Vacation relief

Here, the nurse manager will have to estimate based on past experience of the unit and on hospital policy because one cannot be certain of exactly how much and when vacation time will be taken. Usually, policies place some controls because the hospital wants to avoid paying overtime for vacation relief.

Education differential

1.   Identify staff who meet the requirements for educational differential.

2.   Multiply the number of staff by the appropriate educational differential.

Total all the above amounts to give a yearly projection.

These are just some of the calculations that have to be done. It is now obvious that performing such calculations is indeed a time-consuming process for the nurse manager. All the account details listed in Table 29.1 must be individually calculated. Sometimes each account item may require several calculations to be performed. The manager will often have to repeat the steps for different categories of workers (e.g., staff nurses, nursing assistants, aides, clerks) depending upon the categories of staff working on the unit. The hourly rates and benefits vary with the category. Consequently, one can expect to be adding hundreds of numbers. The good news is that each calculation is a simple mathematical step. Use of computers will make these calculations much easier for nurse managers in coming years, although it will be vital for nurse managers to be involved in the development of the programs for their units so that all the various factors can be included.

Table 29.2 (see page 544) shows an example of a form used to estimate the costs of supplies needed on the unit for a forthcoming budget. Examples of materials and supplies that would be requested might include photocopying, medical-surgical supplies, equipment expenses (but not capital budget proposals), medical instruments, paper and other office supplies, and other regularly stocked items for the unit. To complete the form in Table 29.2, the unit manager will need to know individual prices and the volume of each item that will be used.

Each month throughout the year, the nurse manager should receive from the finance department a budget report that shows actual spending for the year and how this equates with the budget that had been submitted at the beginning of the year. Table 29.3 (see pages 546-547) gives an example of such a report.

In this example, the budget report for December 1992 shows figures for five (out of a real list of 34) categories of items. The figures show the amount that was actually spent in December, followed by

Table 29.2

Example of form to determine budget for supplies.

Waterford Hospital
Budget Request
For Year
Department: (Name of Unit)
Material and Other Supplies

Type of Expense	Details of Estimate	Dollar Amount
	(Examples)	
Medical Supplies	10 boxes of 5-cc syringes (100/box)	$278.89
Instrument	6 stethoscopes	86.59

Prepared By: _____

Source: Reprinted, in part, with the permission of Waterford Hospital, St. John's, Newfoundland (1993). The examples used are fictitious.

the amount that the nurse manager had projected and budgeted for that month. The variance between the two numbers is then shown (with negative variances in parentheses). The next columns show the actual amounts spent compared with the budgeted amounts for the year to date (YTD) and the variance, if any. The final two columns show the total year's budgeted amount and the percentage of that budget that has been spent to the end of December 1992. In the example, where the year is from April 1, 1992 to March 31, 1993, the nurse manager of this unit was absolutely accurate in the projections for "Management—Regular," and had spent 75% of the budget total in three-quarters (75%) of the year. On the other hand, the "Nursing—Overtime" budget was considerably over the amount estimated, and the manager had used 91% of the year's proposed budget in just 9 months.

This form usually is supplied to the unit manager by the finance department of the agency, and it does not require nurse managers to perform detailed calculations. Instead, they must examine the figures on the spreadsheet and be able to evaluate them, particularly the variances and the year-to-date statistics. These monthly spreadsheets are invaluable tools to assist in budget monitoring and controls. The nurse manager can detect any trends, implement any other plans to correct over-budget items, and/or justify any variances. The variances may be either positive (a surplus) or negative (a deficit). For example, the excess spent on overtime may be explained by a sudden increase in sick leave.

The sample forms presented are similar to forms used by other health care agencies at a unit level. The forms are geared toward the development, monitoring, and control steps of the budgeting process. In addition to these, the Waterford Hospital has other forms and mechanisms in place to assist managers and the overall financial performance of the organization. Examples of the other mechanisms include:

- Budgets are on the agenda at management meetings;
- Presentations on each department's performance are given at meetings of the divisional heads;
- Biannual evaluations of the budget are done in addition to the monthly monitoring;
- Special meetings are held to seek input for expense projections as well as for cost-cutting measures;
- Inservice education is held related to the budgeting process.

It is worth noting the impressive process that the Waterford Hospital used during the initial stages of the move to the decentralized budgeting process. Each nursing manager was given one-on-one education. The chief executive officer, chief nursing officer, and chief financial officer met as a group with individual nurse managers. This provided opportunity for any questions or expression of concerns and ideas. This participatory management style paid off. In one year, the nursing department was able to move from a deficit position to one within the budget. Efficient management of $14 million is not a trivial task.

The Waterford Hospital also used successful strategies to address other concepts, such as cost containment. They set up a sub-committee with union and management representatives to discuss areas of concern. Cost awareness information was sent to different units. Float service and annual leave replacement policies were implemented. Sharing within major services increased. Communication about budgetary concerns was increased with all levels of staff. These are examples of strategies and tactics recommended in the literature on the difficult subject of cost containment.

Table 29.3
Budget report.

(Name of Unit)		Budget Report	
Dept. _____ Nursing _____		Responsible _____ (Name of Manager) _____	

Fiscal Year 1992-93

	Actual Dec.'92	Budgeted Dec.'92	Variance
Management—Regular	4 125	4 125	0
Nursing—Regular	21 765	23 886	2 121
Nursing—Shift Diff.	190	212	22
Nursing—Overtime	4 372	3 500	(872)
Nursing—Educ. Allow.	250	250	0
Nursing—In Charge	396	380	(16)

Source: Reprinted, in part, with the permission from Waterford Hospital, St. John's, Newfoundland (1992). The actual form used in the hospital has 34 categories listed and also columns for percentages related to the variances. The figures in this table are fictitious and are used only for illustration.

Cost Containment

Increasingly, governments and health care organizations are looking for ways to contain or reduce costs while at the same time maintaining or increasing quality. Many people view this situation as a paradox. How can one contain costs and yet improve quality? This questioning attitude is often a barrier in dealing effectively with the cost and quality dilemma. People tend to see the two as separate, independent goals and problems—a choice between one or the other—rather than as two interdependent, dynamic, polar opposites to be managed together over time (Hurst, Keenan, & Minnick, 1992).

Managing cost and quality requires the input and involvement of all major players in the health care system—government, agencies, providers, and consumers. The extent of involvement will vary with each respective party.

YTD—Actual Dec.'92	YTD—Budget Dec.'92	Variance	1992/93 Budget	% YTD
37 125	37 125	0	49 500	75
197 775	214 972	17 197	286 629	69
1 886	1 904	18	2 539	74
22 698	18 750	(3 948)	25 000	91
2 250	2 250	0	3 000	75
3 000	2 450	(550)	3 700	82

Governments and agencies are examining ways to restructure the system. Examples of such recent government initiatives include reductions in governing boards, mergers, reallocation of resources, and changes in provincial payment plans. Examples of agency initiatives include bed closures, streamlining services, and changing role statements. These initiatives and others affect the roles and responsibilities of nurse managers.

The first-level nurse manager is responsible for communicating and implementing agency policy and strategic plans at the unit level. As well, this first-level nurse manager is in a position that provides opportunities for communicating the input of employees and consumers to top management.

Managers are also responsible for maintaining costs within an acceptable level. This means that they must find ways to avoid, reduce, or control costs. Cost containment strategies involve cost awareness, monitoring of resources, and effective management. These responsibilities can be fulfilled in a number of ways.

One of the first steps in cost containment is to create an awareness of the various costs encountered in operating a unit. Many nurses are not aware of the exact cost of supplies, drugs, and equipment that they use on a daily basis. Nor are they often aware of the rate at which these expenses increase. They are also often surprised to learn that more than 75% of the unit's budget is related to employees' wages and benefits. The fact is that more education about costs is required. How does a manager increase cost awareness? Examples of activities that assist in meeting this goal include providing cost information at staff meetings, posting information related to costs at the nursing unit, and participating in an organization-wide cost awareness day. A creative measure undertaken by one hospital was the development of cost containment games that generated employee participation (Kelly & Rudh, 1991).

Cost awareness by itself is not always sufficient to meet financial demands. The manager must also implement cost avoidance and cost reduction measures. It has already been emphasized that most of the nursing budget is for wages and benefits. Consequently, most cost containment measures will be directed toward managing the staff. The nurse manager will be responsible for determining the impact on patient care and deciding whether these measures are feasible. Examples of such measures include:

- Postponing or delaying the filling of a vacant position;
- Building in a part-time component for peak periods;
- Staggering shifts to eliminate or reduce overtime;
- Reducing the number of staff;
- Increasing productivity;
- Reducing turnover;
- Using float pools;
- Regulating vacation time;
- Transferring non-nursing activities to support staff.

It is also realized that most managers must operate within the constraints of a collective agreement. This often limits the amount of freedom in choosing cost containment measures. Creativity in generating ideas, however, can be enhanced through encouraging employee participation in the process of brainstorming.

The objective of brainstorming is to generate ideas that reduce resources by having individuals work smarter, not harder. The use of brainstorming around the concepts of reduction in demand for staff, increasing throughput, staffing to demand, and reduction in expenses does generate ideas that can then be analyzed for cost effectiveness, efficiencies, quality improvement, and feasibility of implementation.

The manager can initiate many questions that stimulate the generation of ideas (Smeltzer, 1992).

In addition to cost awareness and cost containment/reduction strategies, the nurse manager is also responsible for monitoring costs. This may be accomplished through review of regular statistical or financial reports. Many agencies provide computerized monthly financial reports that indicate any variances from projected and actual figures. This was illustrated in the Waterford Hospital example. Variance analysis assists the manager in identifying areas of spending that may lead to budget deficits. If such concern is identified, the manager can then attempt to implement measures to counteract the anticipated deficit.

Most of the measures discussed up to now have a direct relationship to costs and the budgeting process. There are also many that have a less obvious relationship to the goal of cost containment. Effective management is one of the strategies suggested for assisting in the achievement of this goal.

Effective management constitutes a broad range of activities. In fact, it can be said that most of the topics covered in this book are linked to effective management and, consequently, all of them are linked to cost containment. Topics such as promoting quality of work-life, leadership, communicating, and program evaluation are just a few areas of nursing management responsibility that have financial implications. The nurse manager must develop an integrated approach to financial management. Only then can the unit hope to achieve the goal of cost-effective quality care.

Applications for Nurse Managers

In today's environment, it is desirable that the financial aspects of nursing management become integrated with the multitude of roles and functions inherent in the domain of nurse managers. To facilitate integration, the following list outlines activities and helpful hints to assist the nurse manager:

- Monitor the use of equipment and supplies;
- Seek input from staff and recommend ways to minimize costs at the unit level;
- Work with staff to identify changing resource requirements;
- Complete forms on time and justify requests for resources;
- Keep current with technological advances and trends;

- Communicate with other departments and parties involved in the budgeting;
- Engage in continuing education related to financial management responsibilities;
- Become familiar with the approach to budgeting and the budgeting policies and procedures used by the agency;
- Become familiar with the respective collective agreements that apply to the unit's staff;
- Develop priority-setting skills;
- Become familiar with nursing costing methods;
- Ensure that quality of care measures do not become lost in the process.

The above list of activities, although not exhaustive, is a tall order for a manager who also has many other responsibilities on a daily basis. Time does not expand, so the manager must be able to set priorities and improve personal efficiencies to meet challenges.

Conclusion

This chapter has provided an overview of the basics related to financial management. It is important that the manager have a working knowledge of the terms associated with budgeting, the budgeting process itself, and cost containment strategies. Nurse managers who resist learning such fundamentals could be sabotaging their effectiveness. An excellent text for those who wish to know more about the subject is Steven Finkler and Christine Kovner's (1993) *Financial Management for Nurse Managers and Executives*.

In an environment characterized by increasing health care costs, increasing demands for health care, and limited resources, the nurse manager is instrumental in leading the way toward cost-effective nursing service.

Acknowledgement

Acknowledgement is given for the assistance and time of Clarrie Case, Assistant Executive Director, Nursing Services, and Joan Rowsell, Director of Planning and Development, two of the nursing leaders at the Waterford Hospital. They provided information and forms to use in the illustrative example in this chapter.

Glossary of Financial Terms for Nurse Managers

Budget. A plan for allocation of resources and a control for ensuring that results comply with the plan. Results are expressed in quantitative terms. Budgets are done for a specific time period, usually a fiscal year, but may be subdivided (e.g., into monthly, quarterly, or semiannual periods). There are many types of budgets and also different approaches to developing budgets.

Capital expenditures budgets. Usually includes expenditures related to physical changes, such as replacement or expansion of the plant, major equipment, and inventories. These items are usually major investments and each agency usually has its own policies and procedures for capital expenditures budgets. The planning is also often more long term than with operating budgets (Marriner-Tomey, 1992).

Cost. Sum of resources (e.g., labour, materials, equipment) used to produce goods or a service.

Cost accounting. Often referred to as *managerial accounting*. This is a subfield of accounting that records, measures, and reports information about costs. The focus is on the performance evaluation and decision-making needs of managers within the organization. Cost data for managerial use need not comply with generally accepted accounting principles (GAAP) as defined by the Canadian Institute of Chartered Accountants. (Barton, 1991).

Cost-benefit analysis. The use of analytical techniques involving a monetary assessment to identify the total costs and benefits of a specific project or intervention. For example, such analysis attempts to answer the question: "Is a project worthwhile?"

Cost centre. A unit (e.g., departmental or geographical) for which costs can be identified and allocated. It is sometimes referred to as a responsibility centre.

Cost effectiveness. Analysis of the benefits of expenditure of resources on a particular intervention to identify whether the resources could be more effectively utilized. For example, such analysis attempts to answer the question: "Is there a less costly alternative method of achieving the same intervention?" (Buchan, 1992).

Expense. A cost that is charged against revenue in an accounting period. (Note: In practice, the terms "costs" and "expenses" are sometimes used interchangeably.)

Financial accounting. The subfield of accounting that records, measures, and reports financial information to external parties. In the case of the health care system, these parties are usually the governing boards and the Ministries of Health. The focus is on the evaluation of the performance of top management and the decision-making needs of the organization as a whole. Cost data for financial accounting must comply with generally accepted accounting principles.

Fixed costs. Costs that are unchanged as volume changes within the relevant range of activity (e.g., manager's salary).

Labour costs. Expenditure on employee pay and benefits.

Operating budget. Indicates how much it will cost to maintain routine operations of the organization during a specified period. Examples of factors that the nurse manager might include are salaries, employee benefits, medical-surgical supplies, and pharmaceutical supplies.

Opportunity costs. The return that could be realized from the best forgone use of a resource. It considers the best comparable use of the resources given up. Accounting systems do not typically record opportunity costs. Unfortunately, they are sometimes mistakenly ignored in decision making.

Revenue. The money coming into the organization or cost centre.

Variable costs. Costs that change with a change in activity (e.g., patient escorts, staffing in case room).

Variance. The difference between what was planned and the actual outcomes (positive or negative).

References

Barton, E. (1991). Introduction to departmental financial management. In S. Ziebarth (Ed.), *Feeling the squeeze—The practice of middle management in Canadian health care facilities* (pp. 267-275). Ottawa: Canadian Hospital Association.

Buchan, J. (1992). Cost-effective caring. *International Nursing Review, 39*(4), 117-120.

Dorman, A. (1991). Budgeting. In S. Ziebarth (Ed.), *Feeling the squeeze—The practice of middle management in Canadian health care facilities* (pp. 276-283). Ottawa: Canadian Hospital Association.

Felteau, A. (1992). Budget variance analysis and justification. *Nursing Management, 23*(2), 40-41.

Finkler, S., & Kovner, C. (1993). *Financial management for nurse managers and executives.* Philadelphia: W.B. Saunders.

Government of Newfoundland and Labrador. (1992). *Budget 1992*. St. John's: Author.

Hodges, L., & Poteet, G. (1991). Financial responsibility and budget decision making. *Journal of Nursing Administration, 21*(10), 30-33.

Hurst, J., Keenan M., & Minnick J. (1992). Managing polarities. *Nursing and Health Care, 13*(1), 24-32.

Kelly, R., & Rudh, S. (1991). Creating cost awareness. *Nursing Economics, 9*(3), 198-200.

Kirby, M. (1992). The economics and politics of health care system ailments. *Alberta Association of Registered Nurses (AARN) Journal, 48*(6), 10-13.

Marriner-Tomey, A. (1992). *Guide to nursing management* (4th ed.). St. Louis: Mosby Year Book.

Smeltzer, C. (1992). Brainstorming: A process for cost reduction. *Nursing Economics, 10*(1), 74-75.

Risk Management

Margaret Mrazek

Margaret Mrazek, RN, BSN, MHSA, LLB (Alberta), is a partner with the law firm of Reynolds, Mirth, Richards, & Farmer in Edmonton, Alberta. Her emphasis of practice is in the areas of health and labour law. A registered nurse who has worked as a general duty nurse, she also taught at a hospital-based school of nursing and later became Director of that school. She held several senior administrative positions in a large acute treatment hospital before beginning to practise law.

Risk management is a concept well known and well developed in industry. The insurance industry has a particularly rich history of risk management; however, its application to the health care field is relatively new (Youngberg, 1984). In the United States, health care risk management arose as a response to the proliferation of malpractice and negligence claims in the 1970s. The increased number of claims resulted in higher insurance costs. As a result, to control costs, some insurance companies insisted that health care facilities which came under their plans have risk management programs to reduce losses. As an incentive to introduce such programs, some insurance companies offered reduced premiums.

In Canada, there has not been the same impetus for the development of risk management programs. It is not clear that Canada has suffered, or will suffer, a similar malpractice crisis as the United States (Dickens, 1993; Picard, 1984). Whether or not a response to a real or perceived malpractice crisis, risk management in Canadian health care was not widely implemented until the 1980s (Stock & Lefroy, 1988). One factor in the growth of risk management programs in Canada was the inclusion of risk management as part of the Canadian Council on Health Facilities Accreditation Program.

This chapter will open with an examination of the basic concept of risk management, including a definition and a discussion of differences and similarities between risk management and quality management. After a brief examination of the legal liabilities of boards and of nurse managers, the structure and process of risk management will be described. The chapter closes with remarks on preventive strategies and comments on the responsibilities of the nurse manager as a witness.

Concept of Risk Management

Although risk management made the transition to the health care field as a reaction to the broadening scope of financial risk of loss, risk management itself is not reactive. Risk management is a proactive process. A risk management system must be both dynamic and expansive.

Definition

A precise definition of risk management is not as essential as commitment to a risk management system. However, a definition does provide a foundation and focus for implementation of a risk management system.

The Canadian Council on Health Facilities Accreditation (CCHFA) (1991) adopts the following definition:

> *Risk management is, as the term suggests, a management system or process. It has four basic steps:*
>
> *• the identification of risk;*
>
> *• risk assessment;*
>
> *• taking actions to manage risks; and*
>
> *• the evaluation of risk management activities.*
>
> *Implicit in the last step is a feedback loop demanding the continuous improvement or correction of action, assessment and/or identification.* (CCHFA, 1991, p. 5)

Risk is defined by CCHFA as "the exposure to any event which may jeopardize the reputation, net income, property, patients/residents/ personnel or liability of the facility" (CCHFA, 1991, p. 1). Poteet (1983) and Stock and Lefroy (1988) also provide definitions of risk management. The definition for risk management used by CCHFA is in essence a definition of the process to be utilized in a risk management program.

The definition used in this chapter for risk management is the following:

> Risk management is the systematic process of identifying, evaluating and addressing (treating or preventing) potential and/or actual risks which are a source of injury or loss of money or reputation.

The purpose of a risk management program is to prevent, or minimize, actual and potential, foreseeable risks that are sources of injury to patients, employees, or visitors, or which result in loss of monies, or which affect the reputation of a health care agency or facility or the professionals and staff providing services therein. Risk management is aimed at achievement of an acceptable standard or level rather than an optimal level or standard of care. In legal terms, risk management is what a lawyer tells a client to do to reduce the likelihood of being sued, or, if the client cannot avoid being sued, how damages can be minimized. As well, from the definitions it can be seen that risk management has a broad application in health care agencies or facilities, as it covers all facets of their operation and management.

Responsibility for such a program is usually delegated to a risk manager or interdisciplinary committee, who may also have responsibility for quality management. In this chapter, the term quality management program includes quality assurance programs.

Risk Management versus Quality Management

Risk management principles are most often implemented in a health care environment that already has in place some form of quality management program. The implementation of a risk management system in an established quality management environment often presents difficulties, as the objectives of the two systems may be incorrectly perceived as incompatible or incongruous.

In fact, risk management and quality management are symbiotic. Ideally, whether as part of two different systems or part of one system, risk and quality management should work together toward the objective of providing a high standard of patient care and a safe health environment.

The fundamental objective of risk management is the provision of an acceptable level of care to protect all assets of the health care facility against loss. The fundamental objective of quality management is the monitoring and continual improvement of health care delivery so as to achieve an optimal level of patient care within the available resources. Quality management is therefore a level beyond the minimal level of a risk management program.

Quality assurance, which is an integral part of quality management, focusses on patient care and requires persons with requisite clinical or professional expertise to establish standards and then determine whether the care provided meets the standards. Risk management, on the other hand, is primarily a managerial responsibility. However, as there are risks of some form in almost every aspect of a health care facility's or agency's operation, everyone has a role to play in a risk management program.

Although the expression of fundamental objectives is quite different between risk and quality management systems, there is a surprising degree of overlap in the processes utilized to achieve the objectives. This is especially true of the long term, as opposed to the short term, processes. For example, when a patient incident occurs, such as an error in administration of medication that causes the patient physical harm, the objectives of both risk management and quality management have not been achieved.

The patient may have legal recourse against the health care providers for the injuries suffered. Such a claim exposes a health care facility or health care agency to the risk of potential liability and a loss of resources. Negative publicity surrounding the event may also adversely affect the ability of the health care facility or agency to obtain future funds, as patients may seek care elsewhere. As well, the reputation of the agency or facility may be permanently affected by a negative event.

The quality of care provided to the patient may also be seriously diminished by an error in the administration of medication. Not only may the patient suffer injury as a result of the occurrence, but the patient's initial recovery may be delayed.

In the short term, the risk manager may respond to the occurrence by:

- Checking the basic facts of the incident;

- Reporting the incident to the administrator;

- Contacting the health care facility's insurers and/or the facilty's legal advisor to report the incident, inquire as to coverage, and seek advice as necessary;

- Reviewing the incident with the individuals involved and arranging to have written statements prepared; and

- Reviewing the patient's chart to determine how the occurrence and response were documented.

In the long term, the risk manager would make recommendations on ways to avoid future occurrences so as to limit claims against the health care facility's resources.

The short term response of the quality manager would be to review the occurrence with staff supervisors to determine whether the cause was human or systemic error. In the long term, the quality supervisor would monitor and adjust the facility's systems so as to ensure that no future occurrences result.

The risk manager's short term response differs from that of the quality manager. Over the long term, however, each manager makes a concerted effort to reduce future occurrences. Such efforts are consistent with the objectives of risk management and quality management systems respectively, and reflect the symbiotic relationship between the two systems.

Legal Liability of Boards of Health Agencies

In Canada, the health agency responsible for a significant portion of the patient treatment and the employment of health care personnel is the hospital. For the most part, the legal liability of hospital boards is similar to that for boards of other forms of health agencies. However, differences may arise between the legislation establishing or authorizing the operation of hospitals and the legislation establishing or authorizing the operation of other health care agencies. Detailed consideration of these differences is beyond the scope of this chapter. Instead, this chapter will examine the legal liability of hospital boards as generally representative of the legal risks associated with most health agencies.

Hospitals are generally operated and managed through a board. Legislation and common law, in turn, govern the authority and obligations of the board. For example, in Alberta the boards of most hospitals are governed by the *Hospitals Act* (1980), chapter H-11. Section 27 of the *Hospitals Act* states:

> *Each approved hospital must have a governing board and, subject to any limitations of its authority imposed by Acts of the Legislature and regulations under it, the board has full control of that hospital and has absolute and final authority in respect of all matters pertaining to the operation of the hospital.*

With this "absolute and final authority" comes legal responsibility. When legal action is commenced against hospitals, it is the board that is named as the defendant. It is the hospital or corporate entity, and not the individual board members, that bears the financial costs of any such legal actions. In some instances, such as human rights, environmental, or occupational health and safety matters, individual board members may be personally liable. Boards or individual members should carry personal director's and officer's liability insurance to cover any such personal liability.

In what circumstances will the hospital or the corporate entity be liable? As large corporations or institutions with varied operations and programs, hospitals must be prepared to address labour, contract, tort, real estate, corporate, environmental, administrative, intellectual property, and even criminal law concerns. From administering collective bargaining contracts to overseeing the proper disposal of medical wastes, hospitals face the full spectrum of legal liability for all these responsibilities.

A major source of liability for hospitals and an area in which risk management can be particularly effective is tort liability (Meagher, Marr, & Meagher, 1986; Picard, 1984). The major risk of tort liability involves patients' claims that the hospital was negligent in its care. Hospitals can be directly responsible to the patient or vicariously responsible to the patient through the actions of hospital employees. A patient may also claim against a hospital for breach of contract, although most actions are on the basis of negligence.

Liability in negligence arises out of the duties owed by the hospital to the patient. These duties include:

- Selecting competent staff;

- Instructing and supervising hospital personnel;

- Reviewing and monitoring the qualifications and competence of professionals performing services within the hospital (i.e., physicians); and

- Establishing and applying policies and procedures so that facilities and equipment are utilized and maintained so as to provide reasonable care to the patient.

These general duties can, in turn, be broken down into department- and employee-specific duties. These duties require employees to act reasonably in such situations as the handling and administration of drugs, the management of infectious substances, and the maintenance of the confidentiality of patient records.

The above sampling of the potential areas for hospital liability underscores the need for preventive approaches to risk management. Substantial claims may arise in an almost unlimited number of areas in a hospital setting. The hospital environment itself is continuously becoming more complex. Advances in knowledge and technology result in specialization, which, in turn, means that hospital departments are simultaneously becoming interdependent and insulated. Hospitals are required to do more with less. In such an environment, the potential for legal claims and financial losses abounds.

Legal Liability and the Nurse Manager

Until recently, nurses have had limited concern for legal liability as, generally, only doctors and hospital boards have been named as defendants in legal actions. However, with the increased knowledge and skill of nurses and the important role nurses play in patient care, more nurses are now also being named as defendants in actions. This has increased nurses' awareness of the legal liability they have for their own actions.

Nurse managers have a very important role in a health care agency or facility as they are responsible for carrying out many of the duties owed by hospitals to patients. Specifically, nurse managers are generally assigned responsibility for:

- Selecting competent nursing staff for their nursing units or departments;

- Instructing such staff to ensure they have the requisite skills to provide the care required by patients;

- Supervising such staff; and

- Continuing review and monitoring of the qualifications and competence of the nursing staff.

If a nurse manager fails to carry out any of these duties and a patient is injured as a result of such failure, the nurse manager could be found liable to the patient for any injuries caused by his or her negligence. However, as an employee of a health care facility or health care agency, the health care facility or agency would normally be vicariously liable for such nurse manager's actions, provided the nurse manager is working within the scope of his or her employment. That is, the nurse manager must meet the standards of a reasonable nurse manager, as failure to do so leaves both the individual and the employer liable. Because of the serious consequences that can arise if a nurse manager does not carry out his or her assigned duties in a reasonable manner, there is an onus on both the nurse manager and the facility or agency to ensure that the nurse manager is competent to carry out the assigned duties and is aware of legal consequences if he or she does not do so.

Although the health care facility or agency, as an employer, is vicariously liable for its employee's actions, this does not necessarily mean that the health care facility or agency cannot pursue an action against a negligent employee to recover monies paid on behalf of an employee in a legal action. A nurse manager should verify that the health care facility or agency will not seek to pursue such an action in the event of a legal action. If an employer will not give such an undertaking, the nurse manager is well advised to ensure that he or she has personal liability insurance that will provide coverage if ever required.

Another area where liability may arise for a nurse manager is a situation where an order left by a doctor is deemed inappropriate by a nurse and/or nurse manager. Although generally nurses are to carry out orders of doctors, with the level of professional training and experience nurses have, how can nurses or nurse managers carry out orders that they deem inappropriate? This creates a dilemma for health agencies and facilities. There is no Canadian case directly on point, although a Canadian court has expressed the view that a physician's instructions should be followed unless the instructions indicate clear and obvious neglect or incompetence:

> *I cannot accept the argument that if any of the nurses or the hospital servants disagreed with the findings or direction of the family doctor, that they should have acted independently or called in other medical advice. Diagnosis is surely not a function of the nurse; and unless there were clear and obvious evidences of neglect or incompetence on the part of the family doctor, it would be unthinkable that the hospital or its agents should interfere with or depart from his instructions. (Serre v. de Tilly et al, 1975)*

As well, the English decision of the House of Lords in Junor v. McNicol indicates that a professional will be liable in negligence only for actions taken on orders of the doctor where the order should have been recognized by a reasonable professional as being manifestly wrong (Picard, 1984, p. 324). The same result is likely to occur in Canada. Therefore, what is required to reduce conflicts that can arise between a nurse manager and doctor in such a situation is to have a mechanism where such disputed orders can be reviewed. Such a mechanism is also an important part of any risk management program.

The nurse manager, in addition to liability from legal action, also could be open to disciplinary proceedings by the nursing profession if he or she carried out an order that he or she knew or ought to have known was harmful to a patient (McCarthy, 1983; Picard, 1984, p. 324).

The nurse manager, as coordinator of patient care, may also become aware of omissions of treatment or inappropriate acts carried out by other health care professionals. As was the case with doctors' inappropriate orders, the nurse manager has a responsibility to pursue these matters with appropriate personnel to ensure that they are reviewed and that necessary actions are taken to counteract the omission or inappropriate treatment. Again, a mechanism is required so that a nurse manager can report such a matter to the proper authorities and have it pursued by qualified personnel.

The increased discussion respecting nurses' carrying out independent practices raises further liability concerns. If a nurse is "self-employed" or enters into a contract with an agency to provide services, such nurse will be personally liable for all his or her actions. As well, in any contract it is likely that the agency will seek to be indemnified by the nurse for any legal action that may arise from services provided by such nurse. In this situation, it is crucial that the nurse have sufficient liability insurance to cover any legal action that may arise from services he or she provides. If serious harm or injury may result to a patient from services provided, then a higher amount of liability insurance should be acquired.

Risk Management:
Structure and Processes

A precise risk management model will not be presented and, indeed, may not be desirable. To be successful, a risk management system must fit within the present systems of the health care facility and it must receive the commitment of the board, senior management, and staff. A certain degree of spontaneity and originality should be encouraged in developing a risk management system appropriate for the specific health care facility or health care agency. This is consistent with the CCHFA program, which neither requires a separate program for risk management nor prohibits setting up a separate program (CCHFA, 1991, p. 10).

Nonetheless, certain key elements of structure and process must be present in any risk management system, whether it is a separate program or combined with other programs such as quality management. These key elements will be explored further below.

Structural Elements

Any risk management system must have a foundational structure around which risk management processes can be developed and implemented. The structure must support processes that permit the identification, assessment, management, and evaluation of risk.

The structure of a risk management system is an amalgam of existing and new structures. The existing or internal structure is borrowed from patient, staff, and other programs already operating within the health care facility. The new or external structure comes from the risk management system itself.

Allen (1986) separates the structure of health care risk management into two programs: individual loss control and organizational elements. The individual loss control programs will already exist within most health care facilities. Allen groups these programs into five headings: patients, medical staff, staff, students, and general programs. Nested within each individual program are further loss control mechanisms. For example, the patient loss control program may include the following elements: patient and visitor safety programs, informed consent, medical record documentation, patient relations and communication, patient identification, and patient search procedures.

These loss control mechanisms all have as their basic goal the prevention of risk to the hospital. The challenge for a risk management system is to utilize, adapt, and adopt the existing structure of these individual loss programs in a coordinated way so as to achieve risk management goals.

The means by which the individual management systems are utilized, adapted, and adopted comprise the structure of the risk management system. The risk management system must import a structure that permits both coordination of the existing individual loss control programs and centralization of responsibility for such coordination, as well as centralization of responsibility for the risk management system itself. Allen (1986) describes this imported structure as the organizational components, and further breaks down the organizational components into three structural components:

Risk manager. Ideally, a person who has the authority and responsibility for developing, implementing, and coordinating the risk management system is required for a program to succeed. The risk manager may involve a new position or a delegation to existing personnel depending on the volume of activity and complexity of the facility or agency.

Risk management committee. A multidisciplinary committee provides both support and advice to the risk manager, if one is appointed, or takes complete responsibility for the program if there is no risk manager. If there is a risk manager, the committee may serve as liaison between the risk manager and senior management or the board. This is an important committee if the program is to function and, therefore, persons on the committee must have authority to make decisions. Further, nursing staff must be represented on this committee.

Risk management policy statement. A statement endorsed by the board of directors is required to provide both support and accountability for the risk management program. This statement can serve as a guiding principle to the risk manager and committee.

At a minimum, a risk management committee consisting of senior facility or agency personnel is required to guide the risk management program. The committee's key role should be to set out the policy or plan for the risk management program and then to have the board's endorsement of such policy or plan.

Process Elements

As defined, risk management is the process of risk identification, assessment, management, and evaluation. Each of these individual elements or components has its own requirements and will be discussed below.

The individual elements should be delineated in a risk management plan or policy. The plan should identify the role and goals of risk management in the health care facility or agency. The plan should identify the task, role and reporting relationships of each of the parties involved. The sources of available information and the reports to be generated should be identified.

Risk identification

Risk identification lies at the heart of risk management and deserves detailed consideration. Identifying areas of risk allows a risk management system to be proactive. Loss is ultimately minimized through a proactive process whereby risks can be identified before they give rise to severe financial consequences. A health care facility or agency must take time and make the effort to identify all sources of information, whether existing or new, that can provide data regarding potential and actual risk in the operation and management of the facility or agency.

There are many different strategies that a health care agency or facility can utilize for the identification of actual and potential risks. The CCHFA (1991, pp. 19-30) discusses four strategies:

Program reporting involves the transfer of reports from individual programs already in existence in a facility to the risk manager or risk management committee. Program reports may be generated from such programs as occupational health and safety, environmental hazards including theft of, and loss or damage to, facility property and/or equipment, infection control, medication administration, security and fire services, chart audits, patient surveys, nursing supervisor and on call reports (if such exist), Workplace Hazardous Material Information System (WHMIS) reports, and such reports from human resources as absenteeism, short and long term disability, staff turnover, and other related reports. These reports should be in a format that identifies the risk and outlines both the frequency with which such risk occurs and the severity of the losses or injury from such risk. The key is to transfer all information in as useful a format as possible so that potential and actual risk identification is maximized.

Generic reports are not identifiable to particular programs but are generated across departments and programs. The most common generic report is the patient incident report. Persons directly involved with a particular event are required to complete an incident report. Such a report serves as the basis from which the risk manager can identify and respond to potential areas of loss. Occurrence reporting is another generic means of identifying risk. Occurrence reporting is limited to specific and limited "occurrences" such as cardiac or respiratory arrests. However, all staff are generally required to complete occurrence reports. Occurrence reporting is therefore narrower in focus but broader in coverage than incident reporting. By involving all staff, the risk manager is more likely to be alerted to those occurrences which have previously been designated as high risk. In some facilities or agencies, either incident reports or occurrence reports will be used, but not both types of reports.

Departmental surveys involve surveying department heads and nurse managers regarding risks in their departments or units. Information from such a survey can provide the risk manager or the risk management committee with invaluable information. This is especially true in the early formation of the risk management program. Department heads and nurse managers have direct knowledge and experience in the daily operation of the health care facility, in general, and their unit or department, in particular. These individuals therefore have knowledge of special vulnerabilities to risk that the facility or agency faces, both from an overall perspective as well as in their particular unit or department.

External reports are those generated from outside the agency. As not all risks will be identified by the risk manager or risk management committee, some risks will first come to the risk manager's or committee's attention from external sources. Such notification may take the form of complaints by a patient or patient's family, or may be a letter from a lawyer, or a statement of claim or report from the Canadian Council on Health Facilities Accreditation. When risks are identified externally, risk management becomes reactive, not proactive. In this sense, the risk management system has failed. The response of the risk manager or risk management committee in this situation must be swift to ensure that no information is lost by a further time delay.

Risk assessment

Assessment serves as the bridge between identification and management (CCHFA, 1991, pp. 31-37). Not every risk that is identified leads to a risk management response. The assessment of risk can relate to a specific incident where a person witnesses a particular event. In this situation, it is the responsibility of all staff to offer appropriate assistance, stabilize the situation, investigate where possible, and then report when necessary. Much of this process, up to the point of reporting, is done intuitively.

The initial report may simply be to a supervisor. At this stage, the most important element in risk management may in fact be to ensure that the event is properly documented. After the initial report and documentation, a formal assessment must be made.

If the risk manager assesses the possibility of a complaint or suit, the risk manager must assume the responsibility of handling the claim in an immediate, reliable, and confidential manner. This assessment may include:

- Gathering evidence so as to determine the facts;

- Notifying the insurer and/or legal counsel;

- Making immediate responses to patients and family, where possible, to discourage claims; and

- Conducting a detailed and objective investigation.

Once these steps have been undertaken, an informed assessment of any long term risk can be made, including the identification of other implications that the incident or complaint may have on the facility or agency, such as the need to establish a policy or a staff educational program to minimize recurrence of the risk. Any data relating to similar incidents should also be reviewed to determine the frequency of such an incident. Further, the consequences of the risk should be reviewed. Could such risk, if unmanaged, reoccur and have serious consequences for a patient, employee, visitor, or the health care facility or agency?

Similarly, the risks identified from program reports, generic reports, incident and/or occurrence reports, departmental or unit surveys, and external reports must be reviewed to determine the frequency and severity of such risks. As well, consideration must be given regarding whether such risks are preventable or can be reduced or minimized. As not all risks will be able to be pursued at the same time, a facility or agency must make decisions regarding which risks should be pursued. Information relating to frequency and severity and whether risks can be prevented or minimized should assist the risk manager and/or risk management committee in setting the priorities the risks that should be pursued. This will ensure that the scarce resources of health care facilities or agencies are expended in an effective manner.

Managing risk

This process involves the actual treatment of the risk through either taking the necessary steps to eliminate or prevent risks from occurring or to minimize the frequency or severity of the risk. For example, for risks such as those arising from defective equipment, it may be possible to eliminate such risks if the equipment is appropriately monitored. However, for risks caused by human error, such as medication administration errors, it may be possible to reduce such risks only through modification of procedures and staff education programs.

The commitment of the board and senior management and support of all staff are required if risks are to be managed (CCHFA, 1991, pp. 37-42). In some situations, a risk may be managed only through a facility-wide plan, while in other situations a department or unit plan may be all that is required. Each risk will, therefore, have to be assessed to determine if and how it can be managed.

Reports should be compiled of the action taken respecting the identified risks. Such reports, although required for the monitoring of risk management programs, do raise concerns; in some provinces, such as Alberta, such reports may not be protected under the *Evidence Act*. Therefore, if a document is relevant to a legal action, it would likely have to be produced or released to the opposing party. As a result, it is important, until existing legislation can be amended, to protect risk management information. The content of risk management reports should be closely monitored to ensure that they contain only factual information. However, despite this concern, it is probably better to have unprivileged reports, as producing no reports will not help to control or manage risks. The courts would likely view such reports as a positive step taken by an agency or facility to try and reduce or prevent injury or losses.

Evaluating risk

A risk management system, to be truly proactive, requires effective feedback. As the risk manager or committee responds to individual risk occurrences, the outcomes of these responses must be fed back into the risk management system. This includes more than just simply posting reports (CCHFA, 1991, pp. 42-44). The risk management system must be carried out with the active participation of the board, as the ultimate evaluator of the system, and the department heads and staff who provide the key inputs into the system.

Each of the above four elements or components is essential for a successful risk management program. As Stock and Lefroy (1988) state: "The success of risk management efforts is dependent on the health care organization's ability to implement each component in a comprehensive and balanced manner" (p. 7).

Incident Reports

Incident reports provide a good source of data relating to risk identification. These reports are generally utilized to document unusual events that occur to a patient in a health care facility. These reports are compiled for the information of management of the facility so it can be aware of such an event and take any steps necessary either to act upon the unusual event or to report such event to an insurer and legal counsel. Although this is an important use for such reports, under a risk management program, such reports, when compiled, also provide useful information to determine the recurrence of the unusual events, the severity of the harm or loss caused by such events, the time when such events occur, and other information that can assist in not only identifying a risk but also assessing and managing it. Therefore, if a risk management program is established, it is important that all incident reports are forwarded to the risk manager, if there is one, or the risk management committee.

However, incident reports, unless appropriately completed, can also pose a risk for a health care facility. The risk relates to the content that may be contained in such a report. As an incident report may have to be produced in court, it should contain only factual information. Such a report should not contain speculations or opinions regarding the event, or outline who was responsible for the event. If information regarding opinions is to be documented, it should be done only in a report that is provided to the facility's legal counsel, as solicitor-client privilege may then be applicable and such document will not have to be produced in court (Picard, 1984, pp. 334-337). Another precaution that should be taken is that such report should not be placed in a patient's medical record, nor should there be a notation in the medical record that such report was prepared, unless there is specific legislation requiring that this be done.

Preventive Strategies

Strategies that prevent risks from occurring are many, but only two will be reviewed in this chapter: documentation, and policies and procedures.

Documentation

Documentation of care or treatment provided to a patient, or regarding a nurse manager's discussion with staff regarding such matters as competency or absenteeism, is crucial. It is important that such care, treatment, or discussions are documented as soon as possible after the care or treatment was provided or the discussion has taken place. All documentation should be dated, written in ink, and signed. Such documentation, if done contemporaneously with the event, will be admissible as evidence in court. Further, factual notes will assist in recalling events if this is ever required. From a risk management perspective, accurate, complete, and contemporaneous notes can assist in reducing risks in the provision of care by ensuring that anyone having contact with a patient is aware of the patient's condition and the care and treatment that was provided. This can, therefore, avoid duplication of treatment and also ensure that all information is available to doctors *and other health care professionals* to ensure that an appropriate diagnosis can be made and treatment ordered.

Nurses often express concern that they do not have time to document things. However, from the perspective of legal liability and patient care, a nurse must make the appropriate time available to document findings and treatment. Such notes may be the only evidence a nurse has that treatment or care has been provided. It is possible for a court to view no documentation as being evidence that no treatment has been provided (Meyer v. Gordon, 1981).

Policies and Procedures

Health care facilities are fairly successful in establishing policies and procedures for staff to follow; this is especially true of nursing staff. However, often after policies and procedures are established they are not reviewed and, therefore, quickly become outdated. As a result, such policies are not followed by staff. The problem that arises and the risk for a facility is that if a patient is injured and an action is commenced, the patient's lawyer will likely request production of relevant policies and procedures. If a policy exists but is not followed, this puts in question both the facility's policy as well as the action of its employees.

If a policy is established and exists, courts would likely look on such a policy as setting out the facility's position on a matter. Then, if the employee did not follow such a policy, the employee would be acting in contravention of the facility's recommended action. It is, therefore, important that if facilities and agencies are to have policies and procedures, they review them to ensure that they are current. All outdated policies should be removed.

Another important matter is ensuring that all staff are aware of a facility's or agency's policies and procedures. Nurse managers have an important role in this area and should ensure that policy and procedure books are up to date and that all staff are acting in a manner consistent with such policies and procedures. Further, staff who act outside of established policies and procedures should have such policies and procedures brought to their attention immediately. If a staff member continues to act outside of an established policy or procedure, appropriate disciplinary actions should be taken by the nurse manager.

Nurse Manager as a Witness

A nurse manager may be called as a witness in an action naming him or her as a defendant or where the facility or agency is named as a defendant, or as a witness for a plaintiff in an action, or as an expert witness.

Witness for Defendant or Plaintiff

A nurse manager who must be a witness in either an action in which he or she or the employer has been named as a defendant, or where the nurse manager is served with a notice to be a witness for a plaintiff in an action, may find this to be a very emotional experience. The nurse manager will be placed in the position of having to recall what was done, when it was done, and any other relevant details regarding the matters in issue. This can be frustrating, as the nurse manager's memory of the event may have faded during the often lengthy period between an occurrence and the trial. The nurse manager, therefore, may have difficulty recalling specifics, unless of course he or she made notes of the matters in issue in the medical record or other documentation that can assist in refreshing his or her memory. This is the reason it is of utmost importance always to document, when an event occurs, all matters of observation of patient, or care provided, or treatment rendered.

As a witness, the nurse manager will initially have to take an oath that all the evidence he or she is about to give will be truthful. The nurse manager will then be asked questions, by his or her lawyer or the employer's lawyer or the plaintiff's lawyer—a process referred to as *examination-in-chief.* The nurse manager should always be prepared by the lawyer prior to giving evidence. The lawyer will be able to review the questions that he or she will be asking the nurse manager at trial, as well as to prepare the nurse manager for cross-examination.

The nurse manager will then be subject to questions from the plaintiff's lawyer, a process that is referred to as *cross-examination.* This experience can be both professionally and personally debilitating (Picard, 1984, pp. 285-287). As well, the judge can also ask questions of the witness.

Although being a witness can be a difficult experience, the following guidelines may assist:

• Always ensure that you are aware of the question being asked. If unsure of the question, ask that it be repeated. If several questions are asked, ask that the lawyer clarify which question he wants answered. The lawyer should ask one question at a time.

• Always speak clearly, slowly, and loud enough so that you can be heard by the judge, jury, and the court reporter, who will be transcribing everything that you say.

• Do not use abbreviations or complex nursing or medical terminology which will not be readily understood by the judge or jury.

• Respond only to questions asked; do not volunteer other information unless it will assist your case. As a witness, you must constantly remind yourself of the question when responding. If you do not know the answer, say so. Also, if you are not absolutely certain of your evidence, you can preface a response with the phrase, "to the best of my recollection," or some similar phrase.

As Gilbert Sharpe (1987) states in relation to physicians as witnesses:

> *The witness who prepares carefully, remains alert, controls his or her temper, answers questions forthrightly, confines answers to what he or she honestly believes to be true and maintains self respect under cross-examination will be pleasantly surprised to find that there is little justification for most of his or her forebodings.* (p. 128)

From my personal experience as a witness for a hospital, such comment is also applicable to nurse managers.

Nurse Manager as an Expert Witness

Initially when a nurse is called as an expert witness in a trial, his or her credentials, including education and experience, will be reviewed by the lawyer calling him or her as a witness. The other lawyer can ask questions regarding the credentials and the area of expertise. The judge will then determine whether, from the evidence, the nurse is an expert in the area in which he or she is to give evidence.

The same process of questioning as set out above will be followed. The evidence the nurse will give, however, will differ in that he or she will not be giving evidence on the facts of the case but rather will be giving evidence relating to nursing or management expertise.

As well, the nurse manager can state personal opinions regarding any matter on which he or she has been declared an expert. An expert has a special role in court. Sopinka and Lederman (1974) set out this special role in the following statement:

> An expert is usually called for two reasons. He provides basic information to the court necessary for its understanding of the scientific or technical issues involved in the case. In addition, because the court alone is incapable of drawing the necessary inferences from the technical facts presented, an expert is allowed to state his opinion and conclusions. (p. 309)

Therefore, a nurse manager called as an expert witness has an important role, as evidence relating to nursing or management, or both areas, will assist the court in interpreting the facts of the case and in reaching its decision. With nursing's increased expertise relating to nursing as an independent practice, as well as the expertise of the nurse manager in nursing unit management, more nurses and nurse managers will be required as expert witness in actions where nursing care or matters relating to management are in issue.

Assistance to Nursing Staff

Nurse managers may also be called upon to assist their staff members if any of them must be a witness in an action. The nurse manager may find it useful to review with their staff the matters set out in the section relating to the nurse manager as a witness. Although the staff will be prepared by the lawyer for the employer or (if a witness for the plaintiff) by the lawyer for the plaintiff, the nurse manager can play an important supportive role in assisting the staff to prepare to give evidence and in listening to their concerns.

If a nurse manager has never been in a court setting, it may be useful to attend a trial before testifying. This can be done at any time the court is sitting. This experience will assist the nurse manager in understanding the courtroom setting and the trial process.

Conclusion

If a board of a facility or agency desires to prevent or minimize actual or potential risks, it must take the initiative to establish and maintain a risk management program. Such risk management program must be structured to meet the needs of the particular facility or agency and include the key components of identification, assessment, and management of potential and actual risks. For a risk management program to be successful, the board and all the management personnel of the facility or agency must be committed to such a program and be prepared to take appropriate action to prevent or minimize potential or actual risks.

Acknowledgement

The author wishes to give special thanks to James Baird, who assisted in both research and preparation of this chapter.

References

Allen P. (1986). *The development of a risk management program*. Ottawa: Canadian Hospital Association.

Dickens, B. (1993). Implications for health professionals' legal liability. *Health Law Journal, 1,* 1-12.

Hospitals Act, R.S.A. 1980, c. H-11 as amended.

McCarthy, S. (1983). Tender loving mercy killing. *Alberta Report, 7,* 26.

Meagher, A.J., Marr, P.J., & Meagher, R.A. (1986). *Doctors and hospitals legal duties*. Toronto: Butterworths.

Meyer v. Gordon (1981), 17 C.C.L.T. 1 (B.C.S.C.).

Picard, E.I. (1984). *Legal liability of doctors and hospitals in Canada* (2nd ed.). Toronto: Carswell.

Poteet, W. (1983). Risk management and nursing. *Nursing Clinics of North America, 18*(3), 457.

Serre v. de Tilly et al. (1975) 58 D.L.R. (3rd) 362 at 367.

Sharpe, G. (1987). *The law and medicine in Canada*. Toronto: Butterworths.

Sopinka, J., & Lederman, S. (1974). *The law of evidence in court cases*. Toronto: Butterworths.

Stock, R.G., & Lefroy, S.E. (1988). *Risk management: A practical framework for Canadian health care facilities*. Ottawa: Canadian Hospital Association.

Youngberg, B.J. (1984). *Essentials of hospital risk management*. Rockville, MD: Aspen Publishers.

C H A P T E R   3 1

Administering Collective Agreements

Judith M. Hibberd

Judith M. Hibberd, RN, BScN (Toronto), MHSA, PhD (Alberta), has broad experience in nursing management and education. She is currently Associate Professor, Faculty of Nursing at the University of Alberta, Edmonton, Alberta.

One of the more challenging aspects of being a nurse manager is working with unionized staff. The majority of non-managerial workers in the Canadian health care system are unionized; about 75% to 80% of all registered nurses belong to unions (Morris, 1991), and so nurse managers play an important role in administering collective agreements. In any one workplace, a nurse manager may have more than one union contract to administer because auxiliary nursing personnel and support staff often belong to separate bargaining units and negotiate contracts independently of nurses' unions.

Effective administration of union contracts requires a basic understanding of the labour relations system and how collective agreements are reached. Nurse managers should also understand the nature of unions, the nature of the employment relationship, and the procedures for resolving union – management conflicts, especially the grievance procedure. Armed with this knowledge, nurse managers should be able to develop appropriate skills and attitudes needed to establish constructive relations with union representatives. Local union representatives often attend labour schools sponsored by their unions. Thus, nurse managers need to be equally well informed in the area of labour relations so that they may deal intelligently with union issues at work.

The objectives of this chapter are to provide an overview of contract administration, and to offer some practical guidelines for dealing effectively with unionized staff. A framework is presented to illustrate the multiple factors that may influence collective bargaining. This is followed by discussion of the union – management relationship and selected terms and conditions of employment; grievance procedure; progressive discipline; and, finally, implications for nurse managers.

Framework for Understanding Collective Bargaining by Nurses

A collective agreement is a contract of employment. In order to understand the processes by which a collective agreement is reached, the reader needs to know something about the industrial relations system.

Scholars frequently view the field of industrial relations from a systems perspective (Anderson, Gunderson, & Ponak, 1989; Craig, 1990). The Canadian industrial relations system is decentralized, somewhat like the health care system, in that responsibility for employment relations rests with the provinces. Although the federal government has a Labour Code governing its own employees and certain national enterprises, each province establishes its own labour legislation. Consequently, there are 11 labour relations systems in the country, which means that procedures relative to collective bargaining tend to vary from province to province. This fact explains why nurses are entitled to strike in some provinces and not in others. Despite this, common elements of the provincial industrial relations systems can be identified. In Figure 31.1, components of these systems that directly or indirectly influence collective bargaining by nurses are presented.

Factors in the environment, such as the state of the economy and the legal system, can be expected to have an impact on the goals of the parties in collective bargaining. For example, in a recession unions are more likely to give priority to job security demands rather than to wage demands, and employers may try to secure wage concessions from unions, as Alberta's nurses discovered in 1988 (Hibberd, 1992).

The principal participants in collective bargaining are the employers and their organizations, and nurses and their unions. But governments play a major part in labour relations in the health field: not only do they fund hospitals and community health care agencies; they also make the rules governing collective bargaining. They are also responsible for protecting the public

Figure 31.1

Framework for understanding collective bargaining by nurses.

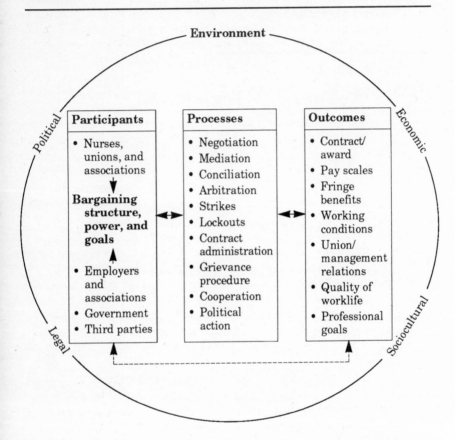

interest. All parties in the collective bargaining process have goals and special interests, and each has various power resources which it brings to bear on the process.

The parties pursue their goals through various processes in which conflict, cooperation, and compromise are anticipated. Figure 31.1 includes various processes and procedures that may be employed in reaching a collective agreement, for example, the negotiating process, mediation, arbitration, strikes, lockouts, and the grievance procedure, to name a few. In the vast majority of cases, collective bargaining results in an agreement without conflict (Craig, 1990), and the principal outcome of these procedures is an employment contract, whether negotiated with or without third party assistance, or imposed by an arbitrator.

In addition to the collective agreement, there are consequences for the continuing relationship of the union and employer. A long and bitter strike, for example, may have a lingering and negative impact on relationships in the workplace and can influence the goals that the parties pursue at the next round of bargaining. As collective bargaining recurs at periodic intervals, this framework may be viewed as a dynamic system in which component parts influence, or are influenced by, each other.

The Union – Management Relationship

The nature of relationships between employers and employees has been defined historically by past practices, common law, and labour statutes. Over the years, total employer domination over employees has been replaced with increasingly progressive laws protecting the rights of employees. All provinces have passed employment standards acts establishing minimum terms and conditions of work for all employees, as well as labour relations acts governing union – management relationships (Morris, 1991). Labour statutes are administered by labour relations boards (or in the case of Québec by labour courts), whose role is to oversee certification procedures, to interpret the law, to make decisions, and to provide third party assistance in disputes between the parties. Employees' rights are further protected by law in the areas of occupational health and safety, human rights, pay equity, workers' compensation, unemployment insurance, and tax and pension provisions.

The union – management relationship is formalized through the process of certification. The union applies to the labour relations board for exclusive right to represent a defined group of employees. The union must file its constitution and bylaws, together with evidence that it represents a majority of a group of employees. Employers are entitled to submit contrary evidence to the labour boards, but they are prohibited from resisting legitimate unionizing activities. Once certified, the union notifies the employer of its intention to negotiate terms and conditions of employment, and the employer must then recognize the collective bargaining relationship.

Successful union – management relations will depend a great deal on how the parties view each other. If they operate from a conflict viewpoint, then the collective agreement will be perceived as merely a temporary "peace treaty" (Giles & Jain, 1989). A more enlightened perspective is to recognize collective bargaining as "a joint decision-making process for determining terms and conditions of employment and spelling them out in collective agreements.

Table 31.1
Typical provisions of nurses' collective agreements.

---

1. Recognition of the parties and purpose of agreement
2. Definitions: nursing personnel covered by agreement
3. Union security: deduction of union dues or the Rand Formula*
4. Management rights
5. Grievance procedure
6. Seniority; promotion; layoff and recall
7. Hours of work; shift schedules; holidays; vacations
8. Fringe benefits: health care benefits; sick leave
9. Compensation and premium payments
10. Committees: professional responsibility; occupational health and safety; agency boards
11. Term of agreement: expiry date of contract
12. Appendices: letters of understanding; salary schedules

* A contractual arrangement in which the employer makes a payroll deduction of an amount equal to union dues from each member of the bargaining unit whether or not the employee is a member of the union.

It is grounded on a dependence or symbiotic relationship between employees and employers" (Fisher & Williams, 1989, p. 185). Such a definition implies a legitimate role for unions in framing the rules by which the parties relate to each other, and is more in keeping with the consultative approach to labour relations taken by professional employees such as nurses and teachers.

Terms and Conditions of Employment

Collective agreements in the health field are becoming more and more complex. Nevertheless, some standard provisions are common to most agreements; these are listed in Table 31.1. The contract usually begins with a preamble. The parties recognize each other and state their intention to work together for the common purpose of providing health care services. Each category of worker covered by the agreement is then defined. In many jurisdictions, first-line nurse managers are excluded from the bargaining unit (i.e., they are out-of-scope) by virtue of their managerial responsibilities. Where nurse managers are in-scope, they may face conflicts of interest, as in the case of a grievance over the application of disciplinary measures. Unions have policies to deal with such situations that generally favour the grievor, although there may be informal discussions between union and nurse manager about the case.

It is important to keep in mind that, whatever provisions the contract contains, they were jointly agreed upon by the parties, albeit reluctantly in some cases, and often in the emotion-laden atmosphere of marathon bargaining sessions. Nevertheless, if the parties have ratified the agreement they have a duty to honour it until such time as the contract is renegotiated.

Management Rights—Implied and Express

Historically, employers have gone to great lengths to protect their common-law prerogatives, and almost all collective agreements contain a management rights clause. The clause (or clauses) may take the form of a broad general statement or a detailed list of specific rights (Cohen, 1989); in either case, the nurse manager must be conversant with these express management rights.

There is considerable debate in the labour relations literature on management rights. Unions argue that once the parties enter a union – management relationship, unilateral discretion by the employer ceases and all decisions become negotiable. On the other hand, employers prefer a residual rights theory "based on management's assertion that all the rights and privileges that employers exercised before unionization must be considered to be reserved to them afterwards except for those specifically limited by the collective agreement" (Giles & Jain, 1989, p. 323).

Much of what goes on in the workplace, however, is not governed by union contracts because, as Giles and Jain (1989) point out, "collective agreements cannot possibly regulate even a small proportion of the issues, tensions, and relationships that spring from the social and physical setting" (p. 340). For this reason, managers need to be aware of the implied rights and duties derived from common law and past employment practices that underlie all employment contracts, whether or not expressed in written contracts (McPhillips & England, 1989). Implied rights and duties (see Table 31.2, page 580) serve as a guide to management practices when the collective agreement is silent on an issue, and they influence arbitrators' decisions when interpreting a collective agreement or judging the merits of a grievance.

The employment relationship is a fiduciary one; in other words, it is based on good faith and trust (Phillips & England, 1989). While the employer retains the right to run the health agency, the employee has an obligation to cooperate with the employer. Any failure to fulfil these rights and responsibilities constitutes a breach of the employment contract.

Table 31.2
Implied employment rights and duties.

Employer
- Provides work and pays compensation for labour
- Responsible for safe workplace
- Responsible for employees' conduct at work
- Gives reasonable notice of termination in absence of just cause

Employee
- Cooperates with employer
- Exercises reasonable skill and care
- Obeys lawful directives
- Is not excessively absent from work
- Behaves in good faith, and does not disseminate confidential information

Source: Compiled from Glasbeek, H.J. (1982), "The contract of employment at common law." In Anderson, J., & Gunderson, M. (Eds.), *Union – management relations in Canada* (pp. 47-77). Toronto: Addison-Wesley.

Conflict between unions and management during the term of the collective agreement, whether or not over the question of management rights, may be resolved informally, or formally through the grievance procedure. Strikes and lockouts are dispute resolution procedures (see Figure 31.1, page 576), but in Canada, they are not allowed during the term of the collective agreement (Sethi & MacNeil, 1989). For this reason, collective agreements must include a grievance procedure.

The Grievance Procedure

A grievance is an allegation that one or more provisions of an agreement have been violated, and a claim for redress (Gandz & Whitehead, 1989). There are three types of grievances: individual, group, and policy grievances (Gorsky, 1981). The type of grievance determines the level at which it can be initiated in the grievance procedure. A policy grievance affecting the union itself, for example, is usually filed directly with the chief executive officer of the agency, whereas an individual or group grievance must first be discussed with immediate supervisors. The subject of a grievance in Canada is confined to the contents of the collective agreement, but in the U.S.A. the subject of a grievance may go beyond the agreement to include violations of a health agency's own rule or past practice (American Nurses' Association, 1985).

Table 31.3
A typical grievance procedure.

Complaint	A nurse discusses a complaint or concern informally with the immediate supervisor and the complaint is satisfied or dismissed within seven working days.
Step 1	The complaint becomes a grievance and is written on the union's grievance form specifying (a) the nature of the grievance; (b) the articles in the collective agreement allegedly violated; and (c) the remedy sought; it is then submitted to the first-level nurse manager within seven working days of the initial discussion. A meeting may be held with the grievor, union representative, and manager. The nurse manager delivers a response in writing to the nurse within seven working days.
Step 2	If the grievance has not been settled, it may be submitted in writing to the director of nursing within seven working days. A meeting of all parties may be convened to discuss the grievance. The director's decision is communicated in writing to the grievor (copy to the union) within seven working days.
Step 3	If the grievance has not been settled, it may be submitted in writing to the chief executive officer within seven working days. A meeting of all parties may be convened. The chief executive officer's decision is communicated in writing to the grievor (copy to the union) within seven working days.
Step 4	If the grievance is not settled, either party may consider whether to proceed to arbitration, or whether to abandon the grievance. Decision to proceed to arbitration is communicated in writing to the other party together with the name of a nominee to the arbitration board within seven working days.
Arbitration	Final, binding decision is made.

Note: If the employer fails to respond within the specified time limits, the grievance automatically moves to the next step in the procedure. If the union or grievor fails to respond within specified time limits, the grievance is abandoned, unless there has been prior mutual agreement to extend the time limits. At each step of the grievance, the employee may be accompanied by a union representative.

Although it is almost impossible to know the entire contract in detail, nurse managers must be thoroughly familiar with the grievance procedure. They must also know the scope of their authority in handling grievances; for example, they need to know at what stage human resources personnel are to become involved in the process. A typical grievance procedure is presented in Table 31.3.

There is not much research on the incidence and pattern of nurses' union grievances. Research in other fields suggests that grievances may serve many functions: they are a means by which unions may communicate with employers; they permit one of the parties to challenge the rights or actions of the other party; they may be a form of continuous bargaining (i.e., a way of forcing a concession that could not be obtained at the negotiating table); or they may be politically motivated by self-serving individuals or groups either within the union or managerial ranks (Gandz, 1982).

Arbitrators have recognized the powerlessness and vulnerability of individuals who choose to challenge an employer's authority, and they uphold the principle of natural justice underlying the grievance procedure. A grievance allows union members to appeal a manager's negative decision at increasingly higher levels of administrative authority, and ultimately to an independent arbitrator or arbitration board, without fear of punishment or dismissal. Even with the protection that a collective agreement affords, a nurse may feel too intimidated to complain. This is why unions have fought for the right to accompany their members throughout the grievance procedure and to receive copies of all written communications about grievances.

The nurse manager plays a critical role at the first step of the grievance procedure. This step is an informal discussion where the grievor and manager determine whether a problem exists. This is where the facts of the situation are carefully and thoroughly investigated; where consultation is sought; and, ideally, where the problem is solved. If the decision is well founded at this point, the nurse manager can expect to be supported by senior administrators should the grievance advance through subsequent steps. To avoid the demoralizing experience of having a decision overturned at a more senior level of the organization, the nurse manager should consult the human resources department and the next level of management before dismissing or allowing a grievance. Senior administrators bring a broader perspective to bear on the procedure and may have handled similar grievances in the past. Nevertheless, what seems like a clear-cut case to unions and employers may be seen in a totally different light by an arbitration board. Indeed, it is often difficult to predict the outcome of arbitration.

Grievance Arbitration

At step 4 of the grievance procedure, either party may refer the dispute to an external arbitration board. Grievance arbitration should not be confused with interest arbitration, which is used to settle disputes arising out of collective bargaining. The two procedures are similar but they deal with different types of disputes. Grievance arbitration deals with disputes arising out of the interpretation, application, or alleged violation of the terms of an existing collective agreement.

Fewer than two percent of written grievances proceed to arbitration, according to Gandz and Whitehead (1989). In a 12-month period from 1991-92, the Staff Nurses' Associations of Alberta, representing 2700 nurses, reported 139 grievances, only two of which went to arbitration (Rogers, 1992). It is, therefore, a relatively rare event for a nurse manager to have to take part in arbitration proceedings.

If a grievance goes to arbitration, union and management each select a nominee to serve on the arbitration board. The nominees jointly select the chair but if they cannot agree on this person the Minister of Labour will appoint the arbitrator. In some cases, the board consists of a sole arbitrator (Rowsell, 1983). A hearing is held at which the parties may be represented by legal counsel. Witnesses may be called and cross-examined, and the parties will formally present their arguments (Gandz & Whitehead, 1989).

Arbitration is time-consuming and expensive; the parties are responsible for the expenses of their respective nominees and witnesses, and they share the fee of the arbitrator. By the time a grievance goes to arbitration, the parties are usually entrenched in their opposing positions and determined to win the case. The arbitration board's decision is final and binding on the parties, and can be appealed only under specific circumstances, for example, if the arbitrator exceeds his or her authority or makes an error in law (Gorsky, 1981).

Appearing at an arbitration hearing is much like attending court, except that the rules of evidence and procedure are not as rigorous, and the hearing may be held in a less formal setting than a law court. In preparation for serving as a witness for management, the nurse manager and other witnesses must be well briefed on their roles at the arbitration hearing, preferably at a meeting with the lawyer or person presenting the case. Because of the potential for every grievance to become an arbitration case, nurse managers must keep meticulous notes of each phase of the grievance process, noting who attended each meeting; what main points were made; what the final decision was; and the underlying reasons for allowing or disallowing the grievance. Moreover, care must be taken with the content and language used in all written communications to the grievor, because these will undoubtedly be filed as exhibits at the arbitration hearing. Even past performance appraisals may be submitted as an exhibit if the grievance involves the discipline of a nurse.

Progressive Discipline

Occasionally it will be necessary to discipline a staff member, and arbitrators in the past have expected employers to apply discipline in a progressive manner (Pearlman, 1991). One might well ask, as Eden (1992) does, whether the application of negative sanctions is an appropriate corporate response to employee misconduct in light of contemporary trends in human resource management. However, as Cannon (1980) notes, the objective of progressive discipline should be to correct behaviour, not to punish it. Nevertheless, if the employee fails to respond to repeated warnings, the ultimate penalty could be dismissal. A typical disciplinary procedure appears in Table 31.4.

Discipline should be used to correct patterns of unsatisfactory behaviour, not to deal with occasional errors or misjudgements. On the other hand, gross misconduct, such as sexual harassment of a patient, would require immediate suspension so that an investigation could take place. Similarly, assaulting a patient would probably be considered just cause for dismissal. Where a staff member has demonstrated unsatisfactory behaviour in more than one area (for example, as in absenteeism and failure to chart narcotic drugs), it would be necessary to apply discipline progressively to both problems. Moreover, a nurse manager has discretion to repeat a step, or to begin the procedure again if there has been a significant time lapse since an earlier disciplinary step. Whatever the situation, the problem must be communicated to the staff member immediately and in private, never in hallways or within earshot of patients or other staff. Discipline that is loudly applied in public is humiliating for the employee, and unprofessional on the part of the manager; it also undermines its objective, namely, to effect a positive change in behaviour.

At every step of the disciplinary procedure, the nurse manager should be prepared for a grievance. The grievance procedure and the disciplinary procedure are similar processes in which increasing pressure is placed on the other party to bring about a change in thinking or behaviour. The disciplinary procedure, however, is the prerogative of management and is not usually spelled out in detail in the collective agreement. Even so, should the case

Table 31.4

Progressive discipline.

Step 1	**Informal discussion.** A private meeting is held between nurse manager and nurse to identify the problem, to discuss it, and to coach or counsel the nurse.
Step 2	**Verbal warning.** Assuming no improvement in behaviour, another meeting is held between nurse manager and nurse. Three points are made: (a) the problem is identified and the desired change in behaviour stated; (b) a time limit is set during which improvement is to occur; and (c) the consequences of failure to improve are stated. The nurse must also understand that he or she has received a verbal warning.
Step 3	**Written warning.** At least 24 hours' notice of a meeting is given to the nurse, who may be accompanied by a union representative. Discussion of the problem follows, with reference to previous verbal warnings. A letter is given to the nurse containing the same three points outlined in step 2. Copies are filed in the employee's personnel record and with the union.
Step 4	**Suspension.** The procedures in step 3 are repeated, but the letter states the length of the suspension, and whether it is to be with or without pay. The nurse must understand that the ultimate consequence of not responding to discipline in the specified amount of time will be dismissal. Copies are filed in the employee's personnel record and with the union.
Step 5	**Dismissal.** A final meeting is held that includes representatives from the Human Resources department and the union. The letter terminating nurse's employment contains final pay cheque and relevant severance papers. Copies of the letter are filed in the employee's personnel record and with the union.

Note: The level at which discipline begins will depend upon the severity of the employee's misconduct or problem and, depending on the situation, steps in the procedure may be repeated. A union representative may be present at each step of the procedure.

go to arbitration, the employer will be required to show that there was sufficient cause to discipline the nurse; that the nurse understood the problem and was given opportunities and assistance to improve his or her performance; that there were no extenuating circumstances; and that the discipline was not arbitrary or unreasonable. As in the grievance procedure, careful documentation is absolutely essential. All evidence that led to the discipline and relevant details of discussions and interviews must be recorded in the employee's file. Such data will likely be used at arbitration. Unions often negotiate time periods beyond which such documentation must be purged from the employee's file. Few managers look forward to using disciplinary measures, but if they are handled thoughtfully, objectively, and in a timely manner, both parties should emerge with their self-respect intact, as well as their respect for each other.

Insubordination

As stated in Table 31.2 (see page 580), an implied duty of employees, whether unionized or not, is to cooperate with lawful directives of the employer. Willful refusal to obey a lawful order is known as insubordination. Employers consider insubordination a serious breach of the employment contract and just cause for discipline. It should be clear that effective management is impossible if the nursing staff no longer respect legitimate orders from the person in charge of a unit.

To be successful in disciplining a person for insubordination, a nurse manager will have to prove that:

- A valid order was given to the employee;
- The order was clearly communicated by a person having the authority to direct the employee; and
- The employee failed to comply with the order (Mrazek & Tumback, 1990).

It is important to note that these cases are not concerned with failure to comply with physicians' orders relative to patient care. Nurses are obligated under professional practice acts to question and, if necessary, to refuse to carry out a physician's order that they know to be erroneous and harmful to patients. Such disputes between professional colleagues fall outside the meaning and definition of insubordination because nurses do not normally report to physicians, but to someone in a line position in the formal structure of the health agency. The concern here is with orders given by nurse managers (as the employer's designate) to their staff members, and this includes patient care assignments that an individual nurse might consider intolerable and unsafe.

Whether or not a nurse can refuse a legitimate order to care for patients is a complex question (Creighton, 1986; Huerta & Oddi, 1992; Northrop, 1987; Wahn, 1979), and nurse managers need to be clear where they stand in such situations. More importantly, a nurse manager must decide if the refusal to obey is serious enough to be defined as insubordination. For example, a nurse may try to avoid working with a particularly difficult client, or may simply forget to carry out a delegated task, neither of which really constitutes insubordination. The most reasonable response of a nurse manager would be to try to negotiate an acceptable compromise with the unwilling nurse, but the problem with this is that precedents can be set, and manipulative employees may be resented by other staff. The nurse manager must be sure of the facts before alleging insubordination.

There are three general circumstances under which an employee is entitled to refuse a supervisor's order: when compliance with an order

1. Constitutes an illegal act;

2. Endangers the health or safety of the employee and co-workers; or

3. Causes irreparable damage (in the case of a union) to the interest of other employees (Mrazek & Tumbach, 1990).

This does not mean that the employee would necessarily escape discipline in such an event; rather, it means that arbitrators likely would rule in favour of the employee for refusing an order under any of these circumstances. There are, however, some requirements of employees who invoke any of these exceptional circumstances. The employee bears the onus of proving the case to the arbitrator, and for this reason the employee must, at the time the order is refused, explain the reason for refusal. As most employees would not be able to articulate their rights and obligations in a case of insubordination, it behooves the nurse manager to explain the seriousness of refusal to comply with a legitimate order, and to help staff articulate their reasons for refusing before administering discipline.

Nurses' refusal to undertake patient care assignments has created some interesting jurisprudence. In the Mount Sinai case in which three nurses were disciplined for refusing to take an additional patient into an intensive care unit (Sklar, 1979a, 1979b), arbitrators did not extend the health and safety exemption (point number 2, above) where, in the nurse's professional judgement, compliance with an order would threaten the health and safety of patients. In other words, the principle established is that "heavy or excessive patient work-loads alone cannot be used as a basis for refusal to carry out an assignment" (Mrazek & Tumbach, 1990). The reason for this is that the employer (including the nurse manager) is vicariously liable for any injuries to patients arising out of a nurse's inability or failure to provide safe care to patients. Hence, employees should more appropriately observe the principle of "obey now, grieve later" (Mrazek & Tumback, 1990).

The principle of "obey now, grieve later" reflects the duty of the employee to cooperate with the employer. Of course, it does not solve the dilemma of the nurse who wishes to refuse a patient assignment on moral and ethical grounds. Such situations can be avoided in part by frank discussions with nurses at the time they are hired, but there appears to be little to protect the conscientious objector (see Creighton, 1986; Peterborough Civic Hospital, 1982). Similarly, nurses who "whistleblow" are largely unprotected at the present time, although there appears to be some movement toward policy changes in this area (Fiesta, 1990; McKenna, 1989). Currently, if a nurse wishes to expose unlawful or hazardous working conditions to the press, he or she would attract discipline from the employer. Nevertheless, when all internal avenues of protest have been exhausted, professional employees have a duty to their clients to ensure that their safety and interests are properly served. Under such circumstances, nurses' professional associations should be consulted, as in the Vancouver General Hospital case (Lovell, 1981).

Nurses' unions have experimented with "disclaimers of responsibility" forms for informing employers that working conditions were not conducive to safe patient care. An arbitrator recently ruled that it was indeed proper for nurses to advise an employer in writing of patient care concerns, but "the inclusion in the professional responsibility form of a disclaimer and a notice to seek indemnification is, at law, a meaningless document and serves only to offend the employer and inflame the situation" (Foothills Provincial General Hospital, 1990, p. 373). To address these issues, the Ontario Nurses' Association negotiated into its contract recourse to an external panel of expert nurses that is authorized to conduct investigations and make nonbinding recommendations to the parties (ONA, c. 1992).

Implications for Nurse Managers

Research on the relationship of unionization and the quality of nurses' work lives is rare. There are, however, several aspects to unionism that can be assumed as valued by nurses. First, Canadian nurses control their own unions and are directly involved in determining terms and conditions of employment.

Second, unionization ensures that there is a direct relationship between seniority and job security—the longer a person stays in a job, the more secure that job becomes. Third, a nurse may launch a complaint against an employer through the grievance procedure without fear of reprisal . Fourth, the collective agreement is periodically renewed, giving nurses opportunities for improving their salaries and terms and conditions of employment. And finally, for nurses who have potential leadership and political skills, union representation provides another avenue for undertaking new roles.

Although managers may regard the collective agreement as a means of restricting their discretion, the existence of a union contract requires managers to be fair and impartial when supervising employees. The contract provides a clear set of rules by which such things as allocation of unpopular shifts and vacation times are decided. If properly administered, the collective agreement ensures standard treatment of staff throughout the health agency, not solely on a particular unit. And finally, joint decision-making committees provide opportunities for nurses to be involved in decisions that affect their work, thereby facilitating organizational change and promoting the quality of their work lives.

It would be naive to ignore the many disadvantages for the employer created by collective agreements. The principle of seniority valued by unions may restrict management's discretion in selecting the most skilled professional nurse for promotion. Also, the practice of "bumping" required by unions during layoffs creates havoc in staffing and staff relations when the more senior union members of the bargaining unit displace their junior colleagues. Restrictions placed on scheduling the hours of work complicate the task of planning shift rotations. Nuisance grievances (i.e., politically motivated or ill-founded grievances) can undermine relationships at work and consume inordinate amounts of time.

Promoting Effective Union – Management Relations

Nurse managers play a key role in promoting effective union – management relations. They will likely be successful if they consider the following: educational preparation for labour relations; development of effective management skills; dealing with local union representatives; recognition of unfair labour practices; and managing during strikes.

- **Preparation for labour relations.** When a nurse is promoted from within union ranks to an out-of-scope position, that nurse becomes aligned with the employer. Nevertheless, intimate knowledge of the goals, values, beliefs, and internal organization of unions learned as a union member will help the new manager recognize the legitimacy of the role that unions play. A working knowledge of the contents of the collective agreement is important, and the nurse manager should be briefed by knowledgeable human resource personnel on changes each time the contract is renewed. Well-developed negotiating and interpersonal skills, especially listening skills, and problem-solving and decision-making skills are essential to the administration of the collective agreement. An open-minded attitude towards unions will be a distinct advantage when dealing with local union representatives.

- **Effective management skills.** Unions have little respect for ineffective managers and may try to take advantage of them, and this applies to senior administrators as well. The frequency of grievances is not necessarily indicative of ineffective management, but there is evidence that organizations with high grievance rates perform more poorly than organizations with low grievance rates (Gandz & Whitehead, 1989). First-level nurse managers need to form networks so that they can support and consult with each other in dealing with unions and to seek out well-informed resource people within the health agency. They must also find out from nurse executives the scope of their authority with respect to contract administration and the grievance procedure. Most health agencies have policies about reporting complaints and potential grievances, and so it is necessary to be aware of such internal guidelines.

   A question of considerable importance is whether the nurse manager will take part in grievance handling at steps 2, 3, and 4 (described in Table 31.3), and whether he or she will write the grievance or disciplinary letters. Nurse managers know their staff better than personnel officers and senior administrators, and they can offer valuable advice at every stage of the grievance or disciplinary procedure. A case can be made for the involvement of nurse managers throughout both procedures, as they have as much interest in the well-being of their staff as does the union. The manager who consistently implements the collective agreement fairly, accurately, and without favouritism, and who communicates

with local union representatives on an equal footing, will
gain the respect of union leaders.

- **Local union stewards and representatives.** Most nursing or health units have a local "shop steward" or union representative. These people may be elected, but usually they
volunteer for these unpaid jobs within the union organization. They work closely with the union's employment relations officers and union leaders. Their role includes the following: to see that the rights of union members are enforced;
to be available to union members during disputes and to
attend their grievance or disciplinary meetings; to help write
out grievances and prepare cases for arbitration; and to collect information for the union (American Nurses'
Association, 1985). Requests by the local union steward to
leave the clinical area during a work day must not be unrea-
sonably denied; nevertheless, such requests are negotiable,
and the needs of patients and clients remain the prime factor in granting permission to leave the clinical area.

    As noted earlier, local representatives may be sent by
their unions to labour workshops in preparation for their
roles, and they bring a wide range of styles, knowledge, and
commitment to their union positions. Some may have political aspirations within the union and will pursue their duties
militantly, challenging every move the manager makes so
that they will be perceived as powerful and effective advocates. Others may be reluctant volunteers and show little
aptitude or enthusiasm for their roles. In the vast majority
of cases, nurse managers and local union representatives
have good working relationships, each acknowledging that
the other has a job to do.

- **Unfair labour practices.** Nurse managers need to know
what constitutes an unfair labour practice. Labour relations
boards have a responsibility to determine whether unions
and employers are engaged in undermining legitimate
labour relations activities. For example, managers must not
interfere with union organization nor seek to circumvent,
with a union member, the provisions of a collective agreement. Similarly, unions have a duty of fair representation—
that is, to represent all members of the bargaining unit fairly and without discrimination (Craig, 1990). For these reasons, it is essential that nurse managers know their own
rights as managers, both implied employment rights, and
expressed rights contained in labour legislation and in collective agreements.

- **Managing during strikes.** Few situations are more divisive and stressful than when a union threatens or actually carries out a strike at a health agency. If it is a nurses' strike, those looking after the most dependent patients will probably struggle with the dilemma of conflicting loyalties—loyalty to patients or loyalty to union colleagues (Hibberd & Norris, 1992). They will very probably agonize over the question of whether to strike or not to strike. Also, members of nonstriking unions will have to decide whether or not to cross the picket lines of the striking union. At such times, nurse managers should remember that unions have the power to discipline members who are considered disloyal to the union. Because solidarity is essential if the strike weapon is to be effective (Hibberd, 1992), extreme peer pressure may be put on nursing personnel who do not wish to abandon their patients. Union penalties can be severe, and ostracism by peers produces a great deal of anxiety and stress (Hibberd & Norris, 1992).

  It is a truism to note that strikes are the result of decisions made on both sides of the bargaining table. In other words, although a strike is the union's weapon, employers also decide whether to allow a strike or to concede to the union's demands.

  Health units and hospitals should all have a strike contingency plan as part of their general emergency strategies. Such plans outline arrangements for rapid downsizing, transferring or discharging patients, and coping with residual populations in the case of hospitals. Community health and home care agencies also require emergency strike plans, although a strike among staff at such agencies may have fewer immediate consequences for care of clients.

  In the event of a labour dispute, a coordinating committee generally issues guidelines for dealing with employees on strike, but it may not offer assistance to nurse managers in coping with the aftermath of a strike. Animosity among staff can linger for weeks and months after the dispute. Poststrike strategies should be designed to speed up resumption of services to clients and patients and normal working relationships. The nurse manager should remain neutral and not engage in arguments with staff; under no circumstances must there be retaliatory practices after the strike. Violence and insults on the picket lines must be dealt with at the time rather than in retrospect. As Rothman (1983) notes: "All workers, union and management, must adopt the attitude that the strike is over and that the issues have been resolved. Arguing about them afterward will only create bitterness" (pp. 161-162).

Staff who continue to provide services to patients and clients during a strike, irrespective of union or management status, work extremely hard, often to a state of exhaustion and at the expense of their health and private lives (Hibberd & Norris, 1992). These people deserve support and encouragement during a strike, and heartfelt appreciation after the strike, not just token rewards. Because the nurse manager is on the front line when striking workers return to work, he or she has an opportunity to serve as a role model in bringing about a peaceful and constructive resumption of the health agency's work.

Conclusion

The impact of reforms and restructure within Canada's health care system is likely to place considerable strain on union – management relations, but it may also stimulate cooperation. Although relations between the parties can vary from outright hostility on the one hand to collusion or apathy on the other, nurse managers should try to promote partnerships with unions rather than assume that the relationship is inherently adversarial. They can do this by recognizing the legitimacy of unions, and by fostering common goals such as promoting high standards of nursing service and job satisfaction among the staff. The challenge for first-level nurse managers is to represent unionized staff and senior management to each other while ensuring that their competing interests do not undermine effective care and treatment of patients and clients.

References

American Nurses' Association (1985). *The grievance procedure.* Kansas City, MO: Author.

Anderson, J.C., Gunderson, M., & Ponak, A. (1989). *Union – management relations in Canada* (2nd ed.). Toronto: Addison-Wesley.

Cannon, P. (1980). Administering the contract. *Journal of Nursing Administration, 10*(10), 13-19.

Cohen, A. (1989). The management rights clause in collective bargaining. *Nursing Management, 20*(11), 24-34.

Craig, A.W.J. (1990). *The system of industrial relations in Canada* (3rd ed.). Toronto: Prentice-Hall.

Creighton, H. (1986). When can a nurse refuse to give care? *Nursing Management, 17*(3), 16-20.

Eden, G. (1992). Progressive discipline: An oxymoron? *Relations Industrielles, 47*(3), 511-528.

Fiesta, J. (1990). Whistleblowers: Retaliation or protection? Part 2. *Nursing Management, 21*(7), 38.

Fisher, E.G., & Williams, C.B. (1989). Negotiating the union – management agreement. In J.C. Anderson, M.Gunderson, & A. Ponak (Eds.), *Union – management relations in Canada* (2nd ed.) (pp. 185-207). Toronto: Addison-Wesley.

Foothills Provincial General Hospital and United Nurses of Aberta Local 115, (1990), 4 L.A.C. (4th), 359-374.

Gandz, J. (1982). Grievances and their resolution. In J. Anderson & M. Gunderson (Eds.), *Union – management relations in Canada* (pp. 289-315). Toronto: Addison-Wesley.

Gandz, J., & Whitehead, J.D. (1989). Grievances and their resolution. In J.C. Anderson, M. Gunderson, & A. Ponak (Eds.), *Union – management relations in Canada* (2nd ed.) (pp. 235-260). Toronto: Addison-Wesley.

Giles, A., & Jain, H.C. (1989). The collective agreement. In J.C. Anderson, M. Gunderson, & A. Ponak (Eds.), *Union – management relations in Canada* (2nd ed.) (pp. 317-345). Toronto: Addison-Wesley.

Glasbeek, H.J. (1982). The contract of employment at common law. In J. Anderson & M. Gunderson (Eds.), *Union – management relations in Canada* (pp. 47-77). Toronto: Addison-Wesley.

Gorsky, M.R. (1981). *Evidence and procedure in Canadian labour arbitration.* Toronto: Richard de Boo.

Hibberd, J.M. (1992). Strikes by nurses Part 2: Incidence, trends and issues. *Canadian Nurse, 88*(3), 26-31.

Hibberd, J.M., & Norris, J. (1992). Strike by nurses: Experiences of colleagues coping with the fallout. *Canadian Journal of Nursing Research, 23*(4), 43-54.

Huerta, S.R., & Oddi, L.F. (1992). Refusal to care for patients with Human Immunodeficiency Virus/Acquired Immunodeficiency Syndrome: Issues and responses. *Journal of Professional Nursing, 8*(4), 221-230.

Lovell, V. (1981). *'I care that VGH nurses care!': A case study and sociological analysis of nursing's influence on the health care system.* Vancouver: In Touch Publications.

McKenna, I. (1989). Whistleblowing and criticism of employers by employees—The case for reform in Canada. In *Papers presented at the Conference Labour Relations into the 1990s.* School of Management, University of Lethbridge, September 10-12, 1987 (pp. 141-184). Toronto: CCH Canadian.

McPhillips, D., & England, G. (1989). Employment legislation in Canada. In J.C. Anderson, M. Gunderson, & A. Ponak (Eds.), *Union – management relations in Canada* (2nd ed.) (pp. 43-69). Toronto: Addison-Wesley.

Morris, J.J. (1991). *Canadian nurses and the law.* Toronto: Butterworths.

Mrazek, M., & Tumback, D. (1990). Insubordination and incompetence—A nurse's dilemma. *AARN Newsletter, 46*(10), 18-19.

Northrop, C.E. (1987). Refusing unsafe work assignments. *Nursing Outlook, 36*(6), 302.

Ontario Nurses' Association. (c.1992). *Full-time collective agreement between participating hospitals and the Ontario Nurses' Association* (Expiry, March, 1993). Toronto: Author.

Pearlman, D. (1991). Progressive discipline: The grievance and arbitration process. In S.A. Ziebarth (Ed.), *Feeling the squeeze: The practice of middle management in Canadian health care facilities* (pp. 185-191). Ottawa: Canadian Hospital Association.

Peterborough Civic Hospital and Ontario Nurses' Association. (1982). 3 L.A.C. (3d), 21-54.

Ponak, A., Gunderson, M., & Anderson, J.C. (1989). Back to the future. In J.C. Anderson, M. Gunderson, & A. Ponak, *Union – management relations in Canada* (2nd ed.) (pp. 465-485). Toronto: Addison-Wesley.

Rogers, L. (1992). AGM Report. *Staff Nurses Association of Alberta Publication, 12*(2), 5,8.

Rothman, W.A. (1983). *Strikes in health care organizations.* Owings Mills, MD: National Health Publishing.

Rowsell, G. (1983). The settlement of disputes. In S. Quinn (Ed.), *Cooperation and conflict: Caring for the carers* (pp. 62-76). Geneva: International Council of Nurses.

Sethi, A.S., & MacNeil, M. (1989). Issues in contract administration and human rights. In Sethi, A.S. (Ed.), *Collective bargaining in Canada* (pp. 317-340). Toronto: Nelson Canada.

Sklar, C.L. (1979a). Saints or sinners? The legal perspective. Part I. *Canadian Nurse, 75*(10), 14-16.

Sklar, C.L. (1979b). Saints or sinners? The legal perspective. Part II. *Canadian Nurse, 75*(11), 16, 18, 20-21.

Wahn, E.V. (1979). The dilemma of the disobedient nurse. *Health Care in Canada, 21*(2), 43-46.

CHAPTER 32

Program Planning and Evaluation

Helen Ready, Bonnie Johnston, Carol Gray, and Sue Paege

Helen Ready, RN, BScN, MHSA (Alberta), is Associate Director of Nursing, Edmonton Board of Health. Bonnie Johnston, RN, BN (Calgary), MHSA (Alberta), is Assistant Program Director, Child and Adult Health, Calgary Health Services. Carol Gray, RN, BN (Calgary), MN (Alberta), is Program Director, Prevention and Promotion Services, Calgary Health Services. Sue Paege, RN, BScN (Alberta), is Regional Supervisor, Clareview Health Centre, Edmonton. The authors have worked together in planning, implementing, and evaluating public health nursing programs in Alberta.

Institutions and community health agencies are being increasingly challenged to be accountable for the delivery and impact of health services within the community in response to current political and economic realities. Sound program planning will be of critical importance in reshaping affordable and accessible health care in Canada because effective, well-designed, and relevant health programs contribute significantly to achievement of optimal health for individuals, families, and populations. First-line nurse managers play a vital role in this area, but to do so they must have the knowledge and skills necessary to carry out the program planning and evaluation process effectively.

The planning process is dynamic and involves continuous analysis of the program planning components: assessment of needs, development of goals and objectives, establishment of an action plan, and evaluation of outcomes. The nurse manager's role, depending on the nature of the project, will range from initiating and implementing programs independently to working with others in the development of collaborative projects.

The objectives of this chapter will be to:

- Define program planning and evaluation;
- Describe the context within which the nurse manager plans;
- Describe a model for program planning and evaluation as it applies to community health settings;

- Provide a case example that illustrates the application of the steps of the model;
- Discuss the implications of all these processes for first-line nurse managers.

Defining Program Planning and Evaluation

In discussing program planning within the context of the health care system and the profession of nursing, it is important to establish the parameters of the terms. Numerous perspectives on how to approach program planning and evaluation are discussed in the literature (e.g., Herman, Morrish, & Fitz-Gibbon, 1990; Posavac & Carey, 1992; Reeves, Bergwall, & Woodside, 1987; Thompson, 1991). They differ with respect to the conceptualization and formulation of the process and the method and rigour of evaluation.

A program, as defined by Stanhope and Lee (1992), is an organized response designed to meet the assessed needs of individuals, families, groups, or communities by reducing or eliminating one or more health problems. Howell (1993) views programs as interlocking sets of activities leading toward a common goal. Programs may be large and encompassing, and contain numerous subprograms, or they may be smaller with a more defined focus. Program planning has been defined as the deliberate and analytical approach to planning which produces carefully detailed programs of action that achieve predetermined objectives (Donovan, 1975). Programs may be planned for the short term or long term. Short term planning has been referred to as "tactical" or "operational," while corporate planning from a long term perspective is referred to as "strategic" (Goodstein, Nolan, & Pfeiffer, 1992). In the midst of today's complex and rapid social change, strategic planning takes place with the expectation that frequent alterations may be required.

Program evaluation is a continuous process, from the initial planning phase until the program is terminated. The major goals of program evaluation are to determine the relevance, progress, efficiency, effectiveness, and impact of program activities on the clients served. The author of this chapter will describe one approach to program planning and evaluation, drawing on relevant references where appropriate.

The scope of nursing practice assists in determining which programs will be developed and how they will be implemented. Although the principles of program planning will be applicable to any area of nursing practice, the focus of discussion in this chapter is specifically related to the field of public health nursing. The following section will provide a brief overview of the fundamentals of public health and the practice of public health nursing. This foundation will contribute to a better understanding of program planning and evaluation within the public health setting.

Characteristics of Public Health Practice

Similarities and differences exist between public health nursing and other areas of nursing practice. The similarities are rooted in a common nursing education, an interest in health as well as illness, and a holistic view of people as physical, social, intellectual, spiritual, and emotional beings. The differences arise from the philosophies and goals of the practice areas and the resulting demand for the development of expert nursing skills particular to that field of practice.

Historically, public health began with the need to attack the scourge of communicable diseases which, until well into this century, caused tremendous disability and loss of life. Throughout the history of public health, it was imperative to employ strategies directed at influencing the political and social will of society to effect the changes to improve health. Unsanitary conditions, care for the sick and poor, and adequate nutrition for mothers and children came about only through social action to improve living conditions and reduce the spread of disease. As a major report noted, "Public health encompasses the promotion, protection, and restoration of health by organized community action" (Howell, 1987, p. 10). It implies the assumption of responsibility by the community and it incorporates the principle of the greatest good for the greatest number.

As health problems began to shift from a primarily infectious and acute nature to those related to an aging population and social and lifestyle influences, the emphasis of public health activities shifted more toward health promotion. Within health care in general, national and international directives for improving health also began to reflect this transition (CPHA, 1990; Epp, 1986).

Public health programs are currently delivered by professionals representing various disciplines, such as public health nurses, nutritionists, dental hygienists, public health inspectors, and health educators. Public health nurses represent the largest number of public health workers in Canada. The Canadian Public Health Association (1990) defines public health nursing as "an art and a science that synthesizes knowledge from the public health sciences and professional nursing theories. Its goal is to promote and preserve the health of populations and is directed to communities, groups, families and individuals across their life span, in a continuous rather than episodic process" (p. 3).

Williams (1992) identified four key characteristics of public health nursing:

- Focus on populations that are free-living in the community as opposed to those that are institutionalized;
- Predominant emphasis on strategies for health promotion, health maintenance, and disease prevention;
- Concern for the connection between health status of the population and the living environment (physical, biological, sociocultural); and
- Use of political processes to affect public policy as a major intervention strategy for achieving goals. (pp. 246-247)

Through outreach activities in the community, public health nurses, together with colleagues and community members, work as a team to define what programs are required to maintain and improve the health of populations and reduce or eliminate preventable illness and injury. Population-focussed programs may be directed to the total population or to particular segments of the population, identified as target groups, or to those considered most at risk for disease, injury, or disability. Figure 32.1 illustrates this concept.

Figure 32.1
Population-focussed programs.

Total population

At-risk population

Target group

For example, media promotions and group teaching on eating well-balanced meals and exercising regularly to protect against heart disease are relevant for all age groups (total population). However, specific teaching related to the risk factors for heart disease may be offered to middle-aged adults (target group). Within this target group there would be at-risk individuals, such as obese males aged 40 to 50 years who smoke, have stressful occupations, and live sedentary lives. Blood pressure and blood cholesterol-level screening, individual counseling, and weight loss support groups may be programs particularly suited and relevant for this at-risk segment of the population.

Program Planning Model

Program planning provides a systematic plan or direction and assists nurses in evaluating when and how well they have met the needs of their clients. It also assists in identifying the resources and activities that are essential in meeting the objectives and clarifies who is responsible for carrying out the designated activities (Stanhope & Lee, 1992).

The four basic components of the program planning process involve: assessment of needs, development of goals and objectives, establishment of a plan of action, and evaluation of outcomes. The program management model thus parallels the nursing process; one is applied to a program whereas the other is applied to clients (Stanhope & Lee, 1992). However, the nurse manager can also view the program planning model as containing some intermediate steps.

We have developed a program planning model (see Figure 32.2) that shows 10 steps that will assist the nurse manager to use the process more effectively. For example, this model shows the distinction between the development of goals, which may be long term and, therefore, difficult to measure, and the definition of objectives, which are relatively short term and can be measured. The scope of nursing practice combined with the specific philosophy, mandate, and stated mission of the health organization sets the context for determining how and what needs are defined, the appropriateness of selected objectives, and the way the strategies will be implemented and evaluated.

The process incorporates the five Ws of planning:

- *Who* will the program serve (population in need)?
- *What* will be the service?
- *Where* will the program function?
- *Why* will the specific services identified be emphasized (program priorities, target groups)?
- *When* is the program anticipated to be implemented? (Norris, 1981).

Figure 32.2
Program planning model.

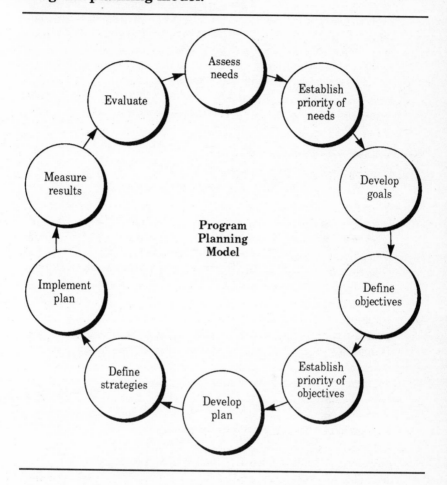

The planning process is applicable and adaptable to every level of practice. It assists the public health nurse in the field who is working to understand and meet the needs of the assigned district, the front-line nursing manager who must deliver programs with limited resources to several communities with competing needs, and senior nursing management personnel who are responsible for focussing on long-range strategic planning within a large rural area, town, or city. The following discussion will describe in further detail each of the four main steps involved in the planning process, but will also show how the intermediate steps are incorporated.

Assess Needs

All planning starts with an understanding or diagnosis of the needs of
the situation. The assessment of need is a systematic appraisal of the
type, depth, and scope of problems as perceived by clients, health
providers, or both (Stanhope & Lee, 1992).

It is important for the first-line manager to establish at the out-
set "Whose health needs are we, or should we be, examining?"
Information may be collected from people already using existing programs and services. In this case, the front-line manager is interested
in knowing:

- How are clients' needs being met with current programs?

- How have the needs of clients changed?

- What unmet needs of clients should be addressed?

Alternatively, the nurse manager may be concerned with identifying and understanding the needs of people not currently served by
the agency's programs and services. The Edmonton Social Planning
Council (1991) suggests that, if this is the case, the manager would
need to:

- Assess overall social and/or health needs in a particular community;

- Assess the needs of a particular subgroup within the community, for example youth, single parents, the elderly, the handi-
  capped;

- Assess people's needs within a particular service area such as
  family life education, daycare, prenatal education.

To ensure a comprehensive understanding and sensitivity to
these needs, it is critical that the nurse manager be extremely familiar
with and knowledgeable about the specific demographic, environmental, and health characteristics of the population in the geographic area.
There are many valuable sources of information available to assist
her in achieving this goal. Table 32.1 lists some of the major ones.

Stanhope and Lee (1992) emphasize the importance of having
client needs identified by both the client and the health provider. If
the client population does not recognize the need, the program will
usually fail. Methods of collecting information may include informal
interviews, participant observation, focus groups, and surveys.
Common characteristics of street people, neighbourhood gathering
places, the rhythm of community life, housing quality, and geographic
boundaries are some of the dimensions that can be observed
(Goeppinger & Schuster, 1992). Given that public health nurses are

Table 32.1
Sources of data about population.

- Epidemiological data, which document the demographic characteristics of the population, major causes of mortality, morbidity, and predicted years of life lost

- Literature reviews, which give results of population-based research at the national and international levels

- Information from social service agencies, school personnel, other human service agencies, physicians in the community, and other community sources

- Public documents, surveys, socioeconomic data, minutes from meetings, and health records

- Expression of need from the people in the community through requests for service and emergence of self-help groups

- Information and suggestions from public health nursing staff who have daily contact with clients and other workers in the community.

mobile around the community, "windshield surveys" are a good start in gaining an understanding about clients and neighbourhoods in public health settings. Many dimensions of a community's life and environment can be readily observed through an automobile windshield.

The first-line nurse manager needs to pull the available information together, identify recurring themes and trends, and determine areas appropriate for nursing involvement. It is important that a distinction is made between clients' needs and their wants or preferences.

The next step in the process (see Figure 32.2, see page 601) is to establish a priority of needs. That is, the nurse manager must decide which needs should be addressed and which needs can realistically be addressed given the mandate of the organization and current resources. As the economy tightens and societal issues become increasingly complex, first-line managers will be constantly challenged with prioritizing needs and deciding how to use most effectively already strained resources. Prior to mobilizing resources to address identified needs, first-line managers must carefully consider many factors, including:

- What needs have been identified by clients or the community? What will be their involvement and commitment to the process?

- Is involvement with the identified needs consistent with the mission and priorities of the agency?

- Are other resources and agencies in the community currently providing the service or considered more appropriate to assume responsibility for addressing the need(s)?

- What will be the costs of addressing the needs? Personnel, facilities, equipment, and financing will all have to be considered.

- Are there identified subgroups that are at greatest risk? For example, single, adolescent pregnant women who are isolated from support in the community would have greater needs than financially secure couples expecting their first child.

- What will be the consequences if the needs are not addressed?

- Will the invested time justify the anticipated outcome?

- What are the "competing" issues and needs from other programs in the agency?

- Do nurses have the necessary expertise and commitment to implement appropriate programs?

- Have programs been implemented in the past to meet similar needs and, if so, how successful have they been?

Consideration of these factors is essential before goals and objectives can be defined.

Develop Goals and Define Objectives

In the program planning process, the nurse manager often finds it helpful to break down this main step into two more manageable intermediate steps. Goals are statements of the outcomes or results to be achieved in carrying out the agency's mission and philosophy. They are generally broad statements of desired outcome and require long-term investments of commitment and resources. An example of a goal would be to reduce the incidence and prevalence of early childhood developmental delays.

Objectives are more precise and are behaviourally stated. An example of an objective related to the goal of reducing the incidence and prevalence of childhood developmental delays could be: to reduce the incidence of developmental delays by screening 100% of infants during the first year of life (to identify any risk condition that would respond to early intervention). The identification of objectives is essential to the organization, implementation, and evaluation of every component of a program. Many approaches and perspectives currently exist describing how to write an objective. For example, Shortell and Richardson (1978) indicate that useful program objectives include a statement of the specific behaviours, accomplishments, and success criteria for the program. A report for the Calgary Health Services (1992) terms a program objective a statement describing a measurable result which is aimed at accomplishing the program goal (health outcome) in total or in part. The requirement for measurability is what most definitions have in common.

The first phase of program evaluation occurs at the objective-setting stage of the program planning process. It is important that consideration be given to the measurability of the objective and the design of appropriate methods to collect data for analysis and evaluation. If this step is missed and evaluation is not considered at this point, the nurse manager may spend considerable resources to implement a program that does not lend itself to manageable, reliable, or cost-effective methods of evaluation.

Objectives, like needs, must be prioritized. A broad goal such as "to eliminate the incidence of unintentional injuries" is so broad that it may produce as many as 10 to 15 different objectives to achieve the optimal outcome. Objectives may range from reducing morbidity and mortality related to falls among senior adults, to reducing the number of injuries related to playground equipment, or to decreasing the number of injuries in childcare settings. It is the nurse manager's responsibility, working with staff nurses and the community, to prioritize the objectives. Collaboration is involved in the mutual selection of goals and objectives. Consideration once again needs to be given to assessing the area of greatest need, staff and community commitment, budget constraints, and overall cost benefits of implementing the program. Once goals and objectives are established and priorities set, intervention activities to accomplish the objectives can be identified.

Develop and Implement Plan

The nurse manager will find it helpful to see this main section as a series of separate steps involving development of the plan, definition of strategies, and implementation. The elements of the program plan or design, the means by which objectives are met, are the strategies that clarify what must be done to achieve the objectives. Strategies are influenced by the type of health problem selected as the focus for intervention and the client or community's readiness to participate in problem resolution. For example, in dealing with self-esteem issues of elementary school children, strategies may focus on the development of skills for teachers to assist them in enhancing children's self-esteem. Strategies for dealing with poor parenting skills may range from organizing and facilitating parenting groups to providing individual consultation and home visits to families identified to be at high risk.

The implementation stage involves a number of further factors and considerations. Adequate resources are required, both in the area of program funding and staff. Of critical importance in this process is the availability of financial resources to support program initiatives. Several alternative methods for reaching designated objectives should be identified and the cost for achieving each outcome determined through cost analysis.

When new funding is not allocated to a new plan or strategy, the first-line manager needs to ensure that other program demands are continuing to be met while incorporating the new initiatives. For instance, the need for drop-in clinics for women who are or plan to begin breastfeeding may be important but not possible to implement because of demand from legislated programs such as communicable disease control. The nurse manager may use creative strategies, such as seeking partnerships with other agencies for delivering programs or utilizing volunteers (Felton & Parker, 1990), or may seek support from other funding sources. This may involve preparing a proposal for research funds. Many projects are initiated through a pilot to "test" the feasibility and gain support and validation of effectiveness to secure future funding.

Health care professionals need to become good facilitators and listeners to involve the public in developing strategies that achieve relevant and practical outcomes. Consistent with current community mobilization and development principles, people need to be involved in solving the problems that affect them. It is imperative that the plan meet the clients' needs and not the professionals' agenda.

Staff must have, or be provided with, the necessary knowledge, commitment, and skill development to carry out the program. It is critical to the success of a program to involve staff at an early stage and benefit from their knowledge and practical sense of what will "actually" work. For example, staff with first-hand knowledge of clients would know that an adolescent drop-in parenting program may be jeopardized without a mechanism to ensure transportation to the program for young mothers and babies.

During this process, it is important to be flexible and open to new ideas that will improve and strengthen the project. It is during this stage that the nurse manager initiates program monitoring for judging the operational performance of the program. Clients' feedback, nurses' observations, and direct observation of operational ease or frustration provides valuable and useful information on what is working and what needs to be changed. For example, suppose that a parenting program is set up for high-risk mothers of children under three years of age. The target group is single, adolescent parents with little or no identified support. Of the eight mothers contacted, only three mothers show up at the health centre for the first two classes.

Reassessment would be in order to determine why the other five mothers were not attending. Did transportation or child care present a problem? Were there any additional barriers preventing their attendance?

Data collection, using previously designed methods and tools, is initiated at the implementation stage and may include, for example, tracking the number of participants attending a seniors' wellness program or the number of referrals received by public health nurses in schools from teachers and parents.

Evaluate Program

Evaluation is the process of comparing the results of the program to the goals and objectives. It also involves the intermediate step of actually measuring the results. For an evaluation to be useful it has to answer questions, offer additional insights, make predictions, and make decision making more rational. When the program is compared with other possible uses of the same resources within this context, the nurse manager wants to understand if the program works, if it is reaching those who need it, and if it is worth doing (Fulton, 1985). As Hawe, Degeling, and Hall (1990) have noted: "There can be no doubt that better quality evaluations... will lead to better interventions and that a systematic approach to evaluation will impose greater discipline to the tasks of needs assessment and program planning" (foreword).

Evaluation design, as has been stated, should begin in the planning phase of a program. There are many aspects to evaluating a program. It is important to evaluate the program *process* (i.e., the program activities and quality) and who the program is reaching. The four main questions to be asked in a process evaluation are whether the program is reaching the target group, whether the participants are satisfied, whether all program activities are being implemented, and whether the materials and components of the program are of good quality. Process evaluation measures include attendance lists, demographic characteristics of those attending, satisfaction surveys, proportion of time spent on various parts of the programs, readability of program materials, and assessment of skill of staff delivering the program.

Evaluating program *outcome* (goals) is, of course, paramount in determining the ultimate value of a program (i.e., the difference it has made to the health status of a population group). However, it can take a long time for a change in health status to become apparent so that it can be described in epidemiological terms. Therefore, evaluation will often take the form of assessing immediate program effect or *impact*. This usually corresponds with the measurement of the program objectives. For example, the goal of a fitness program for the elderly would be to reduce their morbidity and increase their longevity. An effect would be that the participating seniors became more fit and energetic when compared with their previous levels of fitness and energy or when compared to a group of seniors who did not take the program. Program effects are determined by pre- and post-tests of knowledge, attitudes, behaviours, and measures of such factors as health status, quality of life, or social support.

Methods used to evaluate programs' effects can be divided into qualitative and quantitative approaches. Qualitative methods are used to interpret the meaning that the program has for its participants and may make use of open-ended questions and observations. Quantitative measures begin with an idea of the effects one wishes to measure and use a set of standardized measuring instruments that can be applied. For example, a validated and reliable pre- and post-test may be used on the program groups and test results subjected to statistical analysis. Given the nature of many public health programs, it is often necessary to combine qualitative and quantitative methods of evaluation.

Program evaluation results are of great interest to many groups. Program funders (often governments) are interested in program outcome measures and their possible effect on health policy development as well as assessments of the cost effectiveness of the program. Program managers are interested in immediate program effects and also the efficiency of the process (i.e., was the desired effect achieved at the least cost?). In addition, the managers will always be cognizant of the opportunity costs of the program (i.e., whether this program is justified in comparison to other programs over which it received preference). Health workers in other jurisdictions will also be an eager audience for evaluation results, as these may influence their own program plans.

Communication of evaluation findings is the responsibility of those carrying out the program. Presentation of the evaluation report should be designed to meet the information needs of the particular audience being addressed and should be succinct, clear, and interestingly formatted with tables, graphs, and visual depictions used where appropriate (Morris, Fitz-Gibbon, & Freeman, 1987).

As some health needs are addressed, other ones are constantly evolving. The process is dynamic and requires systematic assessment of service delivery to ensure that it is effective, sensitive, and relevant in meeting the needs of the individual and the community.

Case Study:
Planning a School-Based
Program

As the Regional Supervisor of Mid-Town Health Centre, Sharon Sinclair, RN, MN, is a first-line nurse manager. Mid-Town is one of 10 health centres or "suboffices" in a large urban health unit. Sharon supervises a staff of 12 public health nurses (PHNs), each of whom is a generalist; they provide services to all age groups across the life span within a particular geographic area within the region. Sharon and her staff work closely with other public health professionals (dental hygienists, speech language pathologists, environmental health inspectors), all of whom work within the mission statement of the health unit. They also have close connections with other human service organizations in their region of the city and hold regular inter-agency meetings with them (e.g., social services, parks and recreation, mental health services, schools and community leagues).

A basic requirement of a public health professional is the ability to monitor and assess the health needs of the community continuously. Public health nurses come to know the population in their areas through many time-tested contacts. These include meeting virtually all parents of newborns, liaising with personnel in every daycare setting and school, providing immunization and communicable disease services to all age groups, and addressing the health needs of adult and senior groups. Through these contacts in the community setting, the public health nurse has an excellent opportunity to be aware of and identify emerging or special health needs.

Mid-Town Health Centre is located in an area of the city where there are multiple health concerns. This requires frequent reevaluation to determine the kinds of programs that might best meet the needs of the population within this region.

At a regular meeting of Mid-Town Health Centre staff, Lisa Brown, RN, BScN, the public health nurse serving City Core elementary school, stated that "school health" was currently her area of greatest concern. She indicated that the number and complexity of referrals were increasing in her school and included emotional/behavioural problems, poor physical health, and indications of child abuse and neglect. Over the past months, Lisa had discussed many of these concerns with her supervisor,

Sharon, and with the rest of her colleagues. There was general agreement that these concerns required further exploration by Lisa.

Having identified what they perceived to be a need, Sharon and her staff had taken the first step in the program planning process. Sharon knew that there were many steps that must be taken to determine whether and how a new or altered program would result.

The process for this case study will highlight six steps.

Step 1: Assess Needs

- Who has the health need?
- What is the health need?
- What are the sources of information?

To gain a better understanding of the health needs within Lisa's school, Sharon and her staff proposed that a needs assessment should be carried out. This would provide an opportunity to initiate the process of involving the school community in identifying issues of concern to them and determining to what extent Lisa's ideas of health problems in the school differed from or were consistent with that of others. The purpose of the needs assessment was to provide information to facilitate the provision and priority of services based on the identified needs within the school.

Sharon apprised the senior nursing management of the Health Unit of the intent to carry out a needs assessment in City Core elementary school and received approval and support to proceed. Sharon and Lisa next met with the school principal to discuss their proposal for doing a needs assessment, gain support for carrying out the plan, and involve him at an early stage in the planning process. Permission was also obtained from school board authorities to survey school personnel, students, and parents within the school setting.

Questions designed to obtain perceptions of health issues within the school environment were formulated by Sharon and Lisa in consultation with senior nursing management and school personnel. Representatives from the school staff, parents, and students were invited to participate in small group discussions (focus groups) to give their opinion about what they perceived to be barriers to health in the school. Sharon and Lisa worked together to strengthen Lisa's group facilitation skills so that Lisa, in collaboration with the principal and guidance counselor, could guide the process and recording of information.

The data obtained were reviewed by Sharon, Lisa, the principal, and the guidance counselor. Some of the major problems identified in the school included: family problems; stress; frequent illnesses; negative effects of busing; inadequate nutrition (eating habits, food choices); and poor access to appropriate agencies. The major issues identified by participants correlated closely with Lisa's assessment of the health needs within the school. The data also confirmed that there were a multitude of health needs in the school, and that priorities would need to be set to determine the essential problems to be in addressed.

Step 2: Establish Priority of Needs

- Which needs should be addressed?
- Which needs can realistically be addressed?

Sharon reminded Lisa that she could not solve all the problems identified during the data collection phase and that it was important to involve the school community in the identification of both the priorities and the solutions for these issues. Sharon advised Lisa to propose to the principal that a series of consultation meetings be held at the school. This would provide an opportunity to share the data with representatives from the school staff, students, and parents and to obtain feedback on which needs the group perceived to be the most important to address.

It is essential that community members are consulted about health issues they consider important and are involved in the planning of programs designed to resolve or alleviate identified issues. This may be more time consuming, but it produces programs that are more relevant and effective within the community.

The school consultation group identified relationship problems between children and parents and low self-esteem to be the central issues in their school. This information was taken back to the district office and discussed with Sharon. As both areas had relevance for involvement by public health nursing, Sharon would need to work with Lisa to assess the feasibility of the type and extent of Lisa's involvement, given her already extremely busy workload.

Step 3: Develop Goals and Define Objectives

Set the goal:

*   What do we want the situation to be in the future?

Define objectives:

*   What is to be done?
*   How are the objectives to be carried out?
*   How will we know when we have achieved the objectives?

> *A meeting was arranged with some members of the school consul-*
> *tation group to begin the process of deciding how the identified*
> *issues could be addressed. After discussion, the group reached a*
> *consensus that their goal would be to enhance the self-esteem and*
> *coping skills of children attending City Core elementary school.*
> *Objectives proposed included: increasing early identification of*
> *children experiencing emotional or behavioural problems,*
> *enhancing parent-child communication, increasing parents' self-*
> *esteem, improving children's confidence and self-image, and*
> *improving children's problem-solving and coping skills.*

Step 4: Establish Priority of Objectives

*   What factors (e.g., staff and community commitment, time and budgetary constraints) need to be considered?

> *The group knew it would not be practical or reasonable to attempt*
> *resolution of all the objectives at the same time. They considered*
> *existing resources and discussed where they, as a group, felt it*
> *would be important to start. It was decided to address the two*
> *areas of enhancing parent-child communication and improving*
> *children's problem-solving and coping skills. Participants agreed*
> *that any approach, to be effective and integrated, needed to*
> *include strategies that involved both children and their parents.*

Step 5: Develop and Implement Plan

*   What are the strategies to achieve the objectives?
*   What resources and skills will be required?
*   Which alternatives are most feasible?
*   Who needs to be involved in choosing which way is best?

> *During the next month, the group met to discuss how their objec-*
> *tives could be implemented and achieved. They considered sever-*
> *al approaches and reached consensus on what they felt would be*

the most effective and reasonable to implement, given current resources. The improvement of children's problem-solving and coping skills could be addressed by teachers through creative enhancement and adaptation of a component within the health curriculum that dealt with self-esteem. Strategies included helping children identify their strengths, discussing problem situations that children were likely to encounter within their environment, and engaging children in opportunities that facilitated learning effective problem identification and resolution.

To address the objective of enhancing parent-child communication, the group proposed to offer a parenting program. Members within the group were aware that Lisa had facilitated parenting groups in the community and asked if she would be prepared to offer a similar program for parents at the school. Lisa discussed the request with Sharon. One half-day a week for six weeks would be required by Lisa to facilitate the parenting program. Given the current demands on Lisa and the other nurses at the Health Centre, this constituted a fairly heavy commitment of time. The issue was brought back for discussion at a staff meeting. Lisa's colleagues indicated they thought it was important for her to be involved with the parenting program and offered to assist during the six-week period by covering a half-day per week of Lisa's scheduled clinic time.

Planning and preparation for the program was carried out by Lisa with assistance from members of the school consultation group. This included advertising through letters to parents, articles in the local weekly newspaper, and an introductory evening with a keynote speaker and refreshments, selection of appropriate dates and session times, and decisions on how the program would be effectively evaluated.

For the process evaluation, it was decided that a client satisfaction questionnaire would be designed by Lisa and members of the school consultation group for completion by parents at the end of each of the six weekly sessions. During the six-week period, attendance would also be recorded and each session monitored to determine where changes were required to achieve a successful outcome. This careful monitoring of the program necessitated a change following the second session to a later start time to reduce the number of late arrivals. A change from 7:00 to 7:30 p.m. accommodated parents' busy commitments at home and increased the number of parents attending on time from 50% to 95%. A second questionnaire would also be designed and sent to parents three months after completion of the parenting program. The intent of this second questionnaire was to determine the impact of the program (i.e., whether parents had actually used the suggested parenting techniques with their children and whether these strategies had been effective).

Step 6: Evaluate Program

- How well did the strategies and activities work?
- How efficiently were the resources used?
- Were the findings communicated to the appropriate people?

Completed questionnaires were reviewed at the end of the six-week program by Lisa and the school consultation committee. Findings indicated that parents had found the sessions to be extremely useful in providing effective strategies for communication with their children. They were particularly pleased with the opportunity for discussion and support they received from other parents attending the sessions. Teachers working with the children on the self-esteem curriculum reported unprecedented parent interest in their children's work. The school consultation committee recommended the parenting program be offered by Lisa two more times within the next six months to provide an opportunity for other parents to attend. During this time they would attempt to recruit parents who may be interested in facilitating future parent support groups and sessions at the school. This would provide an excellent opportunity to involve interested parents, initiate a peer support system among parents within the school, and re-direct Lisa's role from that of instructor to consultant.

This information was taken back and discussed with Sharon. She approved the plan and was particularly pleased with the school community's commitment to take responsibility for the future development of the parenting program. This direction would allow Lisa the opportunity to re-focus her time and to participate in dealing with the other objectives and needs identified within the school.

The results of the positive evaluation of the process and the immediate effect of the program were shared with all those who had participated in the planning. Sharon and Lisa decided that they would also write an article to submit for publication in a nursing or a public health journal so that the results of their experience could be shared more widely. They knew that the long term outcomes would become apparent only as the health problems that gave rise to the program began to diminish. Lisa resolved to continue to monitor the indicators of health in City Core school on a continuing basis, thus deriving information required toward measuring long term program outcomes.

Conclusion

This chapter has provided an overview of the principles of program planning and some practical examples of operationalizing these principles in public health nursing practice. The principles are familiar—they are the steps of nursing process. It is the multitude of factors that must be taken into account continuously through each stage of the process that often makes program planning and evaluation in public health a real challenge.

In the face of scarce resources and increasingly complex needs, a systematic approach to program planning will assist nurse managers in effectively providing health promotion and prevention services to individuals and groups in their communities.

References

Calgary Health Services. (1992). *Strategic planning*. Unpublished report available from Author.

Canadian Public Health Association. (1990). *Community health—Public health nursing in Canada*. Ottawa: Author.

Donovan, H. (1975). *Nursing service administration: Managing the enterprise*. St. Louis: C.V. Mosby.

Edmonton Social Planning Council. (1991). *Doing it right! A needs assessment workbook*. Edmonton: Author.

Epp, J. (1986). *Achieving health for all: A framework for health promotion*. Ottawa: Health & Welfare Canada.

Felton, B., & Parker, S. (1990). The resource dependence of a country nursing department: Efforts to thrive in the 1980s. *Public Health Nursing, 7*(1), 45-51.

Fulton, J. (1986). *Program evaluation: An introduction*. Unpublished paper, University of Ottawa.

Goeppinger, J., & Shuster, G.S. (1992). Community as client: Using the nursing process to promote health. In M. Stanhope & J. Lancaster (Eds.), *Community health nursing—Process and practice for promoting health* (pp. 253-276). St. Louis: Mosby Year Book.

Goodstein, L., Nolan, T., & Pfeiffer, J.W. (1992). *Applied strategic planning: A comprehensive guide*. San Diego: Pfeiffer & Co.

Hawe, P., Degeling, D., & Hall, J. (1990). *Evaluating health promotion: A health workers guide*. Sydney, Australia: MacLennan & Petty.

Herman, J., Morrish., & Fitz-Gibbon C. (1990). *Evaluator's handbook*. Newbury Park, CA: Sage Publications.

Howell, J.M. (Ed.) (1987). *Think prevention!* (The Report of the Alberta Hospital Association/Health Unit Association of Alberta Joint Committee on Preventive Medicine, Vol. 1). Edmonton: Health Unit Association of Alberta.

Howell, J.M. (1993). *The modern role of public health*. Unpublished paper, Edmonton Board of Health.

Morris, L., Fitz-Gibbon, C., & Freeman, M. (1987). *How to communicate evaluation findings*. Newbury Park, CA: Sage Publications.

Norris, Frances R. (1981). *Program planning manual*. Produced under contract by Family Planning Services, Alberta Social Services & Community Health, Edmonton, AB.

Posavac, E., & Carey, R. (1989). *Program evaluation, methods and case studies* (3rd ed.). Englewood Cliffs, NJ: Prentice-Hall.

Reeves, P., Bergwall, D., & Woodside N. (1984). *Introduction to health planning*. Arlington, VA: Information Resources Press.

Shortell, S.M., & Richardson, W. (1978). *Health program evaluation*. St. Louis: Mosby.

Stanhope, M., & Lee, G. (1992). Program management. In M. Stanhope & J. Lancaster, (1992), *Community health nursing—Process and practice for promoting health* (pp. 201-214). St. Louis: Mosby Year Book.

Thompson, J. (1992). Program evaluation within a health promotion framework. *Canadian Journal of Public Health, 83*(Supplement 1), 567-571.

Williams, C.A. (1992). Community-based population-focused practice: The foundation of specialization in public health nursing. In M. Stanhope & J. Lancaster (Eds.), *Community health nursing—Process and practice for promoting health* (pp. 244-252). St. Louis: Mosby Year Book.

CHAPTER 33

Individual and Organizational Strategies for Managing Available Time

Judith M. Hibberd

Judith Hibberd, RN, BScN (Toronto), MHSA, PhD (Alberta), is Associate Professor, Faculty of Nursing, University of Alberta, where she teaches nursing management at the undergraduate and graduate levels. She has broad experience as a first-line manager and senior administrator, and her research interests are in union – management relations and strikes by nurses.

"We always have time enough, if we will but use it right."
—Johann Wolfgang von Goethe (1749-1832)

The importance of time is reflected in language. Frequent references to time occur in everyday speech, for example, "time is money," "time and tide wait for no man" [nor woman either], and "procrastination is the thief of time." It may seem trite to remark that everyone has exactly the same amount of time, 168 hours per week, but there seems to be a wide range in individual ability to manage available time effectively.

Unproductive use of time in hospitals is one of the underlying forces in the current trend to restructure workplaces (Strasen, 1991). The purpose of this chapter is to examine some ways and means of making good use of time at work. Nurse managers may reflect on their own time management practices and help coach their staff to do the same. More specifically, some practical suggestions are made in three areas where time is often wasted, namely, in organizing the manager's own time, in delegating appropriate work to others, and in running effective meetings.

Wise use of time has potential for reducing personal stress levels, promoting a balanced lifestyle between work and nonwork activities, creating a thoughtful, analytic approach to management, and inspiring others to follow the manager's example.

Individual Strategies for Managing Available Time

Individual managers can often make a real difference in management of their own time through awareness of three simple, but effective, areas: they need to set priorities, be "time conscious," and use some proven time-saving devices.

Setting Priorities

Much has been said in the management literature about the importance of establishing mission statements, long range plans, goals, and objectives for giving direction to the organization (see Chapter 23). Important though these are, it is difficult to focus on long range plans under the daily pressure of the more immediate imperatives of patient care, interruptions, telephone calls, or meetings, to say little of the diverse demands of senior administrators and other disciplines and departments. It may take only one unusual incident to convert an otherwise routine day into temporary chaos, and so it is essential to keep one's priorities in perspective while remaining flexible in the short term.

When setting priorities, it is a matter of deciding what is urgent, what is important, what is routine, and what is nice to do if there is time. Also, when the workload becomes overwhelming, as is often the case, modest goals for the day are advisable. Setting unrealistic goals that are rarely accomplished will contribute to feelings of inadequacy, frustration, and even failure.

The restructuring of health care agencies has led to greater involvement of first-level managers in corporate affairs. This often means long absences from patient care areas. Some nurse managers, however, choose to focus more on the corporate dimension of their roles while delegating much of the professional dimension to staff nurses. Whichever is the case, it is important that the staff understand what the manager's priorities are, as the extent and type of supervision has been identified as a source of dissatisfaction among nurses (Alberta Hospital Association, 1980). Too much time away from the unit on "corporate business" may be resented, and has led to union demands that someone be designated in charge of the unit at all times. Open dialogue about current priorities will help staff to appreciate the full scope and complexity of the manager's role. For example, when the deadline for the unit budget approaches, the nurse manager is likely to need concentrated periods of time in the office. Indeed, many managers schedule one half day, or a whole day, each week for this type of activity.

Time Consciousness

Raising one's awareness about how time is being used is another important step toward taking control of available work time. Some writers advocate that one can start by keeping a detailed log of how work days are spent (Barker, 1990). It is argued that a systematic and detailed analysis of how time is spent on day-to-day activities will reveal whether remedial action is needed. Keeping a time log would no doubt be a useful exercise, but it requires a great deal of self-discipline to do so for more than a couple of consecutive days, raising the question of whether there is a better way of becoming more time conscious.

A rapid way of calculating how one might extract more discretionary time from a seemingly crowded day is outlined in Table 33.1. For example, if the manager could eliminate one nonproductive 20-minute period during each work day, it would theoretically give that manager two extra weeks of discretionary time over one year. This exercise can create time consciousness and stimulate the habit of assessing priorities when planning the day's activities.

Time-Saving Devices

The simplest device for managing time is a pocket diary or day planner. Nurse managers should carry an appointment diary with sufficient space for making notes and reminders. It should become routine practice to enter such events as appointments, meetings, and the dates by which performance reviews are due. The diary should be consulted frequently as a memory aid. Most managers process huge amounts of information each day, and so it is unreasonable to expect memories to operate perfectly under all circumstances. A day planner also provides a record of activities, observations, notes, and frequently used telephone numbers. The task of keeping this day planner up to date can be shared during the day with a clerical person, but clear guidelines need to be established as to how appointments and meetings can be scheduled.

Perhaps the most exciting development in time management for managers is in telecommunications and electronic mail. "Voice

Table 33.1
Time consciousness exercise.

1. Calculate how many days you work per year
    (e.g., 365 days − 25 vacation days + 10 statutory holidays + 104 weekend
    days + 5 sick days = 221 working days).

2. Specify a 20-minute, nonproductive period of time that occurs regularly
    each work day (or two 10-minute periods), such as lingering over coffee;
    chatting on the telephone about the hockey game; waiting for somebody or
    something.

3. Calculate total amount of nonproductive time associated with this
    particular activity per year: 221 days x 20 minutes ÷ 60 = 73 hours and
    36 minutes.

Imagine what you could do if you had almost two additional weeks of
discretionary time per year!

mail" (otherwise known as the telephone answering machine)
should be standard equipment for all nurse managers. Important
communications can now be exchanged without direct interaction
between sender and receiver. Few indications of effective management are as impressive as the prompt return of telephone calls,
and this can be practised if voice mail is checked periodically during the day. Managers can leave recorded messages for each other
without involving clerical intervention. Answering machines do
not obviate the need for secretaries; they allow clerical staff more
time for work that cannot be automated, which in turn allows
managers to make better use of available time.

Electronic mail, or e-mail, is another means of improving the
efficiency of communications and information processing. As
Staggers (1989) suggests, it can virtually eliminate "telephone tag"
and can translate into time savings, not only for managers but for
the entire staff of a nursing division. Because a record of all communications can be kept, and incoming messages or memoranda
printed off the computer screen, it has replaced the need to dictate
and type many written communications. Notices of meetings, conferences, and other announcements can be sent rapidly to dozens

of people throughout the organization. Moreover, nursing staff can send and retrieve their "mail" whenever they have a convenient moment.

Nurses typically spend more than 55% of their time in indirect patient care activities, much of which consists of writing and communicating on behalf of patients (Prescott, Phillips, Ryan, & Thompson, 1991). The use of computers and telecommunications represents a long range investment in increased efficiency and productivity. Similarly, managers and professional staff need to learn how to delegate work that can be safely and effectively carried out by support staff so that they can make more efficient use of their time.

Organizational Strategies for Managing Available Time

In addition to the simple steps that managers can take to manage their own time, they need to be aware of strategies they can use with others. The concept of *delegation* is central to the process of managing organizations because it involves the art and skill of assigning activities to others to achieve the goals and objectives of the health care agency. Managers who can master the challenge of delegation will find that they have more discretionary time to devote to managerial work. Effective delegation requires an understanding of all five of the classical functions of managing: planning, organizing, directing, coordinating, and controlling (Longest, 1990).

Principles of Delegation

No matter how simple or complex the function to be delegated, there is a need to consider five points:

- Define the task to be delegated;
- Choose a capable and appropriately qualified person or persons;
- Give clear directions to the person(s) selected;
- Remain available for consultation and assistance; and
- Give recognition for achievement of objectives.

An example of a complex function currently being delegated to staff nurses is the scheduling of hours of work, which results in self-scheduling (Dechant, 1990; Ringl & Dotson, 1989). This rather tedious and contentious task has been handled by nurse managers in the past, but is now being undertaken by nurses themselves, giving them more control over their hours of work. The example illustrates how the five principles of delegation can be applied.

Define the task to be delegated. A number of implications need to be considered in defining how this self-scheduling is to be managed. For example, what does the collective agreement stipulate about hours of work? No doubt the manager will have to consult with human resources personnel and with union representatives. Will the new schedule include all members of the staff including auxiliary staff? Will the manager be willing to relinquish assignment of vacation time as well as hours of work? What time frame will be considered reasonable for completion of the task? Thus, before proceeding to delegate, the nurse manager must have a clear idea of the scope of the project and the results to be achieved.

Choose a capable and appropriately qualified person. A decision has to be made about who is to take charge of this project and how many nurses should be involved. It will be wise to consult with staff rather than make a unilateral decision, especially if the nursing department is operating from a shared governance perspective. Experience on the unit and willingness to plan self-scheduling are likely to be two of the qualifications to look for in volunteers for this project. Nominations from people possessing these qualifications could be solicited and staff requested to elect their representatives from those nominated.

Give clear directions to the person selected. Although this principle seems obvious, experience suggests that directions are not always clearly communicated. The scope of the project must be spelled out, and the extent of the group's authority explained. Are there any limits to its decision-making power? Will the group have the necessary resources to complete the job? For example, will nurses be permitted to claim overtime for working on this project? Will the volunteers be expected to deal with any interpersonal conflicts arising out of their proposals? When will the group be required to report back to the manager? In the absence of clear objectives, the staff will feel frustrated and they may waste time in defining their task. This is particularly true if the staff elected have little experience in group work.

Remain available for consultation and assistance. This is one of the most important principles of delegation. In asking staff to assume self-scheduling, the manager is not abandoning part of his or her job. In fact, the manager is entrusting this function to someone else while retaining ultimate responsibility for it. For this reason, managers may make the mistake of offering too much supervision, or even worse, undercutting the authority of subordinates by interfering and giving orders. With intelligent and capable staff, all that is needed is assurance that the manager is available if the group requires assistance. Placing trust in staff at this point is probably the best support to offer them.

Give recognition for achievement of objectives. Motivation theory suggests that people respond positively when their efforts are evaluated and their successes acknowledged. Self-scheduling is a time-consuming and difficult task; to promote a spirit of encouragement and cooperation, credit should be given to the people who have done the work. Little respect accrues to managers who publicly give themselves credit for the work of their subordinates.

It is sometimes helpful in understanding the nature of delegation by stating what it is *not*. First, delegation is not simply a matter of giving orders (e.g., sending someone on an errand or assigning staff for coffee breaks). Giving orders is a matter of directing the routine work of people who normally perform that work. Delegation is more than giving orders because it involves transferring sufficient authority to a subordinate to accomplish specific results; in other words, it is empowering someone to make decisions and to solve problems often in nonroutine circumstances. Second, delegation should not be confused with what is known as dumping. Dumping is the habit of indiscriminately assigning an unreasonable number of undesirable tasks to subordinates. Dumping work on others creates a negative impression of managerial work, causes a great deal of resentment among subordinates, and stifles motivation and enthusiasm for work. Finally, delegation is *not* setting people up for failure by assigning them tasks for which they are clearly unsuited or inexperienced. As Poteet (1989) notes, this kind of managerial behaviour will be perceived as unfair and unethical. Indeed, it might also constitute constructive dismissal (Grosman, 1984), which is defined as an attempt by management to bring about someone's resignation, or to generate a case for terminating that person.

Reluctance to Delegate

Newly appointed managers may have difficulty in learning to delegate. There is an element of risk when deciding to delegate a project or task, but, paradoxically, there are also risks in failing to delegate. Managers who immerse themselves in routine tasks can quickly become overwhelmed by a growing backlog of more substantial issues needing their attention, to say little about the stress created by pending deadlines for action. Working longer hours and taking a full briefcase home at the weekend is certainly one response to coping with a heavy workload, but if this habit is sustained over time it will consume personal energy resources and may ultimately lead to burnout. The manager who constantly operates as if there is never enough time to accomplish the work should seriously consider whether part of the problem is a reluctance to delegate.

Strange as it may seem, reluctance to delegate stems largely from fear of loss of control (Poteet, 1984). What follows are six reasons why people may fail to delegate.

The job will not be done as the manager would do it. This problem is typical of inexperienced managers and of managers who have perfectionist tendencies. To expect a job to be done according to exact specifications is to deny the subordinate an opportunity to be creative or to use individual discretion. Perfectionists are likely to hold onto their authority by closely supervising their subordinates, and this in turn creates the impression of lack of confidence and trust in the subordinate.

The subordinate might make a mistake for which the manager would be held accountable. Such fears can be dispelled by choosing the most capable subordinate for assuming the delegated project. More importantly, such fears suggest that the manager has not fully come to terms with the managerial role because accountability for subordinates is a legal, moral, and institutional requirement of people in management positions.

The subordinate might do the work better than the manager would have done it. This fear may stem from personal insecurities or lack of maturity in the manager, and reveals ignorance of one of the principal reasons for delegating, namely to provide opportunities to subordinates to develop additional competencies and to expand their knowledge of the health agency's work.

It will be done faster if the manager carries out the work.
This could well be a rational excuse for not delegating, but it
could also mean that the manager enjoys doing this kind of
work and prefers not to delegate. There is little doubt that
the manager has the right to keep all the enjoyable work for
himself or herself, but, ultimately, it denies opportunities for
job enhancement among the nursing staff and is likely to
generate resentment.

**There is no one with sufficient competence to undertake
the project to be delegated.** Again, this may be the case,
but it suggests that there is a need to assess the inventory of
skills among the staff and to plan a staff development program, or even to review the staffing pattern in the agency or
unit. Managers need competent subordinates in order to survive and ensure succession in the agency. In other words, it
is the manager's responsibility to be developing leadership
potential in subordinates to ensure organizational stability
in the event of such contingencies as illness, resignation, and
even layoff.

**The staff resent delegation, saying they are not paid to do
the manager's job.** This type of excuse for not delegating
suggests a number of problems between manager and staff.
If work is delegated to people already struggling with heavy
workloads, delegation may be perceived as dumping. When
choosing the person to undertake a project, managers may
have to make adjustments in work assignments and help
staff to assess or reassess the agency's priorities.

Encouraging Staff to Delegate

Nurses often complain about the non-nursing duties they assume
(CNA/CHA, 1990; Hibberd, 1987; Premier's Commission, 1988).
Expecting professional people to undertake work of unqualified
staff is clearly an inefficient use of human resources. Nurses tend
to explain that they take on non-nursing tasks (e.g., mopping up
spills or running errands) so that their patients are not inconve-
nienced. Often there are no other workers to whom to delegate
these tasks, particularly on night duty.

Not only must managers understand the principles of delegation, but they also need to help staff nurses become conscious of
how their time is spent and, in turn, of how staff might practise
delegation. Current trends to train nonlicensed personnel and
employ them in intensive care units (Eriksen, Quandt, Teinert, et
al., 1992) make it imperative that nurses understand the job

descriptions of auxiliary workers so that they can plan what to delegate (Hansten & Washburn, 1992).

Many delegated activities involve establishment of committees and task forces and "nowhere is there more danger of unproductive time than in committee work" (Rowland & Rowland, 1985, p. 40). Nurse managers need to have a good understanding of group dynamics and the conventions associated with chairing committees because committee work has become one of the most time-consuming activities of administrators and managers (Beachy & Biester, 1986).

Managing Committees Effectively

Decentralization of decision making and the increasing complexity of health agencies give rise to a need for more meetings. All managerial staff, as well as many rank-and-file health agency workers, are being required to undertake committee work, and many employees have little or no experience of serving on committees. Because learning how to be an effective member of a committee is seldom taught in basic health care programs, the vast majority of employees learn the necessary skills by trial and error and by observing others. The need to learn group work skills cuts across all disciplines and departments, and so educational programs on this topic can be fun (Clarke, 1984) and can also serve as additional means of promoting interdepartmental and interdisciplinary cooperation (see Chapter 27).

Ineffective committees can be costly in view of the labour-intensive nature of these structures. Assuming an average hourly wage of $25 for each member of a committee of 10 people, a two-hour meeting costs $500, and approximately another $150 for fringe benefits. In addition, one must also include whatever it costs to replace nurses drawn from direct care areas to attend the meeting, as well as cost of clerical services and supplies. If coffee or lunch is served, then there are dietary service costs as well. It should be clear that whenever another committee undertakes a project, the agency commits more resources to group work—often without assessing the impact on the budget or on patient care. Moreover, it is a rare event to disband a committee unless, of course, it happens to be a temporary structure such as a task force (Moore & Kovach, 1988). By definition, a task force disbands on completion of its mandate.

All participants in group meetings have a responsibility to contribute to the productivity of committees. Even under the best of circumstances, committees do not reach their full productive potential due to what Charns and Schaefer (1983) refer to as process loss. Process loss is the inherent inefficiencies of meetings, such as waiting until others have finished expressing their thoughts, repeating what has been said before, explaining a point to someone who was not paying attention, or engaging in stress-reduction behaviours such as telling jokes.

Generally speaking, the larger the problem-solving group the less likely it will reach its full productivity potential. Smaller groups, on the other hand, are likely to operate more informally and to reach decisions by consensus. The literature is quite clear on one point: that committees work best when they have between four and nine people (Charns & Schaefer, 1983; Jay, 1982).

In general, there are three types of committees: assemblies and standing committees; special or ad hoc committees; and task forces. Assemblies are large groups of more than 50 people who meet regularly and generally serve as a forum for one-way communication (Jay, 1982). If decisions have to be made, the process is usually formal and is achieved through resolutions and motions that are put to a vote. Standing committees are smaller than assemblies and also meet on a regular basis, but they generally carry out essential corporate functions. This might be an executive board committee or policy-making body. Standing committees often strike subcommittees, either special or ad hoc, to deal more expediently with aspects of the larger committee's work. Special and ad hoc committees are generally composed of experts, and may or may not meet regularly. They are often advisory to the larger standing committee. Task forces may meet regularly or irregularly until the specific tasks assigned to them have been completed. They often conduct inquiries and studies, produce reports, and make recommendations for action to a policy-making body.

There may also be numerous informal and unstructured committees in health agencies, such as patient rounds. The rules for decision making tend to become less and less formal the smaller the group.

Chairing Committees

Sooner or later, nurse managers will find themselves being asked to chair a committee or a particular meeting. A strong chair who fully understands the scope of his or her authority and responsibility is essential if the business of the committee is to be completed effectively and in a timely manner. Common problems observed at meetings are:

- The chair loses control over the direction of the discussion and the meeting itself;
- Too many members talk at once, or subgroups chat and distract others;
- The discussion is dominated by the chair, or by one or two garrulous or high-status individuals
- Members do not contribute to the discussion, are silent, or working on unrelated tasks such as writing reports or reading correspondence;
- Members feel no sense of accomplishment;
- The meeting drones on with many digressions;
- People arrive late, leave early, or drop in for parts of the meeting;
- The chair is uncertain of procedure and appears intimidated by strong members; and
- The agenda is unrealistic and items are routinely deferred.

Almost all these problems can be avoided if the person in the chair is both knowledgeable and confident about his or her role and understands the responsibilities of the chair.

If a nurse manager is asked to assume responsibility for chairing a committee, there are several questions she or he should raise. The first has to do with terms of reference for the committee; if there are no terms of reference, then the first task of the group would be to draft its own mandate. The second question (or questions) involves the scope of authority of the committee (i.e., is it advisory in nature, can it make decisions and issue directives, and to whom does the committee report?). And, finally, the chair should ask about resources available to assist the committee with its work (e.g., is there a budget for the committee, and is there any clerical support for dealing with minutes and correspondence?).

The chair of a committee must have leadership potential because the essence of the role is to facilitate the work of the group. The chair of any meeting has primary responsibility for keeping the members working towards goals and objectives. To accomplish this, the leader must find some middle ground between being an autocrat and being a servant of the group. There will be times when the chair must take a stand, for example either to interrupt a talkative and repetitious speaker, or to bring the group to a decision. There are likely to be as many people at a meeting who are distracted by subgroup chatting as those doing the chatting, and so the chair may bring the meeting to order at such times. Few people want to spend time in poorly run meetings,

Table 33.2

Responsibilities of the committee chair.

1. Sets date, time, and place of meetings
2. Sets agenda for each meeting
3. Circulates agenda, minutes of previous meeting, memoranda, reports, or articles to members in sufficient time for them to prepare for the meeting
4. Prepares self for the meeting, anticipates process and outcome of meeting, and suggests alternative problem-solving approaches as necessary
5. Chairs the meetings, or in a necessary absence, delegates to a competent substitute from among the members
6. Obtains agreement from the members relative to the rules of order; administers the rules consistently, recognizes the absence of a quorum, and defers decisions that require a quorum
7. Establishes an efficient leadership style: starting and finishing on time; promoting effective group dynamics; speaking clearly without dominating the meeting; keeping the group focussed on the task and moving toward goals; encouraging critical thinking; listening to differing ideas; summarizing main points of the discussion; ensuring members understand motions before a vote is taken
8. Acts upon directives and decisions of the committee, or accounts for inaction
9. Ensures minutes are recorded; reviews them before circulation as necessary
10. Reports progress of committee to appropriate person or group; writes annual report
11. Ensures that committee reviews its terms of reference periodically
12. Recommends dissolution of the committee when it has no further reason to meet.

and unless the chair is unduly dominating and autocratic, most committee members are likely to support a chair who acts fairly and diplomatically in keeping the meeting focussed on the task at hand.

The main responsibilities of the chair of a committee are listed in Table 33.2. Some of these responsibilities can be delegated to clerical staff and even to other members of the committee. Chairing a committee provides an excellent opportunity for the nurse manager to exercise leadership skills and to reap the intrinsic rewards of completing a worthwhile project. Committee work is time consuming and labour intensive under the best of circumstances, and this brief overview merely deals with strategies for using time effectively. More comprehensive accounts of the dynamics of groups and committee work can be found in Chapter 27, and in Charns and Schaefer (1983), Cryderman (1991), Jay (1982), and Veninga (1984).

Conclusion

The purpose of this chapter was to suggest some practical ways in which nurse managers might make the best use of both their own and the staff's time at work. Much of the impetus for restructuring workplaces arises from the recognition that much time is wasted in health agencies because of poor design of work structures and processes, and because the nursing workforce is fragmented.

It is clear that the pursuit of efficiency shows no sign of abating. Nurse managers will be required to operate flexibly and innovatively, and they will continue to be evaluated on their ability to maintain high-quality services at the lowest possible cost. In view of the labour-intensive nature of nursing services, the way nurses use their time needs to be managed as carefully as any other scarce resource because time is, indeed, money.

References

Alberta Hospital Association (1980). *Nursing manpower: A study of factors in nursing supply and demand in Alberta hospitals and nursing homes.* Edmonton: Author.

Barker, A.M. (1990). *Transformational nursing leadership: A vision for the future.* Baltimore: Williams & Wilkins.

Beachy, P., & Biester, D.J. (1986). Restructuring group meetings for effectiveness. *Journal of Nursing Administration, 16*(12), 30-33.

Canadian Nurses Association & Canadian Hospital Association. (1990). *Nurse retention and quality of work life: A national perspective.* Ottawa: Authors.

Charns, M.P., & Schaefer, M.J. (1983). *Health care organizations: A model for management.* Englewood Cliffs, NJ: Prentice-Hall.

Clarke, J.I. (1984). *Who, me lead a group?* San Francisco: HarperCollins.

Cryderman, P. (1991). Effective committee work. In S.A. Ziebarth (Ed.), *Feeling the squeeze: The practice of middle management in Canadian health care facilities* (pp. 101-108). Ottawa: Canadian Hospital Association.

Dechant, G.M. (1990). Self-scheduling for nursing staff. *Alberta Association of Registered Nurses Newsletter, 46*(5), 4,6,8.

Eriksen, L.R., Quandt, B., Teinert, D., Look, D.S., Loosle, R., Mackey, G., & Strout, B. (1992). A Registered Nurse-Licensed Vocational Nurse partnership model for critical care nursing. *Journal of Nursing Administration, 22(12)*, 28-38.

Grosman, B.A. (1984). *The executive firing line: Wrongful dismissal and the law.* Toronto: Methuen.

Hansten, R., & Washburn, M. (1992). How to plan what to delegate. *American Journal of Nursing, 92(4)*, 71-72.

Hibberd, J.M. (1987). *Strikes by Alberta nurses: 1977-1982.* Unpublished doctoral dissertation, University of Alberta.

Jay, A. (1982). How to run a meeting. *Journal of Nursing Administration, 12(1)*, 22-28.

Longest, B.B. Jr. (1990). *Management practices for the health professional* (4th ed.). Norwalk, CT: Appleton & Lange.

Moore, C.H., & Kovach, K.M. (1988). Task force: A management technique that produces quality decisions and employee commitment. *Journal of the American Dietetic Association, 88(1)*, 52-55.

Poteet, G.W. (1984). Delegation strategies: A must for the nurse executive. *Journal of Nursing Administration, 14(9)*, 18-21.

Poteet, G.W. (1989). Nursing administrators and delegation. *Nursing Administration Quarterly, 13(3)*, 23-32.

Premier's Commission on Future Health Care for Albertans. (1988). *Caring and commitment: Concerns of nurses in the hospital and nursing home system* (Interim Report). Edmonton: Author.

Prescott, P.A., Phillips, C.Y., Ryan, J.W., & Thompson, K.O. (1991). Changing how nurses spend their time. *Image: Journal of Nursing Scholarship, 23(1)*, 23-28.

Ringl, K.K., & Dotson, L. (1989). Self-scheduling: A practical approach. *Nursing Management, 20(2)*, 42-44.

Rowland, H.S., & Rowland, B.L. (1985). *Nursing administration handbook* (2nd ed.). Rockville, MD: Aspen Systems.

Staggers, N. (1989). Electronic mail basics. *Journal of Nursing Administration, 19(10)*, 31-35.

Strasen, L. (1991). Redesigning hospitals around patients and technology. *Nursing Economics, 9*, 233-238.

Veninga, R.L. (1984). Benefits and costs of group meetings. *Journal of Nursing Administration, 14(6)*, 42-46.

C H A P T E R   3 4

Negotiation—A Skill for Today's Nurse Manager

Lana Clark

Lana Clark, RN, BScN (Alberta), MN (Calgary), is Assistant Executive Director, Patient Care at the Royal University Hospital, Saskatoon. She has several years' experience as a front-line manager and in senior nursing administration.

The Canadian health care system is immersed in a process of reform. Gone are the days when change and conflict were irregular occurrences. Today's health care system is characterized by rapid change, conflict, shrinking resources, and the need for precise, timely decisions. Nurse managers, by nature of their position, often find themselves at the centre of action arising from the outcomes of this reform. In this integral role, the need for nurse managers to incorporate a variety of skills into their leadership style is paramount to their success as health care leaders.

A skill not widely used by nurse managers in day-to-day practice, but described as imperative for contemporary nursing leaders, is that of negotiation (Biggerstaff & Syre, 1991; Smeltzer, 1991). Negotiation is quickly replacing the traditional authority of the leader's coercive power (Biggerstaff & Syre, 1991) and is being recognized as a key strategy in successful conflict resolution (Smeltzer, 1991; Synder-Halpern & Cannon, 1993). Defined as "a process of communicating back and forth for the purpose of reaching a joint decision" (Fisher, Ury, & Patton, 1991, p. 32), negotiation has moved from a rarely used technique to a basic survival skill for nurse managers. This chapter provides an overview of the negotiation process and focusses on the nature of what is encompassed in developing negotiation skills. First, however, there is a need to examine the differences between negotiation for collective agreements and day-to-day negotiation for nurse managers.

Types of Negotiation

Day-to-day negotiation is a process that emphasizes the need to maintain long term interpersonal relationships. It is a continuous process built on trust, creativity, and cooperative decision making. Going beyond the traditional win-lose conflict resolution style and even the contemporary win-win style, day-to-day negotiation attempts to resolve conflict through communication, exchange of ideas, and commitment to a course of action.

In contrast, negotiation associated with collective bargaining has an identifiable time frame that is characterized by start and completion dates. The parties are essentially required to negotiate together and, even if talks "break off," they know that at some point they must return. In this process, the outcome is to attain a settlement with little emphasis on maintaining long term relationships. Indeed, the atmosphere tends to be more "we-they" versus the collaborative problem-solving environment associated with the daily negotiation style.

Why Negotiate?

In the face of rapid change and shrinking resources, conflict in the Canadian health care system is inevitable. As leaders, nurse managers increasingly encounter situations of conflict and the need to resolve these situations has become a significant challenge (Collyer, 1989). Approaches to resolving conflict are discussed extensively in published literature. Thomas (1976) has described five major approaches to conflict resolution. These are avoidance, compromise, collaboration, competition, and accommodation. Contemporary management theory views conflict resolution as a critical process in searching for new methods or solutions to problems (Jones, 1993).

The collaborative approach to conflict resolution has been described in industrial research as the approach most likely to achieve successful outcomes (Citron, 1981). Marriner (1982) found that nurses who used collaborating or compromising approaches were more likely to have successful conflict resolution. In comparison, avoiding or competing approaches were more frequently associated with unsuccessful resolution. A collaborative approach has been associated with the search for integrated solutions and empowerment of others (Kouzes & Posner, 1987), two outcomes characterized within successful health care organizations.

So, why negotiate? Negotiation in day-to-day practice is an effective interactive strategy that allows for the sharing of power and control (Barton, 1991) and emphasizes the need to maintain relationships (Fisher & Ury, 1983). Because it promotes an environment that emphasizes collaboration, negotiation becomes a strategy for conflict resolution. In addition, successful use of negotiation skills may enhance the team spirit of nursing and serve to benefit the organization, the patient, the nurse, and the nursing profession (Smeltzer, 1991).

When to Negotiate?

Negotiation is a fact of life (Fisher & Ury, 1983). It can be used in any situation where there is a desire to affect the behaviour of others (Cohen, 1982). Whether you are negotiating the price of a new car, determining a time when your daughter should be home from the graduation party, or discussing a salary increment with your supervisor, negotiation can help to ensure an effective outcome for all parties. One of the major hurdles to the use of negotiation is the belief that negotiation is used only for collective bargaining. However, Fisher and Ury (1983), with their national best seller, *Getting to Yes,* helped to dismiss this belief and bring daily negotiation to the forefront in conflict resolution and into the daily professional and home life of individuals and groups. Although every negotiation is different, the basic principles are consistent. Once the skill is learned, the daily negotiation process becomes easier with experience (Fisher & Ury, 1983; Fisher, Ury, & Patton, 1991).

How to Negotiate?

The actual "how to" of negotiation consists of two interrelated components: negotiating style and negotiating process.

Style

A negotiating style constitutes a method or manner of approach. The traditional negotiating style is well known and described by Fisher, Ury, and Patton (1991) as "hard" positional negotiation. This style is characterized in the collective bargaining process whereby each party takes a position on certain issues. There is generally a contest of wills where each side, through sheer power, attempts to change the position of the other party (Fisher, Ury, & Patton, 1991). Hard negotiation tends to strain relationships and may even destroy them during the bargaining process.

An alternative to "hard" positional bargaining is a style referred to as "soft" bargaining (Fish, Ury, & Patton, 1991). In this style, positions are still taken, but there is emphasis on being friendly, trusting the other side, making offers and concessions, and avoiding confrontation. Although this style emphasizes the building and maintaining of relationships, it often falls short of providing the best outcome for all parties.

A third negotiation style identified by Fisher, Ury, and Patton (1991) is that of principled bargaining. This style is based on a collaborative process that looks beyond the problem, focussing on interests and mutual gains. The situation of concern becomes depersonalized and energies are focussed on issues rather than on defending positions. Because this style emphasizes the need to maintain relationships and promotes trust and collaborative decision making, principled bargaining is generally the style of choice for nurse managers.

Process — A Blueprint for Nurse Managers

The analogy of an architect's blueprint for a house can be used to help illustrate the process for daily negotiation (see Figure 34.1, page 636). In the centre of the house is a family room. This room brings together all those people involved in the negotiation process. Leading into the family room are hallways. Each hallway extends to another room in the house and each room represents a phase in the negotiating process. The common hallways represent strategies used in negotiation.

Just as the foundation provides overall support for a house, principles are the cornerstone of all negotiation activities, whether they involve individuals or groups. The literature on negotiation (Fisher, Ury, & Patton, 1991; Jones, 1993; Roberts & Krouse, 1988; Smeltzer, 1991; Synder-Halpern & Cannon, 1993) identifies at least 11 key principles:

- Focus on the problem and not the individual or the individual's behaviour.

- Build rapport and maintain communication.

- Build trust.

- Explore interests and gather information.

- Maintain an open mind by searching for creative options. (Techniques such as brainstorming or the Delphi strategy may assist in this process.)

- Focus on issues rather than taking positions. Once a position is taken, there is a tendency to defend the position rather than explore the underlying reason for a problem.

- Use facts and objective standards to shape solutions.

Figure 34.1
A blueprint for negotiation.

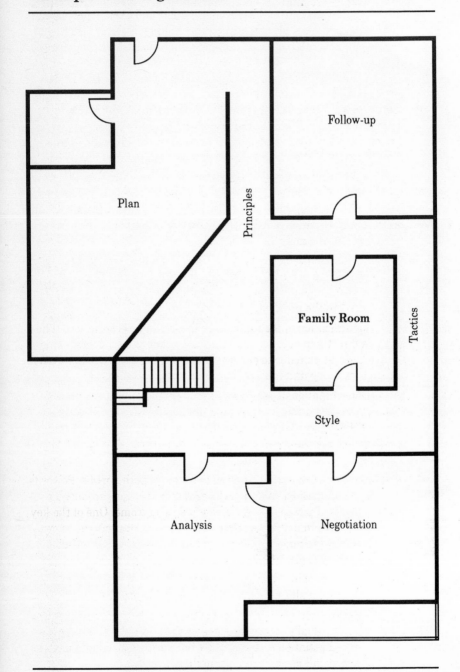

- Be aware of your own values and motives and attempt to understand the perspective of the other person(s).

- Emphasize mutual benefits versus forming options in terms of costs.

- Avoid blaming words, such as "you are late, as usual." Blaming tends to result in defensive behaviour.

- Promote cooperation instead of competition.

These principles are inherent in each of the four phases (the four rooms) of the negotiation process.

Phase 1: Analysis

Before initiating negotiation activities, it is imperative that the nurse manager analyze the context of the situation or problem. A thorough analysis will enhance the possibility of achieving a successful outcome in the shortest period of time. Six major components that should be considered in the analysis include:

- Delineation of the problem or issue. This can be facilitated by separating personal characteristics and behaviour from the issues and identifying all factors contributing directly or indirectly to the problem.

- Identification of the individuals involved in the situation. Who is directly involved and who are the other stakeholders? This information helps to ensure that the right people are involved in negotiation and that stakeholders are kept informed.

- Determination of personal factors that may affect the process. As trust is a major component in the success of negotiation (Fisher, Ury, & Patton, 1991), the nurse manager needs to determine the previous working relationships of the parties involved.

- Identification of the power distribution of both parties. Power is a major consideration in any negotiation because an unequal balance of power may set up a win-lose outcome. One of the key principles in daily negotiation is to strive for collaborative decisions and to maintain relationships. Win-lose situations do not generally facilitate these outcomes.

- Collection of all necessary information. The negotiation will be enhanced if all information is compiled in advance.

- Identification of the environment where negotiation will occur. An individual's or group's power is thought to be enhanced when negotiation occurs in their territories. Selecting a neutral location will dissolve this possibility.

The determination of the power distribution (item 4) is an essential component. One way to determine the power distribution of parties is known as BATNA (best alternative to negotiated agreement) and has been described by Fisher, Ury, and Patton (1991) and Keeney and Raiffa (1991). Simply stated, BATNA is a cutoff point; below that point means no agreement and above it produces agreements (Keeney & Raiffa, 1991). Negotiating power related to BATNA depends primarily upon how attractive the option of not reaching agreement is to each party (Fisher, Ury, & Patton, 1991).

Consider the situation where the nurse manager and a staff nurse are negotiating the nurse's request for a leave of absence when there is a shortage of qualified nurses. In this scenario, the nurse manager's BATNA is high and the staff member's is low. The alternative to a negotiated agreement is less critical to the nurse manager than it is to the staff member. However, the nurse manager who is aware of this unequal power distribution and who wishes to avoid a win-lose solution will need to approach this negotiation so that the outcome is not solely attributed to the manager's power.

Identifying your own BATNA and determining that of the other side allows you to be better prepared for negotiation. In situations of low BATNA, the nurse manager should make every effort to develop greater negotiating power. Developing BATNA may be accomplished through the exploration and refinement of other options than a negotiated agreement (Fisher & Ury, 1983).

Phase 2: Plan

During the planning phase both parties determine a proposed course of action for negotiation. There may be joint discussions to determine meeting times and to arrive at a decision regarding the general approach to negotiation. In addition, individuals will plan their specific strategy and style based on the completed analysis of the problem.

Phase 3: Negotiation

This is the phase when the actions of negotiation are implemented. In any negotiation, there are techniques that enhance the process and those that inhibit the process. The nurse manager needs to optimize enhancing techniques and minimize or eliminate restrictive techniques.

Techniques constructive to negotiation include:

Open communication. This communication technique encourages participation by all involved in the process and allows for an interchange of ideas.

Focus on the task or situation. The use of this technique promotes communication and collaboration while minimizing power struggles. An environment of trust is likely to develop, which in turn facilitates more open discussion of options to resolve the problem at hand.

Mutual responsibility. Communication that requires people to exchange ideas reinforces the belief that the participants can attain resolutions. Mutual responsibility is enhanced by focussing on the benefits of proposed solutions rather than emphasizing the costs.

Techniques that impede negotiation include:

Divide and conquer. This tactic discourages group problem solving and curtails open communication.

Suppression. Pretending differences do not exist does little to promote collaborative decision making or trust.

Majority rule. Setting up competition for votes does not generally enhance successful resolution of differences.

Blaming the other party or implying that the participants lack objectivity and rationality.

Withdrawing before resolution is achieved.

In addition to techniques that enhance or inhibit negotiation, also inherent in the process are a range of negotiating tactics. Tactics are behaviours that can be used individually or in combination to influence negotiation. They may be used by either party. Advantages and disadvantages of each tactic need to be considered carefully prior to their use so as not to compromise the negotiation process. Table 34.1 provides a list of some common negotiation tactics compiled from various sources in the literature (Cohen, 1982; Dolan, 1988; Fisher & Ury, 1983; Snyder-Halpern & Cannon, 1993).

Throughout phase 3, there should be an exhaustive search for solutions or alternatives. The ultimate goal is to reach an agreement that people feel satisfied with and to maintain interpersonal relationships.

Phase 4: Follow-up

Once agreement has been reached, the final phase involves a process of evaluation to ensure successful resolution of the problem. The uniqueness of each negotiation process means that follow-up needs to be tailored to the specific situation. In this phase, there is a need to ensure that the plan of action successfully addresses the problem and that no further intervention is required.

Table 34.1
Negotiating tactics and their use.

Tactic	Rationale for Use
Silence	Encourages the other party to continue to talk, thus revealing more information to you.
Answers that don't answer	To "buy" time or a means to evade the direct answering of a question.
Good guy/Bad guy	Used to attain a specific result; there is a staged quarrel by two members on the same side where one member takes a tough stand and the other appears to do a favour to other side by intervening.
Limited authority	A means of avoiding agreement by indicating that others with greater authority need to be involved in the solution.
Dumb may be smart	May be used to "buy" time or to have the other side further articulate their perspective/concerns.
Nibbling	An approach to get more by breaking a large request into small parts so that it is easier to sell to the other side.
Package deal	A means to achieve concessions—if you give this, I will give that.
Deadline	Forces the other party to make a decision by a designated time.
Trial balloon	Suggesting a position or idea to generate feedback without being committed to the idea. Usually prefaced with a question such as "what if...?"
Change of pace	A means to postpone the need for a decision or to give the impression of a need to escalate the process.
Extreme demands	Begin with options that are known to be extreme so that you eventually attain what you really want.

What to Negotiate?

Day-to-day negotiation can be used in any situation where two or more individuals need to reach an agreement on a particular issue. The negotiation process may take an informal style such as in the case of discussion to change the uniform style worn on a particular unit, the content of an orientation program to ICU, or the topics of a six-month inservice program. A more formal style in daily negotiation may be required in some situations, such as in grievance meetings or when the nurse manager needs to attain an increased operating budget for the unit or for capital equipment that was not included in the yearly budget process.

Regardless of the situation, the blueprint outlined in Figure 34.1 (see page 636) provides a guide to help maximize the chance of a collaborative outcome and maintain the integrity of relationships. Although the steps are consistent, the formality and intensity of the negotiating meeting will vary with the situation.

Conclusion

Negotiation is a skill that involves a process of steps, strategies, and tactics. It can be used in any setting, with individuals or groups, and as an approach for personal or professional problem solving. For nurse managers, who are in a health care environment that is experiencing rapid change and increased conflict, negotiation is a basic survival skill.

References

Barton, A. (1991). Conflict resolution by nurse managers. *Nursing Management, 22*(5), 83-86.

Biggerstaff, R.P., & Syre, T.R. (1991). The dynamics of hospital leadership. *Hospital Topics, 69*(1), 36-39.

Citron, D. (1981). Facing up to conflict. *Nursing Life, 1*(1), 47-49.

Cohen, H. (1982). *You can negotiate anything.* Toronto: Bantam.

Collyer, M.E. (1989). Resolving conflicts: Leadership styles sets the strategy. *Nursing Management, 20*(9), 77-80.

Dolan, J. (1988). *Negotiating skills for attorneys: Workbook.* Boulder, CO: Career Track.

Fisher, R., & Ury, W. (1983). *Getting to yes: Negotiating agreement without giving in.* New York: Penguin.

Fisher, R., Ury, W., & Patton, B. (1991). *Getting to yes: Negotiating agreement without giving in* (2nd ed.). Toronto: Penguin.

Jones, K. (1993). Confrontation: Methods and skills. *Nursing Management, 24*(5), 68-70.

Keeney, R.L., & Raiffa, H. (1991). Structuring and analysing values for multiple-issue negotiation. In H.P. Young (Ed.), *Negotiation analysis* (pp. 131-152). Ann Arbor: University of Michigan Press.

Kouzes, J.M., & Posner, B.Z. (1987). *The leadership challenge.* San Francisco: Jossey-Bass.

Marriner, A. (1982). Managing conflict: Comparing strategies and their use. *Nursing Management, 13*(6), 29-31.

Roberts, S.J., & Krouse, H.J. (1988). Enhancing self care through active negotiation. *Nurse Practitioner, 13*(8), 44-52.

Smeltzer, C.H. (1991). The art of negotiation an everyday experience. *Journal of Nursing Administration, 21*(7/8), 26-30.

Snyder-Halpern, R., & Cannon, M.E. (1993). A framework for the development of nurse manager negotiation skills. *Journal of Nursing Staff Development, 9*(1), 14-19.

Thomas, K. (1976). Conflict and conflict management. In M. Dunnette (Ed.), *Handbook of industrial and organizational psychology* (pp. 899-935). Chicago: Rand McNally.

C H A P T E R 3 5

Issues in Managerial Communication

Donna Lynn Smith

Donna Lynn Smith, RN, BScN, MEd (Alberta), is Manager, Program Development and Special Programs, Long Term Care Branch, Alberta Health. She holds joint appointments with the Faculty of Nursing and the Division of Bioethics in the Faculty of Medicine, University of Alberta.

Organizations of all kinds spend millions of dollars each year in attempts to improve managerial performance. As trends and gimmicks come and go, the importance of interpersonal skills remains a constant theme. But what is effective managerial communication? And how is it achieved?

The purpose of this chapter is to focus upon selected issues of particular importance in communication by first-line or middle managers. The approach will be practical rather than theoretical. Where a prescriptive tone is adopted, readers are encouraged to consult not only the references provided, but a variety of other information sources, including managers who have had experience in more than one organizational environment.

What Is Unique about Managerial Communication?

Nurses have an opportunity to excel in the interpersonal aspects of management. Since the late 1960s, most basic nursing programs have incorporated a significant emphasis on the development of interpersonal or communications skills, and an understanding of factors that can improve or inhibit effective communication. Being able to convey respect for others, to listen effectively, to offer support, to facilitate or participate constructively in problem solving, and to be sincere and genuine are of obvious importance in relationships with clients. They are also important in collegial relationships, and the ability to get along well with others is usually a prerequisite for professional advancement.

As a starting point for this chapter, the assumption is that the present or aspiring first-line nursing manager already possesses basic communications skills, and recognizes the need to use them conscientiously and to improve upon them. However, skills that originally were focussed on establishing relationships with clients, their families, co-workers, and supervisors will be refocussed when used by a first-line or middle manager in the many different types and directions of communication at the heart of this role. There will continue to be some communications with clients and their families, but these will be directed primarily toward quality monitoring, public relations, and problem solving. Conflict resolution and performance coaching involve one-on-one or small group interaction with staff members. Motivational communication regarding the mission, values, and current directions of the organization is a particular challenge when communicating to groups of employees.

The manager must also change the focus of problem identification and definition from one directed toward clinical and peer group concerns to a perspective that encompasses the unit or program as a whole and as a part of the total organization. The manager is accountable for solving many types of problems. Some are dealt with through direct personal intervention. In other instances, the best approach involves developing and empowering members of the work team so that they can prevent problems from arising, or can deal with them effectively through acceptance of personal responsibility. The priority given to staff concerns and the approach to their resolution must be determined in light of their impact on the safety, well-being, and health outcomes of clients. For example, if the nurses on an inpatient unit have been taking turns leaving 15 minutes early on the evening shift, or going to coffee in friendship groups that leave the unit understaffed for periods of time, the manager's hesitancy to frame this as a problem and to deal with it directly could result in an inappropriate response to a clinical emergency. In a community health clinic, traditional working hours of 08:00 to 16:30 hours may be preferred by staff, but may ignore the needs of working families who need services at other times. The first-line manager is spokesperson for professional and organizational values. She or he must accept responsibility for defining problems and developing solutions. In some cases, it will be necessary to obtain support from a supervisor or "champion" at a higher organizational level to achieve a solution.

It is helpful to see the differences between therapeutic and managerial communications in terms of the boundaries of the various interpersonal relationships that managers must establish and maintain.

A belief in participative management approaches should not distract the manager from an obligation to provide leadership and to make decisions. Managers must acknowledge that they hold significant power to influence the job satisfaction, career development, and even the livelihoods of those they supervise.

In most organizations, there are policies that stipulate that an individual cannot have a direct reporting relationship to his or her spouse; however, close friendships or other types of intimate relationships can make it equally difficult for the manager to provide objective performance ratings or recommendations regarding career enhancement opportunities. Boundary considerations also apply in mentoring relationships. Insight into one's own emotional needs and a recognition of the boundaries that distinguish therapeutic, collegial, supervisory, and reporting relationships from close personal relationships is important in achieving effectiveness and credibility as a manager.

A mature and appropriate recognition of boundaries does not require that the manager be aloof, distant, or lacking in spontaneity. Expression of personal qualities of warmth, sincerity, and humour, along with respect for each member of the unit or program team, will be important in creating a climate that enables a group to work productively and to support one another. Injecting humour into the workplace may be an important factor, when it is appropriate. In fact, Burns (1953) has suggested that a joke is a shortcut to consensus in all societies. Recognizing the boundaries of the role will not prevent the manager from developing reciprocal relationships of respect and fondness with staff members, but it will help to avoid pitfalls of judgement that close emotional bonds can sometimes create.

Fundamentals: Good Manners and Common Sense

Sensitivity, courtesy, and discretion are the ingredients of good manners. They are also fundamental to effective managerial communication and performance. As recently as the 1960s, the professional socialization of most nurses included instructions in manners, deportment, and dress. These factors are now considered matters of personal choice; nevertheless, social conformity has been shown to be important for promotion to, and success in, managerial positions. Loyalty, the ability to accept authority, and to conform to a prescribed pattern of behaviour were identified by earlier writers as critical success factors, and Kanter's (1977) classic study, *Men and Women of the Corporation,* confirmed their continuing importance. Kanter points out that conformity pressures arise from the uncertainty surrounding managerial positions. When there is uncertainty and decisions have to be made, the quality of personal discretion is very important:

> *Discretion raises not technical, but human, social, and even communal questions: trust, and its origins in loyalty, commitment, and mutual understanding based on shared values. . . . If conditions of uncertainty mean that people have to be relied on, then people fall back on the social bases for trust.* (p. 49)

Similar social backgrounds and characteristics, or similarity of organizational experience, are two types of homogeneity that can provide a basis for trust. As multicultural workplaces become more common, managers must build trust through use of empathy and respect rather than assume similar backgrounds and values.

Organizational cultures differ, and it is important to be sensitive to the unique traditions and style of the organization as they are communicated through formal corporate image-building, via informal story-telling, and by successful role models. As a new manager, it is often wise to seek advice or coaching before participating in important meetings, making presentations, initiating external or upward communications, or attending work-related social events. This is particularly important if the manager is also new to the organization. In 1970, industrial psychologist Milla Alihan addressed a book entitled *Corporate Etiquette* to aspiring executives. She covered a range of topics including manners, relationships with clerical staff, receiving guests, conducting and participating in meetings, verbal and written communication, appearance, travel, and social functions. Her advice on courtesy is repeated here because of its continuing relevance:

> *Courtesy under all circumstances, even when the tension seems unendurable, should be the young executive's number one guideline. This does not mean that he [sic] has to be servile or fawning. Far from it. It is simply that he must keep his resentments on a leash, his temper under control, and show a willingness to work hard and do his level-best at whatever his superior assigns to him without stepping out of line.* (pp. 9-10)

Readers may be inclined to disagree with this advice on the grounds that the behaviour recommended might inhibit a free exchange of ideas or discourage the acceptance of individual moral responsibility among members of the management team. This is a legitimate concern, and it is dealt with briefly in another section of this chapter. The point here is that within all organizations, managers are judged not only in terms of individual ability and performance, but by their ability to contribute to organizational goals and team performance. Viewed from the perspective of a senior manager, the type of courtesy described above contributes to economy of effort by enabling organizational activities and relationships to operate smoothly and predictably. While good manners and common sense may seem to be basic, it is widely recognized that no amount of specialized knowledge or skill can compensate, in the long term, for deficiencies in these fundamental areas.

Choosing the Medium of Communication

Communication takes many forms and occurs on various levels. For example, procedural instructions that need to be followed by many people are best communicated in writing. Values are best communicated through leadership behaviour, which, of course, includes written communication, but also includes a variety of other interactions. Since rewards or punishment are most effective when they occur in proximity to behaviour, recognition of work well done or feedback about mistakes is most effective if communicated verbally and immediately. A well-known book, titled *The One-Minute Manager* (Blanchard & Johnson, 1982), is devoted to helping managers develop effective skills in providing such instant feedback. The nature of a particular communication and the audience to be addressed should lead the manager to a carefully considered choice from among the many communications media available.

Communicating Values through Leadership Behaviour

Probably the most powerful form of managerial communication is the way in which a manager does or does not recognize and reinforce the behaviours of staff. If a manager spends more time with whiners than with star performers, this communicates a powerful message. If all employees are treated similarly, regardless of obvious performance differences, the "value" of mediocrity will be communicated. If instances of unkindness toward clients or colleagues are tolerated, the manager communicates a lack of conviction about professional values, or an absence of accountability and a need for self-confidence in the leadership role. Body language can be more powerful than words in the communication process, particularly when it is not congruent with what is being said. For example, expressions of concern or appreciation that are not accompanied by eye contact are likely to be experienced as empty or insincere. The strongest advocates of total quality management programs acknowledge that leadership practices must be congruent with the values espoused in the program. The phrase "walking the talk" is used in quality improvement programs to emphasize the need for the manager to match words and actions.

Communicating in Groups

The manager may be a participant in groups convened by others, or may be the chair of a group or committee. Specific skills are involved in each of these roles. A group meeting should be convened during working hours only if there is a valid purpose and framework for its activities. Careful planning and organization are necessary to avoid costly waste of time by participants. Recent research by Kastenbach and Smith (1993) has identified the similarities and differences between work groups and teams. Although work groups present fewer risks than teams and are often an effective vehicle for getting things done, teams are expected to become the primary unit of performance in high-performance organizations. In the role as leader of a program or unit, the manager has the responsibility to be an effective work group leader. Helpful principles for establishing group or team values are suggested in a publication that the Einstein Consulting Group prepared for the American Hospital Association (Leebov, 1990). The principles are:

- Respect people's differences;
- Think positively;
- Acknowledge co-workers;
- Listen;
- Pitch in and help out;
- Live up to your end of the job;
- Respect people's time and priorities;
- Admit your mistakes; and
- Invest in other parts of your life.

If principles such as these are modeled by the leader and presented as norms for the behaviour of a working group, there is some likelihood that the common purpose and mutual accountability that are characteristic of teams will begin to develop. Where leadership skills and individual motivation are present, one or more teams can be developed from the baseline of skills in the work group so that, as Kastenbach and Smith (1993) suggest, teams will enhance existing structures without replacing them.

Collegial Communication

There are many directions and styles of collegial communication. First-line nursing managers communicate downward to those they supervise, and upward to their own supervisors. Many lateral communications are also necessary. These take place between peers in the nursing department and with counterparts in other departments in the organization. Communication between nurse managers and their physician counterparts (that is, department heads or ward chiefs) is now recognized in progressive organizations as lateral and interdependent, with shared responsibility for successful outcomes. The style of communication is determined by a number of factors, including the organizational culture, the objective of the communication, the personalities of the people involved, and the institution. In general, the purpose of lateral communication is to share information, to develop joint definitions of problems and ownership of responsibility for solutions, to give or obtain support, and to improve procedures for getting work done. Most lateral or collegial communication is informal in nature. Occasionally, personal notes of meetings held and the results may sometimes need to be translated into a short memo recording the date, purpose, and subject of a meeting, and the action agreed upon so that follow-up can be monitored.

Upward Communication

Senior executives have demanding and often unpredictable schedules. The time they have for one-on-one communication with subordinates may be limited, not by choice, but by many competing demands. In many organizations, routine meetings are now looked upon with skepticism as being an unaffordable inefficiency. Planning and preparation for all but coincidental meetings with a director or vice-president is therefore an important skill for first-line or middle managers to develop.

Preparation should focus on what needs to be accomplished. Is the purpose to obtain endorsement for a proposed course of action, or to report, verbally, a serious incident and obtain direction about how to proceed? Is there a need to discuss a personal matter? It is helpful to distinguish in one's own mind between urgent and non-urgent matters. If time for discussion is limited, urgent matters should be prioritized, and arrangements made for another time when less pressing issues can be discussed.

Most senior executives routinely deal with incoming mail either early or late in the day. Incoming mail from a manager, or pertinent to the managerial areas of responsibility, may be brought forward by the executive for discussion at the next available opportunity, or answered with a brief comment or instruction. The first-line manager often should prepare written background to precede discussion of a developmental, innovative, or controversial issue. If this is well prepared, it can arouse interest, provide new or relevant information, present a rationale, and suggest a course of action. The executive's initial response to a memo without such background is often a request for more information, or a suggestion that consultation with specialists or peers be initiated and reported upon.

Other types of written communication can be less formal, but equally considerate of the executive's time. For example, a short handwritten note or brief memo could advise the director that a senior employee is retiring, and perhaps offer an invitation to make the presentation at the farewell tea. Secretaries and administrative assistants are important allies in the communication process, and can offer assistance in locating and informing executives of urgent matters that arise unexpectedly, or of sensitive issues that may require discussion.

In general, formal or scheduled communication with directors and vice presidents should be businesslike, constructive in tone, have a clear purpose, and be as succinct as possible. It is not wise for the manager to assume that the director's or vice-president's role is to listen to and to sympathize with problems. Clarkson (1992) offers excellent suggestions for overcoming negative communication behaviours that can be detrimental to professional effectiveness and career success. Proposals, recommendations, or summaries of action taken or in progress are usually more welcome and appropriate than descriptions of problems. Managers should expect to take responsibility for management of their own feelings. This may include taking the initiative in seeking professional assistance for personal difficulties, or to correct behaviour that is dysfunctional in the workplace.

Managers should also make use of informal opportunities to communicate with, and learn from, executives. These may include volunteering for committee work, task forces, or other special assignments, attending social events, or occasionally stopping by to report a small piece of good news.

Confidentiality and Security

Confidentiality and security have always been important issues in managerial communication, and the availability of new technologies has added to the complexities in this area. As recently as the mid-1980s, the major source of efficiency in written communication was use of a dictaphone to produce tapes for transcription by a secretary into memos, letters, and reports. Now, electronic mail enables communication with individuals or groups by entering a message at one computer terminal to be read electronically at another. Facsimile (fax) transmission has turned telephone communication into a form of written communication. Verbal communication can now take place from a variety of locations via cellular phone, as well as by conventional telephone or face-to-face.

Managers have a responsibility to assure the appropriate context and security of communications originating from their offices. To do this, it is necessary to have a clear understanding with the secretary regarding the general procedures for the office, and to provide specific direction when needed. Freiday (1992) offers advice regarding the type of material that should be protected, and its storage, transmission, and disposal.

Several kinds of material require special treatment. Notes or materials that the manager may want to remain privileged (that is, not having to be revealed in a court of law) need to be designated as such. No copies should be made of such material. All materials pertaining to employee performance require special attention in preparation, transmission, and filing. Anecdotal notes and correspondence to employees must be handled according to the advice of the organization's human resource specialists. The existence of more than one personnel file for an employee can lead to serious labour relations problems. A general principle to follow with regard to all written material is to circulate or distribute it only if directed to do so, and to treat all written material regarding legal or human resource matters as confidential.

Legal Considerations

The legislative framework within which communication takes place is generally designed to prevent harm to individuals. The law prohibits everyone from making written or verbal statements that have the potential to damage someone's reputation. Constitutional, human rights, and anti-hate legislation provide guidance as to other types of unacceptable communication. More specifically, provincial health care legislation protects the confidentiality of client information.

Professionalism and skill in managerial communication require scrupulous distinction between facts and opinion. Managers should endeavour to learn as much as they can about the legal issues relevant to various types of managerial communication.

Communicating Bad News

In some respects, the role of a first-line or middle manager is like that of a shock absorber in a vehicle—absorbing impacts from the road below, while functioning as one of many interconnected parts that keep the vehicle moving forward. Health care organizations are experiencing unprecedented numbers and types of changes.

Communicating the purpose of changes, and their effects on a unit program or individual staff members, is an important, and often difficult, task of first-line or middle managers. In more sophisticated organizations, resources may be developed, and specialists made available to assist in this area. In small organizations, or after the specialists have made their contribution, the manager is left to reinforce the message and carry out the activities required to implement the organizational initiative.

During times of change, employees typically experience feelings of loss, insecurity, and anxiety. There may be honest intellectual objections to a course of action being taken by the organization. There may also be expressions of anger directed at or through the manager as the organization's most accessible representative. Leadership and communications skills become inseparable in such situations. As the manager listens nondefensively to staff reactions, it will be especially important to be able to reinforce calmly the available facts and the current reality. If change is occurring rapidly, there will be many unknowns. One of the manager's tasks will be to carry questions and concerns forward, and to obtain and communicate additional information as it becomes available.

At times, managers may be privy to more complete information than they are permitted to share. Managers may have participated in development or discussions of the corporate strategy, but be under instructions to hold it in confidence as part of a corporate implementation strategy. An ethical perspective on lying, and on the dilemmas of concealment and revelation, is found in the two books by Sissela Bok (1979, 1983) cited in the References at the end of this chapter.

Despite uncertainty in changing times, the day-to-day work of the program or unit must continue. The manager must maintain a motivational climate through a presence, an alertness, and a response to signs of individual distress, and by setting limits if necessary. Inexperienced managers should not hesitate to ask for the advice and support they may need in these difficult situations.

Communication of Dissenting Opinions

As mentioned earlier in this chapter, most organizations expect that members of the management team will be loyal representatives of corporate values, goals, and strategies. This does not necessarily require abandonment of critical thinking or humanistic values; rather, in the healthiest organizations, there is concerted effort to tap the intellectual and moral resources of employees in a variety of ways to foster innovation, maximize adaptability, and improve outcomes. In such a climate, managers in the shock absorber role may be more comfortable with uncertainty and ambiguity than their counterparts in organizations where supervisory relationships between corporate management and other levels are authoritarian and nondisclosing.

It is healthy for managers to reflect upon the consequences of the activities they are expected to perform, and to place them in the context of personal values. If moral distress arises, it is important to clarify one's personal objectives and professional obligations before publicly expressing a view that is at odds with the corporate direction. Pronouncements about what is right or wrong, or other confrontational tactics, are generally unwise. However, the skills of principled bargaining discussed by Fisher and Wry (1981) and Wry (1991) may be helpful to managers who want to influence decisions and events (see Chapter 34). In such situations, it is often useful to take some time for personal reflection, and to seek the advice and perspectives of trusted members of one's peer group or of a mentor. Betraying confidences, or refusing to carry out one's duties, can have serious consequences, and the manager should be fully aware of them before considering such action. Sometimes expressing one's feelings or anxieties to a superior can provide an opportunity for receiving needed support or advice. Ultimately, a manager who experiences severe moral distress in the course of carrying out corporate directions will have to consider working in another environment or role.

Summary

In summary, effective managerial communication builds on the skills that nurses learn as part of their basic education. However, accepting a management position has the effect of multiplying the number and complexity of interpersonal roles and relationships. An awareness of the appropriate boundaries of these relationships should be reflected in the manager's behaviour. A number of specific communications challenges for the first-line or middle manager are discussed in other chapters of this book as well.

Managers should expect to engage in reflection and learning throughout their careers. They must seek continuing education and learning resources for the development of specific skills. For individuals and organizations, the domain of interpersonal communication remains one in which lifelong learning is both professionally necessary and personally beneficial.

References

Alihan, M. (1970). *Corporate etiquette*. New York: Mentor Books.

Blanchard, K.H., & Johnson, S. (1982). *The one-minute manager*. New York: Berkeley.

Bok, S. (1979). *Lying: Moral choice in public and private life*. New York: Vintage.

Bok, S. (1983). *Secrets: On the ethics on concealment and revelation*. New York: Pantheon.

Burns, T. (1953). Friends, enemies, and the polite fiction. *American Sociological Review, 18*(6), 654-662.

Clarkson, I. (1992). Project the positive. *Canadian Nurse, 88*(9), 28-30.

Fisher, R., & Wry, W. (1981). *Getting to yes: Negotiating agreement without giving in*. Boston: Houghton Mifflin.

Freiday, R. (1992, October). How to safeguard your company's competitive edge. *Creative Secretary's Letter*, p. 15.

Kanter, R. M. (1977). *Men and women of the corporation*. New York: Basic.

Kastenbach, J.R., & Smith, D.K. (1993, March/April). The discipline of teams. *Harvard Business Review*, pp. 111-120.

Leebov, W. (1990). *Positive co-worker relationships in health care*. Chicago: American Hospital Publishing.

Wry, W. (1991). *Getting past no: Negotiating with difficult people*. Toronto: Bantam.

Assisting the Troubled Employee

Katherine L. Kirk

Katherine L. Kirk, RN, BA, BSN, MN (Saskatchewan), is Associate Professor, College of Nursing, University of Saskatchewan. Her research has focussed on quality of nursing care, beginning with the study of how patients define good nursing care, and now centres on risk management. She participates in promotion of quality care through membership on the Royal University Hospital Nursing Division Quality Management Committee.

In Canada, 33% of women will experience unwanted sexual contact by age 18, 20% will experience sexual assault as adults, and 10% will be physically abused (Moscarello, 1992). The Canada Health Survey (reported by the Working Group on Alcohol Statistics, 1984) found that 3% of females between the ages of 20 and 29 reported daily drinking, while 5.3% of the Canadian drinking population (two-thirds of the total number of adults) are alcoholic. Ten per cent of the current drinking population reported at least one problem related to alcohol in the preceding year. Interestingly, this survey found that incidence of alcohol use is higher in the employed group than the unemployed. Thomas (1993) cited Canadian labour group findings demonstrating that stress-related problems can cause "more economic damage than work stoppages, accidents, or the common cold" (p. 36). Given these prevalence rates, it can be predicted that every nurse manager will at some time have an employee who is troubled by stress, or by substance, sexual, or physical abuse.

The primary role of the nurse manager is to ensure provision of safe client care, consistent with nursing standards and agency policies, and at the same time accommodate the agency's need for fiscal responsibility. To accomplish this task, the manager must have a staff of competent, productive, and safe employees. Impaired performance, which is often manifest in the troubled employee, sets safety of practice at risk and is a financial liability in the form of lost time and low productivity. If significant errors in practice accompany this decreased performance level, costs are increased through client injury and agency liability.

The responsibility of the nurse manager in dealing with the impaired performance of a nurse is described in three of the Standards for Nursing Administration prepared by the Canadian Nurses Association Ad Hoc Committee on Nursing Administration (1988). These are:

> **Standard II:** *Nursing administration participates in the setting and carrying out of organizational goals, priorities, and strategies.*

> **Standard III:** *Nursing administration provides for allocation, optimum use of, and evaluation of resources such that the standards of nursing practice can be met. . . .*

> **Standard VII:** *Nursing administration evaluates the effectiveness and efficiency of nursing services.* (p.10)

These standards require that the manager: identify issues of risk, such as impaired nursing practice; promote quality performance through a formal appraisal system; and ensure that nursing service evaluation is "consistent with a nursing code of ethics, standards of nursing practice, and other relevant documents" (Canadian Nurses Association Ad Hoc Committee on Nursing Administration, 1988, p. 15).

The focus of this chapter will be on sources of problems, identification of the troubled employee, and interventions that may be useful to ensure that standards of care are met while attention is given to the needs of the troubled employee. As well, the chapter will describe strategies that may be used to create an environment where the influence of employee problems on care and team functioning is minimized. The roles of agency administration and of Canadian professional associations will be addressed, in addition to the responsibilities of the nurse manager.

Sources of Problems

Nurses, in common with the general population, are subject to stress related to family caregiving commitments, family violence or abuse, family death, breakdown of family relationships, alcohol and drug abuse, and interpersonal problems. Culver (1991) believes that people who have family histories of abuse and alcoholism often choose to become nurses and implies that this finding directs the hospital's employee-health nurse to "be alert for symptoms which would suggest these serious problems" (p. 203). This finding also has implications for the nurse manager.

Nursing continues to be a female occupation, which means that women's issues are prominent factors in managing staff. Although society is changing, women continue to bear the bulk of the burden of caregiving and homemaking; women who work just add "a second shift" to their days (Hardy, 1990, p. 23). Role overload is a potential cause of employee problems, and the lack of attention given in the literature to the needs of the multiple caregiver as employee (Hardy, 1990) shows that this issue is just beginning to be recognized as significant.

Family violence and nurse abuse are issues that are starting to gain media attention. Added to the potential for these difficulties are the risk of burnout (see Chapter 21) common to the service professions and to the social and physiological effects of shift work. Creighton (1988) describes the requirement of vigorous professional training, accompanied by little time for leisure activities, as an additional stressor inherent in the lives of nurses.

The concern of the nurse manager, in relation to a nurse who suffers from any of the above stressors, is the effect of the problem on the performance of nursing care and the role of a health care team member. The nurse manager needs to be alert to ways to recognize the staff member who might have problems.

Identification of the Troubled Employee

There is a belief that when nurses arrive at work they should leave all personal problems outside the agency door in order to focus effectively on client care. This expectation is unrealistic for the seriously troubled nurse who experiences mood changes and psychosomatic effects as a result of stress and its influence on performance. Early detection of problems is essential to minimize the consequences to the client, agency, and nurse.

Because of the significant legal implications, the literature related to the problem employee has focussed on substance abuse and the nurse who is dependent on drugs or alcohol. However, nurse managers need to be aware of the indicators in both the woman who abuses herself through chemicals (drugs or alcohol) and the woman who is abused by others. Table 36.1 (see page 658) presents a profile of the chemically dependent nurse. Table 36.2 (see page 659) summarizes indicators that might be apparent in an abused woman. Identification of the abused employee is important because the emotional responses and physical needs of the battered woman may interfere with team functioning on the unit.

Indicators of trouble in an employee can be divided into four interrelated categories: decreased productivity, unmet standards of care, impaired interpersonal relationships, and absenteeism.

Table 36.1

Profile of the chemically dependent nurse.

Intrinsic Personality Factors	Behaviour	Psychological Manifestations
Bright	Absenteeism	Irrational thought
Well-liked	Schedule confusion	Poor clinical judgement
Respected	Tardiness	Mood swings
	Inability to meet deadlines	Blames others
	Decreased work quality	Withdrawal
	Excessive errors	Negative outlook
	Incorrect narcotic counts	Decreased attention to appearance
	Deteriorated handwriting	Forgetfulness
		Loss of recent memory
		Blackouts
		Change in level of alertness
		Low self-esteem
		Feelings of worthlessness

Source: Compiled from reports in the literature, especially S. Brennan (1991), Recognizing and assisting the impaired nurse: Recommendations for nurse managers, *Nursing Forum*, 26(2), 12-16, and J. Virden (1992), Impaired nursing: The role of the nurse manager, *Pediatric Nursing, 18*, 137-138.

Decreased Productivity

Decreased productivity commonly results from one or more of three factors. The employee may be "burned out" from attempting to cope with stress and have no emotional energy to care about productivity. There may be physical fatigue from overextension in too many roles, which depletes the energy available for productive work on the unit. Anxiety related to concerns about child care, family illness, or elder care responsibilities may preoccupy the employee. Substance abuse may impair the nurse's ability to identify and prioritize work that needs to be done.

Table 36.2
Indicators of abuse.

Physical Manifestations*	Psychosocial Manifestations
Bone/soft tissue injuries	Depression
Bite marks	Isolation
Old injuries	Fear
Burns	Detachment
Poor nutrition	Hostility
Sleep deprivation	Unrealistic expectations
Vague somatic complaints	Poverty
Miscarriages	Taking responsibility for abuse
Still births	Delay of treatment
Preterm babies	Helplessness
Low birth-weight babies	Anxiety
	Insomnia
	Describes spouse as jealous/impulsive

*Explanation for physical manifestations may be inconsistent with the injury.

Source: Compiled from information in the literature, especially Canadian Nurses Association (1992), *Family violence clinical guidelines for nurses* (Ottawa: Author); P. Jaffe, D. Wolfe, S. Wilson, & L. Zak (1986), Emotional and physical health problems of battered women, *Canadian Journal of Psychiatry, 31,* 625-629; and W. Swanson (1984), Battered wife syndrome, *Canadian Medical Association Journal, 130,* 709-712.

Unmet Standards of Care

Factors involved in unmet standards of care result from the same causes as decreased productivity: lack of physical and emotional energy and impaired ability to think critically. Incomplete or fragmented care, errors in care or in judgement, and poor or inaccurate documentation are examples of infractions in this area.

This manifestation of personal problems in the nurse is the most critical aspect of impaired performance, for it places the client at the greatest risk. For this reason, identification of behaviours in this category requires prompt intervention on the part of the nurse manager.

Impaired Interpersonal Relationships

There are many factors related to problem employees that interfere with interpersonal relationships. Nurses who are, or have been, involved in dysfunctional family relationships may be lacking in self-confidence and have a poor image of themselves. Troubled nurses may withdraw to prevent themselves from being hurt further. Lack of emotional energy may also cause the nurse to become passive, irritable, or curt. Resentment and anger may be expressions of personal problems. Whatever the manifestation of the trouble, it is bound to affect relationships with clients, colleagues, and other health team members.

As well, personal problems may interfere with the satisfaction of clients' emotional needs and communication of important information to clients and families. Informants in a study of patients' perceptions of nursing care stated that a grouchy or mean nurse made them depressed and caused them to wish to leave the hospital (Kirk, 1990). One unproductive nurse with decreased interpersonal skills can adversely influence the morale on the work unit.

Absenteeism

Absenteeism results when a nurse perceives work as a lower priority than other activities. For example, if the caregiving commitments of the nurse's personal life are excessive, he or she may have difficulty complying with the established work schedule. Family dysfunction, substance abuse, and other personal problems are often characterized by higher than average rates of absenteeism.

Absenteeism increases the workload for other staff or, if a replacement is obtained, increases the cost to the unit's budget. Frequent lapses in attendance by the same staff member may generate feelings of resentment in co-workers, who are asked to assume an extra workload to compensate. Quality of care may suffer as a result of increased volume of responsibility per staff member and decreased morale of the nurses.

Absenteeism may be considered in terms of controllable absenteeism and uncontrollable absenteeism (McDonald & Shaver, 1981). Controllable absenteeism results from such factors as decreased motivation of the employee, decreased loyalty to the work place, unsatisfactory emotional and physical environments, and preventable work injuries. Sources of uncontrollable absenteeism include non work-related illness, child or elder care concerns, court appearances, and death in the family. The troubled employee may demonstrate one or both types of absentee behaviour depending on the source of the problem and the individual's coping response.

Intervention by the Nurse Manager

It is important to make the distinction between a nurse manager's responsibility to deal with performance problems and a counselor's responsibility to assist with the management of the stressor of the individual. Although the nurse manager is responsible for minimizing the contributions of the work environment toward stress, it would be a conflict of interest for the manager to become involved in treatment of the troubled staff member. The conflict arises from the manager's power over the staff member's job status in apposition to the vulnerability inherent in a therapeutic relationship.

According to Mynatt and O'Brien (1993), when working with troubled employees the nurse manager can intervene at three levels: primary prevention before the problem is manifest; secondary prevention in dealing with the acute problem; and tertiary prevention to assist the nurse in ongoing recovery from the problem. Policies and system supports must be in place at the professional and agency level to give the manager guidance and resources in dealing with the problem employee.

Primary Prevention

Interventions at the primary level are aimed at preventing stressors from reaching the point where they adversely affect nursing performance (Mynatt & O'Brien, 1993). As well, primary prevention requires early detection of problems. The professional nurses' associations set standards of care to clarify performance expectations. They also set policies and guidelines for dealing with troubled employees to assist agencies with setting their own policies.

One guideline that assists with early detection of trouble is acceptance of the belief that each nurse is a valued member of the profession and, as such, will be assisted to maintain or regain performance levels. Interpretation of this approach at the managerial and staff nurse level creates an environment where staff do not need to fear for a colleague's career if they communicate concern about safety or care quality to the manager. Lee and Eriksen (1990) stress using a positive, rather than punitive, approach in setting sick leave policy; this will decrease staff dissatisfaction. Policies that support nurses by communicating low tolerance for nurse abuse are recommended by Brasen (1993).

Another preventive measure that professional associations, agencies, and managers use is education about issues. For example, the Canadian Nurses Association (1992) has distributed booklets about family violence to all members, and the Saskatchewan Registered Nurses Association (1993) has provided an education day titled "Nurses supporting nurses," which included information about nurse abuse and self-protection. Teaching stress management techniques, providing daycare facilities, sick child care services, elder care information, and allowing flexible staffing are other preventive measures that could be considered.

Secondary Prevention

Secondary prevention is the mode of intervention used once the problem has affected work performance (Mynatt & O'Brien, 1993) and is guided by Value VIII, Obligation 1 of the Canadian Nurses Association (1991) *Code of Ethics for Nursing*: "The first consideration of the nurse who suspects incompetence or unethical conduct must be the welfare of present clients or potential harm to future clients" (p. 15). This statement makes clear the manager's obligation to protect the client by dealing with impaired performance of a staff member.

The first guideline under the above obligation is that the nurse must "ascertain the facts of the situation before deciding upon the appropriate course of action" (Canadian Nurses Association, 1991, p. 15). Klassen and Meredith (1989) identify evaluation criteria that may be used as a framework for identification and documentation of performance problems; the first task is to describe how "the employee fails to meet job criteria, policies, procedures, contractual agreements or employment terms" (p. 26). It is important to document dates and times. Klassen and Meredith state that employee involvement in repetitive accidents, errors, or omissions should be documented. Clarification of the seriousness of the problems, the management implications, the employee's work profile (i.e., the value of the employee's contributions to the agency), and the duration of the behaviour in question is necessary in order to select options for intervention (Klassen & Meredith, 1989).

The ranking of strategies is guided by the second point of Obligation 1, Value VIII: "Relationships in the health care team should not be disrupted unnecessarily...." (Canadian Nurses Association, 1991, p. 15). Options for intervention should be examined using the values clarified in the preceding paragraph as a measure of their worth.

The four major options or alternatives, as identified by Brennan (1991), are: termination, notification to the professional disciplinary committee, consultation with the professional association counseling committee, and referral to an employee assistance program, if the agency has one. Each of these options will be discussed briefly.

Termination. Marriner (1986) lists the following behaviours as grounds for termination of employment: abuse, insubordination, intoxication, possession of drugs, theft, gambling, disorderly conduct, sleeping on duty, or falsification of records. Termination must be weighed in relation to the employee's value and the seriousness of the behaviour. In most cases, termination is not invoked unless the nurse refuses treatment or has a long history of unsuccessful treatment.

Notification of the professional association disciplinary committee. Many managers are reluctant to seek disciplinary action from the professional association because they fear it will jeopardize the nurse's chances of reemployment. However, if the situation is considered serious enough to terminate employment, or if it is a reportable offence in that province (Canadian Nurses Association, 1991), the professional association must be notified to safeguard other clients from the nurse's impaired performance.

Consultation with the professional association counseling committee. Many Canadian provincial professional associations have counseling committees to assist both nursing administration and troubled employees in dealing with problems affecting the quality and safety of nursing care. These committees can provide information about policies, guidelines, and resources.

Referral to an employee assistance program, if available. Many larger agencies participate in employee assistance programs, and these will initiate individualized treatment for a troubled employee. In other agencies, referral for counseling and treatment services may be handled through the occupational health nurse.

Once these options for interventions have been considered, the next step is to confront the nurse with the evidence of incompetent or unethical care, and the need to implement a remedial program. If the manager expects some difficulty with this session, enlisting the support of a colleague may be effective in helping to keep the interview focussed on the behaviour problem and the need for resolution. If the employee is a member of a union, he or she may request assistance from this group. Union contracts specify the guidelines for this type of action.

During this initial interview, the manager should expect denial and anger as responses, although many employees will acknowledge that there is a problem. The interview must remain focussed on the behaviour, but be accepting of the emotions as normal. It is to be hoped that the employee will acknowledge difficulties and participate in a problem-solving process. In order to facilitate this response, the documentation must be explicit in its statement of the problem.

If the employee continues to deny any impairment of performance, the manager must consider other options. One option would be to insist upon treatment, such as compliance with referral to counseling resources as the sole alternative to termination of employment. This strategy is particularly relevant in cases of substance abuse. The progressive disciplinary process may be invoked if the situation is not as serious and more time is available for rectification of the problem. Lachman (1988) states that professional associations can be of further assistance in intervention programs by allowing nurses to be inactive members while undergoing treatment.

Tertiary Prevention

The foci of this third level of prevention are rehabilitation and support of the recovering employee in the work place. Once the nurse has complied with the remediation agreed upon, there is a need to assist this employee to maintain functioning. Strategies that may be beneficial at this stage are: a work contract specifying responsibilities of the employee and the manager; work scheduling responsive to the nurse's needs (e.g., half shifts); a buddy system to give peer support; and attendance at support groups such as Families Anonymous or Alcoholics Anonymous (Abbott, 1987; Lachman, 1988; Robbins, 1987).

Summary

The troubled backgrounds of many problem employees cause a significant lack of self-esteem (Chappelle, & Sorentino, 1993; Lachman, 1988). Intervention programs should attempt to preserve the self-esteem of the employee by focussing on the behaviour rather than the person, and by giving the employee the opportunity to participate in planning the treatment. Esteem-building strategies must be built into all levels of prevention. The work contract can serve this function when used to track improvement and achievement.

Confidentiality is closely related to self-esteem. The employee must be allowed to make the decision to inform peers about the problem. When the employee is attending counseling, the manager needs to know only that the employee is receiving treatment. In the case of a leave of absence or suspension, the manager needs to know only what the terms of the return to work contract will be (Culver, 1991). Foster, Hirsch, and Zaske (1991) recommend that, in the interests of confidentiality, when a troubled employee is receiving counseling, the manager must make decisions "based on the employee's performance and/or behaviour without knowledge of the content of the employee counsellor's work" (p. 86). This recommendation is consistent with the ethical value of "protecting the clients from incompetence" (Canadian Nurses Association, 1991, p. 15). Foster, Hirsch, and Zaske (1991) specify that when a life is at risk or child abuse is evident, legal precedents have been set (in the United States) for breach of confidentiality.

The nurse manager plays a critical role in protecting the client from impaired nursing practice and in reclaiming the valued but troubled nurse for productive practice at all three levels of prevention: trouble prevention, treatment, and rehabilitation or restoration. It is important to treat the troubled employee with sensitivity, recognizing that individual's value and potential for regrowth. However, the ethical value of protecting clients from incompetence (Canadian Nurses Association, 1991) should never be violated to accomplish this task.

Nurse managers have a responsibility to recognize the indicators of trouble in performance and to confront the nurse with accurate data, requesting that lapses in meeting standards of care be rectified. Professional associations provide both guidelines and information about available resources, while many agencies also have access to occupational health or employee assistance programs that may be of use in treating the underlying problem and restoring the employee to competent functioning.

References

Abbott, C. (1987). The impaired nurse: Part II—Management strategies. *AORN Journal, 46,* 1104-1115.

Brasen, T. (1993). Abuse at work. *Occupational Health & Safety Magazine, 16*(2), 7-13.

Brennan, S. (1991). Recognizing and assisting the impaired nurse: Recommendations for nurse managers. *Nursing Forum, 26*(2), 12-16.

Canadian Nurses Association. (1991). *Code of ethics for nursing.* Ottawa: Author.

Canadian Nurses Association. (1992). *Family violence clinical guidelines for nurses.* Ottawa: Author.

Canadian Nurses Association. Ad Hoc Committee on Nursing Administration. (1988). *The role of the nurse administrator and standards for nursing administration.* Ottawa: Author.

Chappelle, L., & Sorentino, E. (1993). Assessing co-dependency issues within a nursing environment. *Nursing Management, 24*(5), 40-44.

Creighton, H. (1988). Legal implications of the impaired nurse—Part I. *Nursing Management, 19*(1), 21-23.

Culver, J. (1991). Employee health nurse counsellors roles in the hospital setting. *AAOHN Journal, 39,* 199-204.

Foster, Z., Hirsch, S., & Zaske, K. (1991). Social work role in developing and managing employee assistance programs in health care settings. *Social Work in Health Care, 16*(2), 81-95.

Hardy, L. (1990). Nursing work and the implications of "the second shift." *Canadian Journal of Nursing Administration, 3*(4), 23-26.

Jaffe, P., Wolfe, D., Wilson, S., & Zak, L. (1986). Emotional and physical health problems of battered women. *Canadian Journal of Psychiatry, 31,* 625-629.

Kirk, K. (1990). *Chronically ill patient's perceptions of nursing care.* Unpublished master's thesis, University of Saskatchewan, Saskatoon.

Klassen, C., & Meredith, S. (1989). The remedial evaluation instrument a new approach. *Canadian Journal of Nursing Administration, 2*(3), 24-29.

Lachman, V. (1988). The chemically dependent nurse. *Holistic Nursing Practice, 2*(4), 34-44.

Lee, J., & Eriksen, L. (1990). The effects of a policy change on three types of absence. *Journal of Nursing Administration, 20*(7/8), 37-40.

Marriner, A. (1986). Problem employees. *Nursing Management, 17*(6), 58,60.

McDonald, M., & Shaver, A. (1981). An absenteeism control program. *Journal of Nursing Administration, 11*(5), 13-18.

Moscarello, R. (1992). Victims of violence: Aspects of the "victim-to-patient" process in women. *Canadian Journal of Psychiatry, 37,* 497-502.

Mynatt, S., & O'Brien, J. (1993). Partnership to prevent chemical dependency in nursing using Neuman's systems model. *Journal of Psychosocial Nursing, 31*(4), 27-32.

Robbins, C. (1987). A monitored treatment program for impaired health care professionals. *Journal of Nursing Administration, 17*(2), 17-21.

Saskatchewan Registered Nurses Association. (1993). Annual report. *ConceRN, 22*(2), insert.

Swanson, W. (1984). Battered wife syndrome. *Canadian Medical Association Journal, 130,* 709-712.

Thomas, G. (1993). Working can be harmful to your health. *Canadian Nurse, 89*(6), 35-38.

Virden, J. (1992). Impaired nursing: The role of the nurse manager. *Pediatric Nursing, 18,* 137-138.

Working Group on Alcohol Statistics. (1984). *Alcohol in Canada: A national perspective.* Ottawa: Health & Welfare Canada.

Index

Note: Index entries that appear in italic type indicate a bibliographic reference.